Tiffany,

A beginning—

M. Erskine

The

WELL-
EDUCATED
MIND

ALSO BY SUSAN WISE BAUER

*The Story of Western Science: From the Writings of
Aristotle to the Big Bang Theory*
(W. W. NORTON, 2015)

The History of the World Series
(W. W. NORTON)

The History of the Ancient World (2007)
The History of the Medieval World (2010)
The History of the Renaissance World (2013)

The Art of the Public Grovel
(PRINCETON UNIVERSITY PRESS, 2008)

The Story of the World: History for the Classical Child
(PEACE HILL PRESS)

Volume I: Ancient Times (2002)
Volume II: The Middle Ages (2003)
Volume III: Early Modern Times (2003)
Volume IV: The Modern World (2004)

The Writing With Ease Series
(PEACE HILL PRESS, 2008-2010)

The Writing With Skill Series
(PEACE HILL PRESS, 2012-2013)

WITH JESSIE WISE

*The Well-Trained Mind:
A Guide to Classical Education at Home*
(W. W. NORTON, 2009)

The

WELL-
EDUCATED
MIND

*A Guide to the Classical Education
You Never Had*

Updated and Expanded

SUSAN WISE BAUER

W. W. NORTON & COMPANY

Independent Publishers Since 1923

NEW YORK / LONDON

Since this page cannot legibly accommodate all the copyright notices, page 471
constitutes an extension of the copyright page.

For information about permission to reproduce selections from this book,
write to Permissions, W. W. Norton & Company, Inc.,
500 Fifth Avenue, New York, NY 10110

For information about special discounts for bulk purchases, please contact
W. W. Norton Special Sales at specialsales@wwnorton.com or 800-233-4830

Manufacturing by RR Donnelly Harrisonburg
Production manager: Louise Mattarelliano

Library of Congress Cataloging-in-Publication Data

Bauer, S. Wise.
The well-educated mind : a guide to the classical education you
never had : updated and expanded / Susan Wise Bauer.
pages cm
Includes bibliographical references and index.
ISBN 978-0-393-08096-4 (hardcover)
1. Books and reading. 2. Best books. 3. Reading. 4. Literature—History
and criticism. 5. Self-culture. 6. Education, Humanistic. I. Title.
Z1003.B324 2016
028—dc23

2015027978

W. W. Norton & Company, Inc.
500 Fifth Avenue, New York, N.Y. 10110
www.wwnorton.com

W. W. Norton & Company Ltd.
Castle House, 75/76 Wells Street, London W1T 3QT

1 2 3 4 5 6 7 8 9 0

For my mother
who taught me to read,
and my father
who gave me all of his favorite books

Contents

PART II
READING:
JUMPING INTO THE GREAT CONVERSATION

Acknowledgments

THE ORIGINAL EDITION of this book would never have been completed without the help of Sara Buffington, who worked on the thankless task of clearing permissions and kept Peace Hill's own publishing efforts running seamlessly along; Justin Moore, who made endless library trips for me (including the ones in which he returned overdue books I was too embarrassed to show up with), checked facts, entered soul-destroying columns of ISBN numbers, introduced me to the music of The Proclaimers, compounded all this with intelligent readings (of the history chapter in particular), and helped me keep my in-box clear; Lauren Winner, scholar and writer, who read the history chapter and offered invaluable help; John Wilson, editor of *Books & Culture;* Maureen Fitzgerald of the College of William and Mary; and my parents, Jay and Jessie Wise, who gave me every moral and practical support imaginable.

For this revision, I'm grateful as always to my editor at W. W. Norton, Starling Lawrence, who keeps reading what I write, and always knows of a better restaurant than the one I'd planned on. Thanks also to Norton's Ryan Harrington, who answers his email promptly, always finds the answers, and does what he says he'll do.

I am deeply indebted to Patricia Worth, executive assistant extraordinaire; Justin Moore (again); Richie Gunn, for the illustrations; the able and charming Michael Carlisle at Inkwell Management; the amazing Julia Kaziewicz, for help with permissions as well as expert advice on many subjects academic; Greg Smith, for his insights on the great texts of science (I didn't take all of his advice, so he gets credit but no blame for Chapter 10); and, as always, my husband Peter.

PART

I

PREPARING

FOR

CLASSICAL

EDUCATION

Chapter 1

Training Your Own Mind:
The Classical Education You Never Had

All civilization comes through literature now, especially in our country. A Greek got his civilization by talking and looking, and in some measure a Parisian may still do it. But we, who live remote from history and monuments, we must read or we must barbarise.

　　　　　　　　　　　　—WILLIAM DEAN HOWELLS,
　　　　　　　　　　　　The Rise of Silas Lapham

THE YEAR I turned thirty, I decided to go back to graduate school. I'd taken years off from school to write, teach literature as an adjunct lecturer, have four children. Now I was back in the classroom, on the wrong side of the teacher's desk. All the graduate students looked like teenagers. And graduate programs aren't designed for grownups; I was expected to stuff my family into the schedule designed for me by American Studies, live off a stipend of six thousand dollars per year while forgoing all other gainful employment, and content myself with university-sponsored health insurance, which supplied bare-bones coverage and classified anesthesia during childbirth as a frill. And I found myself dreading the coming year of classes. I'd been teaching and directing discussions for five years. I didn't think I could bear to be transformed back into a passive student, sitting and taking notes while a professor told me what I ought to know.

But to my relief, graduate seminars weren't lectures during which I meekly received someone else's wisdom. Instead, the three-hour weekly sessions turned out to be the springboard of a self-education process. Over the next year and a half, I was directed toward lists of books and given advice about how to read them. But I was expected to teach myself. I read book after book, summarized the content of each, and tried to see whether the arguments were flawed. Were the conclusions overstated? Drawn from skimpy evidence? Did the writers ignore facts, or distort them to support a point? Where did their theories break down? It was great fun; trashing the arguments of senior scholars who are making eighty times your annual stipend is one of the few compensations of grad-student serfdom.

All of this reading was preparation for my seminars, in which graduate students sat around long tables and argued loudly about the book of the week. The professor in charge pointed out our sloppy reasoning, corrected our misuses of language, and threw water on the occasional flames. These (more or less) Socratic dialogues built on the foundation of the reading I was doing at home. On evenings when I would normally have been watching *The X-Files* or scrubbing the toilet, I read my way through lists of required books with concentrated attention. The housework suffered and I missed Mulder's departure from spook hunting; but I found myself creating whole new structures of meaning in my mind, making connections between theories and building new theories of my own on top of the links. I wrote better, thought more clearly, read more.

I also drove myself into work-induced psychosis. I stayed up late at night to finish my papers and got up early with the baby; I wrote my dissertation proposal on the living room floor, with a Thomas the Tank Engine track in construction all around me; I spent the night before my required French exam washing my four-year-old's sheets and pillows after he caught the stomach flu; I sat through numerous required workshops in which *nothing* of value was said.

Here is the good news: You don't have to suffer through the graduate school wringer in order to train your mind—unless you plan to get a job in university teaching (not a particularly strong employment prospect anyway). For centuries, women and men undertook this sort of learning—reading, taking notes, discussing books and ideas with friends—without subjecting themselves to graduate-school stipends and university health-insurance policies.

Indeed, university lectures were seen by Thomas Jefferson as unnecessary for the serious pursuit of historical reading. In 1786, Jefferson wrote to his college-age nephew Thomas Mann Randolph, Jr., advising him to pursue the larger part of his education independently. Go ahead and attend a course of lectures in science, Jefferson recommended. But he then added, "While you are attending these courses, you can proceed by yourself in a regular series of historical reading. It would be a waste of time to attend a professor of this. It is to be acquired from books, and if you pursue it by yourself, you can accommodate it to your other reading so as to fill up those chasms of time not otherwise appropriated."[1]

---

[1] Thomas Jefferson, in a letter to Thomas Mann Randolph, Jr., in Paris, dated August 27, 1786. This letter is in the University of Virginia Library, where it is titled "Education of

Professional historians might take umbrage at their apparent superfluity, but Jefferson's letter reflects a common understanding of the times: Any literate man (or woman, we would add) can rely on self-education to train and fill the mind. All you need are a shelf full of books, a congenial friend or two who can talk to you about your reading, and a few "chasms of time not otherwise appropriated." (Contemporary critics of university education might add that a Ph.D. doesn't necessarily train and fill the mind in any case; this, sniffs Harold Bloom, is a "largely forgotten function of a university education," since universities now "disdain to fulfill" our yearning for the classics.)[2]

Young Randolph was able to build on the foundation of a privileged education. But his home course in self-improvement was followed by many Americans who were less well schooled—including thousands of eighteenth- and nineteenth-century women, who were usually given much less classroom education than their male counterparts. Limited to the learning they could acquire for themselves once a brief period of formal education had ended, American women of the last two centuries kept journals and commonplace books chronicling their reading, met with each other, and took responsibility for developing their own minds. The etiquette author Eliza Farrar advised her young female readers not only on manners and dress, but also on intellectual cultivation: "Self-education begins where school education ends," she wrote sternly.[3]

Many, many women took this advice seriously. Mary Wilson Gilchrist, a Civil War–era Ohioan who lived at home until her sudden death at the age of 24, could boast only of a single year at Ohio Female College, where she briefly studied trigonometry, English literature, French, music, logic, rhetoric, and theology—hardly time enough to gain even an elementary understanding of this laundry list of subjects, let alone mastery of their principles. But Gilchrist's education didn't cease when she returned home. She kept in her diary a list of the books she read: Charlotte Brontë, William Makepeace Thackeray, Henry Fielding, William Wordsworth, Virgil, Sophocles, and David Hume ("Difficult," she wrote of Hume, hoping that she would "retain some of it"). To keep herself motivated, she set up a reading club with a neighbor. "Mary Carpenter called," one diary entry reads, "and we made arrangements for reading Shakespeare together."[4] Southern teenager Hope Summerell

a Future Son-in-Law," and is archived online at http://etext.virginia.edu/toc/modeng/public/JefLett.html.

[2]Harold Bloom, *How to Read and Why* (New York: Scribner, 2000), p. 24.

[3]Eliza W. R. Farrar, *The Young Lady's Friend, by a Lady* (Boston: American Stationer's Company, 1836), p. 4.

[4]Mary Gilchrist's diary is quoted in Claudia Lynn Lady, "Five Tri-State Women During

Chamberlain wrote in her own journal of reading Humboldt's *Kosmos*, Milton's *Paradise Lost*, Madame de Staël's *Corinne*, and Guizot's *History of Civilization,* among other difficult books; the reading club she helped to organize was, in her own words, "a peace offering to a hungry mind."[5]

What if your mind is hungry, but you feel unprepared, under-educated, intimidated by all those books you know you *should* have read?

"Acquaint yourself with your own ignorance," Isaac Watts advised his readers, in his self-education treatise *Improvement of the Mind* (originally published in 1741). "Impress your mind with a deep and painful sense of the low and imperfect degrees of your present knowledge." This cheerful admonition was intended as a reassurance, not a condemnation: A well-trained mind is the result of application, not inborn genius. Deep thinkers, Watts assures us, are not those born with "bright genius, a ready wit, and good parts" (a relief for most of us). No matter how ignorant and "low" a mind might be, "studious thought . . . the exercise of your own reason and judgment upon all you read . . . gives good sense . . . and affords your understanding the truest improvement."

Today, as in Watts's own time, many intelligent and ambitious adults feel inadequate to tackle any course of serious reading. They struggle to overcome an indifferent education that didn't teach the basic skills needed for mature reading and writing. But Watts's admonition is still true: No matter how incomplete your education, you can learn how to read intelligently, think about your reading, and talk to a friend about what you've discovered. You can educate yourself.

Sustained, serious reading is at the center of this self-education project. Observation, reading, conversation, and attendance at lectures are all ways of self-teaching, as Isaac Watts goes on to tell us. But he concludes that reading is the most important method of self-improvement. Observation limits our learning to our immediate surroundings; conversation and attendance at lectures are valuable, but expose us only to the views of a few nearby persons. Reading alone allows us to reach out beyond the restrictions of time and space, to take part in what Mortimer Adler has called the "Great Conversation" of ideas that began in ancient times and has continued unbroken to the present. Reading

---

the Civil War: Day-to-Day Life," *West Virginia History,* vol. 43, no. 3 (Spring 1982): 189–226. Gilchrist's diary is excerpted on pp. 212–14.

[5]"What's Done and Past," unpublished autobiography, William R. Perkins Library, Duke University.

makes us part of this Great Conversation, no matter where and when we pursue it.

But sustained and serious reading has always been a difficult project—even before the advent of television. Much has been written about our present move away from texts, toward an image-based, visual culture: Schools no longer teach reading and writing properly. Television, movies, and now the Web have decreased the importance of the written word. We are moving into a postliterate age. Print culture is doomed. Alas.

I dislike these sorts of apocalyptic reflections. Streamed entertainment may be pernicious, but reading is no harder (or easier) than it has ever been. "Our post-revolutionary youth," complained Thomas Jefferson in an 1814 letter to John Adams, "are born under happier stars than you and I were. They acquire all learning in their mother's womb, and bring it into the world ready-made. The information of books is no longer necessary; and all knowledge which is not innate, is in contempt, or neglect at least." Jefferson's moan over the stage of modern intellectual culture laments the rise of a philosophy that exalts self-expression over reading. Even before the advent of television, reading that required concentration was a difficult and neglected activity.

In fact, reading is a discipline: like running regularly, or meditating, or taking voice lessons. Any able adult can run across the backyard, but this ability to put one foot in front of another shouldn't make him think that he can tackle a marathon without serious, time-consuming training. Most of us can manage to sing "Happy Birthday" or the Doxology when called for, but this doesn't incline us to march down to the local performing arts center and try out for the lead in *Aida*.

Yet because we can read the newspaper or *Time* or Stephen King without difficulty, we tend to think that we should be able to go directly into Homer or Henry James without any further preparation. And when we stumble, grow confused or weary, we take this as proof of our mental inadequacy: We'll never be able to read the Great Books.

The truth is that the study of literature requires different *skills* than reading for pleasure. The inability to tackle, unaided, a list of Great Books and stick to the project doesn't demonstrate mental inadequacy—just a lack of preparation. As Richard J. Foster eloquently argues in *Celebration of Discipline*, we tend to think (erroneously) that anyone who can read ought to be able to study ideas. "To convince people that they must learn to study is the major obstacle," Foster writes. "Most people assume that because they know how to read words they know how to study." But the opposite is true:

> Studying a book is an extremely complex matter, especially for the novice. As with tennis or typing, when we are first learning it seems that there are a thousand details to master and we wonder how on earth we will keep everything in mind at the same time. Once we reach proficiency, however, the mechanics become second nature, and we are able to concentrate on our tennis game or the material to be typed. The same is true with studying a book. Study is an exacting art involving a labyrinth of details.[6]

Secondary schools don't typically train us how to read seriously, how to *study*. Their task is to produce students who are reading at the so-called tenth-grade level, a fluency that allows readers to absorb newspapers and Stephen King with ease. A university education ought to follow up on this basic literacy by teaching its freshmen how to read seriously, but many college seniors aren't much further along than their high school counterparts. Often, they graduate with a nagging sense of their own deficiencies; as adults, they come back to the task of serious reading and discover that it has not magically become simpler. Homer is still long-winded, Plato still impenetrable, Stoppard still bewilderingly random. Too often, these readers give up, convinced that serious books are beyond them.

But all that's missing is training in the art of reading. If you didn't learn how to read properly in school, you can do it now. The methods of classical education are at your disposal.

The world is full of self-improvement methods. What's distinctive about classical education?

"Some books are to be tasted," wrote the sixteenth-century philosopher Francis Bacon, "others to be swallowed, and some few to be chewed and digested." Bacon, who had a knack for the quotable (he is also responsible for "The remedy is worse than the disease" and "Knowledge is power"), was suggesting that not every book is worthy of serious attention. But the three levels of understanding he describes—tasting, swallowing, and digesting—reflect his familiarity with classical education. In the classical school, learning is a three-part process. First, taste: Gain basic knowledge of your subject. Second, swallow: Take the knowledge into your own understanding by evaluating it. Is it valid? Is it true? Why? Third, digest: Fold the subject into your own understanding. Let it change the way you think—or reject it as unworthy. Taste, swallow, digest; find out the facts, evaluate them, form your own opinion.

---

[6]Richard J. Foster, *Celebration of Discipline* (San Francisco: Harper, 1978), p. 67.

Like Bacon, the classical schoolmaster divides learning into three stages, generally known as the *trivium*. The first stage of education is called the *grammar* stage (in this case, "grammar" means the building blocks, the foundational knowledge of each academic subject). In elementary school, children are asked to absorb information—not to evaluate it, but simply to learn it. Memorization and repetition are the primary methods of teaching; children are expected to become familiar with a certain body of knowledge, but they aren't yet asked to analyze it. Critical thinking comes into play during the second stage of education, the *logic* (or "dialectic") stage. Once a foundation of information is laid, students begin to exercise their analytical skills; they decide whether information is correct or incorrect, and make connections between cause and effect, historical events, scientific phenomena, words and their meanings. In the final stage of secondary education, the *rhetoric* stage, students learn to express their own opinions about the facts they have accumulated and evaluated. So the final years of education focus on elegant, articulate expression of opinion in speech and writing—the study of rhetoric.[7]

Classically educated students know that this pattern (learn facts; analyze them; express your opinions about them) applies to all later learning. But if you haven't been classically educated, you may not recognize that these three separate steps also apply to reading. It is impossible to analyze on a first reading; you have to grasp a book's central ideas *before* you can evaluate them. And after you've evaluated—asking, "Are the ideas presented accurately? Are the conclusions valid?"—you can ask the final set of questions: What do you think about these ideas? Do you agree or disagree? Why?

Classrooms too often skip the first two steps and progress directly to the third, which is why so many elementary texts insist on asking six-year-olds how they feel about what they're learning, long before they've properly had a chance to learn it. This mental short cut has become a habit for many adults, who are ready to give their opinions long before they've had a chance to understand the topic under study. (Listen to any call-in radio show.) And the habit of leaping directly to the rhetoric stage can prevent even mature minds from learning how to read properly. The density of ideas in Plato or Shakespeare or Thomas Hardy frustrates the mind that comes to them ready to draw conclusions. To tackle a course of reading successfully, we have to retrain our minds to grasp new ideas by

[7]A proposal for K–12 education following this pattern is described in detail in Jessie Wise and Susan Wise Bauer, *The Well-Trained Mind: A Guide to Classical Education at Home,* 3rd ed. (New York: W. W. Norton, 2009).

first understanding them, then evaluating them, and finally forming our own opinions.

Like badly taught six-year-olds, we are too quick to go straight to opinion making without the intermediate steps of understanding and evaluation. The British mystery writer Dorothy L. Sayers, proposing a return to classical education for the twentieth century, lamented the loss of the classical "tools of learning" in a speech at Oxford:

> Has it ever struck you as odd, or unfortunate, that today, when the proportion of literacy is higher than it has ever been, people should have become susceptible to the influence of advertisement and mass propaganda to an extent hitherto unheard of and unimagined? . . . Have you ever, in listening to a debate among adult and presumably responsible people, been fretted by the extraordinary inability of the average debater to speak to the question, or to meet and refute the arguments of speakers on the other side? . . . And when you think of this, and think that most of our public affairs are settled by debates and committees, have you ever felt a certain sinking of the heart? . . . Is not the great defect of our education today—a defect traceable through all the disquieting symptoms of trouble that I have mentioned—that although we often succeed in teaching our pupils "subjects," we fail lamentably on the whole in teaching them how to think: they learn everything, except the art of learning?[8]

Grammar, logic, and rhetoric train the mind in the art of learning. But if you never learned how to grasp knowledge quickly and well, to evaluate the validity of arguments, and to present your own opinions with grace and clarity, it isn't too late. You can still learn how to understand, evaluate, and argue with ideas. Like a medieval tutor with a single promising pupil, this book will walk you through each stage of classical education, so that you will have the tools to find the serious contemplation of books a delight rather than a frustration.

How to begin?

Self-educated men and women of the past offer us a few general principles as we start on the project of training our own minds. "Engage not the mind in the intense pursuit of too many things at once," Isaac Watts advises, "especially such as have no relation to one another. This will be

[8]Dorothy L. Sayers, "The Lost Tools of Learning," a speech presented at Oxford University in 1947, reprinted by the *National Review*, 215 Lexington Avenue, New York, NY 10016.

ready to distract the understanding, and hinder it from attaining perfection in any one subject of study." It may seem slow, but study one subject at a time. Begin with this book, which will guide you through the necessary skills of reading and analysis; make this study your sole subject until you've completed it. Once you have learned how to progress through the steps of understanding (grammar), evaluating (logic), and expressing an opinion (rhetoric), *then* turn to the reading lists in Part II. These lists are organized by subject; if you read the books in order, limiting yourself to one field of inquiry (fiction, autobiography, history) at a time, you will find that your earlier reading will set a framework for the books that come later, while your later reading will reinforce and clarify what has come before.

Stick to one list at a time. During this self-study time, avoid the kind of reading that German theologian Friedrich Schleiermacher indulged in during his early years: a wide-ranging and impressive, but unsystematic, devouring of books that left his mind, as he put it in later years, "like Chaos, before the world was created."

Jefferson (always full of advice on every subject) counseled his young nephew to organize this systematic reading around chronology: "Having laid down your plan [of reading]," he tells young Randolph, "the order of time will be your sufficient guide."[9] In other words, read books in the order in which they were written. The nineteenth-century educator Lydia Sigourney agreed; in her *Letters to Young Ladies*, she recommended that reading always be done with the help of a "table of chronology . . . It is a good practice to fix in the memory some important eras—the subversion of an empire, for instance—and then ascertain what events were taking place in all other nations, at the same period of time. A few of these parallels, running through the History of the World, will collect rich clusters of knowledge, and arrange them in the conservatory of the mind."[10] The book lists I include are arranged in chronological order for this very reason; it is easier to understand a subject if you begin with its foundational works, and then read systematically through those books that build, one layer at a time, on this foundation.

When to read?

Lydia Sigourney warned her "young ladies" that systematic reading is "peculiarly necessary" to women "because, dwelling much on the contemplation of little things, [we] are in danger of losing the intellectual

[9]Jefferson, "Education of a Future Son-in-Law."
[10]Lydia Sigourney, *Letters to Young Ladies*, 5th ed. (New York: Harper & Brothers, 1839), p. 138.

appetite."[11] Let's be egalitarian: This is equally true of men. We all juggle multiple jobs, housework, bill paying, paperwork, children and family, and dozens of smaller distractions: meals, groceries, email, the ever-present lure of late-night television. The struggle to keep to a self-imposed schedule of reading is often lost in those moments after dinner when the children are in bed, the dishes done, and we think: *I've been working all day. I just need to vegetate for a few minutes before I try to use my brain.* And three hours later we've watched an hour of TV, signed on to check what emails might have come in since lunch, glanced at a couple of favorite Web sites, put in a load of laundry, and wiped off the kitchen sink.

While avoiding apocalyptic pronouncements on the decadence of modern society, I would still suggest that the biggest difference between modern media and the long-enduring book is the way in which TV and the Internet manage to infiltrate themselves into spare moments and promptly swallow up those "chasms of time." I can't say that I've ever lost myself in Plato and looked up an hour and half later to find that the time I intended to devote to answering my email has suddenly disappeared, but I have often spent the time that I meant to dedicate to reading sorting through email spam, checking out links, and (even worse) playing Spider Solitaire on my computer. ("Just one game," I'll think, "to warm up my brain.")

High language about the life of the mind has to yield, at some point, to practical plans for self-cultivation. The mastery of grammar, writing, logic, analysis, and argumentation—all of which I'll cover in chapters to come—depends on the single uncomplicated act of carving out a space within which they can exist. The first task of self-education is not the reading of Plato, but the finding of thirty minutes in which you can devote yourself to thought, rather than to activity.

THE FIRST STEP: SCHEDULE REGULAR READING AND SELF-STUDY TIME

Your first task in self-education is simple: *Set a time for self-education.*

Remember these principles:

Morning is better than evening. "There are portions of the day too when the mind should be eased," Thomas Jefferson wrote to his nephew Thomas Mann Randolph, Jr. "Particularly after dinner it should be applied to lighter occupations." Late evening is far from ideal for the project of reading seriously. It is usually far better to spend thirty minutes reading before

---

[11]Ibid., p. 133.

breakfast than to devote two hours to it in the evening. As the autodidact Benjamin Franklin famously suggested, early to bed and early to rise is the most effective path to wisdom. (The jury remains out on health and wealth.)

Start short. The brain is an organ, and mental exercise, like physical exercise, has to be introduced gradually. Don't leap ambitiously into a schedule that has you rising at five to spend two hours in reading; you're likely to skip it altogether. Start with half an hour of reading first thing in the morning, and develop the habit of sticking to this shorter time of concentration and thought before extending it. And even if you never extend it, you're still doing more reading than you were before you began the project of self-cultivation.

Don't schedule yourself for study every day of the week. The body begins to drag if exercised every day without a break. Aim for four days per week; this makes it possible to establish a habit of reading while giving yourself the weekend "off" and a "flex morning" for the days when you're still catching up with the previous week's paperwork, the plumber arrives at daybreak, the car battery dies, and the toddler develops stomach flu.

Never check your email right before you start reading. I thought this was a personal problem until I ran across several essays in a row—from the *Chronicle of Higher Education*, our local newspaper, and several other equally varied publications—about the distracting qualities of email. There is something in the format of email (its terseness? the sheer volume of messages? its tendency to reward skimming over deep reading?) that pulls the mind away from the contemplative, relaxed frame so important for good reading. If you get good news, you're distracted by it; if someone writes you a nasty note, you'll spend the next forty-five minutes mentally formulating blistering replies rather than concentrating on your book. If no one writes at all, you'll be depressed because you've suddenly become invisible in cyberspace.

Guard your reading time. We do those things which are rewarding to us, and immediate gratification always seems more rewarding than slow progress toward a long-term goal. We live in a world that applauds visible achievement; it will almost always be more satisfying to *do* something (cleaning the garage, clearing out your email box, checking tasks off your to-do list) than to *think*. The clean garage, the empty email box, the completed list: all of these testify to your productiveness, while reading yields no apparent gain. (All you've done is sit still for half an hour and move your eyes, after all.)

The project of self-education will bring your own sense of what is truly worthwhile into sharp relief. Forced to choose between a chapter of

Uncle Tom's Cabin and some more immediately rewarding task, you will come face to face with your deepest values: What do you prize more, a temporary visible accomplishment or the beginnings of a deeper understanding of racial tensions in the United States? A finished to-do list, or a teaspoonful of wisdom?

This is not a small question. The world that applauds visible achievement is giving you a very strong message about why *you* are worthwhile. When you choose to think, rather than do, you are rejecting production in favor of reflection; you are pushing back against a system that wants to locate your worth as a human being in your ability to turn out a commodity. Reading, rather than working, is a small but meaningful dissent.

So resist other satisfactions or duties that encroach on your reading time.

Take the first step now. On your calendar or day timer, schedule four weekly reading periods of half an hour each now. Next week, use this time period to read Chapter 2 and complete the *Second Step* assignment.

Chapter 2

Wrestling with Books: The Act of Reading

And Jacob was left alone; and there wrestled a man with him until the breaking of the day.

—GENESIS 32:24

THE FUTURISTS HAVE long been declaring it: We are a postliterate culture. Books are outdated forms of communication. Soon the flood of information that is now contained in print will all be presented in multimedia formats.

This prediction is only tangentially related to serious *reading*. Gathering data, which is what you do when you skim news headlines, read *People* at the doctor's office, or use a book on plumbing techniques to fix your sink, has already shifted away from print, toward other media.But gathering data and *reading*—understanding ideas and how people act when they try to live by those ideas—are not the same.

When you gather data from a website or book, you use the same mechanical skill as when you engage in serious reading. Your eyes move; the words convey meaning to your mind. Yet your mind itself functions in a different way. When you gather data, you become informed. When you *read*, you develop wisdom—or, in Mortimer Adler's words, "become enlightened." "To be informed," Adler writes in *How to Read a Book*, "is to know simply that something is the case. To be enlightened is to know, in addition, what it is all about." To be informed is to collect facts; to be enlightened is to understand an idea (justice, or charity, or human freedom) and use it to make sense of the facts you've gathered.

When you read the morning news, you may find out that a suicide bomber has just devastated a Gaza marketplace. This is information—a collection of facts. Whether you gather those facts from an online news site, a print source, or CNN's *Headline News* morning show does not significantly change the information, although the medium may slightly alter your experience of it; a skillful montage of bloody survivors, or a website with links to earlier news reports, may arouse your emotions, or associate this particular bombing with others that have happened recently.

But in order to be *enlightened* about the bombing, you must *read seriously*: history, theology, politics, propaganda, editorials. The ideas that impel suicide bombers cannot be gleaned from brief news reports or interactive media. The causes of such desperate actions cannot be made clear to you through a picture and a moving headline while you eat your toast. These things must be expressed with precise and evocative words, assembled into complex, difficult sentences. To be enlightened—to be wise—you must wrestle with these sentences. Technology can do a great deal to make information gathering easier, but it can do little to simplify the gathering of wisdom. Information washes over us like a sea, and recedes without leaving its traces behind. Wrestling with truth, as the story of Jacob warns us, is a time-consuming process that marks us forever.[1]

But I read so slowly; it will take me forever to get through those lists of Great Books! Reading is a lifelong process. There's no hurry, no semester schedule, no end-of-term panic, no final exam. The idea that fast reading is good reading is a twentieth-century weed, springing out of the stony farmland cultivated by the computer manufacturers. As Kirkpatrick Sale has eloquently pointed out, every technology has its own internal ethical system. Steam technology made size a virtue. In the computerized world, faster is better, and speed is the highest virtue of all.[2] When there is a flood of knowledge to be assimilated, the conduits had better flow fast.

But the pursuit of knowledge is centered around a different ethic. The serious reader is not attempting to assimilate a huge quantity of information as quickly as possible, but to understand a few many-sided and elusive ideas. The speed ethic shouldn't be transplanted into an endeavor that is governed by very different ideals.

Speed-reading techniques are not likely to be of enormous help to you

---

[1]Genesis 32: Jacob, wandering along the banks of the Jabbok river in the dark and dreading the prospect of meeting on the next morning his estranged brother Esau (not to mention all of Esau's well-armed followers), meets a man and wrestles with him there until morning. When day breaks, the man touches Jacob's hip and throws it out of joint, leaving him with a limp. Although the mysterious stranger is never unambiguously identified, he gives Jacob a new name—Israel—just as God renamed Abram, earlier in the book; and Jacob himself says, "I saw God face to face, and yet my life was spared." (As with all great literature, it's best to read the original rather than depend on my summary.)
[2]Kirkpatrick Sale, *Rebels Against the Future: The Luddites and Their War on the Industrial Revolution: Lessons for the Computer Age* (New York: Perseus, 1996).

in any case. They center around two primary skills: proper eye movement (keep your eyes moving forward, and learn how to sweep them
across the page diagonally rather than reading each line individually) and
recognition of important words (look for concrete nouns and verbs, and
allow your eye to move more quickly over "filler" words in a sentence).
Peter Kump, the one-time director of education for the grandmama of all
speed-reading courses, Evelyn Wood Reading Dynamics, offers would-be
speed-readers the following principles:

> Rule One: The more abstract words a passage contains, the harder it is
> to read quickly.
> Rule Two: The fewer ideas a passage contains, the easier it is to read
> fast.
> Rule Three: The more prior knowledge of the subject of a written pas-
> sage the reader has, the easier it is to read fast.[3]

How does Aristotle (here, in the *Nicomachean Ethics*, grading the severity of human misconduct) do on this scale?

> [T]here are three kinds of injury. Those that are done in ignorance are
> Mistakes—when the patient or the act or the instrument or the effect was
> different from what the agent supposed, because he either did not mean to
> hit anyone, or not with that missile, or not that person, or not with that
> effect; but the result was different from what he expected (e.g. he only
> meant to give the other a prick, not a wound), or the person or the missile
> was different. When the injury occurs contrary to reasonable expectation
> it is a Misadventure; but when it occurs not contrary to reasonable expec-
> tation but without malicious intent it is a mistake (for the agent makes a
> mistake when the origin of the responsibility lies in himself; when it lies
> outside him his act is a misadventure). When the agent acts knowingly but
> without premeditation it is an Injury; such are all acts due to temper or any
> other of the unavoidable and natural feelings to which human beings are
> liable. For those who commit these injuries and mistakes are doing wrong,
> and their acts are injuries; but this does not of itself make them unjust or
> wicked men, because the harm that they did was not due to malice; it is
> when a man does a wrong on purpose that he is unjust and wicked.[4]

---

[3]Peter Kump, *Break-Through Rapid Reading* (Paramus, N.J.: Prentice Hall Press, 1998),
pp. 212–13.
[4]Aristotle, *Ethics*, trans. J. A. K. Thomson, rev. Hugh Tredennick (New York: Penguin,
1976), pp. 192–93.

This is not a difficult passage to *understand* (although, granted, it lacks a certain snappy appeal; this particular classic is *not* on your reading list). Aristotle is defining the limits of what we might today call "misdemeanors" or "minor crimes" (he cautions the reader that he is not here discussing deliberate evil or purposeful wrongdoing). Perhaps you've broken your neighbor's nose. Assuming you didn't carefully plan the breaking and lie in wait for him, there are three possibilities. You made a Mistake: You took a light swing at your neighbor, just to scare him, but misjudged your own strength and hit him harder than intended (this is a Mistake because the problem lay inside you, in your poor understanding of your own strength). Or perhaps the nose got broken through Misadventure: You intended to hit your neighbor lightly, but he unfortunately tripped just as you were swinging and fell into your fist. (Alas.) Now the real cause of the broken nose is something outside you (the neighbor's stumble). Or you might have committed an Injury: Your neighbor infuriated you, you hauled off and broke his nose in a fit of temper, but once you cooled down you were heartily ashamed of yourself, made amends, and swore never to do such a thing again.

This is an interesting sort of puzzle: If we take it out of the testosterone-charged nose-punching realm and apply it to something academic, like plagiarism, how do we evaluate the student who copies deliberately? unintentionally? out of desperation? On the weightier side: It is also the foundation of much Western law governing the severity of various offenses. Our distinction between murder and manslaughter hinges on whether the death can be classified as Mistake, Misadventure, or Injury (in which case it may be manslaughter), or whether it lies in the realm of deliberate, purposeful wrongdoing.

Could you speed-read this passage?

No; Peter Kump's principles will be of no help to you. The passage has at least four separate ideas in it, not to mention a whole slew of abstract words (*reasonable expectation, malicious intent, premeditation, unavoidable and natural feelings, wicked, wrong*). And unless you're a lawyer, you probably have no prior familiarity with the classification of injuries.

Generally, fiction is easier to read quickly than nonfiction. Even so, speed-reading fiction works just fine when the plot is the thing (James Patterson, say, or Janet Evanovich) but can cheat you out of understanding character-based fiction. In *Pride and Prejudice*, Jane Austen introduces two of her male romantic leads like this:

Mr Bingley was good looking and gentlemanlike; he had a pleasant countenance, and easy, unaffected manners. His sisters were fine women, with an air of decided fashion. His brother-in-law, Mr Hurst, merely looked the gentleman; but his friend Mr Darcy soon drew the attention of the room by his fine, tall person, handsome features, noble mien; and the report which was in general circulation within five minutes after his entrance, of his having ten thousand a year. The gentlemen pronounced him to be a fine figure of a man, the ladies declared he was much handsomer than Mr Bingley, and he was looked at with great admiration for about half the evening, till his manners gave a disgust which turned the tide of his popularity; for he was discovered to be proud, to be above his company, and above being pleased; and not all his large estate in Derbyshire could then save him from having a most forbidding, disagreeable countenance, and being unworthy to be compared with his friend.[5]

Austen's prose isn't as loaded with abstractions as Aristotle's, but nevertheless Austen introduces two quite separate ideas in this single paragraph: that a man's fortune makes him handsomer to the onlooker, and that manners (themselves a separate idea, defined elsewhere) are even more important than money.

Speed-reading techniques are most useful when pure information is offered, as in (for example) an article from a 2001 *People* magazine, marveling over the actress Jenna Elfman's deceptive youthfulness at the advanced age of twenty-nine:

As she approaches 30, Elfman has found her comfort zone. Her show *Dharma & Greg* is a hit. She and husband Bodhi, 32, have been happily married for six years. And the 5′10″ Elfman likes what she sees when she looks in the mirror. "If you're feeling good about your marriage and career, you're going to look okay," she has said. Elfman definitely does. "She enjoys her life," says her makeup artist Ann Masterson. "She's very secure with who she is." . . . To keep her body toned, Elfman takes ballet lessons at her home three times a week, studies yoga, drinks about 100 oz. of water a day, gets plenty of sleep, and tries to avoid sugar. And if she's sweating getting older, she isn't showing it. "I don't think it matters to her," says . . . director Peter Chesholm. "She still has such a great child within her."[6]

There might (debatably) be an idea (sort of) in that last line, but apart from this the passage is loaded with concrete nouns and verbs (and mea-

[5]Jane Austen, *Pride and Prejudice*, chapter 4.
[6]Susan Horsburgh, Sonja Steptoe, and Julie Dam, "Staying Sexy at 30, 40, 50, 60," *People*, vol. 56, no. 6 (August 6, 2001): 61.

surements). It certainly isn't necessary for you to read every line from beginning to end, and if you glance over it and identify the main words— *30, comfort zone, Dharma and Greg, hit, husband, happily married, mirror, body toned*—you can grasp the passage's import without bothering with the little words.

But in Aristotle and Austen, the little words are *important*. "This does not of itself make them unjust or wicked men, because the harm that they did was not due to malice": Without "of itself" and "due to," the sentence loses its exact meaning.

Three insights offered by the speed-reading experts may be of some use to you. First: The average reader doesn't simply move her eyes from left to right across the page. She continually glances back at what she's already read, and then skips her eyes forward again to find her place. Sometimes this is an important part of understanding; in reading the passage from Aristotle's *Ethics*, you might find yourself glancing back at the definition of Mistake as you read about Misadventure, in order to keep the difference clear in your mind. But often this compulsive backtracking becomes a bad habit that slows you down unnecessarily. Putting your finger on the page and moving it as you read can help you become conscious of whether you've formed this habit; try it first with simple prose, and see whether your eyes tend to leap backward and forward away from the point marked by your finger.

Second: When reading a difficult passage, you may find it helpful to make an initial sweep with your eyes over a paragraph, looking for concrete nouns, action verbs, and capitalized letters, before settling down to read it from beginning to end. When scanning a paragraph in this way, try to follow a Z-shaped pattern down and across the page. A scan of the passage from the *Ethics* would give you the words *Mistake, Misadventure*, and *Injury* (which, in the Penguin edition, are capitalized); the words *ignorance, malicious, premeditation,* and *feelings* might also stand out to your eye. Even before reading, then, you know that Aristotle will be distinguishing three kinds of errors, and that human intention will have something to do with the classification. Now your "slow reading" of the passage will probably be a little more effective.

Third: Peter Kump's Rule Three ("The more prior knowledge of the subject of a written passage the reader has, the easier it is to read fast") should encourage you: serious reading, difficult at the beginning, gets easier and easier. The lists in this book are organized chronologically and by subject, so that whether you choose History or Poetry, you'll begin with the earliest works on the subject. These are likely to be the most difficult because you're not familiar with the conventions of the field, with its peculiar vocabulary, the structure of its arguments, the information it takes for granted. (And neither was anyone else, when those foundational works were written.) But as you continue to read books in the same field, you'll find the same arguments, the same vocabulary, the same preoccupations, again and again. Each time you'll move through them more quickly and with more assurance. You will read faster and with greater retention—not because of a mechanical trick, but because you are educating your mind.

THE SECOND STEP:
PRACTICE THE MECHANICS OF READING

If you have difficulty with the actual act of reading, you may need to do some remedial skill work before tackling the *Iliad*. Try this diagnostic test: Glance at your watch's second hand, note the time, and then read the passage below at your normal speed.

> Books which we have first read in odd places always retain their charm, whether read or neglected. Thus Hazlitt always remembered that it was on the 10th of April, 1798, that he "sat down to a volume of the *New Eloise* at the Inn of Llangollen over a bottle of sherry and a cold chicken." In the same way I remember how Professor Longfellow in college recommended to us, for forming a good French style, to read Balzac's *Peau de Chagrin*; and yet it was a dozen years later before I found it in a country inn, on a lecture trip and sat up half the night to read it. It may be, on the other hand, that such haphazard meetings with books sometimes present them under conditions hopelessly unfavorable, as when I encountered Whitman's *Leaves of Grass* for the first time on my first voyage in an Azorian barque; and it inspires to this day a slight sense of nausea, which it might, after all, have inspired equally on land.[7]

Look again at your watch. How long did it take you to read this passage? Count the unfamiliar words in this passage. How many did you find? If you don't know what a *barque* is, can you figure it out from context? What is Higginson's point?

If it took you a minute or less to read this passage, you are already reading at an appropriate speed for serious prose. If you found no more than ten unfamiliar words in this passage, your vocabulary is already at the so-called tenth-grade literacy level, which means that you are technically capable of reading anything that's written for an intelligent layperson.

---

[7]Thomas Wentworth Higginson, "Books Unread," *Atlantic Monthly*, March 1904.

If you guessed that a barque is a kind of boat, you know how to gather
clues for unfamiliar vocabulary words from context. And if you managed
to figure out (unfamiliar proper names notwithstanding) that Higginson
thinks that the conditions under which you first read a book are likely to
affect the way you remember that book thereafter, you know how to grasp
the main idea of a paragraph.

If it took you more than a minute to read this brief passage, and you
found more than ten unfamiliar words, you would do well to review your
actual mechanical reading skills (see below). Otherwise, you don't need
to do any remedial work.

Did it take you more than one minute to read the diagnostic passage? Extremely
slow readers may be victims of poor early teaching. If you were taught
to read by pure word-recognition methods (in which children learn each
individual word by sight, rather than being taught how to "sound out" the
word by pronouncing each letter or combination of letters), you may be
recognizing the shape of each word as you read.[8] Although many readers
are able to do this fairly quickly, others can't. And since "sight reading"
depends on repeated exposure to a word before you can reliably recognize and remember it, "sight readers" can have great difficulty with more
complex reading that contains a number of unfamiliar words. If you are
both a slow reader and a poor speller, you're probably guessing at the
meanings of words from their shapes, rather than truly recognizing and
understanding them; you're unable to spell because you have no memory of the letters in each word (instead you're just guessing at the word's
meaning because of its shape). You may be able to improve your reading
speed by working through a remedial phonics text such as *Phonics Pathways*, which will retrain you to read words from left to right, decoding
them by sounding them out. This will allow you to recognize unfamiliar
words more quickly (and will probably improve your spelling as well).

---

[8]I have no wish to reopen the phonics versus whole-language debate here; Jessie Wise
and I treat this at greater length in our book *The Well-Trained Mind: A Guide to Classical Education at Home*. Briefly, though: The best reading programs combine phonetic
"decoding" skills (in which children are taught the sounds of letters and letter combina-
tions as the first step in reading) with plenty of reading and oral language work ("whole
language" techniques). However, if you learned to read sometime between 1930 and
1970, you were most likely taught *pure* "sight recognition" with no phonetic decoding at
all (and although phonics began to return to favor in the late 1960s, plenty of classrooms
from 1970 to the present have eliminated phonetic skills completely from their reading
programs). If you learned to read through "sight methods" and are having trouble reading, the method obviously didn't work for you; you will benefit by learning the phonetic
decoding skills that you missed back in first grade.

Use the first fifteen minutes of your scheduled reading time each day to work on remedial phonics skills until you finish the book.

Did you find the vocabulary of the passage overwhelming? A vocabulary-building course will increase your mental store of words and will speed up your reading, since you won't have to pause as often to puzzle over unfamiliar words. *Wordly Wise 3000* (published by the respected educational press Educators Publishing Service) covers over three thousand frequently occurring words, chosen to bring your vocabulary up to twelfth-grade level. Each lesson contains fifteen words, along with exercises aimed to help you use words correctly in context. The series begins at primary level and goes through high school. Most adult readers should probably start with Book 6, although you could back up to Book 5 if you feel truly ill prepared. There is a shift in difficulty between Books 5 and 6; the analogies become more difficult, and the reading exercises much more complex.

The *Vocabulary from Classical Roots* series, also from Educators Publishing Service, is a good follow-up to *Wordly Wise.* As a matter of fact, many readers (not just those doing remedial work) may find this series helpful in preparing to read classic literature. Each lesson gives several Greek or Latin roots, lists of familiar words using those roots, and lists of unfamiliar words along with exercises in proper use. The five books in the series (A, B, C, D, and E) are all on the same level of difficulty, but they progress from the most familiar roots to those less frequently used. In Book A, for example, you'll get *duo,* the Latin root meaning "two," along with *duplicity* and *duplicate*; in Book E, you'll get *umbra,* the Latin for "shade, shadow," along with the vocabulary words *umbrage* and *adumbrate.*

As with remedial phonics, use the first fifteen minutes of your scheduled reading time each day to work on these vocabulary skills.

Do you want to improve your reading speed? Read the first section of Chapter 3 and practice moving your finger from left to right. Do your eyes tend to jump backward from your finger, even when you understand what you've already read? If so, you should spend several weeks using your finger to read, in order to retrain your eyes to move forward. Remember that it's always fine to look back for *content*—but you don't want your eyes to skip backward out of habit.

RECOMMENDED RESOURCES

Dolores G. Hiskes, *Phonics Pathways: Clear Steps to Easy Reading and Perfect Spelling,* 10th ed. (Jossey-Bass, 2011).

Kenneth Hodkinson, Sandra Adams, and Cheryl Dressler, *Wordly Wise 3000: Systematic Academic Vocabulary Development,* 3rd ed. (Educators Publishing Service, 2012). Books 5, 6, 7, 8, 9, 10, 11, 12.

Norma Fifer, Nancy Flowers, and Lee Mountain, *Vocabulary from Classical Roots*, 3rd ed. (Educators Publishing Service, 1998). Books A, B, C, D, and E.

Chapter 3

Keeping the Journal:
A Written Record of New Ideas

Once a day . . . call yourselves to an account what new ideas, what
new proposition or truth you have gained, what further confirmation
of known truths, and what advances you have made in any part of
knowledge.

—Isaac Watts,
Improvement of the Mind

For years I've read Agatha Christie at bedtime. Christie's
prose doesn't exactly sing, and by now I know how every single mystery
ends. But I can read these books over and over again, because I'm using
only half my brain, while the other half recycles the events of the day and
tucks them away, one by one. I don't gain much from the book itself, but
I sleep well.

The same half-attentive method of reading dogs me when I turn to
serious literature. I read; a door slams; my attention wanders to the door,
to the window, to undone jobs, to family dilemmas and work difficulties.
I am not alone in this; our lives are full, and so are our minds. David Denby's lyrical complaint in *Great Books* is true of us all:

I can no longer *submit* to fiction . . . I read and stop, read and stop, a train
halted by obstacles on the track, bad weather, power failures. Everyone
complains that young people, growing up on TV, movies, video games,
and rap music, lack the patience for long, complex, written narratives, and
yet as a child I had not watched all that much television, and I had also
lost my patience in middle age . . . [M]y life had grown much more complex. I was married to a clever and formidable woman, and there were two
kids running around; I had multiple jobs and a lot more to think about

than I had had at eighteen. A much larger experience was now casting up its echoes.[1]

When we sit in front of Plato or Shakespeare or Conrad, "simply reading" isn't enough. We must learn to fix our minds, to organize our reading so that we are able to retain the skeleton of the ideas that pass in front of our eyes. We must not simply read, Isaac Watts tells us, but "meditate and study," an act that "transfers and conveys the notions and sentiments of others to ourselves, so as to make them properly our own."

How is this done? By keeping a journal to organize your thoughts about your reading. What we write, we remember. What we summarize in our own words becomes our own.

For earlier generations, the journal wasn't—as it is in modern times—primarily a tool to reflect on your feelings. Present-day use of the word *journal* tends to imply that you're creating a subjective, intensively inward-focused collection of thoughts and musings. Witness, for example, the ideas and exercises offered in a sample issue of the magazine *Personal Journaling:* travel journaling ("Which traditions or customs are you comfortable with and which make you uneasy? Why?"), dream journaling ("What does this dream tell me about the way I treat myself?"), creative journaling ("Focus on a specific topic and write everything you can think of, never lifting your pen"), and mind-body journaling ("The wise teacher is within you, and through writing you can begin to 'hear' her more clearly"). (*Personal Journaling* also tells you how to make decorative handmade paper with newsprint, dryer lint, and a blender, should you wish to make your journal an *objet d'art* as well as a diary.)

But the journal of self-education has a more outward focus. It is modeled on the last century's "commonplace book," a looseleaf or bound blank book in which readers copied down quotes and snippets that they wanted to remember.

In its simplest form, the commonplace book was a handmade *Bartlett's Familiar Quotations*, a memory aid for the writer. Many commonplace books contained nothing but these quotes. They may be instructive for what the writer chooses to record; Jefferson's college-days *Commonplace Book* contains, among other quotations, Euripedes' observation "Alas, no one among mortals is free; for either he is the slave of wealth or fortune, or else the populace or legal technicalities compel him to resort to practices

[1]David Denby, *Great Books: My Adventures with Homer, Rousseau, Woolf, and Other Indestructible Writers of the Western World* (New York: Simon & Schuster, 1996), p. 47.

that are contrary to his belief." Commonplace books reveal, as Gilbert Chinard remarks on Jefferson's own collections, the extent to which "the study of the classics was . . . an essential part in the moral foundation of many of the men who framed the American institutions."[2] But these traditional commonplace books contain no musings on the collected quotes, no clue to the writer's thoughts as he copied Euripedes or Plato onto the page. The personal aspect is missing.

Occasionally, though, commonplace books took on a more personalized form. Their authors carried them around and jotted in them at odd moments during the day. The commonplace books gathered reflections, scraps of original verse and other creative writing, and summaries of books read, as well as the *de rigueur* bits of copied information. They became artificial memories.

The journal used for self-education should model itself after this expanded type of commonplace book. It is neither an unadorned collection of facts, nor an entirely inward account of what's going on in your heart and soul. Rather, the journal is the place where the reader takes external information and records it (through the use of quotes, as in the commonplace book); appropriates it through a summary, written in the reader's own words; and then evaluates it through reflection and personal thought. As you read, you should follow this three-part process: jot down specific phrases, sentences, and paragraphs as you come across them; when you've finished your reading, go back and write a brief summary about what you've learned; and then write your own reactions, questions, and thoughts.

In this way, the journal connects objective and subjective learning, an ideal described by Bronson Alcott in his own journal of 1834:

> Education is that process by which thought is opened out of the soul, and, associated with outward . . . things, is reflected back upon itself, and thus made conscious of its reality and shape. It is Self-Realization. . . . He who is seeking to know himself, should be ever seeking himself in external things, and by so doing will he be best able to find, and explore his inmost light.[3]

The goal of classical self-education is this: not merely to "stuff" facts into your head, but to understand them. Incorporate them into your mental

[2] Gilbert Chinard, introduction to *The Literary Bible of Thomas Jefferson: His Commonplace Book of Philosophers* (Baltimore: Johns Hopkins University Press, 1928), p. 4.
[3] Amos Bronson Alcott, *The Journals of Bronson Alcott*, ed. Odell Shepard (Boston: Little, Brown and Co., 1938), p. 43.

framework. Reflect on their meaning for the internal life. The "external things"—be they Platonic philosophy, the actions of an Austen heroine, or a political biography—make us more conscious of our own "reality and shape." This, not mere accumulation, is the goal of self-education. The journal is the place where this learning happens.

The first step toward understanding is to grasp exactly what is being said, and the oldest and most reliable way of grasping information is to put it into your own words. To master the content of what you read, summarize.

Lydia Sigourney advises her young female readers to summarize their reading often:

> At the close of every week, abridge in writing, the subjects that you deem most valuable. . . . Write them neatly in a book kept for that purpose—but not in the language of the author. . . . Let this be a repository of condensed knowledge, the pure gold of thought. . . . To strengthen the memory, the best course is not to commit page after page verbatim [as though most of us would!], but to give the substance of the author, correctly and clearly in your own language.[4]

The journal should contain, first, the "substance" of what has been read.

These summaries often provide a jumping-off point for further reflections; E. M. Forster's *Commonplace Book* is just such an autodidact's journal. "Far more than a dictionary-defined compendium of striking 'quotations, poems and remarks,'" writes Philip Gardner, the editor of the version of the *Commonplace Book* published after Forster's death, "[I]t provides a commentary—sharp, wry, and frequently very moving—on the second half of Forster's life." Forster records snippets of his own reading:

> *Proverbs*
> He that blesseth his friend with a loud voice, rising early in the morning, it shall be counted a curse to him. XXVII 14
> As in water face answereth to face, so the heart of man to man. XXVII 19
> Now all is done, save what shall have no end.
> —Shakespeare, Sonnet 110, Tyrwhitt's emendation.[5]

He evaluates his reading, recording his criticisms:

[4]Sigourney, *Letters to Young Ladies*, pp. 54–55, 145.
[5]E. M. Forster, *Commonplace Book*, ed. Philip Gardner (Stanford, Calif.: Stanford University Press, 1985), p. 139.

Hedda Gabler fails because nothing of importance has been changed. . . .
However Ibsen may have known this as well as me and have desired to stage
absolute unimportance as his heroine. He certainly wishes to show her as
cowardly, restless, and weak.[6]

The personal certainly isn't missing in Forster's *Commonplace Book*. In 1947
he jots down, apropos of nothing:

The evening sky behind Fellows' Building. A cone of cloud . . . mottled with pink and gold—both faint, and the word mottled is too strong.
Immensely large aesthetically speaking. I have no idea of its linear measurement.[7]

And in 1953, recovering from a visit to the dentist, he writes:

Writers ought to write and I take up my pen in the hope it may loosen
my spirit. . . . It is 6.45. Feb. 26th. . . .Tony Hyndman has been in. . . . I
was not very friendly to him, I did not want to be bothered, and was not
warm-hearted. . . . It is 7:30. Cannot writers write quicker? I have been
"thinking."[8]

This is very close to the "creative journaling" of *Personal Journaling*. But
more often than not, the personal is anchored to some phrase or idea that
has struck Forster in his reading. He muses, for example, on a line from
Thomas Gray:

When Thomas Gray writes, "I know what it is to lose a person that one's
eyes and heart have long been used to . . ." I recognize an affinity. Laziness
and loyalty have a connection.[9]

And Forster's methods of summarizing and evaluating his reading exactly
demonstrate the purpose of the classical journal. In 1942, Forster has just
finished reading Thomas Hodgkin's *Italy and Her Invaders 376–476*. His
journal entry reads, in part:

Why did Rome fall? . . .

[6]Ibid., p. 36.
[7]Ibid., p. 174.
[8]Ibid., p. 192.
[9]Ibid., pp. 179–80.

Subsidiary causes were

i. *The foundation of Constantinople*, due to fear of Persia: danger from the north never realised. "It was the diffusion of her vital force over several nerve centers, Carthage, Antioch, Alexandria, but above all Constantinople that ruined her. Some of the old tree perished."

ii. *Christianity*—despite St. Augustine's view. For it opposed the deification of the Emperor which consecrated the state. . . ."[10]

He concludes his summary of the reading, and then adds his own thoughts:

My original impulse in this excursion was the discovery of parallels, then I was diverted into interest in the past, now that too is flagging, and I have driven myself with difficulty to finish this analysis. My ignorance and the powerlessness of knowledge weigh on me. . . ."[11]

This is a model of the summarizing that Sigourney recommends. Here Forster restates the main points of his reading in his own words, quotes word for word where Hodgkin supplies a succinct sentence of his own, connects each of Hodgkin's points to the woes of the present day, and then adds a heartfelt commentary on his own emotional reactions to the crumpling of great empires.

Thomas Merton followed a similar strategy in keeping his own notebooks. In *The Asian Journal*, collected from the notebooks kept during the last part of his life, we find, in the span of three pages, quotes copied from T. R. V. Murti's *The Central Philosophy of Buddhism* ("Reflective consciousness is necessarily the consciousness of the false"), a record of Merton's morning walk ("I walked and said Lauds under the croptomeria trees on Observatory Hill, and the chanting came up strong and clear from below. A man was doing vigorous exercises by the shelter that overlooks the valley . . . shimmying in the sun"), and Merton's own summary of his reading, incorporating direct quotes ("Conze comments on the fact that communication between East and West has not so far done much for philosophy. 'So far European and particularly British philosophers have reacted by becoming more provincial than ever before'").[12]

Classical self-education demands that you understand, evaluate, and react to ideas. In your journal, you will record your own summaries

---

[10]Ibid., p. 139.
[11]Ibid., p. 141.
[12]Thomas Merton, *The Asian Journal of Thomas Merton*, ed. Naomi Burton, Brother Patrick Hart, and James Laughlin (New York: New Directions, 1973), pp. 139–41.

of your reading; this is your tool for understanding the ideas you read. This—the mastery of facts—is the first stage of classical education.

THE THIRD STEP: PRACTICE TAKING NOTES AS YOU WRITE AND THEN SUMMARIZING

"If we would fix in the memory the discourses we hear," Watts writes, "or what we design to speak, let us abstract them into brief compends, and review them often." As the next step in your self-education, practice this skill with this book.

1. Invest in a journal: looseleaf notebook, blank book, or other type of journal.

2. Continue to keep to your schedule of reading four times per week. Use this time to read Chapter 4, jotting down notes and then writing brief summaries. Follow these guidelines:

 a. Write the title of the chapter on the first page of your notebook. Read through the entire chapter once without stopping. If any particular ideas, phrases, or sentences strike you, go ahead and jot them down.

 b. Chapter 4 is divided into three major sections. Try to summarize each section in your own words. Ask yourself: What is the most important point that the writer makes in this section? If I could remember only one thing from this section, what would it be? Now, what else does the writer tell me about this important point that I'd like to remember? Make the summary for each section a separate paragraph. Leave very wide margins (two to three inches) on either side of your paragraphs.

 c. When you have done this for the entire chapter, glance back over your summary paragraphs. Now write down your reactions to the information in each summary. Use the margins of your paper for this (a different pen color is also helpful).

Chapter 4

Starting to Read:
Final Preparations

If you are fortunate, you encounter a particular teacher who can help,
yet finally you are alone, going on without further mediation.
—Harold Bloom,
How to Read and Why

IN THE END, there's not much a book can do for you: You must
begin to read.

What a book (like this one) *can* do is hold your hand up to the point
where you start reading. Most of all, a how-to-read book can assure you
that the difficulty you have in reading doesn't necessarily reflect on your
mental ability. Serious reading is hard work.

This should comfort you. If successful reading is a matter of innate
intelligence, you can do little to improve yourself. But a task that is merely
difficult can be broken down into small and manageable steps, and mastered through diligent effort. Reading the Great Books is no different.

The initial small step is simple: Rather than making a sweeping determination to tackle the Great Books (all of them), decide to begin on one
of the reading lists in Part II. As you read each book, you'll follow the pattern of the *trivium*. First you'll try to understand the book's basic structure
and argument; next, you'll evaluate the book's assertions; finally, you'll
form an opinion about the book's ideas.

You'll have to exercise these three skills of reading—understanding,
analysis, and evaluation—differently for each kind of book. If you want
to evaluate a history, you must ask whether the historian's conclusions are
supported by the historical facts he or she offers, whether there is enough
information, and whether this information is trustworthy. If you want to
judge a novel, you should instead ask whether it leads you along a path
whose end is different than its beginning, whether its characters have

motivations and ambitions and hang-ups that are recognizably human, and whether those motivations and ambitions and hang-ups give rise to the novel's crises and situations. To assess a science book, you would ask: What phenomena did the writer seek to explain? How did he observe those phenomena? (With his own eyes, by way of mathematical calculation, by deduction from what *could* be seen?) Is his explanation sufficient? If not, how (or when) does it fall short?

These three sets of criteria stem from the same general impulse: to ask whether the work is *accurate*. Is it *right*? (Or, to use Mortimer Adler's more loaded word, is it *true*?) But they are as different in practice as the criteria used to judge a Renaissance portrait and those used to evaluate a twentieth-century landscape or a twenty-first-century installation.

So consider the following as general principles for reading, principles that will be expanded and altered in the chapters that follow.

1. When you first read through a book, don't feel that you have to grasp completely every point that the writer is making. If you find yourself puzzled by a certain section, or not completely sure what the author means by a particular term, turn down the corner of the page and keep on going. You'll have a chance to come back to that confusing section later on. The secret to reading a difficult book is simply this: Keep reading. You don't have to "get it all" the very first time through.

In the case of fiction, you may feel overwhelmed by a welter of unfamiliar names, but if you persevere (without feeling that you have to stop and sort everything out immediately), you'll find that by the third or fourth chapter you have come to know the central characters, almost imperceptibly; those who are not important will have faded offstage. In a work of serious nonfiction, you will become more familiar as the chapters progress with the author's favorite terms and phrases; you'll begin to gather a broad, vague, even inarticulate idea of what she's up to. Don't stop to look up unfamiliar words unless you absolutely have to. Don't use scholarly editions, packed with critical footnotes that stop you dead every time you hit a little superscript number. Don't fret over missing the nuances. Get the big picture, the broad sweep, the beginning, middle, and end. "Understanding half of a really tough book," writes Mortimer Adler in his classic *How to Read a Book*, "is much better than not understanding it at all, which will be the case if you allow yourself to be stopped by the first difficult passage you come to." In truth, it's impossible to fully understand difficult passages until you know how they fit into the rest of the writer's *schema*.

So the first stage of reading should be a liberating one. Just read, and keep reading.

Your first reading is your handshake with the book; your goal is to finish with a surface acquaintance that will deepen into true understanding as you read again to evaluate and analyze. If you don't understand what you're reading, don't stop; scribble a question mark in the margin, and keep going. You may well find that the earlier chapters of a book, confusing on first reading, suddenly make sense to you as you reach the book's middle or end.

2. Underline in your books, jot notes in the margins, and turn the corners of your pages down. Public education is a beautiful dream, but public classrooms too often train students not to mark, write in, disfigure, or in any way make books permanently their own. You're a grownup now, so buy your own books if you possibly can. In my opinion, a cheap paperback filled with your own notes is worth five times as much as a beautiful collector's edition.

If you know that you can turn down the corner of a confusing page and keep reading, or write a question in the margin and continue on, you'll find it easier to keep going on the first reading. If you have to use library books, invest in adhesive-backed notes (such as Post-its) and use them to mark pages that you'll want to return to; scribble your notes and questions on them. Bits of paper tend to fall out, though, and any good book will soon look like a papery porcupine. Defacing your book is much more efficient.

Ereaders are perfectly fine—but only if you're comfortable with the reader's notation and marking tools. If you find them unusable, go back to the archaic paperback-and-ballpoint-pen method.

3. When you first begin to read a book, read the title page, the copy on the back cover, and the table of contents. This puts you "in the picture" before you begin to read. Do *not* automatically read the preface. In the case of a nonfiction book, the preface may set the book in context for you, summarize the argument, or tell you just why the book is so important—certainly valuable information to have before you begin to read. But the preface can also give you a fully formed interpretation before you even read the book—something to be avoided. For example, E. V. Rieu's preface to his translation of the *Iliad* sums up the plot, tells you about Homer's use of delayed action, and explains briefly how the reader should understand Homer's similes and epithets. This makes the reading of the *Iliad* more rewarding, not less. But Anita Brookner's introduction to the Scribner edition of Edith Wharton's *The House of Mirth*, excellent though it is in itself, gives you a thumbnail sketch of the heroine's charac-

ter and motivations—something you should do yourself before turning to an expert to do it for you.

Generally, you should read the preface only if it has been written by the author (or translator) personally. If the preface or introduction was written by someone else, skip it. Read the first chapter of the book instead, and if you aren't lost or confused, keep on going; save the reading of the preface until you've finished reading the book itself. If the first chapter befuddles you, go back and read the preface before going on.

4. Don't take extensive notes on a first reading. First-reading notes tend to be far too detailed. You'll find yourself writing down many observations that seem important but later prove to be irrelevant, and all the note taking will slow you down. Instead, stop at the end of each chapter (or substantial section) to jot down a sentence—two at the most—in your journal. These sentences should summarize the chapter's content, main assertion, or most important event. But remember: You're constructing a broad outline, not a specific one. You're laying down the strokes of a coloring page, not drawing a careful sketch. Leave out details, even the important ones: "Paris and Menelaus decide to fight a duel to settle the war, but when Menelaus gets the upper hand, Aphrodite whisks Paris back to his own safe bedroom" is a good first-reading summary of the third chapter of the *Iliad*, even though it leaves out plenty of important details. (These summaries also make it easier to come back to a long and complicated book if your reading schedule has been disrupted and you can't remember what happened to Don Quixote in Chapter 7 by the time you reach Chapter 43.)

5. As you read, use your journal to jot down questions that come to your mind. Record your disagreements or agreements with the writer. Scribble down any reflections or connected thoughts that the book brings to your mind. These questions, disagreements, and reflections should be visually distinct from your summary of the book's content. You can write your summaries in a narrow column down the middle of your journal page and jot your remarks on the margins, or use one color pen for summary sentences and another for reflections, or keep separate pages for summaries and remarks. Try to note page numbers beside your comments, since you may want to go back and reread some sections of the book later on.

6. When you've finished your first reading, go back and assemble your summary sentences into an informal outline, an initial "table of contents."

You don't yet have enough information to make a real outline, with some points made subordinate to others; all you need to do is arrange the sentences in order.

7. Now give the book a title (four to seven words) and a subtitle.

These won't be like the titles on the jacket, which were selected at least in part for eye-friendly euphony. Instead, the title should be a phrase that describes the book's main subject, while the subtitle should sum up the book's most important points. Aim for a title and subtitle like those of the seventeenth century: *The pilgrim's progress from this world to that which is to come: delivered under the similitude of a dream, wherein is discovered the manner of his setting out, his dangerous journey, and safe arrival at the desired country.* Seventeenth-century writers knew that a title which told the reader exactly what was about to happen was the best way to guarantee understanding. So give your book a short title—three or four words that seem to sum up the topic—and then write a subtitle that explains exactly what the book does.

Now you've completed the first and most intimidating task of the reader: You've gotten all the way through the book. Your first reading has given you a basic understanding of the book's parts and how they fit together. Don't worry too much if this series of steps seemed laborious and complicated; they will soon become second nature to you, an intuitive first approach to any difficult book.

You're ready for the second and third stages of inquiry.

Although you'll folllow the same basic steps in the grammar-stage (inital) reading of most books, the second stage of inquiry—the logic-stage evaluation—differs enormously from genre to genre. Poetry and history may not be worlds apart, but they're certainly located in different hemispheres, and science may well be orbiting on a minor moon.

The reader needs to approach each *kind* of book—each list in Chapters 5 through 10—with a distinct set of questions, a unique expectation. But the logic-stage *procedure* doesn't change. No matter what questions you ask, you'll always progress into the second stage of inquiry by doing the following:

1. Go back and reread those sections of the book that you identified as difficult. Can you make better sense of them, now that you've arrived at the book's end? Look back through your written comments: Do they tend to cluster around certain parts of the book? If so, glance back through those pages as well. Finally, reread your summaries. Can you identify

which chapter contains the book's climax, the center of the writer's argument, or the author's own summary of his work? Reread that particular section of the book as well.

2. Dig deeper into the book's structure: Answer questions about how the writer has put his words together. The chapters that follow suggest questions for each genre. Jot your answers down in your notebook. Cite particular sentences, even paragraphs. These notes can be more detailed than those first-reading notes, since by this point you should have a clearer idea of which parts of the book are most worthy of your attention.

3. Ask: Why did the author write this book? What did he or she set out to do? Lay out facts, convince you of the truth in a set of deductions, give you an emotional experience? (We'll discuss this for each genre separately.)

4. Now ask: How well did the writer succeed? Did he successfully carry out his intention? If not, why? Where did he fall short? Are his facts unproven, his proofs inadequate, or his emotional scenes flat? What parts of the book did I find convincing; which ones left me unmoved?

As you continue to use your journal for this process, the pages will begin to reflect not only the content of the books you're reading, but the development of your own thought as you grapple with the books' ideas. Remember that the goal of grammar-stage reading is to know *what* the author says; the goal of logic-stage inquiry is to understand *why* and *how*.

The final stage of reading—your rhetoric-stage pass through the book—has a third goal. Now you know *what, why* and *how*. The final question is: *So what?*

What does this writer want me to do?

What does this writer want me to believe?

What does this writer want me to experience?

Am I convinced that I must do, or believe, what the writer wants me to do or believe?

Have I experienced what the writer wants me to experience?

If not, *why?*

Uninformed opinions are easy to come by. But thinking through someone else's argument, agreeing with it for specific, well-articulated reasons, or disagreeing with it because you're able to find holes in the writer's argument, or because the writer left out facts which he should have considered and didn't—that's difficult. The rhetoric stage follows the logic stage for this very reason. The good reader bases his opinion on intelligent analysis, not mere reaction.

The journal is an excellent logic-stage tool. But in the rhetoric stage of inquiry, you need something more. Rhetoric is the art of clear, persuasive communication, and persuasion always involves two people. In your case, one of these people is the book's author: The book is communicating an idea to you, persuading you of something. But for you to articulate your own ideas clearly back to the book, you need to bring someone else into the process.

How can you do this? In her *Letters to Young Ladies*, Lydia Sigourney praises the virtues of "purposeful conversation," talk centered around particular ideas. In the nineteenth century, women often met in "weekly societies" to discuss their reading—the forerunners of today's popular book groups. These discussions, Sigourney suggests, are essential to proper self-education, since they "serve to fix knowledge firmly in the memory."[1]

The problem with book groups (as you know if you've ever been in one) is that the readers who attend them don't always read the book carefully (or at all), and unless someone takes a dictatorial hand during discussion, it's apt to wander off fairly quickly into unrelated chat. For the project of self-education, it's best to find one other person who will agree to read through the Great Books lists with you and then talk with you about what both of you have read.

This reading partner, indispensable in the final stage of reading, can also be useful to you in the first two. During the grammar and logic stages, your partner provides you with some accountability—if you've agreed to finish the first reading of a book by a particular deadline and you know someone else will be checking on you, you're much more likely to make good use of your own reading time to actually finish the book.

During your rhetoric-stage inquiry, when you'll be looking back through the book for answers to questions about the writer's ideas, your reading partner can talk to you about those ideas. Perhaps something that you found troublesome, or illogical, was entirely clear to your reading partner; discuss the differences, and discover which one of you is correct. You may find that the disagreement is only an apparent one, brought about by the use of different words for the same concept. Or you may realize that an apparent agreement between the two of you dissolves during discussion, perhaps because you are using the same words to represent very different things. A reading partner forces you to use words precisely and define your terms.

Ideally, your reading partner will read at more or less the same speed as you do, and can devote the same hours to the project of reading. But

[1]Sigourney, *Letters to Young Ladies*, p. 147.

it isn't necessary for you to come from similar backgrounds, educational or otherwise. As a matter of fact, a reading partner with a very different background can help you to think more precisely, as you discover that you need to explain, clearly, ideas that you've always taken for granted.

If you don't have a reading partner who can meet with you face to face, you can conduct discussions by letter (or email, as long as you treat these dialogues as formal, requiring proper vocabulary, grammar, spelling, and punctuation, not resorting to the shorthand of e-communication). In 1814, Thomas Jefferson, obviously feeling isolated on his Virginia mountaintop, wrote to John Adams that Plato is

> one of the race of genuine sophists, who has escaped the oblivion of his brethren, first, by the elegance of his diction, but chiefly, by the adoption and incorporation of his whimsies into the body of artificial Christianity. His foggy mind is forever presenting the semblances of objects which, half seen through a mist, can be defined neither in form nor dimensions. . . . But why am I dosing you with these antediluvian topics? Because I am glad to have some one to whom they are familiar, and who will not receive them as if dropped from the moon.[2]

Like-minded neighbors are providential, but there are advantages to conducting rhetoric-stage discussions by letter. You can file your letters and their answers as informal essays, and glance back through them to refresh your memory about the books you've read (and publish them once you become president).

A NOTE ON EVALUATION

The chapters that follow will give you guidance in *how* to read different kinds of literature: what structural elements to look for, what techniques to keep in mind, and above all, what questions you should ask of each kind of book. Your answers to these questions show your final understanding of the books you will read.

So how do you know whether you've gotten the answers right?

Getting "the answer" isn't exactly the point of the exercise. In classical education, the question-and-answer process is used as a teaching method;

[2]Thomas Jefferson, *Crusade Against Ignorance: Thomas Jefferson on Education*, ed. Gordon C. Lee (New York: Columbia University Teacher's College Bureau of Publications, 1961), pp. 110–11.

today, we call this "Socratic dialogue." A classical schoolmaster teaches the humanities, not through lectures that tell the student exactly what to think about each book, but through asking selected questions that direct the student's thoughts in the right way. The purpose of answering the questions isn't to provide the "right answer," as you would in a fill-in-the-blank test. You answer them as part of your effort to *think* about books.

This doesn't mean that you won't ever come up with a completely off-base (or what academics call "perverse") answer. Ideally, you would have a classical schoolmaster on hand to listen to your answers and gently steer you away from dead ends, toward more productive ways of thinking. In the process of self-education, you have two safeguards: your reading partner, who will listen to your ideas and tell you whether they're coherent; and the practice of quoting. Whenever you begin to answer one of the questions in the following chapters (for example, in the chapter on autobiography, "For what part of his—or her—life does the writer apologize?"), always quote a sentence or two directly from the work that you're examining. This helps to anchor your ideas, and forces you to be specific instead of abstract (it's relatively easy to make big, general statements, but specifics require thought) and protects you from coming up with "perverse readings." (On the other hand, "perverse" is often in the eye of the beholder, as a glance at any recent journal of literary criticism will suggest.)

Although you should always try to form your own ideas about a book before reading what others think, you can "check up" on yourself by skimming an essay or two of criticism that deals with your reading. Several Web sites offer plot outlines of great books along with very brief essays that survey critical issues: try www.pinkmonkey.com and www.sparknotes.com. Searching Google Books (books.google.com) with the title of the work in question, the author, and a word or phrase such as "critical essays," "criticism," or "critical analysis" can bring up published resources for you to glance over. (Check the publisher of any book that appears in your search results; university presses are much more likely to publish non-perverse criticism than self-publishing "presses" such as Xulon, Lulu, or CreateSpace. If you don't know which publishers are "vanity presses," the Internet is your friend; do a search for "self-publishing presses" and the top twenty will pop up immediately.)

If you live near enough to a college or university to use its library, search its holdings (you can do this online, in most cases, by going to the university Web site and looking for the "Library" link). Look for collections of essays on a particular book, rather than book-length critical works, which are dense and complex. The "Modern Critical Essays" series, edited by

Harold Bloom (*1984: Modern Critical Essays; Anna Karenina: Modern Critical Essays,* and so on) contains essays by a number of well-known critics and will give you a good overview of the critical take on a work.

If you continue to wonder whether your ideas are valid or completely off base, you can use a college or university in another way. Call the department secretary (the English department for novels, autobiographies, poetry, and drama; the history department for history; you're probably out of luck if you're reading science) and ask whether you could make an appointment to visit a faculty member during office hours. Tell the secretary which book you want to discuss; she should be able to direct you to the right instructor. Have your ideas written out before you go (this doesn't need to be a formal "paper," just a string of paragraphs expressing your thoughts). Tell the instructor you've been reading *Moby-Dick,* or the autobiography of Harriet Jacobs, describe your own ideas, and ask what you've missed. Don't overuse this resource (you're not paying tuition, after all), but in most cases an instructor will respond graciously to one or two requests for help. Universities, particular public ones, do have an obligation to "town" as well as to "gown," and asking for an appointment or two is not the same as asking for regular weekly tutorials.

College instructors are generally overworked; you'll get a better response if you call during the summer or over holidays. And don't ask for appointments right at the beginning, middle, or end of a semester, when new class syllabi, midterms, and finals fill every instructor's horizon.

A NOTE ON THE LISTS THAT FOLLOW

The lists that follow allow you to read chronologically through six different types of literature: fiction; autobiography; history and politics; drama; poetry; and science and natural history.

When you read chronologically, you reunite two fields that should never have been separated in the first place: history and literature. To study literature is to study what people thought, did, believed, suffered for, and argued about in the past; this *is* history. And although we do learn from archaeological discoveries, our primary source of information about former times has always been the writings of people who lived in the past. History can't be detached from the study of the written word. Nor should literature be removed from its historical context. A novel can tell you more about a writer's times than a history textbook; an autobiography reveals the soul of an entire society, not just the interior life of an individual man or woman. The sciences suffer when they are treated as a clear lens into "truth," because the theory of the biologist or astronomer or physicist may have as much to do with the scientist's society—and the questions that preoccupy it—as it has to do with pure discovery.

Writers build on the work of those who have gone before them, and chronological reading provides you with a continuous story. What you learn from one book will reappear in the next. But more than that: You'll find yourself following a story that has to do with the development of civilization itself. When you read through the poetry list, for example, you'll begin with the *Epic of Gilgamesh*, progress on through the *Odyssey*, the *Inferno*, John Donne, William Blake, Walt Whitman, T. S. Eliot, Robert Frost, and Langston Hughes (among others). The structure of the poetry will change as each poet moves beyond what former writers have done. But beyond these technical differences, the concerns of the poets shift and change as the world itself hurtles toward modernity: away from the nature of heroism and the quest for eternal life, toward the difficulties of simple existence in a chaotic and planless world. When you've finished with this particular list, you've done more than read poetry. You have learned something about the spiritual evolution of the West.

Although you can choose any of the lists to begin with, they are arranged from the least intimidating form of reading (the novel) on up to the two most intimidating (poetry, difficult because of its highly stylized language, and science, which scares most readers who gave up on math as soon as the SATs were over). The reading techniques suggested for some of the later chapters also build on techniques described earlier. So if you want to skip the fiction list and go straight to autobiography and politics, consider reading through my introduction to the fiction list first.

Do not feel bound to read *every* book on the list. If you read only two or three books on each list, you're likely to miss most of the benefits of reading chronologically. But if you simply cannot wade through a book after a good solid try, put it down and go on to the next book on the list. Don't jettison the whole project because you can't stand *Paradise Lost*. Even literary scholars have books that they have never managed to get all the way through. My *bête noire* is *Moby-Dick*; I know it's one of the great works of American literature, but I have made at least eight runs at it during my adult life and have never managed to get past midpoint. I even took an entire graduate seminar on Melville, did a presentation, and got an A without finishing the book. (Which says something about the state of graduate education, but that's another topic.)

Some books speak to us at one time of life and are silent at another. If a book remains voiceless to you, put it down and read the next book on the list.

You don't have to progress all the way through grammar-stage reading, logic-stage inquiry, and rhetoric-stage discussion for every book. If a book enthralls you, linger over it. If you just barely make it through the first reading and close it with relief, there's no reason to feel that you *must* go on to the next stage of inquiry.

A final disclaimer: List making is a dangerous occupation. No list of "Great Books" is canonical, and all lists are biased; they reflect the interests of the person who drew them up. These particular lists are not meant in any way to be comprehensive. They do not even include all of the "greatest" works in each field. Rather, they are designed to introduce readers to the study of a particular area of thought. In some cases, I have included books because of their popularity or influence, not because they are the "best"; Hitler's autobiography, *Mein Kampf*, is unsatisfying as autobiography and irrational as political philosophy, and Betty Friedan's *Feminine Mystique* has enormous flaws in the way it handles historical data. But Friedan's book started a revolution, and Hitler's started a war. In both cases, these books are important because of their *cultural* influence; they caused readers to look at American marriages, or the problem of national identity, with new interest. Their popularity is part of the history that you are studying when you read chronologically.

You should feel free to add to the lists or to subtract from them. They are intentionally short; expand them. They may not include your favorite author; pencil him or her in. They may include works that you think are trivial or offensive; cross those off.

Make the lists your own. Above all, don't feel that you need to write the list maker and complain.

AN IMPORTANT NOTE ON FORMATS

Many of the older books on these lists are available in multiple editions. I have attempted to find editions that combine readability (decent-sized fonts that don't offend the eye), affordability (so that you can buy the books and *write* in them), and, where possible, an absence of intrusive critical commentary. (Footnoted or marginal interpretations have the potential to distract you from the book's actual content; at worst, they give you the wrong interpretation of a book's meaning before you've had a chance to think about it yourself.)

I have not listed all available ebook editions for each title, but electronic versions are fine as long as you are comfortable making use of the notation and bookmarking tools provided by your particular ereader. It's vital that you write down your thoughts and reactions as you read.

Be careful when ordering ebook versions of books in the public domain. Often, the edition you view is not the one that downloads, and it is very easy to pay money for a sloppy, badly edited ebook that's worse than a free online version.

The same is true of print books. If you're ordering a paperback of a public domain title, be sure to look for one from a reputable publisher, rather than a print-on-demand version (CreateSpace, Lulu, Blurb, Lightning Source, and many others). Anyone can snag the text of a public domain book and throw it up for sale using one of these services, and you're as likely as not to get a smeary, unedited, badly bound pile of pages in exchange for your credit card number.

Many of these books are available as audiobooks. There's absolutely nothing wrong with listening instead of reading for your first read-through. You're still experiencing the text. But make sure that you select an unabridged, non-dramatized version; otherwise, you're getting an interpretation, not the book itself. (And you'll still need a print or ebook version for your second and third levels of inquiry.) I have not listed all available audio versions, but have noted when one is particularly well-done.

Consult this book's website, http://susanwisebauer.com/welleducated mind, for additional recommended editions and links to public domain ebooks.

THE FOURTH STEP: PRACTICING
GRAMMAR-STAGE READING SKILLS

Six principles govern the "first stage" of reading:

1. Plan on returning to each book more than once to reread sections and chapters.
2. Underline or mark passages that you find interesting or confusing. Turn down the corners of difficult sections; jot your questions in the margin.
3. Before you begin, read the title page, the copy on the back, and the table of contents.
4. At the end of each chapter or section, write down a sentence or two that summarizes the content. Remember not to include details (this will come later).

5. As you read, use your journal to jot down questions that come to your mind.
6. Assemble your summary sentences into an informal outline, and then give the book a brief title and an extensive subtitle.

If you completed *The Third Step*, you've already practiced some of these skills in summarizing and reacting to Chapter 4. Now use all of the principles of grammar-stage reading on the first ten chapters of *Don Quixote*. This massive novel is the first work on the Great Books list in the next chapter. Its length may be intimidating, but a first reading of its opening chapters will reassure you: the story is engaging, and the style accessible.

1. Read the title page, back cover, and table of contents. (I recommend the 2003 Edith Grossman translation, or the abridged version done by Walter Starkie.)
2. In the case of *Don Quixote*, Edith Grossman has provided a Translator's Note; read through it and note down in your journal, under the heading "Preface," any important points that you'd like to remember. Personally, I would hold off on reading the introductory essay by Harold Bloom (I'd want to make my own run at the book first).
3. Read the author's prologue. Summarize its main points in two or three sentences.
4. Read Chapters 1–10. At the end of each chapter, write down two or three sentences that will remind you exactly what happened. If you find yourself particularly interested in a passage, bracket it and turn the corner of your page down. Jot any questions or remarks into the margins of your journal.
5. Now go back and make your own table of contents, using your summary sentences from Chapters 1–10. You'll probably want to boil each summary down into a single sentence: what's the central event in each chapter? This should become your chapter title for the table of contents.
6. If this were the entire story of Don Quixote, what would you title it? What would your subtitle be?

Reading:

JUMPING

INTO THE

GREAT

CONVERSATION

Chapter 5

The Story of People:
Reading through History with the Novel

In a certain village in La Mancha, which I do not wish to name, there lived not long ago a gentleman.

A throng of bearded men, in sad-colored garments and gray, steeple-crowned hats, intermixed with women, some wearing hoods, and others bareheaded, was assembled in front of a wooden edifice, the door of which was heavily timbered with oak, and studded with iron spikes.

Call me Ishmael.

The cold passed reluctantly from the earth, and the retiring fogs revealed an army stretched out on the hills, resting.

Mother died today. Or, maybe, yesterday; I can't be sure.

Many years later, as he faced the firing squad, Colonel Aureliano Buendía was to remember that distant afternoon when his father took him to discover ice.

READING THE FIRST words of a novel is like glimpsing the first crack of light along the edge of an opening door. What's inside that invisible room? The reader leans forward, waiting for each detail to take its proper place in the whole. The puzzling pattern just inside the door turns out to be the edge of a screen; the odd dark shape on the floor develops into the shadow of an end table. Finally the door swings open. The reader steps over the threshold, into another world.

Some doors open quickly. That soberly clad throng of bearded men and hooded women are clustered around a Boston jail, waiting for Hester Prynne—the heroine of Nathaniel Hawthorne's 1850 tale of festering guilt, *The Scarlet Letter*—to walk out with her baby in her arms. The summer grass is already warm. The bright sunlight falls incongruously over the iron-banded, rust-streaked boards of the prison. A wild rosebush grows at the front gate, pink blossoms startling against the weathered wood.

The resting army of Stephen Crane's *The Red Badge of Courage* (1895) will soon rise and shake itself. Soldiers in blue coats quarrel, wash their shirts, huddle over campfires. The roads of liquid mud begin to dry under the morning sun. A young private lies on his bed, the smoke from his badly tended fire wreathing around him. Sunlight turns the canvas roof of his tent a bright, diffuse yellow.

Both of these scenes are as clear and immediate as a painting: Read the first paragraphs of either book, and you'll find yourself already over the threshold. But other doors creak open more slowly. The narrator of Albert Camus's 1942 novel *The Stranger* doesn't know exactly when his mother died. The telegram from the Home for the Aged isn't specific. But the matter doesn't occupy his mind for more than a moment or two. His preparations for the funeral are sketchy; he almost misses his bus; when he arrives at the Home for the Aged, the warden shows him into the room where his mother's body lies—but he doesn't bother to look at her face. Why? What's happening? The reader has to suspend these questions, accepting each new bit of information as it drops carelessly from the narrator's thoughts, waiting for the jagged pieces to assemble themselves—late in the book—into a recognizable scene. And Gabriel García Márquez's *One Hundred Years of Solitude* (1967) is even more leisurely, leaping from the colonel's imminent death by firing squad back to the village of Macondo and its unhurried patterns of daily life, back in a distant time when the "world was so recent that many things lacked names, and in order to indicate them it was necessary to point." When will we get back to the colonel's execution? Eventually. (Maybe.) Have patience.

In earlier novels, the doors swing wide almost at once; as the twenty-first century draws nearer, the doors begin to stick, drag open more slowly, a thin millimeter at a time. Even so, you might notice an odd resemblance between the first line—the famous opening words from *Don Quixote*, initially published in Spanish in 1604—and the opening lines from a much later novel, Italo Calvino's 1972 novel-within-a-novel-within-a-novel, *If on a winter's night a traveler*:

You are about to begin reading Italo Calvino's new novel, *If on a winter's night a traveler.* Relax. Concentrate. Dispel every other thought. Let the world around you fade.[1]

All of the opening lines draw you into a new world. But only Cervantes and Calvino remind you, as you step over the threshold, that the *other* world, the one behind you, has never gone away; only Cervantes and Calvino remind you as soon as you begin reading, "This is a book. Only make-believe. Remember?"

Between 1604 and 1972, we have come full circle. This, in a nutshell, is the history of the novel.

Every novel is governed by *conventions*—those expectations which the reader brings to a book. Some conventions are visual. If you pick up a paperback with a pink cover and a half-naked hero on the cover, you expect to read something along the lines of "Evangeline paused at the top of the stairs, gathering the folds of her cream muslin gown around her slim ankles," not "On an exceptionally hot evening early in July a young man came out of the garret in which he lodged in S. Place and walked slowly, as though in hesitation, toward K. bridge."[2]

But novels are also governed by conventions of language. A novel that begins "My father had a small estate in Nottinghamshire; I was the third of five sons. He sent me to Emanuel College in Cambridge at fourteen years old, where I resided three years" is telling you, the reader: *This is a serious and trustworthy account. See how many careful details I'm giving you?* On the other hand, a book that starts out, "It was a bright cold day in April, and the clocks were striking thirteen," is giving you a completely different verbal cue: *This book is not about the world as we know it.*

The well-trained reader shouldn't assume that writers will always use those conventions with a straight face. That serious and trustworthy narrator who tells you that his father "had a small estate in Nottinghamshire" is named Gulliver; next, he's going to tell you about his voyages to Lilliput, where he's captured by people who are six inches tall, and to Laputa, where the natives are so absorbed in thought that visitors have to smack them on the head in order to begin a conversation. In *Gulliver's Travels*, Jonathan Swift uses the conventions of an earlier form of literature, the travelogue,

---

[1] Italo Calvino, *If on a winter's night a traveler,* trans. William Weaver (New York: Harcourt Brace and Co., 1991), p. 3.
[2] This is the first line of Fyodor Dostoyevsky's *Crime and Punishment*, translated by Constance Garnett.

to mock the conventions of his own society. But you won't be able to appreciate Swift's deliberate misuse of careful, verifying detail unless you already know what a travelogue is. This brief (and selective) history of the novel will give you a basic framework of novelistic conventions—so that you can spot them when writers use and change them.

A TEN-MINUTE HISTORY OF THE NOVEL

Cleopatra and Caesar didn't amuse themselves with novels in their spare time, because the long story written in prose didn't exist in ancient times. The novel as we know it today emerged in the eighteenth century, in the hands of Daniel Defoe, Samuel Richardson, and Henry Fielding. Defoe borrowed the conventions of the traveler's tale and produced *Robinson Crusoe*; Richardson used the traditional "epistolary" form (a set of letters written by a character) and turned it into *Pamela*. Fielding, a playwright, found his style cramped by the severe new laws against on-stage obscenity; he wrote *Joseph Andrews* instead. (The "lewd passages" of *Joseph Andrews* are practically invisible to modern eyes, but the story certainly couldn't have been staged in eighteenth-century London.)

These three stories used old conventions but filled them with something new: a glance into the internal life of an individual *person*. Before the eighteenth century, long stories written in prose featured entire chessboards full of static characters, shuffled through series of events in order to tell the story of a nation, explain an idea, or illustrate a set of virtues (as in Spenser's *The Faerie Queene*). But Defoe, Richardson, and Fielding produced a new kind of book: the Book of the Person.

They weren't the first. Over in Spain, a century and a half before Defoe, Miguel de Cervantes Saavedra had already written the first Book of the Person: the story of Don Quixote, the gentleman of La Mancha who decided to become a knight errant. But Cervantes was a lone genius. Defoe, Fielding, and Richardson together began a literary movement that flowered, full-blown, into a new kind of literature: the prose narrative that explores the interior life of a character.

This new form, the "novel," had to compete with another, less respectable literary form, the "romance." The romance was roughly equivalent to the modern soap opera. Romances, in the words of one eighteenth-century critic, involved "exalted personages" in "improbable or impossible situations." Romances were light and escapist, and were thus reading suitable only for women. (Conventional wisdom held that women's brains weren't up to grappling with "real life" anyway, so they might as well read fantasies.) Romance reading was not a manly and respectable pastime.

Novelists, on the other hand, wanted to be taken very seriously indeed. Novels dealt with real people in familiar situations; as Samuel Johnson wrote in 1750, novelists tried to "exhibit life in its true state, diversified only by accidents that daily happen in the world, and influenced by passions and qualities which are really to be found in conversing with mankind."[3] But eighteenth-century readers were a little confused by this distinction between the tawdry "romance" and the noble "novel"—and novelists such as Swift, who insisted on trotting his hero through fantastic landscapes, didn't improve matters. For decades, novels came in for a large share of the general disdain that educated readers felt for romances. Eighteenth-century intellectuals moaned about the corrupting influence of novels in much the same way that organic-food zealots trumpet the dangers of refined sugar. Clergy warned their flocks that novel reading would produce an increase in prostitution, adultery, and (according to the bishop of London in 1789) earthquakes.

Yet the novel prospered. Defoe, Richardson, and Fielding had produced their innovations during a time when the individual *self*, with all its traumas and dilemmas, was of great interest to the public at large. Thanks in large part to the Protestant Reformation, the soul (at least in England and America, the sources of all the eighteenth-century and most of the nineteenth-century novels on our list) was imagined as a lone entity, making its solitary way through a vast and confusing landscape. John Bunyan's Christian, called by Evangelist to forsake his doomed city and find the wicker gate, is called alone. He has to put his fingers in his ears and run away from his wife and children to find salvation, separating himself from every human tie in order to unite himself with God.

Interest in the private self was on the upswing, impelled not only by Protestantism but by capitalism, which encouraged each person to think of himself (or herself) as an individual, able to rise up through society's levels toward wealth and leisure. The self was no longer part of a rigid, unshifting feudal system, with responsibilities beginning at birth and never changing thereafter. The self was free.

Reams have been written on this subject, but for our purposes it's enough to know that this sense of an individual self with a private internal life was central to all the major developments of modern Western life: Enlightenment thought, the Protestant religion, the development of capitalism, and (of course) the novel. Novelists celebrated the individual: Charlotte Brontë's tortured and passionate heroes; Jane Austen's heroines, maneuvering through a society that both protects and hampers them;

---

[3] Samuel Johnson, "On Fiction," *Rambler*, no. 4, March 31, 1750.

Nathaniel Hawthorne's tortured, adulterous clergyman. And the public bought, and read.

Popularity is always a double-edged sword, though. The intellectual elite had already been suspicious of the novel, because of its identification with the "romance." Now they were doubly suspicious. After all, books that everyone reads can't really be worthy of attention by the most educated. (Call it the Oprah effect.) To make things worse, this public readership was mostly female, since middle-class women had the money to buy novels and the leisure to read them, but not the Latin and Greek necessary to appreciate the sterner, more manly "classics." Novels, sniffed the scholar Charles Lamb were the "scanty intellectual viands of the whole female reading public." (Lamb is now primarily remembered as a reteller of Shakespeare for children, which serves him right.)

How did novelists fight back? By playing up their connection with real life. Fantastic tales were scorned. Stories about reality gained critical acclaim.

Fantastic tales didn't disappear, but they were relegated to the scorned realm of the popular. In the nineteenth century, the soap opera of choice was the "Gothic novel," a story of mystery and vague supernatural threat, set in fantastic and menacing places (or in central Europe, which, for most readers, amounted to the same thing). Gothic heroines languished in ruined castles, threatened by ancient spells, insane wives, and mysterious noblemen who avoid sunlight and mirrors. Here is Emily of the wildly popular *The Mysteries of Udolpho*: plucky but not too bright, wandering through the strange echoing castle of Count Morano. Since she's all alone in the dark, she decides that this would be a good time to peer beneath the black veil that covers a mysterious picture in a deserted room. "She paused again," the narrator tells us breathlessly, "and then, with a timid hand, lifted the veil; but instantly let it fall—perceiving that what it had concealed was no picture, and, before she could leave the chamber, she dropped senseless on the floor."

A few brave novelists—notably Hawthorne, who could never resist a touch of supernatural horrors, and Emily Brontë, who had a weakness for ghosts at windows—borrowed Gothic elements to jazz up their tales of adulterous Puritans and unhappy moor residents. But most serious writers rejected the fantastic in favor of the real. The novel even developed a social conscience. Charles Dickens and his American counterpart, Harriet Beecher Stowe, used their stories to kick against the injustices of a market economy that built wealth on the backs of the weak; Dickens protested English society's use of children for labor, while Stowe's *Uncle Tom's Cabin* put a human face on the slave labor that made the southern economy run. (Stowe, quite by accident, turned into an economic dynamo in her own right; *Uncle Tom's Cabin*, according to the historian Joan D. Hedrick, "generated an industry of Uncle Tom plates, spoons, candlesticks, games, wallpapers, songs, and stage spin-offs that ran continuously for the next ninety years.")[4]

The earliest writers had seen nothing wrong with pointing out the fictional nature of their stories ("I would wish this book," Cervantes tells the reader, "the child of my brain, to be . . . the cleverest imaginable"). But later novelists avoided this sort of intrusion into the narrative. They wanted readers to discover a *real* world, not an imaginary one. The late-nineteenth-century novel wasn't supposed to be the child of the writer's brain; it was intended to be an accurate record of ordinary life.

This new philosophy of *realism* turned the novelist into a sort of scientist. Like the scientist, the novelist recorded every detail rather than selectively describing scenes—which tended to make most realistic novels very, very long. The father of realism, the French novelist Gustave Flaubert, was so determined to portray real characters in a real country town that he drew maps and diagrams of his imaginary world. (He got a little lost in the details occasionally; if you're careful, you can catch his heroine turning the wrong direction to go home.) Flaubert's Emma Bovary is the woman eighteenth-century clergymen fretted about, the female reader whose love for romances has blotted out "real life." She is consumed by the desire for romance, that "great passion which . . . hovered like a great pink-plumaged bird soaring in the splendor of poetic skies," and this absorption in fantasy makes her "unable to believe that the tranquility in which she was living was the happiness of which she had dreamed."

Emma Bovary comes to a bad end—she eats arsenic after realizing that she'll never be able to live in a romance—but the realistic novel flourished. Henry James's characters don't run around with Indians in the woods, like the hero of the romantic Leatherstocking tales. Nor do they develop mysterious stigmata and die from guilt, like Hawthorne's anguished clergyman. Instead they go to their jobs, live in their dusty, high-ceilinged rooms, battle consumption, and marry men who are presentable but no great shakes—like most of the "regular" folk in the world.[5]

---

[4]Joan D. Hedrick, "Commerce in Souls: Uncle Tom's Cabin and the State of the Nation," in *Novel History: Historians and Novelists Confront America's Past (and Each Other)*, ed. Mark C. Carnes (New York: Simon & Schuster, 2001), pp. 168–69.

[5]Realism is one of the major movements in English and American fiction. In his 1949 essay "Realism: An Essay in Definition" in *Modern Language Quarterly* (one of the first attempts to define "realism"), George J. Becker suggests that the movement involves: (1) detail derived from observation and documentation; (2) an effort to portray normal experience, not the exceptional; (3) an "objective, so far as an artist can achieve objectivity, rather than a subjective or idealistic view of human nature and experience." For more on this topic, see two

Which brings us, more or less, up to the present. Realism never really goes away. Even today, stories that describe "extraordinary" events (thrillers, science fiction, fantasies, and to some extent religious fiction) tend to be intellectually exiled, dismissed as "popular" genres unworthy of serious critical acclaim. But in the late nineteenth and early twentieth centuries, realism developed offshoots. Dostoyevsky and Kafka perfected a "psychological realism" that pays less attention to physical details and more to psychological details. Rather than giving loving attention to the exact appearance of landscapes or furnishings, psychological realism tries to paint an accurate picture of the *mind*, so that the reader seems to be in direct contact with a character's mental processes. William James (Henry's brother) invented the term "stream of consciousness" in 1900 to describe the unordered but natural flow of human thought, and novelists from Conrad to Virginia Woolf seized on this idea. "Stream of consciousness" writing is the psychological equivalent of the detailed physical landscape description: We are to think that we are seeing, uncensored by the writer's judgment, the "facts" of the mind. "The War was over," thinks Woolf's Mrs. Dalloway as she walks out for the morning's flowers,

> except for some one like Mrs. Foxcroft at the Embassy last night eating her heart out because that nice boy was killed and now the old Manor House must go to a cousin. . . . And everywhere, though it was still so early, there was a beating, a stirring of galloping ponies, tapping of cricket bats; Lords, Ascot, Ranelagh and all the rest of it; wrapped in the soft mesh of the grey-blue morning air, which, as the day wore on, would unwind them, and set down on their lawns and pitches the bouncing ponies . . . and the shopkeepers were fidgeting in their windows with their paste and diamonds, their lovely old sea-green brooches in eighteenth-century settings to tempt Americans (but one must economise, not buy things rashly for Elizabeth), and she, too, loving it as she did with an absurd and faithful passion, being part of it, since her people were couriers once in the time of the Georges, she, too, was going that very night to kindle and illuminate; to give her party.

Too much of this sort of thing is just as wearying as the protracted details of ponds and heaths found in early realism. But early-twentieth-century writers were enthralled by the stream-of-consciousness technique. Faulk-

---

other foundational critical works on the subject: Lionel Trilling's "Reality in America," in *The Liberal Imagination* (New York: Anchor Books, 1957) and Erich Auerbach's *Mimesis: The Representation of Reality in Western Literature* (Princeton, N.J.: Princeton University Press, 1953).

ner's characters rarely come to us by any other means, and James Joyce produced (in *Ulysses*) a famously dense chunk of stream-of-consciousness writing that lasts forty-five pages. (*Ulysses* always ranks at the top of modern Great Books lists, but it isn't on the list at the end of this chapter because it's brutal to read.)

Another form of realism—even more ferociously modern than "psychological realism"—was naturalism. Naturalist writers were convinced that they could write "purely scientific" novels. The individual, the subject of all novelization since *Don Quixote*, was no longer free. The "self" was only the product of inherited traits plus environmental influence. Naturalist writers—most notably Thomas Hardy—gave their characters certain genetic characteristics, plopped them down into a sheer *hell* of environmental factors, and then described the resulting behavior. The naturalist's job (in his or her own eyes, at any rate) was just like the scientist's: Put the rat in the maze, watch what it does, and record the outcome without elaboration.

And so we arrive at the twentieth century. The style of realism, with its careful cataloguing of detail, is still with us. Don DeLillo begins his 1985 novel *White Noise* with his narrator leaning out a window, watching the college kids arrive for the first day of class: "The station wagons arrived at noon, a long shining line that coursed through the west campus. In single file they eased around the orange I-beam sculpture and moved toward the dormitories. The roofs of the station wagons were loaded down with carefully secured suitcases full of light and heavy clothing; with boxes of blankets, boots and shoes, stationery and books, sheets, pillows, quilts; with rolled-up rugs and sleeping bags; with bicycles, skis, rucksacks, English and Western saddles, inflated rafts. . . ." And so on.

But the *ideas* behind the novel have changed since realism's heyday. The novel is generally considered to have moved through "modernity" to "postmodernity." Defining these two terms is tricky, since no one realized that modernity existed until it had been replaced by postmodernity, which simply means "following modernity."

"The dirty secret of higher academics," a colleague told me one day, "is that none of us really know exactly what postmodernism is." It would probably help if critics were able to state in English what modernism is, first; the critic James Bloom, for example, writes that modernism involves "density, the generic ambiguity, and the understanding of . . . [the novelist's] own status as mediated and mediating," which doesn't move us much forward.[6] Most other definitions are just as opaque.

[6]James Bloom, *Left Letters* (New York: Columbia University Press, 1992), p. 7.

More simply, then: Modernism is a type of realism. It too strives to portray "real life." But modernists, writing during and after two world wars, saw that their Victorian ancestors were deluded. The Victorians thought that they could understand what life was all about, but the modernists knew that "real life" was actually beyond understanding. "Real life" was chaotic, planless and unguided, and so the "scientific style" of the modernist is chaotic, refusing to bring novels neatly into any kind of resolution. To quote Dorothy L. Sayers (a good Anglican who responded to modernism by asserting her own belief in God and writing mysteries, an exceedingly unchaotic form of literature):

> Said a rising young author, "What, what?
> If I think that causation is not,
> No word of my text
> Will bear on the next,
> And what will become of the plot?"[7]

Absence of plot made the modernist novel very difficult to read, especially for the common reader who hankered for a *story*.

But the modernists tended to scorn story. One of modernism's most unattractive aspects was its snobbery. Modernist writers distrusted the masses and put all their faith in a small, well-educated elite. Several prominent modernists (most notably Ezra Pound) supported fascism and sneered at democracy. And the most well known were particularly savage about "popular fiction." The novel was an intellectual exercise, not a form of entertainment, and readers who wanted entertainment were welcome to go buy a dime-store Western. Virginia Woolf moaned that the novelist was a "slave" to the necessity of selling books; she longed for a fiction that could be free, with "no plot, no comedy, no tragedy, no love interest, or catastrophe in the accepted style." E. M. Forster wrote that "oh dear, yes—the novel tells a story," but wished with all his heart that the market wouldn't demand "story," that "low atavistic form." (As both Forster and Woolf ended up telling quite interesting stories, the market apparently won out in the end.)

No one likes to be condescended to, so it's hardly surprising that so many high school students develop a loathing for the modernist novels they're forced to read in senior English and go to the movies instead. (Movies have plots, after all.) They're being good postmodernists.

---

[7]Dorothy L. Sayers (with Robert Eustace), *The Documents in the Case* (New York: Harper & Row, 1987), p. 55.

Postmodernism is modernism's teenage child. Postmodernism says to modernism, "Who made you the boss?" (and to E. M. Forster, "Who made you an authority on fiction, you dead white male, you?"). Postmodernism rejects modernism's claim to know the truth about real life. Postmodernism says: There are many ways to portray real life and no single authority can pick which one is right. *Buffy the Vampire Slayer* has just as much intellectual value as *Heart of Darkness*, not to mention a lot more insight into women's lives.

The postmodern novelist considered that all previous attempts to write about the individual self were flawed, because those earlier attempts insisted on seeing the self as essentially free. No, no, says the postmodernist; the private self that we first met in *Don Quixote* and *Pilgrim's Progress* isn't some sort of independent, free being that can find its own path through obstacles, triumphing over society's hypocrisies. Nor was that self formed by nature and genetics. Instead, that private self was *produced* by society. Everything that we think about ourselves—every "truth" we know about our own existence—has been instilled in us, since birth, by our culture. We can't ever get "outside" of society's structures in order to see what is really true. And when we examine our own deepest selves, all we'll find is a collection of social conventions.

Postmodern novelists didn't try to write original stories, since "original" implies some sort of creative ability which is free from the influence of society. Instead, they wrote *about* society, about the flood of information that shapes us from birth. Their careful, lengthy cataloguing of the details of daily life reminds the reader: This is who you are. You're formed and shaped by these details. You can't ever escape them.

In Don DeLillo's *White Noise*, the narrator tries to get some sort of control over the chaos of his life by cleaning out his attic (an impulse we've all felt). But in the end, the details defeat him:

> I threw away picture-frame wire, metal book ends, cork coasters, plastic key tags, dusty bottles of Mercurochrome and Vaseline, crusted paintbrushes, caked shoe brushes, clotted correction fluid. I threw away candle stubs, laminated placemats, frayed pot holders. . . . I threw away my battered khaki canteen, my ridiculous hip boots. I threw away diplomas, certificates, awards and citations. When the girls stopped me, I was working the bathroom, discarding used bars of soap, damp towels, shampoo bottles with streaked labels and missing caps.

Postmodernism can be as heavily didactic as John Bunyan's sermons, and *White Noise* (like DeLillo's later and larger novel *Underworld*) hammers home its point as unrelentingly as any Puritan allegorizer. For folks who reject the idea of "one truth," postmodernists are amazingly loud as they shout their conclusions: *Get it? Get it? You don't have any power. You're pushed here and there by your society. It rules you. It is you.*

Literary postmodernism began to lose some of its steam in the late 1970s, and no single "movement" has replaced it (these things are easier to see in retrospect). But it seems that as the novel passes its four hundredth birthday, we've come full circle, back around to *Don Quixote.* "Sit down," Cervantes tells his readers, "and let me tell you a story. It's just pretend, but that's fine; you'll enjoy it anyway." "Here is my book," the twentieth-century novelist Italo Calvino announces. "Put your feet up and read it."

This technique is called *metafiction.* Rather than creating a fictional world that pretends to be real, metafiction admits, right up front, that it's only a story; the writer is standing behind you as you walk over the threshold into that new world, shouting, "Don't forget where you came from!" Calvino doesn't have to worry about being taken seriously. He can admit that he's writing a novel, because the postmodernists have already shown that the contrast between "real" and "false" is only a product of the realist's quest for a truth that doesn't even exist.

So that tension created in the first years of the novel's existence—the tension between real and fictional, fantasy and reality, novel and romance—has finally begun to ease. Fantastic events are once again possible, and novels that make use of them have their own (intellectually respectable) label: magic realism. Plot has even made a minor comeback; *Possession*, the penultimate novel on the list below, is a love story, a wry reflection on the state of literary criticism, a mystery with a point of view that shifts from present to past, from omniscient narrator to first person, using letters, dreams, critical articles, biographies, bits of tales, excerpts from poems (all written by the author, A. S. Byatt) and old-fashioned storytelling to lead the reader to its center. And the final novel, Cormac McCarthy's Pulitzer Prize–winning *The Road,* deftly combines the quest narrative (one of the oldest plot devices in the world) with post-apocalypticism. In fact, thanks to the solid *stories* at their centers, *Possession* and *The Road* were both bought by production companies and turned into movies.

After four hundred years, the occupation of novel writing has grown up: The best writers of metafiction are happy to be called storytellers. Postmodernism, for all its flaws, loosened the stranglehold of nineteenth-century realism and its related forms, and gave the imagination back some of the power that was usurped in the days of the realists and naturalists.

HOW TO READ A NOVEL

The First Level of Inquiry: Grammar-Stage Reading

The first time you read through a novel, you should look for answers to three very simple questions: Who are these people? What happens to them? And how are they different afterward? As you read, you should also turn down (or bookmark) pages where something significant seems to be happening. Don't worry about what that significance is—you'll return to these sections later, after you do your initial read-through.

Look at the title, cover, and table of contents. With your journal and pencil close by, read the title page and the copy on the back cover. If the book has a biographical sketch of the author and/or translator, read that as well. Remember: it's often best to skip the preface unless it was *written* by the author (or translator); otherwise you may get a full interpretation of the book before you've had a chance to form your own ideas.

Write the title of the book, the author's name, and the date of composition on the top of a blank page. Underneath, note any facts learned from the book's cover or introduction that will help you read the book as the author intended. If, for example, the back-cover copy of *Don Quixote* tells you that Cervantes began his story as a parody on traditional songs and romances about chivalry, you might write "Makes fun of traditional chivalry" (or something similar) as a note to yourself.

Now read the table of contents. *Don Quixote* has many short chapters; the chapter titles ("The prophesying ape," "The puppet show," "The braying adventure," "Concerning a squire's wages") tell you that the story will unfold as a series of separate, brief events. The chapter titles of *The Scarlet Letter* ("Hester and the Physician," "Hester and Pearl," "The Minister in a Maze") introduce you to the story's main characters. In both cases the chapter titles tell you how to approach the book. *Don Quixote* is an episodic adventure; *The Scarlet Letter* an examination of character. If a novel doesn't have chapter titles (*1984, Wuthering Heights, The Great Gatsby*), that also is important; the writer found the various parts of the story too closely related for easy division and labeling. If the chapter titles do give you any clues about the book's contents, you can jot down a sentence or two for reference.

Now start to read Chapter 1.

Keep a list of characters as you read. Somewhere in your notebook (right underneath the title, or perhaps on the open left-hand page), you'll want to keep a list of major characters: their names, their positions, and their relationships to each other. Sometimes (especially in Russian works) characters have two (or more) names; your character list can help keep them straight. If the novel deals with a family, you should put the characters into a genealogical table (otherwise, you'll never keep the relationships in *Oliver Twist* straight).

Briefly note the main event of each chapter.   As you finish each chapter, write one or two sentences describing the chapter's main event in your notebook. These should be memory joggers for you, not a detailed *précis* of the plot. Try to limit yourself to one major event per chapter. "Don Quixote decides to be a knight, so he chooses Aldonza Lorenzo to be his lady and renames her Dulcinea del Toboso" is a perfectly good summary of Chapter 1 of *Don Quixote*. These sentences will help you grasp the book's overall flow—not to mention making it easier to pick your reading back up after an interruption. At some point in your reading, at least one crisis will temporarily derail your study time, and you don't want to have to reread four hundred pages of plot development because you've forgotten what happened before.

Make initial notes on passages that seem interesting.   During this initial reading, don't stop to write down long reflections on the book's content. But if you come across a passage that seems particularly important, bracket it with your pencil, turn down the corner of the page, and write a note to yourself in your journal ("Page 31: Is it important that *books* drove Don Quixote out of his wits?"). Distinguish these notes in some way from your content summaries; write them in the journal margins, on a different page, or in a different-color ink.

Give the book your own title and subtitle.   When you finish reading the book, go back and reread your chapter summaries. Do they provide you with a clear, coherent outline of what happens in the book? If so, you can move on to the next step: titling. If not, rewrite your summaries: delete those details which now seem inessential, add important events or characters that you might have missed.

Once you're happy with your outline, give the book a brief title and a longer subtitle. Before you can do this, though, you'll need to answer two questions:

1. Who is the central character in this book?
2. What is the book's most important event?

If you have difficulty answering these questions, ask yourself: Is there some point in the book where the characters change? Does something happen that makes everyone behave differently? There are plenty of important moments in *Pilgrim's Progress*, but the story's hero changes most drastically right at the beginning, when he hears Evangelist's words and runs through the wicket gate, crying, "Life, life, eternal life!" He is a different man afterward—and although he goes through multiple trials and temptations, his new personality does not alter. Glance back through the list of major events that you've jotted down for each chapter and try to identify the most central and life-changing of them all.

Once you find this event, ask yourself: Which character is the most affected? This is likely to be the book's hero (or heroine). (And don't fret too much about this question; you may change your mind after you've done a second, more intensive reading of the book's important sections.)

Now give your book a title that mentions the main character, and a subtitle that tells how that character is affected by the book's main event. *Christian's Journey to the Celestial City: How an ordinary man responded to Evangelist's invitation by leaving his home and beginning a journey in which he meets various figures that represent biblical truths, faces Apollyon, triumphs over a number of temptations that try to pull him away from the road to the City, and finally crosses over the Jordan to glory*: This sums up the story.

The Second Level of Inquiry: Logic-Stage Reading

Your first reading of the book should give you a sense of the story as a whole—one sweeping tale that you pursue from beginning to end, without stopping to ruminate or look up details. Now you'll narrow your gaze to individual elements of the book. Ideally, you would reread the whole novel at this point, but unless you're independently wealthy and unmarried (like the gentlemen-scholars of previous centuries), you probably won't. Instead, go back through the bracketed or bookmarked sections that you noted on your first read-through. Some will now appear irrelevant; others will suddenly reveal themselves to be central.

If you were reading nonfiction, you would now begin to analyze the writer's argument: What idea is she trying to convince you of? What evidence does he give you for believing this argument?

But fiction has a different end than philosophy, or science, or history. The novel doesn't present you with an argument; it invites you to enter another world. When you evaluate a nonfiction work, you will ask: Am I persuaded? But when you evaluate a novel, you must instead ask: Am I transported? Do I see, feel, hear this other world? Can I sympathize with the people who live there? Do I understand their wants and desires and problems? Or am I left unmoved?

Like any other skill, thinking critically about a novel becomes simpler with practice. The following brief guide to literary analysis isn't meant as a graduate course in literary criticism. Nor is it intended to turn you into a critic. Rather, these questions will begin to guide your thinking into a more analytical mode. As you practice asking and answering them, other questions (and answers) will come to mind.

In your journal, write down answers to the following questions. Not all of them will apply to every novel, of course; if one of the questions doesn't seem to have any good answer, skip it and move on. And remember that there are not, necessarily, "right answers" to these questions. (Critics can argue unceasingly about whether *Moby-Dick* is closer to realism or to fantasy.) But whenever you write down an answer, quote *directly from the novel* in order to support your answer. This will keep you focused on the book. Using a direct quote prevents you from making general—and thus meaningless—assertions, such as "*Moby-Dick* is about man's search for God." That sentence must immediately be followed by, "This can be seen in the scene where . . ." and a description of the scene.

Is this novel a "fable" or a "chronicle"?   Every novelist belongs in one of two camps. Some writers want to draw us into a world very like our own; they tell us how people behave, moment by moment, in lives governed by the same rules that regulate our own lives. These writers convince us that every emotion stems from a cause, every action from a reaction. These writers produce "chronicles"—stories set in our own universe.

Other novelists never try to convince us that the world of the book is real. These once-upon-a-time fables transport us into a place where different laws apply. "I sailed from England," Gulliver remarks, "and was captured by men three inches high." "And then I saw that there was a way to hell, even from the gates of heaven," Christian tells us. The writer of fables begins not with, "At 9 a.m. on a rainy Saturday in June," but rather with "Once upon a time . . ." *Pilgrim's Progress* and *Gulliver's Travels* were written by fable-tellers; *Pride and Prejudice* and *The Portrait of a Lady*, by chroniclers.[8]

This is the first question you must ask of a novel: Is this narrative taking place in a world that is governed by the same rules that govern *my*

---

[8]In contemporary genre fiction, this distinction is most clearly seen in the world of science fiction and fantasy, where science fiction is defined (in the words of Orson Scott Card) as a story with "nuts and bolts." In fantasy, Frodo can put on the Ring of Power and turn invisible; in science fiction, he has to disappear by manipulating the quantum waves in the space-time continuum. Note that the science doesn't have to be *real;* but it has to be at least compatible with present scientific knowledge, with the laws of the universe as we currently understand them.

existence? Or are there fantastic events in the book that don't square with reality as I know it?

Once you've answered this question, you can then consider one of these three questions (again, try to jot down a quote or two from the novel in support of each answer):

1. If this novel is set in our world—a chronicle—*how* does the writer show us reality? Does she try to convince us that her world is real through the careful presentation of physical detail—the meals people eat, the cut and color of their clothes, the landscape that surrounds them? Or does she focus instead on *psychological* detail: the processes of the mind, the rise and fall of emotions, the slow discovery of motivations?

2. If the writer presents a fantastic world, what is his or her intent? Is she writing *allegorically*? In an allegory, the writer establishes a one-to-one correspondence between some part of her story (a character, an event, a place) and some other, literal reality. In *Pilgrim's Progress*, Christian carries a huge burden on his back; this burden represents sin. In *Gulliver's Travels*, Swift's characters war about whether eggs should be cracked at the little or the big end; the bitter dispute between Little-Endians and Big-Endians is an allegorical reference to the controversy over the proper observation of the Eucharist that raged during Swift's century. (A writer's choice of allegory is in itself an expression of opinion, and you can take issue with it: Not everyone finds the debate over the Real Presence as insignificant as the debate over how to crack an egg.)[9]

In the absence of allegory, is the writer of fables *speculating*? In this case, the fantastic elements don't have a one-to-one correspondence to our world; instead, the oddness of the unfamiliar surroundings represents ideas taken to their extreme. George Orwell writes fantastically about a world that doesn't exist, but he doesn't want you to pick out a single parallel between Big Brother and some contemporary politician. In the strange universe of *1984*, certain aspects of modern life are stretched, exaggerated, and expanded to an unthinkable extreme in order to demonstrate their potential danger.

3. Is the novel primarily realistic, but with a few fantastic elements? If so, you cannot simply classify it as a "fable." *The Scarlet Letter* chronicles quite ordinary events—unfaithfulness, the birth of an illegitimate baby— but its climax involves at least one fantastical event. *Jane Eyre* is the story

---

[9]If you suspect allegory but need some cultural or historical details in order to find the parallels, glance through the book's introduction; consult a Norton Anthology, which generally footnotes the most important allegorical elements of a classic work; or Google "Allegory in [title]"(you will probably get better results by using the quotation marks).

of realistic people who live (unhappily) in regular English houses, but Jane hears a ghostly voice at a climactic moment: Is it a dream? When a writer brings fantastical elements into an otherwise realistic tale, he is illustrating a real phenomenon that is too powerful to be described in realistic terms. Can you identify this phenomenon?

What does the central character (or characters) want? What is standing in his (or her) way? And what strategy does he (or she) pursue in order to overcome this block? Almost every novel (even the most modern) is constructed around these basic questions. You can ask them for as many characters as you want, but begin with the person who seems most prominent.

What does Elizabeth Bennet want? This most central of questions often appears to have a straightforward answer. Elizabeth Bennet wants to get married. Christian wants to get to the Celestial City. Heathcliff wants Cathy. Ahab wants the whale.

But generally a deeper, more essential need or want lies beneath this surface desire. You can often get at this deeper motivation by asking the second question: *What's standing in the way?* What destroys Elizabeth Bennet's marriageability, complicates her life, threatens to destroy her happiness? Her family: her wild younger sister, her ridiculous mother, her passive and cynical father. Elizabeth wants to marry, but her deepest want goes beyond matrimony. She wants to abandon the world she was born into and move into another world. She wants to escape. (Asking this question will also keep you from settling on too simple an answer: Ahab *doesn't* just want to catch the whale.)

Now do a little more classification. Is a *person* keeping the heroine from achieving her deepest wants? If so, is that person a "villain" in the classic sense, an evildoer who wishes to do another character harm? (Simon Legree, in *Uncle Tom's Cabin*, is a classic villain.) Or is the "villain" simply another character with a deep want of his own that happens to be at cross-purposes with the heroine's need? (Elizabeth Bennet's mother, father, and younger sister, all pursuing their own needs, are unmindful of their disastrous effect on Elizabeth's struggling romance.)

The block in the heroine's way doesn't have to be a person. A collection of circumstances, a malign force that constantly pushes her in the wrong direction, an impersonal set of events that have united to complicate her life—these can also keep a character from getting what she wants. The novelist's world may demonstrate that human beings are always at the mercy of a flawed, fallen creation—or an uncaring, mechanical universe in which they are as insignificant as flies.

Once you've identified, at least tentatively, a character's wants and the "block" that keeps him from fulfilling them, you can begin to answer the third question: What strategy does a character follow in order to overcome the difficulties that stand in his way? Does he bulldoze his way through the opposition, using strength or wealth to overcome his difficulties? Does he manipulate, scheme, or plan? Does he exercise intelligence? Grit his teeth and keep on going? Buckle under the pressure, wilt and die? This strategy produces the plot of the novel.

These basic questions will take you through even the most modern novels on the list. Characters have always longed for escape, freedom, an ideal existence, control of their lives. Jack Gladney of DeLillo's *White Noise* wants to find the *inherent* meaning of life, not the meaning imposed on him by the corporations that have already constructed the story of his life for him (a story that involves his constant purchase of all the things they manufacture). What keeps him from discovering this meaning? Does he manage to find it in the end? (Three guesses.)

Who is telling you this story? Stories don't just float in the air; they are told by a voice. Whose voice is it? Or, in other words, what *point of view* does the writer adopt?

Point of view, like other aspects of fiction, can be broken into dozens of types, each subtly different. Unless you plan to make a detailed study of the art of fiction,[10] you only need to be familiar with the five basic points of view. Each has its advantages and tradeoffs.

1. First-person point of view ("I") gives a very immediate, but limited, perspective. First person allows you to hear a character's most private thoughts—but in exchange, you can only see what happens within the character's line of sight, and you can only know those facts that the character is herself aware of.

2. Second-person ("You walk down the street and open the door . . .") is uncommon, generally used only in experimental works (and adventure games). Like first-person point of view, second person keeps the reader intimately involved with the story, and brings a sense of immediacy far beyond what first person can produce. But second person also tends to limit the writer to the present tense, cutting off any reflection on the past.

3. Third-person limited (also called "third-person subjective") tells the story from the viewpoint of one particular character, delving into that character's mind, but using the third-person pronouns (*he* or *she*) rather than the

[10]In this case, you might invest in Wayne Booth's *The Rhetoric of Fiction* and Thomas McCormick's *The Fiction Editor*, two classic guides to how (and why) novelists manage to produce the effects that they do.

first-person pronouns. This perspective allows the writer to gain a little bit of distance from the story, but still limits the writer to those events that the viewpoint character can actually see and hear. A useful variant on this—and perhaps the most common narrative strategy in the novels listed below—is "third-person multiple," which allows the writer to use the viewpoints of several different characters, jumping from the "inside" of one character to the "inside" of another in order to give multiple perspectives.

4. "Third-person objective" tells the story from a removed, distant perspective. The narrator can see everything that is happening, as though he were hovering in space above the scene, but can't look into the heart or mind of any character. The writer who uses third-person objective gains a sort of scientific, dispassionate perspective but loses the ability to tell us what the characters are thinking and feeling; we have to deduce this from the characters' actions and expressions. Third-person objective is the filmmaker's point of view.

5. The omniscient point of view—the most popular until the nine-teenth century—puts the writer in the place of God. He can see and explain everything. He can describe both great events in the universe and the thoughts that occupy the most private recesses of a character's soul. The omniscient point of view often—although not always—is the author's point of view as well; it can allow the writer to moralize, to record his own personal ideas about the events of the book. (In Victorian times, the omniscient point of view allowed the writer to address the reader directly: "Gentle reader, what depths of guilt such a woman must suffer!")

Which point of view does the writer choose to use? What does he gain and lose through it? Once you've identified the point of view, try an experiment: retell a crucial passage in the novel from a different point of view. How does this change the story?

Where is the story set?   Every story happens in a physical *place*. Is this place natural, or human-constructed? If natural, do the woods and fields and skies reflect the emotions and problems of the characters? Do clouds cover the sky as the heroine weeps; does the wind rise as tempers fray? Or is nature unresponsive to the hero's struggles? The answers to these questions will tell you how the novelist views the human relationship to the physical world. Is humanity so intimately connected to nature that the earth responds to the human plight? Or is the universe indif-ferent? Are we the center of the universe, or simply bugs crawling on its uncaring surface?

Human-built surroundings—a city, a house, a room—can also reflect the inner life of the characters: bare and clean, cluttered and confused.

"When I was brought back next day," writes the narrator of Camus's *The Stranger*, "the electric fans were still churning up the heavy air, and the jurymen plying their gaudy little fans in a sort of steady rhythm. The speech for the defense seemed to me interminable." The thick, unvarying atmosphere reflects the narrator's own inability to pierce through the fog of confusion all around him.

Look for several sections of description and ask yourself: Who is present in this scene? What are her surroundings like? How does she sense them? What does this say about her state of mind?

What style does the writer employ? "Style" refers not only to the vocabulary a writer uses (simple or multisyllabic?) but also to the general length of sentences. Are they short and terse? Or complex, containing many clauses and subordinate ideas?

At the beginning of the twentieth century, realistic novelists made a concerted effort to move away from complex, complicated sentences—the product of thought and careful pencil work—toward a more colloquial, casual style, closer to what "real, plain people" would use in everyday conversation. This shift away from formal language reflected a change in ideas of "good style."

You can identify whether the writer is using formal or informal language (or *diction*) by using a few simple, mechanical devices. In *Classical Rhetoric for the Modern Student*, Edward Corbett suggests the following:

1. Choose one long paragraph and count the words in each sentence. What's the shortest sentence? The longest? What's the average number of words in a sentence?
2. In the same paragraph, count the number of nouns and verbs which have three or more syllables.
3. How many nouns in the paragraph refer to concrete *things* (people, landscape, animals, clothing, food, etc.), and how many refer to abstract *ideas*?
4. How many verbs in the passage describe physical activity (run, jump, climb, blush) and how many describe mental activity (worry, anticipate, rejoice)?[11]

These mechanical exercises can help you begin to evaluate whether the writer's style is "plain" (short, common words, simple sentences) or more complex and ornamental.

[11]Edward Corbett, *Classical Rhetoric for the Modern Student*, 4th ed. (Oxford: Oxford University Press, 1999), pp. 341–77.

Now take three passages of dialogue from three different characters and compare them, using the above exercise. Do all these characters talk alike? (This is a very common flaw—even in the work of great writers.) Or do their patterns of speech reflect the fact that they have different backgrounds, different jobs, different lives?

Finally, take note of any departures from standard conventions of punctuation and capitalization. Does the writer intentionally make use of fragments or run-on sentences? How are proper names treated? Is dialogue marked traditionally, or set off in some other way? If there *are* departures, how does this change your experience of the book? Try rewriting a sentence or paragraph (or more), re-inserting the conventions you learned in high school English. Compare with the original. What difference does your rewrite make?

Images and metaphors.   Is any particular image repeated again and again? Do the characters find themselves continually crossing water or walking through the woods? Does a particular color (a white dress, a white rose, a white sky) occur more than once? In *The Great Gatsby*, a pair of huge wooden eyes, abandoned by the optometrist who intended to use them as a billboard, looks mournfully out over an ashy plain. A. S. Byatt's *Possession* makes great use of the colors green and blue and their relationship to water and to glacier ice.

Once you've found a repeated image, ask: Is this a metaphor, and if so, what does this represent? A *metaphor* is a physical object or act that stands for something else—an attitude, a situation, a truth. A metaphor is different from an allegory. An allegory involves a one-to-one correspondence between different story elements and the realities for which they stand; an allegory is a *set* of related metaphors, whereas a metaphor is a single image that may bear multiple meanings. The huge wooden eyes in *Gatsby* reoccur several times. Like the eyes of God, they constantly watch the characters, but they are blind and uncaring and bring no meaning to the lives under their gaze. They also look out over a plain that should have developed into a bustling business district but instead turned into a wasteland. So the wooden eyes serve as a metaphor for the absence of God, but also draw our attention to the essential emptiness in the glittering, prosperous lives of Daisy and her circle.

Beginnings and endings.   Now take a moment to examine the opening and closing scenes. The beginning of a novel should draw you immediately into the story's central problem. Does the writer hint at a mystery, begin to sketch out an incomplete scenario you don't immediately understand? If so, perhaps the intent of the book is to show how human beings can triumph over partial knowledge, using their wits and determination to bring meaning to confusion. Does the book begin with violence and color, drawing you in through sheer action? If so, perhaps the intent is to portray humans as busy and effective in their world. Does it begin with passivity and stagnation? Perhaps the intent is the opposite: to show humanity's essential helplessness. "It is a truth universally acknowledged," begins Jane Austen in *Pride and Prejudice*, "that a single man in possession of a good fortune, must be in want of a wife." That single sentence contains all of the novel's major themes: the necessity of marriage, the desire for independent prosperity, and the shifting nature of "universally acknowledged truths," since the characters find their deepest convictions overturned, one by one, as the story unfolds. Henry James begins *The Portrait of a Lady* with a tea party on the front lawn of an English house: "Real dusk would not arrive for many hours," he writes, "but the flood of summer light had begun to ebb, the air had grown mellow, the shadows were long upon the smooth, dense turf." The tranquility and languor of the European scene is soon shattered by the arrival of an energetic American, and this conflict between old and new cultures is James's central preoccupation.

Now that you've considered the beginning, turn to the end. John Gardner suggests, in *The Art of Fiction*, that stories have two kinds of endings. There is the *resolution*, when "no further event can take place (the murderer has been caught and hanged, the diamond has been found and restored to its owner, the elusive lady has been captured and married)." In contrast is the ending of *logical exhaustion*, in which the characters have reached "the stage of infinite repetition; more events might follow . . . but they will all express the same thing—for example, the character's entrapment in empty ritual or some consistently wrong response to the pressures of his environment."[12]

What sort of ending does the book have? The *resolution* that Gardner describes shows a certain faith that we can triumph over our world, control our existence by discovering rules we can follow in order to bring success (or break to court disaster). The ending of *logical exhaustion*, on the other hand, shows that we are trapped, powerless, condemned to repeat the same actions over and over again. Each kind of ending demonstrates a certain philosophy about the nature of human life. Do you agree with that philosophy?

That question (*Do I agree?*) leads us into the third stage of reading: the rhetoric phase.

---

[12]John Gardner, *The Art of Fiction: Notes on Craft for Young Writers* (New York: Knopf, 1983), p. 53.

The Third Level of Inquiry: Rhetoric-Stage Reading

Your answers to the logic-stage questions should begin to reveal the ideas at the core of each novel. During the rhetoric stage, you'll try to decide whether you agree with those ideas or not.

These great novels differ so widely—and your own approach to them will depend so heavily on your own philosophy of life, your religious beliefs, your experience of work and play and family life—that I can't lay down hard and fast "discussion topics" for you. But I can suggest a few topics that will help you begin the process of interacting with the novel's ideas. Remember that your rhetoric-stage examination of a novel should take place in partnership with another reader. You'll begin the dialogue by answering one of the following questions; ask your reading partner to do so as well. If you're conducting your discussion by letter or email, your initial letter can simply consist of a couple of paragraphs in answer to one of the following questions; your reading partner can answer with her own thoughts; and you can then move on to the next question. Even if you're discussing the book in person, write your answers down in your journal, so that your notes can serve as a "history" of the development of your ideas about reading fiction.

What questions should you ask? Most of them will be related to one central query: Is this book an accurate portrayal of life? *Is it true?*

The ideas you'll discuss in the rhetoric stage of novel reading have to do with the nature of human experience: What are people like? What guides and shapes them? Are we free? If not, what binds and restricts us? What is the ideal man or woman like? *Is* there such a thing as an ideal man or woman—or does this idea itself suggest some sort of transcendent "truth" that is only an illusion?

Do you sympathize with the characters? Which ones, and why?   Can you find some point of empathy (emotional or intellectual identification) with each major character? The characters' dilemma, or their reaction to it, must provoke some kind of recognition; even in the oddest and most maniacal character, there should be something that we acknowledge. "Though we can see at a glance that Captain Ahab is a madman," John Gardner remarks, "we affirm his furious hunger to know the truth."

In a great novel, even the evildoers possess some emotion or motivation that also exists in the reader. The novel's bad guy is a villain not because he is a monster, but because some real quality has been distorted and exaggerated until it turns destructive. In the same way, a heroine should not possess undiluted goodness; such a character would be unrecognizable.

Her greatness should result from her triumph over flaws that we recognize, and might even share. If she fails to triumph, like Lily Bart in Edith Wharton's *The House of Mirth*, we should feel that her failure could be our own; were we in her shoes, we too might succumb.

Try to identify the character quality that allows you to sympathize with each character: Ahab's pursuit of truth, Lily Bart's longing for beauty, Huck Finn's craving for freedom. Do you feel this quality in yourself or observe it in others? In the novel, is this quality distorted, or exaggerated, or somehow twisted away from the norm? What opposing tendency destroys it, or stands in the way of its full flowering? Do you recognize that contrary impulse in yourself as well?

And then consider: The writer selected this quality as the character's central defining characteristic. Is the writer making a statement, through that selection, about the human condition—about the universal longings that all humans share, and the opposition that we all face as we try to fulfill those cravings?

Does the writer's technique give you a clue as to her "argument"—her take on the human condition? Point of view, setting, use of detail, stream-of-consciousness reflection: Each technique can imply a certain philosophical commitment on the part of the writer. Consider the implications of point of view. Nineteenth-century narrators were fond of the omniscient point of view, which allowed them (in effect) to take the position of God: to see all, describe all, and issue moral judgments on all. But more than one critic has observed that the slow decline in the use of the omniscient point of view has paralleled a decline in the traditional belief of God as an all-seeing, all-determining being. Without the omniscient point of view, no single, normal, "standard" point of view exists; each character has a different idea about what is happening, and no particular point of view is identified as *true*.

What does the setting of the book tell you about the way human beings are shaped? If the novelist believes that we are produced by our environment—that the place and time in which we live determine who we are—she will pay close attention to physical landscapes. But if she believes man to be a free soul, with power to triumph over his surroundings, she's more likely to concentrate on what's going on inside the characters' heads. Instead of lovingly detailed descriptions of physical setting, she'll produce equally detailed records of emotions, thoughts, and moods.

Is the novel self-reflective? Discovering more about the human condition from a novel: Is this even possible? Can stories about people convey truth? Can written words really communicate something meaningful about existence?

The answer to those questions is not an automatic *yes*. The novelist assumes, as he writes, that his words convey some sort of real meaning to readers; that human existence can be reduced to a page and still remain recognizable. But most writers also feel deep doubt as to whether this will actually happen. Does the novel acknowledge this tension? Does it call attention to itself, or to the acts of reading and writing? Do the characters in it read? What do they gain from their reading? Are some kinds of reading praised while others are condemned? Do the characters write? If so, what do they hope to achieve through their writing? Are they immortalized or destroyed by what they set down on paper?

If the novel is self-reflective, does it affirm that storytelling *can* make a meaningful statement about human existence—or does it question that possibility? The novels *Don Quixote* and *Possession* are nearly four hundred years apart in time. Yet both writers reflect on the acts of reading and writing. Don Quixote loses sight of reality through much reading; the central characters of *Possession* are rediscovered through the stories, poems, and letters that they leave behind.

Did the writer's times affect him?   The common-sense answer to this question would seem to be *yes*. But this was for several decades a highly debated topic, with so-called *formalists* asserting that a novel should be treated on its own terms, as an "artifact" that has nothing to do with its times (or its writer, come to that), and that knowledge of a writer's times can contribute *nothing* to an understanding of the fiction at hand.

It has become increasingly difficult to argue that you can read (for example) *The Great Gatsby* without knowing something about America in the 1920s. But the pendulum has now swung somewhat far over to the other side, with literary critics asserting that a novel is nothing *more* than a product of its times and should be read as a sort of imaginative history, a reflection of social customs—particularly those that oppress a particular race, gender, or class. Thus *The Scarlet Letter* tells us how the Puritans treated adulterous women, *Huckleberry Finn* is about slavery in the mid-nineteenth century, and *Heart of Darkness* reveals the mindset of colonialists toward the native races.

All of these things are true, but these novels are much more than a reflection of their times; to see them primarily as minihistories of culture is to flatten them. The sensible reader should take the middle course: Assume that the writer has been influenced by the accepted wisdom of his times, but also give him the benefit of imagination. Perhaps he was able, in some of the novel's aspects, to make an imaginative leap that took him further than his contemporaries.

As part of your rhetoric-stage discussion, you may want to read a brief history of the times in which the writer lived. This doesn't have to be an enormous project; a few pages from a basic text will give you some sense of the writer's times. The novel list tends to be focused on American and English works, so you might consider investing in Paul Johnson's *History of the American People* or George Brown Tindall's *America: A Narrative History* and Kenneth O. Morgan's *Oxford History of Britain*. A slightly more detailed history—and one that pays a little more attention to social and cultural trends—is *A History of England*, by Clayton Roberts and David Roberts, which comes in two volumes that overlap: *Volume I: Prehistory to 1714*, and *Volume II: 1688 to the Present*. For a broader picture of the world, look for John Morris Robert's *Penguin History of the World*, revised in 2014.

A good rule of thumb is to read twenty years on either side of the work in question, so that when you read *Pilgrim's Progress* you should read about events in England from 1660 to 1700. You may find it helpful to keep a brief timeline of some sort, either along the top margins of your journal or on a separate sheet of paper, so that you can remember momentous events.

If you find yourself getting bogged down, you can skip this part of rhetoric-stage reading. It is better to read the novels and skip the history than to give up on the whole project. On the other hand, you won't fully understand *Huckleberry Finn* without reading about the Fugitive Slave Law; and *1984* won't make complete sense unless you know something about the state of British politics and culture in 1949, when George Orwell wrote his pessimistic screed.

Is there an argument in this book? Now try to bring these different considerations together into a final statement: What exactly is the writer telling you?

A novel is not an argument, and a story should never be boiled down into a syllogism. The primary purpose of a novelist is to lead you through an experience, not to convince you of a point. But in many novels, there *is* an idea. The writer, in describing the life of one particular character, is making a statement about the human condition in general. Jack Gladney, the professor of Hitler studies who stars in DeLillo's novel *White Noise*, is drowning in the ephemera of his culture; and so, DeLillo wants you to know, are all of us. Thomas Hardy's hapless characters struggle against the implacable natural forces that continually push them down into the muck from which they strive to rise. They *always* lose. And so, Hardy wants you to know, will the rest of us.

So think about what happens to the main characters, and *why*. Is there an argument in the hero's (or heroine's) fate—or in the villain's downfall?

Do you agree? Now you can ask yourself that ultimate question suggested above: Is this work *true*?

Here you should consider two senses of the word *true*. A novel that is convincing, vivid, engaging, carefully written so that each detail corresponds to reality, a novel that draws you into its world and keeps you interested in the fates of its characters—that novel is *real*, resonating with our own experience of the world. But a work can be true in this sense and still present an idea about what human experience *should be* that is opposite to our own convictions.

Or a work can vividly portray one aspect of human existence while suggesting that this is the only level on which humans can live.

Or a story can suggest that there *is* no "should be"—nothing to strive for beyond what we see, nothing to believe in beyond what is.

All of these ideas we may strenuously reject while still finding the book itself "believable." So in what sense is the book *true?*

Related to this is one final question: What is fiction *meant* to do? Why are you reading a novel at all? Are you expecting to find out some truth about human nature? Should a novel reveal some difficult, hard-to-face truth about ourselves? Do novels show the inevitable end of certain paths? Or are they, instead, agents of moral change? Do they show us models so that we can amend our ways? This idea—that fiction provides us with a model—itself has a certain assumption behind it: There is some standard of human behavior which applies to all of us, in all cultures, and our quest in life is to uncover it.

The opposing idea was once expressed by Alexander Pope in the phrase, "Whatever is, is right." The novel doesn't set out an ideal, because to assume that there is such a thing as an unchanging standard of behavior governing all people at all times is narrow minded and myopic. The novel has no business in providing models. It simply explores realities: It opens numerous doors for you to peer through, but makes no suggestions as to which threshold you should cross.

THE ANNOTATED NOVEL LIST

Defoe, Richardson, and Fielding helped create the novel, but they're not on this list; literary scholars find them fascinating, but their prose is undoubtedly dated. "And so it fell out to Lady Booby," writes Richardson in *Pamela*, "who happened to be walking arm in arm with Joey one morning in Hyde-Park, when Lady Tittle and Lady Tattle came accidentally by in their coach. *Bless* me, says Lady Tittle, *can I believe my eyes? Is it Lady Booby?"*

Pamela and Fielding's *Joseph Andrews* are both satire, the most quickly dated of all literary forms; Defoe's prose fares slightly better, but long chunks of *Robinson Crusoe* are devoted to minitravelogues, a popular form at the time. ("It happen'd to my farther Misfortune, That the Weather prov'd hazey for three or four Days, while I was in this Valley; and not being able to see the Sun, I wander'd about very uncomfortably, and at last was oblig'd to find out the Sea Side, look for my Post, and come back the same Way I went; and then by easy Journies I turn'd Homeward, the Weather being exceeding hot, and my Gun, Ammunition, Hatchet and other Things very Heavy." And more of the same, in which nothing particular happens.)

So the Annotated Novel List begins with Cervantes, who anticipated those later English writers, and then moves on to Bunyan and Swift. The list is heavily weighted toward those novels originally composed in English (thus American and British literature), although I have tried to include important works of world literature that are available in affordable translations. This list is representative, not comprehensive; the novels on the list were chosen, not just for their enduring value, but also because they illustrate some important stage in the novel's development (the allegorical impulse, in the case of Bunyan) or because their ideas and characters have entered our language.

The annotations that follow are intended to help you enjoy your first reading more. For many of the older novels, I offer a brief plot summary. The joy of these books is not found in the surprise of what happens (as if they were crime dramas on TNT), but rather in the ways that the authors develop and complicate ancient plot structures of love and marriage, ambition and loss, greed and catastrophe. If you'd rather be surprised, you can always skip the annotations and read them afterward.

Read the following list in chronological order:

MIGUEL DE CERVANTES
Don Quixote
(1605)

Best translations: Edith Grossman's energetic 2003 translation brings the tale into a contemporary English voice while retaining much of the original meaning. There are, however, points to reading Tobias Smollett's classic translation of 1755. Grossman attempts to strike a balance between readability and faithfulness to Cervantes's intent (as she sees it); Smollett's translation is closer to a collaboration between himself and Cervantes to produce a popular novel called Don Quixote, *which entered into the English imagination. If you get well and truly bogged down in this lengthy book, try the abridgment by Walter Starkie.*

Alonso Quixada, a poor country gentleman with too much imagination and not enough money, becomes so enthralled with tales of chivalry that he reads day and night, even selling good farmland to buy books. Soon he imagines that he's living in a romantic tale; he renames himself Don Quixote [pronounced *Kee-HO-tay*], claims a village girl as his fair lady, recruits the peasant Sancho Panza as his squire, and sets out on a quest. Cervantes makes use of the literary conventions of the *picaresque* tale, in which a rogue wanders through the countryside, taking advantage of the gullible people he meets. But Don Quixote is the innocent in this journey, and the people he meets (there are 669 characters in *Don Quixote*) are generally hardheaded and intolerant of his fantasies. Don Quixote and Sancho Panza wander from adventure to adventure as Quixote's friends and neighbors scheme to recapture him and bring him back home. Eventually they succeed, and Don Quixote is brought back to La Mancha to be treated for his madness. He's recuperating in a green flannel bedjacket when the young Sanson Carrasco, a neighbor's son, comes home from university with the news that Don Quixote's adventures have been put into a book with more than twelve thousand copies in print! Excited by their fame, Sancho and Don Quixote set off on another adventure; Carrasco, recruited by the village to retrieve the old man yet again, disguises himself as another knight and chases the pair through another whole series of adventures. Finally, posing as "the Knight of the White Moon," he defeats Quixote and orders him home; Don Quixote totters back to his farm, but soon falls ill with a fever and dies. On the surface, *Don Quixote* is a contradiction, an antibook novel. Don Quixote's madness is caused by reading; Sanson Carrasco, the educated university graduate, is vengeful and ineffective. But at the novel's end, the poor country gentleman Alonso Quixada dies and is buried; Don Quixote, the knight created by reading and kept alive through writing, lives forever. Don Quixote's adventures are entertaining, but the real fascination of *Don Quixote* lies in Miguel de Cervantes' constant attention to the ways in which fables become real in the imagination of the reader.

JOHN BUNYAN
The Pilgrim's Progress
(1679)

Best edition: The original English text with modernized spelling is available from Penguin Classics, Wordsworth Classics, and Dover Thrift Editions. Be sure that you don't accidentally pick up an abridged, "retold," "young people's," or "in Modern English" edition.

Both *Don Quixote* and *Pilgrim's Progress* take place within a fantasy that is clearly contrasted to the real world. Cervantes' hero is mad; John Bunyan's tale is a dream. In the dream, Bunyan's ragged hero, Christian, has a burden on his back and a book in his hand; the burden is ruining his life, and the book tells him that he must flee from his home or be destroyed. A mysterious visitor named Evangelist points him toward a narrow wicker gate. Christian finally manages to get through the gate and finds a Cross, at which point the burden on his back rolls away. But this is only the beginning of his spiritual task; now he must travel to the Celestial City. On his way he fights the monster Apollyon, escapes from the goblins who haunt the Valley of the Shadow of Death, resists the temptations of Vanity Fair (a town convinced of the virtues of unbridled capitalism), crosses swords with the Giant Despair, and finally reaches the Dark River, where "great horror" falls upon him. Rescued by Hopeful, he gains the shore and is escorted by Shining Ones into the presence of God. (The sequel to *Pilgrim's Progress*, written six years after the first, is often reprinted as Part II; it tells the story of Christian's wife Christiana and his four sons, who follow his path some years later.) Christian, in the manner of good Puritan divines, is prone to setting out spiritual truths in neatly numbered lists, as though mature spirituality were simply a matter of filling in the correct blanks on a preprinted form. Yet the threat of hell is never absent from *Pilgrim's Progress*; as Christian parades triumphantly into the City, he sees another pilgrim taken to a mysterious door at the city's foot and thrust through: "Then I saw," he ends, soberly, "that there was a way to Hell, even from the Gates of Heaven."

JONATHAN SWIFT
Gulliver's Travels
(1726)

Best edition: Readable basic editions are published by Dover Thrift Editions and Penguin Classics. The Norton Critical Edition, edited by Albert J. Rivero, provides extensive annotations; these can distract from the story, but since so much of the tale is intended as political or cultural satire, they can also help you make sense of what would otherwise be very puzzling episodes.

Ship's surgeon Lemuel Gulliver keeps trying to sail from Point A to Point B, but bad navigation, pirate attacks, mutinies, and storms push him off course every time. First he ends up shipwrecked on the island of Lilliput, where he is imprisoned by people six inches high (no mean feat). When he finally manages to escape to England, his countrymen strike him as grotesquely huge. On Gulliver's second voyage, he winds up on an island of giants, where he is treated like a pet. This time he is rescued by an eagle that snatches him up and drops him into the sea near an English ship. But back in England, he suffers from the same unpleasant change in perception; his fellow Englishmen now look like midgets. Restless, he plans another voyage away from home and discovers Laputa, a flying island where the men are obsessed by music and mathematics, while the women long for the less preoccupied men from a neighboring island. Gulliver's fourth and final journey lands him on an island inhabited half by barbarian, humanlike creatures called Yahoos, and half by graceful, intelligent horses called Houyhnhnms. When he finally returns to England for good, Gulliver is so revolted by his fellow countrymen (who now appear to be Yahoos) that he buys two horses and moves into the stable to live with them. Poor Gulliver: Travel is supposed to broaden the mind, but living with exaggerated versions of human behavior has narrowed him into a settled hatred of the entire human race. *Gulliver's Travels* is an adventure in perception and (partly) in the power of propaganda; Swift leads you to see through Gulliver's eyes and to accept his version of events—which, without your noticing, will often veer far from the "truth."

JANE AUSTEN
Pride and Prejudice
(1815)

Best edition: Thanks to the last two decades of Austen movies and miniseries, her novels have been reprinted by a whole slew of publishers, including Dover Thrift Editions, Vintage Classics, and Penguin Classics. The novel reads beautifully without explanations, so give the over-edited and unwieldy annotated editions a miss.

Pride and Prejudice deals not with the male world of quests and sea voyages, but with the indoor world of women, thus anticipating by a couple of hundred years the Oprah boom in women's fiction. "It is a truth universally acknowledged, that a single man in possession of a good fortune, must be in want of a wife," the novel begins. A wife is the icing on the cake for Charles Bingley and Fitzwilliam Darcy, single men with plenty of money and an unassailable position in the world. But without husbands, the five daughters of the impoverished Bennet family can look forward only to a slow decline into poverty. When Charles Bingley rents a house in the neighborhood, Jane, the mild and sweet-tempered oldest daughter, falls in love with him. But his friend Darcy is appalled by the vulgarity of Mrs. Bennet and the low position of the rest of the family, and convinces his malleable friend to give Jane up. Meanwhile Darcy, against his will, finds himself attracted to the second daughter, Elizabeth, and finally proposes to her in the most obnoxious manner possible. Elizabeth rejects him indignantly. But then a profligate rake who was once Darcy's childhood friend seduces Elizabeth's wild and uncontrollable youngest sister, Lydia—and Darcy sets out to make the situation right. He also steers Bingley back toward Jane, and Elizabeth, softened by these proofs of a changed heart, agrees to marry him. Her father consents ("He is the kind of man, indeed," Mr Bennet remarks, "to whom I should never dare refuse anything which he condescended to ask"), and the novel closes with a double wedding. *Pride and Prejudice* is one of the most satisfying romances in literature, but it ends with an unasked question: Elizabeth, resentful of a world in which appearance is everything, has now moved into its center by marrying one of the richest (and most conservative) men in England. How will her new life change her?

CHARLES DICKENS
Oliver Twist
(1838)

Best edition: The 1838 three-volume version with George Cruikshank's original illustrations is available online, as well as in the paperback Modern Library edition (2001). As with Pilgrim's Progress, *be sure that you don't accidentally pick up an abridged or adapted version of this novel, which for some reason (perhaps we should blame the musical) is often thought suitable for children.*

An unknown girl gives birth in a workhouse and then dies without revealing her identity; her baby, minutes old, lies gasping for breath on a grimy mattress. If the baby had been "surrounded by careful grandmothers . . . and doctors of profound wisdom, he would most inevitably and indubitably have been killed in no time." But since no one is present but an overworked doctor and a drunken matron, the baby lives. This caustic reversal of fortunes introduces us to Oliver Twist, the orphan child who deserves love and care, but is instead used by adults from his infancy on. The matron who raises him steals his charity handout; the parish rents him to a coffin maker for five pounds; when he runs away to London, the stolen-goods fence Fagin teaches him to pick the pockets of passersby. Oliver is rescued from the streets by the prosperous Mr. Brownlow, but two other thieves, Monks and Sikes (with the help of Sikes's working-girl lover Nancy), kidnap him back and force him to help with a robbery. The house's owners, Mrs. Maylie and her niece Rose, catch Oliver in the act and decide to adopt him, but Monks and Sikes are determined to kidnap the child back again. Nancy, who has begun to regret her involvement, warns Rose and Mrs. Maylie of the kidnap plot; when Sikes discovers her treachery, he beats her to death. (Dickens is a shrewd observer of phenomena for which there were no clinical labels: "I must go back," Nancy tells Rose, who tries to convince her to leave Sikes. "I am drawn back to him through every suffering and ill usage; and I should be, I believe, if I knew that I was to die by his hand at last.") Oliver introduces Rose and Mrs. Maylie to his previous benefactor, Mr. Brownlow, and the three adults plan to trap Sikes and Monks when they make their kidnap attempt. Sikes hangs himself accidentally while trying to escape the ambush. Monks is captured and turns out to be Oliver's illegitimate half-brother; his pursuit of Oliver has been an attempt to steal the younger child's inheritance. In two of the book's more staggering coincidences, Rose turns out to be Oliver's aunt, and Mr. Brownlow realizes that Monks and Oliver are both the sons of his old school friend Edward Leeford. Dickens's unlikely plot (and I've left out three quarters of it) is meant to demonstrate that children who survive in London do so by pure chance, because benevolent individuals happen to take pity on them. *Oliver Twist* was originally subtitled *The Parish Boy's Progress* in a satirical play on Bunyan's title. Christian is a grown man who can pursue his own destiny, but Oliver Twist is entirely dependent on the kindness of strangers.

CHARLOTTE BRONTË
Jane Eyre
(1847)

Best edition: Available from Wordsworth Classics, Dover Thrift Editions, Everyman's Library, and as an Audible audiobook (you have your choice of several readers, but remember to opt for an unabridged single-performer reading rather than an abridged or "full cast performance").

Jane Eyre, an orphan raised by an aunt who dislikes her and cousins who torment her, escapes first to school, then to a position as a governess at the estate of Thornfield. Her employer, the dashing but manipulative Mr. Rochester, persuades Jane to marry him; she agrees, but on her wedding day discovers that the strange maniacal laughter and weird happenings in the Rochester household are caused by Mr. Rochester's wife Bertha, who went insane shortly after their marriage and is confined to the attic. Rochester, prevented from committing bigamy, tries to convince Jane to live with him; but she flees away over the moors and stumbles onto the cottage of distant relations, the Rivers family. She stays with the two sisters, Diana and Mary, and is courted by their brother, the reserved and ascetic St. John Rivers. But when St. John proposes, telling Jane that God has called her to be both his wife and his assistant on his missionary voyages, Jane declines. Fortunately, she inherits a small sum of money from a distant uncle, which gives her a certain amount of independence. Pondering her next move, Jane has a sudden and vivid vision of Mr. Rochester, calling to her. She returns to Thornfield only to find it blackened and ruined. Rochester's mad wife burned the house, herself inside it; Rochester is now free to remarry, but has been blinded and scarred in the fire. Jane marries him anyway ("Reader," she announces in one of the novel's most famous lines, "I married him"), takes care of him, and, as the novel closes, bears him a son. Rochester is one of literature's great rascals: sexy, charming, rich, and disreputable. In Jane, Charlotte Brontë creates the perfect woman for him; she refuses to marry him until she, not he, can be the dominant partner.

NATHANIEL HAWTHORNE
The Scarlet Letter
(1850)

Best edition: Published by Dover Thrift Editions, Penguin Classics, and Vintage Classics.

Hester Prynne becomes pregnant well after her husband is lost at sea. Her Puritan community threatens to execute her for adultery, but when the village minister, Arthur Dimmesdale, intervenes on her behalf, the village elders allow her to live—as long as she wears a scarlet cloth *A* sewn onto the front of her dress. Hester gives birth to her daughter Pearl and lives quietly until a stranger appears in town. This weather-beaten man has spent years living with the Indians; he calls himself Roger Chillingworth, but Hester recognizes him as her missing husband. Humiliated by Hester's pregnancy, Chillingworth refuses to reveal his real identity to the town. Instead he scrapes up a friendship with Arthur Dimmesdale, whom he suspects (quite rightly) of being Pearl's father. Under the guise of manly comradeship, he subjects Dimmesdale to mental torture until the minister climbs up onto the scaffold, confesses his sin to the whole town, rips open his shirt to reveal a bizarre stigmata (an *A* which has formed itself on the flesh of his chest), and then dies. Chillingworth, deprived of the mouse in his cat-and-mouse game, dies too. Hester moves away with Pearl, but unexpectedly reappears some years later, still wearing the scarlet *A* on her gown, and goes on living quietly in Massachusetts until

her death. Pearl, who is born outside of society's moral constraints, manages to escape all social pressures and live happily ever after; but she only
achieves this freedom by leaving the Anglo-American world altogether to
marry some mysterious nobleman. (No one ever sees him, but letters with
a coat of arms that is "unknown to English heraldry" arrive for Hester
with regularity.)

HERMAN MELVILLE
Moby-Dick
(1851)

*Best edition: The Penguin Classics paperback has a large, readable font, and
a durable binding (important in such a thick book). The Wordsworth Classics
edition is also high quality. The Norton Critical Edition, edited by Hershel
Parker and Harrison Hayford, has plenty of enlightening footnotes about
whaling, but it's easy to get lost in the biographical details about Melville.*

A schoolmaster (whose true identity is never revealed, although he asks
us to call him "Ishmael") decides, restlessly, to change his life. He signs
onto the whaling ship *Pequod* along with the harpooner Queequeg, a tat-
tooed cannibal from the South Seas. The *Pequod* is captained by Ahab,
a maniacal whaler with a scar that runs the whole length of his body
and a wooden leg. Ahab is determined to find and kill the huge white
whale Moby-Dick. When the whale is finally spotted, boats are lowered
from the ship to chase it down; Ahab is in the lead boat, but Moby-Dick
charges his boat and destroys it. Ahab is rescued, and once again the crew
pursues the white whale. On the third day of the chase, the whale rams
the ship itself and splinters it; the rope from Ahab's harpoon coils around
his neck and drags him down into the water; and the crew all die except
for Ishmael, who is rescued by a passing ship.

This may sound fairly straightforward, but the novel is one long exercise in symbolism. What is it *really* about? The human impulse to "create and destroy gods and heroes" (Eric Mottram); God's "inscrutable
silence" in the face of man's pursuit of spiritual truth (James Wood);
language, which has "so many meanings offered that we end up with
meaninglessness" (Wood again); man's quest for knowledge, which
brings "misery as well as wonder" (James McIntosh); the rejection of
cultural authority and the subversion of accepted cultural truths (Carolyn Porter); heterosexual anxiety and homosexual identity (too many
critics to cite). It's also about obsession; the fruitless quest for a truth that
is often sighted but never found; the essential isolation and loneliness of

the human self, even when surrounded by company; the conflict of natural, savage, uncomplicated man (Queequeg) and educated, confused, uncertain man (Ishmael); and (oh, yes) what it's really like to chase, harpoon, and cut up a whale.

HARRIET BEECHER STOWE
Uncle Tom's Cabin
(1851)

Best edition: The Modern Library Classics paperback, which has beautiful large print and plenty of white space. Usable editions with smaller print are published by Signet Classics (200th Anniversary Edition) and Dover Thrift Editions.

Uncle Tom is a slave on Arthur Shelby's Kentucky plantation. Shelby is a conscientious master, but he is still a slaveowner, and Tom is still an asset. So when Shelby gets into debt, he sells Tom "down the river" to the slave markets in the Deep South, dreaded by slaves because of the greater cruelty, the hot, humid living conditions, and the grueling field labor. Selling Tom, who has been with the family for years, is bad, but Shelby also sells the five-year-old Harry away from his mother, Eliza. When his indignant wife protests, Shelby insists that his debts leave him no choice. But Mrs. Shelby, who is a woman and therefore possessed of greater moral sensitivity than any man, argues with her husband. Eliza overhears, snatches her child, and runs away. She tries to convince Uncle Tom to come with her, but he stays behind out of loyalty, knowing that Shelby needs the money from his sale. For this misguided identification with the aims of white people Tom eventually pays with his life. He travels down South, but on the way saves the life of Little Eva St. Clare, an impossibly good, golden-haired, consumptive child. Little Eva convinces her father to buy him, and on her deathbed pleads with Mr. St. Clare to set Tom free. St. Clare agrees, but before he can keep his promise he is accidentally killed; his wife sells Tom to pay her debts, and Tom is beaten to death by his new master, the drunk and vicious Simon Legree.

Eliza reaches Ohio after a dangerous passage across a river jammed with floating ice cakes. She finds refuge at the home of a proslavery senator who, moved by her plight, changes his mind and sends her to a Quaker community, which in turn helps her escape to Canada. Meanwhile, Arthur Shelby, haunted by his decision to sell Harry and Tom, decides to look for his slaves. When he discovers the circumstances of Tom's death, he meets two other slaves who are running away from Simon Legree's brutal treatment; one of them, Cassy, turns out to be Eliza's mother. Shelby goes back to Kentucky and frees all his remaining slaves; Cassy and her companions go to Canada and find Eliza there; and all of the fugitives decide to relocate to Liberia, the new colony for ex-slaves. Like Dickens, Stowe wants her readers to feel the emotions of the wretched. But while Dickens may find hope in benevolent individuals, Stowe sees them as ultimately helpless in the face of an unjust system. She wants a complete social reformation, and she borrows highly evocative themes (children in peril, bereaved mothers, saintly females) from contemporary "women's fiction" in an attempt to enlist her audience's emotions (and thus their wills) in this project.

GUSTAVE FLAUBERT
Madame Bovary
(1857)

Best translation: Adam Thorpe's 2011 translation, published by Vintage Books, beautifully echoes the rhythms of the original, while also deftly avoiding post-1857 English vocabulary and expression.

Gustave Flaubert, the "father of realism," kills his heroine off because she tries to live in a romance novel. Emma Rouault marries the village doctor, Charles Bovary, because she likes the idea of being the doctor's wife. But the reality is so boring that she becomes ill. Her husband gives up his rural practice and moves her to the town of Rouen, where she has a daughter. But motherhood doesn't fulfill her yearning for romance; when the baby drools on her (certainly one of the great realities of life), Emma recoils in horror. Instead she yearns for the law clerk Léon—until he leaves town—and incurs the wrath of her mother-in-law, who complains that Emma is too busy reading novels: "books, bad books, works that are against religion and where they make fun of priests." Longing for romance, tired of her dull husband with his dirty fingernails and peasant ways, Emma is ripe for the attentions of the town bachelor Rodolphe Boulanger, who has "frequented women a great deal." Boulanger has an affair with Emma, promises to carry her off, and then ignores their appointed meeting ("I cannot . . . have a child on my hands!" he thinks to himself. "The fuss, the expense!"). Emma, disappointed, begins an affair with Léon, who has just returned to town; she goes deep into debt, spending her husband's money without telling him until the sheriff comes to confiscate their property. Neither Léon nor Rodolphe will help her, so she poisons herself. Even here, romance and reality war: "How pretty she still is," an attendant sighs over her beautifully dressed corpse, until a "torrent of black fluids" pours out of Emma's mouth "like a vomiting" and stains her flounces. Charles Bovary dies of grief, leaving their daughter an orphan who has to work in a cotton mill—surely a guarantee that she won't share her mother's failings, which required a regular source of money for their indulgence.

FYODOR DOSTOYEVSKY
Crime and Punishment
(1866)

Best translations: The Vintage Classics paperback, translated by Richard Pevear and Larissa Volokhonsky. The classic translation by Constance Garnett, available in a Dover Thrift edition, is more dated than the Pevear/ Volokhonsky translation, but still well respected.

Raskolnikov commits a murder that even he doesn't understand. His family is poor, and his sister Dunya needs a dowry, so Raskolnikov murders an elderly pawnbroker and her sister for the jewelry in their room—even though the jewelry is poor stuff, hardly enough to make them wealthy. Raskolnikov slowly comes to the attention of the police inspector Porfiry Petrovich. When he realizes that he's under suspicion, Raskolnikov briefly considers turning himself in, but he abandons this plan when he becomes interested in the prostitute Sonya, the devout daughter of a dead clerk and a consumptive mother.

Meanwhile, Raskolnikov's sister Dunya has managed to become involved with three men at once. She breaks off her engagement with the petty bureaucrat Luzhin and becomes involved with Raskolnikov's friend Razumikhin instead; Luzhin, bitter over his rejection, plants money on Sonya and then accuses her of stealing it. (Fortunately, a neighbor sees him and exonerates her.) Dunya has also attracted the attention of a former student of hers, the sinister Svidrigailov, who follows her to St. Petersburg. When Raskolnikov finally confesses the murders to Sonya, he is overheard by Svidrigailov, who then lures Dunya to his room and locks her in. He promises to help save Raskolnikov if she will marry him, but she refuses; finally, Svidrigailov releases her and kills himself in despair. All of this twisted love stands in contrast to the love offered to Raskolnikov by Sonya, Dunya, and his mother. When they all exhort him to clear his conscience, Raskolnikov finally turns himself in and is sentenced to eight years in Siberia. Dunya and Razumikhin marry; Sonya follows Raskolnikov to Siberia, where she lives near the prison camp and helps care for its inmates. Imprisoned in Siberia, Raskolnikov suffers from wounded pride: "Oh, if only I were alone and no one loved me, and I myself had never loved anyone!" he thinks to himself. *"None of this would be!"* But under his pillow he keeps a copy of the Gospels that Sonya has given him. When he takes them out, the story of his crime ends, and a new story begins—but Dostoyevsky makes no attempt to tell it. "Here begins a new account," he writes, "the account of a man's gradual renewal . . . his gradual transition from one world to another, his acquaintance with a new, hitherto completely unknown reality. It might make the subject of a new story—but our present story is ended." Dostoyevsky's careful account of Raskolnikov's growing uneasiness over his crime is a classic description of the stages of guilt; it strikes a contemporary note even today, a century and a half later.

LEO TOLSTOY
Anna Karenina
(1877)

Best translation: The 1901 translation by Constance Garnett, revised by Leonard J. Kent and Nina Berberova in 2000 (Modern Library Classics), remains the most lyrical English version; more recent translations, while sometimes more faithful to Tolstoy's idioms, have not done the novel justice.

Stepan Arkadyevich is in trouble—he's been caught cheating on his wife, Dolly. Fortunately, Stepan's sister Anna is coming to town. She negotiates a truce between her brother and his wife and meets Count Vronsky, who has been paying halfhearted attention to Dolly's younger sister Kitty. When Vronsky sees Anna he falls in love with her; Anna, despite her husband and eight-year-old son, carries on an increasingly obvious liaison with Vronsky until she becomes pregnant with Vronksy's child and runs away with him. Meanwhile, Kitty pines for Vronsky but is slowly comforted by another suitor, the solid and worthwhile Levin. They marry and work together to run Levin's estate.

But Anna and Vronsky tear at each other. Anna is cut off from her son by her husband's decree; she is nagged by grief, guilt, and "an inner irritation, grounded in her mind on the conviction that his love had diminished." For his part, Vronsky begins to "regret that he had put himself for her sake in a difficult position." Their liaison degenerates; they quarrel; Anna rushes to the railway station, intending to run away. As she looks at the tracks, she thinks, "There . . . and I shall punish him and escape from everyone and from myself." She throws herself under the train. Vronksy, devastated, goes into the army.

Levin and Kitty aren't blissful either; Levin goes through a crisis of faith that almost drives him to suicide. But the two are held together by more than romantic love—they have the formal structure of family that Anna and Vronsky lacked. Levin's responsibilities to his family and estate force him to endure. And as he continues, doggedly, "laying down his own individual and definite pattern in life," he is given the gift of faith. Spiritual strength fills the empty structures of his existence. At the book's end, he reflects: "I shall go on in the same way. . . . [B]ut my life now . . . is no longer meaningless, as it was before, but it has an unquestionable meaning of the goodness which I have the power to put into it." Tolstoy's novel ends with a deft mixture of hope and realism; Levin's new strength doesn't depend on circumstances, but on his decision to believe in the spiritual dimensions of his everyday life.

THOMAS HARDY
The Return of the Native
(1878)

Best editions: Available from Penguin Classics, Modern Library Classics, and Signet Classics. Alan Rickman narrates the unabridged audiobook from Audible.

The Return of the Native begins, not with a hero or heroine, but with an entire chapter about the landscape: Egdon Heath, a natural force in its own right, a "sombre stretch of rounds and hollows . . . singularly colossal and mysterious in its swarthy monotony." Eustacia Vye lives on Egdon Heath. She is a forceful girl, with "instincts toward social nonconformity" and plans for life that show "the comprehensive strategy of a general" rather than "the small arts called womanish." She longs to escape Egdon Heath, and when Clym Yeobright, hometown boy made good, returns to the small village, she sees him as her deliverer. They marry—but she's infuriated by his decision to stay in Egdon Heath and become a schoolmaster. And things get worse. Clym reads too much and ruins his eyesight, and philosophically becomes a woodcutter. Trapped in this peasantlike existence, at the mercy of forces beyond her control, Eustacia begins an affair with her old suitor Damon Wildeve. When Clym's mother hears of the affair, she visits the Yeobright house to intervene. But Eustacia is entertaining Wildeve (in Clym's absence) and doesn't answer her mother-in-law's knock. Clym's mother goes away across the heath—where she stops to rest and is promptly bitten by a snake (Eustacia isn't the only character at the mercy of hostile natural forces). Clym, returning from his woodcutting, stumbles across his dying mother. He learns from villagers that she has been seen coming away from his home, demands an explanation from his wife, and discovers her affair. Eustacia runs away to elope with Wildeve, but on her way to meet him in the middle of the night, she falls (or jumps) into the nearby millpond and drowns. Damon plunges in after her and is drowned as well. Like water, the forces of nature and society bubble, pool, and flow all around the characters in *The Return of the Native*, ultimately submerging them in their fruitless attempts to escape. Hardy is the greatest "landscape writer" in the English language; his moors, fields, and hills are real enough to touch and taste; his dark woods and deep pools bristle with menace.

HENRY JAMES
The Portrait of a Lady
(1881)

Best editions: Available from Penguin Classics, Signet Classics, and Oxford World's Classics, as well as in a no-frills Dover Thrift Edition.

Isabel Archer is an American girl with a very American suitor—Caspar Goodwood, a tall, brown businessman with a resolute jaw. But Isabel's aunt, who has lived with her husband and son on an English country estate for years, decides to rescue Isabel from uncouth America and show her Europe. In England, Isabel is courted by the noble Lord Warbuton and is half inclined to fall in love with her cousin Ralph. Meanwhile her American friend Henrietta Stackpole, an independent and persistent reporter for an American publication, arrives in England. Troubled by the appeal of old (and in her eyes, decadent) Europe for Isabel, Henrietta invites Goodwood to visit—but Isabel, determined to make her own way, orders Goodwood to go away.

Fortunately Isabel doesn't have to stretch her self-reliance too far, since her uncle dies and, at Ralph's request, leaves Isabel half of his estate. With money in her pocket, Isabel makes the acquaintance of a sophisticated widow, Madame Merle, and goes traveling. Madame Merle introduces her to Gilbert Osmond, an oddly untrustworthy American with a fifteen-year-old daughter, Pansy. Isabelle agrees to marry Osmond, but Ralph objects that Isabel is giving up her liberty: "You were meant for something better than to keep guard over the sensibilities of a sterile dilettante!" he cries. Isabel refuses to listen. But three years later, she has been diminished by her marriage: She has less wit, less curiosity, less brilliance. When she discovers that Madame Merle is actually Pansy's mother and has been in contact with Osmond, her lover, all along, she is sickened by her husband's deception. She announces that she will travel to England (against Osmond's will) to see the dying Ralph. After her cousin's death she meets Caspar Goodwood again; the American begs her to leave Osmond and come back to America with him. She refuses, but the novel ends ambiguously, with Goodwood finding out from Henrietta Stackpole that her friend has gone back to Rome: "Look here," Henrietta says, "just you wait." Does Isabel finally return to him? We don't know, but in her efforts to be free she has consistently wound herself into chains; why would marriage to Goodwood bring her any greater liberty?

MARK TWAIN
Adventures of Huckleberry Finn
(1884)

Best editions: Available from multiple publishers (Dover Thrift Editions, Penguin Classics, Bantam Classics, Signet Classics), and also as a public domain ebook. Elijah Wood's unabridged audio recording for Audible captures Huckleberry Finn's voice beautifully. Be careful not to pick up a "young reader" or expurgated edition.

After he discovers six thousand dollars in a cave, Huckleberry Finn is suddenly in demand. Tom Sawyer wants him to join a robber's band, the Widow Douglas and her sister Miss Watson plan to civilize him, and his drunkard father kidnaps him and hauls him off to a cabin in the woods. Huck appreciates the freedom to smoke, cuss, and live in dirt, but doesn't enjoy being beaten daily, so he fakes his own gory murder and runs off. In the woods, he meets Miss Watson's slave Jim, who has also run off to avoid being sold. Huck and Jim set off on the Mississippi, headed for freedom. Along the way they explore a wrecked riverboat (Huck pretends to know the owner); meet up with a crowd of boastful raftsmen (Huck pretends to be the son of a riverman); take part in a bitter family feud (Huck pretends to be an orphan); and finally join up with two con men who claim to be the exiled King of France and the Duke of Bridgewater.

Huck tags along while the Duke and the King pretend, in turn, to be evangelists, actors, circus performers, and the long-lost heirs of a rich tanner. Meanwhile Jim stays on the raft, fearful of capture. When the Duke and the King—broke and exposed as frauds—sell Jim to a local farmer for a few extra dollars, Huck plots to free him. He pretends to be Tom Sawyer; Tom Sawyer, showing up to help, pretends to be Huck Finn; Jim, who could perfectly well get away on his own, pretends to be in a dungeon so that the two boys can mount an elaborate rescue. All three are caught, but Tom Sawyer shouts out that Jim has been free all the time. Miss Watson died two months before and set him free in her will, but Tom wanted to stage his false rescue for "the *adventure* of it."

"I reckon I got to light out for the Territory . . . ," Huck complains at the book's end, "because Aunt Sally she's going to adopt me and sivilize me and I can't stand it. I been there before." Huck's flight to freedom— the quintessential American quest—forces him to change identities again and again, never settling; as David F. Burg writes, Huck understands "that to keep moving is as near as one can ever come to freedom."[13]

STEPHEN CRANE
The Red Badge of Courage
(1895)

Best editions: Now in the public domain, this very short novel is available as a free ebook online, as well as in paperback from Dover Thrift Editions, Puffin Classics, and (in a collection with four other stories) Signet Classics. Multiple single-reader audio versions have been produced by Audible.

Henry Fleming, a farm boy fighting in the Civil War, worries over his ability to be brave. When his first battle starts, he finds himself in the middle of a confused and chaotic mass of soldiers, all shooting wildly; he starts shooting too, pleased and relieved to find himself already fighting. (Crane's battle scenes are fascinating for their extreme realism and limited point of view; he is the nineteenth-century equivalent of the handheld video camera, offering a nonprofessional, man-in-the-street view of events.) The soldiers around Henry retreat. Henry follows their example as he did before—but this time his crowd-following leads him into cowardly flight. Guilty and ashamed, Henry rejoins his regiment, trailing woefully along behind the honorably wounded: "He felt that he was regarding a procession of chosen beings. . . . He could never be like them." He imagines that the other soldiers are jeering at him as he passes. Suddenly the column of wounded is overwhelmed by a wave of men that pours past them in full retreat. Henry grabs a passing soldier to ask him what has happened, but the panic-stricken man clubs him with his rifle and runs away. Now wounded, Henry finally makes his way back to camp and tells them that he was injured in the battle. ("Ah," his

[13]David F. Burg, "Another View of *Huckleberry Finn*," *Nineteenth-Century Fiction*, vol. 29, no. 3 (December 1974): 299–319; 319.

corporal tells him, examining his head, "yeh've been grazed by a ball. It's raised a queer lump jest as if some feller had lammed yeh on th' head with a club.") But soon the regiment is once more engulfed in battle. Henry hides behind a tree and keeps on shooting blindly ahead of him. When the smoke clears, he discovers (to his surprise) that he's been at the forefront of the fighting: He's a hero, no longer a coward. Stephen Crane called *The Red Badge of Courage* a portrayal of fear, but fear and bravery have little relationship to Henry's reputation; his heroism is purely chance.

JOSEPH CONRAD
Heart of Darkness
(1902)

Best editions: Republished by Modern Library Classics, Everyman's Library, and Oxford World's Classics. Kenneth Branagh narrates the unabridged Audible audiobook.

Five old friends have gathered on a yacht in the Thames. One of them—Marlow, a seaman and wanderer—tells the story of his journey into the Congo. Hired by a trading company to check up on their ivory-production center, Marlow makes his slow and difficult way deep into Africa. As he travels, he hears again and again of the mysterious Mr. Kurtz, another employee of the trading company. Mr. Kurtz sends out magnificent shipments of ivory and also takes good care of his native workers, enriching the company and educating Africans at the same time. But as Marlow gets closer and closer to the heart of Kurtz's operation, he finds run-down ports, broken equipment, and hostile Africans. When he finally finds Kurtz, the man is dying; he's become more savage than the natives and has ruined an entire section of the Congo in his attempts to ship out more ivory. Before Marlow can bring him back to England, Kurtz dies, muttering, "The horror! The horror!" Like Bunyan's Christian, Marlow has made a pilgrimage. His journey into Africa has been a journey into the innermost recesses of the human soul, but instead of a Celestial City he has found only confusion, illusion, lack of clarity, lack of meaning, lies, and death. Back in civilization, Marlow meets Kurtz's fiancée, who asks about Kurtz's last words; Marlow lies, telling her that Kurtz died with her name on his lips. Kurtz's last words reveal the only truth he has discovered about human existence—but it's a truth no one can face. Nor is the darkness only in Africa. As Marlow finishes his story, the men on the yacht look up and see "a black bank of clouds . . .

an overcast sky . . . the heart of an immense darkness" hovering over the English landscape.

EDITH WHARTON
The House of Mirth
(1905)

Best editions: Available from Signet Classics, Dover Thrift Editions, and Penguin Classics. Avoid the multiple critical editions, which provide you with far too much interpretation. The unabridged audio version by Anna Fields is my favorite (Audible), although I suggest that you skip over the extended introductory essay.

The New York socialite Lily Bart is twenty-nine and (horror!) still unmarried; with no money of her own, she depends on grudging hand-outs from her aunt and taps her friends for the luxuries that satisfy her sense of beauty. Afraid that her days as perpetual houseguest will end when she's no longer young and lovely, Lily tries, reluctantly, to snare a rich husband. Her options are limited: Simon Rosedale, the Jewish finan-cier whose cash is making a place for him in high society, has already asked her to marry him, but she cannot bear to sink so low (Wharton's easy anti-Semitism is symptomatic of her times). Lawrence Selden, an attractive and sympathetic lawyer, is unfortunately too poor for her tastes. Her best choice is Percy Gryce, a heavy, colorless millionaire who col-lects Americana and always obeys his mother. But Lily despises her own marital ambitions, and her halfhearted schemes fall through, ruining her reputation in the process. No longer an "unsoiled beauty," Lily descends with startling rapidity through the strata of Gilded Age society; finally, she tries wage labor as a milliner, but can't keep up the ten-hour work-days. Fired from her job, reduced to living in a cheap boardinghouse while her savings dwindle away, and plagued by insomnia, Lily takes a double dose of chloral to help her sleep and never wakes up. Perhaps there are things that money can't buy, but in Wharton's America, you can't live without it.

F. SCOTT FITZGERALD
The Great Gatsby
(1925)

Best edition: The Scribner Classics paperback reprint. Jake Gyllenhaal's unabridged audio reading for Audible is well done.

Nick Carraway moves away from his innocent midwestern hometown and rents a house on Long Island Sound. His beautiful cousin Daisy lives across the water; the mysterious millionaire Jay Gatsby lives in a sparkling, brand-new mansion right beside him. Gatsby has loved Daisy since his college days. His desire is draped with romantic phrases, but what he really adores is Daisy's embodiment of wealth; she gleams "like silver, safe and proud above the hot struggles of the poor." When Daisy's husband Tom begins an affair with Myrtle Wilson, his mechanic's wife, Jay Gatsby convinces Nick to play matchmaker between himself and Daisy. Nick himself falls into a passionless relationship with socialite Jordan Baker. As all three affairs run in parallel, tensions tighten between the five central characters (the mechanic's wife apparently doesn't count). During a disastrous dinner at the Plaza, Tom sneers at Gatsby and accuses him of adultery. Daisy and Jay Gatsby leave together and drive back to the Sound in Gatsby's car—and accidentally run over Myrtle, who rushes into their way. Daisy was driving, but Jay Gatsby takes the blame. Myrtle's husband discovers Gatsby's identity, breaks into Gatsby's mansion, and shoots both Gatsby and himself.

Nick organizes the funeral service, but no one comes. Daisy and Tom drift away, Jordan Baker marries someone else. And finally Nick moves back to his midwestern town, abandoning New York and its deceptive beauty for the dark, solid worth of middle America.

VIRGINIA WOOLF
Mrs. Dalloway
(1925)

Best edition: The Harvest Book paperback. The unabridged audiobook read by Annette Bening is available from Audible.

Clarissa Dalloway steps out of her door in the morning to buy flowers for her party that same evening—and instantly we are plunged into the disjointed, image-bright stream of her thought. *Mrs. Dalloway* follows the thoughts of three main characters over the course of a single day in 1923. Clarissa Dalloway, a London society woman in her early fifties, remembers the long-ago days when she was courted by Peter Walsh, before she rejected him. Peter Walsh, now in love with a much younger woman, also muses about those days and recollects his first introduction to Clarissa's husband. Septimus Warren Smith, a shell-shocked soldier on the edge of complete disintegration, replays the events of the war and sees his friends dying in flames. The physical lives of the three only intersect twice; once, when Peter Walsh strolls past Septimus and his weeping wife in the park; and again at the end of the day, when Septimus's physician comes to Clarissa's party and remarks, casually, that his young patient committed suicide just hours before. But the story actually takes place not in the physical world, but in a different kind of universe: a mental reality, where the laws that govern time and space are different, where characters who never meet in person intersect, mysteriously, in their thoughts, and where Septimus and Clarissa, unacquainted with each other, are mirror images. Septimus is unable to cope with disrupted, shattered, post–World War I England; Clarissa Dalloway survives, but only because she refuses to think deeply ("She knew nothing," Woolf writes, "no language, no history; she scarcely read a book now, except memoirs in bed").

FRANZ KAFKA
The Trial
(1925)

Best translation: Breon Mitchell's translation, published by Schocken Books, is clear and captures Kafka's use of legal gibberish well.

"Someone must have been spreading lies about Josef K.," *The Trial* begins, "for without having done anything wrong he was arrested one morning." It's the morning of his thirtieth birthday, and at first Josef thinks that the arrest is a joke. But an Inspector appears and assures him that it is no joke; he is undoubtedly guilty, but until his trial he can go about his business. Josef K. keeps attempting to refute the accusation, but since he never finds out what it is, all his attempts end in confusion. He defends himself in front of spectators, only to discover that they are all in fact officers of the court; he discovers that the warders who first arrested him are being flogged for their conduct and tries to intervene; he tries to engage a lawyer, finds the lawyer on a sickbed, is tempted away from the sickbed by the lawyer's nurse (who seduces him), and then returns to find that the Chief Clerk of the Court has arrived in his absence. These dreamlike, irrational attempts to defend himself continue for a full year. On the morning of his thirty-first birthday, two more warders show up and order Josef K. to go with them. He realizes that they mean to execute him—but although he has the opportunity to escape, he allows himself to be killed. Kafka's opening words suggest that Josef K. lives in a rational world; "must have" implies some sort of cause and effect, "false accusation" assumes some existing standard of justice. But this reasonable order is an illusion. None of the court proceedings make sense; eventually the words that stand for those proceedings (*accusation, trial, crime, guilt*, even Josef K.'s name itself) become emptied of meaning as well. At the end, K.'s executioners lead him to his trial in silence. The rational order of the universe, and the words that express it, have both been shown to be phantasms.

RICHARD WRIGHT
Native Son
(1940)

Best edition: The Harper Perennial paperback.

Bigger Thomas lives in a rat-infested Chicago apartment controlled by wealthy Mr. Dalton; the Daltons charge their black tenants enormous rents and then give some of the money to black schools, which makes them feel enlightened. When Bigger gets a job as chauffeur on the Dalton estate, Mary Dalton—the daughter of the house—and her socialist boyfriend Jan treat Bigger as a peer. Bigger finds this oddly infuriating. ("Why didn't they leave him alone?" he thinks, when Jan shakes his hand. "He was very conscious of his black skin and there was in him a prodding conviction that Jan and men like him . . . made him feel his black skin by just standing there looking at him.") In a further egalitarian gesture, Jan and Mary invite Bigger to drink with them. All three get drunk. Bigger takes the staggering Mary home, back to her room. He kisses her, and then, hearing her mother in the hallway outside, puts a pillow over her face to keep her quiet. Afterward he's startled to find that Mary is dead. Panicked, Bigger stuffs her body into the furnace and then convinces his girlfriend Bessie to help him write a false ransom letter implicating Jan. Bessie starts to lose her nerve, though, and Bigger finally murders her in her sleep with a brick. Bessie's murder goes unnoticed. But the police decide that Bigger has murdered Mary Dalton and mount a manhunt for him, raiding black homes all along the South Side. Arrested and put on trial, Bigger becomes an icon for all that whites fear in blacks: strength, sexuality, and vengefulness for past mistreatment.

Jan, uneasily aware that somehow he bears responsibility for Bigger's plight, hires the lawyer Max to defend his girlfriend's murderer. ("I was . . . grieving for Mary," he tells Bigger, "and then I thought of all the black men who've been killed, the black men who had to grieve when their people were snatched from them in slavery.") Max admits Bigger's guilt, but argues that Bigger's life had been "stunted and distorted" by white mistreatment. Despite Max's plea for life imprisonment due to these extenuating circumstances, Bigger is sentenced to death. Wright's novel is a groundbreaking exercise in naturalism written from the black perspective; white Americans may struggle against natural forces, but black Americans were the physical tools of this struggle.

ALBERT CAMUS
The Stranger
(1942)

Best translation: Matthew Ward's translation, published by Vintage Books, captures the intentional stylistic differences Camus uses; be sure to read the translator's preface.

Like *Native Son, The Stranger* is about a murder that, insignificant in itself, demonstrates some truth about human existence. The murder of Mary Dalton shows the hopeless distortion of black-white relations in America; the murder of the Arab in *The Stranger* demonstrates that the events of life have no ultimate meaning. The actions of Meursault, the novel's central character, are presented in a flat, unemphasized sequence, so that no action has more importance than any other. Meursault's mother dies, so he goes to her funeral because everyone seems to expect him to. The day after the funeral, he meets Marie by chance, and the two sleep together. Meursault reads an old newspaper, sees spectators returning from a football game, decides to eat his supper, and tells Marie he'll marry her if she thinks it would give her pleasure: "It had no importance really," he thinks. Meursault's upstairs neighbor Raymond asks Meursault to help him humiliate his girlfriend. Meursault agrees ("I'd no reason not to satisfy him"), but this infuriates the girl's brother, who assaults Raymond with the help of an Arab friend. Walking on the beach later, Meursault sees the friend sleeping in the shade of a rock, and fires five shots into the man's body for no particular reason. He is arrested at once and put on trial. Refusing to show any emotion, he is judged to be a dangerous and unfeeling criminal and sentenced to death. But Meursault looks forward to execution, since death is the one certainty of life; he feels that he is "on the brink of freedom . . . I laid my heart open to the benign indifference of the universe."

In Camus's philosophy of "the absurd," there is no significance to life; all humans are condemned to death, facing the inevitable end. The only possible response is to admit that death will come and then to live actively in the present, making choices without regret. Camus writes in "The Absurd Man" that anyone who comes to terms with this truth is "imbued with the absurd." Actions have no meaning, but they do have consequences, and "those consequences must be considered calmly . . . There may be responsible persons, but there are no guilty ones."[14] Meursault's decision to kill the Arab is acceptable because he is willing to suffer the consequences of his choice; in his willingness to act, and in his calm acceptance of death, he is the model "absurd man."

GEORGE ORWELL
1984
(1949)

Best edition: The Signet Classic edition. Simon Prebble narrates the unabridged audio version from Audible.

Orwell's *1984* gave us the phrases "Big Brother" and "thought police," not to mention a whole new set of fears about the invasion of our private lives. Winston Smith lives in a London apartment where a two-way television screen monitors his every movement and word. Posters of Big Brother, the leader of the Party, remind him that he is constantly under surveillance by the Thought Police. Winston works for the Ministry of Truth, which continually rewrites books and newspapers so that Big Brother will appear to have predicted all political developments ahead of time. The Ministry of Truth aims to reduce all languages to Newspeak, the official language, with a vocabulary that gets smaller every year: "In the end," an official explains, "we shall make thoughtcrime literally impossible, because there will be no words in which to express it."

Winston rebels against the Party by starting a diary. Soon his rebellion takes more active forms: He begins an affair with his coworker Julia, and he accepts an invitation from his superior, O'Brien, to join a secret brotherhood that fights against the Party. But O'Brien turns out to be a Party spy, and as soon as Winston and Julia join the brotherhood they are arrested. O'Brien takes charge of Winston's rehabilitation, convincing him that Winston must believe only what the Party dictates: "Whatever the Party holds to be truth *is* truth," O'Brien lectures. "It is impossible to see reality except by looking through the eyes of the Party." Eventually Winston begins to break; he sits in his cell and writes "Freedom is Slavery. Two and Two make Five." But O'Brien wants him to love Big Brother, not simply to obey. The final step in Winston's forcible conversion takes place when O'Brien threatens to strap his head into a cage filled with starving rats, so that the rats can eat his face. At this, Winston screams, "Do it to Julia!

[14]Albert Camus, "The Absurd Man," in *The Myth of Sisyphus and Other Essays*, trans. Justin O'Brien (New York: Vintage Books, 1991), p. 67.

Not me! Julia!" His love for Julia has been broken; now he can love the Party. Orwell's hell on earth didn't come about in 1984. But in his chilling, detailed vision of a world where both mind and will can be manipulated by large and powerful institutions, he was decades ahead of the postmodernists and their condemnation of our advertisement-driven society.

RALPH ELLISON
Invisible Man
(1952)

Best edition: The Vintage International paperback.

In *Invisible Man*, the unnamed narrator exists beneath a veil that reflects back to the reader's eyes a white man's picture of what a black man should be. He wins a white-sponsored scholarship to a southern college for Negroes by fighting other black students in a boxing ring. Because he is articulate and presentable, the college asks him to show a visiting white trustee around the campus. The trustee insists on being driven into a rural slum and then to a bar that serves black veterans. At the bar, a shell-shocked black veteran attacks the trustee. When the college president discovers this adventure, he expels the narrator and sends him North to work, with "letters of reference" that advise employers not to hire him. Eventually the young man finds work in a paint factory known for its bright white paint. He gets into a fight, leaving his paint cans unattended; they explode and knock him unconscious, landing him in a hospital where he is forced to take part in shock-treatment experiments. Finally he escapes from the hospital and collapses in the street, where he is rescued by other blacks and given a home. He becomes a spokesman for the "Brotherhood," an organization working for oppressed blacks, and is put in charge of their Harlem agenda. But after a falling-out with the Brotherhood leadership, he realizes that they see him only as an instrument for their cause. Caught in the middle of a Brotherhood-incited riot, the narrator falls down a manhole. Two policemen cover the manhole. So the narrator takes up residence in a secret basement room, which he has lined with 1,396 bulbs that burn on stolen electrical power. He has been viewed by others as a bright black boy, as a guide into the seaminess of black life, as unthinking labor, as an experimental subject, as a useful spokesman, as a rioter, but never as himself. Everyone around him, the narrator muses, "see only . . . themselves, or figments of their imagination—indeed, everything and anything except me." Under the ground, the Invisible Man is now literally invisible, as he has been metaphorically invisible all his life; yet Ellison's brilliant novel has made him visible to the alert reader.

SAUL BELLOW
Seize the Day
(1956)

Best edition: The Penguin Classics edition.

Tommy Wilhelm, staying in a hotel because he's separated from his wife and sons, relies on his irascible, elderly father to pay his hotel bill. Tommy's broke and hopes to make a fortune in lard with the help of Tamkin, a doctor who claims to be an expert in the stock market—but who disappears, mysteriously, when lard falls precipitously and wipes Tommy's investments out. The novel takes place during a single day, but Tommy spends a good part of it thinking about the past, remembering all of his attempts to remake himself into a new man. He tried to be an actor but failed. He changed his name from Wilhelm Adler to Tommy Wilhelm ("Wilhelm had always had a great longing to be Tommy. He had never, however, succeeded in feeling like Tommy"). He bragged to his friends that he was about to become a vice president at his firm but didn't get the promotion. Too ashamed to stay and admit his failure, he quit his job but allows his father to boast about his position as vice president, even though both know that the title is a myth. Each reinvention of himself fails, including his final attempt to turn himself into an investor, since he insists on trusting the advice of Dr. Tamkin even though he half suspects him of being a fraud. At the end of the day, Wilhelm finds himself at the funeral of a stranger, where he is mistaken for the dead man's relative: "He, alone of all the people in the chapel, was sobbing. No one knew who he was. One woman said, 'Is that perhaps the cousin from New Orleans they were expecting? . . . It must be somebody real close to carry on so.'" As he weeps, Wilhelm finds happiness in his tears. Here at least he finds that importance in the eyes of others which he has always sought—even though it is based on a false identity.

GABRIEL GARCÍA MÁRQUEZ
One Hundred Years of Solitude
(1967)

Best edition: The Harper Perennial Classics paperback, translated by Gregory Rabassa. John Lee narrates the unabridged Audible audio verson.

José Arcadio Buendía and his wife Úrsula are cousins; Úrsula is afraid that she'll have a baby with a pig's tail, so she bars her husband from her bed. When a neighbor jeers at his unconsummated marriage, José Arcadio Buendía kills him in a duel and visits Úrsula's room in a passion of unproven manhood. Úrsula's baby, when born, doesn't have a pig's tail, but the dead neighbor insists on wandering through his house at night, so that he can wash the blood off his throat in the bathroom. So José Arcadio Buendía takes his wife and children off to found the new town of Macondo.

Macondo, isolated at first, is eventually opened to the outside world by tribes of gypsies—one of whom, Melquiades, bears a mysterious manuscript written in Sanskrit. Outside trade brings both prosperity and troubles. José Arcadio Buendía's oldest son runs off with the gypsies; his second son Aureliano becomes a colonel and fights bloody battles in a vague civil war until his mother threatens to kill him with her own hands. ("It's the same as if you'd been born with the tail of a pig," she snaps.) Eventually Aureliano retreats to his workshop to make little gold fishes, and his great-nephew Aureliano Segundo comes to the center of family life. Segundo marries a beautiful, pretentious, and hysterical woman but carries on an affair with the villager Petra Cotes, who makes him prosperous by wandering around his property, spreading her aura of fertility. Even magical prosperity, though, pales in the face of economic progress: a railroad opens into Macondo, and Yankee traders arrive on the train to sell bananas. This banana company introduces all sorts of trouble to Macondo: disorder, violence, assassination, and more family troubles. ("Look at the mess we've got ourselves into," Segundo's brother, Colonel Aureliano Buendía complains, "just because we invited a gringo to eat some bananas.") Led by Aureliano Segundo, the banana-company workers go on strike; infuriated, the Yankee traders call up a four-year rain that eventually beats the soggy proletariat into submission.

As Segundo's grandson, Aureliano Babilonia, grows to adulthood, he develops two obsessions. He has an incestuous passion for his aunt and fathers a baby with a pig's tail. And he is enthralled by the mysterious gypsy manuscript that arrived in Macondo generations before. After years of translation, he discovers that the manuscript tells the whole story of the Buendía clan, right down to himself—not "in the order of man's conventional time, but . . . in such a way that [the events] coexisted in one instant." Gabriel García Márquez follows the same narrative strategy, juxtaposing normal events with magical ones and casting doubt on the possibility of "realistic" fiction that accurately records some sort of "objective history" of humanity. In *his* family history, imagination and fact exist side by side, indistinguishable from each other.

ITALO CALVINO
If on a winter's night a traveler
(1972)

Best edition: The Harvest edition, translated by William Weaver.

Salman Rushdie called this "the most complicated book you . . . will ever read," but you won't get too lost as long as you know that this novel has eleven beginnings and only one end. Calvino's narrator speaks directly to you, the reader; you begin to read, only to discover that your novel (apparently a spy romp having to do with exchanged suitcases) has been bound wrong at the printers so that the first thirty-two pages repeat themselves again and again. You take it back to the bookstore and there meet the Other Reader, a beautiful girl who is also in search of the rest of the misbound novel. The bookseller gives you a new copy of your book—but this novel turns out to be a completely different story. And just as you become engrossed in it, you find that the rest of the pages are blank. So it goes for the rest of the tale; each story you begin leads you into another beginning. These ten opening chapters are linked by your quest to find each novel's ending—and, finally, to discover who is responsible for the chaotic state of these books. Lingering in the background is a third question: Why is Calvino doing this? In each novel's beginning, he mocks a fiction formula (the spy novel, the adventure, the coming-of-age tale). And in your quest between the tales to find the "real" novel, he continually (and clearly) tells you that any "reality" you might find is as much an illusion as each novel that you find. "I want you to feel," one novel begins, "around the story, a saturation of other stories that I could tell . . . a space full of stories . . . where you can move in all directions, as in space." Any "order" you might find in this book (or in life) has been imposed by the will. It has nothing to do with reality.

TONI MORRISON
Song of Solomon
(1977)

Best edition: The Vintage reprint edition. Don't substitute the abridged audiobook version from Audible for reading the entire novel, but since Morrison herself narrates, it's worth a supplemental listen.

Milkman Dead is born in the charity hospital of a Michigan town. His father, Macon Dead, is a rent collector, an exile: a black man living in the North whose American ancestors are in the South and whose African ancestors are entirely unknown. Macon has a sister, Pilate, who was born after their mother died in labor; Pilate, mysteriously, has no navel. As children, Pilate and Macon saw their father murdered and ran away to hide in a Pennsylvania cave. An old harmless white man was sleeping there; full of rage, Macon murdered the man and then discovered sacks of gold nuggets in the cave. Pilate refused to let Macon take the gold, and then disappeared (along with the gold) while Macon was out of the cave. She tried to work in Virginia, but was ostracized because of her missing navel. Eventually she traveled back to the cave, collected the bones she found there, and came to live in the town where her brother Macon had settled, along with her illegitimate daughter Reba, Reba's daughter Hagar, and a mysterious green sack which (Macon thinks) has the gold nuggets in it.

Milkman has a twelve-year affair with Hagar, but he grows tired of her and instead turns for company to his friend Guitar, "the one person left whose clarity never failed him." But Guitar has become politically active; he has joined a society called the "Seven Days," which executes a white person whenever a black man, woman, or child is murdered. Milkman finds politics boring, but when Guitar needs money to carry out one of his revenge killings, Milkman offers to help him steal Pilate's gold. But the green sack in Pilate's basement holds bones, not gold. So Milkman sets out on a quest to Pennsylvania to find out what happened to the gold nuggets. He doesn't find the gold, but he does find his roots: he meets the characters who populate Pilate's stories about her childhood, and realizes that the nonsense songs the children sing on the streets contain the names of his grandfather and grandmother, aunts and uncles. He also realizes that Guitar is following him—and that Guitar has become his enemy. As the novel ends, Guitar shoots Milkman for the sake of the gold. Milkman's quest from North to South goes in the opposite direction from the flight of the escaped slave; it is the quest of the freedman who must return South and face the remnants of a slave-holding culture in order to reclaim his family ties.

DON DeLILLO
White Noise
(1985)

Best edition: The Penguin Classics edition.

Jack Gladney is a professor of Hitler Studies at the College-on-the-Hill; his wife, Babette, pathologically afraid of death, is taking black-market "psychopharmaceuticals" from a shady medical research firm that advertises in supermarket tabloids; their motley mass of children (produced from six separate marriages) battle various odd insecurities. Gladney, trying to find some sort of order in all this chaos, is interrupted by a chemical spill that sends a huge black toxic cloud across the landscape. The residents are all evacuated until the cloud finally disperses. Back home, Gladney sets himself to track down his wife's pill supplier. When he finds the man and has a gun battle with him (in imitation of older heroes), nothing in partic ular comes of it. Gladney and Babette and their children end the book in the supermarket, shopping (again) as they have every week: Nothing has changed. White Noise is like *1984* with no Big Brother; it convinces us that our lives have no real meaning. A certain order is imposed on the chaos of events by the media and by companies that want us to buy their goods. They invent for us stories that seem to make sense out of our lives, but that actually convince us that we must have their products.

A. S. BYATT
Possession
(1990)

Best edition: The Vintage International edition. Virginia Leishman narrates the unabridged audiobook from Audible.

Roland Mitchell is an academic without job offers, a browbeaten ex–graduate student who pays the rent by working for his former dissertation advisor, James Blackadder. Blackadder is Britain's foremost authority on the prolific Victorian poet Randolph Henry Ash, and Roland spends his days digging through Ash's correspondence. One day in the London Library, Roland discovers a forgotten letter from Ash to a mysterious lady love. Joined by his fellow scholar Maud Bailey, he steals the letter and sets out to discover the lady's identity—and finds Christabel Mott, also a Victorian poet and the darling of American feminists. Maud and Roland chase Christabel and Randolph Henry through an engrossing labyrinth of letters, journal entries hinting at unrevealed mysteries, brilliant poems, critical articles, biographies, and stories, each adding another detail to the story of unlikely love. They are in turn pursued by Blackadder's bitterest enemy, the American scholar Mortimer P. Cropper, who wants to buy up all of Ash's letters with his limitless wealth and take them out of Britain. Along the way, Maud and Roland fall reluctantly in love with each other. And when they discover the center of the maze, they discover a startling secret—which, as Byatt relies on plot to move the last pages of her novel to the end, I won't reveal.

CORMAC McCARTHY
The Road
(2006)

Best edition: The Vintage International edition.

An unknown catastrophe has swept over the human race, leaving the earth wrecked, ash-covered, and criss-crossed by bands of cannibalistic savages. Only a few survivors have managed to keep their humanity; two of them, an unnamed man and his son, travel along melted highways and through shattered cities, battling starvation and human predators, hoping to find something better when they reach the sea. McCarthy's Pulitzer Prize–winning novel deftly combines one of the most enduring forms of world literature, the quest narrative (*Don Quixote* and *The Pilgrim's Progress*), with the extremely American genre known as the "road narrative," a journey through open spaces toward an undefined horizon where, possibly, better things await (*Huckleberry Finn* and *Moby-Dick*). Presenting itself as grimly realistic and postmodern ("He pulled the blue plastic tarp off of him and folded it and carried it out to the grocery cart and packed it and came back with their plates and some cornmeal cakes in a plastic bag and a plastic bottle of syrup. . ."), the novel slowly reveals a deep vein of magic. Washing his son's hair, drying it beside the fire, the man realizes that his actions are "like some ancient anointing. So be it. Evoke the forms. Where you've nothing else construct ceremonies out of the air and breath upon them." Throughout, McCarthy points out the human compulsion to categorize our world in ways that we understand: good and bad, heroic and villainous, divine and demonic. But the categories continually break down; in the end, the riddle of existence is beyond our comprehension. "All things," the novel concludes "were older than man and they hummed of mystery."

OTHER RECOMMENDED RESOURCES

Johnson, Paul. *A History of the American People.* New York: Harper Perennial, 1999.

Morgan, Kenneth O., ed. *The Oxford Illustrated History of Britain,* updated ed. Oxford: Oxford University Press, 2009.

Roberts, Clayton, David Roberts, and Douglas R. Bisson. *History of England: Volume I: Prehistory to 1714,* 6th ed. Upper Saddle River, N.J.: Pearson, 2013.

Roberts, Clayton, and David Roberts. *History of England: Volume II: 1688 to the Present*, 6th ed. Upper Saddle River, N.J.: Pearson, 2013

Roberts, J. M *The Penguin History of the World*, 6th ed., ed. Odd Arne Westad. New York: Penguin, 2014

Tindall, George Brown. *America: A Narrative History*, brief 8th ed. New York: W. W. Norton, 2009.

Chapter 6

The Story of Me:
Autobiography and Memoir

"WHEN I WAS your age . . ."

People have always told stories about themselves. Augustine (theologian, scholar, African heir of Roman civilization) and Harriet Jacobs (slave, mother, African fugitive from American culture) both wrote autobiographies. Yet Augustine's skill at putting words on paper makes his tale of conversion no "better" than Jacobs's chronicle of poverty and flight. No one needs to be an expert to write autobiography.

But the autobiographer is possessed of an odd conviction: that the details of his life will be of interest to unknown, random readers. It's a conviction that goes against every rule of good party behavior: *Don't drone on about yourself.* Yet the autobiographer tells you about his parents, his second-grade classmates, his complicated misgivings over marriage, in the sublime confidence that you will be enthralled.

Why on earth does he think that you'll keep reading?

WHY AUTOBIOGRAPHY IS MORE COMPLICATED
THAN YOU MIGHT THINK

In the beginning, there was Augustine.

Augustine, born in North Africa at the tail end of the Roman empire, is the first "autobiographer." He wasn't the first writer to jot down details of daily life; diaries and journals have been kept since humans have had a sense of the passage of time and have possessed written language. But Augustine was the first writer to tell the story of his life.

Turning life into story is not as straightforward as it might seem. A diarist notes the events of each day, without bothering to fix them into an overall pattern. But the autobiographer has to put his life into order, explaining thoughts and events which appear important only in hindsight. And this hindsight is itself shaped by the overall purpose that the autobiographer has chosen for his life.

So the autobiographer's backward gaze doesn't just tell events—it sees them as part of a design that exists only because the writer has decided that one explanation (and no other) makes sense of his life.

Skip forward in time from the fourth century to the twentieth; to Richard Rodriguez, born to Mexican parents, growing up in California. As a child, Rodriguez spoke English at his Sacramento elementary school, but Spanish in private ("These sounds said . . . *I am addressing you in words I never use with* los gringos. *I recognize you as someone special, close, like no one outside. You belong with us. In the family*"). But when Rodriguez's teachers suggested that he needed more practice in English, his parents insisted that English be used at home as well. In his autobiography *Hunger of Memory*, Rodriguez writes:

> One Saturday morning, I entered the kitchen where my parents were talking in Spanish. I did not realize they were talking in Spanish, however, until, at the moment they saw me, I heard their voices change to speak English. Those gringo sounds they uttered startled me. Pushed me away. In that moment of trivial misunderstanding and profound insight, I felt my throat twisted by unsounded grief. I turned quickly and left the room. . . . Again and again in the days following, increasingly angry, I was obliged to hear my mother and father: "Speak to us *en inglés*." (Speak.) Only then did I determine to learn classroom English. Weeks after, it happened: One day in school I raised my hand to volunteer an answer. I spoke out in a loud voice. And I did not think it remarkable when the entire class understood. That day, I moved very far from the disadvantaged child I had been only days earlier. The belief, the calming assurance that I belonged in public, had at last taken hold.[1]

Did this happen just as Rodriguez describes? No, of course not. The grown man's awareness is layered over the child's memory at every point. The child was angry; only the adult knows that this was a "moment of trivial misunderstanding and profound insight." The child asked a question in English; only the mature Rodriguez sees the connection between this question and the brief exchange in the kitchen, weeks before. And this particular story has importance only because Rodriguez sees the story of his life as the story of his entrance into American public life. "I turn to

[1] Richard Rodriguez, *Hunger of Memory: The Education of Richard Rodriguez* (New York: Bantam, 1982), pp. 21–22.

consider the boy I once was," he writes, "in order, finally, to describe the
man I am now. I remember what was so grievously lost to define what was
necessarily gained." Had he decided that his life was about the emergence
of his sexuality, or the development of a great creative talent, the event in
the kitchen would have assumed another meaning entirely.

In other words, Rodriguez's story of the event in the kitchen isn't an
objective reconstruction of the past. Instead, it is part of a tale constructed
by a writer who has much in common with a novelist; Rodriguez is making a point and marshalling his plot points so that they lead to a climactic
interpretation. This is what the autobiographer does. And so Augustine
is the first autobiographer because he chooses a meaning for his life and
arranges the events of his life to reflect this meaning. Rodriguez becomes
an American; Augustine becomes a follower of God.

But Augustine's *Confessions* make at least four other innovations as well,
which is why his story has itself become a pattern by which other autobiographers (whether they know it or not) shape their own lives. Unlike
earlier writers, Augustine chooses to tell only those events which belong
to the schema he is sketching out. So he ignores the fathering of a child,
and instead spends pages on an adolescent theft of pears from a garden,
an incident that provides him with a nice echo of Adam and Eve's original sins and shows that their flaw is also in him. Unlike earlier writers,
Augustine sees decisions and thoughts, not big external events, as the true
landmarks of a life; like the hero of an ancient epic, he journeys toward a
new shore, but his journey is an internal trek from corruption to holiness.
Unlike earlier writers, Augustine puts his private self at the center of the
universe; his story is not about a Roman, or a North African, or even a
church member, but about *Augustine*, an individual whose hidden, private life has enormous supernatural significance. Unlike earlier writers,
Augustine sees a single moment of his life—his conversion—as the pivot
around which all else spins. Choosing a meaning for the past, relating all
else to it, describing the *inner* life of the private self, finding that "water-
shed" event of the past that made the self what it is today: all of these
become, after Augustine, the conventions of the autobiography.

And Augustine is the first writer to answer that annoying question:
Who wants to hear about my life, anyway? For Augustine, as for Margery
Kempe, Teresa of Ávila, John Bunyan, Thomas Merton, and an unbroken
line of spiritual autobiographers who stretch right up to Charles Colson, the answer is: *all those who, like me, are sinners* (by any measure, a
wide intended readership). If the purpose of autobiography is to point sinners to grace, the autobiographer can be both humble and self-centered.
Minute, individual self-examination (a most satisfying activity) has enor-

mous importance to thousands of readers. After all, the same divine image sleeps in them; they must perform the same self-scrutiny and encounter the same God.

"Confessional" autobiography never disappears, but another kind of life story grows up beside it. The Godward focus of the Middle Ages begins to blur, and the men of the Enlightenment decide that they are not *sinners*, but *humans*. It is, after all, the age of invention, and a brilliant Venetian glassmaker has created a mirror in which people can see their own faces without the distortion caused by polished bronze. And thinkers of the sixteenth and seventeenth centuries become convinced that they can glimpse their private selves with as much clarity as they can see their own faces.

So Michel de Montaigne, René Descartes, and Jean-Jacques Rousseau steal Augustine's invention, the autobiography, and run away with it. They tell stories of their private selves journeying through a secular conversion toward a new shore—not holiness, but self-knowledge.

This creates a whole new knot at the center of the autobiography. For Augustine and his fellow religious autobiographers, the journey toward holiness *is* a journey toward self-knowledge. It's a straightforward argument: Holiness is God's most essential quality. So the holier the self becomes, the more it becomes like God. And since the self is the image of God, the more it becomes like God, the more it becomes itself; it draws closer and closer to *reality*.

But when the Enlightenment autobiographer peers into his center, he doesn't see the face of God reflected there. He sees a *self* that exists independent of God, independent of society, independent even of his own will (the technical term is "autonomous"). The reality of this free, autonomous being depends only on—well, on it*self*.[2]

In the absence of a relatively concrete definition of the self as the "image of God," autobiographers found themselves forced into skepticism—the admission that they didn't know exactly what was down there in their centers. Montaigne, the first "post-Augustinian" autobiographer, announced in his collection of essays (first published in 1580) that, since he could not know for sure what this mysterious "self" was, or what it knew, he would only "assay" (examine) himself in an effort to tell the reader who he *thought* he was. Descartes concluded, in 1641, that he could not be

[2]In his chronology in *Autobiography: The Self-Made Text* (New York: Twayne, 1993; p. xvi), James Goodwin pinpoints the "earliest recorded use of word *self* in the modern philosophical sense of intrinsic identity that remains the same through varying states of mind and experience" as occurring in 1674, in the *Poetical Works* of the minor poet Thomas Traherne: "A secret self I had enclos'd within / That was not bounded by my clothes or skin."

sure of his existence as a "sensing self" (since his senses might be deceiving him) or as a "feeling self" (emotions being equally unreliable) or even as a "religious self" (since his knowledge of God was no more certain than either sense or emotion). He knew only that he was *thinking* about the problem, and so the only statement he could make with any assurance was that "'I am, I exist' is necessarily true whenever it is stated by me or conceived in my mind."

So if these autobiographers don't know exactly who they are, what is the purpose of autobiography?

As it turns out, skepticism doesn't actually change the purpose of autobiography. The story of a life *still* serves as an example for readers, a model by which they can understand their own lives. But the skeptical autobiographer doesn't assume that readers are pursuing holiness above all else; knowledge of God, after all, is no longer the journey to self-knowledge. Instead, the skeptical autobiography demonstrates how the writer has shaped his (or her) story so that he is able to define his (or her) *self* in the absence of certainty—in the absence of the God who gave concrete shape to Augustine's journey. The skeptical autobiography tells the reader: *Here is the meaning I chose for my life. I discovered that my elusive* self *was a thinking being. Might this be a meaning that you too could choose?*

That elusive self might not prove to be a thinking being, as it did for Descartes. Instead, the self might turn out to be an American, as in Richard Rodriguez's autobiography. (You too can find a balance between your heritage and your present national identity.) Or it might prove to be a woman struggling against the pressure to be domestic, as in Jill Ker Conway's autobiography *The Road from Coorain*. (You too can discover your self to be a scholar, even though all around you are telling you that your self's identity is simply *daughter*.) Or your self might turn out to be an entrepreneur who can make it big in America despite humble beginnings, as in Benjamin Franklin's tale of his life in the New World. But whatever the self is discovered to be, the writer argues for its genuineness, its authenticity—and offers it as an example for you to follow.

This sort of autobiography may be post-Augustinian, but Augustinian autobiography didn't go away. John Bunyan published the story of his life, *Grace Abounding to the Chief of Sinners*, to an enormously receptive public in 1666; it went through six editions in two years, and spiritual autobiographies abounded for the next two centuries. Every book on the list at the end of this chapter is either spiritual or skeptical, a guide to God or a guide to self-definition. The two types of autobiography remain cousins, with a certain family likeness that they owe to their common ancestor, Augustine.

These cousins have continued to lend to and borrow from each other. The skeptical autobiography often indulges in a kind of confession, very like the confessions of sin found in spiritual autobiography. In skeptical autobiography, though, confession is not a path to God's favor. Instead, the willingness to expose yourself, warts and all, becomes a mark of sincerity, a further reason for your readers to believe you and (perhaps) adopt your way of life. Nor does spiritual autobiography escape from the skeptic's need to justify the ways of the self to readers who question its sincerity. Teresa of Ávila offered her story to God, but she also wrote to defend herself (and her plans to establish a convent) against her superiors, who doubted the reality of her religious visions. Charles Colson's *Born Again* may offer readers a path to God, but Colson has certainly not forgotten all those *other* readers who would prefer to know exactly what went on at the Watergate.

A FIVE-MINUTE HISTORY OF AUTOBIOGRAPHICAL CRITICISM

Like novels, most autobiographies have plots: beginnings, middles, and ends. But while novelists are aware of themselves as craftsmen (and women), autobiographers are often "accidental writers" who would never consider themselves professionals. Novelists think about the conventions and difficulties of writing fiction, and sometimes even write long essays about how novels should be constructed. But most autobiographers put down the events of their lives without consulting experts or discussing theories of autobiographical composition. Novels can be assigned to schools or movements, such as *realism* and *naturalism*; autobiography doesn't have convenient literary labels.

But the artlessness of autobiography is an illusion. Writers of autobiography do use technique. Not only do they restructure the past so that it brings meaning to the present, but they follow certain conventions as they retell their lives. They may do both unconsciously—but this is still *craft*.

Consider the most classic of all autobiographical openings, the one used by Benjamin Franklin in his *Autobiography*: "I was born," Franklin writes, "in Boston, in New England. My mother was . . . daughter of Peter Folger, one of the first settlers of New England." When the American ex-slave Frederick Douglass sets down the story of his life, he too begins with his birth and ancestry. "I was born in Tuckahoe," he tells us. "I have no accurate knowledge of my age. . . . I never saw my mother, to know her as such, more than four or five times in my life. . . . She left me without the slightest intimation of who my father was."

But although family provides Franklin with a prototype for himself (his ancestors were free men who valued reading and writing and refused to kowtow to unreasonable religious authorities), family has no part in the rest of Douglass's story. Why, then, does he begin with his birth and parentage? Because, although he has never studied a book about writing autobiography, he has read other life stories, and his reading has made him aware that a "proper" autobiography begins with birth and family ancestry.

This is a convention of autobiography.

These conventions went more or less unexamined until the 1950s, when academics finally turned an interested eye toward life stories. Autobiography had always been considered a sort of second-class literary undertaking, slightly indulgent, requiring no skill other than an endless fascination with yourself. But during the fifties, a cluster of books and articles suggested that autobiography was in no way the simple, straightforward activity it had seemed. Rather, the autobiographer, as Roy Pascal wrote in 1960, "half discovers, half creates a deeper design and truth than adherence to historical and factual truth could ever make claim to."[3]

Why autobiography should suddenly become a topic of critical inquiry in the 1950s has never been explained, but—like most midcentury phenomena—this new interest probably had something to do with post–World War II trauma. Roy Pascal claimed that autobiography can be a way of discovering a truth that is more true than historical fact, because he lived in a time when sensible people longed to triumph over historical facts (that bare record of inexplicable slaughter and holocaust). The notion that the critic, viewing those facts through the lens of a life story, could find a deeper truth beyond them must have seemed beautifully, unbelievably promising.

By the 1950s, Freudian psychology had also become completely popularized. The idea of the *subconscious* had entered our language, and had irrevocably dyed our ideas about that elusive *self.*

Freud explained that our subconscious directs us even when we're not entirely aware of it, and must be excavated if we ever hope to act with any sort of freedom, rather than as puppets of unexplained impulses. Saint Paul, of course, had provided an explanation of the conflict between conscious and subconscious a couple of thousand years earlier, when he lamented, "What I would not do, that I do; and that which I must do, I would not do." But Paul's model of two opposing selves required a belief in the Augustinian view of the authentic self as the image of God. Freud's model was much more congenial to the scholars and theorists who had long accepted the skeptical, Enlightenment view of the self as self-designing, self-governing, and (in the end) self-understanding. So Freud was a bet-

[3]Roy Pascal, *Design and Truth in Autobiography* (Cambridge, Mass.: Harvard University Press, 1960), pp. 61–83.

ter fit than Paul when it came to explaining inexplicable human acts. He offered a solution that required, not submission to some external divine power, but rather a greater and greater understanding of the space within. Autobiography, like an extremely useful psychotherapy session, examined the space within and ordered it, identifying and classifying each urge.

So in the Freudian era (and we're still in it), critics become increasingly interested in the strategies that the "I" of an autobiography uses to organize that space within. How does the conscious mind (the *ego*) justify its acts? How does it account for those impulses rising out of the subconscious? The autobiographer tries to figure out *why* she has always resented her older brother and uses the autobiography as a way to explain.

Like the conscious mind, the *self* who sits down to create an autobiography has been pushed, pulled, and driven by forces it has never fully understood. This *self* begins to set her life down on paper—and, as she reflects on past events, begins to discover her own motivations, her own subconscious impulses. She writes in the first person—as "I"—but the *I* of the autobiography lives through those past events with a knowledge denied to the *self* when those events took place. In the end, the *I* of the autobiography turns out to be a very different person than the self it represents.

This was not a brand-new insight. An occasional autobiographer had reflected on this paradox, all the way back to Montaigne, who wrote in 1580: "In modelling this figure [the "I" in his essays] on myself, I have had to fashion and compose myself so often to bring myself out, that the model itself has to some extent grown firm and taken shape. Painting myself for others, I have painted myself with colors clearer than my original ones. I have no more made my book than my book has made me." But Freud supplied a language that allowed literary critics to discuss the paradox as a *theoretical* problem. The initial burst of books and articles in the mid- to late 1950s led to an ongoing critical discussion that still prospers: any university library will yield titles ranging from the simple to the unintelligible, from Robert Sayre ("The person who can write his own story can rise from the status of the unknown and inarticulate") to Rodolphe Gasche ("Autobiography is not to be in any way confused with the so-called life of the author, with the corpus of empirical accidents making up the life of an empirically real person").[4]

This ongoing critical discussion (besides winding itself into unintelligibility fairly frequently) has also produced, somewhat after the fact, *genre*

---

[4]Robert Sayre, *The Examined Self: Benjamin Franklin, Henry Adams, Henry James* (Princeton, N.J.: Princeton University Press, 1964); Rodolphe Gasche, quoted in Jacques Derrida, *The Ear of the Other: Otobiography, Transference, Translation*, trans. Peggy Kamuf, ed. Christie V. McDonald (New York: Schocken Books, 1985).

labels for autobiography. Sometime in the early 1970s, scholars realized, with great surprise, that women think of their lives differently than men do. Augustine, the first autobiographer, was raised on the tales of Greek and Roman heroes, men whose virtues he was to emulate. And so his spiritual journey took on the flavor of an epic spiritual quest.

But Margery Kempe was never given the option of modeling herself after an epic hero. Like most women, she was uneducated; rather than epic tales, she heard stories of domestic fulfillment. Besieged by her husband and fourteen children, she was unable to think of her life as a solitary journey. So why should Augustine's experience shape *her* life story?

As a *genre*, women's autobiographies seemed to be distorted by an intractable literary tradition that insisted they view their struggles and achievements through male eyes. Told that they should be patient, quiet, and devoted to the men in their lives, women produced autobiographies in which the *I* was patient, yielding, and passive. The spiritual autobiographies of women dealt not with an active grappling with sin, but the difficulties of passive submission to the male God. Through the nineteenth century, the *I* in a woman's autobiography was more likely to confess her inadequacy than to act vigorously in the face of opposition. As Patricia Spacks observes, the autobiography shows a public face, but while the "face a man turns to the world . . . typically embodies his strength," a woman's public face must show a "willingness to yield."[5] Even in the case of social activists such as Jane Addams and Ida Tarbell, this publicly yielding face persists. In her study of women's stories, Jill Ker Conway points out that the personal correspondence of these women is forcible and full of conviction, but that their autobiographies portray them as passively called to activism, sought out by causes rather than seeking them.

The genre of "black autobiography"—particularly in the United States, with its slave-holding past—suffers from the same sort of distortion. African American autobiographers found themselves copying the forms practiced by whites, even when those forms didn't suit the shape of their lives. In the earliest African American autobiographies (the "slave narratives"), the writer inevitably begins with birth and parentage, just as a white writer would. But the real beginning of the story comes slightly later, in an event that becomes a convention of black autobiography: the recognition of blackness. Each African American writer views herself as, simply, a *person*—until a point at childhood where she is suddenly gazed at, by someone else, with disdain or horror. At this moment, the *I* sees itself, no longer as "normal," but as something different: as *black*. From

---

[5]Quoted in Carolyn G. Heilbrun, *Writing a Woman's Life* (New York: Ballantine Books, 1988), p. 22.

this moment on, the African American autobiographer struggles with double vision. Like the white autobiographer, she tries to create herself in the pages of her book, but as she does so she cannot help seeing herself through the hostile eyes of others. Blackness becomes (in the words of Roger Rosenblatt), both identity and tragic fate, a "condition that pre-scribes and predetermines a life."[6]

A second convention marks almost all African American autobiogra-phy: entry into a world of reading and writing. When Frederick Douglass was a child, his mistress began to teach him to read. But her husband halted the lessons: "Learning will do him no good, but a great deal of harm," he told his wife sternly. "If you teach him how to read, he'll want to know how to write, and this accomplished, he'll be running away with himself."[7] So the instruction ceased, but Douglass convinced his young white acquaintances to explain the ABCs. Learning to read was Doug-lass's conversion, the point at which he stepped over into a new world. Through reading, he gained a vocabulary that (as Douglass himself puts it) "enabled me to give tongue to many interesting thoughts which had often flashed through my mind and died away for want of words in which to give them utterance."[8] And through writing, he entered the white world not just as victim, but as witness and activist. Writing gave him power even over his enslaved past, since he could now record his days as a slave and fill them with moral judgment on the slaveholders. "It did not entirely satisfy me to *narrate* wrongs—I felt like *denouncing* them," he writes. "I could not always curb my moral indignation for the perpetrators of slave-holding villainy long enough for a circumstantial statement of the facts."

Autobiography allows a writer to recreate his own life, to read meaning back into past events, to give shape and sense to what has been meaning-less. So how is it different from fiction? (And should we get upset if the facts appear to have been stretched just a bit?)

As autobiographical criticism began to gain steam, more academics began to question the line between fact and imagination. Faith in the existence of cold, hard facts—knowledge that can be *proved* by observa-tion or experimentation or some other scientific method of establishing truth—became part of our Western point of view around the time of the Renaissance; this reliance on scientific proof as the ultimate test of

[6]Roger Rosenblatt, "Black Autobiography: Life as the Death Weapon," in *Autobiography: Essays Theoretical and Critical*, ed. James Olney (Princeton, N.J.: Princeton University Press, 1980), p. 171.

[7]Frederick Douglass, *Narrative of the Life of Frederick Douglass, an American Slave: Written by Himself* (1845), chapter 6.

[8]Frederick Douglass, *My Bondage and My Freedom* (1855), chapter 11.

truth separates the "modern era" (which began sometime around Copernicus) from what came before. But in the last third of the twentieth century, thinkers began to question the infallibility of scientific proof. They pointed out that there are many different types of certainty, and that "proof" in the modern sense exalts scientific certainty above all others. They pointed out that scientists were people too, and were apt to find facts that they hoped for, as well as facts that existed. They pointed out that a "fact," particularly in autobiography, is a slippery object. If two historical personages write down two different accounts of the same event, might *both* accounts be true—depending on point of view?

These questioners of modernism were labeled *postmodernists*. (Modernism and postmodernism are slightly different, in this context, from the literary modernism and postmodernism discussed in the last chapter.) Postmodernism helped autobiography to prosper, since postmodernists generally resist labeling one point of view as more "worthwhile" than another, which means that the suburban mechanic has just as much right to tell his life story as the president. But in praising each individual point of view as worthwhile ("Both accounts of that battle are true—the writers were standing on opposite sides of the field, that's all!"), postmodernism gradually released its hold on the "normative" point of view: that which is true for everyone. You no longer read an autobiography to find out the truth about past events (an assumption that governed the memoirs of political retirees for decades). Rather, you read autobiography to find out what it's like to see the world from another point of view, from inside the skin of another person. If the point of view is vividly drawn, so that you *understand* life as a woman or an ex-slave or a second-generation Mexican immigrant, does it really matter whether the *events* are "accurate"?

Like many questions posted by postmodernism, this one remains unanswered. But in most cases, the reader who peruses autobiography is a practicing postmodernist, even if he doesn't realize it. He's not searching for the "facts" so beloved by modernists. He's demonstrating (in James Olney's words) "a fascination with the self and its profound, its endless mysteries and, accompanying that fascination, an anxiety about the self, an anxiety about the dimness and vulnerability of that entity that no one has ever seen or touched or tasted."[9] The reader of autobiography (whether spiritual or skeptical) is hoping for a map through trackless waters, a hand-

[9]James Olney, *Autobiography: Essays Theoretical and Critical* (Princeton, N.J.: Princeton University Press, 1980), p. 23.

book to the deep interior spaces. And if he *does* happen to discover exactly what happened at the Watergate, this is simply an unexpected bonus.

HOW TO READ AN AUTOBIOGRAPHY

The First Read-Through: Grammar-Stage Reading

In your first reading of an autobiography (the "grammar stage" reading), you're asking a simple question: What happened? Take the writer's assertions at face value. You won't be able to see the overall shape of the life until you've read the entire work, so don't begin to criticize the author's interpretation of the past until your second read-through. Remember to mark in some way—by turning down a page, or making a note in your reading journal—passages that seem to carry some extra significance. Although you don't yet know what this significance is (and the passages may, on second reading, turn out to be unimportant), these notes will simplify your search for answers to the analytical questions that I'll suggest later on.

Look at the title, cover, and table of contents. This initial survey of the book is always your first step. Follow the same process as you did with the novels you read for Chapter 5: With your journal and pencil close by, read the title page and the copy on the back. Write the title of the book, the author's name, and the date of composition on the top of a blank page. Also write a short sentence saying who the author is (scholar, nun, politician, slave).

Glance through the table of contents. Many autobiographies don't have chapter titles, but those that do will give you a preview of the shape that the writer is giving to his life. *Mein Kampf*, for example, begins with "In the Home of My Parents," and continues on to "Why the Second Reich Collapsed," "Race and People," "The Strong Is Strongest When Alone," and "The Right to Self-Defence," which gives you a foretaste of Hitler's take on himself: He identifies himself with the German people, so that his own "suffering" and rise mirror those of the German nation. (This also allows him to do pretty much anything he pleases in his rise to power, since, in his own eyes, he *is* Germany.) If you do get an overview of the writer's purpose, write a brief sentence or two about what this purpose might be.

What are the central events in the writer's life? When you did your initial reading of the novel, you jotted down the main events of each chapter to provide yourself with a brief outline of the plot. When you first read an autobiography, you should note the events of the writer's life. Although the writer's focus may be on intellectual development or a change in mental state, the physical events of a life nevertheless provide a framework to hang internal developments on. List these events in order, down the left-hand side of a page. Try to limit your list to a single page; an autobiography may be crammed with incident, but you don't need to record all of these incidents in your initial outline. Pick out the central happenings. For each chapter, ask yourself: Out of all of these happenings, which two are the most important? (This is a somewhat mechanical narrowing device, so if there seem to be three important events in a single chapter, don't feel bound to eliminate one—and for a long autobiography with many short sections, such as Gandhi's, you'll need to eliminate entire chapters.) Birth, education, traveling, marriage, taking on an occupation, catastrophe (a plunge into poverty, imprisonment, divorce, death of a loved one), parenthood, great achievement, retirement—these form the "skeleton" of a life. As you list these events, try also to note what makes them unique—not "Took first job" but "Began work as a lawyer, hated the job at first."

An occasional autobiography (such as those written by Descartes and Nietzsche) have very few (or no) external events; in Descartes' *Meditations*, "I cleared my schedule today so that I can sit down and write all this in one sitting" is all the physical event you get, and Nietzsche has no "happenings" at all. In this case, try to note the primary *intellectual* events—the conclusions that the writer comes to as he marshals his evidence. Look for the words "Therefore" or "I concluded" or "Clearly" (or some synonym) in order to identify these conclusions; these "terms of conclusion" tell you that, having put together a number of facts, the writer is ready to tell you what those facts mean.

What historical events coincide—or merge—with these personal events?   As you list personal events on the left-hand side of your page, keep your eyes open for historical events—those great happenings in the *outside* world (outbreak of war, a change in laws that affects the narrator's rights, natural catastrophes). List these down the right-hand side of the page, across from the personal events with which they coincide.

The part that history plays in the retelling of a life varies. Sometimes historical events directly affect the writer's life: the passage of the Fugitive Slave Act makes Douglass's position in the North precarious; Gandhi's life in India is changed forever by the unrest caused by a British crackdown on indigenous freedoms; Maya Angelou's childhood is shaped by Jim Crow. Sometimes wars and catastrophes just echo dully in the background; sometimes historical events are referred to only obliquely, because in the writer's time they formed part of a common knowledge that has faded in the present day. In Chapter 5, I suggested that a one-volume world history would set the novel in perspective; you might want to refer to it now, in order to get more details about events that seem blurred in autobiography. You might also make use of *The Timetables of History*, a reference work that lists major events for each year of recorded history in seven different categories (politics, art and music, literature, and so on). You can easily scan the years that cover the writer's life and make notes of happenings that seem significant. (The absence of an important historical circumstance from a writer's autobiography may be as meaningful as its presence.)

You can jot down this additional information on the right-hand side of the page as well, but write it in a different color—or in some other way distinguish it from the historical information provided by the *writer himself*.

Who is the most important person (or people) in the writer's life? What events form the outline of that story? Human beings define themselves against others: We find our self-definition in our uniqueness. Uniqueness is that which no one else has. As we tell the story of what makes us unique, we must tell others' stories too, in order to show that our story is different.

So every autobiography outlines more than one life. Each autobiographer tells at least one other story that plays counterpoint to his own. Often, this story is that of a parent; Jill Ker Conway's autobiography is largely the story of her relationship with her mother. In the telling, she sketches a compelling portrait of this tragic figure, a woman of energy and talent who is kept from exercising her gifts, and so sinks into paranoia and instability. The story runs side by side with Conway's and informs it with a certain fear: What if Conway, energetic and talented like her mother, is also unable to overcome the restrictions her society places on women?

Nietzsche talks about his father, Harriet Jacobs about the master who torments her, Gertrude Stein about the painters of Paris, Elie Wiesel of the small sister who disappeared into the concentration camps and who comes to symbolize all helpless Jewish children destroyed by hatred. As you read, try to identify the figure who stands at the center of the writer's life. On another sheet of paper, make a brief list of events that shaped *this* life—as told by the autobiographer at one remove.

Give the book your own title and subtitle. As you did with the novels, try titling and subtitling each autobiography after you've finished it. This title will serve as a memory hook for you as you move into the stage of analysis and try to discover the writer's purposes. If you're having difficulty, use this format:

A _____ *'s Story: In Which [Writer's Name]. . . .*

To fill in the first blank, use a single noun that best describes the author; in the second sentence, list one or two of the writer's most notable achievements. So Franklin, the father of American autobiography, appears as:

A Businessman's Story: In Which Benjamin Franklin Manages to Rise to Wealth and Prominence Through Determination and Hard Work, Despite Starting With Absolutely Nothing.

Or, alternately:

An American's Story: In Which Benjamin Franklin Frees Himself From All Oppression and Creates Exactly the Life He Wants.

There are many ways to title an autobiography, since lives have many facets; don't get hung up on wondering whether you're doing it "right" or not. You'll return to this titling again later, and decide whether the title you've settled on is still your first pick.

The Second Level of Inquiry: Logic-Stage Reading

Now that you've identified the autobiography's main events, you need to discover the overall plan (the *theme*) that ties the work together. Go back to those passages that you marked as interesting or confusing and reread them. Glance back over your outline as well; reread those sections of the autobiography that seem most central to the writer's life.

Then use your writing journal to make notes of your answers to the following questions. Each aims to help you answer the most central question of all: *What pattern has the writer discovered in his or her own life?*

What is the theme that ties the narrative together?   Begin by making a hypothesis: Form a first theory about the autobiography's *theme*.

First, determine whether the autobiography is primarily *spiritual* or *skeptical* in orientation. Spiritual autobiography has the writer's relationship with the divine as its organizing plan. True knowledge of God, or a change in spiritual state, serves as the life's climax. But this movement toward religious fulfillment might take different forms: a journey; a battle; the facing of a trial that must be endured; a psychological revelation that uncovers the true nature of the self. What sorts of metaphors does the writer use to represent this spiritual movement? And what does this reveal about her understanding of the divine? Is the knowledge of God a new world to be discovered, a territory to be conquered by force, or a mirror where we see our own true faces?

If the autobiography is *skeptical,* the writer is trying to understand her

own story without spirituality as its primary organizing theme. "Skeptical" doesn't necessarily mean "secular"; religious experience can still play
a role, but some other theme gives the story its beginning, middle, and
end. What is this theme? Is it "relational," describing the writer's slow
resolution (or dissolution) of relationships with parents, siblings, lovers? Is
it "oppositional," presenting the life as a conflict between two different
possible choices? For women, this may involve choosing between domestic and professional lives, between a conventionally feminine life and a
life of intellectual or social activism. For men, this opposition might take
the form of conflict between an expected career and a desired career; or
perhaps between existence as a public figure and happiness as a private
figure. Is it "heroic," casting the writer in the mold of a mythic hero
or heroine, conquering difficulties and overcoming obstacles? Is it "rep-
resentational," transforming the writer into a symbol for all other men
or women who share the same condition? (Harriet Jacobs represents the
enslaved mother, Benjamin Franklin the young American man seeking
wealth and freedom.) Or is it "historical," describing a historical movement (the emancipation of women, for example) through the lens of one
writer's experience? These themes can serve you as starting points for your
own thinking, but you shouldn't feel bound by them; you can create your
own categories as you read.

When you've settled on a possible theme, write a couple of sentences
describing it. You'll come back and revise the theme at the end of your
analysis.

Where is the life's turning point? Is there a "conversion"? "Conversion"
is the point at which the writer comprehends a great truth about herself
and changes the direction of her life, or experiences something so shattering, or so magnificent, that she is never the same afterward. Even skeptical autobiographies contain conversions. Transformation from one state
of being to another is *necessary* for autobiography; if the writer had always
been the same, she would have no purpose in laying out the chronological events of her life. She could simply write a history, with herself as
an objective, unchanging narrator. But autobiography isn't history; it is
the story of a growing, changing life. Look for the change. As we saw
above, African American writers often trace their change to a first recognition of blackness, when they see themselves, for the first time, through
the eyes of another. Many female autobiographers come to a slow understanding of themselves as independent, powerful people, not as adjuncts to
someone else. Spiritual autobiographers see the divine and find their vision
permanently altered.

Glance back at your outline. Is there a chapter in which important events seem to cluster? This cluster might occur just before or just after a transition point. Can you find the key words "For the first time"? Frederick Douglass is raised by his grandmother and surrounded by "kindness and love"—until she takes him to his master's plantation and leaves him there. When he looks around, his grandmother is gone. "I had never been deceived before," Douglass reflects, "and something of resentment mingled with my grief at parting with my grandmother . . . [T]his was my first introduction to the realities of the slave system."

An autobiography may contain more than one turning point; there are other transitions in Douglass's story (his mastery of the alphabet, his battle with the slave master Covey), although this is the first and most fundamental. You may be able to finger one transition as most central, or it may seem that two different points in the story are equally important. You may also find that although a definite change takes place between the beginning and the ending of an autobiography, so that the "I" who narrates the first chapters seems quite different from the "I" at the end, the change is more gradual. Make a note of whether the "conversion" is immediate or slow, and how the narrator is changed.

For what does the writer apologize? In apologizing, how does the writer justify?   "I am an ornery character," writes poet May Sarton, "often hard to get along with." But she adds immediately, "The things I cannot stand, that make me flare up like a cat making a fat tail, are pretentiousness, smugness, the coarse grain that often shows itself in a turn of phrase. I hate vulgarity, coarseness of soul." Well, who doesn't? That makes us *all* hard to get along with. Since no life is blameless, every autobiography contains an accounting of faults. And since humans find it psychologically impossible to live with guilt, apologies for these faults are almost always followed by justifications.

If you can find and mark these confessions and justifications, they will help to bring the pattern of the writer's life into view. Apologies appear differently in spiritual and skeptical autobiography. Spiritual autobiography *requires* confession of fault without self-justification; the writer is able to pour out her faults before God, because the grossness of the sin doesn't affect God's forgiveness. The presence of the divine eye makes honesty possible. (As a matter of fact, in some spiritual autobiographies, the worse the sin, the better the forgiveness.) In the Christian tradition, forgiveness means that the soul is reborn, becomes new. So the writer who tells, postconversion, of her preconversion life, is in effect writing about a different *person*—which allows even more devastating self-criticism.

On the other hand, the writer of spiritual autobiography is perfectly well aware that readers (not counting God) are finding out about these faults too. So even as the writer confesses to God, she may justify herself to you, the reader. Does this happen? If so, where?

In skeptical autobiography, confession of faults takes a different form. Honest confession is difficult—perhaps impossible—when a writer unfolds his soul to an unknown mass of listeners. Honest acknowledgment of fault requires that the confessor be sure of the listener's sympathetic ear. In the absence of assured forgiveness, the writer has to hedge confessions about with explanations, so that readers who might not be inclined to gracious forgiveness cannot dismiss his entire life as unworthy. Very typical of such a confession is Gandhi's explanation of his failure to provide his own sons with a decent education: "My inability to give them enough attention and other unavoidable causes prevented me from providing them with the literary education I had desired, and all my sons have had complaints to that . . . the artificial education that they could have had in England or South Africa . . . would never have taught them the simplicity and the spirit of service that they show in their lives today, while their artificial ways of living might have been a serious handicap in my public work." In admitting his fault, Gandhi not only hedges it ("unavoidable causes"), but provides a reason why his fault led to a better outcome.

What is the model—the ideal—*for this person's life?*   The autobiographer apologizes for her life at the point where the story she is telling diverges from the one she *wishes* she could tell. She apologizes because she has fallen short of some *ideal*. What is this ideal? The perfect scholar, the ideal wife/daughter/mother, the dynamic leader?

Whatever it is, the autobiographer is always measuring herself against it. "One senses a straining toward perfection in all autobiography," writes Roger Rosenblatt, "perfection of a kind that connects the individual with a cosmic pattern. . . . There is for every autobiographer an absolute ideal. Falling short of it is perhaps what inspires the autobiography in the first place; but if we are to understand the lives detailed before us, we must know this ideal as fully as we know the 'realities' given us."[10]

Look again at your title, subtitle, and theme. Glance back over the apologies that the writer makes. Ask yourself: If this writer could be perfect, who would she be? What characteristics belong to that ideal figure that she seems to be comparing herself to? And is there any hint where this ideal may have originated? The mother who feels guilty over losing

[10]Rosenblatt, "Black Autobiography," p. 176.

her temper with her children has absorbed an image of the Ideal Mother (always patient, always cheerful, able to entertain a three-year-old for hours with only two Popsicle sticks and glue). The autobiographer who apologizes for her failings as wife, as daughter, has also absorbed an image of what she *should* be. Perhaps it has come from her reading, from her parents, or from her religious community. Or perhaps from that vague thing we call "society," which encompasses the media, schooling, and the opinions of random acquaintances. Can you trace the ideal image back to its source?

What is the end *of the life: the place where the writer has arrived, found closure, discovered rest?*   It is a peculiarity of autobiography that the writer must bring the story to an end before it has ended. As Montaigne remarked in his *Essays*, no life can be fairly evaluated until after death; because of "the uncertainty and mutability of human affairs which lightly shift from state to state . . . [All] the other actions in our life must be tried on the touchstone of this final deed. . . . The assay of the fruits of my studies is postponed unto death."

But the self-written story of a life can't wait until the author's death. So the autobiographer *creates* an end, a stopping point. "Many more of the dealings of God towards me I might relate," Bunyan concludes in *Grace Abounding to the Chief of Sinners*, "but these out of the spoils won in battle have I dedicated to maintain the house of God." *Won in battle*: Although the "real" John Bunyan continued to fight doubts and temptations for the rest of his life, the "autobiographical" John Bunyan—the *I* who tells this story—has found final victory.

This "stopping point" question, perhaps more than any other, highlights the difference between the narrator of autobiography and the actual person who stands behind that narrator. How can any living person know the final shape of her life? In the absence of this certainty, she must create a final meaning for her life and set it down for us to see.

Reread the final chapter of the autobiography. Look for statements of conclusion, which often (though not always) are introduced with "time words" such as *so* or *from then on* or *now* or *during*. (Darwin's memoirs, for example, end with the statement, "I am not conscious of any change in my mind during the last thirty years," which places the end of his *written* life startlingly early.) Remember that the writer has selected this particular chapter as a vantage point from which he can look back and see his whole life spread out in a meaningful pattern behind him; the last chapter usually contains the final puzzle piece, the one that makes sense of all else.

Write a brief paragraph (two or three sentences) describing the writer's position at the end of the autobiography (where is she? what is she doing?), and quote any evaluation that the writer herself supplies.

Now revisit your first question: What is the theme of this writer's life?   Look back at the theme you suggested at the beginning of this evaluative process. Does it still ring true, now that you've examined transitions and endings, apologies and ideals? Each of these elements should have clarified the theme: You should now have a better idea of how the writer is constructing herself on paper, how the *I* of the story is formed. If your ideas have changed, revise your description of the autobiography's theme. Then revisit your title and subtitle. Do these, too, need revising in the light of your deeper study?

The Third Level of Inquiry: Rhetoric-Stage Reading

Your evaluative reading of the autobiography centered on the individual life portrayed. As you move into your third and final stage of reading, broaden your point of view beyond the single written life. What broader conclusions does the writer draw about the group he or she belongs to (men, women, immigrants, activists), or even more broadly, about human nature in general?

Remember that this stage of reading is best done in the company of another reader. Answer the first question (in writing or in conversation), and ask your reading partner to respond. Then have your partner answer the second question; you supply the response. This dialogue allows each of you to play the part of devil's advocate in turn.

Is the writer writing for himself, or for a group?   Does the writer see himself as a solitary soul, unique to the point where he cannot be imitated? This is very rare; much more often, the autobiography represents a pattern that could be adopted by a larger group of people—or a way of life that certain classes of humans are forced into.

Does May Sarton write for the creative soul; Frederick Douglass, for the black man; Harriet Jacobs, for the enslaved mother; Richard Rodriguez, for the Hispanic American? If so, which ones? Beware of overgeneralizations. Which readers can truly identify themselves with the situation of the autobiographer? Rodriguez describes an experience that, perhaps, is recognizable to most second-generation Hispanic Americans—but which parts of his story are unique to him, to his particular family and education? Does he make the mistake of assuming a universality to his experience that others might not share?

Ask these questions for each autobiography. What parts of the writer's experience does he assume to be universal? Which does he view as unique to himself? Are you part of the "group" which might be expected to identify most closely with the writer's experience? If so, does it ring true for you? And if not, what parts of the story *do* resonate with your own experience?

Finally, make a moral judgment. If the writer is laying down a pattern for others to follow, do you find this pattern to be good? And be sure to define what you mean by *good*. Does "good" mean "socially constructive" ("If everyone behaved that way, society would run smoothly")? Or "ethically consistent" ("This pattern lines up with the laws of morality, or of God, as I understand them")? Or "self-fulfilling" ("Anyone who behaved in this way would reach their highest potential as a human being")? These are three very different meanings of the word *good*, although we tend to use such common words without thinking carefully about which meaning we intend. But think now. Precise use of language marks an educated reader.

What are the three moments, or time frames, of the autobiography?   Remember that each autobiography has three distinct time frames: the time during which the events actually happened; the time during which the writer is putting the events on paper; and the time in which the autobiography is read.[11] In your first stage of reading, you became familiar with the first time frame, when you listed the happenings of the writer's life. Now take some time to think about the second and third frames.

The second time-frame moment, during which the autobiographer writes, is an intriguing one. *Why* does the writer sit down, at a particular point in time, and decide to put down his life? Did a child request family information? (This is Benjamin Franklin's stated purpose for writing.) Is death approaching? Has a political or cultural event shoved the narrator into the spotlight, so that the public is demanding details? Has he been arrested, jailed, elected president?

Find the writer's stated reason for putting down his life in writing. (Only the most maniacal ego—Nietszche springs to mind—assumes that it is intrinsically interesting.) Ask whether this reason rings true. (Did Franklin's son really ask for his father's entire life to be set down in writing? We never hear about the son again after the first paragraph, after all.) And then ask: Was the writer at a high or low point when writing?

---

[11]I am indebted to Erik H. Erikson's *Gandhi's Truth: On the Origins of Militant Nonviolence* (New York: W. W. Norton, 1993) for this insight.

Was the story written in a three-month burst, or over twenty-five years? An autobiography written in prison (as Bunyan's was) creates a different pattern for past events than one written at the high point of a life, after immense achievement and public acclaim. An autobiography written in a short period encapsulates the narrator's attitude at one brief time in life; one written over years may show more perspective, as the writer revises and returns to the pattern again and again.

Finally, how has the autobiography been changed by the years that have passed since its publication? Books are living objects; they change from reader to reader, from decade to decade, from age to age. Hitler's autobiography, published before World War II, sounds to our ears both pathetically deluded and weirdly threatening. Franklin's autobiography has limitless confidence in hard work and thrift and their ability to launch even the poorest immigrant to the highest level of American society; in today's world, this confidence sounds naive. Margery Kempe's visions, which begin right after the birth of her first child, can be easily diagnosed as postpartum psychosis; Booker T. Washington's appeal to ex-slaves to forget about political power, at least for now, grates on contemporary ears.

You will never rid yourself of your contemporary glasses, but you can at least be aware that you have them on. Beware of chronological snobbery: People in the past were not more ignorant or less insightful than people today. A good dose of antidepressants might have put an end to Margery's visions, but they would not have solved most of the underlying difficulties in her life, and modern medical science hasn't dealt with postpartum psychosis any better than Margery's confessors—who confirmed her religious calling, and thus gave her permission to retreat from a life which she found literally unendurable.

Make an effort to understand each autobiography on its own terms—and *then* put it into the frame of your own time. Ask yourself that most characteristic rhetoric-stage question: *Do I agree?* Which is more valid, our own contemporary understandings, or those of the time? In the sixteenth century, Margery walked away from her fourteen children, abandoning them for a life of religion. In the twenty-first century, a Texas woman under similar stresses took drugs prescribed by her psychiatrists, stayed home with her five small children, and drowned them all in the bathtub. Who acted more responsibly?

Where does the writer's judgment lie?   In the "Note to the Reader" that prefaces Thomas Merton's autobiography, *The Seven Storey Mountain*, William H. Shannon remarks that it contains three levels of meaning:

First, there is the *historical* level: what actually happened in his life. Second, there is the *remembered* level: what Merton was able to recall of the events of his life. Memory is often selective, which means that the remembered past may not always coincide with the historical past. Finally, there is the level of *monastic judgment*. . . . [Merton's] monastic commitment colors the way Thomas Merton (his religious name was Father Louis) tells the story. *The Seven Storey Mountain*, I believe it can be said, is the story of a young man named Thomas Merton being judged by a monk named Father Louis [and judged very severely, Shannon notes].[12]

These same levels of meaning can be found in every autobiography. Each story has a historical dimension, a "remembered" dimension, and a dimension of *judgment*. What, or whom, does the writer judge? Is his critical eye turned on himself, or on others? If he criticizes himself, what basis does he use for judgment? (Remember that Ideal from your logic-stage reading?) If he judges others—society, family, God—is his criticism valid? Who is ultimately responsible for his successes and failures: society, family, God?

Do you agree? Does the writer, in your view, shift blame—or judge himself too harshly?

Do you reach a different conclusion from the writer about the pattern of his life? As you glance through the outline of events that you sketched out on your first reading, and then at the evaluations you jotted down on your second reading, you may see two very different patterns. The autobiographer's life may seem self-destructive to you, or petty, or vindictive; yet the *writer* sees a pattern of generosity and victimization. Or you may see great self-sacrifice and courage, but the autobiographer sums up with: *How wretched and unworthy I am!*

If *you* were finding a pattern to the events presented, what pattern would you find? This is a difficult exercise, since you haven't necessarily been given all the information you need; remember that the writer includes those parts of his life which fall into a pattern, and eliminates those which don't seem to fit.

But you can ask a related question: What's missing? What might you expect to find in this work that *isn't* there? And why did the writer choose to gloss over it?

You can get at the "missing element" in two ways: through your knowledge of the writer's life gleaned from other sources (you know that he was

[12]William H. Shannon, "Note to the Reader," in *The Seven Storey Mountain*, by Thomas Merton (New York: Harcourt, 1998), pp. xxii–xxiii.

married to the same woman for thirty-five years, yet he never mentions her; why?), or through hints that the writer himself drops. Thomas Merton refers to a "past" that barred him from entering a religious order on the first try, but never writes of what that past is (although Shannon spills the beans in the "Note to the Reader"). Franklin remarks that he committed only three past actions that were less than perfect (somewhat hard to believe). May Sarton writes of a love affair so obliquely that you might miss it on a first reading. Why? How would the missing elements throw the pattern that the writer is assembling off balance? Would it produce a different pattern altogether?

Do you agree with what the writer has done? Has he been honest, according to his lights—or, on reflection, do you feel misled?

What have you brought away from this story?   What expectations did you bring to the story? Did you hope to find out how genius worked, or how a difficult marriage can be endured, or how madness was overcome? And did the recounting of the author's life help you to understand this? Or are you still peering at Rousseau's tales of adolescence and thinking, Yes, but that still doesn't explain why a man gives all of his children away to a foundling hospital.

Lying behind this question is an assumption worth examining: that scientific brilliance, or literary glory, or a new system of philosophy can be explained if we examine the life of the man or woman who achieved it. Each of the autobiographies in the following list was written by a man or woman of accomplishment; this accomplishment justified the writing of the autobiography. Yet how far do the events of a life go toward explaining what a man or woman has accomplished?

In an autobiography, you can see, however tentatively, a successful human being groping for the secret of success. But you may come away wondering how far even a genius understands the workings of his own mind. Sometimes autobiography seems very much like dating. The people involved are incapable of making any sort of objective evaluation—but no one else can make this evaluation for them.

So finally: Do you understand more about creativity, or about slavery, or about the experience of God, than you did before you began to read? Or do you remain on the outside?

THE ANNOTATED AUTOBIOGRAPHY LIST

AUGUSTINE
The Confessions
(A.D. C. 400)

Best translations: There are several good choices for reading the Confessions *in English. Henry Chadwick's 1991 translation (Oxford World's Classics) is perhaps the most widely read, particularly by academics; it tends toward the literal, but also makes use of modern English structures to keep the narrative flowing forcefully forward. Maria Boulding's 1997 translation (*The Confessions, Revised: The Works of St. Augustine: A Translation for the 21st Century, Vol. 1*) is slightly less literal, more dynamic, and so occasionally moves a little too far toward paraphrase, but also in many places gives a more faithful sense of Augustine's own rich prose style. Frank J. Sheed's 1948 translation, republished by Hackett, is still preferred by many, particularly within the Catholic community, since it is the most poetic and lyrical of the three.*

How does a rebel against God become a man who has God as the "light of my heart"? Augustine's account of his life lays out the answer: He finds that, as a baby, he already had memories of God, his Creator. But his will and intellect did not know God. As a boy, he studies only for self-glorification; as a young man, he indulges his "habits of the flesh" and takes a mistress. Aware of a certain "poverty of mind," he tries to fill this empty place through becoming a teacher (in Carthage), and through becoming a follower of the radical prophet Manes. He stays in the Manichean sect for nine years, awaiting the arrival of an expert who can answer all of his deepest questions about good and evil. But when the expert finally arrives, Augustine discovers that he is "ignorant of the liberal arts" and has only "knowledge . . . of a very conventional kind." His intellect unsatisfied, his enthusiasm for the sect starts to dwindle. So does his enthusiasm for teaching, since his students become rowdier and more ignorant every year. "Here I was already thirty," Augustine writes, "and still mucking about in the same mire."

In an effort to regularize his life, he rejects his long-term mistress (and their son), goes to Milan to teach, and studies first Neoplatonism, and then Paul's Epistle to the Romans. Both offer more intellectual satisfaction than Manichean theology—but although his mind becomes convinced of the truth of Christianity, his will lags behind.

Sitting in his Milan garden, "weeping in the bitter agony of my heart," he hears a child's voice saying, "Pick up and read, pick up and read." He picks up the Epistle to Romans and reads, "Put on the Lord Jesus Christ and make no provision for the flesh in its lusts." He writes then, "At once, with the last words of this sentence, it was as if a light of relief from all anxiety flooded into my heart. All the shadows of doubt were dispelled." He stops teaching, becomes baptized, and goes back home.

So how did the rebel become a saint? His will finally joined his memory and his intellect in the knowledge of God. Augustine is the first autobiographer to divide man into three; since man is made in the image of God, who is Three in One, human beings consist of memory (reflecting the Father), intellect (reflecting Christ, the "Logos" or Word), and the will (the Spirit). These three parts are independent of each other—in fact, they battle with each other. God is in man's memory from birth; any questing mind, searching for truth, will also encounter God; but for conversion to come about, the *will* must also come into line with the will of God—as it finally does, for Augustine, in the garden at Milan. But even as he divides man into three neat parts, Augustine laments the inadequacy of the scheme: "I find my own self hard to grasp," he writes, "I have become for myself a soil which is a cause of difficulty and much sweat."

MARGERY KEMPE
The Book of Margery Kempe
(c. 1430)

Best translations: John Skinner's translation into contemporary English (Image, 1998) is both readable and faithful to the original. Barry Windeatt's 1986 translation for Penguin Classics is slightly more archaic sounding, but still accessible. The 2001 Norton Critical Edition, The Book of Margery Kempe: A New Translation, Contexts, Criticism, *translated and edited by Lynn Staley, offers additional helps by footnoting all unfamiliar geographical, historical, and theological vocabulary. (Remember to save the critical essays until you've done your own first reading.)*

Margery Kempe dictated her autobiography to a townsman in 1432, just before her death at the age of fifty-nine; four years later, a priest transcribed these notes into a third-person narrative which refers to the narrator as "this creature." Although Kempe's words have been through two sets of male hands, they show a wholly female life, fenced in by constant pregnancy and the demands of domesticity. Like Augustine, Margery Kempe is torn by desires; unlike Augustine, Kempe isn't free to wander about the medieval world looking for satisfaction. Nevertheless, she is constantly tugged toward the divine. After the traumatic birth of her first child, she sees "devils . . . all inflamed with burning flames of fire," ordering her to abandon her faith. Her family, afraid she will do herself an injury, keeps her "bound" until she has a vision of Christ sitting beside her bed. At this, she is "stabled in her wits," goes back to daily life, and becomes first a brewer and then a miller.

Both of these businesses fail, and Margery has a vision telling her to live without the "debt of matrimony" so that she may understand heavenly mirth. Mr. Kempe, unconvinced, replies that he will give up sex when God appears to him also. So Margery goes on paying her matrimonial debt, giving birth to fourteen children. She also begins to have mystical visions, traveling through time and space in the company of an angel. When Margery prays that her husband will be chaste, he's stricken with impotence ("You are no good wife," he protests plaintively). Eventually they come to an agreement: If he promises not to "meddle" with her, she will pay his debts with her own money.

Kempe's spiritual calling is finally recognized by the archbishop of Canterbury, who gives her permission to wear nun's clothing. Despite opposition, she becomes more and more prominent as a "holy woman," making pilgrimages to Jerusalem and Rome and meeting with the famous female mystic Julian of Norwich. But even as she becomes a public figure, she is pulled back toward domesticity; her aging husband sinks into senility, and Kempe returns home to care for him. "And therefore," Kempe writes, "was her labor much the more in washing and wringing, and her expense in making fires; and hindered her full much from her contemplation."

MICHEL DE MONTAIGNE
Essays
(1580)

Best translation: The Penguin Classics paperback edition of The Complete Essays, *translated and edited by M. A. Screech (1993).*

Because Montaigne continued to revise these essays up to the year of his death in 1592, there is, as Screech notes in his foreword, "no such thing as a definitive edition." This Penguin edition follows the fairly common practice of marking chunks of the essays with A (for the first edition), A1 (for the 1582 edition), B (for the 1588 edition, which made enormous changes to the original essays and added an entire new book), and C (for the final edition being prepared at the time of Montaigne's death). Screech also adds '95 to mark additions from the first posthumous edition. These letters in the text are slightly distracting at first, but once your eye becomes accustomed to them you can simply ignore them and read the text as a coherent whole.

The external events of Montaigne's life appear only obliquely in his essays; he attended college and became a lawyer; married and had several children (only one, a daughter, lived); inherited the family property and sold his law practice to devote himself full-time to study. But his study was disturbed by a slide into "melancholy humor" and disordered "ravings." In order to control his disorderly thoughts, he set about writing the *Essays*; without political or academic qualifications, he chose to write about what he knew: "I am myself the matter of my book," he tells the reader. At a time when only the powerful and famous wrote about the splendid events of their lives, Montaigne claimed that the real interest of a life lay not in outward events (which are public), but in the thoughts, habits, and emotions that make up the private self.

You need not read every essay unless you're particularly interested in sixteenth-century French warfare. Begin with Montaigne's direction "To the Reader." In Book I, read Chapters 2–4, on the power of emotion and grief to shape (and distort) the self; Chapter 9, on memory; Chapters 19–21, on the shape of a life that looks inevitably forward to death; Chapter 26, on education (for boys); Chapter 28, "On affectionate relationships" (this has elsewhere been titled "On friendship" and is the best known of Montaigne's essays); Chapter 29, on man's relationship to society; and Chapter 51, on the untrustworthy nature of words.

In Book II, read Chapter 1 and Chapters 5–8, on the various qualities that make up what we think of as our "core" or "true" self; Chapter 10, on the value of studying the lives of great men (Montaigne winks at the reader here, encouraging us to view his own life as "great"); and Chapters 17–21, 29, and 31, which complete Montaigne's musings on the virtues and vices that make up the "self." Finally, in Book III, read Chapters 1–2, on the difference between "useful" actions and "good" actions; and Chapter 13, "On Experience." Here Montaigne ponders the nature of truth: can the mind think its way to certainty? Drowning in speculation, Montaigne casts a lifeline around the details of everyday life; he chooses, willingly, to limit his vision for the sake of sanity, placing a border around the too-wide world. "If you have been able to examine and manage your own life," he concludes, "you have achieved the greatest task of all."

TERESA OF ÁVILA
The Life of Saint Teresa of Ávila by Herself
(1588)

Best translations: The excellent Penguin Classics edition, translated by J. M.
Cohen (1998). The 1946 translation by E. A. Peers, which is slightly dated
but still readable, has also been republished in a Dover edition as The Autobiography of St. Teresa of Avila *(2010).*

Written in Castilian Spanish and first translated into English in 1611,
Teresa's autobiography begins in childhood. Like Augustine, she knows
the goodness of God, but rejects it. But while Augustine yields to intellectual temptations, Teresa is seduced by physical vanity; she tries to
"attract others by my appearance . . . using perfumes and all the vanities
I could get." Sent to school in a convent, Teresa learns that "the world
is vanity, and will soon pass away." She is afraid that she will go to hell
and so forces herself to become a nun, taking the habit through sheer
self-determination, without any true love of God. God rewards her
with joy in her vocation, but she soon realizes that lax observance of
the Rule within the convent allows her too much freedom to indulge
her vanity. She wanders from God, but he reproves her and teaches her
to return to him in prayer. (Here Teresa stops her narrative to describe
the four states of prayer and their place in the soul's experience of
God.) As her story resumes, Teresa tells of her greatest vision (of the
torments of hell) and her calling to establish a convent in which the
Rule would be kept "with the greatest possible perfection." With the
help of a "widowed lady" of means, Teresa founds the House of St.
Joseph, where the nuns can live a more penitential life. She is opposed
by her superiors, who think that her visions are delusions. But in fighting this "severe persecution," Teresa is given a revelation: "a spiritual
transport of a kind which I cannot describe . . . a truth which is the
fulfillment of all truths." This nonverbal truth—greater than the truths
of "many learned men"—is a rapture in which she glimpses the truth
of the Trinity. Augustine anchors himself in Neoplatonism and the
New Testament, and Montaigne in the certainties of daily life; but
Teresa finds truth neither in the intellect nor in physical existence.
She points her readers toward a direct, mystical experience of God, a
"state of ecstasy" in which the soul can receive "true revelations, great
favours and visions." And she tells her readers, again and again, to trust
their own visions—even, perhaps, when learned men condemn them
as illusory.

RENÉ DESCARTES
Meditations
(1641)

Best translations: Readers have a number of good options, including the Penguin Classics paperback, Meditations and Other Metaphysical Writings, *translated by Desmond M. Clarke (1999); Hackett's* Meditations, Objections, and Replies, *edited and translated by Roger Areiw and Donald Cress (2006); and the Cambridge University Press translation by John Cottingham,* Meditations on First Philosophy, *with Selections from the Objections and Replies (rev. ed., 1996). The last is probably the most contemporary sounding of the translations, and also includes the most scholarly apparatus.*

Perhaps Descartes envied Teresa's certainty; he was a deeply religious man, but temperamentally incapable of accepting divine truth without question. In the *Meditations*, Descartes doesn't tell the story of his physical life ("I was born . . .") but rather the tale of his intellectual life, which "begins" on the day when he sits down to arrange his thoughts and discover which ones are actually trustworthy. He begins with his senses, asking, Do I know that my experience of the physical world is true? No, he answers; sometimes, his senses have deceived him (telling him, for example, that a distant object is nearer than it actually is). If his senses deceive him in one thing, it is possible that they deceive him in all, and that all his ideas of the outside world are wrong. Nor can he prove, without a doubt, that God (whom Descartes believes, rather than knows, to be powerful and good) would not allow him to be deceived; it is possible that some evil force has intervened and is holding him in a state of deception.

Descartes may be deluded about the things that he perceives, but one thing is certain: he is *thinking about* the problem. And if he is thinking, he must *exist*. So he concludes, "I certainly did exist, if I convinced myself of something. . . . Thus, having weighed up everything adequately, it must finally be stated that this proposition 'I am, I exist' is necessarily true whenever it is stated by me or conceived in my mind."

Having settled this problem, Descartes can turn to other questions— the existence of God, the nature of truth, the relationship between the mind and the body. "I will now close my eyes," he continues, "block my ears, and shut down all my senses. I will erase from my thought all images or physical things . . . addressing only myself and looking more deeply into myself. I will try to make myself gradually better known and more familiar to myself. I am a *thinking thing*. . . ." Augustine, Margery

Kempe, and Teresa attach their sense of self to their relationship with God; Montaigne, to his daily existence. But Descartes finds himself in his mind. He does not exist as a sensing thing (this could be deceptive) or as a feeling thing (emotions being equally deceptive) or as a religious man (since his knowledge of God is also full of doubts); he exists, without debate, only as a thinking thing. This vast change in the way that the self considers itself echoes throughout all later autobiographies, which continue to excavate the mind, assuming that what we think will reveal who we are.

JOHN BUNYAN
Grace Abounding to the Chief of Sinners
(1666)

Best editions: Now in the public domain, Bunyan's memoir has been republished by Penguin Classics, Oxford World's Classics, and Vintage (as the joint volume The Pilgrim's Progress and Grace Abounding to the Chief of Sinners). *It is also available in multiple places online as a free ebook.*

As a Nonconformist, Bunyan rejects the Church of England—its rites, its doctrines, its authority, and its congregations. And this makes him very much alone. He longs to join other believers; when he hears "three or four poor women sitting at a door in the sun, and talking about the things of God," he longs to enter into a brand new life. But the women, he writes, seem to be "on the sunny side of some high mountain . . . while I was shivering and shrinking in the cold." Between the women and himself, Bunyan sees a wall; he can't find a way through, until he discovers "a narrow gap . . . [A]t last, with great striving, methought I at first did get in my head, and after that by a sideling striving, my shoulders, and my whole body; then I was exceeding glad, and went and sat down in the midst of them, and so was comforted with the light and heat of their sun."

Finally in the company of others who also believe, Bunyan should be secure and full of grace. But the temporary comfort and hope that he feels is followed by an obsessive desire to blaspheme, and the cycle continues; Bunyan fights off temptation, is "put into my right mind again," is assaulted by temptation again, understands grace, struggles against guilt again. Finally he grasps that his righteousness is not his own, but that of Jesus Christ. "Now did my chains fall off my legs indeed." Is this the final act? Not quite; darkness descends again on his soul, until God assures him with a final scripture: *You are come to Mount Zion, to the city of the living God*

. . . to the general assembly of the first-born . . . to the spirits of just men made perfect. At last Bunyan has found his company, where others stand with him in the presence of God. He is no longer alone. Has he reached salvation at last? Perhaps, but for Bunyan, conversion is not a single shining moment, but a long path down which he walks, with an eye always cautiously behind: Like Christian in *Pilgrim's Progress*, Bunyan was threatened by the "door to hell, even at the gates of heaven."

MARY ROWLANDSON
The Narrative of the Captivity and Restoration
(1682)

Best editions: The narrative can be found in the collections The Account of Mary Rowlandson and Other Indian Captivity Narratives, *ed. Horace Kephart (Dover, 2005), and* American Captivity Narratives, *ed. Gordon M. Sayre (Houghton Mifflin, 2000). The St. Martin's Press standalone volume,* The Sovereignty and Goodness of God, Together With the Faithfulness of His Promises Displayed: Being a Narrative of the Captivity and Restoration of Mrs. Mary Rowlandson, *is edited by Neal Salisbury; published in 1997, it is now out of print but widely available secondhand.*

Captivity narratives were a peculiarly American form of autobiography in which white settlers, trying to tame the American wilderness and beset by thorns, weeds, plague, and storms, are (as a last straw) kidnapped by hostile Indians—who become an embodiment of spiritual evil, determined to wipe out colonists who are trying to establish God's kingdom on earth.

In Mary Rowlandson's narrative, Indians attack the little settlement of Lancaster, Massachusetts, while Mary's husband—the town minister—is away in Boston, asking the governor of Massachusetts to station soldiers in Lancaster to protect its residents. Mary sees her oldest sister and her nephews killed, but she is captured alive, along with her young daughter (wounded by an Indian musket ball) and her other children. Nine days later, the little girl dies. The Indians bury her, and Mary and her surviving children are kept for ransom. To avoid reprisals, their captors march them into less populated areas. Mary records each day's march in her journal; throughout, she reflects on the similarity between her own plight and the plight of Old Testament characters who also suffered. Her experience is always compared with theirs, with God's possible response charted in the same terms. Threatened with death if she stirs from the wigwam where she is confined, Mary laments, "Now may I say with

David, II Sam. xxiv. 14, *I am in a great strait.* . . . This distressed condition held that day and half the next; and then the Lord remembered me, whose mercies are great."

Put to work, Rowlandson encounters both kind and unkind Indian masters (the women are particularly disagreeable to her). Finally she is ransomed and meets her husband in Boston. Although their children are still held captive, eventually they are redeemed and reunited with their parents. "I have learned to look beyond present and smaller troubles," Mary writes, "and to be quieted under them, as Moses said, Exodus xiv. 13, *Stand still and see the salvation of the Lord.*"

JEAN-JACQUES ROUSSEAU
Confessions
(1781)

Best translations: The Oxford World's Classics translation by Angela Scholar, edited by Patrick Coleman (2000), remains the most readable and energetic contemporary version. J. M. Cohen's 1953 translation (Penguin Classics) sounds very slightly dated, but is still accessible; it has also been recorded unabridged by Frederick Davidson for Audible.

Rousseau's autobiography is roughly modeled on Augustine's; like Augustine, Rousseau announces that all men are alike in their sinfulness. "Assemble about me, Eternal Being, the numberless host of my fellow-men," he writes, "Let each of them, here on the steps of your throne, in turn reveal his heart with the same sincerity; and then let one of them say to you, if he dares: *I was better than that man.*" Unlike Augustine, though, Rousseau claims sinfulness as the quality that makes him human; he celebrates it, rather than lamenting it. He tells us of his perverse sexual tastes, his propensity to steal ("I decided that stealing and being beaten went together and constituted in some sense a contract. . . . On the strength of this idea I began to steal with an easier mind than before"), his decision to put all five of his children into a foundling hospital (he refers to the birth of his second child simply as an "inconvenience"), his feuds, his hatreds, his failings. And he claims all of these as an essential part of a *self* that was formed, not by God, but by a random set of childhood influences and social strictures. Rousseau paints no picture of the self he *should* have; he merely lays out the self that he *is,* refusing to apologize for it.

Without any "ideal" self to use as a pattern, Rousseau is unable to bring order to the tale of his life. "The further I advance into my narrative," he writes, "the less order and sequence I am able to introduce into it." But ultimately he triumphs over this muddle by simply announcing, *I am*, like God in the desert. (The echo of Exodus is intentional; Rousseau is not the image of God, or a thinking being, but simply *himself*.) And, like God, he cannot be judged. The *Confessions* ends with Rousseau's account of a public reading of this autobiography before several prominent citizens. He ended this reading, he tells us, with a challenge: "As for me, I hereby declare publicly and without fear: that anyone who . . . examines with his own eyes my nature, my character, my morals, my inclinations, my pleasures, my habits, and can think me a dishonorable man, is himself a man who ought to be choked." In the face of this declaration, his audience falls silent, refusing to speak; Rousseau is as he is, and no one dares to judge him.

BENJAMIN FRANKLIN
The Autobiography of Benjamin Franklin
(1791)

Best editions: This has been in the public domain for years and is available in multiple editions, as well as online as a free ebook. The Autobiography and Other Writings, *ed. Kenneth Silverman (Penguin, 1986), contains the* Autobiography, *selections from Franklin's letters, and excerpts from* Poor Richard's Almanac. *Other editions have been published by Oxford World's Classics, Dover Thrift Editions, and Signet Classics. Ten different unabridged audio versions are available from Audible.*

With his *Autobiography*, Benjamin Franklin invents the American Dream: The poor boy from Boston succeeds in business without the help of family connections or inherited wealth. And Franklin's character is as self-made as his fortune; he decides what virtues he ought to have and sets out to achieve them through sheer hard work: "Humility," he writes. "Be like Jesus and Socrates." He also deals with flaws *sans* outside help; Franklin marks faults on an ivory tablet with a lead pencil, and wipes them away with a wet sponge once they are overcome. Throughout his *Autobiography*, Franklin consistently refers to his mistakes (and his sins against others) as *errata*, printer's errors that are unintentional and easily corrected in the next edition; he is able to make himself flawless just as easily as he makes himself rich. But this picture of a self that prospers all alone is an illusion; Franklin's family *gave* him the invaluable skills of reading and writing, and his oldest brother gave him his first job. And Franklin's rejection of his faults is equally suspect; his reluctance to admit serious error introduces a note of arrogance to the character of the self-made American man. For the next two hundred years, this character takes its clue from Franklin's aside in Part I: "So convenient a thing it is to be a *reasonable creature*, since it enables one to find or make a reason for everything one has a mind to do."

FREDERICK DOUGLASS
Narrative of the Life of Frederick Douglass, an American Slave
(1845)

Best editions: Douglass wrote his autobiography three separate times. The first version, Narrative of the Life of Frederick Douglass, An American Slave, *was published in 1845; the second,* My Bondage and My Freedom, *in 1855; and this third and final version in 1881. Each autobiography retells and alters stories from the previous version. Although you can simply read the earliest* Narrative *(available from Dover Thrift Editions and Penguin Classics), the Library of America version edited by Henry Louis Gates (*Frederick Douglass: Autobiographies: Narrative of the Life of Frederick Douglass, an American Slave/My Bondage and My Freedom/Life and Times of Frederick Douglass*) contains all three.*

Born to parents he never knew, Frederick Douglass is raised by his grandparents; they are loving and kind, skilled at fishing and gardening, well respected by their neighbors. But when he is old enough to work, Douglass is taken to his master's plantation and abandoned amid a crowd of other children. Stripped of his family identity, he is treated like an animal (the children eat from a trough "like so many pigs"). But Douglass refuses to be an animal, instead struggling toward a new understanding of himself. He learns to read despite his master's objections ("If he learns to read the Bible it will forever unfit him to be a slave," the man declares) and begins to consider himself a thinking, speaking human being. When he is beaten and abused by the brutal slavemaster Covey, Douglass wrestles Covey to the ground—and is finally able to think of himself as a *man*. "This battle with Mr. Covey," writes Douglass, "revived a sense of my own manhood. I was a changed being after that fight. I was nothing before—I was a man now." Equipped both mentally and emotionally for life as a freedman, Douglass runs away to Massachusetts and is recruited by abolitionists to tell white northern audiences about his experiences as a slave. Again he remakes himself, this time as a speaker and thinker—too successfully for his abolitionist friends, who advise him to keep "a little of the plantation speech . . . [I]t is not best that you seem learned." Their fears come true when Douglass is denounced as an imposter; his audiences begin to say that he does "not

talk like a slave, look like a slave, or act like a slave." "They believed,"
Douglass writes, "I had never been south of Mason and Dixon's line."
In answer to this accusation, he sets down the entire story of his life as a
slave in writing—thus reclaiming, as an essential part of his *new* identity,
the years spent in bondage.

HENRY DAVID THOREAU
Walden
(1854)

*Best editions: Published as a stand-alone by Dover Thrift Editions, and in
collections with other essays by Modern Library Classics, Signet Classics, and
Bantam Classics.*

Thoreau is the anti-Franklin; Franklin's story tells American men how
to make themselves into men of wealth, but Thoreau sees the American
economy as a morass that traps all men, rich and poor together. Even
those who inherit land become slaves to it, they are forced to work like
"machines" in order to make property pay. "The mass of men," Thoreau writes, in his most famous line, "lead lives of quiet desperation." So
Thoreau offers a new pattern for American lives. He retreats to a hand-
built cottage on the shores of Walden Pond; this withdrawal from the
American economy is purely symbolic (the cottage is only a mile and a
half from the center of the nearby village), but it allows him to construct
a temporary identity as a man free from economic necessity, rejecting the
need to buy, sell, or work.

Thoreau's descriptions of his simple life at Walden are not an economic solution (he knows perfectly well that all of America cannot
retreat to the woods) but a form of protest. His essays don't progress
chronologically; rather, they discuss different aspects of his life at the
pond—life in solitude, how to treat visitors, the value of reading, his
attempts to grow food. "Simplify, simplify," Thoreau preaches. "The
nation itself . . . is . . . an unwieldy and overgrown establishment . . .
ruined by luxury and heedless expense, by want of calculation and a
worthy aim, as the million households in the land; and the only cure
for it as for them is a rigid economy, a stern and more than Spartan
simplicity of life and elevation of purpose." Thoreau sets himself up
as an example of this simplicity; his months at Walden are a pattern
for us to follow. *Walden* demonstrates the possibility of a new kind of
existence, a "beautiful and winged life" that must break out from the
dry husk of the old.

HARRIET JACOBS
Incidents in the Life of a Slave Girl, Written By Herself
(1861)

*Best editions: Available from Dover Thrift Editions and Penguin Classics;
also published by Modern Library Classics in a collection along with* Narrative of the Life of Frederick Douglass, an American Slave *(ed. Kwame
Anthony Appiah), the earliest version of Douglass's autobiography (see above).*

Raised by a strict grandmother to be virtuous, Harriet Jacobs is faced with
an insoluble dilemma: Her master, "Dr. Flint," is determined to make
her into his mistress. When he forbids her to marry the black man of her
choosing, Jacobs is faced with a difficult choice: not between keeping her
virtue and giving it away, but rather between giving it away by choice or
surrendering it to the master she hates. So in order to protect herself, she
begins an affair with a white neighbor and bears two children by him.
This relationship with "Mr. Sands" serves as temporary protection, but
Dr. Flint continues to be obsessed by her; he refuses to sell her, and eventually Mr. Sands marries a white woman and ends the connection with
Jacobs. Several times given the chance to escape, Jacobs refuses because
she would have to leave her children behind. Finally, desperate to avoid
Dr. Flint's attentions, she fakes an escape—and lives for seven years in a
crawlspace in her grandmother's attic. Eventually Jacobs and her children
do escape, but the Fugitive Slave Act means that they can be arrested,
even in the North. At last Jacobs is bought by a sympathetic white friend
and set free, but she finds this a bitter victory: "A human being *sold* in the
free city of New York! . . . I am deeply grateful to the generous friend
who procured [my freedom], but I despise the miscreant who demanded
payment for what never rightfully belonged to him or his."

Jacobs knows that her use of fictional names (she calls herself "Linda
Brent"), her good English prose, and her seven-year existence in an attic
make her story difficult to believe, so her autobiography includes letters
from respectable whites, vouching for its credibility. White voices thus
become an inextricable element of Jacobs's story, reflecting the reality
of slavery itself: "Slavery is a curse to the whites as well as to the blacks,"
Jacobs writes. "It makes the white fathers cruel and sensual; the sons
violent and licentious; it contaminates the daughters, and makes the
wives wretched. And as for the colored race, it needs an abler pen than
mine to describe the extremity of their sufferings, the depth of their
degradation."

BOOKER T. WASHINGTON
Up from Slavery
(1901)

Best edition: The Oxford World's Classics paperback, edited by William L. Andrews (2000).

Slavery ends during Washington's childhood, but in the post–Civil War economy, jobs for freedmen are scarce and unpleasant. Washington, his mother, and his stepfather go to West Virginia to work in the salt mines there. Although Washington isn't a slave, he is imprisoned by poverty. Education becomes for him, as it was for Douglass, the way to form a new identity. Washington remakes himself as a scholar and teacher. He works his way through night school and then through Hampton University, goes on to do graduate work, comes back to Hampton University as a teacher, and in 1881 heads up a "normal school" for black students at Tuskegee. The school aims to teach practical skills; in Washington's view, Negroes can form a new racial identity for themselves—as citizens, not slaves and victims—through patience, education, hard work, and good manners. Forget about political power for right now, he advises his readers; improve your hygiene, your table manners, and your ability to handle money, and whites will eventually grant you political power out of respect.

Washington appears, in his autobiography, as a humble, hardworking, and thoroughly admirable man, an ideal leader for a troubled people. But his "accomodationist" view of race relations brings Washington into conflict with other black intellectuals, who accuse him of ignoring the need for equality in favor of peace. But Washington sees himself as a model for his race. Throughout his autobiography, Washington refers to his own experience as the ideal for other young black men. He works in the salt mines and goes to school at night; so, too, can they. He is willing to wear a homemade cap as a child, rather than insisting that his mother spend precious money on a new one; they should be content to scrimp and save toward economic independence, rather than splashing money around in an attempt to be like whites. He rose to prominence and power through the same patient persistence he recommends to others.

FRIEDRICH NIETZSCHE
Ecce Homo: How One Becomes What One Is
(1908)

Best translation: Duncan Large's translation, republished as an Oxford World's Classic in 2009, makes Nietzsche as accessible as possible while retaining his idiosyncratic style and punctuation. The unabridged audio version from Audible is the older Anthony M. Ludovici translation; it is a perfectly fine rendering, but sounds a little more dated and archaic than the Large version.

Although Nietzsche announces a conventional autobiographical purpose (he is going to trace the influences that have made him into the man he is in 1888, at the age of forty-four), his chapters (beginning with "Why I Am So Wise" and "Why I Am So Clever") are neither chronological nor logical. As autobiography, *Ecce Homo* parallels Descartes' attempt to find his "self" in his intellect, or Bunyan's attempt to find his "self" in the love of God—or Washington's attempt to find his "self" in hard work and education. But Nietzsche finds his "self" elsewhere. Nutshelling Nietzsche's philosophy is impossible, since he was an existentialist, and since existentialism is a rejection of all systems of philosophy and all explanations for human existence. Instead, each human action (and each human life) must create its own meaning. Each man is completely free to choose his own path. Existence is so infinitely varied that it cannot be reduced to any sort of system. There is no "moral code" in the universe—no "right" or "wrong." There are simply choices, with consequences that must be endured after the choices are made.

So Nietzsche's autobiography is a hymn to the uniqueness of his own existence; it is a record of his choices and their consequences. At its end, he rails against the "concept of the *good* man," who is "weak, sick, ill-constructed . . . an ideal made in opposition to the proud and well-constituted, to the affirmative man"—the man who boldly chooses and in the act of choice finds meaning. Nietzsche wrote *Ecce Homo* in three weeks and then went mad, two weeks after sending the manuscript to the printer; the title is drawn from the New Testament, where Pilate uses it to point out Jesus Christ to the masses before his crucifixion. But for Nietzsche, Christ is not "the man"; *he* is. He does not offer himself as a model (that would set up a standard, an "ideal" that applies to all), but rather as an example— a man who finds meaning in making his choices and living with their consequences.

ADOLF HITLER
Mein Kampf
(1925)

Best translations: The earliest translation into English was sponsored in 1938 by the American publishing company Reynal & Hitchcock. It was closer to a paraphrase than a translation in many places, so the 1939 translation by James Murphy—the only one approved for accuracy by the Third Reich—is preferable. It is not easy to find in print, although several ebook versions are available. The slightly later translation by Ralph Manheim (1943) has been republished by Houghton Mifflin (1998) and is just as accurate, although it lacks the historic interest of the "approved" English translation. Avoid the so-called "Ford translation," which (despite aggressive marketing) appears to be a self-published effort by an uncredentialed translator.

Hitler wrote *Mein Kampf* ("My Struggle") while in jail for a failed attempt to prevent Bavaria from seceding from the German republic. In Hitler's account of his own life, every choice that he makes is dictated by his attempts to restore Germany to its previous glories; he is Every(German) man; his defeats represent Germany's humiliations, and his rise to power parallels Germany's return to glory.

Even as a child, Hitler writes, he wonders why all Germans did not have "the good luck to belong to Bismarck's Empire." He believes that Bavaria's defeat by France and its following subjection to French rule (which Hitler continually calls "the time of Germany's deepest humiliation") could have been avoided if the German people had been united. So from his earliest days he is determined to restore the divided parts of Germany to the "great German Motherland." He refuses to become a government official and turns to painting, not for personal reasons, but because he cannot bear to be part of a government that serves French, rather than German, interests. His study in Vienna, his initial involvement in politics, his service in the Bavarian army during the First World War, his membership in the German Labour Party, and his impatience with the "faulty and ineffective" German government are all motivated by an "intense love" for the German people and a "profound hatred for the [French-dominated] Austrian State." Hitler sees himself as the only man able to "employ any energetic and radical methods" to restore German power; his ravings on the demonic influence of Jewish blood and the "loss of racial purity" that "will wreck inner happiness forever" are eerily combined with constant calls to end tiresome bureaucracy that sound perfectly reasonable. Plowing through all the vituperation is tiring, so you need not read the entire biography. In Part I, read Chapters 1–6 and Chapter 11; in Part II, read Chapters 2–4, 10, 11, and 15, which clearly demonstrate Hitler's fantastic understanding of propaganda techniques. The twenty-first century may have rejected Hitler's doctrine of racial purity, but his techniques of propaganda are still much in use—although they have been turned to the service of the market, rather than the nation-state.

MOHANDAS GANDHI
An Autobiography: The Story of My Experiments with Truth
(1929)

Best translation: The Beacon Press paperback, translated by Mahadev Desai (1993).

Gandhi's autobiography is a life in borrowed clothes: he is an Eastern thinker using a Western form to tell the West of his search for spiritual truth. "I know of nobody in the East having written [an autobiography]," a friend tells him, as he begins the task, "except those who have come under Western influence. And what will you write? Supposing you reject tomorrow the things you hold as principles today . . . ?" So Gandhi's autobiography is, in part, an apology for *being* autobiography at all. He writes that he intends to describe his arrival at the spiritual truths which then shaped his political actions, and "as my life consists of nothing but those experiments, it is true that the story will take the shape of an autobiography."

Gandhi is born in India, under British rule; he marries at thirteen (an Indian custom, for which he feels he must apologize), and at nineteen travels to England (without his wife and young son) to study law. He then returns to India as a barrister, but finds himself without much work. Taking a temporary position in South Africa, he discovers that the Indian population, classed as "colored," suffers from discrimination. He stays in South Africa for almost twenty years, working for Indian rights. Finally returning to India in the middle of post–World War II unrest, he finds the British overlords tightening restrictions on their Indian subjects. His nonviolent protests against this repression culminate in a countrywide eruption of civil disobedience, which finally forces the British to take notice. Throughout the story, Gandhi examines himself to find spiritual principles that will govern his political actions. Chief among these is the principle of *Ahisma*, or nonviolence, which becomes the directing principle of Gandhi's life; a "votary of *Ahisma*," Gandhi writes, "remains true to his faith if the spring of all his actions is compassion, if he shuns to the best of his ability the destruction of the tiniest creature." And he discovers this spiritual truth through "deep self-introspection"; he has, he tells us, "searched myself through and through, and examined and analysed every psychological situation. . . . For me [my conclusions] appear to be absolutely correct, and seem for the time being to be final."

GERTRUDE STEIN

The Autobiography of Alice B. Toklas

(1933)

Best edition: The Vintage Books paperback (1990).

Gandhi borrows an unfamiliar form, but Gertrude Stein borrows someone else's life; her autobiography is, in the words of Estelle Jelenik, "a disguise of the self in words."[13] She uses the voice of her companion, Alice B. Toklas, but only the first few pages deal with Toklas's life; the tale then turns to Stein herself. The autobiography begins with the classic "I was born," chronicling Toklas's birth in California and takes her up through her late twenties in a mere three pages, when the (apparently) transitional point of her life occurs: she meets Gertrude Stein, and writes that she has "met a genius." From this point, Stein adds in Toklas's voice, "my new full life began." This mockery of the standard autobiographical "conversion" shifts the tale to Gertrude Stein, her life in Paris, her friendship with the painters Pablo Picasso, Pierre Matisse, and Paul Cézanne; the German offensive that forces her to leave Paris; and her work in a war hospital. The narrative runs constantly away into capsule biographies of other personalities; the cumulative effect is something like one of those portraits made up of hundreds of colored squares that, when examined closely, each turn out to be a picture of something else. At the end, the reader has been given a portrait of Gertrude Stein, made up of dozens of portraits of other people.

Stein's autobiography displays characteristics that critics have labeled "typically feminine" (as opposed to the "typically masculine" autobiographies that came before): She writes anecdotally, telling stories of people rather than politics; and her story is told nonchronologically (were the chapters in chronological order, Chapter 4 would be the first, followed by Chapters 3, 1, 2, 5, 6, and 7). This disregard for order turns Stein's autobiography into a game, something close to a literary version of *Clue*; to get any glimpse of Stein's true self, the reader has to reorder the clues and find out what's missing.

---

[13]Estelle C. Jelinek, *The Tradition of Women's Autobiography: From Antiquity to the Present* (Boston: Twayne Publishers, 1986), p. 39.

THOMAS MERTON
The Seven Storey Mountain
(1948)

Best edition: The Mariner Books anniversary edition (1999).

Thomas Merton became a new man when he entered the Trappist order; his autobiography tells the story of the "old" Merton, a selfish and self-centered intellectual who is now (figuratively) dead. So he judges his own life very harshly indeed, accusing himself of lacking love, that central virtue of the Christian life, from his earliest days. His exclusion of his small brother from his childhood games, he writes, is "the pattern and prototype of all sin: the deliberate and formal will to reject disinterested love for us for the purely arbitrary reason that . . . it does not please us to be loved." Merton's story of his youth, education, and time at Cambridge aims to show us that his sin did indeed follow this pattern, as he continually rejects God's love.

Merton's mind begins to accept God before his will does. When he reads a book on medieval philosophy, he begins to realize that his ideas about God—"a noisy and dramatic and passionate character, a vague, jealous, hidden being"—come, not from God, but from images made by other men. Freed from this distorted idea of God, Merton begins to read theology to find out who God is and is drawn to the Catholic Church and its theology—"a tremendous, profound, unified doctrine." This intellectual understanding, though, does not bring Merton much closer to accepting the love of God; he condemns himself for talking "for hours about mysticism and the experimental knowledge of God" while "stoking the fires of the argument with Scotch and soda." In the end, he is able to submit to the love of God only by surrendering to the institution of the church, and accepting, with humility, its dictates. "The conversion of the intellect is not enough," he writes, a theme that echoes in conversion stories from Augustine to Colson; "as long as the will . . . did not belong completely to God."

C. S. LEWIS
Surprised by Joy: The Shape of My Early Life
(1955)

Best edition: The Harcourt Books reprint of the 1955 edition. Audible publishes the unabridged audio version.

Lewis's autobiography is partly the story of his intellectual and imaginative development, and partly the tale of his coming to grips with Christian faith. This double tale is haunted by the possibility that the two might conflict, perhaps fatally. The title of Lewis's story comes from his attempt to discover the source of Joy, a piercing experience that he is not entirely able to describe in words: "It was a sensation, of course, of desire; but desire for what? . . . Something quite different from ordinary life . . . something, as they would now say, 'in another dimension.'" Lewis's pursuit of Joy turns out to be the thread that binds his intellect and his faith together. At first, he chases Joy with his intellect, studying Norse mythology and other subjects that have brought him that unexpected stab of Joy in the past. The middle section of the book traces Lewis's education, painting a delightfully vivid portrait of his life at school, the tutor who introduces him to Greek, and his delight in finding book after book that speaks directly to his longing for Joy.

But as Lewis's delight turns "imperceptibly into a scholar's interest," he realizes that Joy has flown. Around the same time, he becomes convinced of the intellectual truth of theism; "I gave in," he writes, "and admitted that God was God, and knelt and prayed: perhaps, that night, the most dejected and reluctant convert in all England." But Lewis's will is not yet God's. He is still determined "not to be 'interfered with' . . . 'to call my soul my own.'" Joy, imagination, and intellect do not come together until the story's end, when Lewis's *will* is finally converted in a way that is completely inaccessible to his reason: "I know very well when, but hardly how, the final step was taken. I was driven to Whipsnade one sunny morning. When we set out I did not believe that Jesus Christ is the Son of God, and when we reached the zoo I did. Yet I had not exactly spent the journey in thought." Only then does Lewis again find himself able to experience Joy—not as an end in itself, but as a signpost pointing him to the divine.

MALCOLM X
The Autobiography of Malcolm X
(1965)

Best editions: Available from both Ballantine Books and Penguin Modern Classics.

Malcolm X's autobiography was written by someone else: Alex Haley, who convinced Malcolm X to tell him his thoughts on an ongoing basis, while Haley shaped those thoughts into an autobiography. This collaboration with another writer introduces a different voice into the core of the story, and in the end changes its entire form. Haley began work on the autobiography while Malcolm X was still a follower of Elijah Muhammad and the chief spokesman for the Nation of Islam (which preached the need for reparations and the establishment of a separate black nation inside America). In 1964, Malcolm broke with Muhammad and the Nation of Islam, disillusioned over Muhammad's extramarital affairs ("I had always taught so strongly on the moral issues," he writes, sadly, "I had discovered Muslims had been betrayed by Elijah Muhammed himself") and uncomfortable with the Nation's increasingly violent rhetoric. (After the break, he discovers that the Nation has approved his assassination.) He forms his own organization and begins to preach the "spiritual force necessary to rid our people of the vices that destroy the moral fiber of our community." But although Malcolm wanted to go back and rewrite the earlier parts of his autobiography, which speak glowingly of the Nation of Islam, Haley protested. In the end, the completed sections of the autobiography remained unchanged, so that *The Autobiography of Malcolm X* shows with unusual clarity a "conversion" from one state of mind to another. It also shows a weird prescience: In the opening chapters, Malcolm writes, "It has always been my belief that I, too, will die by violence." In the final chapter, he sums up his life as "a life that has, as it were, already ended . . . now, each day I live as if I am already dead." In the epilogue, Haley tells of Malcolm's assassination, which happened after the autobiography's completion but before its publication.

MAYA ANGELOU
I Know Why the Caged Bird Sings
(1969)

Best edition: Ballantine Books (2009). I Know Why the Caged Bird Sings *is the first (and most central) of Angelou's seven autobiographies; it is collected, along with five others, in the Modern Library edition,* The Collected Autobiographies of Maya Angelou *(2004). The unabridged audio from Audible is read by Angelou herself.*

The autobiographies of African American women, writes critic and scholar Joan Braxton, are "a tradition within a tradition"; black men may have re-invented the tradition of white male autobiography to fit their own lives, but black women have had fewer models, along with a very different experience to relate. *I Know Why the Caged Bird Sings,* the story of Angelou's life until the age seventeen (when she gave birth to her son) tells of a series of deprivations: her childhood innocence (taken from her at the age of seven in an assault by her mother's boyfriend), her racial identity ("I was really white," she thought as a child, "[but] a cruel fairy stepmother . . . had turned me into a too-big Negro girl, with nappy black hair, broad feet and a space between her teeth"), her family ties (absent father, enigmatic grandmother, and elusive mother), even her name (her white employer insists on calling her "Mary," objecting that her given name is "too long"). The arrival of puberty reveals that her sexual identity too has been stolen from her: "The Black female is assaulted in her tender years," Angelou writes, "by all those common forces of nature at the same time that she is caught in the tripartite crossfire of masculine prejudice, white illogical hate and Black lack of power." In this trackless waste, Angelou finds a faint path leading out: not in written words, as Douglass did, but in the power to speak. "Words mean more than what is set down on paper," an older woman tells her. "It takes the human voice to infuse them with the shades of deeper meaning." Encouraged, Angelou begins to rediscover her own voice—but the autobiography does not simply end with her ability to read, write, and speak. Taught since childhood to view her own physical being as not white enough (and so not feminine enough), Angelou must also find a way to reclaim her body. At the book's close, she discovers her natural ability to protect her baby son, even in sleep; her ability to mother is the beginning of her reconciliation to her own femaleness.

MAY SARTON
Journal of a Solitude
(1973)

Best edition: The trade paperback from W. W. Norton (1992).

Poet and novelist May Sarton wrote a series of journals for publication; each tries to make sense of a particular section of Sarton's life. This journal is an attempt to understand the nature of solitude, at a time when Sarton is suffering through the end of a romantic relationship. Struggling to find meaning in her isolation, Sarton tries to define the value of her work, which demands that she be alone. She airs her frustrations over her inward suspicion (common to creative women) that she is shirking her responsibilities by being alone with her books, rather than caring for people. As she writes, she realizes that love—the wish to be with another person—has the potential to wreck her work. "It is harder for women, perhaps," she laments, "to be 'one-pointed,' much harder for them to clear space around whatever it is they want to do beyond household chores

and family life. Their lives are fragmented." This journal is full of darkness and fragmentation, but Sarton continually tries to bring sense and
meaning to her chaos. "The darkness again," she notes, one Monday. "An
annihilating review in the Sunday *Times* . . . Now it is the old struggle
to survive. . . . On a deeper level I have come to believe (perhaps that is
one way to survive) that there is a reason for these repeated blows—that
I am not meant for success and that in a way adversity is my climate. . . .
Somehow the great clouds made the day all right, a gift of splendor as they
sailed over our heads." Do we really believe that the clouds make Sarton's
wretchedness irrelevant? No, but we can believe that she *wants* them to.

   At the end of her book Sarton continues to feel guilt over her decision
(part made, part thrust on her) to live in isolation. But she concludes, "I
begin to have intimations, now, of a return to some deep self that has been
too absorbed and too battered to function for a long time. That self tells
me that I was meant to live alone, meant to write the poems for others."

ALEKSANDR I. SOLZHENITSYN
The Gulag Archipelago
(1973 in English)

Best edition: The Gulag Archipelago *is a massive, seven-volume work that
appeared in English (translated by Thomas P. Whitney and Harry Willets)
between 1973 and 1985. Most of those single volumes are now out of print.
However, the unabridged work—all eighteen hundred pages of it—is full of
details of Russian history and Soviet society that aren't necessary to the student of autobiography. The best way to read* The Gulag Archipelago *is to
use the authorized Perennial Classics abridgment of the entire seven-volume
memoir, translated by Whitney and Willets, abridged by Edward E. Erick-
son, Jr., and approved by Solzhenitsyn himself (Harper Perennial Modern
Classics, rev. abridged ed., 2007). In addition, the first three unabridged volumes have been recorded by Frederick Davidson for Audible.*

Solzhenitsyn's autobiography moves from first to second to third person as it conveys the nightmarish, absurd quality of arrest and imprisonment under the Soviet system. "They take you aside in a factory corridor
after you have had your pass checked—and you're arrested," Solzhenitsyn
writes. "You are arrested by a religious pilgrim whom you have put up for
the night 'for the sake of Christ.' You are arrested by a meterman who has
come to read your electric meter. You are arrested by a bicyclist who has
run into you on the street, by a railway conductor, a taxi driver, a savings
bank teller. . . ." Solzhenitsyn ascribes the submissiveness of the Russian

people ("Almost no one tried to run away") to "universal ignorance . . . Maybe they *won't take* you? Maybe it will all blow over?" But this memoir, written as a call to action, was intended to convince its readers that it would not, in fact "blow over." Solzhenitsyn leads the reader through arrest, interrogation, and deportation to the "corrective labor camps" where men, women, children survive for decades, working at hard labor in subzero cold, subsisting on grits and gruel.

Solzhenitsyn's autobiography is the story not just of himself, but of all these prisoners, told in clear detail to make the abstract idea of imprisonment concrete, so that the rest of the world will finally take notice. But Solzhenitsyn the man changes throughout the story as well. He learns that he too is evil: "In the intoxication of youthful successes I had felt myself to be infallible, and I was therefore cruel. In the surfeit of power I was a murderer, and an oppressor. . . . And it was only when I lay there on rotting prison straw that I sensed within myself the first stirrings of good." In his imprisonment, Solzhenitsyn learns that revolution is the wrong solution to oppression. "Even in the best of hearts," he concludes, "there remains . . . an unuprooted small corner of evil. Since then I have come to understand the truth of all the religions in the world: They struggle with the *evil inside a human being*. . . . And since that time I have come to understand the falsehood of all the revolutions in history: They destroy only *those carriers of evil contemporary with them*."

CHARLES W. COLSON
Born Again
(1977)

Best edition: The Chosen Books paperback (2008).

Colson, Richard Nixon's "hatchet man" during the Watergate years, tells his story, as Augustine does, by locating his central flaw and exposing it in public confession. But this flaw has *nothing* to do with Watergate, which comes and goes fairly early in the book—and which, Colson continues to insist, involved *no* wrongdoing on his part. As a confessional, *Born Again* is endlessly intriguing in its ongoing tension between honesty and PR; the sins Colson confesses are all spiritual, since he denies that any "legal" crimes ever occurred. His crime is his personal pride: "Pride had been at the heart of my own life," he writes, "as far back as I could remember. . . . Of course, I had not known God. *How could I?* I had been concerned with myself. *I* had done this and that, *I* had achieved, *I* had succeeded, and *I* had given God none of the credit, never once thanking Him for any

of His gifts to me." Like Augustine, Colson makes an effort to understand his new belief with his reason: "All my training insisted that analysis
precede decision." Like Augustine, he shares his belief at once with a
friend—businessman and entrepreneur Tom Phillips, who has climbed to
the top of his company by "shrewd wits and raw ability" and who assures
him that his experience is perfectly valid. Like Augustine, Colson comes
to faith through a book—in Colson's case, one of C. S. Lewis's works on
theology. But unlike Augustine, Colson finds a very public dimension
in his conversion. "Could there be a purpose to all that had happened to
me?" he asks, in his introduction. "And then I began to see it. The nation
was in darkness; there was anger, bitterness, and disillusionment across the
land. While my inclination was to think in terms of grandiose reforms,
God seemed to be saying that the renewal of our national spirit can begin
with each person—with the renewal of individual spirit." Throughout his
story, Colson connects personal spirituality with national revival.

For Americans, Colson's autobiography has probably been the single
most influential post-Augustinian *spiritual* autobiograpy. Colson clearly
positions his conversion story, not just as the tale of one man's fall and rise,
but as a blueprint for the "fixing" of America; like Booker T. Washington, he sees in his own story a model for an entire nation. And his interpretation of "born again" helped to fuel an entire cultural and political
movement which continues to hold up individual holiness as the key to
national renewal.

RICHARD RODRIGUEZ
Hunger of Memory: The Education of Richard Rodriguez
(1982)

Best edition: The Bantam paperback (1983).

The opening chapter of *Hunger of Memory* sets the stage for Rodriguez's
own understanding of himself, the child of Latino immigrants living in
America: "My writing is political because it concerns my movement away
from the company of family and into the city," he writes. "This was my
coming of age: I became a man by becoming a public man." Language
becomes the symbol of this movement away from family identity toward
public identity; Rodriguez learns to speak English in the classroom only
when his parents refuse to speak Spanish to him at home. This is both
great gain and shattering loss; Rodriguez is no longer "the disadvantaged
child," but there is now a new quiet at home: "[As] we children learned
more and more English, we shared fewer and fewer words with our par-

ents." The very words that give Richard Rodriguez a public voice silence him at home. But for Rodriguez, the tradeoff is a necessary one. His story serves as a model for other Spanish-speaking children; his autobiography is in part an apology for English education and a rejection of bilingual education, which deprives children of the chance for full public participation. "In public," he writes, "full individuality is achieved, paradoxically, by those who are able to consider themselves members of the crowd. . . . Only when I was able to think of myself as an American, no longer an alien in *gringo* society, could I seek the rights and opportunities necessary for full public individuality." As he continues to tell his story, Rodriguez explores other tensions between public and private selves: the conflict between his public achievement in academics, and his private intellectual life; his relationship with the Church, which through its sacraments and public rituals, "relieved [me] of the burden of being alone before God"; and finally, the very process of writing private scenes in his own life into public autobiography.

JILL KER CONWAY
The Road from Coorain
(1989)

Best edition: Vintage Books (2011). Barbara Caruso narrates the unabridged audiobook from Audible.

Conway's autobiography begins, not with her birth, but with a fourteen-page meditation on the harsh beautiful Australian landscape. It is this landscape—and the demands it makes on those who try to live in it—that shapes Conway's childhood and adolescence. She is born on a remote Australian sheep farm, the unexpected youngest child in a family of boys, and from her earliest days carries the image of the "ideal woman" as thrifty, tough, unemotional, a good manager who "was toughened by adversity, laughed at her fears, knew how to fix things which broke in the house, and stifled any craving she might have for beauty." Her mother is this ideal woman. But as Conway grows, she sees drought, natural disaster, and tragedy deprive her parents of their treasured farm. Determined to escape this hard world, she relies on her intellectual achievement to make a new life for herself as a scholar. But she is still haunted by her mother, who—stripped of her outback farm, the world within which she can do meaningful work—becomes instead a manager of her children, overcontrolling, paranoid, and irrational. Conway writes, "I was seven before I even laid eyes on another female child," and the story of her life is laced through with her attempts to figure out how women can find a place in the world when that world does not allow them to exercise their talents freely.

ELIE WIESEL
All Rivers Run to the Sea: Memoirs
(1995)

Best edition: The Schocken Books paperback (1996). Although the audiobook version from Audible is abridged, it is narrated by Wiesel himself and is worth adding to your first read-through.

Wiesel's remembrances of the Holocaust are torn between the wish to find answers, and the knowledge that those answers will forever elude him. "Auschwitz," he writes in this first painful volume of his autobiography, "is conceivable neither with God nor without Him." Taken into the camps, Wiesel loses his family; liberated, he discovers that no country will welcome him. Finally Charles de Gaulle invites a group of refugees, including Wiesel, to France. Here, at the age of sixteen, he has to learn again what "normal" life is like. Every certainty, even the ritual certainties of his faith, have become meaningless: "How long would we recite the prayer for the dead? The mourning period normally lasts for eleven months after a relative's death. But what if you don't know the date of death? Halachic scholars weren't sure how to resolve our situation." Eventually Wiesel is reunited with two of his sisters who survived the camps, goes back to school, and begins his work as a journalist at the Yiddish paper *Zion in Kamf.* He goes on to describe his continuing involvement in journalism, political speech, and public protest through the establishment of the state of Israel and on into the 1960s. This would seem to close the story nicely, but Wiesel instead ends his memoir with an account of the dream he had just before his wedding: "Of what does a man dream when he is forty years old and has made the decision, consecrated by the Law of Moses, to make a home with the woman he loves? He sees himself as a child, clinging to his mother. She murmurs something. Was it something about the Messiah? He feels like telling her, 'You died, and He didn't come. And even if he does, it will be too late.' He walks with his father to Shabbat services, and suddenly finds himself in the ranks of a procession toward death. . . . He soundlessly calls to a gravely smiling, beautiful little girl and caresses her golden hair. His thoughts scale mountains and hurtle down steep pathways, wander through invisible cemeteries, both seeking and fleeing solitude and receiving stories already told and those he has yet to tell." Wiesel's autobiography is an attempt to tell these stories and to bring, for a moment, all of those doomed children, women, and men back to life. His mother becomes all Jewish women, ripped from her children without the chance to say goodbye; his little sister becomes all massacred children; his father becomes all Jewish men, removed from the community of the living before their lives were finished.

ADDITIONAL RECOMMENDED RESOURCE

Grun, Bernard, and Eva Simpson. *The Timetables of History: A Horizonal Linkage of People and Events*, 4th rev. ed. New York: Touchstone Books, 2005.

Chapter 7

The Story of the Past:
The Tales of Historians (and Politicians)

History is above all else an *argument*. It is an argument between different historians. . . . Arguments are important; they create the possibility of changing things.

— JOHN H. ARNOLD

ICTURE A HISTORIAN at work. You might imagine him in the archives of a university library, paging through old records: letters, inventories, bills of sale. You might picture him crouched over dusty artifacts: coins, pottery, inscriptions on bits of stone. Or reading old chronicles of battles, deciphering Greek accounts of victories and reconstructing the chronology of a war.

In truth, he's just as likely to be in his office, reading another historian's most recent book with his feet up on the desk. Since history is (in part) the investigation of past events, historians *do* study the evidence left behind by those who lived long—or not so long—ago. This evidence includes papers of all kinds: invoices, bills, and receipts, as well as diaries and letters. How do we know how the southern plantation economy worked? Through the painstaking categorization of paperwork recording sales of slaves, purchase of supplies, prices paid for crops. Physical traces left by settlements, travelers, and advancing armies are also vital. How do we know how far the Romans progressed into Britain? From traces of Roman camps and remains of Roman roads and walls, crumbling beneath the grass.

But this is only a part of what the historian does. "Most practising ancient historians," remarks Neville Morley in his primer on studying ancient history, "don't actually spend all their time studying such 'primary' sources; they are more often concerned with studying the arguments of other historians."[1] The overall task of the historian isn't just to tell you what happened, but to explain *why*: not just to construct a bare outline of facts, but to tell a story about them. And this project is generally done in a give and take with other historians, not simply by meditating on the evidence itself. The historian never sits down with a collection of documents or artifacts with a "fresh mind." His mind is already full of other people's theories as to why Rome fell, or how African Americans in slavery developed an energetic culture of their own. When he examines the evidence, he is already asking: Do the theories I already know explain this? Or can I come up with a better interpretation?

The tales told by historians have much in common with the tales told by novelists. Like the novel, the history tells a story about a "hero," an individual, or a country, or perhaps a particular group within a country: working women, soldiers, slaves. Like the hero of a novel, this "historical hero" grapples with a problem (poor wages, the demands of war) and finds a strategy for coping with it. A history's conclusion, like a novel's climax, pronounces a final judgment on the hero's choice of strategy.

Unlike the novelist, though, the historian has to shape his plot around certain historical givens. To use a ridiculously simplified metaphor: It's as though both writers are painting a portrait of a woman sitting at a table. But while the novelist is painting from imagination and can give the woman any features, any race, any age, any dress, the historian is looking at an actual young, white woman sitting at a sidewalk table outside a St. Louis eatery. He can paint her so that her background fades and her individuality stands out; he can paint her as a dreamlike figure against a colorful and busy scene; he can paint her so that we notice her race and age and her worried expression, but not her clothes; he can blur her face but paint her shabby dress and peeling handbag with great detail. But he cannot make a young white woman into a middle-aged Asian matron or into an African American man.

In this obligation to adhere to what they see in front of them, historians actually share the task of autobiographers. Both shape "real" events into a design that leads the reader forward to a final interpretation, one that fills those events with meaning. But until very recently, historians have rejected any comparison with autobiographers. Autobiography, after all, cannot possibly be objective. As Georges Gusdorf remarks, "it reveals . . . the effort of a creator to give the meaning of his own mythic tale." Objec-

[1]Neville Morley, *Ancient History: Key Themes and Approaches* (New York: Routledge, 2000), p. ix.

tivity, Gusdorf adds, is the task of the historian, who must "discern" the *facts* beyond the myth.[2]

For generations, objectivity has been the single most important quality of the historian. A historian who has *personal* involvement with a topic has traditionally been viewed as untrustworthy and unprofessional. Autobiography, as the epitome of personal involvement in past events, has ranked at the bottom of scholarly endeavors. Even as a source for information about the past, autobiography rates little attention. As the historian Jeremy Popkin points out, "standard manuals for students caution them against reliance on these 'least convincing of all personal records.'"[3]

Where did this ideal of the perfectly objective historian come from?

A FIFTEEN-MINUTE HISTORY OF HISTORY

Historical writing—which you will sometimes see referred to as "historiography" (*graphos* is the Greek word for "writing")—developed over the course of several thousand years and thus has its own history. My attempt to outline this enormous, complicated "history of historiography" should be considered as a beginning for your own understanding. It draws simple connections where connections are in fact multiple and complex. It suggests direct causes ("Impatience with rationalism led to romanticism") where many factors actually came into play, and where the "result" may have existed alongside the "cause" for many years. It simplifies great philosophical insights by examining them *only* as they apply to the writing of history. This is why I've capitalized such words as Relativism and Postmodernism in this chapter, turning them into labels for certain types of historical writing.

Think of yourself as a beginning history reader. Beginning readers need simplicity before they progress to complexity. When you first teach a child her letter sounds, you tell her that *a* makes the sound heard in *cat*. The truth is that *a* makes many other sounds as well, but if you tell the beginning reader all of the possible *a* sounds at the same time, she might give up in sheer confusion and refuse to learn to read, so she learns only the simplest sound first. Once she begins to read, she can begin to under-

[2]Georges Gusdorf, "Conditions and Limits of Autobiography," in *Autobiography: Essays Theoretical and Critical*, ed. James Olney (Princeton, N.J.: Princeton University Press, 1980), p. 48

[3]Jeremy D. Popkin, "Historians on the Autobiographical Frontier," *American Historical Review*, vol. 104, no. 3 (June 1999): 725–48; Popkin is quoting G. Kitson Clark's manual *The Critical Historian*.

stand the additional complexities of the letter *a*. The following outline provides an "easy primer" approach to history; as you continue to read historical writing, you will find yourself adding new complexities to its simple structure.

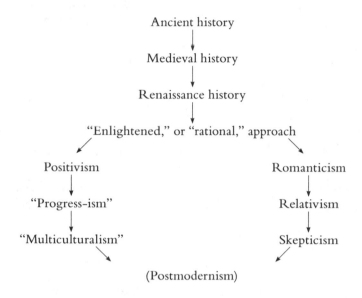

Ancient history
↓
Medieval history
↓
Renaissance history
↓
"Enlightened," or "rational," approach
↙   ↘
Positivism   Romanticism
↓   ↓
"Progress-ism"   Relativism
↓   ↓
"Multiculturalism"   Skepticism
↘   ↙
(Postmodernism)

Ancient History

History illuminates reality,
vitalizes memory,
provides guidance in daily life.
—CICERO

The earliest forms of historical writing are the accounts kept by ancient kings of their victories (not, generally, of their defeats). These military chronicles have historical value, but they are not "historical writing" because they have a single, limited purpose: the immortalization of one particular king. In present-day terms, the ancient chronicles are more like press releases than history. When the Assyrian ruler Sennacherib boasts that his invasion of Judah destroyed "forty-six . . . strong walled towns and innumerable smaller villages," and that Judah was "overwhelmed" by "the awful splendor of my lordship," he is not trying to enlighten inquisitive Assyrian readers. He's crowing.

"History," in the sense of a coherent story written to illuminate the past, first appeared among the Greeks. The great Greek triumvirate of historians—Herodotus, Thucydides, and Xenophon—took a slightly wider view of history. Rather than simply boosting the prestige of a king or leader, they tried to write the story of *men* (primarily Greek men). Their purposes went beyond puffery: Thucydides writes for "those who desire an exact knowledge of the past as a key to the future, which in all probability will repeat or resemble the past." And the Greek historians defined, for the first time, the border between myth and "history." Herodotus draws a careful line between truth and absurdity; this line doesn't always stretch through territory that a modern historian would recognize (Herodotus is quite impressed with accounts of a country full of one-eyed people who steal gold from griffins), but he is conscious that such a line *exists*. In their efforts to record what *really happened*—in Thucydides' own phrase, an "exact knowledge of the past"—the Greek historians were innovators.

In other ways, though, their histories bore a family resemblance to the ancient chronicles that came before. Greek histories are hero-centered, much concerned with kings and generals. "History," for the ancients, happens when great men exercise their ambition, plan, scheme, fight, triumph, or show themselves wanting. "Cyrus," begins the historian Xenophon, "set about planning that he might be king. . . . When any of the King's court came to visit him, he treated them all in such a way that when he sent them back they were more devoted to him than to the King." Cyrus's wily diplomacy set into motion an entire string of events, and Cyrus became the greatest Persian king because of his own ambitions, not because some great pattern had decreed it. History had no "great pattern." History was a swarm of interlinked tales, each telling of a great man's life, each life story bearing within itself its own causes. No single "purpose" shaped the tales of these Greek historians into a great Plan; the Plan came into view only with the advent of Christianity.

Medieval History

Thus says the Lord to His anointed,
to Cyrus, whose right hand I have held,
to subdue nations before him and remove the armor of kings. . . .
I will go before you and break in pieces the gates of bronze.
—ISAIAH 45:1–2

Medieval historians transformed history from a series of interlinked stories to one long, sequential story, with a beginning and an ending decreed by God. The interlinked stories of ancient historians were joined by odd and unpredictable connections; with Christianity, the links were shaken into a straight chain, a line pointing forward, unbending as an arrow, to the End. Cyrus became king because God had planned it long before, not because of his own driving ambition.

The first medieval historian is (naturally) Augustine, whose *City of God* proved as central to the idea of Western history as his *Confessions* was to the idea of the Western self. After the Goths sacked Rome in 410, there were widespread mutterings that the Christians had caused the catastrophe by deserting the old gods. In response, Augustine set out on a thirteen-year writing project, a "theoretical history" arguing that all of history records the doings of two separate political entities—the kingdom of God and the kingdom of men—existing side by side, in the same space and time. The members of the two kingdoms share certain goals (the desire to live in peace, for example), but in the end, they pursue different purposes: the one seeks power, the other worships God. This side-by-side existence creates the tensions and conflicts of history, in which God is bringing his kingdom to perfection, while unbelieving man fights and resists him.

This sense of history as God's unfolding plan was a Christian reworking of the method of Hebrew historians, who saw all of Israel's past (and future) as the outworking of God's plan to form a "holy people" on the earth. By shifting the ultimate home of this "holy people" from earth to heaven, medieval historians could now tell the story of the entire universe, from Creation on, in one unbroken line; all of God's acts in history pointed to the birth of Christ, and then past it to the time of Christ's return. This was enormously clarifying to historians, who could now make sense out of what had previously seemed shapeless. Faith in the eternal God and reason—that faculty that shapes chaos into order and arranges unsorted heaps of information into patterns—joined together to lead historians into a story with creation at its beginning and the world's remaking at its end. Finally, the events of history made sense.

But visualizing history as God's eternal workshop did little to impress on medieval historians the difference between ancient times and their own. If all men are made in the image of God, they are essentially alike; if they are all part of one story, there is not much more difference between ancient times and the present than between the first act of a play and its end. So medieval history is marked, not only by its providentialism, but by its tendency to view ancients and contemporaries in exactly the same way. (Medieval art inevitably dresses biblical characters in medieval dress, and places fifteenth-century weapons in the hands of Hebrew kings.) The sense of the past as a foreign country (where, in L. P. Hartley's famous phrase, they "do things differently")[4] began to develop only with the Renaissance.

Renaissance History

History is the intellectual form in which
a civilization renders accounts to itself of its past.
—JOHANN HUIZINGA

"Between the fifteenth and eighteenth centuries," historian Joyce Appleby remarks, "the Christian scheme of history steadily lost credibility. Certainty and conviction about God's purposes in human affairs gave way to growing doubts."[5]

This is true. Yet the popular picture of an enormous breach between a Christian Middle Ages and a secular Renaissance is oversimplified. For one thing, "Christian history" never actually went away; for every new European colony in the Americas, there was a historian who claimed that God had personally planted that particular settlement in order to bring his kingdom on earth at last. But even more central to the Renaissance practice of history was a developing sense of the past as a faraway and alien place, removed from the present not by geography, but by *time*. That sense of time (which allows us, in the present day, to draw a straight line that goes from left to right and call it a "time line") depended on the Christian hypothesis that time was a progression, an arrowlike reality with an undeveloped beginning and a perfected end.

Sometime around 1600, Europeans began to use the word "primitive" to mean "undeveloped" or "not yet modern"; as John Lukacs points out,[6] this idea of primitive (inferior because it is far away in time) replaced the Greek idea of "barbarian" (inferior because it is distant in space, far away from Greek land). The concept of "primitive" was followed closely by the idea of "anachronism," something happening out of the correct order in time. A sense of historical difference didn't arrive full-fledged;

---

[4]The opening lines of Hartley's 1953 novel *The Go-Between*: "The past is a foreign country. They do things differently there."

[5]Joyce Appleby, Lynn Hunt, and Margaret Jacob, *Telling the Truth About History* (New York: W. W. Norton, 1995), p. 58. This is an excellent text on the practices and problems of North American historians, and I am indebted to it for its sharp insights on the ongoing relationship between history and science. Appleby herself qualifies this statement later, although she does continue to speak of the two eras as radically different.

[6]John Lukacs, *A Student's Guide to the Study of History* (Wilmington, Del.: ISI Books, 2000), p. 16.

Shakespeare's Romans are unmistakably Elizabethan ("The clock hath stricken three!" Cassius cries, although no clocks existed in ancient Rome), and were acted in knee breeches and powdered periwigs as late as the eighteenth century. But during the Renaissance, linear time became an accepted reality. The Renaissance historian looked at what men had done, within this framework of linear time, and asked, Why? And in finding the answer, he pursued a strategy markedly different from that of the medieval writer.

Reason was not suddenly "discovered" during the Renaissance, as though every earlier generation had had its collective brain on ice. Rather, what changed during the Renaissance was the material on which reason exercised its powers. A medieval historian, faced with a historical question ("Why did the barbarian Angles invade Britain and slaughter native Britons?") was likely to tussle with deep theological questions about the purposes of God and the puzzling ways in which his will was carried out. A Renaissance historian, faced with a similar challenge, turned to the study of *men*: their desires, fears, and ambitions. In this, Renaissance history was much more like Greek history than like its medieval counterpart, which is hardly surprising since Renaissance scholars idolized the classical past.

But the Greeks were happy to ascribe certain events to the workings of divinity. For the Renaissance thinker, the gate to this avenue of explanation was slowly swinging closed. The Renaissance was shaped by a philosophy that found its clearest expression in Descartes, who (as we saw in his *Meditations*) looked for a sure place on which to stand, a way to know that his conclusions were *true*. Descartes believed in God, but distrusted God's ability to communicate unambiguously with man. And technological innovations—most notably the telescope—had already revealed that explanations given by medieval thinkers who claimed to reason straight from their knowledge of God were likely to be incorrect. The only way to be assured of a *true* conclusion was to reason your way to it without taking divine revelation or divine purposes as your starting point. The mountain of God was no longer the vantage point with the best view; man's own mind provided the higher peak.

The medieval historian sought to find out what God intended, and to illuminate this purpose through the writing of history. The Renaissance historian instead reasoned his way through a chain of past events to find out why a civilization rose or fell. And these reasons had immense present importance. If God had not decreed the pattern of history, it could be altered and controlled. Find out why Rome fell in the past, and you might well save your own civilization from a similar fall in the near future. Machiavelli scoured the past for examples of successful leadership; from this historical foundation he reasoned his way to a prescription for effective present-day rule. Thomas More, outlining the ideal society, retained those past ideas of the Greeks which he thought might solve the problems of the English in the future.

For the first time, history became a matter of *becoming*, not of being; of trying to account for the way that countries develop, rather than simply describing them as they *were*. And the very word *becoming* implies a sense of progress, of movement toward an end point. The Renaissance historians didn't raze the foundation of linear time that Christian historians had laid. Instead, they knocked down a few walls and built patchwork buildings on the old cornerstones. Ironically, the Christian sense of time as a linear progression from a less realized time toward a more complete reality made it possible for later scholars to suggest that life might evolve, over time, from a primitive to an advanced state.

The "Enlightened," or "Rational," Approach

To study history means submitting to chaos
and nevertheless retaining faith in order and meaning.
—HERMANN HESSE

Enlightenment scholars didn't just build patchwork buildings. They erected huge enormous glittering temples to Reason all over the landscape. Given a chance, Enlightenment thinkers might well have chosen a Darwinian metaphor instead: They were finally walking from the primordial, God-ridden ooze of the Middle Ages, onto the solid beach of rationalism, to bask in the sunshine of free thought.

Descartes had already suggested (in the early seventeenth century) that reason, not divine revelation, was the one true source of knowledge. Now John Locke, in the mid-seventeenth century, proposed that man comes into the world with nothing *but* the capacity to reason. No innate knowledge of God, no instincts, no natural patriotism: just the ability to see and touch and feel and hear the physical world, and to reason about it. Everything that man knows, he has learned by analyzing the evidence of his senses. *This* is the source of all knowledge, and man's reason—dealing with tangible, physical evidence in a way that is completely reliable and unbiased— becomes the ultimate source of truth. Man's mind is the "enlightener."

The Christian impulse to look for an overall meaning to historical events remained. But historians now sought this meaning through exercising their reason freely. If unreasonable, illogical factors—religious belief, say, or patriotism—influenced the historian, his pure and reliable reason had been corrupted; he no longer wrote truth. And in the same way, truth could not be discovered if historians were pressured by church or state to come to certain conclusions: "If we are asked, 'Do we now live in an enlightened age?'" Immanuel Kant wrote in 1784, "The answer is, 'No,' but we do live in an age of enlightenment. . . . [T]he field has now been opened wherein men may freely deal with these things." Freedom meant no preconditions; no preexisting belief in God, no fear of state reprisals. History was not meant to serve any sort of ideological end. It was meant to find the *truth*.

This idea that a historian could find *truth* through the scientific examination of the past depended on a new understanding of the cosmos. In the late seventeenth century, Isaac Newton's "natural science" had proposed something startling: Universal, cosmic laws governed every level of the universe's functioning, from the greatest planetary bodies down to the tiniest fragment. These laws could be proved through mathematics—and they were constants throughout the universe.

Now Enlightenment philosophers had a model for reason: Reason was like gravity. Like gravity, it was a mathematical certainty. Like gravity, it was a constant throughout the universe. Like gravity, it always brought the same conclusions. Just as an experiment, if conducted properly, led to one and only one result, so history, if approached properly, would yield one and only one correct conclusion: the *truth*.

Newton's laws served as a model not only for reason, but for history itself. Like scientists, historians could discover historical laws that were just as real and predictable as physical laws. Newton observed objects fall, and from this reasoned his way to the law of gravity; historians observed nations fall, and from this reasoned their way to the laws that govern empires. These historical laws, like scientific laws, were universally applicable to all nations—just as the law of gravity governs every object, large or small.[7]

The search for universal historical laws wasn't simply an academic exercise. It had real, present urgency. All over Europe, the power of the monarchy was fraying at the seams; in France, it pulled apart entirely in 1789. Monarchs had claimed to rule by divine right, to hold authority over others because they were chosen by God. But now men saw themselves as equal to the king, possessing an equal capacity for reason, and an equal ability to govern themselves. A monarch's claim to God-given authority was as dead as a universal belief in the apocalypse.

---

[7]Appleby, Hunt, and Jacob are among the many historians who have noted the connection between the development of Newtonian science and the development of modern historical writing (see *Telling the Truth About History*, pp. 52–76).

But without a divinely ordained pattern for government, how should nations run themselves? To answer, historians combed the past to find those universal historical laws that govern human communities. Locke concluded that men govern themselves by entering into a contract with their government; Rousseau, that they enter into a contract only with themselves. In explaining this new commitment to republicanism, historians relied increasingly on the idea of historical evolution. Not only individual nations, but history itself was evolving toward maturity. Monarchies had been for children, but republics were for adults. That idea of "primitive" versus "advanced" has continued to shape the way we think about history today: it allows us to talk about the "ancient" world, about the "Dark Ages," about "premodern" times and about "modernity," about the "end of history."

The Enlightenment (like literary realism) never really goes away. It shaped the identity of the modern West. And like any coherent system of belief, it has its own creed, which is still recited today:

Reason is "autonomous" or independent of any other part of man. The truth about the world can be discovered not by faith, not by intuition, but through the exercise of the single most important element of the human person: the mind. And the mind is capable of escaping bias in order to see what really *is.*

Institutional authority is suspect. Authority isn't primarily concerned with truth but with power. So it tends to insist, blindly, on ideas which will help it keep its power, rather than truly exercising its reason in an unbiased way. (In modern academic circles, you are only allowed to say this part of the creed once you leave the graduate program.)

Every effect has a cause, and that cause can be discovered. There is no ultimate mystery in the world; there is always an explanation. Arthur C. Clarke, best known for *2001: A Space Odyssey,* once wrote, "Any sufficiently advanced technology is indistinguishable from magic." An Enlightenment motto if ever there was one: Anything that may seem miraculous to us simply has causes and effects that we have not yet discovered.

Historians of the Enlightenment did their best to remove the mystery from the past by putting it under scientific scrutiny. The Greek sense of history as a set of stories, linked together by the passions of great men, had given way to the medieval understanding of history as the single story of God's work in time. During the Renaissance, this single story had become the story of men, not the story of the deity. Now historians viewed history as an expanse of physical phenomena that had to be explained.

The Enlightenment gave birth to two families of historians. One set of children worshiped their parent; the other set hated it. Like battling siblings who finally hit their fifties, both families end up (after four hundred years or so) sitting in the same living room.

From Positivism to "Progress-ism" to "Multiculturalism" (and Thence to Postmodernism)

Positivism[8]

History is a science, no more and no less.
—J. B. BURY

Positivism, the Enlightenment's eldest child, was a nineteenth-century infatuation with one particular Enlightenment ideal: the historian as scientist. The originator of the term *positivism*, the French sociologist Auguste Comte, was much enamored with the idea of the scientist as synthesizer of knowledge, able to observe the facts about human existence and draw from them laws that would coalesce into one Grand Theory explaining all.[9] In Comte's view, historians were co-laborers at this noble task.

Positivists held, quite logically, that since both historians and scientists pursue the same magnificent end they should pursue it in the same way. Despite the move toward "scientific history" during the Enlightenment, for most of the eighteenth century history had been an amateur's occupation. David Hume, Edward Gibbon, and Mary Wollstonecraft were writers and scholars, but none of them had been "trained" to be a historian. Certainly no eighteenth-century historians made a living out of history. But the nineteenth-century Positivists began to assemble a system of professional, scientific training for historians: university seminars, a period of apprenticeship, the publication of a dissertation or some other scholarly work in order to gain "entry" into the ranks of the qualified.

A large part of this scientific training involved the proper handling of sources. Nineteenth-century German historians were the first to draw a line between "primary sources" (directly produced by the person or during the time under study) and "secondary sources" (secondhand evidence or other scholarly works). "Scientific historians" modeled their use of sources after the scientist's use of evidence. They would no more go

---

[8] *Positivism* is a technical term in law, linguistics, philosophy, and historiography, and has a different meaning in each field. Here I am using it only in its narrow historiographical sense as referring to those historians who saw their task as scientific and rational.

[9] Appleby, Hunt, and Jacob use the wonderful phrase *heroic science* in their discussion of Comte and positivism in *Telling the Truth About History*.

on hearsay (as Herodotus was quite willing to do) than a scientist would. They had to weigh, measure, and validate their evidence firsthand.

"Evidence," then, came to mean that which could be weighed, measured, and validated. For the Positivist, great natural forces were much more worthy of study than great men. Historical events came about not because of men's ambitions, but because of physical factors: the distribution of metals in a particular country, or the soil in which certain crops grew, or the mountains that protected its cities. People's passions as explanation for historical change were suspect—as suspect as God's providential hand.

"Progress-ism"

> History itself is nothing but the activity
> of men pursuing their purposes.
> —Karl Marx

"Progress-ism"—faith in forward progress, the belief that history always marches toward a better world, always advancing, always improving—was the natural sequel to Positivism. After all, scientists were progressing from great discovery to great discovery, each one bringing with it the chance to transform the world. Historians would do the same.

The syllogism was simple: If historians do their work with meticulous scientific accuracy, they will discover historical laws. Since historical laws are universal and unchanging, they can prescribe future actions that will bring about a more perfect existence. Because reason is the most powerful part of man (much more powerful than the will), the recommendations will be carried out as soon as people are convinced of their necessity. To convince the intellect of the rightness of a particular course is always to convert the will, since the (weaker) will is always under the control of the (stronger) intellect. (In present-day political usage, "progressive" is sometimes interchangeable with "liberal," which explains why "Education is the answer" is both supremely progressive and quintessentially liberal as a strategy for social change.)

Augustine, who found his sinful will to be much stronger than his reason, would have thrown up his hands in dismay. But Augustine lived in a different world. In his universe, the Garden of Eden stood as the high point; since the first sin, the human condition had headed steadily downward, and only direct divine intervention could make things better. But Progress-ism offered a golden future spread out ahead, as the poor, the criminal, and the wrong-headed were inexorably converted by the rhetoric of Reason. History became a tool for change: "If history is ever to help us solve . . . the great and grievous riddle of life," the historian Jacob Burkhardt told his German listeners in the late nineteenth century, "we must [understand] . . . the true nature of life on earth. . . . [F]ortunately for us, ancient history has preserved a few records in which we can closely follow growth, bloom and decay in outstanding historical events."[10] Those ancient patterns would reveal principles that historians could use to perfect the world.

Faith in progress took several different forms, some more optimistic than others. In the practice of English history, historians who saw the past as an inexorable progression toward perfection were said to write "Whiggish" history. In American history, the progressive movement saw history as a constant struggle between "the people" (honest workers) and "aristocrats" (corrupt and dishonest tycoons) to preserve the American dream. After a time of fierce struggle, this conflict would lead to a more perfect American democracy. American progressivism drew on the work of Karl Marx, perhaps the most famous evangelist of the progress-in-history gospel.

Marx looked at the ancient pattern of class struggle throughout all of human existence and in this struggle found the historical principle that—he believed—could guide man into a more perfect existence. "The history of all hitherto existing society," *The Communist Manifesto* begins, "is the history of class struggles. Freeman and slave, patrician and plebian, lord and serf, guildmaster and journeyman, in a word, oppressor and oppressed, stood in constant opposition to one another." As a Positivist, Marx believed that the key to history was the analysis of the tangible, material conditions under which people lived. As a believer in historical progress, he was convinced that this analysis revealed a historical law that could be used to reshape the future: The workers of the world must be given control over the "means of production" (the raw materials and equipment needed to produce goods). This would bring utopia: the "worker's paradise."

Marx saw the constant struggle between two hostile classes of people as the engine that drove history toward perfection. Rationalist that he was, Marx nevertheless borrowed this idea from the mystical philosopher Georg Hegel, who wrote long and largely incomprehensible tracts about history as the self-realization of the divine; as history progresses forward, Hegel explained, the "divine Spirit" reveals itself more and more, making the meaning of existence gradually clearer. Marx jettisoned Hegel's esoteric

[10]Jacob Burckhardt, *Reflections on History* (taken from lectures delivered by Burckardt in Germany in 1868–71, first published in German in 1906; this quote is from the first English edition, published by Allen & Unwin, 1943), p. 21.

musings about the World-Spirit Made Manifest (along with Hegel's conviction that the process had come to complete fulfillment in Prussia in 1805), but he retained Hegel's description of how history progresses forward: two opposing forces (in Hegelian terms, "thesis" and "antithesis") struggle, and from their struggle a new and more perfect reality ("synthesis") arises.

Marx's particular brand of Progress-ism altered Progress-ism forever. It treated the underclass (which struggled with the overclass) as a vital element in the forward movement of history. The laborers were the antithesis of the bourgeoisie (the people who control the factories and the production of goods—what Americans would consider "upper middle class"). Without the struggle between antithesis and thesis, between underclass and overclass, there was no *synthesis*, no forward progress, no communist state. The workers became important in their own right: They were no longer simply the poor, criminal, and wrong-headed who needed to be converted by reason, but people with their own power ("agency"), their own values, their own patterns of life.

Multiculturalism

"History, real solemn history, I cannot be interested in. . . .
The quarrels of popes and kings,
with wars and pestilences in every page;
the men all so good for nothing,
and hardly any women at all."
—CATHERINE, IN *NORTHANGER ABBEY* BY JANE AUSTEN

The Marxian revolution in historiography altered the historian's universe irrevocably. Early Progress-ism tended to be elitist, exalting the work of the well educated (who also tended to be well bred and well heeled) and ignoring conflict in history. But after Marx, the poor and oppressed, and their struggle against domination, became essential parts of the historical equation.

After Marx, historians gradually began to study not just the economically oppressed, but *all* oppressed and dominated people: women, whom Marx himself apparently didn't notice, African Americans, Native Americans, and then Hispanics, urban dwellers, "subalterns" (peoples who have been colonized by foreign invaders, as in British-occupied India), and so on. The study of these multiple cultures was the first stage of a movement that expanded beyond the realm of historiography and, some time later, acquired the nickname "multiculturalism."

This study of previously ignored people was sometimes called "history from below"—described by the historian Jim Sharpe as "rescuing the past experiences of the bulk of the population from . . . total neglect by historians."[11] Historians who worked "from below" realized that focusing *only* on "movers and shakers"—kings, generals, and politicians—gave only a partial picture of the past. "History from below" (also known as "social history") used nontraditional sources such as personal diaries, oral histories, and interviews to build an alternate history, one that described what "real people" were doing as great events rolled over their heads. Some historians turned to quantitative analysis: wealth distribution, census results, population movements, birth rates, causes of death, and a hundred other sets of figures. The social historian could draw conclusions about the rights of women, for example, by examining hundreds of tax records, finding the instances in which women were listed as owners of land, and calculating the conditions under which they had gained their property.

Positivists would have applauded. But social historians didn't use quantitative methods primarily because they were scientific. As a matter of fact, social historians tended to be ambivalent about science, which was produced by those well-educated elites to trample on the lives of others. Rather, social historians who wanted to write about "the anonymously downtrodden" (to use Laurence Veysey's phrase) found themselves faced with a problem: Traditional "primary sources" such as letters and memoirs were almost always written by elite, educated people—which skewed the focus of history toward the relatively small and well-to-do segment of the population who were literate and leisured enough to write. So historians turned to new sources, piecing together the stories of ordinary people from tax records, inventories, birth and death records, advertisements, wage stubs, and other kinds of evidence.

Social historians tended to be wary of drawing conclusions from those stories that would apply to the rest of the human race. After all, "traditional history" had made the error of assuming that the lives of the "ordinary" could be explained by studying events at the highest level of society. The social historian wanted to avoid the same trap, instead giving each life its proper weight as unique. Laurel Thatcher Ulrich's *A Midwife's Tale* tells us every detail of midwife Martha Ballard's life, but Ulrich avoids making statements about "eighteenth-century midwifery," let alone about "women in colonial New England"; she aims instead to tell us of this one woman's life, a life that would never have been known without the diary, since even Ballard's headstone carries her husband's name rather than her own.

[11]Jim Sharpe, "History from Below," in *New Perspectives on Historical Writing*, 2nd ed., ed. Peter Burke (University Park: Pennsylvania State University Press, 2001), p. 27.

In its most extreme forms, social history focused *exclusively* on those anonymously downtrodden, dismissing any larger unifying themes that might link the lives of the downtrodden and their putative tramplers together. But even more moderate forms of "history from below" show that the Enlightenment vision of universal historical laws that apply to all men (and women) had begun to break down. Many social historians rejected the validity of a "Story of Mankind," in favor of a multiplicity of separate histories. Any attempt to unite those histories into a coherent whole, they objected, would inevitably flatten all those unique stories, reducing them back into anonymity.

So the social historian resisted generalizations, instead keeping her eyes firmly on her own small patch of the world and explaining only the truths governing that particular culture. She rejected the ideal of one objective, preferred point of view that would reveal the truth. Instead, she saw multiple points of view, each arising within a particular culture, each yielding a different version of the truth. "Generalizations," in the words of the social historian Edward Ayers, "numb us to . . . the emotional shadings of historical experience, the subtle and shifting contexts in which people had to make choices . . . the instability of even the most apparently permanent structures."[12]

Which leads us to Postmodernism. But before we complete the journey through history, let's go all the way back to the Enlightenment again, and meet that *other* family of historians.

From Romanticism to Relativism to Skepticism (and Thence to Postmodernism)

Romanticism

Genuine historical knowledge requires nobility of character,
a profound understanding of human existence—
not detachment and objectivity.

—FRIEDRICH NIETZSCHE

Although every eighteenth-century thinker was affected by Enlightenment thought, not every eighteenth-century thinker welcomed the Enlightenment creed with joy. Romanticism accepted some Enlightenment ideas more or less uncritically; like Progressives, the optimistic

---

[12]Edward L. Ayers, "Narrating the New South," *Journal of Southern History*, vol. 61, no. 3 (August 1995): 555–66.

Romantics believed that man was destined to triumph over his environment, rising steadily to greater and greater heights. But Romantics saw man boosted to those peaks by warm gusts of imagination and creativity—not conveyed there by the cold calculations of reason.

For one thing, the exercise of reason was limited to the physical world. Many Romantics rejected the traditional Christianity of the Middle Ages. But many retained a pantheistic belief in God, seeing the presence of the divine in nature. They worshiped a glorious invisible reality that man could glimpse beyond the tangible and the physical; Hegel's theology of the mystical Divine slowly revealing itself in the progress of history was quintessentially Romantic. Against the flattening Enlightened insistence on what could be tasted, touched, and seen, the Romantics insisted on the presence of mystery in the world. They refused to find single, explicable causes for historical events, or simple, rational answers to great questions. The complexity of the world demanded multiple answers; Edward Gibbon lays out so many complexities and multiple explanations for the decline and fall of Rome that he never does arrive at a final interpretation.

Human beings were just as complex. For the Romantic, to classify man solely as a rational creature was to take away what makes him distinctively human: creativity, intuition, emotion, religious feeling, patriotism. Against Positivism, the Romantics claimed Immanuel Kant as their own; Kant emphasized the freedom to think, and freedom was central to the Romantic rejection of Positivist logic. The Positivists had turned man into a cog, a calculator, a "machine made of meat" (in Marvin Minsky's phrase), whose actions could be calculated with certainty from an examination of the factors around him.

The Romantic historian wanted to bring emotion and creativity, the passions and ambitions of men, back into the study of the past. Enlightenment thinkers had emphasized man's sameness, those universal laws which govern all human beings. But the Romantics exalted man's uniqueness and infinite variety.

The Enlightenment had scorned patriotism as an irrational corrupter of reason, but the Romantic respect for diversity produced an increased respect for national identity. Romantic historians followed instead the arguments of eighteenth-century philosopher Johann Gottfried von Herder. Herder was willing to believe that historical events had causes, but he was skeptical about man's ability to discover those causes with any certainty, since they were most likely not single and simple, but multiple and difficult to discern—or perhaps psychological, driven by passions that remained hidden even to the historical actors themselves. Human beings were deep wells of mystery, and history was an even deeper well; some of its reaches and crannies would always remain inaccessible to the historian.

Herder's insistence on the ultimate mystery of man, rather than humanity's essential sameness, could have led to a skepticism in which no one could make any general conclusions about mankind at all. (Indeed, Herder wrote, the job of "ordering together . . . many occurrences into a plan" was beyond reason; it was an act that belonged instead to the "creator, . . . painter, and artist.")[13] But Herder, like thinkers since the Middle Ages, was impelled to look for some principle that governed this ordering together. He wanted a unified history, not a fractured one, and he found his organizing principle in *nationalism*.

For Herder and the Romantic historians who followed him, national identity was something that all people had in common, and yet allowed them individuality. National identity, Herder wrote, was partly determined by physical landscape, partly by circumstance, and partly "by the inborn and self-nourishing character of the peoples. . . . As man originates from and in one race, so his body, education, and mode of thinking are genetic."[14] This nationalism seemed to combine the best insights of science (the study of physical factors such as landscape, for example) with a Romantic respect for that intangible, personal *something* that makes people different. Historians discovered a new interest in the writing of national history. Scholars investigated native languages and collected national folktales—as did the Brothers Grimm, linguists who were forty-odd years younger than Herder.

Some Romantic nationalists developed a less charming interest in racial purity. Herder, German by birth, quotes approvingly from the ancient historian Tacitus, who wrote that "[t]he tribes of Germany, who never degrade themselves by mingling with others, form a peculiar, unadulterated, original nation, which is its own archetype." Herder adds, ominously, "Now look about you. . . . The tribes of Germany have been degraded by mingling with others." It was a short step from the glorification of national identity to the belief that the progression into perfection demanded the mastery of other, less worthy nations.

[13]Johann Gottfried von Herder, *Older Critical Forestlet* (1767–68). Quoted in Michael N. Forester, "Johann Gottfried von Herder," *The Stanford Encyclopedia of Philosophy* (Winter 2001 edition), ed. Edward N. Zalta, available online at http://plato.stanford.edu/archives/win2001/entries/herder.
[14]Johann Gottfried von Herder, *Materials for the Philosophy of the History of Mankind* (1784), e-text edition (ed. Jerome S. Arkenberg) published in *Internet Modern History Sourcebook*, at www.fordham.edu/halsall/mod/1784herder-mankind.html.

Relativism

Nothing capable of being memorized is history.
—R. G. COLLINGWOOD

In 1957, Karl Popper dedicated his book refuting Romantic nationalism to "the countless men and women of all creeds or nations or races who fell victims to the fascist and communist belief in Inexorable Laws of Historical Destiny."[15]

Popper argues that logic prevents anyone from predicting the course of human history "by scientific or any other rational methods." History, he writes, is affected by the growth of scientific knowledge itself. But the growth of knowledge can't possibly be predicted: "If there is such a thing as growing human knowledge, then we cannot anticipate today what we shall know only tomorrow." So history cannot be predicted either.

Romantic nationalism had proved to be a bloody dead end, but there was no retreating backward into "Progress-ism," let alone Positivism, for the Romantics. The first half of the twentieth century had destroyed not only man's faith in glittering forward progress but also some of the unquestioning faith in the power of science to reveal truth. Popper's use of reason (and, later in his book, the principles of quantum physics) to deny the existence of the very "universal laws" that Enlightenment historians had so proudly proposed shows a growing realization of the limits of science. Widespread questioning of science's role as the sole and central revealer of truth would take another twenty years, but as scientific knowledge had recently been used to kill millions of people as efficiently as possible, it no longer held quite its old glamour.

Wary of any claims to absolute truth, historians moved cautiously toward Relativism. Like Positivism, Relativism has slightly different meanings in ethics, epistemology, and other philosophical fields. But for historians, Relativism suggested that the quest to find "absolute truth," either in history or *about* history, was misguided. In the last century, dozens of opposing voices had shouted their version of absolute truth, and had backed it up with both evidence and bloodshed. Which one of those voices had the absolute truth? None, the historian answered; each had the truth only *as it appeared from his position.*

Relativism was similar to the multicultural approach taken by social historians, but it was rooted, not in the study of a particular underprivileged group, but rather in disenchantment with the entire Enlightenment

[15]Karl Popper, *The Poverty of Historicism* (New York: Basic Books, 1957).

construct. The Enlightenment was built on a conviction that two kinds of objects existed in the world: that which was studied, and those who studied it. This allowed for objectivity, since scholars could remove themselves entirely from the object of their study and view it from a safe and neutral distance. Now, Relativists rejected the difference between scholar and object. In Relativism, a scholar had no neutral space to stand, no inert, objective truth to be studied. No matter where the scholar stands, he touches, affects, changes, and takes part in the subject of his own research.

Faithful to its Romantic heritage, Relativism puts the individual and his own experiences right at the center of all knowledge. Now the task of the historian was not objective study, but the exploration of the past from his or her own particular perspective. The historian no longer tried to find some grand intellectual synthesis, since this would require him to take a position on "truth." He wanted only to put himself into the place of individuals who lived in the past.

Relativism led history away from its traditional focus on politics, military history, and economics—all fields that require the historian to come to a general conclusion about a whole country—and instead directed the historian toward the experiences of those who might have a different story to tell about historical events. "This book," wrote Sarah B. Pomeroy in her study *Goddesses, Whores, Wives, and Slaves: Women in Classical Antiquity*, "was conceived when I asked myself what women were doing while men were active in all the areas traditionally emphasized by classical scholars."[16] If women were excluded from political, military, economic, and intellectual life, as they were for centuries, how could intellectual history, or political history, or military history tell anything close to the true story of a civilization?

Intellectual or political historians might claim to tell *the* story of a nation, but the Relativist saw that they told, simply, *a* story: a story that was true only relative to certain members of that society.

Skepticism

> Our deepest thinkers have concluded
> that there is no such thing as History—
> that is, a meaningful order to the broad sweep of human events.
> —FRANCIS FUKUYAMA

As a historical method, skepticism—a doubtful habit of mind toward those who claim to know the absolute truth—had been around since (at least)

---

[16]Sarah B. Pomeroy, *Goddesses, Whores, Wives, and Slaves: Women in Classical Antiquity* (New York: Schocken Books, 1975), p. 3.

Peter Abelard, who wrote in 1120, "By doubting we come to inquiry; and through inquiry we perceive truth." All scholars utilize a certain degree of skepticism.

But skepticism as a historical method and Skepticism as a settled philosophy about the very nature of history were two very different things. Historical Skepticism was the logical end to Romanticism, since the Skeptical historian rejected entirely the power of the reason to come to any overarching conclusions about human existence. He simply presented his version of the past as one among many possible versions. Nor did he pronounce any part of the past to be either good or bad. After all, moral judgment on any part of history depends entirely on the point of view of the judge; another historian might see the issue differently; those who lived in the past would have had another perspective still.

In its worst forms, Skepticism produced perverse history; in its best forms, it motivated historians to new and complex scholarship. As John Arnold points out, the Skeptic who asks "Why did the Holocaust happen?" and yet refuses to believe the conventional answer of "Adolf Hitler" may end up denying the Holocaust altogether—or may be forced to delve deeply into the "the anti-Semitic and fascist elements within other countries of the period," too much ignored by traditional historians of World War II.[17]

Yet in all its forms, Skepticism leads every scholar to renounce the "myth of objectivity"—to admit that the ideal of the scientist-historian is flawed, since no human being (scientists included) actually possesses the mythical Enlightenment brand of reason that can always arrive at truth, regardless of national identity, race, class, gender, religious conviction, ambition, greed, or all those other competing and jostling parts of the human personality.

Which brings us, once again, to Postmodernism.

POSTMODERNISM

History is an argument without end.
—PETER GEYL

Postmodernism means "after the modern age," but although modernity preceded Postmodernism, it still exists alongside it. Modernity began with Galileo and his confidence that he could reason out the laws which governed the heavens. Modernity covers the whole period of the

[17]John Arnold, *History: A Very Short Introduction* (Oxford: Oxford University Press, 2000), p. 118.

Enlightenment and beyond; modernity promised that nature could be understood and mastered, and that science would improve life; modernity announced that "better" meant "faster" and "more efficient." The West entered modernity first and spread the gospel of the modern age along with its colonies and exports. So the modernization of the world is synonymous with its westernization: along with modernity, the rest of the globe is offered Western capitalism, Western democracy, freedom of the press, human rights, gender equality, Windows-based operating systems, and cheap hamburgers. Modernity is the ultimate expression of that Enlightenment drive toward the discovery of historical laws that are universally applicable to all nations; modernity's innate drive is to establish one, "modern" way of life on every patch of earth.

Postmodernism protested that modernity was not *the* way of life, but *a* way of life. Postmodernism pointed out that, all the way back in the Renaissance, when the pronouncement of Descartes became the center of Enlightenment thought, the conclusion "I think, therefore I am" had been masquerading as a neutral place to stand. Setting reason at the center of inquiry determined where the scholar would end up—just as starting with "I believe in God, therefore I am" would dictate a certain type of conclusion. According to the Postmodernist, the self can no longer say, "I think, therefore I am," because human beings do not have a single, central identity. They are made up of various, sometimes contradictory impulses and elements: mind, emotions, beliefs, prejudices, gender, sexual preference, class, spiritual leanings. Multiculturalism, Relativism, and Skepticism were all forms of Postmodernism. According to Postmodernism, there may indeed be one truth about history (Postmodernist historians are agnostic on this point), but there is absolutely no way that the historian can be sure he's uncovered it.

So how do Postmodernists do history? Very, very cautiously. Since there are, theoretically, no statements that they can make which will be true for everyone (or even a significant subset of "everyone"), Postmodernist historians don't make universal statements or sweeping generalizations. They focus carefully on individual lives, and veer away even from little affirmations. Reading Postmodernist history can leave the reader longing for a synthesis—or just a simple conclusion. As the historian Jeremy Popkin remarks, Postmodernism has brought a great strength to the practice of history by showing that "apparently trivial events, such as the death of an utterly unknown Chinese woman of the seventeenth century, can provide important insights into historical process," but these "studies of single lives often . . . leave historians frustrated: the evidence is never complete and conclusive enough to answer all our questions about life in the past."[18]

---

[18]Popkin, "Historians on the Autobiographical Frontier," p. 729.

Postmodernism tends to be the scholarship of younger historians, often those working on underprivileged groups. Traditional scholars view it with some alarm. Popkin's lament is an example of the primary *objection* to Postmodernism: It avoids asking the *really* difficult questions, and its refusal to formulate truths about human existence is (traditional scholars complain) just plain sloppy scholarship. Some Postmodernists have called on historians to abandon altogether linear narratives, which connect causes with effects, in favor of different models. Elizabeth Deeds Ermarth, for example, recommends that historians take a page from the visual arts and think in terms of a "collage . . . shaking together their kaleidoscopic facts of past, present, and future, and fashioning them once more into an agreeable pattern. . . . That model of collage has the virtue of liberating historians from the constraints of linearity, or from . . . the conventional representation of time."[19] Traditional historian Gertrude Himmelfarb (among many others) retorts that although Postmodernism "entices us with the siren call of liberation and creativity . . . it may be an invitation to intellectual and moral suicide."[20] Many practitioners of "history from below," put off by the more extreme pronouncements of Postmodern historians, have rejected the Postmodern label altogether, preferring to call themselves simply practitioners of "microhistory," "women's history," "subaltern studies," or some other topic.

The battle between traditional and Postmodern history is still rumbling on, with acrimony unabated on both sides.

The End of History

> Our knowledge of the past is something we struggle for;
> it comes from somewhere,
> is created, fought over, and changed.
>
> —NATALIE ZEMON DAVIS

In the Star Trek universe (a strange and illogical place that occasionally manages to make a philosophical statement in fifty-five minutes, minus commercial breaks), one villainous race is more vicious than all the rest: the Borg. The Borg are a collective. The Borg want every other civilization to be part of their collective too. They bulldoze through the uni-

---

[19]In *History: What & Why? Ancient, Modern, and Postmodern Perspectives*, by Beverly Southgate (London: Routledge, 1996), p. 123.
[20]Gertrude Himmelfarb, "Postmodernist History," in *Reconstructing History: The Emergence of a New Historical Society*, ed. Elizabeth Fox-Genovese and Elizabeth Lasch-Quinn (New York: Routledge, 1999), pp. 71–93.

verse, droning with monotonous regularity, "We are Borg. Resistance is futile. You will be assimilated." No Borg ever thinks of itself as *I*.

At least not until the episode "I, Borg," when Captain Jean-Luc Picard and his crew discover an injured adolescent Borg and plan to infect it with a computer-type virus, which it will then spread to the rest of the collective. But then the young Borg develops a sense of individual identity and begins to call itself Hugh. So Picard and the rest decide to skip the virus; they believe that this sense of the individual self—a single, separate soul with its own identity and dignity—is so powerful that it will, itself, infect the Borg collective and make it discontent with its collective existence.

Implicit in all this is a value judgment: Those who see themselves *first* as members of a community, rather than as individuals, have not yet fully developed. They are still children, incomplete, not as mature as those who have a Western sense of the self as individual. Furthermore, all human history is moving toward this idea of individuality. It is so powerful that it need only be introduced in order to conquer. This is the "end of history"—not the apocalypse, but history's final goal.

The phrase "the end of history" comes from Francis Fukuyama, who argues that all nations inevitably evolve toward modern liberal democracy. Fukuyama illustrates a truth about Western historical writing: We have never shaken off the medieval Christian inheritance that causes us to look for a meaning, an "end" to the process of history. Linear history has become part of our identity in the West; the diagram at the beginning of this section shows my own inevitable tendency to see time as a line that points forward. And even Postmodernists have an "end of history" in mind: a paradisiacal time of toleration, when every point of view will be accepted without condemnation.

HOW TO READ HISTORY

As you read history, you'll ask yourself the classic detective (and journalist) questions: Who? What? When? Where? Why? At the first level of inquiry, ask these questions about the story the writer tells: Who is this history about? What happened to them? When does it take place, and where? Why are the characters of this history able to rise above their challenges? Or why do they fail? On the second level of inquiry, you'll scrutinize the historian's argument: What proof does she offer? How does she defend her assertions? What historical evidence does she use? Finally, on your third level of inquiry, ask: What does this historian tell us about human existence? How does the history explain who men and women are, and what place they are to take in the world?

The First Level of Inquiry: Grammar-Stage Reading

Look at the title, cover, and table of contents. This initial survey of the book is always your first step. Follow the same process as you did with the novels you read for Chapter 5: With your journal and pencil close by, read the title page and the copy on the back cover. Write the title of the book, the author's name, and the date of publication or composition on the top of a blank page. (These are not always the same.) Also write a short sentence about the author (scholar, nun, politician, slave). If you are able to glean from the table of contents any sense of the work's overall structure, make a note of this as well. (For example, Jacob Burckhardt's *The Civilization of the Renaissance in Italy* has an immensely detailed table of contents divided into six general sections: "The State as a Work of Art," "The Development of the Individual," "The Revival of Antiquity," "The Discovery of the World and of Man," "Society and Festivals," and "Morality and Religion." You might list these six topics under your title, as a general guide to the development of Burckhardt's argument.)

Does the writer state his or her purpose for writing? Begin by reading the author's preface or introduction; if there is no introduction, read the first chapter. (Remember to save critical prefaces written by *other* scholars until after you have read the book itself.) Look for the writer's purpose, which is often found in these early pages. Bede, for example, begins his *Ecclesiastical History* by writing, "Should history tell of good men and their good estate, the thoughtful listener is spurred on to imitate the good; should it record the evil ends of wicked men, no less effectually the devout and earnest listener or reader is kindled to eschew what is harmful and perverse, and himself with greater care pursue those things which he has learned to be good and pleasing in the sight of God." In other words, Bede intends, through his history, to teach his readers to imitate what is good and avoid what is harmful. When you find the writer's purpose, note it down in your own words (or copy it, if it's brief enough).

What are the major events of the history? What concrete happenings does the historian build his story around? Make a chronological list of these events. Try not to include too much detail; if necessary, use an arbitrary measure and write down only the most important event in each chapter or section.

Who is this story about?   As you read, note down the main characters that you meet. Are they individuals, groups of people ("women," for Mary Wollstonecraft; "working-men," for George Orwell), or entire nations? If they are individuals, is the history focused on a single person, or on a network of individuals who may be related by blood or some other tie? If the historian is describing a group of people, how does she distinguish them: by nationality, gender, age, class, job, economic status? And in both cases: Is the historian telling you a "top-down" or "bottom-up" history? In other words, is she focusing on those who have wealth, influence, and/or political power? Or on "ordinary" people and their daily lives? If the historian is telling the story of nations, what is distinctive about each nation? How do its people envision themselves: as warriors, men of learning, farmers, free people? And how (in the historian's eyes) is this nation better (or worse) than other nations? (In works such as Locke's *The True End of Civil Government* or Niccolò Machiavelli's *The Prince*, you may find that the central "characters" are the ruler or the government on the one hand, and a very broadly defined group of "men who are ruled" on the other.)

What challenge did this hero/ine face?   Once you've discovered the identity of the central character or group of characters, ask yourself the same basic question you asked in your first reading of the novel: What is the *problem*? What challenges the ability of the central character(s) to lead full lives? In Eugene D. Genovese's *Roll, Jordan, Roll*, there are two sets of central characters: slaves and slave owners. Both groups are warped and imprisoned by the institution of slavery. The middle-class housewives of Betty Friedan's *The Feminine Mystique* are imprisoned by the mystique itself—the perception that tending home and children is the only feminine aspiration worth fulfilling. You may find more than one answer to this question: Barbara Tuchman, who writes about the quite sizable group "fourteenth-century people," lists plague, taxes, war, robbery, and half a dozen other challenges.

Who or what causes this challenge?   Once you've identified the challenge faced by the character, ask yourself: What explanation does the writer give? Who or what is responsible for this? In some cases, the answer will be a system: In *Roll, Jordan, Roll*, Genovese attributes the challenges faced by both whites and blacks to the system he defines as "paternalism." In others, it will be much more concrete: The invading D-Day forces in Cornelius Ryan's *The Longest Day* fought, obviously, against the Nazis. In many cases, the writer will suggest more than one cause, in which case you'll need to make a list.

Identifying the cause or causes of historical problems is at the center of the writing of history. In David Hume's *History of England*, why did the House of Commons call the monarch to be accountable to Parliament? In Jean-Jacques Rousseau's *The Social Contract*, why do men decide to enter *into* the social contract? The historian's task is to answer this question; does he succeed in doing so?

What happened to the historical "hero/ine"?   If you were to sum up the history in a paragraph (as though it were a movie plot), how would you do so? You can start by using the answers to the character and problem questions above. Say to yourself: "Faced by the problem of [the challenge], [the central character] . . ." How should the sentence end? What *action* does the character take; how does he (or she) struggle against historical odds; how does he (or she) plan to overcome a historical problem? If the character is essentially passive, what has he failed to do? (One aspect of Mary Wollstonecraft's *Vindication of the Rights of Women* might be summed up as, "Faced by the problem of their lack of education, women failed to realize that they needed to think more and feel less.") If there is more than one central character or more than one explanation, you may need to construct more than one of these sentences. For the more theoretical works, such as Thomas Paine's *Common Sense*, you will need to put the sentence in the form of a recommendation: "Faced with a brutal and tyrannical monarchy, the citizens of the colonies ought to . . ."

This exercise can be carried out on a number of levels. You might make a very brief restatement of one overall idea: For Jacob Burckhardt's *The Civilization of the Renaissance in Italy,* for example, you might simply write, "Faced with new scientific discoveries and new ideas about what nations should be, citizens of Italy developed a new picture of themselves as individuals rather than members of a group." Or you might make a very detailed list. Each section of Burckhardt's book offers a different challenge that the Italians of the Renaissance faced, and a different analysis of their response to each challenge.

Allow your interest in the book to guide you. If the topic interests you, you may want to write a page or more, listing the various problems that the historian tackles and the ways in which his central characters respond to each; if you find the book less than inspiring, a broader summary is sufficient. In a book such as Plutarch's *Lives*, in which each separate chapter stands on its own as a mini history, you will need to write a sentence or two for each biography that you read.

Do the characters go forward, or backward—and why?   In the most basic terms: Has there been movement in the history? Are the characters better off or worse off by the book's end? Have the events of the history improved their lot or made it more dire? Or are the characters in essentially the same place on the last page as on the first? If so, is the historian suggesting that change must take place in the future?

When does the story take place? This is a basic question, but certainly not irrelevant to the writing of history. It has four parts: What dates does the historian cover in his study? What time frame does this encompass—ten years, the lifetime of one person, several hundred years? If the historian is writing theoretically, as Rousseau and Locke do, what time frame do his recommendations cover: Are his suggestions for government intended as universal, for all times, or for a particular point in human history? When did the historian live? And how much time separates him from his subject?

Jot down the answers to these questions—but you may find that you'll benefit from keeping a time line as well. This doesn't have to be elaborate (you can keep a running time line on a sheet of notebook paper, a piece of posterboard, a long strip of newsprint, etc.), but you should mark on it the dates covered by each history, the birth and death dates of the author, and, if appropriate, the two or three most significant events highlighted by each historian. One time line, containing this information for all histories read, will help you to keep historians and their works in chronological order.

Where does the story take place? What part of the world is being described? Where is the writer in relation to it? Is he describing his own country in the past, or a place removed from his in both time and space? How far away is his own country—and culture? A "sense of place" is as central to history as a sense of time. Consult a map or atlas as well as a globe; if you have a shaky sense of geography, checking the physical place of each history that you read will help you begin to order the physical world in your mind.

The Second Level of Inquiry: Logic-Stage Reading

Once you've grasped the content of the history, you can move on to evaluate its accuracy. When you analyzed the novel, you asked yourself: How well developed are these characters? Do their actions match the personae that the novelist has constructed for them? This was a question of internal logic: How well did the writer follow his own rules? But in reading a history, you need to make an additional critical step. The historian is using outside evidence to build an argument. Does the story told by the historian make good use of that outside evidence? Or does it distort the evidence in order to shape the story in a particular way?

Look for the historian's major assertions.   Check the last two paragraphs of each chapter and the final chapter of the book. These tend to be the places where the historian will give a summary statement—two or three sentences that briefly review the interpretation of the stories (or other evidence) that she has presented. Often the next-to-last paragraph will contain the summary statement while the last paragraph polishes it off with a rhetorical flourish. In *The Souls of Black Folk*, for example, W. E. B. Du Bois concludes his chapter "Of Mr. Booker T. Washington and Others" with this statement in the next-to-last paragraph: "The South ought to be led, by candid and honest criticism, to assert her better self and do her full duty to the race she has cruelly wronged and is still wronging. The North—her co-partner in guilt—cannot salvage her conscience by plastering it with gold. We cannot settle this problem by diplomacy and suaveness, by 'policy' alone." This is the core of Du Bois's argument in all the preceding pages: that the South and the North together are responsible for the black plight, and that "the Negro race" must call them to responsibility, not wait patiently for reform. The final paragraph is a call to his listeners to do just that.

When you find these summary statements, highlight them; then jot them down, in order, in your own words. Leave an extra space between each statement, so that you can fill in the next part of the analysis.

What questions is the historian asking?   The act of writing history requires the historian to answer questions about the past. Look at your paraphrased summary statements and ask: What questions do these statements answer? In the example above, Du Bois is asking, "Should the black man be an activist, or should he improve himself and wait for recognition?" He answers this by asserting the guilt of North and South and calling for activism.

You won't necessarily need to find a question in every chapter of the history. As you look over your summary statements, you will see that a historian may spend several chapters answering the same question. But once you've formulated your question, write each question down above the summary statements that propose an answer.

What sources does the historian use to answer them?   Does the historian identify his sources? Laurel Thatcher Ulrich, who bases her study of Martha Ballard on Ballard's diary, describes her primary source in great detail. But more often, you will need to scan footnotes. Does the historian use mainly written source documents (letters, journals, bills of sale, etc.), oral sources (interviews, folktales), or the arguments of other historians? What use does he make of media: magazines, newspapers, advertisements? Does he use quantitative analysis of information drawn from tax records or sim-ilar sources of raw data? Does he make any use of nonwritten cultural sources such as songs, architecture, clothing styles, or images? If he does use visual sources (paintings, emblems, flags), does he merely describe them, or does he furnish an illustration? If he doesn't, does he describe color, tex-ture, features, the place where a visual source appeared, who saw it? Does the historian ever express doubt or reservation about any part of his source material? You may want to note down the primary types of evidence used. Is this evidence drawn from a broad base? Or does the historian put too much reliance on one or two narrow sources?

Does the evidence support the connection between questions and answers?   Now that you have questions and answers, it's time to look at the evidence the writer provides to connect the two. If W. E. B. Du Bois asks, "Should the black man improve himself and wait for recognition?" and answers, "No, because the North and the South are responsible for his plight," he ought to provide two kinds of evidence. In the first place, he should demonstrate the guilt of North and South by giving historical facts about what they have done to the black man; in the second place, he should support his condemnation of "patient endurance" by showing that North and South have responded by becoming more hostile, rather than less. And in fact he does exactly this: He writes that for fifteen years, the ex-slaves have been asked to "give up . . . three things—first, political power, second, insistence on civil rights, third, higher education of Negro youth—and concentrate all their energies on industrial education, the accumulation of wealth, and the conciliation of the South. . . . As a result of this tender of the palm-branch, what has been the return? In these years there have occurred: the disfranchisement of the Negro, the legal creation of a distinct status of civil inferiority for the Negro."

Sometimes a historian will make the connection between question and answer simple for you by making a clear causal statement. As you glance through the chapters you've already read, look for explicit links between facts and interpretations, introduced by the following phrases or construc-tions:

Because of [historical factor], the [historical character acted in a certain
    way].
Since [historical factor], the [historical character acted in a certain way].
Therefore . . . [you'll find a historical factor before this word, and an
    explanation afterward]
It is clear, then . . .

It follows, then . . .
It is hardly surprising that . . .
As a result . . .

Once you've asked yourself what sort of evidence the historian gives you
to connect question and answer, take some time to examine this evidence. You probably won't be able to pinpoint errors of fact; this would
require you to look at the actual sources the historian uses. But you can
evaluate how the historian is *using* the evidence he cites. Using rules of
argument, you can decide whether or not the historian is treating his evidence fairly—or whether he is playing fast and loose with it in order to
come to a hoped-for conclusion. As you evaluate the evidence, look for
the following common errors:

1. Misdirection by multiple proposition: Look at those summary statements and see whether there is more than one "proposition" in each. A
proposition is a single statement of fact; Du Bois makes four propositions
in the summary above: The North is guilty; the South is guilty; activism will work; patient endurance won't work. Although there's nothing
wrong with statements that contain multiple propositions, a historian may
present evidence that explains one proposition and then wrap up with
a statement that tosses one or two additional propositions into the mix.
Because you've been convinced that the first proposition is true, the others may slide by your eye. Du Bois does give convincing historical evidence that patient endurance has not worked in the South, but what about
those assertions that the North is as guilty as the South? What evidence
does he suggest for these?

2. Substituting a question for a statement: The rhetorical strategy of
substituting a question for a statement is more common in spoken arguments than in written ones, but historians who hope to rouse their readers
to action will sometimes resort to this technique. But a question does not
give information; it implies a statement of fact, but if it were turned into a
statement, it would often appear exaggerated or obviously untrue. "Ye that
tell us of harmony and reconciliation," Thomas Paine fumes, in *Common
Sense*, "can ye restore to us the time that is past?" This question is obviously
meant to convince the reader that reconciliation is as impossible as returning to the past. But Paine doesn't state, baldly, "Reconciliation is impossible," because he would then have to support that statement with evidence.

3. Drawing a false analogy: Paine follows up his rhetorical question
with another: "Can ye give to prostitution its former innocence? Neither
can ye reconcile Britain and America." The analogy is meant to illustrate

the impossibility of reconciliation, but that isn't all it does; it draws another partial comparison, and (without directly saying so) implies that reconciliation would be a moral evil. An analogy is meant to illustrate one part of an argument; it should never be treated as an exact parallel. A popular eighteenth-century analogy makes this clear: To say that the universe is like a clock set into motion by a Clockmaker makes one very specific point about the relationship between God and his creation—he is responsible for its existence, but doesn't need to keep his hand on it constantly to keep it running. But the analogy should not then be carried out to imply that the universe will "run down"; that is not its purpose. A historian who, like Paine, is also a skillful rhetorician will sometimes choose an inflammatory analogy in order to imply a conclusion (the moral evil of reconciliation) that he would find difficult to support were he to make it directly.

4. Argument by example: Telling a story is not the same as proving a point. Betty Friedan, arguing in *The Feminine Mystique* that women were barred from certain intellectual pursuits in the 1950s, writes, "Girls would not study physics: it was 'unfeminine.' A girl refused a science fellowship at Johns Hopkins to take a job in a real-estate office. All she wanted, she said, was what every other American girl wanted—to get married, have four children, and live in a nice house in a nice suburb."[21] The first phrase may be true, but the second doesn't prove it. Did she apply for this fellowship? Was it offered to her out of the blue? (That would seem to disprove Friedan's argument.) Did any other girls accept these fellowships? How many, in what proportion? No matter how vivid it may be, the example of a woman who is convinced that she must stay home and raise her children in order to be truly feminine does not prove a systematic, national conspiracy to send women home; this must be demonstrated by a much wider sampling of American women.

5. Incorrect sampling: Whenever a historian cites a number of particulars and then draws a conclusion from them, you should look to see whether the conclusion is warranted. How many examples does the historian use? Is this a significant number? Are they "representative"—that is, drawn from the group about which the historian wishes to make a conclusion? (Women's historians, for example, have pointed out that early feminist scholars tended to sample white women, and then draw conclusions from them about women generally, without using a representative sample of black women as well.) If the sample isn't representative of the historian's conclusion, what group *does* it represent—and should the historian's conclusion be rephrased to cover this group?

---

[21]Betty Friedan, *The Feminine Mystique* (New York: Dell, 1984), p. 73.

6. Hasty generalizations: Using particulars in history is both necessary and complicated; although historical theories have to be rooted in historical realities, it is often tempting to draw a conclusion too quickly. Consider this argument:

Women were oppressed in ancient Greece.
Women were oppressed in ancient Britain.
Women were oppressed in ancient China.
Therefore, women were oppressed in every ancient civilization.

The conclusion seems likely, but the historian can't actually state it with confidence unless she has done an exhaustive survey of every ancient civilization. She can actually only conclude from this that women were oppressed in ancient Greece, Britain, and China. This historian has drawn a hasty generalization. She could have avoided the error with a qualification: "Women were oppressed in the ancient cultures for which we possess the most historical evidence."

7. Failure to define terms: *Oppressed* is also problematic in the conclusion above. Does it mean "denied the vote but allowed to hold property"? "Allowed to vote and hold property but paid lower wages for doing the same job as men"? "Not allowed access to abortion"? "Kept in holes and fed scraps"? Terms—and abstractions in particular—should always be defined. It is simple to use a concept word (*freedom, quality, oppression, virtue*) without defining it; but the exact ideas attached to each one of these words changes over time. Aristotle and Augustine mean two very different things when they use the word *virtue*; Rousseau and Friedan mean very different things when they speak of *equality*. Glance over your summaries of the historian's argument. Does the argument lean heavily on abstract terms? If so, does the writer define those terms—telling you, for example, exactly which "human rights" he's arguing for? "A state of equality," John Locke writes, carefully, "[is one] wherein all the power and jurisdiction is reciprocal, no one having more than another." This is a political definition, not a social or economic one; equality means something quite different for Mary Wollstonecraft.

8. Backward reasoning: Backward reasoning finds a causal connection where none exists; it takes a description and finds in it a cause. If a historian were, for example, to state, "Every empire that has relied on mercenary armies has disintegrated" (something which may be historically true, although it involves a hasty generalization), he might be able to support this statement with historical evidence. If, however, he then concludes, "Empires disintegrate because they rely on mercenary armies," he may be

ignoring other contributing causes. Even if it could be proved without a doubt that the first statement were true, it would be illogical to conclude that the mercenary armies were the cause of disintegration. It could be equally true that an empire that finds itself disintegrating hires mercenaries in a desperate attempt to beef up its defenses—in which case the mercenaries would be just a symptom, not a cause. Because two facts are simultaneously true does not mean that one arises from the other; it may, but the historian needs a great deal more proof to be even partially sure.

9. Post hoc, ergo propter hoc: Looking for causation is always tricky, and historians are particularly prone to the *post hoc, ergo propter hoc* fallacy— literally "after that, therefore because of it." This is the fallacy of thinking that because one event comes after another in time, the first event caused the second event. So without supplying more information, the historian cannot write:

Rome recruited its army from mercenaries.
Then Rome fell.
Therefore, the army of mercenaries caused the fall of Rome

The relationship between the mercenaries and the fall could be a coincidence. It might also indicate cause and effect—but the coincidence in time should be a starting place for the historian's investigation, not a statement of conclusion. Even if the historian can find a number of different cases in which this sequence occurs, he should still continue to investigate the relationship. After all (in a classic statement of the *post hoc, ergo propter hoc* fallacy) night always follows day, but no astronomer would ever claim that day causes night.

10. Identification of a single cause-effect relationship: Predicting causation is tricky, and the *post hoc, ergo propter hoc* illustrates a wider fallacy: oversimplification. No historian should hang *any* historical event on a single cause; all historical events have multiple causes. Even if the historian can identity a perfectly good cause of Hitler's rise to power (Germany's depressed and desperate state), she should continue to search for contributing causes: Does that depression account for the focusing of German hatred onto their Jewish compatriots? Although it is perfectly acceptable for a historian to spend most of her time investigating one particular cause-and-effect relationship, it is too simplistic for her to conclude that she has discovered the *single* cause.

11. Failure to highlight both similarities and differences: Whenever a historian draws parallels between events that happen in different cultures, or different times, does he also account for the differences that divide them? It is relatively simple to pick out commonalities between (say) the

French Revolution and the American Revolution, but historians must also be careful to treat each as unique, coming from a different cultural background. So: Does the historian properly understand the differences, or does he flatten the variations between times, reading the priorities and problems of the present back into the past?

Can you identify the history's genre?   Now that you have examined the historian's questions and answers, the sources he's used and the use to which he's put the sources, you should be able to identify the genre, or branch, that he is pursuing. Historians have generally agreed on a three-part division in historical theme: political, intellectual, and social.

Political history is the oldest of the traditional branches of history; it tells the stories of nations and of leaders, of wars and of treaties, of those who control governmental power. Political history focuses on leaders; it encompasses traditional biography (the biographies of the famous and powerful), diplomatic history, international history, and military history. Bede did "political history." So did David Hume, and so does James M. McPherson.

Intellectual history is rooted in the early part of the twentieth century; in American historical writing, it came into its own in the 1940s and '50s. Intellectual history focuses on the ideas that may have led to a particular social movement or set of events. Perry Miller's history of New England is an intellectual history, because it is organized around the changing Puritan idea of the covenant and the effects that this idea had on Puritan life. Intellectual history assumes that people share patterns of thinking, and that those patterns change the way they act. It assumes that the content of the mind can be known and analyzed with some certainty; it puts an Enlightenment-era importance on thinking as the most important part of the human being; it assumes that science, philosophy, politics, economics, and (to some degree) religion begin in the mind and spread outward to affect the rest of the world.

Social history arose in reaction to intellectual and political history, which were seen as elitist and hyper-rational, focusing on leaders to the exclusion of the vast majority of people on earth, and on ideas to the exclusion of religious belief, emotion, class identity, and a hundred other factors. Social historians try to examine those patterns of life which apply to the majority, not the minority. They are more likely to use nontraditional sources, on the grounds that traditional sources reflect the lives and opinions of a tiny, well-educated elite. Social historians are concerned with how "ordinary people" live, and how the patterns of those lives have changed over time. They examine politics, economics, wars, treaties, and great events as they affect individual lives.

There can be significant overlap between these three fields. Influenced by social historians, intellectual historians are more likely than they once were to study popular ideas and their manifestation in popular (not elite) culture, and the study of economic trends can combine the methods of traditional political history with those of social history. However, there is a certain commitment here to a priority of importance: Which has more effect on history, great leaders or "the masses"? In your reading of each history, can you identify its basic genre? Does it fall more securely into the political, intellectual, or social camp? Does it do history from above, or from below?

Does the historian list his or her qualifications?   Now that you've identified the bent of the history, spend a few minutes on the historian: What is his bent? First check to see whether he explains his own qualifications. Thucydides, writing in the days before professional historians, explains that he is well suited to write about the Peloponnesian Wars because he fought in them; later historians are more likely to cite some aspect of their training or research. If the historian doesn't remark on his own qualifications, check the jacket flap or the back of the book for academic training, personal experience, or other titles. Occasionally a historian will explain his theoretical stance in his introduction. Sometimes you may find it interesting to do a Web search on the author's name. You will often come upon a review of one historian's work, written by another historian, which will shed light on the purposes of both.

Academic qualifications aren't necessarily the mark of a good historian. But historians who have been trained within the university are more likely to identify themselves with a particular school of historiography than nonacademic historians (such as Cornelius Ryan). Understanding a historian's training and background can help you understand more clearly how a historian's work might fit into the categories above.

The Third Level of Inquiry: Rhetoric-Stage Reading

Once you've understood the historian's methods, you can reflect on the wider implications of her conclusions. What does the historian say, then, about the nature of humans and their ability to act with purpose—to change their lives or control the world around them?

What is the purpose of history?   After you have grasped the basics of a historical argument, you should step back and consider its conclusions against the backdrop of the whole project of history writing: What purpose does this history serve? Does the historian see himself as laying out an objective, true relation of past events—perhaps for the first time? Is the history intended to create a sense of national pride? To impel a group of people to action, or to reform? Is it meant to explain the present-day state of some modern phenomenon by analyzing its roots? Does it stand as a pattern for present-day people, either as an ideal to copy, or as a warning to avoid? Does the historian intend to correct previous exaggerations, or to amplify previous understatements? Can you draw, from the purpose of this particular history, any conclusions about the historian's understanding about the nature of historical writing generally?

Does this story have forward motion?   Does the history show traces of linear movement toward an end? If so, is the writer telling a story of advancement from a less developed state toward a more developed state? Or of declension, from a high point down into conflict and chaos? What sort of advancement or decline is traced: political, intellectual, or social? Or, conversely, does the story show a lack of forward movement? After you have come to a conclusion, ask again: What does the historian believe about human existence generally? Does it progress forward, or are we treading water? Are we destined to climb, or doomed to slide downward?

What does it mean to be human?   A history always highlights one particular aspect of human beings as central. For John Locke, man cannot be truly human unless he is free; for Mary Wollstonecraft, woman cannot be truly human unless she is educated; for Jacob Burckhardt, men cannot be truly human unless they recognize themselves as individuals first and as members of a community *second*. In these histories, how are men and women portrayed? Are they essentially workers, patriots, members of families, businessmen, rational animals, children of God? What is their central quality? To what must they aspire in order to be human?

Why do things go wrong?   A historian's explanations for evil reveal his true understanding of man's nature. In the history you've just read, what causes one set of people to be challenged or persecuted by another? What motivates the oppressors? Why do people live in squalor? What motivation does the historian give to his wrongdoers? Are people inept? Psychologically warped by outside factors? Well meaning, but helpless in the face of natural forces that push them into misdeeds? Are they greedy, in rebellion against God, convinced of their own superiority?

What place does free will have?   Are the people in this story in charge of their own fates? Are they powerful or powerless? If they can affect their own worlds, is this because they are well-to-do, well educated, in positions of power? Or are the poor and uneducated just as capable, in their own way, of shaping their lives? (We call this by the technical term *agency*.) Are rich and poor alike helpless in the tide of impersonal historical events?

Every historian makes a central assertion, somewhere, about responsibility: about human ability or helplessness in the face of historical challenges. Or he may attempt to take a middle ground. In *The Prince*, Machiavelli writes, "It is not unknown to me how many have had and still have the opinion that because the things of the world are in a mode governed by fortune and by God, that men in their prudence are unable to correct them. . . . I judge that it could be true that fortune is the arbiter of half our actions, but that she lets the other half, or nearly that, be governed by us." (Which half is which?)

What relationship does this history have to social problems?   Whether or not historians should be involved in current policy is an ongoing debate between historians. Some feel that historians, with their perspective on the past, should be involved in present-day politics and in the formation of social theory; others are horrified by this "lack of objectivity." William E. Leuchtenberg points out that historians, aiding the counsel in *Brown v. Board of Education*, "made it possible for counsel for black pupils to parry the argument that the framers of the Fourteenth Amendment did not intend it to empower the national government to desegregate schools"; this "public history" is an important part of the historian's role. Richard Hofstadter warns, on the other hand, "The activist historian who thinks he is deriving his policy from his history may in fact be deriving his history from his policy, and may be driven to commit the cardinal sin of the historical writer: he may lose his respect for the integrity, the independence, the pastness, of the past."[22]

A historian may follow one of three paths in her attitude toward social events. She may show disengagement, a commitment to the past for its own sake, making no efforts to draw parallels between past and present. She may go to the other extreme and follow a policy of advocacy (as Paine, Locke, and Friedan do), writing history in order to bring about a social change. Or she may pursue a middle path of "indirect advocacy," connecting the past with the present but refraining from making direct recommendations for social change. Can you identify the path that each historian chooses?

What is the end of history?   If the writer is telling a story of historical progress—of ascension toward a higher, more enlightened state of being—

---

[22]Both quotes from William E. Leuchtenberg, "The Historian and the Public Realm," *American Historical Review*, vol. 97, no. 1 (February 1992): 1–18.

what does that "higher state" involve? Are the subjects more aware of themselves, more aware of their community, better able to see themselves as independent actors, more loyal to their country? Or (if this is a story of declension), how is the end different from the beginning? How has the civilization, or group, or subjects declined? How are they worse off at the end?

In other words, what is the goal of the historical story? What does the historian see as the ultimate shape and form of humanity?

How is this history the same as—or different than—the stories of other historians who have come before? A historian interacts with the facts of history, but also with the ideas of other historians. As you progress through the reading list, compare your answers to the above questions as they apply to each historian. Do you see an overall development in the way history is done?

Is there another possible explanation? Finally: Given the same facts, would you come to a similar conclusion?

This is an incomplete question, because you don't have all of the historian's sources; you don't know what he might have left out because he found it unimportant, what facts have been eliminated which, in the hands of another historian, might have produced an entirely different interpretation. But exercise your creativity: Do the facts you know allow for another interpretation? Lytton Strachey writes of Queen Victoria that she "fell more and more absolutely under [Prince Albert's] intellectual dominance" until he became "the actual controller of the forces and the functions of the Crown. . . . Albert had become, in effect, the King of England." Do the actions of Albert and Victoria (stripped of Strachey's commentary) admit any other interpretation? As you become more familiar with the process of history, practice doing history yourself.

THE ANNOTATED HISTORY LIST

Your goal in reading through the following list is to understand the ways in which the writing of history has changed over time. So these books are organized by chronological order of composition, not in order of the subjects studied. It doesn't include all of the "great books" of history— or even a good sampling of them. Such a list would take years to work through (if any agreement could even be reached about what should be on it). The list that follows is compiled for the lay reader, not the professional historian, so it doesn't focus exclusively on those books which academics would consider most important. Rather, it combines academic histories (such as *Roll, Jordan, Roll*) with those popular histories (such as *The Longest Day*) which have had a hand in shaping our pictures of the past. Since philosophy is a field that requires its own peculiar reading skills and background knowledge, the list veers away from the works of Hegel, Herder, and others whose focus was primarily on the philosophy of history, rather than on the writing of history itself. It does include works on politics (Machiavelli's *The Prince*, John Locke's *On Civil Government*, and so on), since these essays, which describe how a country should be run, influence the ways in which later historians analyze the governments of the past.

When reading the more ancient works on the list, don't feel obliged to read every single word. The histories of Herodotus and Thucydides are quite long and detailed; you need not master every detail of the wars of the Greeks to understand the basic nature of the conflicts. Later works, constructed as arguments, should be followed from beginning to end; but in histories that offer sets of connected incidents, one or more sets can be dropped without significant loss of understanding. Because it isn't necessary for the amateur historian to read every word of Augustine, Hume, Gibbon, or Tocqueville, the list suggests several places where you can read abridged editions instead.

HERODOTUS
The Histories
(441 B.C.)

Best translations: Despite a handful of new translations since 1999, Robin Waterfield's translation for Oxford University Press (Oxford World's Classics reprint, 2008) remains my favorite; it successfully balances readability with literalism. Tom Holland's 2014 translation, published by Viking, is much more contemporary and accessible, but too often buys its appeal by sacrificing the original meaning (although it might be an excellent choice for high school students who will, we hope, revisit the text later in life). Aubrey de Sélincourt's 1954 translation (rev. ed., Penguin Classics, 2003) is accurate and has aged well, but the Waterfield translation is particularly pleasant to read.

At the beginning of Book II of *The Histories*, Herodotus solemnly tells the story of two newborn babies who, brought up in silence, both say their first words in Phrygian—thus proving that the Phrygians are the oldest race on earth. "I heard this version of the story from the priests of Hephaestus in Memphis," Herodotus informs us, "but the Greek version includes . . . many other absurdities." This attempt to separate truth from fiction demonstrates Herodotus's wish for accuracy, which earns him the title "father of history." Using travelers' tales, priests' stories, and eyewitness accounts, Herodotus treats the past not romantically, but realistically, evaluating past kings and heroes as actual people rather than legendary heroes.

Herodotus has a broader purpose than previous historians: "I will cover minor and major human settlements equally," he declares, but his primary aim is to recount the conflict between the Greeks and the Persians, whose King Cyrus first set his sights on the Greek peninsula. But Herodotus promises that he will go beyond a mere description of the war: He will reveal the roots of the whole conflict. Croesus of Lydia, a fabulously rich king who is worried about the increasing power of his Persian neighbor Cyrus, thinks that he might benefit from some additional divine intervention, so he sacrifices to Apollo in order to get the Greek gods into his camp. He then attacks Cyrus, who trounces him and whisks him off to Persia to be burned alive. When Apollo rescues Croesus, Cyrus transfers his wrath to Greece. In his efforts to divide truth from legend, Herodotus doesn't eliminate divine intervention from the realm of "truth," and in his evaluation of trustworthy evidence he puts stories told by priests at the top of his list. And his sense of historical difference is undeveloped (three Persians argue, in very Greek terms, about the superiority of democracy, oligarchy, or monarchy as a form of government). But he does make a new distinction: between the use of *literary* resources such as epics (which have to do with heroism, ambition, and other humanistic qualities) and the use of eyewitness accounts, which reveal *facts*.

In the rest of his history, Herodotus goes on to describe Cyrus's rise to power, the subsequent reigns of Cambyses and Darius, and the details of the war which began under Darius. His accounts of the battles of Marathon, after which a messenger runs twenty-six miles with news of the Greek victory and then dies; Thermopylae, where a band of heroic Spartans sacrifice themselves to cover the Greek retreat; Salamis, the war's decisive naval battle; and Plataea, the final Athenian victory over the Persian foot soldiers, became the central source for all later histories of the Greeks and their wars, and his careful attention to military strategy became the model for centuries of military history.

THUCYDIDES
The Peloponnesian War
(c. 400 B.C.)

Best translations: The best way for the nonspecialist to read Thucydides is probably The Landmark Thucydides: A Comprehensive Guide to the Peloponnesian War, *ed. Robert B. Strassler (Free Press, 1998). The text*

*itself could be more contemporary (it is an updated version of the nineteenth-
century, although still elegant, translation by Richard Crawley), but the maps
and notes give much-needed context for this name-and-place-heavy history.
In terms of translations alone, Steven Lattimore's 1998 translation for Hackett
is more contemporary, and supplies a brief and very clear summary before each
section—invaluable for the reader unfamiliar with ancient history. Martin
Hammond's recent translation for Oxford University Press (Oxford World's
Classics, 2009) is equally accessible and provides plenty of explanatory notes.*

With the Persian threat suspended, the Greek city-states of Athens and
Sparta turned on each other, in a series of devastating conflicts known
collectively as the Peloponnesian War. The aristocrat Thucydides was an
Athenian general until 424 B.C., when he lost an important battle and was
exiled. From exile, he began to write the tale of the ongoing conflict;
although the war had not yet ended, Thucydides had already heard legends and distortions, and wished to set the record straight. "The absence
of romance from my history," he wrote, sternly, "will, I fear, detract
somewhat from its interest; but if it be judged useful by those inquirers
who desire an exact knowledge of the past . . . I shall be content" (I:22).
Thucydides sees his work, and the practice of history generally, as a pattern for life, since (as he writes) this exact knowledge of the past can serve
as "a key to the future, which in all probability will repeat or resemble
the past."

Thucydides, like Herodotus, begins well before the war in order to
trace its genesis, but he is aware of the difficulties involved in writing
about the distant past: "Because of the amount of time that has gone by,"
he writes, "I have been unable to obtain accurate information about the
period that preceded the war. . . . [But] I do not consider those times to
have been very important as far as either war or anything else is concerned." This wholesale dismissal of the early history of the Greek peninsula might cause modern historians to gasp, but Thucydides does not
see the Greek civilization as dependent on anything that came before; it is
unique and without ancestors.

Unlike Herodotus, who sets down an immense variety of material,
Thucydides picks and chooses his stories and shapes his final tale into a
deliberate form: He is an Athenian, and even in exile shows a clear par-
tiality to the Athenian cause. In *The Peloponnesian War*, Athens fights first
with Corinth after intervening in a dispute between Corinth and several
Corinthian colonies, and then is drawn into conflict with Corinth's ally,
Sparta. Unlike Herodotus, Thucydides refuses to attribute any historical events to the intervention of the gods, instead describing long polit-

ical negotiations between the parties, the complicated web of alliances between Greek city-states, and the shaky condition of Greece since the end of the Persian war. His account shows a slowly declining Athens, weakened by the loss of its great statesman Pericles, by the plague, and by a disastrous defeat in Sicily. Athens recalls its most famous disgraced general, Alcibiades, to try to reverse its decline, and Thucydides infuses this development with a note of hope. But then the history breaks off, Thucydides died without bringing it to an end. Athens (as we know from other accounts) was forced into surrender.

PLATO
The Republic
(c. 375 B.C.)

Best translations: At least four new translations have appeared in the last fifteen years alone, giving readers plenty of choice. R. E. Allen's 2006 translation for Yale University Press (paperback, 2008) and C. D. C. Reeve's 2004 translation (Hackett) are probably tied as the best renderings for nonspecialists, balancing faithfulness to the original text and readability. (Reeve has also reworked a 1974 translation by G. M. A. Grube, so look for the 2004 version instead.) I am personally fond of Robin Waterfield's translation (Oxford World's Classic, 2004); it has been criticized by some philosophers as being a little too free with Plato's original text, but as a (non-philosophizing) historian I find it readable and entirely usable.

Plato's picture of the ideal civilization served as a template for scores of later historians, who held their own nations up against Plato's prototype. *The Republic* uses real, historical figures as mouthpieces for Plato's own arguments; it begins at a festivity where Socrates and several other noted philosophers are discussing the makeup of human societies, which should (above all) be just. They define justice as a compromise that the State enforces in order to keep the citizens safe, but Socrates, who would prefer justice to be natural rather than constructed, leads them on to describe what a just society would look like. They concoct a country whose rigid class divisions are willingly accepted by the citizens, who know the place to which they are born; in which education is universal (for men, at least); in which citizens act for the good of their country, rather than for their own pleasure (since the latter always leads to boredom and dissatisfaction); and in which the rational practice of eugenics encourages the strong and intelligent to have children, while the sickly are quietly removed from view.

The leader of this country would be a philosopher-king, a man with both power and wisdom, who understands that all we see is only a shadow of the Real; as he governs, he tries to guide his nation into conformity with the Real, rather than listening to the will of the masses. His task is to grasp the Real, and through this to discover justice, which is itself an Ideal. And this conclusion, of course, bears the stamp of Socrates' authority.

Few present-day historians would dare to copy this method, but Plato's willingness to put words into Socrates' mouth demonstrates his own view of history: Historical writing involves the discovery of ideas, not of "historical facts," which are (after all) mere shadows. If Plato expresses the Ideal (which exists independently of either Plato or Socrates) and does so in a way that Socrates could have used, he is doing accurate history; he is holding to truth. Plato's use of Socratic dialogue to reveal his conclusions also can be considered "historical"; after all, Socrates contributed to our knowledge of the Real through his invention of the dialogue technique, and in this sense is still taking part in the search for the Ideal.

PLUTARCH
Lives
(A.D. 100–125)

Best translations: There are two simple ways to read Plutarch in English. You can read the entire set of biographical sketches in the 2001 Modern Library Classics edition, Plutarch's Lives, Vol. 1 *and* Plutarch's Lives, Vol. 2. *The translation is by the seventeenth-century poet John Dryden, revised in 1864 by the poet-historian Arthur Hugh Clough; it has become an English classic in its own right, but the slightly archaic prose does add an extra level of difficulty to the work. As an alternative, you can read selected lives in a more engaging modern translation by Robin Waterfield, published by Oxford World's Classics (reissue edition, 2009). This too comes in two volumes:* Roman Lives: A Selection of Eight Roman Lives *and* Greek Lives: A Selection of Nine Greek Lives.

Plutarch is the first biographer in the modern sense; he chronicles the life of men as men, rather than treating them as elements in a larger scheme of historical events. For Plutarch, the lives of great men *are* the larger scheme. History is formed by the famous, the powerful, and the privileged. Plutarch began a tradition of biographical writing that allowed Thomas Carlyle, hundreds of years later, to remark that "the history of what man has accomplished in this world, is at bottom the history of the Great Men who have worked here."

As he writes, Plutarch links together the public accomplishments and private life of each of his subjects. "The most glorious exploits," he writes, "do not always furnish us with the clearest discoveries of virtue or vice in men; sometimes a matter of less moment, an expression or a jest, informs us better of their character and inclinations." Furthermore, the public and private are inextricably mixed; private life reveals character, and character determines the course of history. So we are told of Romulus's great battles, but also of his supreme will to conquer, which made those battles into victories—a quality that led him, in his later years, to insist on being accompanied everywhere by young men who carried leather thongs, so that he could instantly command any bystander to be arrested and bound.

Plutarch tells the stories of Greek and Roman heroes in pairs, with an eye to similar virtues and vices. For Plutarch, history is a moral enterprise, and historical figures are models to be emulated or shunned. So in the pairing of Alcibiades (the Athenian hero) and Coriolanus (who later appears in a Shakespearian tragedy), we learn that Alcibiades was graceful and charming but warped by "ambitions and a desire of superiority," and that Coriolanus had a "generous and worthy nature," but due to a lack of early discipline was slave to "a haughty and imperious temper." Both men had checkered careers because they were prone to being governed by their faults. But Plutarch gives Coriolanus the moral edge, since (bad temper notwithstanding) he was a straightforward and upright man, while Alcibiades was "the least scrupulous . . . of human beings." Herein lies the lesson: A short fuse is a drawback, but unscrupulous behavior is a fatal flaw. These biographies are fables to guide moral development; as Plutarch himself writes, "The virtues of these great men . . . [serve] me as a sort of looking-glass, in which I may see how to adjust and adorn my own life."

AUGUSTINE
The City of God
(completed 426)

Best translations: Although scholars of religion and political philosophy will want to read the unabridged work (the most standard is the Penguin Classics translation by Henry Bettenson, edited by G. R. Evans, weighing in at 1184 pages), the amateur historian is probably better off with an abridged edition. The easiest to locate is the Image Classics abridgment (1958) of the translation by Demetrius B. Zema and Gerald G. Wash.

Augustine, born in North Africa, is known for his elaboration of the doctrine of original sin, which says that all men inherit the sin of Adam from birth, and remain self-centered unless called by God to worship him. *The City of God* argues that the community of self-worshipers (the city of earth) and the kingdom of God-followers (the city of God) live inextricably mixed together on earth. The tensions of history come because the two cities, which have different ends, are forced to live side by side.

Augustine is careful to explain that the city of God is not identical to the Church, since not every Church member truly worships God. Nor is this city simply made up of Christian individuals, since the church itself is the place where God chooses to work on earth. In the same way, the city of man is not simply made up of people who don't follow God; nor is it identified as any particular government. Instead, the city of earth is the place where men are driven by their lusts, and the most powerful lust is the lust for power. In the city of earth, Augustine writes, "the princes and the nations it subdues are ruled by the love of ruling." Unlike Plato, Augustine sees no way that an earthly state can be just, since it can only enforce justice through the exercise of power, and since that power is always flawed. "True justice," Augustine remarks, "has no existence save in that republic whose founder and ruler is Christ."

However, the city of God can coexist with some earthly states more easily than with others. Augustine defines a state, or "commonwealth," as a group of people bound together by common love for an object. Such a commonwealth will be "a superior people in proportion as it is bound together by higher interests, inferior in proportion as it is bound together by lower." The city of God is the highest type of commonwealth, since it is bound together by the love of God, but those earthly states that are bound together by a love of peace are much superior to those which are bound together by a lust for power. Members of the city of God, who also wish to live in peace, can cooperate with an earthly state that pursues peace, but will always find themselves in opposition to a state run by a tyrant. "The earthly city," Augustine concludes, "which does not live by faith, seeks an earthly peace. . . . The city of God makes use of this peace only because it must, until this mortal condition which necessitates it shall pass away. . . . Thus, as this life is common to both cities, so there is a harmony between them." So while keeping his eyes firmly focused on the ultimate, unearthly fulfillment of the city of God, Augustine still lays out principles by which an earthly state can be governed.

BEDE
The Ecclesiastical History of the English People
(731)

Best translation: The Oxford World's Classic translation, done in 1994 by Judith McClure and Roger Collins (republished 2000).

Bede's history is one of the first to tell the story of a *nation*—a political entity, as opposed to an ethnic group such as "Greek." Bede uses the past to build a sense of national identity, which is no mean feat, considering that England began as a patchwork of Danish kingdoms and wasn't united under one king until two hundred years after Bede's death. But even though the "English" spoke five languages and had a dozen minor kings, Bede sees them as having one identity: "At the present time," he writes, "there are five languages in Britain, just as the divine law is written in five books, all devoted to seeking out and setting forth one and the same kind of wisdom."

Bede borrows from Augustine in seeing the kingdom of England as having spiritual rather than physical borders (perhaps because the physical borders were rather difficult to define in the mid-eighth century). Thus his history is the "Ecclesiastical History" of the English people; it recounts the growth of the City of God in England. Bede begins by describing the earliest inhabitants of Britain and Ireland (the Picts, who originally came from Scythia), continues on through the Roman occupations of Britain, details the ongoing battles between the native Britons and the invading Angles, and finally arrives at the coming of Augustine (of Canterbury, not to be confused with Augustine of Hippo, who wrote *The City of God*), which is the turning point of his narrative. Augustine establishes the *ecclesia anglorum,* the distinctively English church, which links together all of the various races of England into a spiritual unity. After this point, English kings get relatively short shrift (Aelfrith, who was "ignorant of the divine religion," gets one paragraph) and Augustine, the spiritual king of England under the spiritual emperor Pope Gregory, becomes the star (he gets nine long chapters). The *Ecclesiastical History* continues in this pattern, alternating brief descriptions of kings with lengthy tales of bishops.

Gregory's advice to Augustine shows a concern to establish a common practice for the faith that now unites the English. "Make a careful selection [of the customs from the various churches]," he orders Augustine, "and sedulously teach the Church of the English, which is still new in the faith, what you have been able to gather from other churches. . . .

And when you have collected these as it were into one bundle, see that the minds of the English grow accustomed to it." This is exactly the story that Bede tells; England is a country full of many different peoples, who are nevertheless united in their knowledge of God. The *History* concludes with a national celebration of Easter, which symbolizes the "ending point" of the national progression; bickering over the exact date of this festivity has finally been resolved (there is a long and detailed discussion of the process), and by falling in with the rest of Christendom, the English have demonstrated their maturity not only as a nation, but as citizens of the kingdom of Christ.

NICCOLÒ MACHIAVELLI
The Prince
(1513)

Best translations: Both Harvey C. Mansfield's translation (2nd ed., University of Chicago Press, 1998) and Peter Bondanella's more recent translation for Oxford World's Classics (2008) are readable, fair to the original, and contain useful explanatory footnotes.

In the political chaos of Renaissance Italy, with the city-states of Venice, Milan, Naples, and Florence struggling to advance their own interests, Niccolò Machiavelli offers his own primer on political technique. He is not writing a history, but his method is historical. Each technique is supported by historical proof, a demonstration from times past that shows his conclusions to be true.

Machiavelli begins by surveying the different kinds of territories, states, and kingdoms that a prince might rule. Although his musings on the different kinds of Renaissance states (principates, hereditary or acquired; mixed principates; kingdoms; and so on) may seem irrelevant, he is using these highly particular forms of government to make general statements about the nature of massed men. In Chapter III, for example, "Of Mixed Principates," he progresses from a description of the mixed principate to an all-important statement of political philosophy: "Men willingly change masters when they believe they will better themselves." Far from feeling loyalty, subjects are glad to change their governor, as long as they believe that a new and better order will follow.

After explaining the character of the governed, Machiavelli goes on to describe the qualities of a governor, giving historical examples for each quality he recommends, in a return to the biography-as-fable approach of Plutarch: "A prudent man ought always enter into the ways beaten by great men," he writes, "and imitate those who have been most excellent, so that, if your virtue does not reach up to there, at least it gives some odor of it." Machiavelli's historical references go all the way back to Moses: "It was necessary for Moses to find the people of Israel . . . enslaved and oppressed by the Egyptians, so that they, in order to escape their servitude, would be disposed to follow him." This becomes the first of his principles: The efficient ruler will always appeal to the wickedness of his people in order to improve his moral authority over them.

For Machiavelli, "good" means "effective," which has led to his reputation as a conniver free of morality. But he does have a morality. The "good," in Machiavelli's scheme, is that the country would prosper. (He ends *The Prince* with a plea to Lorenzo de' Medici to come and rescue his ailing city.) And since the prosperity of the country benefits the individual members of it, actions taken by the prince that might seem "wicked" actually become "good" if they benefit the state and its people. As a matter of fact, Machiavelli sees sustained wickedness as a bad option both for prince and for country. A single cruel action, he notes, may be necessary "at one stroke for the necessity of securing oneself," but continual cruelty means that the prince must always rule "knife in hand; nor can he ever rely on his subjects." In *The Prince*, politics are based, not on the "ideal" but on the "real"—and remaining in power is the greatest reality of all.

SIR THOMAS MORE
Utopia
(1516)

Best editions: Available from several publishers, including Penguin Classics (ed. Paul Turner, 2003), Dover Thrift Editions (1997), and Norton Critical Editions (3rd ed., 2010; read the introduction, which includes brief historical background, but save the critical essays for afterward).

Plato describes an ideal society, Machiavelli the society that actually exists; Thomas More writes instead an "imaginary history," proposing a society which *might* work. He puts himself into this history, telling the story of a character named Thomas More, who after Mass one day meets the traveler Raphael Hythloday (the name is invented from a combination of Greek words and means something like "talented teller of nonsense"). Hythloday describes his travels in a distant land called Utopia (or "Noplace"). Like a novelist, More uses the old form of the travelogue satirically, following Hythloday through this imaginary land, which embodies an eclectic collection of classical and New Testament principles. Utopia has fifty-four identical cities, all the same, exactly twenty-four miles apart. All citizens have the same living conditions. Everyone takes turns doing the farm work, with all land held in common. Value is based on usefulness, not scarcity (so that gold is worth nothing). Everyone believes in a Divine Power of some kind, but no one religious sect is allowed to proselytize, since "if one religion is really true and the rest are false, the true one will sooner or later prevail by its own natural strength, if men will only consider the matter reasonably and moderately." This "moderation" is at the center of More's *Utopia*, which is based on the ability (and willingness) of all men to exercise both reason and selflessness, doing the right thing by choice. More, like Augustine, seems to be skeptical about the possibility of a Christian state (which would need threats and violence to enforce faith), but he describes a state where an unspoken Christian ethic undergirds every law: "No man," More writes, "should conceive so vile . . . an opinion of the dignity of man's nature as to think . . . that the world runneth at all adventures governed by no divine providence. And therefore they believe that after this life vices be extremely punished and virtues bountifully rewarded." Without this shared religious context, Utopia—like Bede's England—would have no coherence.

JOHN LOCKE
The True End of Civil Government
(1690)

Best editions: Available as a public domain ebook, as well as from Cambridge University Press as the second part of Locke: Two Treatises of Government, *third edition (Cambridge Texts in the History of Political Thought, 1988). It can also be found in* Two Treatises of Government and A Letter Concerning Toleration, *ed. Ian Shapiro (Yale University Press, 2003), and in the Dover Thrift Edition,* The Second Treatise of Government and A Letter Concerning Toleration *(2002).*

John Locke lived during a time of growing hostility toward monarchies, but nevertheless found himself defending a pair of monarchs. Decades before, Parliament and the English had executed the Stuart king in favor of Oliver Cromwell's English republic, but eventually tired of Cromwell's draconian measures and brought the Stuarts back to England. Unfortunately, the Stuart male heirs proved so incompetent that, in 1688, the

English put a Stuart daughter on the throne instead: Mary, who, with her Dutch husband William, was allowed to be queen only on condition that she cooperate with Parliament. This "Glorious Revolution" (glorious because bloodless) established a contractual monarchy, in which power began to shift away from the monarch toward Parliament, which was (theoretically) representative of the people.

Locke writes in support of this revolution. Political authority, Locke argues, should only be exercised to protect property. When man is in a "state of nature," he must protect his own property, which forces him into a constant state of war; instead, men can join together into a "commonwealth" and form a government, to which they delegate the job of preserving each man's right to his own property.

This contract between men and their government does require that men "give up . . . liberty of a kind," but Locke sees this as necessitated by the greed of men: "For if men could live peaceably and quietly together, without uniting under certain laws and growing into a commonwealth, there would be no need at all of magistrates or politics, which were only made to preserve men in this world from the fraud and violence of one another." Furthermore, it is a very limited surrender, since government should only concern itself with property issues; it is "a power that hath no other end but preservation, and therefore can never have a right to destroy, enslave, or designedly to impoverish the subjects."

Yet Locke has little faith that government will limit itself to such a narrow field. So he suggests that government have three branches: a legislative group that makes laws protecting property, an "executive" branch to oversee their enforcement ("It may be too great a temptation to human frailty, apt to grasp at power, for the same persons who have the power of making laws to have also in their hands the power to execute them"), and finally a third branch, called the "federative," to deal with foreign powers. But if this separation of powers doesn't keep a government from overstepping its limited responsibilities, the government can be dissolved. The commonwealth gave it power, and the commonwealth can take that power away, instead "erecting a new legislative . . . as they shall find it most for their safety and good." Locke's essay ends without answering at least one vexing question: Since this common authority is appointed by those who have property, and since the government is responsible to those who appoint it, what of those who have no property?

DAVID HUME
The History of England, Volume V
(1754)

Best editions: Hume can be read online at Project Gutenberg. His entire
six-volume history was republished by the Liberty Fund in the mid-1980s; it
was numbered chronologically, so that Volume I details Roman Britain to the
death of King John in 1216; Volume II deals with the early monarchy until
1485; Volumes III and IV cover the Tudors; and Volumes V and VI chronicle
the Stuart kings—the most recent royal house). But Hume actually wrote
his accounts of the Stuart kings first. Volumes V and VI were the first writ-
ten and were published in 1754 and 1757 respectively; Hume then continued
backward with his work. You need only read Volume V of the Liberty Fund
edition (David Hume's History of England, Volume 5: 1603–1649) in
order to understand Hume's methods and aims, but you can continue on with
the whole series if the urge strikes you.[23]

David Hume set out to write a history of England that would, in good
Enlightenment fashion, demonstrate a bias-free exercise of reason. Like
Locke and many others, he preferred to see Parliamentary limits on
royal power. But he rejected the arguments of contemporary historians,
who insisted that the English had always been free, and that tyrannical monarchs had seized rights historically belonging to the people. A
scientific analysis of the past, Hume insisted, would show that English
kings generally acted without consulting Parliament or any other body
of advisors, and (in fact) were strongest when they did so. When Parliament demanded accountability from the monarch, it set a historical
precedent.

So Hume began his history of England with the Stuart kings; it was
at this point, he wrote, that the increasing aggression of the House of
Commons forced the monarchs to react. In his view, flaws in Parliament
did just as much to produce unrest in England as any defect on the part
of the Stuart kings: "The meetings of Parliament were so precarious,"
he writes, "their sessions so short compared to the vacations, that, when
men's eyes were turned upwards in search of sovereign power, the prince
alone was apt to strike them as the only permanent magistrate invested
with the whole majesty and authority of the state. . . . By a great many,

---

[23] The volumes are listed at $12.00 each; the ISBNs are Volume I, 0-86597-022-X; Vol-
ume II, 0-86597-027-0; Volume III, 0-86597-029-7; Volume IV, 0-86597-031-9; Volume
V, 0-86597-033-5; Volume VI, 0-86597-035-1. The ISBN number for the entire paperback series, which costs $50.00, is 0-86597-020-3.

therefore, monarchy, simple and unmixed, was conceived to be the government of England; and those popular assemblies were supposed to form *only the ornament* of the fabric, without being in any degree essential to its being and existence." Hume was immediately accused of "Tory prejudice," of supporting the right of the monarchy to do as it pleased. But in fact Hume, skeptic as he was, rejected any royal pretensions to divine privilege. On the other hand, he had a low opinion of the masses, and thought that whatever government could best keep the country peaceful and prosperous should be in power, never mind philosophical arguments for or against it (the "utilitarian" point of view).

Hume did not pursue scientific research methods or sort his sources carefully, so the *Histories* are full of minor (and sometimes major) errors of fact. His history is "enlightened," not because of his method, but because of his aims: He did not intend to prove any particular point of view, but rather to take whatever story the past told and relay it to a large audience. "The first Quality of a Historian is to be true and impartial," he wrote in a letter to a friend; "the next is to be interesting."

JEAN-JACQUES ROUSSEAU
The Social Contract
(1762)

Best translation: Maurice Cranston, for Penguin Classics (1968).

Locke and Rousseau both see government as a contract—but Rousseau, unlike Locke, believes that men come to this contract with innate goodness. For Rousseau, man in his natural state has a moral sense (he is a "noble savage," uncivilized but naturally ethical). However, although man may be naturally good, his social structures are bad, particularly those that encourage property ownership. Ownership is society's original sin: everything began to go downhill the first time a man said, "This is mine." But salvation is possible through the social contract.

This social contract is an association that men enter into by mutual agreement. Rousseau's model for this is the family; he argues that fathers and children (mothers seem to have dropped out of the picture) both give up a certain amount of liberty "for their own advantage": The children get protection, the father gets love. In the same way, the "state" is an association in which the members get protection, and the state gets (rather than love) the enjoyment of ruling. In this association, freedom is preserved because all of the members give up the same rights to join: "Since each gives himself up entirely, the condition is equal for all. . . . [N]o one has any interest in making it burdensome to others." Every member has

power over every other member, which is the essence of the social contract: "Each of us puts in common his person and his whole power under
the supreme direction of the general will. . . . [T]his act of association produces a moral and collective body . . . called by its members State when it
is passive, Sovereign when it is active."

Rousseau goes on to define laws as the will of the whole people, drafted
by the legislature and imposed by the general will of the people. He does
see a possible flaw, though: "Of themselves, the people always desire what
is good," but unfortunately they "do not always discern it." Therefore, the
people need a Legislator—a "great man" who is able to see clearly what
the people need even if they don't see it themselves. But this great man is
not a dictator, because, although he writes the constitution of a state, he
has no role in enforcing it. Rather, the people will enforce the laws—pre-
sumably, because they recognize in it that "good" which they desired but
were unable to articulate on their own. Rousseau's efforts to explain how
this will work in real life lead him into multiple contradictions. However,
in *The Social Contract* he is himself taking on the role of the Legislator; he
is the "great man" who can discern what the masses cannot, and he can
comfortably leave its execution in other hands.

THOMAS PAINE
Common Sense
(1776)

*Best editions: This brief essay can be purchased by itself from Penguin Classics
(ed. Isaac Kramnick, 1982) and Dover Thrift Editions (1997). The Library
of America edition (1995), edited by Eric Foner, also includes a number of
Paine's other essays, such as "Rights of Man" and "The Age of Reason."*

Continuing the trend of the age away from an active and powerful state,
Thomas Paine remarked that the best government was the one that governed the least (a principle which became known as *laissez-faire*). Writing
at the time of the American Revolution, Paine was less political philosopher than propagandist, determined to convince the colonists (and Penn-
sylvanians in particular) that monarchy was dead.

Paine starts out by drawing a distinction between government and society. Society, he writes, "is produced by our wants, and government by
our wickedness. . . . The first is a patron, the last a punisher. Society in
every state is a blessing, but government even in its best state is but a necessary evil; in its worst state an intolerable one." Society is what people join
together to do; government is made necessary in society because of "the

inability of moral virtue to govern the world." For Rousseau, society and the state were the same. For Paine, the "state" is society's unwelcome guest, the policeman who has to stay in the guest room to protect "life, liberty, and property," even though none of the family really wants him there.

This "policeman" government should not be a monarchy. To prove this, Paine sketches out a history of the world in which idyllic equality once ruled. In "the early ages of the world," he writes, "according to the scripture chronology, there were no kings; the consequence of which was there were no wars; it is the pride of kings which throw mankind into confusion." Paine holds this vague early time of equality as his ideal (referring to the quiet rural lives of the patriarchs, and ignoring the violent details of Genesis). In order to reinstitute this pastoral innocence in the present, delegates from each colony should attend a yearly assembly where they would cast lots to find out who would be president for a year. This president is simply a chairman for the assembly, which will pass only those laws approved by at least three-fifths of the assembly. This will restrain vice, since, all together, the delegates will serve to check each other's ambition. Paine fears that, if any one man gains power for too long (four years being an unthinkable period), he will inevitably become a tyrant—like the English monarch, who is now too busy protecting his own power to protect the life, liberty, or property of the American colonies. Only God is free from this impulse to tyrannize: "But where says some is the King of America? I'll tell you Friend, he reigns above, and doth not make havoc of mankind like the Royal Brute of Britain."

EDWARD GIBBON
The History of the Decline and Fall of the Roman Empire
(1776–88)

Best editions: Penguin and Everyman's Library both publish the unabridged six-volume version of Gibbon's massive history. Reading all of Gibbon is a long-term project: Horatio Hornblower, C. S. Forester's fictional naval captain, survived three-year voyages with the History *as his only reading material. A one-volume abridged edition is probably best for most readers. Penguin's abridged version (2001) is edited by David Womersley; the Modern Library abridgment (2003) is edited by Hans-Friedrich Mueller (introduction by Daniel J. Boorstin).*[24]

[24]The ISBNs for the unabridged Penguin paperbacks, each with a cover price of $24.95, are as follows: Volume I, 0-14-043393-7; Volume II, 0-14-043394-5; Volume III, 0-14-043395-3.

Gibbon's great achievement was to write a history that attempted, in good Enlightenment style, to analyze *all* of the possible causes of his immensely large and complex effect, the decline and fall of Rome. He also returned to the original Latin sources, although not the original documents themselves. The scientific analysis of primary sources suggested by those who professionalized history would come after his death.

Gibbon's interest in Rome reflected his interest in the present; Rome, a noble experiment in just government, failed despite its centuries of success. Lying behind the efforts to understand Rome's fall is a subtext: Perhaps, next time, a civilization can achieve Rome's greatness without its fall. "In the second century of the Christian era," Gibbon's history begins, "the Empire of Rome comprehended the fairest part of the earth, and the most civilised portion of mankind. . . . The image of a free constitution was preserved with decent reverence; the Roman senate appeared to possess the sovereign authority, and devolved on the emperors all the executive powers of government." Yet this separation of powers did not preserve the empire. Why?

In the *Decline and Fall*, Gibbon excels at uncovering all of the factors that led to the decline: the state of its economy, the effect of various technologies, geography, class warfare, the rise of new cultural and religious ideas, flawed forms of government, and more. He is not quite so successful in recapturing the mindset of ancient peoples; indeed, he leans heavily on blanket characterizations of large groups of people. In his chapter on the formation of the Christian church, for example, he writes, "While [Christians] inculcated the maxims of passive obedience, they refused to take any active part in the civil administration or the military defence of the empire. . . . But the human character, however it may be exalted or depressed by a temporary enthusiasm, will return by degrees to its proper and natural level. . . . The primitive Christians were dead to the business and pleasures of the world; but their love of action, which could never be entirely extinguished, soon revived, and found a new occupation in the government of the church. . . . The catholic church soon assumed the form, and acquired the strength, of a great federative republic." Here Gibbon footnotes various church fathers, including Tertullian and Origen, and adds a number of facts about the accomplishments of church councils. But his interpretation rests on his assumption that he can categorize a large group of ancient people as essentially the same as contemporary people; he does not, in other words, manage to put himself back into the minds of the ancients.

MARY WOLLSTONECRAFT
A Vindication of the Rights of Woman
(1792)

Best editions: This public-domain text can be read online at a number of sites. Paperback editions are also published by Dover Thrift Editions (1996), Longman Cultural Editions (2006, includes lots of commentary along with contemporary responses), and Oxford University Press (2009, includes Wollstonecraft's additional essay "A Vindication of the Rights of Men").

As a young woman, Wollstonecraft tried to establish her financial independence by working first as a companion, then as a school administrator, a governess, and finally a professional writer. She published *A Vindication of the Rights of Woman* in 1792, the same year that Thomas Paine published *The Rights of Man.* Locke, Paine, and Rousseau had claimed that men should rule themselves; Wollstonecraft asserts that women should do the same. But Wollstonecraft has a low opinion of women's ability to do so, not because their minds are inferior, but because they have never been trained. Instead of being taught to use their reason, they have been taught an "artificial weakness," which "gives birth to cunning" and "those contemptible infantine airs that undermine esteem even whilst they excite desire." Wollstonecraft argues that three qualities—reason, virtue, and knowledge—make us capable of happiness and allow society to function. But women are not allowed to train their reason, because they are denied education. They are taught to be deceptive, not virtuous: "Women are told from their infancy, and taught by the example of their mothers, that a little knowledge of human weakness, justly termed cunning, softness of temper, *outward* obedience, and a scrupulous attention to a puerile kind of propriety, will obtain for them the protection of man." And they are encouraged to exalt feelings rather than knowledge: "Their senses are inflamed, and their understandings neglected, consequently they become the prey of their senses . . . and are blown about by every momentary gust of feeling. . . . [T]heir conduct is unstable, and their opinions are wavering." These are harsh words, but Wollstonecraft blames an educational system that teaches "one half of the human race" to live in "listless inactivity and stupid acquiescence." Society, she argues, trains women only to be wives. A real education, which would train women to think and be strong, would transform society itself: Without so much practice in tyrannizing women, men would no longer turn so quickly to tyranny.

Wollstonecraft directs her screed at middle-class women and at men. In her introduction, she explains that the aristocratic woman is so dissipated by great wealth that she cannot be redeemed by education. (She doesn't explain why poor women are excluded.) Men are included in her audience because she must convince those who are responsible for legislation to carry out her reforms. And, in any case, Wollstonecraft was perfectly aware that she was writing primarily for men: Paradoxically, her essay would have been too difficult for most women, who had not been taught to follow a logical argument—or in many cases, to read at all.

ALEXIS DE TOCQUEVILLE
Democracy in America
(1835–40)

Best translations: Democracy in America *was published in two volumes, the first in 1835 and the second in 1840. The 2000 translation by Harvey Mansfield and Delbe Ainthrop (University of Chicago Press, paperback 2002) is the most readable; Arthur Goldhammer's 2004 translation for the Library of America (2004) is slightly more demanding but also more literal. An excellent one-volume abridgment (you don't have to read the entire massive work), translated by Stephen Grant and abridged by Sanford Kessler, is published by Hackett (2000).*

The French politician Alexis de Tocqueville had aristocratic blood but liberal inclinations; believing that modern governments (including his own) were inevitably evolving toward democracy, he traveled through America to examine how democracy looked in practice. There, he found a vexing contradiction: The citizens of this great democracy often displayed a "peculiar melancholy . . . in the bosom of abundance" and a "disgust with life . . . in the midst of an easy and tranquil existence. . . . I saw the freest and most enlightened men placed in the happiest condition that there is in the world; it seemed to me as if a kind of cloud habitually covered every visage, and I thought them grave and almost sad, even in their pleasures."

Tocqueville attributes this *ennui* to the very freedom and equality at the center of democratic practice. Freedom allows citizens to indulge in "the single-minded pursuit of the goods of this world"; equality fills them with "a kind of ceaseless trepidation" because each citizen is competing with every other citizen, and "has but a limited time at his disposal to find, to lay hold of, and to enjoy" those material benefits. In this, Tocqueville is echoing Plato's cautions in *The Republic*: Plato warned that the man who is devoted to the pursuit of pleasure, rather than virtue (which includes acting on behalf of the state rather than on behalf of self) will find himself searching, unceasingly, for new amusements. The very freedom on which democracies depend—the freedom of citizens to participate in their government—ironically tends to produce a preoccupation with pleasure, rather than with civic duty: in America, Tocqueville remarks, it is quite difficult to convince citizens to take part in their own assemblies. Constantly drawn by the pursuit of goods, feeling the pressure of others all around pursuing the same goods, the weary citizen of the democratic society has little energy left for participation in government.

Tocqueville sees in action the principles that Locke and Rousseau proposed in the abstract; he sees the flaws in Locke's focus on property (materialism makes citizens uninterested in the general welfare) and Rousseau's proposal of complete equality (it produces competition and can lead to a tyranny of the majority). Materialism and undifferentiated equality are the two thorny problems of a democracy: "Men who live in democratic times have many passions," he writes, "but most of their passions end in love of wealth or issue from it. . . . When fellow citizens are all independent and indifferent, it is only by paying them that one can obtain the cooperation of each; this infinitely multiplies the use of wealth and increases the value of it. . . . ordinarily, therefore, one finds love of wealth, as principal or accessory, at the bottom of the actions of Americans; this gives all their passions a family resemblance, and is not slow to make of them a tiresome picture."

KARL MARX AND FRIEDRICH ENGELS
The Communist Manifesto
(1848)

Best edition: Since 1910, most English editions of The Communist Manifesto *have used the translation made by Samuel Moore, in consultation with Friedrich Engels. This version has been published by Penguin Classics (2002), Dover Thrift Editions (2003), Verso (with an introduction by Eric Hobsbawm, 2012), and Norton Critical Editions (with commentary, 2012).*

The Communist Manifesto was first published in 1848, when Karl Marx was twenty-nine and Friedrich Engels was twenty-seven. In the composition of this manifesto, the two moved from socialism (which implied a utopian and ultimately peaceful commitment to shared property) to communism (which had a more aggressive ring to it, suggesting that a revolt would bring this sharing into existence).

In the *Manifesto*, Marx and Engels argue that history must be studied in terms of *material goods*: In order to understand how people live, you must first understand how they earn their livelihood. Their own examination of history through this lens reveals that one class of people, which they label the *bourgeoisie*, now controls the means to produce goods on a large scale. This control of the "means of production," which requires the investment of capital, has "put an end to all feudal, patriarchal, idyllic relations . . . and has left remaining no other nexus between man and man than naked self-interest, than callous 'cash payment.' . . . It has converted the physician, the lawyer, the priest, the poet, the man of science, into its paid wage-labourer . . . [and] has reduced the family relation to a mere money relation." In short, our modern economic system has "alienated" men and women from their work; rather than treating their work as a way of life, they labor only for the cash payment at the end.

This has come about because the bourgeoisie, needing "a constantly expanding market for its products" continually revolutionizes the "modes of production" (the way goods are produced) so that products can be made faster and in greater quantities. In response, a working class has developed—the proletariat, who "live only so long as they find work, and who find work only so long as their labour increases capital. These labourers, who must sell themselves piecemeal, are a commodity . . . exposed to all the vicissitudes of competition." Because the workman is a commodity, he can attract only that sum of money that he needs for his maintenance. Wages go down, skill is no longer essential because the factory system divides tasks into meaningless parts, and "the small tradespeople, shopkeepers, and rentiers, the handicraftsmen and peasants . . . sink gradually into the proletariat, partly because their diminutive capital does not suffice for the scale on which Modern Industry is carried on . . . partly because their specialized skill is rendered worthless by new methods of production." It's difficult to argue with this description, in a world where every family restaurant cowers before the Golden Arches. But the *prescription* that follows—remove the capital from the hands of the bourgeoisie and put it into the hands of the state, which is the proletariat "organized as a ruling class"—ignores the corrupting effects of power so feared by Locke and Paine.

JACOB BURCKHARDT
The Civilization of the Renaissance in Italy
(1860)

Best translation: The Penguin Classics translation by S. G. C. Middlemore, with introduction by Peter Burke (1990). Part II, "The Development of the Individual," is most central to Burckhardt's argument.

It is to Jacob Burckhardt that we owe the popular conception of the Renaissance as the time when man began to be modern. Burckhardt writes, "In the Middle Ages both sides of human consciousness—that which was turned within as that which was turned without—lay dreaming or half awake beneath a common veil. The veil was woven of faith, illusion, and childish prepossession, through which the world and history were seen clad in strange hues. Man was conscious of himself only as member of a race, people, party, family, or corporation—only through some general category. In Italy this veil first melted into air: an objective treatment and consideration of the State and of all the things in this world became possible. The subjective side at the same time asserted itself with corresponding emphasis: man became a spiritual individual, and recognized himself as such."[25]

Burckhardt's chronicle of the Renaissance turns on this analysis of these years as the "first modern" age. Frederick II, for example, is described as "the first ruler of the modern time . . . early accustomed . . . to a thoroughly objective treatment of affairs." War itself became a "purely rational" activity. Italy began to "swarm with individuality." This "perfecting of the individual" led, in Burckhardt's analysis, to the modern idea of fame; the modern forms of wit and satire; the form of the modern university; modern humanism; and a dozen other traits recognizable as belonging to modern life. For Burckhardt, the Italian city-states of the Renaissance stand as the first modern, republican governments based on classical ideals; Italy's use of the ancient city-state model, "strengthened in turn the republican ideal and contributed mightily to its triumph later in modern nations and primarily in our own." And although various scholars have questioned this pivotal role of the Italian Renaissance (Burckhardt tends to flatten the difference between Renaissance times and his own), this interpretation became a standard and is still widely held.

W. E. B. DU BOIS
The Souls of Black Folk
(1903)

Best editions: Available from Dover Thrift Editions (1994) and Oxford World's Classics (2007), as well as in a collection with Narrative of the Life of Frederick Douglass *and* Up From Slavery *(Dover, 2007).*

Du Bois, a Harvard-trained sociologist who taught at Atlanta University, begins his book by stating that "the problem of the Twentieth Century is

[25]Jacob Burckhardt, *The Civilization of the Renaissance in Italy*, trans. S. G. C. Middlemore (New York: Albert & Charles Boni, 1928), p. 143.

the problem of the color-line"—an observation that shapes the work of almost all later writers of African American history. Du Bois's work is a combination of history, autobiography, and cultural study, ranging from the history of African American education, the failings of Reconstruction, the meaning of African American "sorrow songs," to the place of Booker T. Washington as an African American leader. Du Bois's sharp disagreements with Washington's accommodationist policies (Washington believes that "the Negro's future rise depends primarily on his own efforts") highlight Du Bois's own analysis of American society as fatally flawed for its black citizens.

Central in all of his writings is Du Bois's concept of "double consciousness," which he explains through the metaphor of "the Veil." Black Americans, he argues, see themselves with double vision: with their own self-vision, but also through the eyes of hostile whites. "It is a peculiar sensation," he writes, "this double-consciousness, this sense of always looking at one's self through the eyes . . . of a world that looks on in amused contempt and pity. One ever feels his two-ness—an American, a Negro; two souls, two thoughts, two unreconciled strivings. . . . The history of the American Negros is the history of this strife. . . . [The Negro] simply wishes to make it possible for a man to be both a Negro and an American, without being cursed and spit upon by his fellows, without having the doors of Opportunity closed roughly in his face." Like the black autobiographers of the last chapter, Du Bois has single vision until a childhood moment when a girl at his school refuses to take his visiting card: "Then it dawned upon me with a certain suddenness that I was different from the others," he writes, "shut out from their world by a vast veil."

Existence within this veil gives the Negro one advantage, though. Comparing it to the "caul" which marks a newborn baby as having second sight, Du Bois says that this removal from the mainstream of American society gives the Negro truer sight, a perspective that reveals its flaws. The veil is more hindrance than benefit, though; so much so that when Du Bois's baby son dies, he writes that his grief is mixed with relief: "The Veil, though it shadowed him, had not yet darkened half his sun. . . . Fool that I was to think or wish that this little soul should grow choked and deformed within the Veil." Perhaps finally despairing of seeing the Veil lifted, Du Bois—an admirer of Marx—ended his life in Ghana, after becoming an active member of the Communist party.

MAX WEBER
The Protestant Ethic and the Spirit of Capitalism
(1904)

Best translations: Stephen Kalberg's translation, published by Oxford University Press, rev. ed. (2010); another good translation is found in the collection The Protestant Ethic and the Spirit of Capitalism and Other Writings, *translated and edited by Peter Baehr and Gordon C. Wells, Penguin 20th Century Classics (2002).*

Weber's argument—that the Calvinist Protestantism of America's Puritan settlers was a foundation for capitalism—rests on a theological syllogism. In Calvinism, the saved are not brought into the kingdom of God by their own efforts, since all men by nature are helpless to do anything good (or even turn to God on their own). Instead, some are "elect," chosen by God out of his good favor and grace. Because this choice of salvation (or damnation) belongs to God's secret councils, no man can presume to know who is elect and who isn't. But since man without God is capable of nothing good, those who do plenty of good works and display God's blessing on their lives prove to others—and to themselves—that they belong to the elect. This, Weber says, produces a strong psychological drive to work, work, work, as a way of self-assurance (after all, no one wants to be damned).

Weber appends to this the theological concept of the "calling," which he sees as unique to Protestantism: The highest kind of life was *not* renunciation of the world and withdrawal to a monastery, but rather excellence and achievement within the world, in whatever place God has "called" you to. For the Calvinist, Weber writes, the "elected Christian is in the world only to increase this glory of God by fulfilling His commandments to the best of his ability. . . . The span of human life is infinitely short and precious to make sure of one's own election. Loss of time through sociability, idle talk, luxury, even more sleep than is necessary for health . . . is worthy of absolute moral condemnation. . . . Thus inactive contemplation is also valueless, or even directly reprehensible if it is at the expense of one's daily work. For it is less pleasing to God than the active performance of His will in a calling."

This valuing of every moment of time helped to support Western "rationalization": a commitment to the most efficient methods of accomplishing every task in politics, economics, and daily life. Rational activity wastes no time. And the most certain way to advance in a Western capitalistic society is to adopt rational methods—to become more efficient. Advancing becomes not only economically necessary but philosophically essential, since the acquisition of goods becomes a mark of God's favor.

Leisurely work, or remaining in the same stratum of society to which you were born, becomes a mark of failure—and possibly of damnation. "The religious valuation of restless, continuous, systematic work in a worldly calling," Weber concludes, "as the highest means of asceticism, and at the same time the surest and most evident proof of rebirth and genuine faith, must have been the most powerful conceivable lever for the expansion of . . . the spirit of capitalism."

LYTTON STRACHEY
Queen Victoria
(1921)

Best edition: Mariner Books (2002).

In *Queen Victoria*, Strachey portrays a middle-class housewife who happens to sit on a throne. "Discretion is not the better part of biography," Strachey once said, but his portrait of Victoria is adulatory. Despite a hot temper, the child Victoria was "very truthful; whatever punishment might follow, she never told a lie," and her governess Fräulein Lehzen made sure that she was taught "the virtues of simplicity, regularity, propriety, and devotion. The little girl, however, was really in small need of such lessons, for she was naturally simple and orderly, she was pious without difficulty, and her sense of propriety was keen." As queen, Victoria was devoted to "unremitting industry" and with the help of her consort, Prince Albert (who showed "indefatigable perseverance" in opening museums, founding hospitals, collecting art, and making speeches to the Royal Agricultural Society) toiled unceasingly for her country. She grew to be "very short, rather stout, quite plain," and dressed "in garish middle-class garments." To the end of her life, Strachey writes, she was accessible to her people, who "felt instinctively Victoria's irresistible sincerity . . . vitality, conscientiousness, pride, and simplicity." These middle-class virtues, not brilliance or political acumen (or any of the virtues ascribed to Renaissance rulers), made Victoria a good queen; she was an ordinary person, not a monarch claiming divine power and authority.

Furthermore, Victoria—even though a queen—shows herself to be such a perfect Victorian *woman*: adoring wife, mother of a large brood (nine children), occasionally irrational and never intellectual. As a girl, Strachey's Victoria does make an effort to break from this mold; she announces that she will never marry, and her expression moves from "ingenuous and serene" to "bold and discontented." Fortunately, though, she falls in love with her cousin Albert, marries him, and becomes truly feminine. She is happiest when she is living a quiet domestic life at her country house, Balmoral; Albert, the more intelligent of the two, arranges her papers and duties for her, while "Victoria, treasuring [his] every word, preserving every letter" is "all breathless attention and eager obedience." She is a woman, and Strachey loves her because she doesn't commit the impertinence of being a prince.

GEORGE ORWELL
The Road to Wigan Pier
(1937)

Best edition: Mariner Books (1972).

Orwell's project began as a documentary report; he was asked by the board of editors of the Left Book Club (devoted, according to its own literature, to "the terribly urgent struggle *for* World Peace & a better social & economic order & *against* Facism") to write about the daily lives of the unemployed in the north of England. Orwell traveled north and documented the lives of both the unemployed and the working poor. His descriptions of daily life are unstintingly realistic, detailing both the squalor of the working poor ("Sink in living room. Plaster cracking and coming off walls. No shelves in oven. Gas leaking slightly. . . . Bugs, but 'I keeps 'em down with sheep dip' ") and the psychology of poverty ("The basis of their diet, therefore, is white bread and margarine, corned beef, sugared tea, and potatoes. . . . Would it not be better if they spent more money on wholesome things like oranges and wholemeal bread? . . . Yes, it would, but the point is that no ordinary human being is ever going to do such a thing. . . . When you are . . . underfed, harassed, bored, and miserable, you don't *want* to eat dull wholesome food. You want something a little bit 'tasty' ").

So what is to be done about this poverty? In Orwell's view, English socialism hasn't managed to bring reform because it is divided from within. English socialists are alienated from the proletariat, which they theoretically support, by a gap of culture and manners. When a white-collar Englishman becomes a socialist, Orwell writes, he remains "vastly more at home with a member of his own class, who thinks him a dangerous Bolshi, than with a member of the working class who supposedly agrees with him; his tastes in food, wine, clothes, books, pictures, music, ballet, are still recognisably bourgeois tastes. . . . He idealises the proletariat, but . . . he is still responding to the training of his childhood, when he was taught to hate, fear, and despise the working classes." Furthermore,

Orwell adds, those white-collar workers who *do* belong to the proletariat don't recognize it; they think of themselves as middle-class. He asks, "How many of the wretched shivering army of clerks and shopwalkers, who in some ways are actually worse off than a miner or a dock-hand, think of themselves as proletarians? A proletarian—so they have been taught to think—means a man without a collar. So that when you try to move them by talking about 'class war,' you only succeed in scaring them; they forget their incomes and remember their accents, and fly to the defense of the class that is exploiting them." English socialists, Orwell concludes, must learn how to explain the exact ways in which English workers are exploited, rather than simply borrowing rhetoric from the communists: "[T]he essential point here is that all people with small, insecure incomes are in the same boat and ought to be fighting on the same side."

PERRY MILLER
The New England Mind
(1939)

Best edition: The reprint edition breaks this work into two volumes, both published by Belknap Press (1983): Volume I, The New England Mind: The Seventeenth Century, *and* Volume II, The New England Mind: From Colony to Province. *You can choose to read only the first volume if you prefer, although both are fascinating.*

Like Max Weber, Perry Miller writes about the intersection of Puritan theology with the new American project. Unlike Weber, Miller is not particularly concerned with economics; he is an "intellectual historian," meaning that he focuses on ideas and how they change *actions*. For Miller, the central idea in Puritan New England is the covenant between God and man. Since God chooses to "elect" only on the basis of his sovereign will, his grace is unpredictable. Puritan piety was thus full of doubt over whether or not believers have truly been selected, despair over sin, and anguish over God's inscrutability—which the Puritans managed to contain by constructing a logical and entirely reasonable set of doctrines. In the doctrine of the covenant, men can be sure of salvation because God has entered into an unbreakable agreement with them.

This covenant between God and man became the model for Puritan society generally; as Miller writes, covenant theology "was of tremendous value to the leaders of Massachusetts, not only in the realm of faith and personal conduct, but just as much in the realm of politics and society."

Miller describes how Puritans entered into church membership by publicly testifying about their experience of grace. This membership was itself a covenant entered into by a sacred oath, and this covenant granted full citizenship in the civil community to each member who entered it. The children of church members were admitted provisionally; as they came of age, they too had to enter the covenant through testifying about their experience of grace. But although the first generations of Puritans were scrupulous in pursuing membership, fewer and fewer children applied for full membership. Concerned at this decline—which affected both community and church—the Puritan leaders instituted the Halfway Covenant, which allowed provisional members to be baptized into church membership and to be full citizens—although not to take part in the central sacrament of the church, the Lord's Supper.

In Miller's history, this Halfway Covenant and the developments that followed it (a later Puritan divine even opened the Lord's Supper to those who had not made a profession) indicate a decline in piety—a secularization, a diminishing of the concern with God's approval. The Puritan "city on a hill," the place where God's kingdom on earth had finally found a place to settle, began to crumble from within; doctrinal agreement ("the first three generations in New England paid almost unbroken allegiance to a uniform body of thought") gave way to disagreement and fracture. "Compared with the founding generation," Miller writes, "there had been a notable falling off and lessening of zeal." Although recent scholars of Puritanism have taken issue with this fairly simple pious-to-indifferent story of declension, Miller has remained the single most influential Puritan historian of the twentieth century.

JOHN KENNETH GALBRAITH
The Great Crash 1929
(1955)

Best edition: The Mariner Books reprint edition (2009).

Galbraith wrote his history in 1954 and revised it twice afterward; the later editions reflect on developments in the 1970s and afterward that seem to echo those of the 1920s. In his preface, Galbraith writes that, although the story of the Great Crash is worth telling "for its own sake," he also has a "more somber purpose. As a protection against financial illusion or insanity, memory is far better than law." Galbraith's purpose is a moral one, then, or at least a social one: He aims to preserve culture through creating a common agreement among its members, rather than legislating from the top down. "For protecting people from the cupidity of others and their own," he concludes, "history is highly utilitarian. It sustains memory and memory serves the same purpose as the SEC and, on the record, is far more effective."

Galbraith's lively history of the Great Crash centers around the year before the crash, when interest in the stock market swelled and then crested. Although he pays a certain attention to purely economic factors, his main interest lies in the characters who acted in the drama; the crash is rooted in their motivations. In 1928, Galbraith writes, the American people were "displaying an inordinate desire to get rich quickly with a minimum of physical effort." To do so, they bought shares in companies that had been formed for the sole purpose of buying shares in other companies. They put blind trust into financial experts who boasted of their "professional financial knowledge, skill, and manipulative ability." "One might make money investing directly in Radio, J. I. Case, or Montgomery Ward," Galbraith writes, "but how much safer and wise to let it be accomplished by the men of peculiar knowledge, and wisdom." Objectivity is not Galbraith's aim; "fiscal incest" is the least provocative term he uses for the advice given by these experts, who relied on a "hocus pocus of lines and areas on a chart," and he has none too high an opinion of the investors who bought into their advice either. They were willing to be convinced, he suggests, because they simply wanted to be rich; and as the stock markets nosedived, experts and investors alike were willing to deceive themselves: "If one has been a financial genius," he concludes, "faith in one's genius does not dissolve at once. To the battered but unbowed genius, support of the stock of one's own company still seemed a bold, imaginative, and effective course. . . . They bought their own worthless stock. Men have been swindled by other men on many occasions. The autumn of 1929 was, perhaps, the first occasion when men succeeded on a large scale in swindling themselves."

CORNELIUS RYAN
The Longest Day
(1959)

Best edition: The Simon & Schuster reprint edition (1994).

Ryan's account of D-Day uses the techniques of microhistory—the close examination of one part of history in an attempt to illuminate the whole.

The Longest Day aims to illuminate World War II through a detailed and scrupulous recounting of the events of June 6, 1944. (The book was also made into a John Wayne movie in 1962.) Ryan, a war correspondent who also flew bombing missions with the U.S. Air Force, examines events on both sides with a reporter's eye: "In the ground-floor room he used as an office," Chapter 2 begins, "Rommel was alone. He sat behind a massive Renaissance desk, working by the light of a single desk lamp." Later, we meet Eisenhower, struggling to decide whether or not to invade on June 6: "The American who had to make that great decision wrestled with the problem and tried to relax. . . . Eisenhower's trailer, a long low caravan somewhat resembling a moving van, had three small compartments serving as bedroom, living room, and study." Ryan maintains this same calm, detailed tone as he describes the wave of invasions on the beaches on D-Day: "Caught by a sudden swell, the craft swerved sideways, lifted and crashed down on a series of mined steel triangles. Jones saw it explode with a shattering blast. It reminded him of a 'slowmotion cartoon—the men, standing to attention, shot up into the air as though lifted by a water spout. . . . [A]t the top of the spout bodies and parts of bodies spread like drops of water.'" He widens his point of view only occasionally, as in the book's final paragraph: "Soon this most occupied of all French villages would be free—as would the whole of Hitler's Europe. From this day on the Third Reich had less than one year to live." But even here, Ryan returns almost at once to his narrower focus; the paragraph concludes, "In the Church of St. Samson the bell tolled midnight."

Ryan used 383 oral interviews to construct his soldier's-eye view of D-Day, but an academic historian would find the result to be less than pure "microhistory." Although Ryan does focus on the experiences of individual soldiers on June 6, he places their stories within a preexisting understanding of D-Day and its place in the whole war, which he constructed not from soldiers' stories, but from more traditional sources. In an interview about his technique, Ryan remarked that he used the oral interviews "to place the individual into the overall significance of the big picture"[26] whereas a "professional" historian would have allowed the oral interviews to determine the shape of the whole.

[26]Quoted in Roger Horowitz, "Oral History and the Story of America and World War II," *Journal of American History*, vol. 82, no. 2 (September 1995): 617–24.

BETTY FRIEDAN
The Feminine Mystique
(1963)

Best edition: The 50th Anniversary Edition was published in 2013 (W. W. Norton), with an introduction by Gail Collins and an afterword by Anna Quindlen. Read the text itself before you read either.

Friedan describes an American world ruled by the "feminine mystique," the powerful idea that "truly feminine women do not want careers, higher education, political rights. . . . All they had to do was devote their lives from earliest girlhood to finding a husband and bearing children." She echoes the complaints of Mary Wollstonecraft, but she doesn't picture women as imprisoned in the home for the last three hundred years. Rather, she writes, "old-fashioned feminists" were making progress until the 1950s, when something strange happened: Women began to go backward. The average marriage age dropped. The proportion of women attending college dropped. Women "who had once wanted careers were now making careers out of having babies." And these women tried to accept home and family as the fulfillment of all their dreams, stifling their longing for wider horizons: "If a woman had a problem in the 1950s and 1960s, she knew that something must be wrong with her marriage, or with herself. . . . What kind of woman was she if she did not feel this mysterious fulfillment waxing the kitchen floor?" To build this picture of housewives trying to be content as they slowly wither away, Friedan depends on interviews (*The Feminine Mystique* began as a questionnaire to Friedan's Smith classmates) and women's magazines. "The image of woman that emerges from this big, pretty magazine," she writes, after examining the table of contents for a 1960s issue of *McCall's*, "is young and frivolous, almost childlike; fluffy and feminine; passive; gaily content in a world of bedroom and kitchen, sex, babies, and home. . . . Where is the world of thought and ideas, the life of the mind and spirit?"

Friedan offers an explanation which is partly social (after the war, women magazine writers went back home, "started having a lot of children, and stopped writing," while "men, back from the war, who had been dreaming about home, and a cozy domestic life" took over the media), partly Freudian (American culture accepted Freud's description of women as "childlike dolls, who existed . . . to love man and serve his needs"), and partly economic ("[T]he really important role that women serve as housewives is *to buy more things for the house.* . . . [T]he perpetuation of housewifery, the growth of the feminine mystique, makes sense (and dollars) when one realizes that women are the chief customers of American business. Somehow, somewhere, someone must have figured out that women will buy more things if they are kept in the underused, nameless-yearning, energy-to-get-rid-of state of being housewives"). Friedan's conclusions are as energetic and convincing as her methods are flawed: Who *is* that "someone" who figured out that women must buy, and what were black, Hispanic, and working-class women doing while Friedan's white suburban housewives languished in their plush houses? But Friedan, like Thomas Paine, is more evangelist than historian; she too has a revolution in mind. "When enough women make life plans geared to their real abilities," she concludes, "[they] can fulfill a commitment to profession and politics, and to marriage and motherhood with equal seriousness."

EUGENE D. GENOVESE
Roll, Jordan, Roll: The World the Slaves Made
(1974)

Best edition: The Vintage Books paperback (1976).

In his groundbreaking work of African American history, Genovese argues that the history of slavery cannot be understood unless slaves and masters are seen as interdependent: Slaves shaped the world of the whites just as surely as whites shaped the world of the blacks. He rejects the widely accepted idea that slavery rendered the slaves completely dependent, defenseless, and without family relationships. Instead, Africans in slavery developed their own customs, their own *world*; this "separate black national culture" formed as the slaves "struggled to survive spiritually as well as physically—to make a livable world for themselves and their children within the narrowest living space and harshest adversity." Genovese's new emphasis on slave "agency" (the power to resist) put a revolutionary spin on the independence and strength of slaves, who were no longer viewed as passive victims. Slave religion is a prime example of the African American ability to resist white control: Although white Christianity told slaves to obey their masters, the slaves developed their own unique, particular form of Christianity, which instead emphasized God's vengeance on oppressors and the promise of freedom after death.

But Genovese doesn't fall into a simplistic analysis of slaves as directing their own destinies—or of masters as entirely evil. He argues instead that whites and blacks were "organically" related. Slaves and masters changed each other's worlds in a relationship based on paternalism: White plantation owners acted as "authoritarian fathers who presided over an extended and subservient family, white and black." This paternalism mixed evil and good. It "brought white and black together and welded them into one people with genuine elements of affection and intimacy"; it obliged whites to care for their slaves out of a "strong sense of duty and responsibility," but also allowed them to treat them with cruelty and hatred. Paternalism led blacks to serve their masters out of genuine obligation and affection, but also warped them so that they accepted white authority over blacks as somehow natural. The role of the plantation mammy is, for Genovese, emblematic of this complicated relationship: "To understand her is to move toward understanding the tragedy of plantation paternalism. . . . Primarily, the Mammy raised the white children and ran the Big House either as the mistress's executive officer or her *de facto* superior. . . . In general, she gave the whites the perfect slave—a loyal, faithful, contented, efficient, conscientious member of the family who always knew her place; and she gave the slaves a white-approved standard of black behavior. She also had to be a tough, worldly-wise, enormously resourceful woman." And yet, in wielding this power, she became dependent on her white "family," unable to establish authority among her own people. Genovese's refusal to trace simple oppressor-oppressed relationships acknowledges the slaves' power and independent culture, even as he refuses to gloss over the horrors of slavery.

BARBARA TUCHMAN
A Distant Mirror: The Calamitous Fourteenth Century
(1978)

Best edition: The Random House paperback reprint (1987).

Tuchman's study of the fourteenth century assembles the century's details into a pattern that resembles our own: "After the experiences of the terrible twentieth century," she writes in her preface, "we have greater fellow-feeling for a distraught age whose rules were breaking down under the pressure of adverse and violent events. We recognize with a painful twinge the marks of a period of anguish when there is no sense of an assured future." She examines this fourteenth-century "period of anguish" from the point of view of Enguerrand de Coucy VII, a minor nobleman who advised two French kings and married an English princess.

Tuchman illustrates the decline of chivalry, in which the knights, who were supposed to protect the weak, became a tyrannical class in their own right. She rejects any romantic ideas of a pastel-colored knights-and-ladies society, instead describing late-night drinking sessions in castle halls as late-medieval biker-bar brawls in which knights groped ladies, insulted them, and scuffled with angry husbands. She describes Christianity's power over every aspect of daily life ("Christianity was the matrix of medieval life: even cooking instructions called for boiling an egg 'during the length of time wherein you say a Miserere'"), but is pessimistic about its ability to bring peace or virtue ("The Church, more worldly than spiritual, did not guide the way to God"). She tells of the Black Death, but finds this only to be one disaster in a time that was "a succession of wayward dangers; of the three galloping evils, plague, and taxes; of fierce and tragic conflicts, bizarre fates, capricious money, sorcery, betrayals, insurrections, murder, madness, and the downfall of princes; of dwindling labor for the fields, of cleared land reverting to waste; and always the recurring black shadow of pestilence carrying its message of guilt and sin and the hostility of God."

Tuchman is more interested in politics than in ideas, and her history focuses on the complicated (and ultimately destructive) attempts of the English and French to make peace while simultaneously stealing each other's land, rather than the development of philosophy and science. She details the lives of the warrior class, but doesn't pay much attention to the peasants; her concern instead is to describe a time of political crisis and disorder, in which English invasions, French weakness, predatory knights, and corrupt clergy shaped the course of events. In describing the violence and unrest of the fourteenth century, and in comparing it to our own times, Tuchman is arguing for a certain historical uniformity, rejecting both a simple "progress-ism" (which would see the twentieth century as naturally better than the fourteenth) and a pessimistic sense of decline (which would view the twentieth century as spiraling downward into unheard-of dangers).

BOB WOODWARD AND CARL BERNSTEIN
All the President's Men
(1987)

Best edition: Simon & Schuster reissue edition, 2014.

Woodward and Bernstein's book on Watergate is based on the reports they filed with the *Washington Post*, news stories that played a large part in Nixon's eventual resignation. In a twist that postmodernists might applaud, *All the President's Men* keeps its writers in full view; it begins not with Nixon or with any of the president's men, but with Woodward.

"June 17, 1972. Nine o'clock Saturday morning. Early for the telephone. Woodward fumbled for the receiver and snapped awake. The city editor of the *Washington Post* was on the line. Five men had been arrested earlier that morning in a burglary at Democratic headquarters, carrying photographic equipment and electronic gear. Could he come in?"

The history of Watergate is one of slow discovery by the American people of high-level misdeeds. In their slowly unfolding chronicle, Woodward and Bernstein stand in for "typical Americans," understanding a complicated and disgraceful sequence of events one tiny fragment at a time. The style is immediate and unadorned: "Woodward told Stoner that the *Post* had a responsibility to correct an error. No comment. If an apology was called for, it would be given. No comment. Woodward raised his voice to impress on Stoner how serious it was when a newspaper made a mistake. Finally, Stoner said he wouldn't recommend making any apology to Bob Haldeman." That prose won't win any awards, but it matches the purpose of the book: to uncover, as clearly and nonsensationally as possible, the "truth."

All the President's Men begins with the Watergate break-in and ends with the indictments of the president's men. Its last paragraph recounts the president's speech to the American people on January 30, 1974: "The President said, 'I want you to know that I have no intention whatever of ever walking away from the job that the American people elected me to do for the people of the United States.'" *All the President's Men* was completed in 1974 and came out just before Nixon's resignation on August 9, 1974; it is thus not only a history of the break-in and its investigation, but part of history itself. (You can still read the original Woodward-Bernstein story on the break-in, published in the *Washington Post* on June 19, 1972, online at the *Washington Post* website.)

JAMES M. McPHERSON
Battle Cry of Freedom: The Civil War Era
(1988)

Best edition: The Oxford University Press trade paperback reprint (2003); originally published as a stand-alone volume, McPherson's text has now been incorporated into the Oxford History of the United States series.

"Both sides in the American Civil War professed to be fighting for freedom," McPherson's preface begins—thus summing up the difficulty of "compressing[ing] the war and its causes into a single volume." Faced with a South that claimed to be taking up arms to protect "political rights . . .

and State sovereignty" and a North that insisted it was fighting to preserve the "last, best hope . . . of republican freedoms in the world," McPherson sets out to balance political and military events (and rhetoric) with the social and economic developments that helped to fuel the war.

McPherson's initial chapter surveys the condition of the United States at mid-century: its unrestrained growth, especially in the West; the state of the southern economy, including its dependence on cotton and on the low-cost slave labor that made cotton production economically feasible; the growing gap between rich and poor; ethnic conflict; the fast growth of urban population; the improved transportation that allowed goods to be sold far away from their point of manufacture; labor protests; and the evolution of the "child-centered nurturing family." These widely varied descriptions all set the stage for McPherson's narrative of the Civil War, which begins in Chapter 2 with James K. Polk's presidency and the spark that ignited the war: the argument over whether, in this rapidly expanding United States, the new territories admitted to the Union would be slave-holding or free. From this point on, McPherson unfolds a detailed military and social history of the Civil War. He is careful to outline all the groups that took different positions on the war, avoiding lumping all Union or all Confederate sympathizers together.

McPherson's achievement lies, not in a particularly unique or startling take on the Civil War, but on his ability to pull together into one coherent whole the bewilderingly varied details of the war and the unendingly disparate theories on how and why the war progressed as it did. McPherson's story ends with the Union victory, which "destroyed the southern vision of America and ensured that the northern vision would become the American vision." But in this new America, many problems remain. McPherson's history ends with a question: "What would be the place of freed slaves and their descendants in this new order?"

LAUREL THATCHER ULRICH
*A Midwife's Tale: The Life of Martha Ballard,
Based on Her Diary, 1785–1812*
(1990)

Best edition: The Vintage Books paperback (1991).

The narrow subtitle of Ulrich's history points out a new direction in history: the study of the individual, the small, and the particular. Perry Miller could write about all of New England; sixty years later, Ulrich focuses on one woman, one diary, and a span of time that covers one generation.

Although Martha Ballard's diary hints at larger social developments—
for example, the encroachment of professionally trained male doctors on
obstetrics, formerly the province of midwives and nurse practitioners—
Ulrich is very careful not to draw sweeping conclusions. Her method is
to examine the past for particularity, not for universality; to highlight the
unique, not to look for connections. This discomfort with generalizations
reflects a postmodern distrust of truth that applies to all social classes, as
well as Ulrich's discontent with "traditional" sources of history. "Martha Ballard's diary," she writes, in her introduction, "connects to several
prominent themes in the social history of the early Republic"—but it is
essentially *different* from those records left by men in positions of power.
The diary restores "a lost substructure of eighteenth-century life" and
"transforms the nature of the evidence upon which much of the history
of the period has been written." For example, when Ephraim Ballard,
Martha's husband, goes to debtor's prison, Martha runs out of wood. This
problem aggravates her tense relationship with her older son, on whom
she is now forced to rely—the "axis of her life," Ulrich writes, has been
"tipped" toward her son. Martha's relationship with her son and her son's
wife, who eventually decide to take over the family home and relegate
Martha to a single bedroom, becomes increasingly difficult, producing in
Martha's diary a "peculiar mixture of self-righteousness and self-sacrifice,"
in which Martha continues to cook for her son's family while refusing to
ask him to gather wood. "Most historians have studied imprisonment for
debt as an aspect of economic and legal history," Ulrich writes. "Martha's
diary shifts the focus from mortgages and lawyers to wood boxes and sons,
showing how family history shaped patterns of imprisonment in an era of
political and social transformation."

These "forgotten" family records tell a history that sometimes comple-
ments and sometimes contradicts the traditional histories of the period.
This new focus is highlighted in Ulrich's conclusion, where she writes,
"To celebrate such a life is to acknowledge the power—and the poverty—
of written records. Outside her own diary, Martha has no history. . . . It is
her husband's name, not hers, that appears in censuses, tax lists, and mer-
chant accounts for her town. . . . Without her diary even her name would
be uncertain. . . . Martha lost her given name as well as her surname at
marriage. For 58 of her 77 years, she was known as 'Mrs. Ballard.' . . . No
gravestone bears her name, though perhaps somewhere in the waste places
along Belgrade Road there still grow clumps of chamomile or feverfew
escaped from her garden."

FRANCIS FUKUYAMA
The End of History and the Last Man
(1992)

Best edition: Free Press reissue edition (2006).

Fukuyama's book, an expansion of his 1989 essay "The End of History," argues that History with a capital *H* (that is, not a sequence of events, but a "single, coherent, evolutionary process") inevitably moves toward the modern, liberal democratic, industrialized state. Modern science is at the center of this movement; it has had "a uniform effect on all societies that have experienced it" because it "makes possible the limitless accumulation of wealth, and thus the satisfaction of an ever-expanding set of human desires." Because of modern science, "all human societies, regardless of their historical origins or cultural inheritances . . . must increasingly resemble one another."

The power of science explains the modern movement toward industrialization, but not the phenomenon of spreading democracy (after all, plenty of industrialized countries have operated under other forms of government). So why is democracy also transforming the modern world? Fukuyama explains that while animals merely want food, shelter, and safety, men are driven by an additional need—the desire to be "recognized" by others as having worth and dignity. This "desire for recognition," Fukuyama argues, is what impels all societies toward democracy: Liberal democracy treats its citizens as adults, not children, "recognizing their autonomy as free individuals. Communism is being superseded by liberal democracy in our time because of the realization that the former provides a gravely defective form of recognition." He spends a great deal of time defining and illustrating this "desire for recognition," which he calls *thymos*, and discussing how it interacts with love of country, nationalism, ethnicity, religion, and other "irrational" (by which he means "unsystematized," not "ridiculous") desires of the human soul. Finally, he asks: Is the liberal democratic state truly the *end*—the highest goal—of history? Does it "adequately satisfy the desire for recognition," or would a better, future form of society satisfy this desire in a more thorough manner?

By the end of his final section, "The Last Man," Fukuyama has concluded that liberal democracy is the "best possible solution to the human problem." And since the move toward liberal democracy is strengthened by "the homogenization of mankind . . . as a result of economic development," soon humanity will appear, not like "a thousand shoots blossoming into as many different flowering plants," but rather like "a long wagon train strung out along a road"—some "pulling into town sharply and crisply" (having arrived at the blessing of democracy), some stuck in the mud along the way, and some "attacked by Indians . . . set aflame and abandoned along the way." Which are these failed societies (and who the Indians might be) is left for the reader to decide; in a style of historical writing diametrically opposed to that of Ulrich, Fukuyama describes a Hegelian history that rolls on toward a glorious end, with historical details submerged in the swelling tide of fulfillment.

Chapter 8

The World Stage:
Reading through History with Drama

To *read* a play is a contradiction in terms. . . . Plays are to be seen and heard and responded to as one responds to a rite or a spectacle. They cannot be simply *read*, as one reads a novel.
—EDWARD PARTRIDGE, critic

Plays are literature and exist as complete experiences on a page, and are not *made* a complete experience in performance. Reading a play . . . is as thrilling an experience as seeing it.
—EDWARD ALBEE, playwright

A comfortable room, tastefully but not expensively furnished. Upstage right, a door leading into the hall, upstage left, a door leading to Helmer's study.

"The cold passed reluctantly from the earth, and the retiring fogs revealed an army stretched out on the hills, resting."

These opening lines, written within two years of each other, affect the reader differently. The comfortable room, tastefully but not expensively furnished, appeals to the eye but to no other sense; it is a blank background, ready to contain any event from murder to marriage. But the second landscape reveals not just a physical place, but also a mood and an expectation. The scene is one of malingering, of reluctance, of slow revelation; the fog rises only grudgingly from the ground, and the stretched-out army, like a dragon, might at any moment wake up, rise, and scorch the ground.

The first opening lines—from *A Doll's House*, written in 1897—are those of a play by Henrik Ibsen; the second opening lines belong to Stephen Crane's short novel *The Red Badge of Courage*, published in 1895. The play and the novel have a certain family likeness: Both move characters through a scenario. Both use dialogue to advance the plot and develop the characters. Both deal with the same basic conflict: Crane's hero discovers his manhood, Ibsen's Nora realizes that her femininity imprisons her. And both stand at the same historical point in the development of storytelling; Ibsen and Crane are both realists, writing lifelike accounts of a point of psychological transition in a character's life.

Yet the two stories are very different. Like novels, autobiographies, and histories, plays follow the same basic trajectory we've already traced three times: from an ancient fascination with heroism and fate and a medieval preoccupation with the plan of God, through a Renaissance interest in humanity's limitless quest for knowledge and an Enlightenment conviction in the power of reason, to a modern preoccupation with realistic, "scientific" explanations, and a postmodern disgust with that same scientific obsession. But plays and novels cannot be read in the same way. Crane the novelist provides you with every impression he wants you to have; Ibsen the playwright supplies only one dimension of his story. He must leave sight, sound, mood, and expectation in the hands of the directors, lighting technicians, scene designers, costumers, and actors who will put *A Doll's House* on stage.

The stage imposes other restrictions on the stories told by plays. Novels can sprawl across vast landscapes; plays must fit on stage and within an audience's attention span. Novels wander into the pathways of the characters' minds; plays tell you what characters say and do, not who they are. The subject of the play is not the life of the mind, but human action. Even patterns of speech change, from page to stage. As the novelist Joyce Carol Oates writes, "What shimmers with life on the page may die within minutes in the theater . . . prose is a language to be spoken to an individual, recreated in an individual reader's consciousness, usually in solitude, while dramatic dialogue is a special language spoken by living actors to one another, a collective audience overhearing."[1]

The dialogue found in a novel echoes only in the mind of the individual reader, who recreates it in private. The dialogue of a play is heard in the company of a crowd of listeners—and as any teacher will tell you, a crowd of listeners has a weird, unpredictable personality of its own. What's more, the playwright has no control over the presentation of the story to that crowd. The novelist keeps watch over sentences, shaping and polishing them in the knowledge that every reader will read the same words. But the words of a play are mediated by (at least) two separate sets of people: the director who stages and interprets the play, perhaps even cutting it into a

---

[1] Joyce Carol Oates, "Plays as Literature," *Conjunctions*, vol. 25 (Spring 1995): 8–13; 9.

different final form, and the actors who lend their own faces and personalities to the characters. A play is the polar opposite of autobiography: Autobiography takes what is private and controls it by shaping it into an acceptable form before allowing a reader to peep at it; the play gives itself to unknown handlers, trusting them with the job of setting it before its audience.

If the play is such a collaboration, why bother to *read* it?

Because *you* can act as director, allowing the play to take shape in your mind. Think for a moment of *Hamlet*. Hamlet, the prince of Denmark, is preoccupied (haunted, we might even say) by his father's recent death. "I see my father," he muses to his friend Horatio, referring to his memories of the dead king. But Horatio, unknown to Hamlet, has already seen the ghost of Hamlet's father stalking around the battlements, and he wheels around to look for the specter: "Where, my lord?" "In my mind's eye," Hamlet snaps, thinking this to be self-evident.

Hamlet's father may have a poignant existence in his son's mind, but Hamlet doesn't do anything about his father's death until the ghost makes a visible, on-stage appearance to him as well. Only then is Hamlet spurred to take action. And this action leads, ultimately, to the death of everyone he loves (not to mention several unfortunate bystanders). If Hamlet had been able to exercise his imagination a little more competently, drawing his own conclusions from his father's haunting presence in his memory, the ghost's appearance (and all of the deaths that unspool from this physical manifestation) wouldn't have been necessary. But once the ghost appears in a particular form—once Hamlet's idea of his father is forced by necessity to "take flesh," once the ghost issues final orders to his son—a chain of particular events is set into motion and can't be stopped.

What's the lesson for the reader? Once staged, a play takes on an irrevocable reality, an inevitable outcome imposed on it from without. But while it is still in a reader's mind, subject only to her imagination, it is full of limitless potential; it is richer than any staged version.

More than any other form of literature, the play is placebound. It is designed to be performed on a stage, so it is shaped by the possibilities and limits of staging which the playwright has in his mind as he writes. And the play is written not for the world, but for a particular, local audience (one way in which the "play proper" differs from the movie or TV script). Greek comedies were written for Athenians; medieval morality plays for illiterate churchgoers; English comedies of the Restoration for upper-middle-class Londoners; modern plays for Broadway or Chicago or London. Although these plays can speak to a much wider audience, they draw their form from the conventions that local audiences understand.

Shakespeare wrote his tragedies with the restless groundlings in the pit in mind, knowing that they might hurl things at the stage if they weren't entertained with "low humor" between noble soliloquies. This changed the final form of his plays.

Since the development of drama is so intensely affected by local theaters, local histories, local customs, and local dilemmas, the only way to write a decent "history of the drama" would be to treat each country and tradition separately. Each country has its own ancient plays and rituals, its own path into postmodern times. So the brief theatrical history that follows is focused on one particular part of the world: the English-speaking part. Ancient Greek dramas and European plays in translation do appear, but primarily because of their influence on English-language playwrights; I could not do justice to German expressionism, Russian symbolism, and French absurdism without covering German, Russian, and French history (which would require, among other things, better fluency in German, Russian, and French than I possess).[2]

A FIVE-ACT HISTORY OF THE PLAY

Act I: The Greeks

Aeschylus, Sophocles, Euripides, Aristophanes, Aristotle

Women and men have probably acted out stories for thousands of years (a whole subfield of cultural anthropology has grown up around the play-like rituals of ancient cultures), but the earliest written plays come from ancient Greece. The first Greek playwright was a poet named Thespis, who lent his name to the entire theatrical enterprise. In the early days of Greek drama, poets usually recited their works alone on stage. Thespis appears to have introduced the innovation of a chorus that sang, danced, and spoke dialogue with him in a back-and-forth interchange. Since all of Thespis's plays have disappeared, it's impossible to be sure of this, but the "chorus"—a "group character" that converses with the plays' heroes—appears in all later Greek drama.

The great Greek playwrights who followed Thespis composed their

---

[2]Readers who are interested in investigating these traditions could consult a complete theater history as a starting place. *History of the Theatre*, 8th ed., by Oscar Brockett (Boston: Allyn & Bacon, 1998), is a standard text; the paperback *Oxford Illustrated History of the Theatre*, edited by John Russell Brown (Oxford: Oxford University Press, 2001), is a briefer, more affordable history.

plays for enormous outdoor stadiums that held as many as twenty thousand spectators; the plays were performed at festivals where the actors began at dawn and shouted out their lines for hours, and where the audience was likely to spend the intervals between plays feasting (and drinking). In such a setting, acting was not a matter of conveying emotion by a turn of the head, an expression, or a graceful gesture. The spectators were too far away (and probably too intoxicated) for subtleties.

Instead, the actors wore heavy masks, each expressing a single emotion, and relied on their speeches to carry the play forward. Special effects were limited; the most elaborate visual effect was provided by a crane that creakingly lowered an actor playing Zeus or Apollo to the stage (thus the phrase *deus ex machina*, "god from the machine," to describe the unexpected appearance of a deity). The most elaborate actions—sea battles, earthquakes, stabbing deaths, and boiling children—tended to happen out of sight of the audience, with the Chorus (a group of fifteen or so men, picked months ahead of time and given special training in singing, dancing, and physical fitness) describing the action as it peered offstage.

Given the setting, the Greek plays were constructed as spectator sports: They retold mythological stories in a familiar form, so that the audience already knew what events to expect and when to expect them. A Greek play typically had five parts (which later served as the model for the traditional five-act English play); the *prologue*, during which the audience hears about the "backstory" of the play; the *parados*, the entry of the Chorus during which it chants or sings an introduction to the action that will follow; the *episodes*, which consist of several different "scenes" between the play's main characters; the *interludes*, which come between the scenes, indicating a change in action or in place, and which consist of recited commentary or explanation (these *interludes* might have required the Chorus to move from one side of the stage to the other, in a ritualized progression known as *strophe* and *antistrophe)*; and finally the *exodus*, the last climactic scene. As the episodes built toward the exodus, the spectators would follow along, waiting for the moment of crisis and the denouement, or resolution, that came after. The whole process required sympathy with the play's hero, something like the emotion found in a football stadium during a home game; ancient Greek drama, with its arena performances, its ritualized costumes and victory gestures, and its demand for audience empathy, probably resembled the Super Bowl more than it did a modern-day Broadway production.

Aristotle, who followed the great Greek dramatists in time, codified their conventions into law in his *Poetics*. The purpose of the play, Aristotle writes, is *mimesis*—an imitation of life that grants the viewer greater understanding of the truths of existence. To be effective, this mimesis should be tightly focused on a narrow section of life; thus every play should have three "unities." Unity of time decrees that a play should take place during "a single circuit of the sun" (centered on the moment of highest significance, in other words, rather than on an entire life); unity of action means that the play should focus all of its events around a single great event or theme; unity of setting dictates that the action should take place, as far as possible, in a single physical place. Tragedy, the most powerful form of mimesis, is the story of a hero who is "worthy of respect (*spoudaois*) and who makes a significant intellectual (not moral) error which leads to his downfall from happiness to misery."[3] Oedipus, with the best of intentions, makes the error of trying to avoid his destiny; Agamemnon, forced to choose between two evils, picks the wrong one. Tragedy succeeds, Aristotle writes, when it evokes pity (the emotion we feel when we see undeserved evil happening to someone else) and fear (which comes when we consider that this undeserved evil might happen to us too). The implication is clear: Moral missteps are relatively easy to avoid, but even the most upright man can make an honest mistake that will lead to catastrophe: You too could be Oedipus. If the tragedy is to be mimetic, offering the watcher (or reader) greater understanding, it must contain *katharsis*—a clear explanation as to why the hero encountered disaster.[4]

Aeschylus, Sophocles, and Euripides wrote tragedies; Aristophanes wrote comedies. Comedy, depending as it does on contemporary manners and morals to set up the jarring contrasts at its center, always dates more quickly than tragedy; a joke about politics loses its kick (try watching a Jay Leno monologue from the Bill Clinton era), but the danger of wrong choices never goes away. The Romans, who came after the Greeks and stole most of their literary principles, wrote more comedies than tragedies—which is why neither the Roman playwrights nor Aristophanes are so widely read today as the Greek tragedians.

But even the tragedies of the Romans were inferior to those of the Greeks. Drama generally held a lower place in the Roman social scheme. Roman theater groups, like Greek troupes, acted at festivals. But while the

---

[3] Leon Golden, "Othello, Hamlet, and Aristotelian Tragedy," *Shakespeare Quarterly*, vol. 35, no. 2 (Summer 1984): 142–56.

[4] *Katharsis*, a word used only once in the *Poetics*, is a hotly debated term, but many scholars now agree that it refers, not to an emotional "purging" felt by the audience, but rather to the clarity that comes within the play when the reasons for the hero's fall come sharply into focus. George Whalley writes, "It is the incidents within the action itself (not the emotions of the audience) that are purified, brought into a sharp focus specific to tragedy" ("On Translating Aristotle's *Poetics*," the introductory essay to Whalley's translation of *Aristotle's Poetics* [Montréal: McGill–Queen's University Press, 1997], p. 27).

Greek festivals tended to be centered around play performance, Roman dramas had to compete with the more spectacular performances of lion fights, chariot races, and stadium sea battles. (In one of his prefaces, the tragedian Terence complains that the first two performances of his play were canceled because the audience left halfway through to go see the gladiator shows.) The Romans made no innovations in dramatic themes; these would come during the Middle Ages, when the Greek dramas had entirely slipped from view.

Act II: Mystery and Morality

Everyman

College theater-appreciation texts notwithstanding, Christianity didn't bring an end to classical drama; the barbarians who invaded Rome did. Classical drama needed physical space for its spectacles, players who could devote weeks to rehearsal and training, and spectators who had time to sit and watch. Without a leisured and prosperous population, classical drama (like professional football) had no space to exist. Acting didn't disappear, since traveling bards, wandering acrobats, and clowns wandered through England and Europe all through the Middle Ages, but the *theater* crumbled.

But just as Christianity gave history a new shape—turning the linked episodes of the Greeks into a straight line pointing toward apocalypse—so the Christian church gave drama a new physical space within which it could remake itself. The church as an institution was not particularly enthusiastic about acting as such. The wandering bards, acrobats, and clowns were known for their loose morals, and the church's bishops and theologians were suspicious of classical dramas composed in worship of Zeus, Apollo, Athena, and other "demons." But the drama itself was remarkably compatible with the Christian view of the world. After all, plays were structured around action, and Christianity was all about God's meaningful acts in history. Plays were built with a beginning, a middle, a crisis, and a resolution; Christianity found the beginnings of its story in the Garden of Eden, the middle in Israel's existence as a nation, the crisis in the Crucifixion, and the resolution in the Resurrection. And Christianity had its own classical hero in Christ-Adam, a composite figure who made the wrong intellectual choice in the Garden of Eden and suffered catastrophe on the cross. All of human history, post-Resurrection, was a *denouement*, a working out of the rippling effects of this one central event.

Furthermore, the rituals of the church were themselves theatrical, relying on a constant retelling of the Creation-Crucifixion-Resurrection tale. Church services even included dialogue. The reading of the Old Testament, the gospels, and other portions of the New Testament out loud in each service, an attempt to bring the sacred Word to a largely illiterate populace, often involved conversations between different biblical characters. Although no one knows for sure when different "actors" were assigned to the different parts of scriptural dialogue, a chanted portion of the Easter service that recounts the dialogue between the angel at the tomb and the three Marys who came to anoint Christ's body was probably dramatized first. Initially, the parts were read by different voices; eventually (perhaps) costumes and props were added. Maybe this additional entertainment tended to increase Mass attendance. We can only speculate, but we do know that other scriptural stories were soon acted out as well. These "mystery plays" ("mystery" here takes its oldest, biblical sense of something once hidden, now revealed and explained) retold the stories of Creation, the Fall, Cain and Abel, Noah's Flood, the raising of Lazarus, the Last Supper—the central scenes of the Bible, all the way through to the Last Judgment.[5]

At some point (driven, perhaps, by an increasing audience, or by the church's wish to evangelize), the drama went outside. The mystery plays moved from the center of worship to the center of village activity—the marketplace. In the process, mystery plays acquired the first corporate sponsors. The water-drawers' guild supplied the flood for the Noah's Ark mystery play while the carpenters built the Ark; the bakers' guild cooked up an elaborate Last Supper, and the goldsmiths created jewelry for the Three Kings to offer to the Christ Child. At one point, the guild use of the plays for product placement grew so shameless that the city of York put a ban on guild emblems. The "secularization" of the plays extended to attention-grabbing subplots as well; the Noah's Ark mystery play incorporates a subplot about Noah's wife and her unwillingness to enter the ark; the Second Shepherd's Play is mostly about sheep stealing, although the Christ Child makes an extremely brief appearance right at the end.

These mystery plays are not direct descendants of the Greek tragedies; their origin is entirely different. Yet there are certain lines of continuity. Like the Greek dramas, the mystery plays offer illustrations of truths about existence, not psychological studies of individual characters. Noah's wife, a medieval shrew who scolds her husband and swears by Jesus Christ, is a walking anachronism, but her place in the story illustrates God's gracious redemption of the undeserving. Mystery plays were filled with types and generalizations, designed to illustrate *qualities*, not *personalities*.

---

[5]Since evidence is scant, this is speculation. Some scholars have suggested that the mystery plays might instead have grown out of secular roots (folk dances, mummers' plays, and so on), but that's speculation too.

In time, the *morality play*—the allegorical exploration of character qualities—became detached from its Bible-story foundation and stood on its own. Morality plays told the story of a character representing man, wrestling with abstractions made concrete: Lust, Ambition, Greed, Sloth. He is advised in his struggle by Good and Bad Angels, who encourage him to choose such companions as Friendship, Confession, and Penance instead. *The Castle of Perseverance* stars Mankind and his (successful) temptation by Lust-liking, Flesh, and Pleasure; after Mankind dies, Mercy, Justice, Peace, and Truth (the "four daughters of God") argue about whether he should be allowed into heaven. *Everyman*, the best-known medieval morality play, brings Death on stage to inform Everyman of his impending demise. Everyman's companions, from Wealth to Friendship, soon desert him, leaving him with only Good Works at his side.

By the fifteenth century, the acting of plays had been entirely removed from the physical space of the church. Companies loaded their scenery onto wagons and traveled from town to town with their morality and mystery plays; the drama gained its own place as outdoor theater. Actors spoke their lines, close to their audiences, where the emotions on their unmasked faces could be clearly seen.

Act III: The Age of Shakespeare

Christopher Marlowe, William Shakespeare

"Oh, what a world of profit and delight, of power, of honor, of omnipotence!" exclaims Dr. Faustus, Christopher Marlowe's discontented hero. "All things that move between the quiet poles / Shall be at my command!" The possibility of controlling the world was new to the Renaissance; increasing knowledge of the physical universe seemed to promise a new dominance over it. For the first time, man was not merely a soul poised between heaven and hell, waiting out his days on earth so that he could begin his real life in heaven. He was a *personality*—in the words of Jacob Burckhardt, a "many-sided man," a free individual with power to act in the world and to change it. The flat, allegorical Everyman of medieval drama had become a *person*, full of complexities, ambitions, and potential.

Shakespeare dominates the Renaissance, but the first "person" in English drama belongs to Christopher Marlowe. Marlowe, two months older than Shakespeare, was already writing in the 1580s, ten years before Shakespeare's first "dramatical histories" came to the stage. His early play *Tamburlaine*, about the fearsome Mongol conqueror who called himself the "scourge of God," rejects the notion that Tamburlaine might be an instrument of divine purpose; he is instead an active, thinking human. "Nature," Tamburlaine tells one of his victims,

> Doth teach us all to have aspiring minds;
> Our souls, whose faculties can comprehend
> The wondrous architecture of the world
> And measure every wandering planet's course,
> Still climbing after knowledge infinite,
> And always moving as the restless spheres,
> Wills us to wear ourselves and never rest.

In *Doctor Faustus*, Marlowe takes Everyman and turns that flat character into an *individual*. Faustus, restlessly climbing after "knowledge infinite," is faced with the same choice that Everyman is given: knowledge and wealth on earth or bliss in heaven. Unlike Everyman, Faustus chooses earth; like any good Renaissance scholar, he is unable to turn his back on the unfolding knowledge of the physical world, even if it means his damnation.

And at the play's end, Faustus has both knowledge and hell. The Renaissance (and later, the Enlightenment) praised human ability to act: to survey a situation, analyze it, decide on a course of action, and carry it out triumphantly. Yet the two greatest Renaissance playwrights are skeptical of simple Renaissance optimism. Shakespeare writes comedies, tragedies, and histories—but he never writes victories. Even the happy endings of his comedies are bittersweet, spiked through the heart by past misunderstandings and the possibility of future dissolution. Shakespeare's heroes are thoughtful and able to act, but they are also unhappy, conflicted, divided against themselves.

Greek literature (and architecture) was rediscovered during the Renaissance, and Shakespeare is obviously aware of Aristotle's laws for dramatic form: He writes his plays in five acts and makes a half-hearted attempt to maintain the unities. But he asks his audiences to empathize with his heroes, not because they are morally upright, but because their motivations are psychologically credible. Lear's demand that his daughters love him more than their husbands is twisted but pathetically real. We grit our teeth over Hamlet's indecision, but his unwillingness to throw a match into the bonfire piled up in the middle of his family is perfectly comprehensible. Richard III is a moral monster but an efficient politician, an individualist who looks first to his own end, rather than the larger good, quite different from the Oedipus who tries nobly to do what is best for his people, even in the face of private catastrophe.

And, of course, all of these men come to sad ends. The Renaissance saw man as free to choose his own path, rather than bound into God's preordered design; Shakespeare's heroes are free, but they are far from happy. "All the world's a stage," Shakespeare wrote, in the most quoted lines of *As You Like It*:

> And all the men and women merely players;
> They have their exits and their entrances,
> And one man in his time plays many parts,
> His acts being seven ages. . . .
> Last scene of all,
> That ends this strange eventful history,
> Is second childishness and mere oblivion,
> Sans teeth, sans eyes, sans taste, sans everything.

Greek drama had acted out, ritually and with stylistic gestures, the place of man in a world governed by immovable forces; man could not always avoid breaking the universe's rules, but at least he knew why the resulting chaos descended on him. Medieval drama had acted out, ritually and with the Bible as its playbook, the place of man in a comprehensible universe where God had already determined his beginning, middle, and end. But in this third act of the human drama, a time of constant discovery, when no one knew what the astronomer might see in the heavens next, the players on stage were acting out a play without a predestined end. Renaissance scientists and philosophers might see this undetermined end as a glorious one, brought about by man's increasing power over the universe; Shakespeare is not so sure.

The age of Shakespeare was brought to an end not by an intellectual movement, but by politics. The theater—not to mention England's economy—flourished under Elizabeth I and her heir, James I. But the powerful Puritan wing of Parliament found James's son Charles I to be insufficiently Protestant; they started a civil war, exiled the king (and later executed him), and campaigned against all things Catholic and all things libertine. Sculptures and all art that bore the taint of the icon were destroyed; the theaters, centers of public immorality, were closed down; England lay under the rule of Oliver Cromwell. The English playwrights fled to France or retired; actors got other jobs; the "spirit of Elizabethan drama was largely extinguished."[6]

---

[6]Albert Wertheim, "Restoration Drama: The Second Flowering of the English Theatre," in *500 Years of Theatre History*, ed. Michael Bigelow Dixon and Val Smith (Lyme, N.H.: Smith and Kraus, 2000), p. 82.

This great disruption illustrates, more clearly than any theoretical argument, how different the drama is from the novel, or the autobiography, or the work of history. If a government declared novels to be immoral, novelists would go right on scribbling in secret; memoirists have written their stories in prison camps, under repressive regimes, in hiding. But plays cannot be held in a secret room. They must have a space to inhabit, or else they die.

Act IV: Men and Manners

Molière, William Congreve, Oliver Goldsmith,
Richard Brinsley Sheridan, Oscar Wilde

Until his death in 1659, Cromwell went on trying to "fix" society by running it according to Puritan principles, and banning (among other things) horse races, dancing, and Christmas. But in 1660, Parliament rejected the Puritan commonwealth and brought Charles's heir, Charles II, back out of exile. And there was great rejoicing, not so much over Charles II—who was inclined to figure prominently in brothel brawls, street riots, pub fights, and all sorts of other disruptive messes—as over the absence of Cromwell's government. The theater made a strong return. Charles II issued royal licenses for two theater companies, which he declared to be the only legal theaters in London (thus the birth of the term "legitimate theater"). The playhouses were rebuilt—but with a difference. The theater of Shakespeare's time had developed from the marketplace, grass-roots drama of the Middle Ages. The theater of the "Restoration" was an elite institution, run by aristocrats and licensed by the king himself. Shakespeare's Globe had seated fifteen hundred, with plenty of cheap tickets for anyone who wanted to stand in front of the stage. The new London playhouses held five hundred at the most, with no standing room for the working-class "groundlings."

And the plays which the prosperous audiences came to see were very different from the plays of the Renaissance. The late seventeenth and early eighteenth centuries were times of political uncertainty, during which philosophers were laying down arguments against the old hierarchies that had governed society for centuries. England's monarchy, unlike others, had survived its crisis, but the old order was not what it had been; Charles II was a trifler, ruled by his mistresses, and his court—those aristocrats theoretically given, by God, the task of ruling their inferiors—was even worse. Nor did the monarchy fare well in the years that followed. Charles's heir, the Catholic James, unexpectedly fathered a child, at which point the English, unable to bear the prospect of a Catholic dynasty, got rid of him and imported the Dutch William, hemming him about with restrictions. It was an age of lofty political ideals and of practical compromises, of rhetoric about man's freedom combined with real constraints on man's existence, of an enormously high respect for the common man combined with a down-to-earth distrust of what that common man might do if he were actually allowed to take over.

In the absence of old certainties and old gods, Restoration and eighteenth-century society turned to new stabilities, combining a new passion for classical art and architecture (structured, symmetrical, stable, and ruled by unvarying laws) with an unending respect for manners, which became a way of mastering the uncertainties of a rapidly shifting society. Manners reinforced the existence of an upper (and upper-middle, middle, lower-middle, and working) class, in a world where philosophers were rejecting hierarchy; Rousseau might write about radical equality, but the man in the street was snickering at his neighbor's inability to tie a cravat properly.

Restoration and eighteenth-century dramas held to classical forms— but mocked society's obsession with manners, especially those that hedged sex and marriage. And the greatest Restoration and eighteenth-century dramatists are, like Shakespeare, pessimists about human nature. In the plays of Oliver Goldsmith and Molière, characters use manners as weapons which allow them to do as they please; a power-hungry, savage face snarls beneath the mask of manners. Locke and Rousseau may debate calmly about man's nature, but Goldsmith and Molière are the hecklers, shouting from the corners, "You think man is ruled by reason? Come and see what human beings are *really* like."

In an age in which scientists, politicians, historians, and novelists were announcing that man was ascending to the stars, playwrights—those who actually had to put people on stage so that they could *act*—were not convinced. Their plays are full of compromise, stupidity, crassness, malice, evil, and all uncharitableness. Their upper-class heroes are tyrants and triflers; Goldsmith's Mr. Marlow announces proudly that he can enjoy himself only in the company of common women, whom he can seduce without feeling guilty. Goldsmith goes so far as to put his "low" hero Tony Lumpkin at the center of his story. Lower-class characters, he argued, had a greater range of emotions and qualities, because fashion did not make them the same by smoothing their characters into uniformity. Did his upper-crust audience get the joke against them? Apparently not; they laughed at Tony Lumpkin and applauded when Marlow got the girl.

"Manners," that artificial shape given to the ultimate chaos of life, were ordained by a society that believed in rules and in the smooth, scientific, clockwork functioning of the universe. The comedy of manners satirized the rules, and in doing so displayed a certain distrust for man's ordering of the world. But these comedies still held to the classical conventions of the play itself—the five-part structure, the unity of time and place and action. This "neoclassical" structure transformed playwriting into a rational activity; in good Enlightenment fashion, reason, the most important part of man, was in firm control of the imagination.

Act V: The Triumph of Ideas

Henrik Ibsen, Anton Chekhov, George Bernard Shaw, T. S. Eliot,
Thornton Wilder, Eugene O'Neill, Jean Paul Sartre, Tennessee Williams,
Arthur Miller, Samuel Beckett, Robert Bolt, Tom Stoppard

The nineteenth-century Romantics revolted against this Enlightenment vision of humans as thinking machines. Romantics rated emotion and creativity much higher than rationality; the playwright was not an artisan, but a genius unlimited by conventions and rules. By the late nineteenth century, playwrights began to shake off those Aristotelian ideals in favor of wilder, freer, and more anguished forms.

The Romantics rejected, not only the ordered classical play structure, but also the Enlightenment optimism which announced that the world could be classified, ordered, and dominated. The Romantics wrote in the clear knowledge that man's reach would always exceed his grasp, and that no knowledge would ever satisfy his deepest longings.

Romantic poets were prey to angst, depression, and self-slaughter, and their plays were "poetical dramas," wild, fantastic poem-plays that could not physically fit onto the nineteenth-century stage. Straining against the Enlightenment framework, these poets were still imprisoned by the conventions of the stage—until the early part of the twentieth century.

Modern dramatists, led by Bertholt Brecht (born just before the century's turn), had an epiphany: They rejected the "realistic conventions" of the stage in order to portray life with more truth. "Theatrical realism"—preserving the illusion that the action on stage is "real" through traditional sets, natural dialogue, and the observance of an invisible "fourth wall" between audience and actors—was now seen as complicit in the illusion of order, a false structure that (like the manners of the eighteenth century) found imaginary rules in a world which was actually made up of chaos and disorder.

Brecht, probably the most influential theorist of the drama since Aristotle, rejected the idea that some inexorable destiny governs human existence and leads us toward a meaningful end. In his plays, he also rejected the traditional play structure leading to a climax; in Brechtian "epic theater," there is no more "decreed end," no "resolution" resulting from the characters' actions. Instead, these plays are sets of linked episodes; they concern, not heroes or men of action, but (in the words of Brecht's friend and interpreter Walter Benjamin) the "Untragic Hero," a thinking man making his way from episode to episode.

In his effort to shake the audience from its preoccupation with order, Brecht prescribed the insertion of intervals to "destroy illusion" and "enable the spectator to adopt a critical attitude." The "fourth wall" also disappears: "The stage is still elevated," Benjamin writes. "But it no longer rises from an immeasurable depth: it has become a public platform."[7] In other words, there *is* no "stage," no exalted point from which any member of society has any right to make pronouncements about what is right and what is orderly; the actors and audience are grappling together with the play's ideas. In a Brechtian play such as Tom Stoppard's *Rosencrantz and Guildenstern Are Dead*, or Peter Schaffer's *Equus*, the audience might be seated partially on stage; the actors might wander down to sit with the audience. Thornton Wilder's Stage Manager speaks directly to the audience, introducing the players by their real names. He doesn't want the onlookers to become lost in the story of Emily and George; he wants them to keep themselves firmly in mind throughout.

In English-language drama, two "Brechtian" movements have been particularly widespread: symbolic drama, and the "theater of the absurd." Symbolism is based in part on the work of the French poet Stéphane Mallarmé, who wrote that drama should be "evocative rather than descriptive, and relying upon suggestion as opposed to statement."[8] Mallarmé went a step further than Brecht (who had no particular objections to scenery or costumes); he wanted the stage to be stripped and "detheatricalized," reduced to bareness, so that the playwright could offer the audience obvious *symbols.* For the symbolist, the orderly appearance of the world is a veil that hides real truth; the only way past the veil is through the use of symbols, which can momentarily lift it and give us a glimpse of what lies behind. Symbolist drama (such as Samuel Beckett's *Happy Days*, which features a woman buried up to her waist in sand but only aware of her

[7]Walter Benjamin, "Studies for a Theory of Epic Theatre," in *Understanding Brecht*, trans. Anna Bostock (London: NLB, 1973), pp. 15–22 (first published in German in 1939).
[8]Haskell M. Block, *Mallarmé and the Symbolist Drama* (Detroit: Wayne State University Press, 1963), p. 103.

predicament in fleeting glimpses) features oblique, nonrealistic dialogue, long disruptive pauses, and little action.

"Theater of the absurd" rejects theatrical realism, not so much because the conventions of the theater are inadequate, but because traditional explanations of the meaning of life are themselves inadequate. To quote the playwright Eugène Ionesco, man is "lost in the world, [and] all his actions become senseless, absurd, useless." So absurdist drama eliminates cause and effect, turns characters into types rather than portraits, and reduces language to a game which has no power to convey meaning. Samuel Beckett's *Waiting for Godot*, published in 1952, is "theater of the absurd." It lacks plot, character development, and (for that matter) setting, and guides the audience toward the conclusion that life, too, lacks plot, character, setting, and any possibility of meaningful communication. Dramatists who use the principles of the "theater of the absurd" belong to no particular school, since they insist that any shared agreement between minds is an illusion; each writer is, by definition, "an individual who regards himself as a lone outsider, cut off and isolated in his private world."[9] But they do share an attitude: All certainties have disappeared, be they religious, political, or scientific. "Absurd," writes Ionesco, "is that which is devoid of purpose. . . . Cut off from his religious, metaphysical, and transcendental roots, man is lost."[10]

Theater of the absurd was one expression of modern despair, but not every modern playwright is sunk in despair—and not all have chosen to express their doubts about life through symbols or absurdity. Tennessee Williams, Arthur Miller, Robert Bolt, and others may borrow from Brecht (Bolt's Common Man in *A Man for All Seasons* is not so very different from Wilder's Stage Manager), but they allow their stories to unfold within a particular place and time: Tudor England, the New York of the 1940s, a hot apartment in a Polish neighborhood. Playwrights who maintain a level of dramatic realism in their dramas find truth in the actions of characters; they believe that an audience can recognize a human likeness in the actions and motivations of another person. Tom Stoppard makes a statement about language by allowing Rosencrantz and Guildenstern to disappear into a whirl of confusion and absurdity at his play's end; but Arthur Miller tells us about American capitalism in his detailed psychological portrayal of Willy Loman, sixtyish salesman, and Tennessee Wil-

[9]Martin Esslin, *The Theatre of the Absurd* (Woodstock, N.Y.: Overlook Press, 1973), p. 4.
[10]Quoted in *A Century of Innovation: A History of European and American Theatre and Drama since the Late Nineteenth Century,* by Oscar G. Brockett and Robert Findlay, 2nd ed. (Boston: Allyn & Bacon, 1991), p. 312.

liams writes about despair through his portrait of an alcoholic southern belle. Realistic drama, in the words of Anne Fleche, "provides a motivation for dialogue, a reason for being. It promises a fullness of meaning, a logic that connects character. . . . Thoughts are *connected* through dialogue; they become lucid and perceptible."[11] Symbolism and absurdism reject the possibility that words can reveal any truth about human existence; dramatic realism retains its faith in language. Both kinds of drama continue to exist side by side.

THE PURPOSE OF DRAMA (OR, WHY BUY A TICKET?)

In 1959, the dramatist Harold Habson—faced with plays full of symbols and absurdities—wrote indignantly, "It is time someone reminded our advanced dramatists that the principal function of the theater is to give pleasure. . . . It is the duty of the theater, not to make men better, but to render them harmlessly happy."[12]

The debate about what theater ought to do has continued ever since. "Serious" theater—whether realistic or not—has continued to attract a sizable audience, but since Restoration times and the elimination of cheap tickets for groundlings, "popular" and "serious" theater (read "entertainment" and "exploration of ideas") have continued to diverge. Brecht and his followers stripped the stage and sent actors out into the audience. But the "popular" theater developed a quite different form: melodrama, which sold hundreds of thousands more tickets than the serious theater. In melodrama, good and evil were clearly defined, and the villain got what he deserved while the audience cheered. The melodrama, with its affirmations of married love, patriotism, motherly affection, and the dangers of debt, gambling, and drinking, was what most people saw while the intellectuals were attending performances of *No Exit*. In America, *Uncle Tom's Cabin* became one of the most successful melodramas ever, with over five hundred touring companies presenting it ("Many actors spent their entire professional lives playing in *Uncle Tom*," remarks Daniel Gerould).[13] *Under the Gaslight* introduced audiences to London poverty and ended with the poor working girl rescuing a bound victim (a one-armed

[11] Anne Fleche, *Mimetic Disillusion* (Tuscaloosa: University of Alabama Press, 1997), p. 26.
[12] Quoted in G. W. Brandt, "Realism and Parables (from Brecht to Arden)," in *Contemporary Theatre* (London: Edward Arnold Publishers Ltd., 1962.), p. 33.
[13] Daniel C. Gerould, *American Melodrama* (New York: Performing Arts Journal Publications, 1983), p. 14.

veteran) from the path of an oncoming train (an image which became emblematic of the melodrama).

Melodrama was entertainment, but it also represented a third path toward truth; as Peter Brooks writes in his well-known study *The Melo-dramatic Imagination*, melodrama was born in a time of "radical freedom," when audiences needed "the promise of a morally legible universe to those willing to read and interpret properly its signs." Realistic drama claimed that human beings could find truth in careful psychological portraits, making the mind the place where connections between people are possi-ble; nonrealistic drama claimed that no connections between people are possible at all; melodrama asserted that ultimate good and evil exist, and that "even when facing an abyss, man may choose to believe in good and evil."[14] Melodrama is no longer performed today, but that's not because no one believes in good and evil anymore; the function of melodrama has shifted to the summer blockbuster movie with its good guys, bad guys, and victorious endings.

Serious theater, battling both the movies and *Cats* for spectators, remains perpetually in crisis. At its best, a serious play provides what Peter Brook calls the "Holy Theatre"—a place where the audience can see "the face of the invisible through an experience on the stage that transcended their experience in life. They will maintain that *Oedipus* or . . . *Hamlet* or *The Three Sisters* performed with beauty and with love fires the spirit and gives them a reminder that daily drabness is not necessarily all."[15] This doesn't always happen in serious theater, which has been justly accused of unintelligibility and bleakness.

In *Equus*, the last play on this particular annotated list, Peter Shaffer expresses his own yearning for some connection with the ineffable that can't be conveyed only with words but requires speech and action. How this will be conveyed in the future (the techniques of symbolism and the-ater of the absurd have become somewhat dated) is still an open question. Netflix and Hulu, not to mention the movies, will not kill the theater any more than the ebook has killed the paperback; it is worth noting how many playwrights (most notably David Mamet, whose plays may well end up in a future list of dramatic classics) cross over into screenwriting while still fully engaged in the theater.

But there's no particular agreement among contemporary playwrights as to what degree of realism is necessary for an audience familiar with the

[14]Peter Brooks, *The Melodramatic Imagination* (New Haven: Yale University Press, 1976), p. 204.
[15]Peter Brook, *The Empty Space* (New York: Atheneum, 1983), pp. 42–43.

conventions of film. Like the novel, the drama has seen something of a move away from abstraction: "If I read one more article about how we all have to steer ourselves away from narrative and realism because TV and film do that, and our job is to 'push the envelope,'" writes the playwright Theresa Rebeck, "I'm just going to throw up. This elitism is driving audiences away."[16] "The audience needs to be clear about what's up on stage," the playwright Marsha Norman insisted:

> Television does such a great job with social issues, with personal family drama, the kinds of things that were the mainstay of a certain segment of theater writers; Arthur Miller, for example. . . . Those things are actually better done on television. . . . What we look for in the theater are things that only theater can do, not what TV and film can do better.[17]

What theater can do better than TV is to *imagine*. Norman's dialogue is realistic, but her sets are bare (her play *Trudy Blue* operates "at mental speed," the character imagining herself from set to set while the actors use only five chairs and a table) and Norman identifies this "getting to pretend" as theater's strength. But it is notable that her pretending involves character development; although it has retained some elements of dramatic nonrealism, contemporary theater seems to be shifting away from the symbolic, philosophical "idea play," back to the exploration of the human personality.

HOW TO READ A PLAY

Compared with novels and autobiographies, plays are generally quite short. This may allow you to add one extra step to your reading process: Before the "first level of inquiry" reading, consider scheduling a block of time in which you can sit down and read the play straight through in one sitting, without stopping or looking back. After all, a play is constructed to be acted during a single evening; and since acting takes place in time, the production always moves forward, never backward. Novels, autobiographies, and histories are designed to be read slowly, with time for meditation, and with the freedom to turn back and compare a writer's

[16]Theresa Rebeck, *Theresa Rebeck: Collected Plays 1989–1998* (New York: Smith and Kraus, 1999), p. 9.
[17]Interview in *BOMB Magazine* (New York), January 1999, online at www.bombsite .com/norman/norman12.html and www.bombsite.com/norman/norman13.html.

conclusions with the premises. But a playwright knows that the audience won't have the luxury of looking back. Your first reading should reflect this reality.

If you cannot take the time to do this (with some longer plays, such as Shakespeare, you may simply find it too cumbersome), you can progress directly to the first level of inquiry.

The First Level of Inquiry: Grammar-Stage Reading

Just as you did when reading the novels, ask these basic questions as you read: Who are these people? What happens to them? And how are they different afterward? As you read, if you sense that one particular scene is essential—even if you're not quite sure why—make a note of it or turn down the corner of the page, so that you can glance back at it after you've finished your first-level reading.

Look at the title, cover, and general organization of the play.   Read the title page and back copy; write the play's name, the author's name, and the date of composition on your blank page. Beneath, make a note about the general historical era that the author belongs to. Is he an ancient Greek, an Englishman of the Restoration; is she a post–World War II American? If you gather any useful information about the author or about the play's structure, make a note of that as well; it may help you to read intelligently: "Reality and illusion intermix. . . . [F]ate leads our two heroes to a tragic but inevitable end" reads the back of *Rosencrantz and Guildenstern Are Dead*; if you know this, you won't expect realistic scenes, and you'll be able to look out for "inevitabilities" as you read.

Then, glance at the play's divisions. Note the number of acts: three, four, five, one? Does the play keep to classical structure, or is it episodic, like a Brechtian play? Does it divide symmetrically into two halves? If so, look for a "cliffhanger" toward the end of the first part. Is there a separate prologue or epilogue? These are probably locations for an introductory or final statement of purpose. Arthur Miller's two-act *Death of a Salesman* closes with a separate scene, the Requiem: "He only needed a little sal-ary!" the salesman's wife cries, but her son answers, "No man only needs a little salary"—which is one of the play's organizing themes.

When you encounter stage directions, read them carefully.   As you begin to read, pay attention to stage directions, both descriptions and notes about the movements of actors across the stage. Older plays often contain very little (or nothing) in the way of stage directions: "Enter Oedipus" is about all the direction you'll find in *Oedipus the King*, and even this was inserted by the play's translator. However, if you read with attention to what the characters are doing, you will find clues in the characters' speeches that will help you to picture their actions on the stage. "Hamlet in madness hath Polonius slain," the king announces, "And from his mother's closet hath he dragged him." Hamlet has just slain Polonius, but without the king's speech, we wouldn't know what action he took afterward.

More recent scripts are more likely to lay out the scene with great detail: "At a plain strong oak table," writes George Bernard Shaw in *Saint Joan*, "seated in chair to match, the captain presents his left profile. The steward stands facing him at the other side of the table, if so deprecatory a stance as his can be called standing. The mullioned thirteenth-century window is open behind him. Near it in the corner is a turret with a narrow arched doorway leading to a winding stair which descends to the courtyard." Shaw could hardly be more specific.

What conclusion can you come to? The setting of *Oedipus* is not central to the play's meaning; it has been played in modern dress, in the South before the Civil War, in Japanese masks, as an African American gospel production (as has *Hamlet*, with varying degrees of success). *Saint Joan*, on the other hand, can only be played in fifteenth-century France. When a playwright provides you with this level of detail, he intends you to take note. Don't simply skim past the description and move on to the dialogue. Instead, take the time to picture the scene in your mind; when you find a clue such as the king's speech above, pause for a moment to visualize the action it describes.

You may find it helpful to sketch the stage and the furnishings, and then to trace in pencil, as you read, any movements indicated by the playwright. Whenever the writer takes the time to write such directions as [*Rising*] in front of a character's dialogue, or [*Crosses stage left*], he is emphasizing that action in order to draw attention to something on stage: the speech, the actor, another character. If the character "crosses stage left," does she cross to another character, to an empty space, to the shadow of a tree, to the threshold of a door?

Keep a list of characters as you read. Unlike the novel, which introduces you to each character in turn, the play generally lays out the *dramatis personae* right up front. Glance down the list; if you wish, you can make a note of each character in your own journal, so that you can jot identifying sentences after each one. (You may feel more inclined to do this if the list seems confusing or too large.) In contemporary plays, the *dramatis personae* will sometimes include the names of the actors who premiered the part.

So, in *A Streetcar Named Desire*, you'll find that Marlon Brando was the first actor to play Stanley Kowalski, with Jessica Tandy as Blanche Dubois. Sometimes this can help you to visualize a part, since the director undoubtedly cast an actor who seemed to be physically "right" for the role in its first performance.

Watch for physical descriptions of the characters, or "tags" explaining emotion. Shaw provides both: Joan, he writes, has an "uncommon face; eyes very wide apart and bulging as they often do in very imaginative people, a long well-shaped nose with wide nostrils, a short upper lip, resolute but full-lipped mouth, and handsome fighting chin." Later, Captain Robert de Baudricourt makes a speech which is prefaced with the following tag [*his irresoluteness now openly swamping his affected decisiveness*].

As with stage directions, if the writer inserts these tags, she means you to pay attention to them; make notes of the physical description of the characters, and of any hints of the character's emotional makeup that the tags might provide.

Briefly note the main event of each scene.   As you finish each scene, write down a simple sentence describing the primary action and the characters who take part in it. As you write, don't forget that other characters may be on stage as well. It is simple, when reading, to imagine the characters, not on stage, but in the actual place where the writer puts them: a courtroom, a living room, a basement. But in actuality they are sitting on a raised platform in front of people who are staring at them. The playwright, as the critic Ronald Hayman remarks, has the problem of giving them something to do: "Whenever there is more than one character on stage," Hayman counsels, "the reader needs to keep them all in mind. The temptation is to concentrate exclusively on whoever is speaking. A character who is listening—or not listening—may be contributing no less to the theatrical effect. . . . If they are not speaking, what are they doing?"[18]

Can you identify a beginning, middle, climax, and resolution?   A play, no matter what it treats, has to ask an initial question, or set before you a scene which has in it some kind of tension. *What is the initial question or tension?* The curtain rises; you see Oedipus the king, standing at the top of the temple steps while his people stream up them to ask the gods why Thebes has been struck with plague, blight, miscarriage, crop failure. Oedipus doesn't know, and neither do we; we need the answer to this question. Tom Stoppard begins *Rosencrantz and Guildenstern Are Dead* with an entirely different

[18]Ronald Hayman, *How to Read a Play* (New York: Grove Press, 1977), p. 14.

kind of tension: Two well-dressed Elizabethans are sitting on a bare stage, flipping coins—but the coin toss has turned up heads eighty-six times in a row. Why?

A playwright, no matter how avant garde, has an audience sitting in front of his stage. He has to keep their interest; he cannot simply tell them what he thinks about life, as though he were writing a philosophical essay. He has characters on that stage, and he needs to make the audience care about their actions, if he is to attract their attention and keep it through the rest of the play. In Thornton Wilder's *Our Town*, Wilder creates tension by hinting at his characters' ends: "There's Doc Gibbs comin' down Main Street now," the Stage Manager remarks, "comin' back from that baby case. And here's his wife comin' downstairs to get breakfast. Doc Gibbs died in 1930. . . . Mrs. Gibbs died first—long time ago in fact. . . . She's up in the cemetery there now." As he speaks, Mrs. Gibbs comes on stage and starts to fix breakfast, and the audience watches her. Normally, watching someone fix breakfast isn't all that interesting, but knowing that someone is going to *die*: That puts you in the position of the immortals. You know something Mrs. Gibbs doesn't. And you're wondering: Is her death going to be part of the plot? When will it happen?

Where is the point of greatest tension? Somewhere in the play, events will reach a point where the problems seem most intractable, or when emotion is at its highest peak. This is the play's "middle"; it may not be the exact middle of the performance, but it is the *structural* middle that sets us up for the play's climax and resolution. In *A Streetcar Named Desire*, the tensions between the four central characters—Stanley and his wife Stella, Stella's sister Blanche and Stanley's friend Mitch, who is courting her—reach their highest point in the first scene of Act III, when Stella discovers that Stanley has warned Mitch away from her sister. It is at this point that the characters are the most estranged from each other; here, they seem unlikely to ever come to an agreement.

Where does the play's action reach its climax? At what point does the tension result in an action that changes the characters or their situation? Generally, the "middle" is not the same as the climax: *A Streetcar Named Desire* reaches its climax—its highest point—when Stanley assaults Blanche in the fourth scene of Act III. The assault is the playing out of the tension in that "middle" scene, in which Stanley (acting out of mixed hatred and lust) ruins Blanche's romance and alienates his wife; when he attacks Blanche near the play's end, he is making physical his hatred and lust, and potentially ruining his relationship with his wife forever.

Identifying the "middle" and the climax is a tool to help you understand the playwright's use of tension and resolution; it isn't an exact science, and you shouldn't fret about finding the "right" scene. Simply look for the point at which the play's tensions become very clear, and then ask yourself: What action do these tensions produce? Sometimes, you may find that the "middle" and the climax happen back to back. In *Our Town*, you can make a good argument for the "middle" occurring at the end of Act II, when Emily and George both panic just before their wedding, insisting that they don't want to "grow old"—"Why can't I stay for a while just as I am?" Emily wails, feeling with keenness the passing of time. The "climax" then comes at the end of Act III, when Emily—dead and buried—goes back to relive her twelfth birthday and breaks down into weeping: "I can't go on," she sobs. "It goes so fast. We don't have time to look at one another."

But you could also make a good argument that in this case the "middle" occurs when Emily decides to revisit her childhood, against the warnings of the other dead, and that the climax follows in the same scene. Don't get too obsessed with this: choose a "middle" and climax that make sense to you.

Where is the resolution? What happens after the climax? What results does it bring; what happens to each character afterward? The last scene of *A Streetcar Named Desire* shows Blanche's madness, Stella's grief, and Stanley's complete lack of regret. *Our Town* ends without resolution for the characters: "They don't understand," Emily says, hopelessly, of both the living and the dead, and the Stage Manager reappears to close the action with the flat remark, "Eleven o'clock in Grover's Corners.—You get a good rest, too. Good night." You, the reader, are supposed to find the resolution of *this* play yourself.

Which "act" of the drama does the play belong to?   Is the structure Aristotelian, separated into acts that build toward an end? Or is it Brechtian, divided into episodes that lead you gradually toward the acceptance of an idea?

What holds the play's action together?   Is the play given coherence through its plot—a set of events leading toward a resolution? Or is it held together through the study of a character's mind? Do you keep reading because you want to find out what happens, or because you care about what happens to a particular character? Is the play united by an idea that the author is exploring? Does it try to elicit an emotion from you, or is it attempting to lead you toward a conclusion? Do the last speeches express an intellectual conclusion, or an overwhelming emotion? If you're unsure, pretend that someone has walked through the room where you're reading and asked, "What's the book about?" If you're reading *The Importance of Being Earnest*, you might answer, "It's about a lot of mix-ups in identity." Mistaken identity: Oscar Wilde is writing to make you laugh, but also to make you think about how people assign identity to each other.

It's fine to answer the question, "What is this book about?" with "I have no clue." Sometimes that's the point of an "idea" play that explores meaninglessness.

Write a two- or three-sentence explanation of the play's title. Books are inevitably retitled by publishers (T. S. Eliot's original title for the book-length poem *The Waste Land* was *He Do the Policemen in Different Voices*), but playwrights tend to get to keep their own titles; plays are generally performed before they are published, and the title of the play is part of the script. So you can assume that the play's title sums up, describes, or in some way adds to the play. What is the title's relationship to the play? Does it refer to characters, plot, ideas, emotion? Does it refer to a climactic event (*Death of a Salesman*), a place (*The Cherry Orchard*), a person (*A Man for All Seasons*)? What was the playwright implying through the choice of title?

The Second Level of Inquiry: Logic-Stage Reading

As you move into a more detailed criticism, reread the play. Try to come to a final decision about the play's coherence: Does it come from a connected plot, from the psychology of a particular character, or from the exploration of an idea? The playwright may use more than one kind of coherence (plot often involves character), but which do you think to be central? Did you answer the question, "What is it about?" with a person, an event, or an idea?

Once you've answered this question, move on to one of the three options below.

If the play is given unity by plot . . . List the events that lead up to the play's climax. Each event should lead into the next; can you find the connections between them? Ask, "Why does this event produce the next event?" Jot down a brief sentence describing each connection; this will give you a glimpse of the play's "bones."

Now ask yourself: What genre does this resemble? Is it a romance, in which two characters are held apart by circumstance or misunderstanding until they manage to connect? Is it an adventure, progressing from one excitement to another? Is it purely comedic, centered around incongruous and bizarre happenings? Is it "tragic," telling the tale of the fall of a hero? Is it a mystery? The slow revelation of facts unknown to the main characters is an effective way to advance the plot. Peter Shaffer's *Equus* borrows absurdist techniques, but in form it is much like a mystery: Why does Alan Strang blind the horses at the stable where he works?

Many plays are a mixture of genres, but if you're able to identify one that dominates, go on to ask: Why did the playwright choose this particular set of techniques to move the play along? Is there some match between the genre and the subject of the play? What techniques does he borrow from other genres? "Genre" is an infinitely flexible term, so don't worry too much about whether you're "getting it right"; your goal is to try to discover how the playwright moves the action along: through suspense, by revealing facts, by building an ominous sense of looming catastrophe?

If the play is given unity by character . . .   Ask, for each major character, the same basic questions you asked for the novel in Chapter Five: What does each character want or hope to accomplish? What blocks each character from getting what he or she wants: Her own failings or flaws? Another character? Circumstances? What strategy does a character follow in order to get what he or she wants? Is she successful? Does he suffer defeat?

If the play is given unity by an idea . . .   Can you state the idea? Read again any prologue or epilogue, read the last two pages in each act. See if you can formulate the idea into a sentence. What does each character stand for? In an "idea play," you need not analyze the characters as though they had real wants, needs, and plans; they "stand for" something else. What does each major event do to the characters? Compare their state at the beginning and end of the play; what change has there been? Does that change help to illustrate the playwright's idea? At the beginning of *Rosencrantz and Guildenstern Are Dead*, the two central characters are flipping coins and arguing about their tendency to come up heads every time. At the end, all the characters in both plays (Stoppard's, and Shakespeare's *Hamlet*, which has been running along in the background) die—except for Rosencrantz and Guildenstern, who disappear in a cloud of sentence fragments. What movement has there been? At the beginning of the play, Rosencrantz and Guildenstern are assuming that there must be an explanation for the phenomenal run of heads; they are still operating under the "old" idea of order in the world. At the play's end, they have given up the idea of explanations.

No matter what unifying factor the play uses, go on to answer the following questions.

Do any of the characters stand in opposition to each other?   Contrasts are a powerful rhetorical strategy, and particularly powerful when they are visual. Are there oppositions of character in the play? Oppositions of class? Physical oppositions? In Goldsmith's *She Stoops to Conquer* Tony Lumpkin and his cousin's lover Hastings are at opposite ends of the social spectrum, as are Lumpkin's beloved Bet Bouncer and Hastings's love, the refined Miss Neville; they are physical opposites as well in every possible way. Of Shakespeare's aristocratic pair of ladies in *A Midsummer Night's Dream*, one is very tall and the other very short. In *Rosencrantz and Guildenstern Are Dead*, the two central characters present very little contrast; in fact, they call each other by the wrong names, which is part of Stoppard's point.

If you can find contrasts in character, class, setting, physical type, speech, or some other element of the play, list the contrasting elements on two sides of your journal and write a very brief description of each. How does this strategy on the part of the playwright add to the play's coherence?

How do the characters speak?   Read the speeches of each character out loud, several times. Read several speeches from the same character in a row. Then read another set of speeches from another character. Do their speech patterns differ?

If the characters are individuals, developed as unique people with their own backgrounds, wants, and needs, you should see a difference in speech. In Arthur Miller's *Death of a Salesman*, the sixtyish Willy Loman has one pattern of words ("The street is lined with cars. There's not a breath of fresh air in the neighborhood. . . . Remember those two beautiful elm trees out there? When I and Biff hung the swing between them?") and his desperate, thirtyish son Biff has another ("This farm I work on, it's spring there now, see? And they've got about fifteen new colts. . . . And it's cool there now, see?")

In an "idea play," all speeches may sound the same. In T. S. Eliot's *Murder in the Cathedral*, a fable about the corrupting effects of power, Thomas Becket says: "You think me reckless, desperate and mad. / You argue by results, as this world does, / To settle if an act be good or bad." The Chorus, responding to him, chants, "We did not wish anything to happen. / We understood the private catastrophe, / The personal loss, the general misery, / Living and partly living." The two voices are identical.

This exercise may help you to clarify further the question of coherence: If the characters all sound the same, either the playwright has slipped up, or this is not a character-driven play.

Is there any confusion of identity?   In a novel, which often gives you the privilege of hearing the characters' thoughts, the characters know who they are. In drama, which presents a character to the gaze of an audience, there is much more room for deception: The gap between what (or who) a character appears to be, and what (or who) he ultimately proves to be, may be immensely wide. From Oedipus on, confusion over identity stands as a constant element in drama—which, by its very form, has to do with *how an outside observer views characters.*

Mark any aspects of identity confusion in the play and ask: What purpose does this identity confusion serve? Identity is the most essential element of human existence; what statement about the human condition does this confusion make? In the case of Oedipus, identity is essential: Oedipus has tried to become someone else, but his attempts to change his identity are doomed to failure. *Rosencrantz and Guildenstern Are Dead* demonstrates the opposite; identity is a matter of chance, a meeting of elements by coincidence to form a whole. A different meeting of elements, a different set of coincidences, would result in an entirely different identity. What purpose do the confusions of identity serve in *A Midsummer Night's Dream, She Stoops to Conquer, The Importance of Being Earnest?*

Is there a climax, or is the play open ended?   Does the playwright lead you into a satisfying resolution, with the plot wound up, the fate of the characters settled, an idea neatly stated? Or does the play illustrate a dilemma, some problem which intrinsically resists a solution? A playwright will generally allow the form of a play to reflect the possibility—or impossibility—of resolving the problem that he has presented.

What is the play's theme?   Be very careful when you reduce a play to a "thematic statement." After all, a playwright is writing a play, rather than a philosophical essay. If he could state his "theme" easily in prose, he'd write the essay instead. Thomas Merton, who was a poet and critic as well as a monk, once warned, "The material of literature and especially of drama is chiefly human acts—that is, free, moral acts. And, as a matter of fact, literature, drama, poetry, make certain statements about these acts that can be made in no other way. That is precisely why you will miss all the deepest meaning of Shakespeare, Dante, and the rest if you reduce their vital and creative statements about life and men to the dry, matter-of-fact terms of history, or ethics, or some other science. They belong to a different order."[19]

However, even Merton adds, "Nevertheless, the great power of something like *Hamlet, Coriolanus*, or the *Purgatorio* or Donne's *Holy Sonnets*

---

[19]Thomas Merton, *The Seven Storey Mountain* (New York: Harcourt, 1998), p. 197.

lies precisely in the fact that they are a kind of commentary on ethics and psychology and even metaphysics, even theology." When the playwright sat down to write, something vexed him, nagged at him, and demanded expression. What was it? Can you try to sum it up? This answer should not be the same as your answer to "What is this play about?" *Hamlet* is about a man of thirty who can't bring himself to accuse openly his uncle/stepfather of murder, but that is not its theme.

There may be a number of good answers to this question; I have seen at least fifteen thoroughly respectable statements of the theme in *Hamlet*. Try to come up with one. State, in three or four sentences, what problem the playwright is tackling—and what answers he may have found.

The Third Level of Inquiry: Rhetoric-Stage Reading

In the "rhetoric stage" level of inquiry, you can ask many of the same questions of the play that you asked of the novels: How does the writer create sympathy between you and the characters? How does he reflect on the human condition? What is humanity's central problem in this play? (You can refer back to the chapter on "Reading the Novel" for a full list of these questions.)

These are useful questions, but remember: A play is not a novel. A play is centered on visible action. So in your rhetoric-stage reading of the play, take a more active role. Begin to see the play not just vertically (creating a relationship between you and the characters) but horizontally, as something that has been presented and re-presented over time, each time creating a new set of relationships between the characters and an audience which occupies a different place—and perhaps, a different time.

How would you direct and stage this play? Depending on your enthusiasm for the play, you can carry out this project for one scene, for one act, or for the whole play. Consider writing out answers to these questions:

1. Who will play the main characters? Assign the main characters to actors: imaginary actors (describe them), real actors (draw on your knowledge of TV, movies, or local theater), or even people you know (members of your family, friends; if Blanche Dubois reminds you of a disturbed second cousin, write in that cousin's name). Putting a face and body, mannerisms and a tone of voice to each character will immediately begin to shape the play in your mind.

2. What sort of stage will you use? Will it be a raised platform, or on the same level with the audience? Will it be a "picture stage" (flat, behind

curtains) or a stage that juts out into the auditorium? Will the audience be on two, three, or four sides ("theater in the round")? How large is your auditorium? Do you see this play as most effective in a small studio theater that seats fifty, a college auditorium that seats four hundred, a huge theater with balconies? Will you use a curtain or not?

Will the actors ever breach the "fourth wall"—the barrier between audience and the stage? Will they be drawn into the audience—entering for one scene, perhaps, from the back of the theater and walking down the aisles? If so, what will you be intending to accomplish through this? And what relationship will the play create between itself and the audience? Will the onlookers be passive, active, part of the action, removed from it?

3. What scenery and costumes will you use? Will you be recreating a historical period or setting your actors in the present day? Will the scenery be realistic or impressionistic—suggested, rather than elaborately developed? Will a certain color or shape dominate? If so, why?

4. Mark the sound effects and visual effects. How will you carry them out? Are there crowd noises, ringing bells, traffic sounds, battle noises? How do you hear these? Reading is a silent activity, but a play demands sound. Will the sound be subdued in the background, overwhelming and surrounding the audience? How does each player on the stage react to the sound?

If the play calls for visual effects that are out of the ordinary (such as transparent walls, the appearance of a ghost, a dream sequence), how will you light or stage this? How do the actors react to the appearance? Do they all see it, or does only one react while the others remain blind to it? If so, how do they react to the *player* who reacts?

Remember that often sound and visual effects are found, not in stage directions, but in the dialogue of other characters. "It faded on the crowing of the cock," gasps one of Denmark's frightened soldiers, watching the ghost of Hamlet's late father fade away—something we would otherwise not have known.

Will the play have music? What sort of music, and when? With your imagination and a CD collection, you have a vast resource for selecting background music.

In most cases, if you're going to do this for an entire play, it's simplest to be able to write directly into the script.

5. Can you write out stage directions? You can do this for one or two scenes—or for more. Mark each character's movements. What are they doing the entire time they're onstage? If the playwright has given you very specific directions, what has she left for you to add? If you stage a scene in two different ways, does the meaning of the scene change?

All of these are beginning questions for direction; if you find yourself interested in the process, investigate one of the books on the reference list at the end of this section (see page 312).

6. Does your staging emphasize the play's theme? How will you use costume and setting, music and visual effects, movements, speech and silence, to bring out the theme which you've identified in the play?

7 How have other directors interpreted this play? Watch several staged productions of the play, live or on film. This, obviously, will be limited to productions from the last fifty or sixty years, but even this should give you some idea of how these plays have been presented. Do they emphasize the same theme, or shift it from production to production? If you can, watch two different stagings fairly far apart in time. How are the productions different in costumes, in staging, in style of dialogue, in emphasis? (A list of plays available to watch follows on pages 313–16.)

THE ANNOTATED DRAMA LIST

The following list of editions certainly does not encompass all the good editions and readable translations of these works, but I have tried to indicate the translations I found the most readable and accurate, as well as those editions that combine affordability and helpful footnotes with decent-sized type. Many of these plays (including the Greek ones) are available in Dover Thrift editions for under $3.00. These cheap paperbacks are often a good way to read the English plays, but in the case of the Greek plays and those modern plays originally written in a foreign language, the Dover editions are usually public domain translations— often outdated or anonymous, which more often than not means archaic and inaccurate.

A thorough list of dramatists worth reading would also include John Dryden, John Webster, Ben Jonson, Edward Albee, Eugène Ionesco, David Mamet, Harold Pinter, Sam Shepard, John Guare, Margaret Edson, Marsha Norman, and many more. This particular list was chosen because the plays on it are readable, and because they serve as good representatives of the development of drama from ancient Greece to modern times.

What plays from the last forty years will endure? Perhaps Marsha Norman's Pulitzer Prize–winning *'Night, Mother* (although a Pulitzer isn't necessarily a guarantee of immortality). Perhaps the plays of Harold Pinter or Sam Shepard, although it's impossible to say which ones. And David Mamet's stylish dialogue will most certainly be marked—but whether his plays or screenplays will best demonstrate it is still an open question.

AESCHYLUS
Agamemnon
(c. 458 B.C.)

Best translations: The Penguin Classics paperback, The Oresteia: Agamemnon, The Libation Bearers, The Eumenides *(1984), uses Robert
Fagles's excellent but somewhat formal translation. Another fine translation,
more colloquial and free-flowing than Fagles, is found in the Penn Greek
Drama Series volume,* Aeschylus, 1: The Oresteia: Agamemnon, the
Libation Bearers, the Eumenides *(University of Pennsylvania Press,
1997), trans. David R. Slavitt. Slavitt, a poet himself, reinterprets as often as
he translates, but the result is highly enjoyable.*

Agamemnon is the first of a trilogy of plays known as *The Oresteia*; the other
two plays, *The Libation Bearers* and *The Eumenides*, complete the story of
Agamemnon's unfortunate family. A little background is necessary: The
Trojan War has already started. The Trojan warrior Paris stole Helen,
wife of the Greek king Menelaus, and carried her off to Troy;[20] Menelaus
recruited his brother Agamemnon (who happened to be married to Hel-
en's sister Clytemnestra) to be commander in chief of an enormous Greek
army. But the goddess Artemis, who loved Troy, blew great winds on the
fleet to keep the Greeks from sailing. Agamemnon, knowing that the
expedition was the will of Zeus, consulted the prophet Calchas, who told
him that Artemis could only be appeased by the sacrifice of Agamemnon's
daughter Iphigenia. Agamemnon performed the sacrifice against the wild
objections of his wife. The wind died, the Greeks sailed for Troy, and the
battle dragged on for ten years. Troy finally fell, and messengers set out to
carry the good news back to Greece.

As *Agamemnon* begins, the Watchman, Agamemnon's loyal servant, is
standing on top of Agamemnon's palace, watching for news of Troy's
defeat. The Chorus, made up of men too old to fight, enters and fills in
the story of Iphigenia's sacrifice (which the Chorus condemns as an act
of "utter ruthlessness . . . impure, unholy"). Clytemnestra then arrives

---

[20]The play also assumes that the audience knows how the Trojan War began: The goddess of discord, Eris, offered a golden apple to the fairest of the goddesses. Aphrodite,
Hera, and Athena asked Zeus to decide which one was the most beautiful, but he (wisely)
declined to judge and sent them to Paris instead. Paris chose Aphrodite, not for her
beauty, but because she promised to reward him with the most beautiful woman in the
world. With the competition over, Aphrodite helped Paris to magic Helen away from
Menelaus and back to Troy.

and hears that Troy is indeed fallen; Agamemnon is on his way home. (Menelaus, it appears, has been lost at sea.) She spreads sacred tapestries on the ground to welcome her husband, but when Agamemnon arrives (bringing with him the captive Trojan princess and prophetess Cassandra, Paris's sister), he refuses to walk over them. Only a god should walk over the tapestries, he tells her; he is simply a man. But Clytemnestra finally persuades him to come in.

Cassandra, remaining behind, is overcome by the god Apollo and pours out a confused and bloody tale about slaughter and a bathtub—in the middle of which she reveals that Agamemnon carries a curse on him. His father, Atreus, punished Agamemnon's brother Thyestes for sleeping with Atreus's wife by roasting Thyestes' children and serving them to his brother. Cassandra sees the children's ghosts ("What do they carry in their hands? O piteous sight! / It is their own flesh—limb and rib and heart they hold, / Distinct and horrible, the food their father ate! / I tell you, for this crime revenge grows hot"). Sure enough, Clytemnestra stabs both Agamemnon (in his bath) and then Cassandra, claiming that Agamemnon deserved to die because he sacrificed her daughter.

Agamemnon did sacrifice Iphigenia—but only to please Zeus, who wanted the Greeks to conquer Troy. So why did he deserve death? Because Zeus gave him two wrong choices (displease the king of the gods, or sacrifice his daughter) as punishment for Atreus's wrongdoing. Agamemnon was thus forced into an act that was simultaneously evil and good because of his father's sin; in its portrayal of the effect of a parent's evil on a child, *Agamemnon* keeps its immediacy even today.

SOPHOCLES
Oedipus the King
(c. 450 B.C.)

Best translations: Several good translations of Sophocles are available. Sophocles I: Antigone, Oedipus the King, Oedipus Rex, ed. Mark Griffith and Glenn W. Most (University of Chicago Press, 3rd ed., 2013), was originally done by David Grene and Richmond Lattimore in the 1950s, but has been updated and revised to remove dated vocabulary and expressions. The Oxford World's Classics translation, Sophocles: Antigone, Oedipus the King, Electra, translated by H. D. F. Kitto and edited by Edith Hall (reissue ed., 2009), was done with performance in mind and is particularly good for reading aloud. Robert Fagles's readable translation for Penguin Classics, Sophocles: The Three Theban Plays (1984), is the most literal of the three.

When King Laius of Thebes was mysteriously murdered by a highway-man, Oedipus took over both his throne and his wife. But now the king must discover why Thebes is plagued with sickness, disaster, and blight. He sends his brother-in-law Creon to ask the oracle of Apollo at Delphi for answers; Creon comes back with the news that Thebes is harboring the criminal who killed King Laius.

Oedipus promises to find this criminal, calling the prophet Teiresias to help him. But when Teiresias accuses Oedipus himself of the crime, the king grows angry. Creon, he shouts, has put the prophet up to this to take the throne away from him. Creon denies any design on Oedipus's crown ("If I were king," he objects, "I would have to do things which I did not want. / So why should I seek the crown rather than the pleasant untrou-bled life I now lead?"). But Oedipus exiles him anyway.

At this rash act, Oedipus's wife Jocasta tries to reassure her husband. Prophecies don't always come true, she tells him; back when she was mar-ried to Laius, the oracle at Delphi predicted that their three-day-old baby would someday kill Laius, so Laius sent a man out to expose the baby on a hillside. "We knew then," she says, "that the son would never kill his father. / The terror of the prophecy would die there on the hills. / That is what the prophet said, my king. / Pay it no mind. God alone shows us the truth." Laius, she adds, was not killed by his son, but at a place where three roads meet. Oedipus is horrified. He remembers, years ago, blundering into a hostile party of travelers at a three-road junction, killing the oldest member of the party, and fleeing. He never knew the identity of his victim. But he orders his men to find the old servant who was supposed to expose Jocasta's baby son. When the servant is finally found and brought back to the palace, he admits that he gave the baby to a shepherd in Oedipus's home country; Oedipus realizes that he is both Jocasta's son and the murderer of King Laius, his natural father. The Chorus enters to describe the final scene, in which Jocasta hangs herself, and Oedipus blinds himself. Creon returns from exile, assumes the throne, and grants Oedipus's wish: that he must now in turn be exiled. Oedipus's fate comes about, despite valiant attempts to avoid it—and he has been brought low by the intellectual and moral integrity that impelled him to seek out the truth about his parentage. "The power that made you great," Creon concludes, "was your destruction."

EURIPIDES
Medea
(C. 431 B.C.)

Best translations: The Oxford World's Classics paperback, Euripides: Medea and Other Plays *(reissue edition, 2009), is translated by James Morwood into readable, contemporary prose. The Cambridge Translations from Greek Drama translation by John Harrison,* Euripedes: Medea *(Cambridge University Press, 1999), has extensive explanatory notes on facing pages. The well-regarded 1950s translation by David Grene and Richmond Lattimore,* Euripides I: Alcestis, Medea, The Children of Heracles, Hippolytus, *has been updated by Mark Griffith and Glenn W. Most (University of Chicago Press, 3rd ed., 2013).*

Medea opens with the Nurse on stage, ready to tell us Medea's backstory: When the hero Jason came to Medea's country to steal the Golden Fleece from her father, she helped him, and then ran away with him. Now they live in exile in Corinth—but Jason has deserted Medea and her two sons in order to marry the daughter of Creon, Corinth's king. "I'm afraid she's dreaming up some dreadful plan," the Nurse warns. "She is dangerous. . . . But here come the boys, back from their game. / They have no idea of their mother's troubles / Young minds are still untouched by grief."

This ominous foreshadowing precedes bad news: King Creon arrives to banish Medea and her sons from his country. He tells Medea that she will die if she stays in Corinth even one more day; when she begs him, he grants her twenty-four more hours. Jason arrives to confirm Creon's banishment; even though Medea pleads with him to remember his oaths, he rejects her. So Medea pretends to repent of her earlier bitterness and sends Jason's new wife a beautiful robe—imbued with poison, so that the princess dies horribly as soon as she puts it on. Creon, who tries to help her remove it, dies as well.

Medea waits to hear of the deaths and then, reciting a chilling and contradictory list of reasons (her boys will be killed in revenge, and it is better that she should kill them than another; her boys will remain in Corinth while she is in exile, and they will miss her; she will make the children suffer "to hurt their father," although she will "suffer twice as much myself"), takes her two boys into her house and murders them. They scream for help, but the Chorus hesitates ("Shall we go in? / This is murder. / I'm sure we should help the boys.") and in the end remains outside. Jason arrives, furious and frightened, but Medea refuses to let him

see the boys' bodies; she will bury them in secret so that her enemies cannot desecrate the graves. Medea's confused self-justification, her decision
to kill the children whom she both loves and hates, Jason's desertion, and
the Chorus that hesitates when it should act: All strike a weirdly contemporary note, in this story of a woman who is mistreated by men and kills
her own children in response.

ARISTOPHANES
The Birds
(c. 400 B.C.)

*Best translations: Paul Muldoon's translation for the Penn Greek Drama
Series, Aristophanes, 3: The Suits, Clouds, Birds, ed. David R. Slavitt
and Palmer Bovie (University of Pennsylvania Press, 1999), is modern and
colloquial; it includes stage directions, which are not in the original, but which
help clarify the action. The Oxford World's Classics translation by Stephen
Halliwell, Birds and Other Plays (2009), is more literal but still readable.
The Peter Meineck translation, Aristophanes I: Clouds, Wasps, Birds
(Hackett, 1998), is both readable and contains explanatory footnotes.*

The surviving Greek comedies have a fairly standard structure: the prologue introduces a "happy idea," the Chorus discusses the idea, and a series
of scenes shows how the "happy idea" would work out in real life. In *The
Birds*, the "happy idea" is a civilization without unnecessary bureaucracy
or false prophets. Two Athenian men—Peisthetaerus and Euelpides—leave
Athens. "It isn't that we've anything against the city as such," Euelpides
remarks, "it's as grand and happy a place as ever a man paid a fine in. But
the Athenians yammer away in the lawcourts for the whole of their lives."
Led by their pet crow and pet jackdaw, they find their way to the Kingdom
of the Birds. The birds (played by a singing, dancing chorus of twenty-
four men in feathered costumes) plan to peck them to death for human
crimes against birds, but the Hoopoe suggests that the humans might be
able to advise them on self-protection: "It wasn't from their friends that
cities learned to perfect their fortifications," the Hoopoe points out, "it
was from their enemies."

So the Athenians teach the birds how to gather their fragmented peoples together into one state. The result is Cloud-cuckoo-land, the great
and happy city of the birds, which immediately begins to attract humans
who want to "feather their nests" by creating bureaucracies: the Oracle
Man arrives, offering to sacrifice for them, the Inspector insists that he
must be paid a fee to look over the new city, and the Statute-Seller offers

to make laws for a fee. All are turned away. Finally, the birds manage to wall off Olympia and intercept the savor of all sacrifices; the gods, helpless in the face of so much bird resourcefulness, send Prometheus, Poseidon, and Heracles to offer Peisthetaerus the goddess Sovereignty ("the very beautiful girl who looks after Zeus's thunderbolts for him") in marriage, if only he will ask the birds to unwall their frontier. The birds agree, and the play closes with a wedding song and dance. Written in a time when Athens suffered from far too many lawmakers, clerks, and prophets, *The Birds* is a utopian vision of a land which has none.

ARISTOTLE
Poetics
(C. 330 B.C.)

Best translations: The Penguin Classics translation by Malcolm Heath (1997) and the newer translation by Anthony Kenny for Oxford World's Classics (2013) are both literal and clear, if rather dry. The St. Augustine Press edition, Aristotle on Poetics, *translated by Seth Benardete and Michael Davis (2002), is slightly more colloquial and provides explanatory footnotes.*

Aristotle's essay on the art of dramatic poetry is partially concerned with the technique of drama, but the center of his argument has to do with the purpose of poetry. Like all art, poetry must be *mimetic*—it must imitate life in a way that brings greater understanding to the listener. Imitation, Aristotle points out, is man's natural way of learning; he is imitative by nature from childhood, and good imitations bring pleasure. Tragedy is the imitation, or *mimesis,* of noble characters; comedy of inferior persons. Aristotle never returns to a further discussion of comedy, although part of the *Poetics* has been lost (and perhaps his prescriptions for comedy along with it).

Tragedy is the *mimesis* of a particular kind of life: the hero of noble character suffers through a *peripeteia,* a sudden downturn in his fortunes. This reversal should lead him to *anagnorisis* ("recognition"), an understanding of why this change in fortunes has come about. Tragedy succeeds, Aristotle writes, when it evokes two emotions. Pity is the emotion that we feel when we see a catastrophe coming upon someone else. (The German idea of *Schadenfreude,* a pleasurable shudder when you hear that something bad has happened to someone else, is not unlike Aristotelian "pity," although Aristotle does not see pleasure as part of the experience.) Pity is a somewhat removed emotion; fear, on the other hand, comes when we recognize that catastrophe might equally well happen to us. A good tragedy is not only *mimetic,* offering the watcher (or reader) greater understanding, it must contain *katharsis*—a clear explanation to the *audi-ence* as to *why* the hero encountered disaster.

For Aristotle, tragedy is always a moral enterprise: Capable men, he writes "should not be shown changing from prosperity to disaster because that is not terrible or pitiful, but simply repulsive; and dissolute men should not be shown changing from bad fortune to good, because it doesn't engage even sympathy, let alone pity or terror." Pity and terror are best aroused when a good man is shown going from good fortune to bad; and the most pitiable things of all are acts done by blood relations to each other.

Everyman
(FOURTEENTH CENTURY)

Best editions: Everyman and Medieval Miracle Plays, *edited by A. C. Cawley (Random House, 1993), contains a selection of other biblical plays from medieval times as well. Standard texts of* Everyman *are also available in the Dover Thrift edition,* Everyman and Other Miracle and Morality Plays *(1995), which includes versions of four mystery plays (including* The Second Shepherd's Play, Abraham and Isaac, *and* Noah's Flood*), and the New Mermaids drama series volume,* Three Late Medieval Morality Plays, *ed. G. A. Lester (Bloomsbury Methuen Drama, 2002).*

In *Everyman*, the first character onstage is God, who announces that he will require a "reckoning" of every man's person because his creatures are so spiritually blind. He summons Death and sends him to Everyman (which is to say, the whole human race). Everyman himself is going hap-pily about his everyday life when Death arrives; in a panic, he begs Death for a reprieve, but only wins the right to look for a companion on his voyage. He tries Fellowship and Family, but neither will go with him; Fellowship points out, reasonably enough, that if he were to go with Everyman, he would never again come back; Kindred and Cousin plead that they have toe-cramp. He then tries Wealth and Riches, but this is no good either, since (as they explain) their "condition is man's soul to kill." Eventually Everyman is forced to turn to more ethereal companions— Discretion, Strength, Beauty, Knowledge, and Good Deeds (who is lying on the ground, so weakened by Everyman's sinful neglect that he cannot stand). They agree to accompany him, but as Everyman approaches the grave, all of his companions desert him—except for Good Deeds, who remains by him as he descends into the world below. "They all at the last do Everyman forsake," says the Doctor, the "learned theologian" who delivers the epilogue, "Save his Good Deeds there doth he take." It's a somewhat unexpected ending: Why is Good Deeds the only character able to pass between the two worlds, when Knowledge and Discretion are left behind?

Good Deeds is a fusion of the spiritual and the physical. Every listener, the Doctor warns, should "make his account whole and sound" so that he too can ascend to God. The financial, earth-bound metaphor is no mistake: To ignore the spiritual is to be blind, but to be "enlightened" is to see the spiritual and physical bound together into one whole. And this respect for the physical aspect of life is seen in the form of the allegorical form of the play itself—with every spiritual reality represented by a character of flesh and blood.

CHRISTOPHER MARLOWE
Doctor Faustus
(1588)

Best editions: The Oxford World's Classic edition, Dr. Faustus and Other Plays, ed. David Bevington and Eric Rasmussen (reissue edition, 2008), and the Dover Thrift edition, Dr. Faustus (1994), are both straightforward presentations of the play. The Norton Critical Edition, Doctor Faustus, ed. David Scott Kastan (2005), provides two different texts of the play (1604 and 1616) along with explanatory annotations (and twenty-five different interpretations).

Faustus already has degrees in divinity, law, and medicine, but although he has all the knowledge that any good medieval man could wish for, he wants more. Browsing through a book of magic, he decides to make a deal with the devil. Good and evil angels appear at once, the good angel begging him to forsake knowledge ("O Faustus, lay that damned book aside"), the evil angel promising, "Be thou on Earth as Jove is in the sky, / Lord and commander of these elements." His mind is made up: Faustus raises up Mephistopheles, the devil's servant, agrees to his terms, and signs the pact with his blood (which congeals as he tries to write).

With all the power in the world and twenty-four years of life left, Faustus at first demands explanations for the great questions of the universe. But as time goes on, he begins to trifle his power away. He turns invisible to play tricks on the famous, flies around the world, and demands to have Helen of Troy brought back from the dead for his own. As death draws near, he begins to panic, but each time he tries to pull back from the deal, Mephistopheles offers him another temptation. As he descends into hell at the play's end, Faustus mourns, "See, see where Christ's blood streams in the firmament! One drop would save my soul. . . . Ah, rend not my heart for naming of my Christ; Yet will I call on him—O spare me, Lucifer!"

Despite his pleas, Faustus never *does* call on God, although he has ample opportunity. Faustus is a Renaissance man—a seeker after great knowledge, set free from theological restrictions—yet in finding knowledge, he loses something. Marlowe is not recommending a simple return to medieval faith; Faustus cannot simply call on God. But a deep ambivalence about the new order comes through: If God is removed from the center of life and man is put in His place, what will the world be like? With no company but his own, man might find himself speaking the words of Mephistopheles, the devil's servant, who describes hell in the new order as a state of mind:

> Hell hath no limits, nor is circumscribed
> In one self place; for where we are is hell,
> And where hell is, there must we ever be.

WILLIAM SHAKESPEARE
Richard III
(1592–93)

Best editions: There are dozens of Shakespeare editions. The Folger Shakespeare Library edition contains detailed annotations on facing pages (ed. Barbara A. Mowat and Paul Werstine, Simon & Schuster, 1996). Signet Classics (1988) and Dover Thrift Editions (1995) offer no-frills text.

Two branches of the royal family, the Yorks and the Lancasters, are battling over England's throne. The Yorks murdered the Lancaster king, Henry VI, and his heir, Prince Edward; the York king Edward IV took the throne. But Richard, Edward IV's younger brother, wants to be king. He murders his other brother Clarence (a possible contender for the throne) and marries Anne (the wife of the murdered Prince Edward). When Edward IV dies, Richard ascends the throne, poisons his wife Anne, and sends his nephews Edward and Richard—Edward IV's rightful heirs—to the tower, where they are murdered. But Richard has been cursed by Queen Margaret, Henry VI's widow, and Nemesis, in the shape of yet another Lancastrian cousin named Henry, arrives and challenges him to battle. Haunted by the ghosts of all he has killed, Richard III goes into the Battle of Bosworth Field shaken; he is killed after losing his horse (and crying out the play's most quoted lines: "A horse! A horse! My kingdom for a horse!").

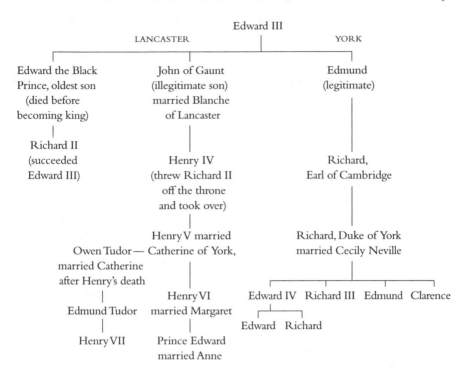

It's easy to be confused by the multiple Henrys, Richards, and Edwards casually mentioned by Shakespeare. Use the following chart to sort them out as you read. The common ancestry of Lancaster and York goes all the way back Edward III, who had five sons and thus produced way too many royal personages; he was the common great-great-grandfather of both Henry VI and Richard III. The Lancasters are in the middle of the chart below, the Yorks on the right side; the war between them ("The War of the Roses") erupted after Henry IV, an illegitimate descendant of Edward III, claimed the throne; the Yorks could claim descent from a legitimate son of Edward's.

The Richard of Shakespeare's play is a mesmerizing figure: evil, compelling enough to convince Anne to marry him even though he is responsible for her husband's death, charming when necessary, hypocritical, with just enough conscience to be afraid of ghosts. He is marked by his willingness to change his speech, his plans, and even his body to each occasion: "I'll be at charges for a looking glass," he muses, when Anne first rejects him, "And entertain a score or two of tailors / To study fashions to adorn my body." Richard is an intelligent, practical, effective, Machiavellian ruler who uses any means to gain his own ends. Yet he can only exert so much control; Queen Margaret's curse haunts him. Richard is caught in a cycle of history in which "every murder is both crime and punishment for crime, until at the end Richard pays the final penalty."[21]

WILLIAM SHAKESPEARE
A Midsummer Night's Dream
(1594–95)

*Best editions: The Oxford School Shakespeare edition (Oxford University Press, reprint edition, 2009) is designed for students but is useful for all readers; it contains explanatory footnotes, illustrations, and notes on staging. The play alone is also available from Signet Classics (1998) and Dover Thrift Editions (1992). Dover also publishes the play in an edition with Arthur Rackham's wonderful illustrations (*Shakespeare's A Midsummer Night's Dream, Illustrated by Arthur Rackham, *2003).*

The plot of Shakespeare's most famous comedy centers around three groups of characters: four young lovers, a group of rustic players, and a tribe of fairies. We meet the lovers first. Hermia wants to marry Lysander, but her father wants her to marry another suitor, Demetrius. He appeals to the local nobility—Duke Theseus, who is himself getting ready to marry Hippolyta, the vanquished warrior queen. Theseus tells Hermia that she has to marry her father's choice, so Hermia and Lysander make plans to run away. Hermia tells no one but her best friend Helena, who (since she is in love with Demetrius herself) immediately runs to Demetrius and tells him that his intended is running off with another man.

Meanwhile, the rustics, led by Bottom the weaver, are meeting in the palace woods to practice the play that they will perform for Theseus on his wedding day. But the woods have fairies in them—Oberon the fairy king and Titania the fairy queen, who are in the middle of a marital tiff. To improve his wife's temper, Oberon sends his servant Puck to gather magic nectar which will cause Titania to love whomever she sees when she wakes up. In the middle of this, Demetrius storms into the woods, looking for Hermia; he is followed by Helena, weeping pathetically. Oberon feels sorry for Helena and tells Puck to put the nectar on Demetrius's eyes as soon as he falls asleep; unfortunately, Puck gets confused when Lysander and Hermia show up as well and puts the juice on Lysander's eyelids instead. When Lysander wakes, he sees Helena, still

[21]Wolfgang H. Clemen, "Tradition and Originality in Shakespeare's *Richard III*," *Shakespeare Quarterly*, vol. 5, no. 3 (Summer 1954): 247–57.

trailing after Demetrius, jumps up, and runs after her—leaving Hermia all alone.

Oberon, who has decided to revenge himself on Titania, finds her bower and puts juice on her eyelids himself. The rustics blunder in and start their rehearsal; Puck, hovering mischievously in the wings, gives Bottom a donkey's head. When Titania wakes, she falls madly in love with the ass-headed weaver and takes him to her bower. Oberon finds this funny, but he is annoyed when he finds that Puck has anointed the wrong young man; now Lysander is chasing Helena, Helena is chasing Demetrius, Demetrius is chasing Hermia, and Hermia is sobbing pathetically after Lysander, who has forgotten all about her. Oberon tells Puck to blot the scene out with a fog and anoint everyone's eyes correctly; he himself goes to find Titania and takes the spell off her. The play ends with a triple wedding: Theseus and Hippolyta, Demetrius and Helena, and Hermia and Lysander (since Hermia's father, finding that his prospective son-in-law is now in love with another woman, agrees to let Hermia marry her choice). The rustics perform their play (very badly), and Oberon and Titania show up to bless the wedding.

All is well, but only because of chance and fairy intervention, and even the wedding has its dark side; Hippolyta is only marrying Theseus because he conquered her, and Demetrius, at least, is still enchanted. At the play's end, Puck concludes:

> If we shadows have offended,
> Think but this, and all is mended,
> That you have but slumber'd here,
> While these visions did appear

The happiness at the play's end is just as illusory as any shadow.

WILLIAM SHAKESPEARE
Hamlet
(1600)

Best editions: The Oxford School Shakespeare edition (Oxford University Press, 2009) for notes and staging; the play alone is available from Oxford World's Classics (2008) and Signet Classics (1998).

Hamlet is a hero, but he isn't an *active* hero; unlike Oedipus, who goes to some pains to deliver Thebes from plague and to discover the truth of his birth, Hamlet broods, hesitates, and regrets that he must act: "The time is out of joint. O cursed spite / That ever I was born to set it right!" His greatest desire is not simply to avoid action, but to avoid existence; in his most famous speech ("To be, or not to be, that is the question. . . .") he wishes to "dissolve into a dew."

Told, in a visit from his father's ghost, that his uncle Claudius (now married to his mother) killed him by pouring poison into his ear, Hamlet frets over what to do. He pretends madness to disarm his uncle (and as part of his act, brutally rejects Ophelia, the daughter of the lord chamberlain, Polonius). He then seizes on the chance visit of a group of players to stage a retelling of the murder in front of Claudius. Frightened, Claudius plots to get rid of Hamlet. Hamlet, on the other hand, is given a perfect opportunity to kill his uncle during prayer, but declines, making the excuse that the king would go straight to heaven were he killed in a state of grace.

Polonius, sure that the prince is insane, hides in the queen's rooms when her son goes in to speak with her. But Hamlet, hearing the old man behind the draperies and thinking him to be Claudius, finally acts—at the wrong time and place. He stabs Polonius through the curtains and then discovers his mistake. Conscience stricken, he agrees to leave Denmark and go to England; Claudius has arranged for him to be killed, but he escapes and returns to Denmark, sending ahead of him a letter announcing his intentions.

Ophelia, her father dead, loses her wits and drowns herself. Her brother Laertes returns for her funeral; Claudius convinces him to challenge Hamlet to a duel with a poisoned sword, and, just to be on the safe side, puts poison in a cup as well. When Hamlet arrives they fight; Laertes wounds Hamlet, but Hamlet (not realizing the sword is poisoned) scuffles with him and wounds him with it as well. Meanwhile the queen drinks the poisoned drink; Laertes, dropping to his knees, confesses that he too is dying, and that Hamlet is doomed. Hamlet grabs the poisoned sword, kills Claudius, and dies himself—finally brought to action by a series of coincidences beyond his control.

MOLIÈRE

Tartuffe

(1669)

Best translations: Richard Wilbur's witty 1961 translation, Tartuffe, *renders the play in rhymed couplets (Harvest Books, 1992). A more recent translation by Maya Slater, also in rhymed couplets, can be found in the Oxford World's Classics volume,* Molière: The Misanthrope, Tartuffe, and Other Plays

(2008). Curtis Hidden Page's unrhymed 1908 translation has held up well; it can be read at Project Gutenburg. Constance Congdon's recent rendering of the play into iambic pentameter is also worth reading (Broadway Play Publishing, 2014).

The pious hypocrite Tartuffe meets Orgon, a Parisian gentleman, in church, and by pretending piety convinces Orgon to take him into his home. Tartuffe is a great favorite of Orgon and his mother, but the rest of the household is not deceived. When Tartuffe gives the maid a handkerchief and orders her to cover her bosom because "such sights . . . evoke sinful thoughts," she remarks, "You are mighty susceptible to temptation. I could see you naked from top to toe, without being in the least tempted." And Orgon's brother-in-law Cléante warns him that he has been taken in: "There are hypocrites in religion," he says. "I know nothing more odious than the whited sepulchre of a pretended zealot, than those downright impostors . . . who, from motives of self-interest, make a trade of piety."

Instead of listening, Orgon accuses Cléante of becoming a freethinker. And worse is to come: he decides that his daughter Mariane, in love with Valère, should marry Tartuffe. ("I had promised you to Valère," he sighs, "but beside his being inclined to gamble, as I am told, I also suspect him to be somewhat of a free-thinker; I never notice him coming to church.") Elmire, Orgon's wife, tries to convince Tartuffe to leave her daughter in peace, but instead the "holy man" tries to seduce her. ("Men of our stamp love discreetly," he assures her.) Her son Damis overhears Tartuffe's attempts and runs to Orgon with this tale—but Orgon disinherits him, accusing of slandering the "saint," and makes over his estate to Tartuffe instead. "All the world's goods have but few charms for me," remarks Tartuffe, while accepting the gift.

So Elmire arranges for Orgon to hide under a table while she meets with Tartuffe and persuades him to renew his addresses; when Tartuffe does so, Orgon tries to throw him out. But since Tartuffe now owns the estate, the king's officers have to remove him by force. "I renounce all pious people," Orgon cries. "Henceforth I shall hold them in utter abhorrence and be worse to them than the very devil." "You exaggerate again!" Cléante reproves him. "You never preserve moderation in anything. You never keep within reason's bounds; and always rush from one extreme to another." But lack of balance is not Orgon's only flaw; the truth is that he has been able to exert complete control over his household through Tartuffe, using the holy man's manners as a mask for his own tyrannical desires.

WILLIAM CONGREVE
The Way of the World
(1700)

Best editions: Available from Dover Thrift Editions (1994), Penguin Classics
(The Way of the World and Other Plays, *ed. Eric S. Rump, 2006).*

The Way of the World is crammed with incident, even though it holds to
the Aristotelian unity of time (taking place over the course of only one
day). Intrigues and subplots boil from every act, but the skeleton of the
plot is constructed around Mirabell, a gentleman who once pretended to
be in love with Lady Wishfort but who is now in love with the heiress
Mrs. Millamant; Lady Wishfort, who now hates Mirabell for pretending
to love her; and Mrs. Millamant herself, who happens to be Lady Wishfort's niece (and ward).

Mirabell may love Millamant now, but he used to keep Lady Wishfort's
daughter as a mistress, before she married his best friend Fainall. Fainall
(who also keeps a mistress) would like Millamant to marry Mirabell, since
Lady Wishfort would then get angry, disinherit Millamant, and pass that
money along to her natural daughter—Fainall's wife. But Millamant has
not quite made up her mind to marry Mirabell, keeping him at a distance with witty remarks. "A man," Mirabell complains, "may as soon
make a friend by his wit, or a fortune by his honesty, as win a woman
with plain-dealing and sincerity." This lack of plain dealing continues.
Mirabell has his servant pose as an imaginary rich uncle to convince Lady
Wishfort of his worth as a suitor, but Lady Wishfort decides to court the
"rich uncle" herself. When Lady Wishfort's nephew, Sir Wilfull Witwoud, arrives and begins to woo Millamant (very awkwardly), Millamant
and Mirabell manage to reach an agreement of marriage.

Meanwhile, Fainall has decided to take a more direct route to Lady
Wishfort's money; he tells her that he will publicize her daughter's pre-
marital affair with Mirabell unless she hands Millamant's inheritance
over. But Mirabell foils this by blackmailing Fainall in turn, threatening
to reveal his present mistress. Sir Wilfull Witwoud, seeing that Millamant loves Mirabell, tells Lady Wishfort that he has no wish for Millamant and would rather travel to foreign parts; Lady Wishfort sighs "I can
hold out no longer. . . . I am ready to sink under the Fatigue" and agrees
to the marriage. The characters (none of whom are admirable) are moral
insofar as they are successful. Fainall turns out to be the villain at the
end, less because he is evil than because he has been outwitted. The play
is famous for its conversations; the characters talk, talk, and talk, using

wit and words to conceal their true feelings far more often than they do to reveal them.

OLIVER GOLDSMITH
She Stoops to Conquer
(1773)

Best editions: Available from Dover Thrift Editions (1991) and Oxford World's Classics (She Stoops to Conquer and Other Comedies, *ed. Nigel Wood, Michael Cordner, Peter Holland, and Martin Wiggins, 2008).*

Goldsmith's play, which involves two well-bred young men on their way to propose to two well-bred young women, has none of these well-bred people at its center; the true power of the play is Tony Lumpkin, an "awkward booby." Mr. Hastings and Mr. Marlow, two gentlemen of education and wealth, set out to visit the Hardcastle household. Marlow is supposed to court the daughter of the house, although the two have never met; their parents have arranged the meeting, unaware that Marlow is incapable of speaking to a woman of his own class and can only be at ease with servants and barmaids. Hastings, Marlow's friend, has volunteered to come along because he is already in love with the household's resident niece, Miss Neville. The Hardcastles intend Miss Neville to marry Tony Lumpkin, Mrs. Hardcastle's son from her previous (low) marriage—which will keep Miss Neville's fortune in the family. But Tony is unwilling; he is in love with Bet Bouncer, a country girl with "cheeks as broad and red as a pulpit cushion."

When Marlow and Hastings stop at the local alehouse to ask for directions to the Hardcastle estate, they accidentally insult Tony Lumpkin, who by way of revenge tells them that they will never reach the Hardcastle estate by nightfall—but that an inn is right around the corner. This "inn" is, however, the Hardcastle house itself. Hastings and Marlow storm into it, treating the bewildered Hardcastles like servants and innkeepers. When Hastings meets Miss Neville, he realizes his mistake—but the two decide to keep the joke going as cover for their own plans to elope. They tell Marlowe that Miss Hardcastle, by a great coincidence, is also visiting this "inn," and introduce the two. But Marlowe is too frightened of this aristocratic lady to look her in the face. So she dresses as a barmaid and sashays past him (this is the "stooping to conquer" of the title), awakening his interest. Eventually, all mistaken identities are righted. Miss Neville marries Hastings; Marlow proposes to Miss Hardcastle and then discovers that she is the daughter of the house; Tony renounces his claim to Miss Neville in favor of Bet Bouncer. Goldsmith's play casts into question the

idea of "low"; who is lower, the honest Tony, or Marlow, who is ready to
seduce a barmaid on first meeting?

RICHARD BRINSLEY SHERIDAN
The School for Scandal
(1777)

*Best editions: Available from Dover Thrift Editions (1990) and Oxford
World's Classics (The School for Scandal and Other Plays, ed. Michael
Cordner, 2008).*

Sir Peter Teazle is newly married to the daughter of a country squire; he
has a lovely young ward, Maria; and he has acted as "a kind of guardian"
to two young men who lost their father in childhood—the Surface brothers, Joseph and Charles.

In public, Joseph appears to be "amiable . . . and universally well-spoken
of," while Charles is "the most dissipated and extravagant young fellow in
the kingdom, without friends or character." But appearances are deceiving. Charles is actually good natured, although spendthrift; and Joseph is
actually "artful, selfish, and malicious." Charles is in love with Maria, but
Joseph (who is favored by Sir Peter) wishes only for her fortune.

Charles and Joseph's uncle, Sir Oliver Surface, arrives from Australia;
he has been hearing contradictory reports about his nephews, so he poses
as a moneylender ("Mr. Premium") and calls on Charles. Charles tries
to borrow from him on the strength of his possible inheritance from Sir
Oliver himself: "Though at the same time," Charles adds, "though at the
same time the old fellow has been so liberal to me that I give you my word
I should be very sorry to hear that anything had happened to him." "Not
more than *I* should, I assure you," Sir Oliver remarks. Charles offers to sell
the family portraits to raise money, and, in one of the play's most famous
scenes, auctions them off to "Mr. Premium" and two other moneylenders.
But he refuses to sell the portrait of Sir Oliver—and Sir Oliver himself,
touched, decides to pay off his nephew's debts.

Meanwhile, Joseph is in his own library, carrying on an affair with
Sir Peter Teazle's young wife. While they are engaged in intimate conversation, Sir Peter arrives and Lady Teazle leaps behind a nearby screen.
What follows is a "screen scene," a convention of manners plays, in which
characters overhear private conversations from a hidden place. Lady Teazle overhears Sir Peter telling Joseph his suspicions that Charles is having
an affair with his wife, but Sir Peter then hears Charles arriving and leaps
into a closet himself. When Charles comes in, he begins to describe how

he once found Joseph and Lady Teazle together. To stop him, Joseph opens the closet door and reveals Sir Peter; Charles knocks the screen down and finds Lady Teazle, who begs her husband for forgiveness. Sir Peter collects his wife and marches out, giving Charles (now debt free) permission to marry Maria. All has been "righted" (despite Charles's shaky character), but only because "manners" were breached in the two pivotal scenes: Sir Oliver and Sir Peter both hear speeches not intended for them.

HENRIK IBSEN
A Doll's House
(1879)

Best translations: Frank McGuinness's translation (New York: Faber & Faber, 1996) is contemporary and readable; it opened on Broadway in 1997. Another excellent translation, by James McFarlane and Jens Arup, is found in the Oxford World's Classics edition (2008).

Nora Helmer has broken the law. Needing money for her husband's medical expenses, she forged her father's signature in order to borrow it from the bank. (It is illegal for women to borrow money without authorization from a husband or father.) Her friend Mrs. Linde is shocked to hear this, but Nora has been able to pay the loan back regularly through saving part of her dress allowance and doing copywork jobs late into the night. ("Oh, sometimes I was so tired, so tired. And yet it was splendid to work in that way and earn money. I almost felt as if I was a man.")

But now Nora's husband, Torvald, has become a director at the bank where she took out the loan—and the officer who approved it, Mr. Krogstad, is about to lose his job. He asks Nora to intervene for him. When she refuses, he tells her that he knows her secret: Her father's signature was dated three days after her father's death. If he loses his job, he will reveal her crime.

Nora tries to avert the crisis—but Torvald refuses to listen to her pleas for Krogstad. The man loses his job, and Torvald receives a letter from Krogstad describing Nora's crime. "You've been my pride and joy," Torvald bellows at Nora, "and now I find you're a hypocrite and a liar and worse, worse than that . . . a criminal!" Torvald is afraid that Krogstad will broadcast Nora's sins through polite society unless he's given his job back: "It'll have to be hushed up," Torvald decides. "We shall have to make it look as if nothing has changed between us. . . . I mean, you'll obviously have to stay on in the house, but you won't be allowed to have anything to do with the children." Then, in the midst of his diatribe, he receives another letter from Krogstad, who has decided to marry Mrs. Linde and no longer wishes to hold any threat over Nora's head. Relieved of the threat of public humiliation, Torvald immediately reverses himself: "Poor little Nora, I understand. . . . For a man there's something intensely reassuring and pleasurable about *knowing* that he's forgiven his wife. . . . It's as if she becomes somehow doubly his possession, as if he's allowed her to be reborn, so that in some way she becomes both his wife and his child."

At this, Nora packs up to leave. "I've been your doll-wife," she tells him, "just as I was Daddy's doll-child when I was at home." It would take a miracle, she tells her husband, for their relationship to become a marriage; she walks out and leaves him. Nora loves her husband, as society demands, but this very love leads her into an act condemned by those same social laws. Caught in this paradox, she finds her home ruined and her husband's love for her revealed as, simply, an extension of his own self-respect.

OSCAR WILDE
The Importance of Being Earnest
(1899)

Best editions: The play is widely available as a public domain ebook, as well as from Dover Thrift Editions (1990), Prestwick House (with explanatory notes, 2005), and with four other plays in the Oxford World's Classic edition, Oscar Wilde: The Importance of Being Earnest and Other Plays *(2008).*

In London, Jack Worthing calls himself Ernest; when he is at his country estate, where his eighteen-year-old ward Cecily lives, he calls himself Jack and attributes all his city doings to his (nonexistent) brother Ernest. Jack is in love with Gwendolen Fairfax, the cousin of his friend Algernon Moncrieff. He proposes to her in town, using the name Ernest, and she agrees, since it has always been her dream to marry a man named Ernest. Her aunt, Lady Bracknell, demands to know Jack's family background; when Jack reveals that he was discovered in a handbag in Victoria Station, Lady Bracknell refuses to consent to the match. Gwendolen promises to write to Jack at his country address. Algernon, overhearing (and knowing that Jack's ward Cecily, an extremely pretty girl, lives at this address along with her governess, Miss Prism), decides to visit.

He arrives at the estate before Jack and introduces himself as Ernest, Jack's brother. Cecily falls in love with him at once and promises to marry him (since she has always wanted to marry someone named Ernest).

Unfortunately, Jack has decided that his dual identity has gotten too complicated; he arrives in black and announces the death of his brother Ernest to the bewildered Cecily. Gwendolen then arrives in a fury, having heard that Cecily has become engaged to Mr. Ernest Worthing. To straighten things out, Jack and Algernon admit their real names; both girls threaten to break off their engagements unless Jack and Algernon are both rechristened Ernest immediately. Lady Bracknell, arriving for the christenings, recognizes Miss Prism as the nursemaid who, twenty-eight years before, accidentally left Lady Bracknell's baby nephew at Victoria Station in a handbag. Jack is this nephew, Algernon's older brother—and he was christened Ernest. "Gwendolen," he says solemnly, "it is a terrible thing for a man to find out suddenly that all his life he has been speaking nothing but the truth." Wilde, who was convicted of homosexuality in the courts and sentenced to two years at hard labor, mocks conventions of heterosexual marriage. The dual identities of his male characters (Ernest-Jack, Algernon-Ernest) are the more remarkable since his female characters are undivided; all that frothy comedy stems from more serious uncertainties about the nature of identity.

ANTON CHEKHOV
The Cherry Orchard
(1904)

Best translations: Sharon Marie Carnicke's contemporary, lyrical version is published by Hackett (trade edition, 2010). The Penguin Classics translation by Peter Carson in Anton Chekhov: Plays (Penguin Classics, rev. ed., 2002) contains four other Chekhov plays as well. Perhaps most interesting is the version done by Tom Stoppard, a brilliant playwright in his own right, for Grove Press (2009); his work is based on a literal translation by Helen Rappaport.

Lopakhin, once a peasant, is now a rich man. He is waiting at Madame Ranevsky's elaborate family estate for her return from Paris. The estate has been under the management of her adopted daughter Varya and her brother Gaev, but Madame Ranevsky's extravagances have run it into debt. When Madame Ranevsky arrives with her daughter Anya, Lopakhin tells her that the estate will have to be auctioned—unless she raises money by dividing the land and renting it to weekend vacationers. "Forgive me, you appear not to understand," she says. "If there is one truly remarkable thing in this entire region it is my cherry orchard." Unable to face the gradual dismantling of her aristocratic way of life, Madame

Ranevsky ignores the debts; Varya, more realistic, frets over her unsettled relationship with Lopakhin. ("He's too busy with his . . . business," she tells Anya. "There's great talk about the impending wedding. . . . [B]ut there's nothing, it's just . . . a dream.") Anya, who once loved the cherry orchard "like a person," is courted by Peter Trofimov, a socialist who hates what the orchard represents. "Why do I care less about the cherry orchard than I used to?" Anya says to Peter, and he answers, "Your orchard is all of Russia. Your father's father, and his father, and his, were owners of serfs. They owned human lives. From every tree in your orchard there are people hanging, they peer at you through the branches, you can hear their voices moaning in the leaves."

Finally the family decides that the money sent to them by an aged relative will suffice to buy the place back, and Gaev goes cheerfully off to the auction. But the estate sells for six times Gaev's money—to Lopakhin, who now owns the place where his father was a serf. "The dull and lowly Lopakhin will take his axe to the cherry orchard and send the trees whistling to the ground!" he shouts, drunkenly. Although they weep, the family promptly makes new plans. Gaev finds a job at a bank, Madame Ranevsky plans on returning to Paris, Anya decides to go to university and promises her mother that she will soon support both of them. At the play's end, the sound of axes is heard offstage as the cherry orchard is chopped down. There are no villains or heroes in *The Cherry Orchard*, and Chekhov offers no answers. Instead he shows us the world of the aristocrats, now passing away, as simultaneously beautiful and oppressive, wistfully desirable and fatally flawed; the complexities are carefully painted, not resolved.

GEORGE BERNARD SHAW
Saint Joan
(1924)

Best edition: The Penguin Classics (2001).

Shaw's own preface lays out his twin preoccupations: to deal fairly with the medieval belief in the miraculous ("In the Middle Ages people believed that the earth was flat, for which they had at least the evidence of their senses: we believe it to be round . . . because modern science has convinced us that nothing that is obvious is true"), and to write a tragedy with "no villains . . . If Joan had not been burnt by normally innocent people in the energy of their righteousness her death at their hands would have no . . . significance." The play continually returns to this question of perspective: Truth and falsehood depend on the position of the observer.

As the play begins, Joan arrives at the fortress of the soldier Robert de Baudricourt to convince him to give her a horse and a company of soldiers so that she can help the Dauphin regain his throne (now held by Henry VI). Robert is skeptical, but his friends have already agreed to accompany Joan; "What is the good of commonsense?" they ask. "Nothing can save our side now but a miracle." So Robert sends Joan to the Dauphin, who eventually gives command of his army to "the Maid." Joan leads the army against the English, who are besieging Orleans; the wind miraculously changes direction, allowing her soldiers to sail across the river, and the English are defeated.

The English then meet with the French bishop of Beauvais. The English chaplain insists that Joan is a witch, and the earl of Warwick is afraid that loyalty to Joan might distract the masses from loyalty to their own feudal lords. The bishop believes that Joan's nationalism is a threat to the church; "the Catholic Church knows only one realm, and that is the realm of Christ's kingdom." He is at first reluctant to cooperate with the English: "You great lords are too prone to treat the Church as a mere political convenience," he snaps. "I am no mere political bishop." But he finally agrees to help turn Joan over to Warwick and his soldiers, who burn her at the stake. The tragedy of this ending is lightened, though, by the epilogue, in which Joan and her enemies appear to Charles in a dream. "The burning was purely political," Warwick tells her pleasantly. "There was no personal feeling against you, I assure you." "I bear you no malice, my lord," Joan says politely. A 1920s clergyman then enters the dream to announce that Joan has been made a saint; when they laugh at him for his "extraordinarily comic dress" he retorts stiffly, "You are all in fancy dress: I am properly dressed." This is Shaw's summation: Each character in the play thinks himself "properly dressed," doing what is right in his own eyes. And the play itself leaves the final judgment on Joan's life to the audience.

T. S. ELIOT
Murder in the Cathedral
(1935)

Best edition: Harcourt (1964).

Eliot's priest, Thomas Becket, shares the reservations of Shaw's bishop: He too worries that political ambition will distort his service to God. But while *Saint Joan* employs a slightly tongue-in-cheek theatrical realism (Shaw's medieval Frenchmen speak like twentieth-century gentlemen),

Eliot's play is impressionistic, featuring symbolic characters (Tempters, Assassins, and a Chorus that speaks in unison) and written in verse.

The play's central character is the archbishop of Canterbury, the "turbulent priest" Thomas Becket, who has spoken against Henry II's extension of royal powers into areas that he believed should belong to the church. Afraid of the king's anger, Becket has fled to France. As the play begins, he is returning to England, in a scene reminiscent of Palm Sunday as the people line the road and throw down their capes before him. The people of Canterbury are ready to welcome him ("He . . . was always kind to his people"), but unresolved tensions between Becket and the king remain. Three priests worry about the dangers of Becket's return: He, like the king, is a proud and powerful personality, resentful of all earthly authority, answering only to God.

In another echo of Christ's story, Tempters come to Becket, promising him wealth, influence, and peace if he will only satisfy the king. Becket rejects each temptation, musing that, since he holds the spiritual authority to grant or withhold "heaven and hell," he has no need for earthly power. But Becket's final temptation leads to a severe psychological struggle, one with no resolution: He is tempted to become a martyr willingly, and so to have even more glory. No matter what decision he makes, Becket sees corruption *in himself.*

At the play's end, the Knights sent by Henry chase Becket, murder him, and then step forward to address the audience directly, explaining in prose that they are "four plain Englishmen who put our country first." Becket may lose himself in anguished contemplation of his own sin, but these knights are convinced that they are acting rightly. Eliot, like Chekhov and Shaw, refuses to resolve his conflicts, but the struggle he presents is an internal one—taking place not primarily between Henry and Becket, but within the mind of Becket himself.

THORNTON WILDER
Our Town
(1938)

Best edition: Harper Perennial Modern Classics (2003).

Our Town begins by drawing our attention to its unreality; the Stage Manager comes onto the scene and introduces us to the actors who play each character. This story of the small-town residents of Grover's Corners is meant to be a philosophical reflection, a set of illustrations revealing a truth about human existence. Emily Webb and George Gibbs meet as children, marry ("Almost everybody in the world gets married," the Stage Manager remarks, as they prepare for the wedding), and have children; Emily dies and enters the community of the dead. The play's climax comes when Emily decides to relive her twelfth birthday. She sees her parents and brother (now dead), and tries to go through the day as she did when she was twelve, but she grows frustrated with the blindness of ordinary people: "Oh, Mama," she bursts out to her mother, "just look at me one minute as though you really saw me. Mama, fourteen years have gone by. I'm dead. You're a grandmother. . . . Wally's dead, too. . . . Don't you remember? But, just for a moment now we're all together. Mama, just for a moment we're happy. *Let's look at one another.*" Mrs. Webb, unheeding, goes on cooking, and Emily breaks down. "It goes so fast," she sobs. "We don't have time to look at one another. . . . Do any human beings ever realize life while they live it?—every, every minute?" "No," the Stage Manager answers. "The saints and poets, maybe—they do some."

Our Town shows the details of those lives that go "so fast"; it aims to illustrate the particular value of each moment of ordinary time. In the end, the play is hopeful about the human condition. "We all know that *something* is eternal," the Stage Manager remarks. "And it ain't houses, and it ain't names, and it ain't earth, and it ain't even the stars. . . . [E]verybody knows in their bones that *something* is eternal, and that something has to do with human beings." Wilder is a humanist: We may have little control over our world, over our decisions, and over the passage of time, but what we do within that world is *meaningful* in some eternal sense. *Our Town* is a tragedy, but a tragedy that recognizes humanity's essential worth—*not* its essential insignificance. (Wilder is the only American to win Pulitzer Prizes for both drama and fiction, for the plays *Our Town* and *The Skin of Our Teeth* and the story *The Bridge of San Luís Rey*.)

EUGENE O'NEILL
Long Day's Journey into Night
(1940)

Best edition: Yale University Press (2nd ed., 2002).

O'Neill (1888–1953) wanted this play, written in 1940, to remain unpublished for twenty-five years after his death, but it was first produced in 1956.

James Tyrone, his wife Mary, and their two sons—Jamie, in his mid-thirties, and Edmund, ten years younger—have just finished breakfast on an August morning. But amid the trivial family exchanges, tensions grow: James and Jamie quarrel, Jamie sneers at Edmund, Edmund coughs, and Mary begins to yearn for the morphine to which she is addicted. By lunchtime, when the doctor calls to tell Edmund that he is consumptive, Mary has taken her first shot of morphine and James has started to drink. In midafternoon, Mary makes an effort to reconnect: "James!" she cries. "We've loved each other! . . . Let's remember only that, and not try to understand what we cannot understand. . . . [T]he things life has done to us we cannot excuse or explain."

But James is unable to respond. Each member of the family, isolated and dreading this solitude, tries to form alliances with the other members, and these alliances continually shift and change, creating anger and bitterness.[22] Mary mourns over the death of the child born between Jamie and Edmund, blaming both James and Jamie: "If I hadn't left him with my mother to join you on the road," she accuses her husband, "because you wrote telling me you missed me and were so lonely, Jamie would never have been allowed, when he still had measles, to go in the baby's room. . . . I've always believed Jamie did it on purpose. He was jealous of the baby." "Can't you let our baby rest in peace?" James asks wearily. But Mary can find peace only by retreating further into her drug addiction and pretending a return to her girlhood. "You go back," she muses, "until at least you are beyond [pain's] reach. Only the past when you were happy is real."

Night finally falls. Edmund, who has left the house in anger, returns at midnight to find his father, drunk, sitting at the table. He drinks with his father, quoting Baudelaire: "If you would not feel the horrible burden of Time weighing on your shoulders and crushing you to earth, be drunken continually." Jamie enters, drunk as well; Mary descends from her room, high on morphine. Edmund tries once again to connect with his mother. But she is trapped in the past. "I remember," she says, slowly. "I fell in love with James Tyrone and was so happy for a time." And the play ends.

O'Neill shows the slow building of tension partly through dialogue, but largely through the characters' faces and voices; he uses dialogue tags to reveal this hidden dimension of the drama (*He gives her a quick apprehensive glance*, reads one dialogue tag, *but if his suspicions are aroused her tenderness makes him renounce them and he believes what he wants to believe for the moment. On the other hand, Jamie knows after one probing look at her that his suspicions are justified. His eyes fall to stare at the floor, his face sets in an expression of embittered, defensive cynicism*).

---

[22] I owe this insight to Stephen A. Black, "O'Neill's Dramatic Process," *American Literature*, vol. 59, no. 1 (March 1987): 58–70.

JEAN PAUL SARTRE
No Exit
(1944)

Best translation: The Stuart Gilbert translation in No Exit and Three Other Plays *(Vintage, reissue edition, 1989).*

Garcin, newly dead, enters hell and finds himself in a French drawing room, with no bed (so that he cannot sleep), no mirrors (so that he cannot reflect on his own identity), no windows (so that he cannot connect with the outside world), and no toothbrush (no personal possessions)—just a weird bronze ornament on the mantelpiece, too heavy to lift, and a paper knife for cutting the pages of books (although no books are in the room). In Sartre's version of hell, humans are incapable of taking any action—and also barred from any oblivion, even the briefest. The lights never turn off, and the valet who shows him to his room never even blinks. "Ah," Garcin says, "it's life without a break. . . . One has to live with one's eyes open all the time." And there is no escape; outside the room are only passages, more rooms, more passages, and stairs.

Two more characters enter the room: Inez, a lesbian whose lover killed both of them ("For six months I flamed away in her heart, till there was nothing but a cinder. One night she got up and turned on the gas while I was asleep"), and Estelle, a society woman who ran away with her lover, killed their baby, and then died of pneumonia. Estelle laments the lack of a mirror: "When I can't see myself I begin to wonder if I really and truly exist. I pat myself just to make sure, but it doesn't help much." "You're lucky," Inez answers, "I'm always conscious of myself—in my mind. Painfully conscious." Each character wants something from the others; Inez wants Estelle, Estelle wants Garcin to affirm her desirability to men, Garcin wants Inez to recognize him as brave and courageous. But in hell, each character has lost the capacity to *act*. Exasperated with each other, they manage to get the door open—but can't bring themselves to leave the room. "Hell is—other people," Garcin concludes, "we are together forever, and ever, and ever. . . . Well, well, let's get on with it. . . ."

Those are the play's last words, but of course they cannot "get on with it." Sartre's existential philosophy found meaning only in what man is able to *do*; when action is impossible, man is in a meaningless hell. *No Exit* points out a contradiction in existentialism itself: Meaning only comes when man is able to act with some control to change his future. Yet this action must always involve other people—and whenever man is dependent on the actions of others to validate his own, he lacks control and is caught in a cycle that never ends. The only meaningful choice that remains is death. And when man cannot choose death, he is truly in hell.

TENNESSEE WILLIAMS
A Streetcar Named Desire
(1947)

Best editions: The New Directions paperback (2004) or the Signet mass market paperback (1984).

Blanche Dubois, a southern lady, arrives at her sister's house with nothing but her suitcase; she has lost the family estate in Mississippi, Belle Reve ("Beautiful Dream"), and has nothing left. Her sister, Stella, is married to the blue-collar Stanley Kowalski. Blanche finds Stanley common and "ape-like"; Stanley finds Blanche snobbish, affected, and dishonest. The two battle for Stella's loyalty. Blanche's weapons are her gentility, the memories of their shared past, and guilt. "I stayed and struggled!" she tells her sister. "You came to New Orleans and looked after yourself!" Stanley's hold over Stella is sexuality; "There are things that happen between a man and a woman in the dark—that sort of make everything else seem—unimportant," Stella tells Blanche. She becomes pregnant, and Stanley's hold over her is strengthened. In a fight over a poker game, Stanley wrecks the apartment's living room and hits Stella; Blanche carries her off to a friend's apartment, but Stella returns as soon as Stanley calls her. "The only way to live with such a man," Blanche snaps, "is to—go to bed with him! And that's your job—not mine!"

Blanche is tentatively courted by Stanley's friend Mitch. But Stanley, snooping through Blanche's past, discovers that she is notorious for her drunken promiscuity. He tells the idealistic Mitch of Blanche's reputation, and Mitch rejects her. When she realizes what Stanley has done, Blanche begins to scream at him—but Stella goes into labor and Stanley takes her to the hospital. Mitch arrives, driven to see Blanche one more time, and Blanche admits that she has lied about her past: "I don't tell the truth, I tell what *ought* to be the truth." When Mitch refuses to marry Blanche but tries to seduce her anyway, Blanche throws him out. Stanley, coming back to the apartment from the hospital, high with excitement, finds Blanche alone there and rapes her. She goes insane; in the play's last scene, a nurse and doctor arrive to take her away. She goes with them, puzzled but accepting, while Stella weeps in Stanley's arms, distraught and guilty, but not moving away from her husband's body. The play is realistic psychological drama: Stanley hates Blanche but also desires her; she loathes him but finds his sexuality compelling. It is also social commentary: There is no place for Blanche, the genteel southern lady, in this new urban world.

ARTHUR MILLER
Death of a Salesman
(1949)

Best editions: Available from Penguin Classics (2000), or with explanatory notes and interpretive essays from Viking Critical Library (1996).

Willy Loman, sixtyish salesman, lives in a tiny New York house, trapped and caged by the buildings all around him and by his own insufficiencies. He has just returned from a fruitless attempt to drive up to his sales territory "beyond Yonkers"—"I suddenly couldn't drive anymore," he tells his wife Linda. "The car kept going off onto the shoulder, y'know." He is losing his sales territory, reduced from his salaried position at the company to working on commission, suffering from confusion between past and present. Willy's two sons, Happy and Biff, in their thirties and unsuccessful, are both home; their presence exaggerates Willy's confusion. As he speaks to them in the present, he imagines the past, and these scenes play out on stage. He sees himself encouraging the young Biff's athleticism, overlooking his tendency to cheat and his failing grades in math.

When Biff and Happy realize that their father is borrowing money to pay his bills, they plan to ask Biff's former boss, Bill Oliver, to invest in a new sporting goods business. They tell Willy that they will meet him in the evening for dinner, after getting the money from Oliver. Willy, inspired, goes himself to ask his own boss for a salaried position: "Selling was the greatest career a man could want," he muses, while his employer waits impatiently for him to be done. "In those days there was personality in it, Howard. There was respect, and comradeship. . . . Today, it's all cut and dried, and there's no chance for bringing friendship to bear—or personality. . . . I put thirty-four years into this firm, Howard, and now I can't pay my insurance! You can't eat the orange and throw the peel away—a man is not a piece of fruit!"

But Willy is "thrown away"—he is fired. Meanwhile Biff sees Bill Oliver but doesn't dare ask for money, suddenly realizing what a failure he was in his previous job for Oliver. When Willy arrives at the restaurant, the three quarrel over the past. The young Biff appears on stage. He has just failed his senior math class and won't be able to take up his college athletic scholarship. He searches out Willy to ask for help, but finds his father in a motel room with another woman. The young Biff storms out, giving up on college; the older Biff accuses his father of ruining his life.

They leave the restaurant separately. Back home, Willy realizes that his life insurance (twenty thousand dollars) would set Biff up in his new business. "That boy—" he cries out, "that boy is going to be magnificent!" He leaves the house and crashes the car, killing himself. In the epilogue, Linda stands at Willy's grave with her sons and Willy's only friend, their neighbor Charley: "I can't understand it," she laments. "He only needed a little salary." "No man only needs a little salary," Charley replies. Miller himself called the play a tragedy—one about "the common man," who is "as apt a subject for tragedy in its highest sense as kings were," because the psychology of all men is the same. In this psychological tragedy, Miller adds, the "tragic feeling is evoked in us when we are in the presence of a character who is ready to lay down his life, if need be, to secure . . . his 'rightful' position in his society. . . . There are among us today, as there always have been, those who act against the scheme of things that degrades them."[23] Twentieth-century capitalism degrades Willy: "The competition is maddening!" he complains at the play's beginning, but his efforts to resist the market are doomed.

SAMUEL BECKETT
Waiting for Godot
(1952)

Best edition: The Grove Press paperback (2011).

In the first act of *Waiting for Godot*, two tramps—Vladimir and Estragon—arrive on stage and stand beside a tree, waiting for Godot to arrive. They chant back and forth, trying to figure out what they've asked Godot for, what he said he would provide, why they're waiting.

But no more information is ever provided. Two other travelers—Pozzo and his slave Lucky—arrive on stage, chat for a while, and then leave. A boy arrives and tells the two that Godot won't be coming, but will come the following day. They decide to go, but don't budge. ("Well, shall we go?" "Yes, let's go." *They do not move.*) In the second act, the exact same events occur: Lucky and Pozzo arrive again, although they have changed roles, and don't remember meeting Vladimir and Estragon the previous day. Vladimir makes an effort to change the situation: "Let us not waste our time in idle discourse!" he suddenly exclaims. "Let us do something

---

[23] Arthur Miller, "Tragedy and the Common Man," *New York Times*, February 27, 1949, section II, pp. 1, 3.

while we have the chance!" But they keep on waiting. The boy shows up again and says that Godot will not be coming, but doesn't remember delivering the identical message the day before. Vladimir and Estragon debate hanging themselves, but don't have a strong enough cord. "I can't go on like this," Estragon says. "That's what you think," Vladimir retorts. They again decide to leave, again fail to leave, and the curtain falls.

Godot never arrives (asked what Godot "means," Beckett once remarked, "If I knew, I would have said so in the play"). But *waiting*, not Godot, is at the center of the play. Beckett is a symbolic writer, and the two tramps waiting for some vague and undefined end are symbols for the human experience: in Martin Esslin's words, "the act of waiting as an essential and characteristic aspect of the human condition."[24] Every human being waits out the period between birth and death, unable to perform any significant act, to understand the world, or even to communicate meaningfully with another human being.

ROBERT BOLT
A Man for All Seasons
(1960)

Best edition: The Vintage Books paperback (reissue edition, 1990). The preface, by Bolt himself, is an essential part of the play and suggests Bolt's own preferences for sets, costumes, and so on.

Thomas More is under pressure from Henry VIII to sanction his divorce from Catherine of Aragon, so that he may marry Anne Boleyn; but More refuses. Cardinal Wolsey wants More to agree with the king. "If you could just see facts flat on, without that horrible moral squint," he says, "you could have been a statesman." But Wolsey displeases the king; More succeeds him and comes under even greater pressure from Henry VIII, who wants More's public blessing because "you are honest. What's more to the purpose, you're known to be honest." When the king commands More to swear on oath that the marriage is legal, More refuses and is imprisoned. No one can find grounds for executing him, but Thomas Cromwell, Secretary to the Council, is determined to smooth the way for the king. He offers More's pupil Richard Rich the gift of a position as Collector of the Revenue, collects from him seemingly innocent "tidbits of information," and dangles the possibility of public recognition before the younger man. Rich is susceptible to this temptation. (Early in the play Rich complains

---

[24]Esslin, *The Theatre of the Absurd*, p. 29.

that the only recognition he's ever had is "one half of a Good Morning delivered at fifty paces by the Duke of Norfolk. Doubtless he mistook me for someone else." "Be a teacher," More counsels him, advising him to avoid the quest to be well known. "You'd be a fine teacher." "And if I was, who would know it?" Rich objects. "You, your pupils, your friends, God," More replies. "Not a bad public, that.") Trapped by his increasing wealth and prominence, unable to give either up, Rich agrees to lie about More in public, accusing him of treasonous statements. More, condemned, turns to Cromwell: "What you have hunted me for is not my actions, but the thoughts of my heart," he says. "It is a long road you have opened. For first men will disclaim their hearts and presently they will have no hearts. God help the people whose statesmen walk your road."

"Thomas More," wrote Bolt in his own preface, "knew . . . what area of himself he could yield to the encroachments of his enemies, and what to the encroachments of those he loved. . . . At length he was asked to retreat from that final area where he located his self. And there this supple, humorous, unassuming and sophisticated person set like metal." More's identity is located in his integrity before God; the oath which Henry demanded of him would have identified his most private self with a lie. Like *Saint Joan* and *Murder in the Cathedral*, Bolt's play combines historical truth with nonrealistic elements (the Common Man, a choruslike figure who comments on the action and takes minor roles) in order to investigate a psychological problem: the location of the self.

TOM STOPPARD
Rosencrantz and Guildenstern Are Dead
(1967)

Best edition: The Grove Press paperback (reprint edition, 1994).

Two minor characters from *Hamlet*, Rosencrantz and Guildenstern, are trying to figure out why they have been summoned to Elsinore, but they keep getting interrupted—first by the Players, arriving to perform at Claudius's court, and then by Ophelia charging through, pursued by Hamlet. Rosencrantz and Guildenstern are helpless to direct their own lives; they can't act, because they can't make up their minds about what to do next. "Set loose to find our own way," Guildenstern mourns. "We are entitled to some direction. . . . I would have thought."

All of the actions of the play are determined by *Hamlet*, which (running offstage) turns into a theatrical version of Fate, providing an inevitable sequence of events, but no meaning to accompany them. Rosencrantz and Guildenstern try to get rid of Polonius's body, take a sea voyage with Hamlet to England, are attacked by pirates, and discover that Hamlet has ordered their deaths. To their surprise, they discover that all of the Players are (improbably) on board as well. "Pirates could happen to anyone," the chief Player says, comfortingly, but the two are inconsolable over the letter. When the Player adds, "Most things end in death," Guildenstern stabs him: "No one gets up after death!" he screams but the Player, after dying spectacularly, hops up to take a bow. All the Players then kill each other, leaving Guildenstern and Rosencrantz among the bodies. "There must have been a moment at the beginning where we could have said— no," Guildenstern says. "But somehow we missed it." Both disappear from view as lights come up to show the final scene from Hamlet, with the last speech of Horatio slowly drowned out by music and darkness. There is no cause and effect in the play; the two occupy a world they cannot understand; they have nothing to help them interpret the actions around them. Language is useless, their efforts to take action end in absurdity, and the form of the play itself reflects the impossibility of reaching true understanding.[25]

PETER SHAFFER
Equus
(1974)

Best edition: The Scribner paperback (2005).

Equus, told as a Brechtian series of numbered scenes, follows an extended psychotherapy session between psychiatrist Martin Dysart and his seventeen-year-old patient Alan Strang, who has blinded six horses with steel spikes. Strang, isolated from his family and from his society, is a worshipper of a great, strange, elemental god he calls "Equus." Equus is a force compounded from his love of horses, sexual desire, a warped sense of religion, isolation, disappointment, and (above all) his sense that something great, overwhelming, transcendent, and beyond his control occupies the universe. Alan's worship of Equus torments him, but it also serves to protect him from the banalities of a world filled with chattering consumerism: "Remington ladies' shavers!" customers shout at Alan, as

---

[25]Roger Ebert, who saw the play in its original theatrical run and later reviewed the film, provides several intriguing comments on the differences in form between the two in his 1991 review of the film in the *Chicago Sun-Times*, available online at www.suntimes.com/ebert/ebert_reviews/1991/03/639806.html.

he desperately tries to fulfill his duties as a shop attendant. "Robex table-ware? Corydex? Volex? Pifco automatic toothbrushes?" The psychiatrist Dysart discovers this belief, but is reluctant to remove it: "He'll be deliv-ered from madness," Dysart cries out at the play's end. "What then? . . . I'll give him the good Normal world where we're tethered . . . blinking our nights away in a non-stop drench of cathode-ray over our shrivelling heads!" He may "cure" Alan Strang, returning him to the twentieth-century world of materialism and irrelevance by taking away his delusions of the cruel, powerful, beautiful, mocking god Equus. But Dysart himself knows that some great inexplicable force lies hidden in all men "crying out, 'Account for Me!' "

Shaffer argues for the irreducible complexity of human beings, their ultimate mystery. His play deals with the internal, not the external, land-scape, and so he sets *Equus* on an abstract stage, where the actors sit on benches on the stage (and sometimes in the audience) while waiting to perform their scenes. The action is both internal and clearly symbolic, standing for some part of man which is in danger of being eliminated altogether by "normality." The "gods" have returned in Shaffer's play; but this time they dwell in the deep reaches of the mind, not on Olympus.

ADDITIONAL RESOURCES FOR
RHETORIC-LEVEL READING

Ball, William. *A Sense of Direction: Some Observations on the Art of Directing.* Hollywood: Drama Publishers, 2003. A good guide to all the basics of directing scenes.

Bloom, Michael. *Thinking Like a Director: A Practical Handbook.* London: Faber & Faber, 2001. Begins with the first reading of the play and takes you right through rehearsals.

Brook, Peter. *The Empty Space: A Book About the Theatre: Deadly, Holy, Rough, Immediate.* New York: Touchstone, 1995. The director of the Royal Shakespeare Company analyzes the issues every director must face when staging a new play.

Gillette, J. Michael. *Theatrical Design and Production: An Introduction to Scene Design and Construction, Lighting, Sound, Costume, and Makeup,* 7th ed. New York: McGraw-Hill, 2012. This standard textbook covers all aspects of staging for beginners.

Ingham, Rosemary. *From Page to Stage: How Theatre Designers Make Con-nections Between Scripts and Images.* Portsmouth, N.H.: Heinemann, 1998. A little more detail on designing sets and scenery.

MOVIE VERSIONS OF THE PLAYS

The versions below are only a few of those available; search the Internet Movie Database at www.imdb.com for more.

Most of these can be purchased in DVD or watched online through streaming services (Netflix, Amazon, Hulu, etc.). Many can be viewed in part, or whole, on Youtube. Use the title, director or stars, and date in in your online search.

Agamemnon
1983, directed by Peter Hall for the BBC National Theatre; translation by Tony Harrison.

Oedipus Rex
1957, directed by Abram Polonsky and Tyrone Guthrie; translation by William Butler Yeats; starring Douglas Campbell and Eleanor Stuart.
1968, *Oedipus the King,* directed by Philip Saville, starring Christopher Plummer, Orson welles, and Donald Sutherland.

Medea
1959, adapted by Robinson Jeffers, starring Judith Anderson; this is the black-and-white film made from the Broadway production.
1970, directed by Pier Paolo Pasolini, starring Maria Callas in a nonsinging role. In Italian, but you can sometimes find it with subtitles.
1988, directed by Lars von Trier, starring Udo Kier, Kirsten Olesen, and Henning Jensen.

Doctor Faustus
1968, directed by Nevill Coghill, starring Richard Burton and Elizabeth Taylor.
2012, directed by Matthew Dunster, starring Charlotte Broom, Michael Camp, Paul Hilton, and Arthur Darvill; a production from the Globe Theatre.

Richard III
1955, directed by and starring Laurence Olivier; long considered one of Olivier's best performances.
1995, directed by Richard Loncraine, starring Ian McKellen and Annette Bening; set in the 1930s.

A Midsummer Night's Dream
1936, directed by William Dieterle and Max Reinhardt, starring James Cagney, Olivia De Havilland, and Mickey Rooney; includes Mendelssohn's music.
1969, directed by Peter Hall, starring Ian Holm and Judy Dench; a Royal

Shakespeare Company production that also includes Ian Richardson, Diana Rigg, and Helen Mirren.

1996, directed by Adrian Noble; a video adaptation of a staged Royal Shakespeare Company production.

1999, directed by Michael Hoffman, starring Michelle Pfeiffer and Kevin Kline; set in late nineteenth-century Italy.

Hamlet

1948, directed by and starring Laurence Olivier; significantly but thoughtfully cut, this film won four Oscars.

1964, directed by Bill Colleran and John Gielgud, starring Richard Burton; a staged Broadway performance.

1969, directed by Tony Richardson, starring Nicol Williamson and Judy Parfitt.

1990, directed by Franco Zeffirelli, starring Mel Gibson; heavily cut and very quick moving.

1996, directed by and starring Kenneth Branagh; Branagh set out to film the entire play, cutting nothing.

2000, directed by Michael Almereyda, starring Ethan Hawke and Kyle MacLachlan; set in modern-day New York City.

2009, directed by Gregory Doran, starring David Tennant and Patrick Stewart; a Royal Shakespeare Company production.

Tartuffe

1978, directed by Kirk Browning, starring Donald Moffat, Victor Garber, and Tammy Grimes.

She Stoops to Conquer

1971, starring Ralph Richardson and Trevor Peacock; a British television production.

2008, directed by Tony Britten, starring Roy Marsden, Ian Redford, and Susannah Fielding.

2012, directed by Jamie Lloyd, starring Sophie Thompson, Steve Pemberton, and Timothy Speyer; a National Theatre production.

The School for Scandal

1959, produced by Hal Burton, starring Joan Plowright, Felix Aylmer, and John Saunders.

2003, directed by Michael Langham and Nick Havinga, starring Bernard Behrens, Blair Brown, and Pat Connolly.

A Doll's House

1959, starring Julie Harris and Christopher Plummer; a stage performance, broadcast for television.

1973, directed by Patrick Garland, starring Claire Bloom and Anthony Hopkins.

1992, directed by David Thacker, starring Juliet Stevenson and Trevor Eve; a televised version.

2015, directed by Charles Huddleston, starring Ben Kingsley, Julian Sands, and Michele Martin.

The Importance of Being Earnest

1952, directed by Anthony Asquith, starring Michael Redgrave and Joan Greenwood.

1988, directed by Stuart Burge, starring Joan Plowright and Paul McGann.

2002, directed by Oliver Parker, starring Rupert Everett, Colin Firth, and Judy Dench.

The Cherry Orchard

1959, directed by Daniel Petrie, starring Helen Hayes and John Abbott.

1962, directed by Michael Elliott, starring Peggy Ashcroft and John Gielgud.

1971, directed by Cedric Messina, starring Jenny Agutter, Peggy Ashcroft, and Edward Woodward.

1981, directed by Richard Eyre, starring Judi Dench and Bill Paterson.

1999, directed by Mihalis Kakogiannis, starring Charlotte Rampling and Alan Bates.

Saint Joan

1957, directed by Otto Preminger, starring Jean Seberg and John Gielgud.

1967, directed by George Schaefer, starring Theodore Bikel and Genevieve Bujold.

Murder in the Cathedral

1951, directed by George Hoellering, starring John Groser and Alexander Gauge (with T. S. Eliot as the Fourth Tempter).

Our Town

1940, directed by Sam Wood, staring William Holden and Martha Scott; significantly different from the Wilder play.

1977, directed by George Schaefer, starring Ned Beatty, Hal Holbrook, and Glynnis O'Connor.

1989, directed by Gregory Mosher, starring Spalding Gray and Penelope Ann Miller; a PBS-filmed version of a Lincoln Center performance.

2003, directed by James Naughton, starring Maggie Lacey, Jeffrey DeMunn, and Jane Curtin.

Long Day's Journey into Night

1962, directed by Sidney Lumet, starring Katharine Hepburn and Ralph Richardson.

1973, directed by Peter Wood, starring Laurence Olivier and Constance Cummings; originally aired as Episode 20, Season 5, of ITV Sunday Night Theatre.

1987, directed by Jonathan Miller, starring Peter Gallagher, Jack Lemmon, and Kevin Spacey.

1996, directed by David Wellington, starring Peter Donaldson and Martha Henry; the full title of this Canadian film is *Eugene O'Neill's Long Day's Journey into Night.*

No Exit

1964, directed by Philip Saville, starring Harold Pinter; a BBC production.

A Streetcar Named Desire

1951, directed by Elia Kazan, starring Vivien Leigh and Marlon Brando.

1984, directed by John Erman, starring Ann-Margret and Treat Williams.

1995, directed by Glenn Jordan, starring Alec Baldwin and Jessica Lange.

Death of a Salesman

1966, directed by Alex Segal, starring George Segal, Gene Wilder, and Lee J. Cobb; a television version, abridged from the play.

1985, directed by Volker Schlondorff, starring Dustin Hoffman and Kate Reid.

Waiting for Godot

1961, directed by Alan Schneider, starring Zero Mostel and Burgess Meredith; first aired as Episode 28, Season 2, of the Play of the Week.

1988, directed by Samuel Beckett himself, starring Rich Cluchy and Lawrence Held; the full title of this television production is *Beckett Directs Beckett: Waiting for Godot by Samuel Beckett.*

2001, directed by Michael Lindsay-Hogg, starring Barry McGovern and Alan Stanford; an Irish production.

A Man for All Seasons

1966, directed by Fred Zinnemann, starring Paul Scofield and Wendy Hiller.

1988, directed by and starring Charlton Heston, also starring John Gielgud and Vanessa Redgrave.

Rosencrantz and Guildenstern Are Dead

1990, directed by Tom Stoppard himself, starring Tim Roth, Gary Oldman, and Richard Dreyfuss.

Equus

1977, directed by Sidney Lumet, starring Richard Burton and Peter Firth.

Chapter 9

History Refracted:
The Poets and Their Poems

ALL POEMS ARE about God, love, or depression.

> Who would have thought my shriveled heart
> Could have recovered greenness? It was gone
> Quite underground; as flowers depart
> To see their mother-root, when they have blown,
> Where they together
> All the hard weather,
> Dead to the world, keep house unknown.
> These are thy wonders, Lord of power,
> Killing and quickening, bringing down to hell
> And up to heaven in an hour.
> Making a chiming of a passing-bell.
> We say amiss
> This or that is:
> Thy word is all, if we could spell. . . .
>
> And now in age I bud again,
> After so many deaths I live and write;
> I once more smell the dew and rain,
> And relish versing. . . .
> —From "The Flower," by George Herbert

depression: an area lower than the surrounding surface
love: that state of feeling arising from sympathy or natural ties
God: what is invoked
—Adapted from *The Oxford English Dictionary*

"Poem" is an impossibly broad word. It embraces arrangements of words
that may be sensibly direct, as in Robert Frost's "Birches":

> When I see birches bend to left and right
> Across the lines of straighter darker trees,
> I like to think some boy's been swinging them.
> But swinging doesn't bend them down to stay
> As ice storms do. . . .

obscurely allusive, as in John Donne's "Air and Angels":

> Twice or thrice had I loved thee,
> Before I knew thy face or name,
> So in a voice, so in a shapeless flame,
> Angels affect us oft, and worshipped be;
> Still when, to where thou wert, I came,
> Some lovely glorious nothing I did see.

or an evocation of physical sensation in syllables, as in Walt Whitman's "I Sing the Body Electric":

> The continual changes of the flex of the mouth, and around the eyes,
> The skin, the sunburnt shade, freckles, hair,
> The curious sympathy one feels when feeling with the hand the naked
>   meat of the body,
> The circling rivers the breath, and breathing it in and out,
> The beauty of the waist, and thence of the hips, and thence downward
>   toward the knees,
> The thin red jellies within you or within me, the bones and the marrow
>   in the bones,
> The exquisite realization of health. . .

The poem can chronicle some aspect of the past, as history does; the poem can tell us a story about a character, copying the function of the novel. Like autobiography, the poem can reveal the poet's own developing sense of self; like drama, the poem can bounce dialogue back and forth between speakers, demanding that the onlooker take a part in imagining the scene. But poems are not history, or autobiography, or fiction. They are written in *poetry*.

Novels, autobiographies, histories, and most plays are written in *prose*. Poetry and prose are words which define each other; as a literary label, "poetry" most commonly means "that which is not prose" (and vice versa). So how are the two different? Most poets—and critics—would probably answer, "I know poetry when I see it"—a useful cop-out that can also be applied to great art and pornography. As you read poetry, you too will develop an eye and ear for that mysterious, ethereal dividing line between poetry and prose. But as you begin the project of poetry reading, consider using this simple definition as an early guide: Poetry is like a periscope. It always involves a watcher (the reader), peering through the periscope at something being watched, the "thing" that the poem is about—a sensation, or mood, or problem, or person, or tree, bush, or river. But the poem's subject does not imprint itself directly on the watcher's eye; it bounces from one mirror to another first, and each mirror becomes part of the image that eventually strikes the eye's lens.

The two mirrors in this "periscope" are the poet and the language of the poem. In a poem, the poet never disappears; his mind, his emotions, and his experiences are part of the poem. The novelist or playwright will often try to stay out of sight, so that the reader can experience the story or play without continually remembering its author. But a poem is an expression of the poet's presence. Compare these two scenes, both set in eighteenth-century groves, by the novelist Jane Austen and her contemporary, the poet William Wordsworth. In Austen's *Pride and Prejudice*, Elizabeth Bennet has just turned down Mr. Darcy's arrogant proposal of marriage. The next morning she goes for a walk to clear her head.

> After walking two or three times along that part of the lane, she was tempted, by the pleasantness of the morning, to stop at the gates and look into the park. The five weeks which she had now passed in Kent had made a great difference in the country, and every day was adding to the verdure of the early trees. She was on the point of continuing her walk, when she caught a glimpse of a gentleman within the sort of grove which edged the park; he was moving that way; and fearful of its being Mr. Darcy, she was directly retreating. But the person who advanced was now near enough to see her, and stepping forward with eagerness, pronounced her name. She had turned away, but on hearing herself called, though in a voice which proved it to be Mr. Darcy, she moved again toward the gate. He had by that time reached it also, and holding out a letter, which she instinctively took, said with a look of haughty composure, "I have been walking in the grove some time in the hope of meeting you. Will you do me the honour of reading that letter?"—And then, with a slight bow, turned again into the plantation, and was soon out of sight.

This is prose; Elizabeth and Darcy meet in the grove, he gives her a letter and Jane Austen herself is nowhere to be seen. But William Words-

worth's "Lines Written in Early Spring" put the poet right in the middle
of the grove:

> I heard a thousand blended notes,
> While in a grove I sat reclined,
> In that sweet mood when pleasant thoughts
> Bring sad thoughts to the mind.
>
> To her fair works did Nature link
> The human soul that through me ran;
> And much it grieved my heart to think
> What man has made of man.
>
> Through primrose tufts, in that green bower,
> The periwinkle trailed its wreaths;
> And 'tis my faith that every flower
> Enjoys the air it breathes.
>
> The birds around me hopped and played,
> Their thoughts I cannot measure:—
> But the least motion which they made
> It seemed a thrill of pleasure.
>
> The budding twigs spread out their fan,
> To catch the breezy air;
> And I must think, do all I can,
> That there was pleasure there.
>
> If this belief from heaven be sent,
> If such be Nature's holy plan,
> Have I not reason to lament
> What man has made of man?

The reader (peering through the periscope) sees the twigs, the birds, and
the primrose tufts—and Wordsworth himself, reclining right in the middle of the grove and lamenting what man has made of man. *His* sensations,
his perceptions, and *his* conclusions are woven right through the fabric of
the scene. We see the grove through his own eyes; and although we also
see Elizabeth and Darcy through Jane Austen's eyes, we are not *made aware*
of it, as we are in Wordsworth's poem.

The presence of the poet is an essential part of the poem—even in those poems where the poet makes a conscious effort to express his own absence, as Mark Strand does in his 1980 poem "Keeping Things Whole":

> In a field
> I am the absence
> of field.
> This is
> always the case.
> Wherever I am
> I am what is missing.

Mark Strand may be missing a strong sense of his own presence (he defines himself entirely by negations), but he is standing, large as life, right in the middle of this poem.

Because of this presence, the poem always reminds you that the poet is not neutral toward the subject of her work. Rather, she takes one of three positions. She is "depressed," alienated from the world of the poem, struggling to find her place in it or pushing it away, uneasy and not at home; she is "in love," embracing the poem's subject, speaking out of sympathy and affection for it; or she is invoking something from outside herself, channeling some transcendent truth beyond her capacity to understand, something that exists independently from her own ease or discomfort in the world; an outside force to which she stands as witness.

> Let the light of late afternoon
> shine through chinks in the barn, moving
> up the bales as the sun moves down. . . .
>
> Let the fox go back to its sandy den.
> Let the wind die down. Let the shed
> go black inside. Let evening come. . . .
>
> Let it come, as it will, and don't
> be afraid. God does not leave us
> comfortless, so let evening come.
> —Jane Kenyon, "Let Evening Come"

All poetry is about God, love, or depression.

The second "mirror" of the telescope is language. The language of poetry is self-consciously *formal*—meaning that the *form* of each poem (its words, their arrangement and sequence) can't be separated from the poem's ideas. In prose, words and ideas have a slightly looser relationship. Almost any novel or autobiography can be made into a movie. A play can be turned into a musical or a one-person show; a history can be transformed into a special for the Learning Channel. In each case, the work keeps its essential identity even though its words are altered.

But a poem is only a poem as long as it retains its original words. The six-hour movie version of *Pride and Prejudice* is still Jane Austen, but a paraphrase of "Keeping Things Whole" is no longer Mark Strand. The poet's language never becomes a transparent window through which meaning can be seen: In a poem, the language *is* the meaning. A poem cannot be written in any other way. Its form, its function, and its meaning are all one. And the more "poetic" a piece of prose is, the more it resists paraphrase; Italo Calvino's poetic novel *If on a winter's night a traveler* has never been dramatized, while Harriet Beecher Stowe's prosy masterpiece *Uncle Tom's Cabin* has been turned into a movie, a play, a musical, a minstrel show, and a comic book series.

DEFINING THE INDEFINABLE

When forced into corners and ordered to cough up definitions of poetry, poets almost always resort to metaphors.

"Poetry is a way of taking life by the throat" (Robert Frost).

"Poetry is like making a joke. If you get one word wrong at the end of a joke, you've lost the whole thing" (W. S. Merwin).

"Poetry is above all a concentration of the power of language, which is the power of our ultimate relationship to everything in the universe" (Adrienne Rich).

"Poetry is like ice skating: you can turn quickly. Prose is like wading. It also has a lot of good. You can see your toes, for example" (Robert Pinsky).

"Poetry is like love—easy to recognize when it hits you, a joy to experience, and very hard to pin down flat in a satisfying definition" (Marie Ponsot).

"A poem is like a radio that can broadcast continuously for thousands of years" (Allen Ginsberg).

"Poetry is like shot-silk with many glancing colours, and every reader must find his own interpretation according to his ability and according to his sympathy with the poet" (Alfred, Lord Tennyson).

None of these definitions say anything about rhyme, meter, stresses, or tropes. Although poetry makes use of all of these techniques (and more), poems are not characterized by any poetic technique in particular, since conventions of poetic language change from century to century. Ancient listeners knew that they were hearing poetry when they heard an *epic simile*, a dramatic comparison which implies a connection between two events. Homer's Penelope, mourning her son's flight, asks:

> Why did my son leave me?
> What business had he to go sailing off in ships
> that make long voyages over the ocean like sea-horses?[1]

Horses carried men into battle, just as the ship will carry her son away; Penelope is losing Telemachus to the aftereffects of the Trojan war, just as she lost her husband to the war itself. The epic simile is a *structural marker* of ancient poetry.

But by medieval times, the epic simile has been replaced by other structural markers: the division of each poetic line into two halves, with at least two words in each line *alliterating*, beginning with the same sound. Beowulf, we learn, ruled his land for fifty years in peace until a new threat began

> to dominate the dark, a dragon on the prowl
> from the steep vaults of a stone-roofed barrow
> where he guarded a hoard; there was a hidden passage
> unknown to men, but someone managed
> to enter by it and interfere
> with the heathen trove. He had handled and removed
> a gem-studded goblet; it gained him nothing. . . .[2]

This too is poetry, but it uses different conventions and different structural markers. Medieval listeners (or readers) knew that they were in the presence of poetry as soon as they heard those alliterative syllables: *gem, goblet, gained*. (Seamus Heaney's translation, quoted above, preserves this alliteration.) But the ancient listeners might not have understood this to be poetry at all.

If you rely on structural markers to identify poetry, you'll be hard-pressed to understand why the *Iliad* and Allen Ginsberg's *Howl* are both labeled "poetry." My own "Poetry is like a periscope" metaphor (a somewhat unpoetic one, especially compared with Voltaire's "Poetry is the music of the soul") is meant to help you begin to understand poetry apart

---

[1] Homer, *The Odyssey*, trans. Samuel Butler (London: A. C. Fifield, 1900), book IV, lines 706–10.
[2] *Beowulf*, trans. Seamus Heaney (New York: W. W. Norton, 2001), lines 2, 212–18, p. 151.

from obvious structural markers such as end rhymes or stanzas, which change from generation to generation. The *Iliad* and *Howl* are both self-conscious about language, although in wildly dissimilar fashion; Allen Ginsberg and Homer are both present in their works—although in completely different ways. The very brief history of poetic practice that follows isn't designed to make you into a critic (or a poet). Rather, it assumes a basic grasp of the ancient-medieval-Renaissance-modern-post-modern progression of thought outlined in the previous chapters; against that background, it aims to lay out the most common features of self-conscious, poetic language, and to introduce you briefly to the changing ways in which poets have thought of their own job.

A SEVEN-MINUTE HISTORY OF POETRY

The Age of Epics

The earliest Western poetry is that of the Greeks, and the earliest Greek poetry is *epic poetry*—sprawling oral tales of heroes and battles, finally written down by Homer around 800 B.C. In the *Iliad*, the warrior Achilles falls out with his commander, Agamemnon, and manages to turn Zeus against his own army; in the *Odyssey*, Odysseus tries to get home after the Trojan War has ended. Incident-filled, plot-driven, centered around the failings and strengths of men and women: These epics seem much more like novels than poems. Why, then, are they considered the first great *poems*, rather than the first great *tales*? And where is the "personal presence" of the poet in these stories of bloodshed and sea adventure?

Poetry, for the Greeks, was a term that covered a much broader territory than it does today. "Poetry," wrote Aristotle, "is more philosophical and more worth-while than history, for poetry speaks in general terms, while history concerns itself with detail." In other words, poetry was language that sought to demonstrate universal truths; poetry described reality. *Mimesis*, Aristotle's term for the poetic process, is the "imitation" or depiction of real life in a way that brings understanding to the listener. The poet was not at the margins of society, as he tends to be today. Rather, he was a combination historian, librarian, and philosopher—rather like the "public intellectual" of the twentieth century, crossed with an archive.

This archive function was particularly important in the earliest days of Greek civilization, when all poetry and history were oral: memorized and passed down from poet to poet, repeated around the fire weekly, resung at each telling in slightly different words. The poet was a reshaper of tales. He took the details of history that had been passed down to him and "re-created" or "made" it for his listeners, putting it together with other facts into a coherent whole, using his own style of language and description. The *Iliad* begins with a fact, probably an actual historical event: A warrior kidnapped the daughter of a priest and refused to give her back when her father arrived with the required ransom. Homer takes this fact and weaves it into a story, so that it becomes the pivotal conflict in a tale about a clash of wills between two strong and proud men, neither of whom will back down and risk public humiliation. Homer, like the ideal poet Aristotle describes in his *Poetics*, is a "maker," a creator; he creates not just a story, but an entire universal system of cause and effect.

So where is the poet in the *Iliad* and the *Odyssey*? He is *speaking*; remember that these epics were oral for centuries, so that the poet was always before the eyes of his audience. He wasn't hidden behind paper. They could see and hear him; they knew that he was the maker of the poem, constructing a whole theory of human existence around the "bare facts" of history.

The demands of oral composition shaped the language of Greek epic poems. Instead of writing his work down for readers, the poet composed as he spoke, weaving the details of his story together into a fresh version each time he performed. But the basic series of events remained the same. To keep his story in order, the poet made use of formulaic "plot skeletons," stringing his details into an accepted, familiar sequence. These included: the hero, far from home, struggling to return; the withdrawal of a hero from a conflict, a resulting disaster, and the hero's return; the death of a much-loved friend, followed by a search for some way to gain immortality and defeat death.

Other memory aids included an oral "table of contents," a prologue that outlined what the poet was about to do (something which was as helpful to the audience as to the speaker), as well as occasional halts to recap the action before proceeding on to new scenes. Long speeches, complicated descriptions, and flashbacks were often introduced and concluded with the same words; this "ring composition" gave the poet a verbal marker, a way to wrap up the speech or flashback and get back into the action. Scenes that occur often (feasts, battles, insults) were told with the same repetitive structure. If the poet didn't immediately recollect the details of one particular battle, it made little difference; he could simply follow the already-established pattern.

To keep this repetition from growing wearisome, poets would vary it with extended comparisons, or epic similes. In one battle scene, a commander might fight like a "hill-bred lion, ravenous for meat"; another commander in another battle would instead tread "catlike, compact behind his shield," while a third would turn on his enemies like a "boar on wild dogs."

In order to work out the meter of each line correctly on the fly, the poet could drop a "formula phrase" into a line whenever necessary. Greek meter was based on the length of vowels, so poets had a stock of descriptive adjectives ("well-built," "well-found," "wine-dark") and phrases ("of the silvery feet") of various lengths that could be inserted as needed. (Which explains why the "flowing-haired Achaians" are sometimes "battle-hardened" and sometimes just plain "brave," depending on how many syllables the rest of the line was lacking.)

The First Lyrics

Epics were the earliest Greek poems, but lyric poetry (all poetry that was nonnarrative and nondramatic) reached its peak three centuries after Homer. Like epic poetry, lyric poetry was written to be performed; *lyric* meant "accompanied by the lyre."

And like the epic poet, the lyric poet was seen by his audience. This poetry is still primarily oral, not written; as a matter of fact, all of the Greek lyric poetry that survives is in bits and fragments.

The bits and fragments fall into two categories: choral poetry, performed by a chorus, and "monodic" poetry, recited by the poet or by a trained soloist. Choral poetry was often performed as part of a religious ritual; the *paean* was a song of worship to Apollo, a *humnos* was a general worship song, a *threnos* was a dirge (from these, we get the English words *paen, hymn,* and *threnody*).

> Then too the god whose splendour bright
> Glads mortals with his radiant light. . .
> And to the goddess every rite divine
>   With prompt submissive reverence pay!
>   —Pindar, "Seventh Olympic Ode" (a *humnos*)[3]

Monodic poetry had a wider range of subject: love, hate, loss, longing. The elegy was a solo poem with a particular type of meter; the *iambos,* from which we derive the English meter iambic, was an invective against an enemy. These lyric poems didn't have the same sweep as the epic poems, but their goal was at once smaller and more innovative. They painted scenes of private emotion, vignettes of personal experience.

> Overcome with kisses her faintest protest,
> Melt her mood to mine with amorous touches,

---

[3] Quoted from *Pindar,* trans. C. A. Wheelwright (New York: Harper & Brothers, 1837), p. 53.

Till her low assent and her sigh's abandon
　　Lure me to rapture.
　　　—Sappho, "Ode to Anactoria" (a monodic poem)[4]

The individual voices of the poets shone through, in the verse itself, for the first time. (And eventually, Greek lyric poetry became the model for the seventeenth-century explosion of English "lyric poetry," which borrowed both its techniques and its technical terms.)

Greek lyric poetry started to lose steam with the invention of writing. Written prose began to gain on spoken poetry as the language of argumentation, or "rational discourse." At the same time, the Greeks were building larger and more elaborate amphitheaters for the spoken word, which led to an increased emphasis on drama (with its spectacle and costume) rather than recited poetry. The lyric poet, already shoved to the edges of Greek culture, suffered further from Plato's pronouncement in the *Republic* that "all poetical imitations are ruinous to the understanding of the hearers," and that lyric poetry, by inflaming the emotions, drove out "law and the reasons of mankind." Pressed in on by prose, drama, and Plato, the lyric poet folded meekly and devoted his time to epigrams: the succinct, proselike statement of a truth.

Epigrams, which first appeared as inscriptions on tombs, were brief and straightforward. (If you have to carve a poem on granite, you're likely to make it a short one.) Greek epigrams soon evolved away from tombstone inscriptions toward *bon mots* of truth, good for all occasions:

　　　　No man desires to be
　　　　A friend with you in time of doom.[5]

Roman Odes

Roman writers borrowed Greek forms of poetry just as they did Greek drama. But like Latin drama, Latin verse never quite achieved Greek heights—except, perhaps, for the odes of Horace.

The ode form used by Horace follows a fairly standard pattern: It describes a scene and then reflects on it in the light of life's brevity and death's inevitable approach.

---

[4]Quoted from *The Poems of Sappho: An Interpretative Rendition Into English,* trans. John Myers O'Hara (Portland: Smith & Sale, 1910), p. 7.
[5]Quoted from *Ancient Greek Epigrams: Major Poets in Verse Translation,* trans. Gordon L. Fain (Berkeley: University of California Press, 2010), p. 16.

Tomorrow and its works defy;
          Lay hold upon the present hour,
And snatch the pleasures passing by
          To put them out of fortune's power;
Nor love, nor love's delights disdain—
Whatever thou gettest today is gain.
—Horace, Book 1, Ode 9 (translated by John Dryden)[6]

In his odes (which were translated by English poets from John Milton to A. E. Housman), Horace took the position of the experienced, salty, slightly cynical but good-hearted observer of life; he is best known for his exhortation *Carpe diem* (generally, and somewhat inaccurately, translated as "Seize the day!"), which encapsulates his whole philosophy: Enjoy life in the present day, because death is on its way. In these odes, he brings to maturity the individual, personal voice of the poet that first appeared in the Greek lyrics.

Strain your wine and prove your wisdom; life is short; should hope be
     more?
In the moment of our talking, envious time has ebbed away.
Seize the present;
trust tomorrow e'en as little as you may.
—Horace, Book 1, Ode 11 (translated by John Conington)[7]

Medieval Poetics

Medieval poetics, like medieval history, doesn't descend in a straight line from ancient times; thanks to barbarian invasion and general cultural disintegration, classical poetry (like classical drama) ceded its place, for a time. Writing faded; Greek and Latin lost their immediacy; and the poetry that emerged from the Middle Ages owed more to Germanic oral tradition than to the Latin odes.

Beowulf, the earliest medieval epic, features a beleaguered Christian community living on a hill, in a place of light and feasting, while a prowling monster—a "God-cursed" descendent of Cain—lives in the swamps below and storms up the hill occasionally to eat the inhabitants, driven by a jealous rage of their eternal security. The epic was probably performed

[6]Quoted from *Horace: The Odes, Epodes, Satires, and Epistles, Translated by the Most Eminent English Scholars and Poets* (London: Frederick Warne and Co., 1889), p. 15.
[7]Quoted from *The Odes and Carmen Saeculare of Horace,* trans. John Conington (London: Bell and Daldy, 1863), p. 13.

orally long before it was written down, sometime around A.D. 800, in Old English, and it makes use of techniques familiar from Greek oral epics— formulaic phrasings ("God-cursed Grendel") and metaphoric descriptions that fill out the meter. In Old English, these metaphors are called *kennings*. They describe an object in terms of its characterstics, often using a hyphenated phrase to do so:

> Before long
> the battle-dodgers abandoned the wood,
> the ones who had let down their lord earlier,
> the tail-turners, ten of them together.
> —*Beowulf,* trans. by Seamus Heaney (ll. 2845–48)

Each line of Old English poetry was divided into two half lines; every half line contained at least two stressed (emphasized) syllables. Often those stressed syllables were also *alliterated* (they began with the same opening sound).

> Nor **did** the **crea**ture / **keep** him **wai**ting
> but **struck sud**denly / and **start**ed **in**;
> he **grabbed** and **mauled** / a **man** on his **bench,**
> **bit** into his **bone** lappings, / **bolt**ed down his **blood,**
> and **gorged** on him in **lumps,** / **leav**ing the **bod**y
> **utt**erly **life**less, / **eat**en **up.** . . .
> —*Beowulf,* trans. by Seamus Heaney (ll. 738–43), stresses and line
>   divisions mine

Sir Gawain and the Green Knight, a slightly later tale of courtly love and honor, probably originated as a written, not an oral, composition, but the anonymous author copied *Beowulf*'s poetic conventions; *Gawain* too makes use of alliterative formulas ("Guinevere the goodly queen," "the most noble knights") and a pattern of half-lines with alliterative syllables:

> And in **guise** all of **green,** / the **gear** and the **man:**
> A **coat** cut **close,** / that **clung** to his **sides,**
> And a **mantle** to **match,** / **made** with a **lin**ing
> Of **furs** cut and **fit**ted— / the **fab**ric was **no**ble. . .
> —*Sir Gawain and the Green Knight,* trans. by Marie Boroff (ll. 151–78),
>   stresses and line divisions mine

Like *Beowulf, Sir Gawain* also has its hero confronting a supernatural being from an earlier time: a Green Man who can pick up his severed head and walk away with it. In both cases, the poet (like the Greek epic poet) serves both as entertainer and as historian, while dutifully glorifying God; in both epics, the Christian hero triumphs over paganism—but just barely.

Later medieval poems—Dante's *Inferno,* Chaucer's *Canterbury Tales*—continued to be driven by Christian themes. Like the epic poet, the medieval poet had a prophetic role: He revealed truth, often by telling a tale of pilgrimage, a spiritual quest for a great heavenly treasure. Yet medieval poetics inherited from Augustine a certain reservation about how truthful these poetic tales could actually be. After all, language—like the rest of creation—was fallen, inherently corrupt, and so could not come into direct contact with the divine.

Instead, the poet told truths at one remove, as reflected in a dream. Language might reveal the divine, but at the same time it had the potential to obscure it from view. Words, which were part of the physical realm, could point to falsehood as easily as to truth. "The art of rhetoric," Augustine wrote, in his formative *On Christian Doctrine,* is "available for the enforcing either of truth or falsehood. . . . To strive about words is not to be careful about the way to overcome error by truth, but to be anxious that your mode of expression should be preferred to that of another. . . . [T]he man who cannot speak both eloquently and wisely should speak wisely without eloquence, rather than eloquently without wisdom."[8]

This ambivalence about words reflects an even deeper suspicion of poetry. The self-conscious language of poetry seemed, inevitably, to imply that the poem might be more preoccupied with the language of the poem than with the truth that lies behind it, and this preoccupation with language is the "eloquence" that Augustine warns of. So Dante's *Inferno* takes place in a dream, the narrator seeing the truth at one remove, and Chaucer ends his stories of pilgrimage with a retraction of everything he has just said, assuming (ironically) the character of a pilgrim tempted away from the right path by eloquence, turned to wrong ends by the wrong use of language.

For our Book says, "all that is written, is written for our edification," and that is my intention. Wherefore I beseech you meekly for the mercy of God to pray for me, that Christ have mercy on me and forgive my sins; and especially for my translations of worldly vanities, which I revoke . . . the

---

[8]Saint Augustine, *On Christian Doctrine,* trans. J. F. Shaw (1873), book IV, chapter 2, section 3, and book IV, chapter 28, section 61; available online at www.ccel.org/a/augustine/doctrine /doctrine.html.

Tales of Canterbury, which tend toward sin . . . and many a song and many a lecherous lay, that Christ in his great mercy forgive me the sin.[9]

Medieval theologians suggested that words were so malleable that they might well contain four levels of sense. Every story in Scripture bore four meanings: the literal (the actual story or surface meaning); the allegorical (sometimes also known as "typological," an illustration of a spiritual truth having to do with Christ or the heavenly realm); the tropological (the "moral" of the story, an application to the actual life of the Christian); and the anagogical (which inevitably had to do with the last times: death, judgment, and eternal destiny). Joshua's conquest of the Promised Land, for example, was interpreted as revealing a literal truth about Israel's history; an allegorical truth about Christ's leadership of his people in a fight against the kingdom of Satan; a tropological truth for the believer, who needed to destroy "strongholds" of Satan in order to achieve a moral life; and an anagogical foreshadowing of the Christian's final triumphant entry into heaven (symbolized by the Promised Land).

This multilevel interpretation—based on an Augustinian suspicion of the ability of words to convey simple unvarnished truth and laid out by Thomas Aquinas in his *Summa Theologica*—became not just a way of interpreting Scripture, but a poetic method. Dante, trained in medieval hermeneutics, himself understood the Bible as containing these four distinct levels of meaning: "If we consider the letter [literal meaning] alone," he wrote of Psalm 113, which contains an account of the Exodus from Egypt,

the thing signified to us is the going out of the children of Israel from Egypt in the time of Moses; if the allegory, our redemption through Christ is signified; if the moral sense, the conversion of the soul from the sorrow and misery of sin to the state of grace is signified; if the anagogical, the passing of the sanctified soul from the bondage of the corruption of this world to the liberty of everlasting glory.[10]

And so Dante's pilgrim, literally lost in a dark wood, is also, allegorically, lost on the way to heaven, between the kingdom of God and the reign of Satan; he is, tropologically, grappling with the moral demands of

[9]Geoffrey Chaucer, "Retraction," from *The Canterbury Tales,* trans. Nevill Coghill (New York: Penguin, 2000).
[10]In *Epistolae: The Letters of Dante,* trans. Page Toynbee (Oxford: Oxford University Press, 1966), p. 199.

daily life; and, anagogically, is heading toward his final and eternal desti-
nation—Inferno or Paradise.

Renaissance Verse

The Renaissance saw a shift in this skepticism about language; the new
science of the Renaissance understood the world (and its language) not
as essentially flawed, needing to be cleansed by fire, but as a puzzle to
be solved by the intellect. Renaissance and Enlightenment scholarship
depended on a post-Augustinian reliance on language as a clear means of
communication. The poet could become, not a mystic, but a word scientist; he could reveal truth not through ecstatic experience, but through
the careful, exact choice of syllables. "Is there in truth no beautie?" protested the English poet-parson George Herbert. "Must all be veiled, while
he that reads, divines, / Catching the sense at two removes?"

So Renaissance poetry became increasingly precise in metaphor, vocabulary, meter, and rhyme. Strict and inflexible meters forced the poet to
account for every single syllable; particularly popular was iambic meter,
an artificial alternation of stressed and unstressed syllables:

> When **in** dis**grace** with **for**tune **and** men's **eyes**
> I **all** a**lone** be**weep** my **out**cast **state**,
> And **troub'l** deaf **heaven with** my **boot**less **cries**,
> And **look** up**on** my**self** and **curse** my **fate**. . .
> —William Shakespeare, Sonnet XXIX

In the sixteenth and seventeenth centuries, poetry was understood to be
more precise than prose. In fact, because it forced its writer to choose words
so carefully, poetry was seen as the *best* way to speak truth; Sir Philip Sidney, writing his enormously influential essay *The Defense of Poesy* around
1580, concludes, "Of all sciences . . . is our poet the monarch. . . . He
beginneth not with obscure definitions, which must blur the margin with
interpretations and load the memory with doubtfulness; but he cometh to
you with words set in delightful proportion."

This respect for words had something to do with science, but
also something to do with Protestantism; new efforts to translate
the Bible into "reliable prose," rather than relying on the interpretation of the Holy Spirit speaking through churchmen, put a high premium on the ability of plain words to reveal God. "In this milieu,"
writes Barbara Lewalski in *Protestant Poetics and the Seventeenth-Century
Religious Lyric,* "the Christian poet is led to relate his work not to inef-

SONNET FORMS			
	Form	Rhyme scheme	Example
Petrarchan (Italian)	An 8-line octet poses a question, idea, or argument; a 6-line sestet resolves, responds to, or illustrates the octet. Octet and sestet are connected by the volta, the turning point, where the shift between problem and resolution occurs.	Octet: *abba abba* Sestet: *cd cd cd* OR *cde cde* OR some variation	John Donne, Holy Sonnet 10, "Death, be not proud"
Shakespearian (English)	Three quatrains present three parallel ideas or develop a related three-point argument; the final couplet links, explains, or concludes the argument.	Quatrains: *abab* *cdcd* *efef* Couplet: *gg*	William Shakespeare, Sonnet 116, "Let me not to the marriage of true minds"
Spencerian	Three quatrains develop each other (rather than standing in parallel); the final couplet states a final overarching concept or idea.	Quatrains: *abab* *cdcd* *efef* Couplet: *ee*	Sir Edmund Spenser, Sonnet 75, "One day I wrote her name upon the strand"

fable and intuited divine revelation, but rather to its written formulation in scripture."[11]

The sonnet, the queen of all Renaissance poetic forms, displays this faith in the power of precise words to convince and to demonstrate. Written in iambic pentameter (five pairs of syllables per line, each following the pattern "unstressed STRESSED"), the sonnet always contained four-

[11]Barbara Lewalski, *Protestant Poetics and the Seventeenth-Century Religious Lyric* (Princeton, N.J.: Princeton University Press, 1979), p. 6.

teen lines, followed a rigid rhyming pattern, and developed its argument according to a strict logical scheme. Petrarchan sonnets posed a question in the first eight lines (the *octet*) and resolved it in the concluding six (the *sestet*); Shakespearian sonnets used three quatrains (sets of four lines) to develop related ideas, and then concluded with a couplet making a final conclusion about the grand implications of those ideas; Spenserian sonnets also contained three quatrains and a concluding couplet, but the quatrains tended to develop a single idea with more and more complexity.

No matter what its scheme, the sonnet had the power to take the most complex and baffling aspects of human existence—the inevitability of death, the unruliness of love, man's fear of the unknown—and resolve it, neatly, by the final couplet.

The Renaissance and Enlightenment also saw a return to classical forms, as the West rediscovered classical civilization. The mark of an Enlightenment scholar was a familiarity with the classics, and an ability to use classical poetic forms. John Milton used Greek conventions to produce what C. S. Lewis labeled a "secondary epic"—a form that copies the conventions of the oral epic, but which has its birth in writing, not in speech. In imitation of Homer, Milton's *Paradise Lost* invokes the Muse, makes a formal statement of its theme, chronicles grand battles between fallen and heavenly demons, and even catalogues demons just as Homer catalogued his ships.

But *Paradise Lost,* which assures us that it will "justify the ways of God to man," reflects a very different reality than the Homeric chaos of competing divine and human ambitions. Milton chronicled an orderly and ordered world, neatly hierarchical and bound together by a Great Chain of being. His story of rebellion against God is both theology and social commentary: order is all important, and rebellion against authority is always devastating.

Romanticism

William Blake, the first Romantic poet, rebelled.

Lashing out not only against authority (governmental, religious, and educational) but against institutions and against the Enlightenment reduction of man to a "thinking machine," Blake aimed to bring humanity's mysterious, inexplicable, spiritual side back into focus. He wrote his own mythologies (long, odd sets of poems: *The Marriage of Heaven and Hell, The Book of Urizen*); in *Songs of Innocence and of Experience* he wrote against reason, against rational education, against theological precision, all of which destroyed creativity and caged the unfettered human soul.

I went to the Garden of Love,
And saw what I never had seen:
A Chapel was built in the midst,
Where I used to play on the green.

And the gates of this Chapel were shut,
And "Thou shalt not" write over the door;
So I turned to the Garden of Love
That so many sweet flowers bore;

And I saw it was filled with graves,
And tomb-stones where flowers should be;
And Priests in black gowns were walking their rounds,
And binding with briars my joys & desires.
—William Blake, "The Garden of Love," *Songs of Experience*

Blake and the Romantic poets who came after him had at least two lasting effects on poetry. Rationality certainly didn't disappear, but (as in early Greece), it shifted sideways into written prose. The poet spoke for the less rational, more emotive, more imaginative side of humanity—a role poets continue to fill today. Regaining their role as prophets, the poets reached for contact with the divine.

But this divine was not a godlike Muse, separate from humanity and greater; it was a Divine that infused both humanity and nature, a sublime force that reason could not explain away. With the publication of their *Lyrical Ballads* in 1798, William Wordsworth and Samuel Taylor Coleridge offered a mysticism less "religious" than Blake's, and a little more mainstream; an impersonal Divine Force, a Sublime that resided both in the beauties of the world and in the human soul. Like Blake, Wordsworth and Coleridge rebelled against the logical, the orderly, and the hierarchical; they were antieducation (education simply quenched the divine spark born into each man), seeing men as containing at birth a diverse spark of the divine which society did its best to flatten into uniformity. "Our birth is but a sleep and a forgetting," Wordsworth wrote,

The Soul that rises with us, our life's Star,
Hath had elsewhere its setting,
And cometh from afar:
Not in entire forgetfulness,
And not in utter nakedness,
But trailing clouds of glory do we come

From God, who is our home:
Heaven lies about us in our infancy!
Shades of the prison-house begin to close
Upon the growing Boy. . .
—From William Wordsworth, "Ode: Intimations of
    Immortality from Recollections of Early Childhood"

Ironically, many Romantics (Lord Byron being a notable exception) led somewhat stodgy personal lives; Wordsworth even ended up as Stamp Distributor for his home county, a quintessentially bureaucratic position. And although they rejected the rules of taste imposed by reason, Romantic poets tended to retain the classical forms (the odes, lyrics, epigrams).

But even within the limits of these forms, the *I* in the poem became ever more present. Sometimes the *I* is identical with the poet, as in Wordsworth's "Lines Written in Early Spring" ("I heard a thousand blended notes, / While in a grove I sate reclined") or Coleridge's equally famous "This Lime-Tree Bower My Prison," written as he sat in the garden with a sprained ankle while his guests went off for a walk: "Well, they are gone, and here must I remain," the poet sighs, conversationally, "This lime-tree bower my prison!" Occasionally the "I" is an imaginative, mythical persona, identified with the poet's imagination. "As I was walking among the fires of hell," Blake writes in the introduction to his poem "Proverbs of Hell," "delighted with the enjoyments of Genius, which to Angels look like torment and insanity, I collected some of their Proverbs."

Rather than "I think, therefore I am," the Romantic poets substituted, "I imagine, therefore I am." Sometimes this imagining *I* was active, exercising its creative power to produce myth and legend; sometimes it was passive, receiving truth from the mystical, infusing Divine.

Since the Romantics saw nature and the human soul as the two most likely locations for the divine, their poems tended to begin with either natural scenes or emotional states. The scene, or emotion, is described with care, and then connected to a larger, more cosmic idea (the pleasant garden idyll of "Lines Written in Early Spring" spirals rapidly into, "Have I not reason to lament / What man has made of man?"). Romantic poets also made heavy use of the *monologue*, a single-speaker dramatic poem with the psychology of the speaker as its primary focus.

My genial spirits fail;
And what can these avail
To lift the smothering weight from off my breast?
—From Samuel Taylor Coleridge, "Dejection: An Ode"

American "Romanticism" (The American Renaissance)

Romanticism, the great flowering of English poetry, was in essence a European phenomenon. A similar flowering, some decades later, happened in the United States, just after the Civil War. This so-called American Renaissance, late in the nineteenth century, saw American poets incorporating the ideas of the Romantic—the divine presence in nature, the supremacy of the imaginative, the speaking *I* as the poetic voice, the focus on mood and experience rather than on argument and reason—but trying to do so within an American context. The English Romantic tradition, speaking as it did with a peculiarly English voice, did not suit the Americans; Walt Whitman, Emily Dickinson, Edgar Allan Poe, and others had their own "I" to speak of.

Given the intense individualism of the American democratic experience, it is perhaps inevitable that these poetic voices should be self-absorbed. "I sing myself, and celebrate myself," announces Walt Whitman, and Emily Dickinson asks anxiously, "Why—do they shut Me out of Heaven? Did I sing—too loud?" This poetry of the American Renaissance went one step beyond the English Romantics: *Self*-discovery (rather than a discovery of the world through the eyes of the self) became the primary purpose of the poem. Autobiography was its most dominant theme; both Whitman's *Leaves of Grass* and Dickinson's poems explore the identity of the common, uncelebrated, ordinary American man or woman. The poetry of the "American Renaissance" grapples with the implications of English Romanticism: If everyone is unique, diverse, bearing a spark within him- or herself, then no one can give guidance on how we are to think of ourselves; we must each struggle to an understanding of who we are alone.

The poets of the American Renaissance show varying degrees of faith in the ability of language to actually *express* this understanding. Walt Whitman, with sheer confidence that he will be heard and understood, writes in free-flowing verse that borrows prophetic biblical cadences and epic lists, and often possesses neither rhyme nor meter:

This is the city and I am one of the citizens.
Whatever interests the rest interests me,
        politics, wars, markets, newspapers, schools,
The mayor and councils, banks, tariffs, steamships, factories, stocks, stores,
        real estate and personal estate.
—From Walt Whitman, "Song of Myself"

But Emily Dickinson writes carefully, formally, finding words barely adequate for what she has to say. She fits her thoughts neatly into metered, rhythmic lines, but distorts them with nontraditional capitalization, strained syntax, and dashes to show uncertainties she cannot convey in any other way.

> 'Tis Coronal— and Funeral—
> Saluting— in the Road—
> —From Emily Dickinson, "Upon concluded lives"

Modernism

The end of the nineteenth century and the beginning of the twentieth saw the rise of irony in poetry. "Irony," in the words of James Kincaid, comes about when "every life becomes tragic, and the element of the special case is removed. . . . Catastrophic disillusionment and destruction are not the lot of the godlike hero, invoking by his stature the terrible laws of retribution, but of every ordinary person going about the business of common life. . . . We are all victims."[12]

Modernist poetry remains autobiographical, exploring the self and the self's place in the world, but the uneasiness of the American Renaissance has settled into a pervasive worry: The self is under attack, constantly pushed in upon from the outside, looking for a firm place to stand in a world where cosmic certainties have begun to break down and where chaos seems more likely than order.

In this chaos, the poet is consumed by an effort to find some sort of harmony among the discords of existence. But as they searched for order, modernist poets rejected many of the certainties held by earlier writers. Logical thought was unreliable: "The use of logic in place of perception is hostile to principles," Ezra Pound wrote in 1931. "The logician never gets to the root." This suspicion of logic led naturally to a dismissal of cosmic theories produced by deduction: Intellectual concepts, the great overarching *theories* that gave previous generations a way to place themselves within the world, were no longer usable.

William Carlos Williams instead chose to find meaning in the physical and unique existence of *things*, their "quiddity." "No ideas except in things," Williams wrote, and made it his job to immortalize the quiddity of things (a red wheelbarrow, a plum) on the page. William Butler Yeats ("Things fall apart; the centre cannot hold; / Mere anarchy is loosed upon the world") chronicled chaos and despair, but held on to

---

[12]James R. Kincaid, *Tennyson's Major Poems: The Comic and Ironic Patterns* (New Haven: Yale University Press, 1975), p. 1.

metrical patterns; his "accentual verse" is a new kind of meter, counting only stressed syllables rather than the total number of syllables in a line (a method that allowed him to keep the form of a metered poetic line, while stretching or compressing it at will). T. S. Eliot chose to find order by making careful connections between experiences—experiences in the past and in the present, experiences in the poet's daily life. The poet, Eliot once remarked, is always "amalgamating disparate experience; the ordinary man's experience is chaotic, irregular, fragmentary. The latter falls in love, or reads Spinoza, and these two experiences have nothing to do with each other, or with the noise of the typewriter or the smell of cooking; in the mind of the poet these experiences are always forming new wholes."[13]

Like poets of the Romantic era and the American Renaissance, modernist poets seemed to believe wholeheartedly in the potential of the human *self*. Adrift in anarchy, unable to reason its way to a governing explanation of life, the self nevertheless possessed the ability to find, in some mysterious and half-understood way, a firm place (however tiny) to stand in the middle of whirling disorder.

For many of the modernist poets, this firm place could be found only in a specific image. Pound, Williams, and other modernists were influenced by Japanese haiku, which took a strict syllabic structure (three lines, the first with five syllables, the second with seven, the third with five) and combined it with a tight thematic strategy: The poem opens by focusing in on a particular detailed image and then, after the fifth or twelfth syllable, opens out to consider a larger, more general idea. Without holding to the strict syllables of haiku, a subgroup of Modernists (known, after 1912 or so, as Imagists) focused in on this careful anchoring of the poem in a precise visual picture. Often, the picture itself stood for the rest of the poem, without the subsequent turn to the cosmic. The Imagist poets aimed to render particular, specific images, not vague generalities; to write clear "hard" poetry, not blurred or vague verse; to distill poetry down to its most comcentrated forms.[14]

> Grass, and low fields, and hills,
> And sun,
> Oh, sun enough!

[13] Quoted in *Modernism: 1890–1930*, eds. Malcolm Bradbury and James McFarlane (New York: Viking, 1991), p. 83.
[14] These are three of the six Imagist goals found in Amy Lowell's *Some Imagist Poets* (1915).

Out and alone, among some
Alien people!
—From Ezra Pound, "Plunge"

"Modernism" is an enormously broad label for a group of poets who saw themselves as *sui generis*, and who often did their best to kick each other (or themselves) out of the modernist fold ("Modernism," T. S. Eliot complained in 1929, is a "mental blight"). Nevertheless, these poets were linked most strongly by two common suspicions. They were suspicious of the human community; the speakers of their poems are profoundly alone, alienated from other men. And they were skeptical of language's capacity to express both the reality of chaos and the attempt to find order. "You have no cosmos until you can order it," Ezra Pound wrote, in an early draft of his massive work *The Cantos*, but as he aged he grew less and less convinced that poetic language could order anything. The idea of the poem as a "place to stand," a solid spot in quicksand ("A poem is a momentary stay against confusion," in Robert Frost's phrase) stood in tension with the growing modernist conviction that language itself was distorted and fractured beyond any repair. "A rose is a rose is a rose," wrote modernist poet Gertrude Stein, celebrating the quiddity of a thing while stretching syntax to its limits in order to demonstrate its inadequacy.

Alienation

Modernism too had its dissenters.

In England, a group of younger poets known as the "Movement" turned away from a modernist, fragmented poetry, toward a neo-Romantic style which returned to plainer syntax and style, to poetic form, to the exploration of nature and the acts of everyday life. Movement poets such as Philip Larkin turned their focus away from psychological explorations, back toward the physical world and the actual lives of real people.

In America, slightly later, the beat poets expressed their own alienation by focusing, not on the insufficiencies of language, but on the evils of the military-industrial complex. Beat poets, led by Allen Ginsberg (and also including the writers Jack Kerouac and William Burroughs) set out to create a subculture, a neo-Romantic alternative society that rejected the conventions that shaped American culture. Ginsberg, a homosexual and a communist at a time when neither was socially acceptable (or even legal) strikes out, as Blake did, against the authorities. Like Blake, Ginsberg—who once had had a vision of William Blake talking to him, in his Spanish Harlem apartment, in a voice that had "all the infinite tenderness and anciency and mortal gravity of a living Creator speaking to his son"—rejected discipline, order, and theology in favor of a wild mysticism. ("The soul is holy! The skin is holy! The nose is holy!" he howled.)[15]

Meanwhile, modernism was dying—but as a poetic movement, modernism was almost too fractured to have a coherent "after." Modern poetry had been dominated by white, upper-class, well-educated males; now women and African American poets attempted to find their own path into the modern age. African American poets, building on the early poetry of Paul Laurence Dunbar and later on the work of Langston Hughes, struggled to find a balance between "white" styles of speech and the black folk tradition. Women, writing in a poetic tradition that was overwhelmingly male, often found themselves pigeonholed as "feminist poets."

> The pact we made was the ordinary pact
> of men & women in those days.
>
> I don't know who we thought we were that our personalities
> could resist the failures of the race. . .
> —Adrienne Rich, from "From a Survivor"

But there is no sense in which women, or African American poets, or poets from other cultural groups, or white male poets formed a unified literary movement after the death of modernism. Modernism's legacy had been the intensely inward, individualistic character of the late-twentieth-century poet; the poet, like the madman, was a solitary figure, not following "schools." The closest thing to a poetic "school" in late twentieth-century poetry is Postmodernism, which celebrates fragmentation to the point of incoherence. John Ashbery, self-declared Postmodernist, illustrates the difficulty of reading "postmodern poetry":

> The "second position"
> Comes in the seventeenth year.
> Watching the meaningless gyrations of flies above a sill
> Heads in hands, waterfall of simplicity
> The delta of living into everything.
> —John Ashbery, from "The Skaters"

as does Leslie Scalapino, a generation Ashbery's junior.

---

[15]From Allen Ginsberg, "Footnote to *Howl*." In *Howl and Other Poems* (San Francisco: City Lights Books, 2006).

> "There" is neither—by simply bypassing existing — by
> observation occurring at the same time (one is outside literally
> looking, seeing is more passive, within one's own husk at dye — at
> the moment then — is not observation which is sole, itself)
> > nor is it experience —as it is occuring
> > —Leslie Scalapino, from "As: All Occurence in Structure,
> > > Unseen—(Deer Night)"

The late twentieth century saw an ongoing struggle not between competing poetic visions, but between poetry written by and for poetic specialists, and poetry written for the "common reader." The poet Vernon Scannel complained that "much contemporary poetry seems to be written for specialist exegesists in the universities in order that they may practise their skills in 'deconstruction.'" "I gave up on new poetry myself thirty years ago," remarked journalist Russell Baker, a thirty-year veteran of the *New York Times* op-ed page, "when most of it began to read like coded messages passing between lonely aliens on a hostile world."

In 1983, Philip Larkin, reflecting on the growing abstruseness of "academic" poetry, remarked that poets—thanks, in part, to the impossibility of earning any money *writing* poetry unless they also teach and write *about* writing poetry—have become critics and professors, and thus pass judgment on poetry as well as writing it. The result is that poetry is in danger of becoming the province of experts: "It is hardly an exaggeration," Larkin writes, "to say that the poet has gained the happy position wherein he can praise his own poetry in the press and explain it in the classroom, that the reader has been bullied into giving up the consumer's power to say 'I don't like this, bring me something different.'"[16] John Ashbery's career (he won the Pulitzer Prize and became both a critic and a professor) seems to confirm the truth of Larkin's remarks; the *Times Literary Supplement* called Ashbery's poems "sophisticated, thickly referential and almost totally impenetrable," an admiring remark that illustrates the ongoing preference of the literary elite toward abstruse poems that must be decoded, rather than coherent poems that must be interpreted.

Postmodernism continues strong, and yet in the last decades, poetry has been partially rescued from the postmodern; in the United States, the Poet Laureate position has become more visible; new translations of classic poetry have brought poets such as Robert Pinsky and Seamus Heaney to a larger audience; Jane Kenyon writes comprehensible poetry, Mark Strand

---

[16]Philip Larkin, *Required Writing: Miscellaneous Pieces*, 1955–1982 (Ann Arbor: University of Michigan Press, 1999).

incomprehensible poetry with strong narrative threads, Billy Collins conversational and witty poems that are much simpler on the surface than in their subtexts, Adrienne Rich poetry that connects with political and social issues.

In the meantime, the careful reader of poetry should be willing to work hard at understanding poetry: to take it on its own terms, chew it over, reflect on it, and analyze its forms, and then to praise it or to conclude, "This is a disorganized mess" and put the book down.

HOW TO READ A POEM

The First Level of Inquiry: Grammar-Stage Reading

> It's wonderful to discover and read a poem when you know nothing
> about the poet, have never read critical commentary on the work, and
> have to figure out what the poet is doing with language.[17]
> —Herbert Kohl

The first step in reading poetry is to begin reading.

Poetry is a meeting between reader and the poet. Sometimes, arming yourself ahead of time with too much information on technique, historical milieu, and the poet's biographical background can keep you from meeting the poet; the background information serves to keep the poet at arm's length.

Consider the following poem:

> We wear the mask that grins and lies,
> It hides our cheeks and shades our eyes,—
> This debt we pay to human guile;
> With torn and bleeding hearts we smile,
> And mouth with myriad subtleties.
>
> Why should the world be overwise,
> In counting all our tears and sighs?
> Nay, let them only see us, while
> We wear the mask.

---

[17]Herbert R. Kohl, *A Grain of Poetry: How to Read Contemporary Poems and Make Them a Part of Your Life* (New York: HarperFlamingo, 1999), p. 3.

We smile, but, O great Christ, our cries
To thee from tortured souls arise.
We sing, but oh the clay is vile
Beneath our feet, and long the mile;
But let the world dream otherwise,
We wear the mask![18]

Now read the poem again, slowly. Make an imaginative effort; put yourself into the place of the one who wears the mask; picture yourself smiling and mouthing "subtleties" while you feel the exact opposite of what your face shows. Imagine the "world" before which you are putting on this act. Who is in it; why are you forced into such false happiness?

Have you exercised your imagination?

The poem is by Paul Laurence Dunbar, an African American poet who wrote "We Wear the Mask" in the late nineteenth century, in the days of Jim Crow. Now you know, a little better, why Dunbar chose this image; he is writing about the "veil" that W. E. B. Du Bois also described, the "double vision" forced on African Americans by a world that requires them to view their own blackness through white eyes.

If you're an African American reader, perhaps you immediately identified with Dunbar's problem in just the way that he intends. But what if you are white, Hispanic, Asian? You should still be able to make the imaginative leap into Dunbar's difficulty. At some point in your life, you too have worn a mask; perhaps you've had the serious, life-shaping experience of constructing a whole life around someone else's image of who you are; maybe you've only had the fleeting experience of behaving one way at a party while thinking something else entirely. But even if your "mask" experience seems trivial and unimportant, in light of Dunbar's more comprehensive complaint, *it is important for you to identify with the problem of the poem.* Then you can make an emotional identification with Dunbar. That initial jolt of emotional recognition ("Yes! I know what it's like to wear a mask—even if it's only for an evening!") connects you to the poet. Without that connection, you might as well read a sociological description of the problem of black double consciousness; there's no reason for you to read a *poem.*

If you know, before reading, that Dunbar is an African American poet of the early twentieth century, that he was the only black student at Central High School in Dayton, Ohio, that his color kept him from attending college, and that he died an alcoholic at age thirty-three, it

[18]Paul Laurence Dunbar, "We Wear the Mask." In *Selected Poems,* by Paul Laurence Dunbar (New York: Dover Publications, 1997), p. 17

may hamper your emotional understanding of the lyric. You may feel that your own jolt of identification is trivial. (After all, what are your problems in comparison?) Or, if you already know something about African American life at the turn of the century, you may gloss over the unique experience Dunbar is trying to share, putting your own previous knowledge in its place, and missing Dunbar's own particular twist on the subject.

Coming to a poem without background knowledge, then, can actually be a plus; it helps you to identify with a familiar emotion or experience, before grappling with its difference. The exception to this rule is poetry that seems completely foreign in subject or form; if, for example, you tackled the *Inferno* with no understanding of the Christian distinction between heaven and hell, you might legitimately give up before reaching the end. But in most cases, you'll find that an initial try at a poem will yield you a surprising level of understanding; even Homer's epics, crammed with unfamiliar names and odd conventions, tell a fairly straightforward story full of recognizable emotions.

Read 10–30 pages of poetry.   So your first step in reading a poem is simply to *read*, without preparation. If the poem is a lengthy epic, try to read at least the first section, or "book." If you are reading a number of shorter poems, aim to read five to ten poems (anywhere from ten to thirty pages of poetry). As you read, jot down your initial reactions in your reading journal. Can you find a familiar emotion, experience, or mood? If the poem is a narrative tale, note down the two or three major events that happen in the first book, and write a sentence describing the tale's hero.

Read the title, cover, and table of contents.   Now that you've had an initial chance to connect with the poet and the poem, go back and do a little bit of elementary background work. Read the title page, the copy on the book's back cover, and any biographical sketches provided. Jot down in your journal the title, the author's name, the span of time over which the poems were composed, and any other facts you might find interesting.

Glance at the table of contents. For a narrative poem, the table of contents may read like a list of chapters in a novel, giving you a preview of the plot; for a poetry collection, the titles of poems may provide an overview of the poet's preoccupations. (The first thing you'll notice about the table of contents in W. H. Auden's *Selected Poems*, for example, is that none of the poems have titles; each is listed by its first line, and those lines are very often directed straight at the reader: "Watch any day his nonchalant pauses," "Will you turn a deaf ear," "Consider this and in our time," "What's in your mind, my dove.")

Read the preface.   In most cases, prefaces to poetry collections give you valuable information about the poet's techniques and ideas. In the case of modern poems the preface can give you a leg up on understanding the poet's preoccupations (you may discover, for example, that Mark Strand is particularly interested in absence, and is prone to write about the ways in which he is not present; or that Jane Kenyon wrote her last collections of poems while ill with leukemia, which adds to the meaning of "Let evening come"). In the case of an older work, you may discover information that the original audience would already have known: "The stylistic tradition represented by *Sir Gawain and the Green Knight*," writes Marie Boroff in the preface to her translation, "calls for the frequent use of such explicitly qualitative adjectives as *noble, worthy, lovely, courteous,* and—perhaps most frequent of all—*good.* These adjectives may be used frequently and freely because, within the traditional world portrayed in this poetic style, knights are inevitably noble and worthy, ladies lovely, servants courteous, and indeed everything, aside from monsters and villainous churls, ideally good."[19] The medieval listener would have known that Gawain inhabited such a fairy-tale world, and would have taken this information for granted.

Finish reading.   Now that you've had a chance to make an initial emotional identification and then to fill in some background information, go back to reading. As you read, follow these steps:

I. For narrative poems (poems that tell a story), make a quick list of major characters as you read, and jot down the main events, just as you did when reading the novel. You'll find this particularly helpful in the epic poems, which are longer than some novels and boast dozens of characters. For a long poem (the *Odyssey, Paradise Lost*), try to limit yourself to two or three major events per section; otherwise you'll end up with an outline so long and detailed that it won't serve to jog your memory. You'll also find this outline helpful for such works as Frost's "Death of the Hired Man," in which the major events are implied through the dialogue.

2. For nonnarrative poems, simply make notes on the poem's *ideas, moods,* or *experiences* as you read. Is the poem describing a scene, portraying a mood, investigating a thought? Use the process of writing as a way to reflect on the poem's content. Don't worry about making these notes complete sentences; poems do not always propose complete, well-rounded thoughts for your intellect to grasp. A poem may put evocative

[19]Marie Boroff, preface to *Sir Gawain and the Green Knight*, trans. Boroff, p. x.

words close together to create a reaction or build a sense of fear, or exhilaration, or foreboding, or peaceful repose. Write down whatever words or phrases seem to capture your response to the poem.

3. As you read, circle phrases or lines that catch your eye or ear; turn down the edge of your page, or write the phrases and lines in your journal. You can return to these later.

4. Mark any section of the poem that you find confusing or obscure— but don't give up. Keep reading.

The Second Level of Inquiry: Logic-Stage Reading

Now that you've read the poem (or poems) once, you'll need to pay a little more attention to the poem's form; remember that the shape of the poem is essential to its meaning. Poetry analysis can be a highly technical activity; the full analysis of rhythm alone requires you to learn *scansion*, the graphing out of a poem's meter. What follows is a nonspecialist's guide, a broad outline of basic poetic techniques meant to increase your appreciation of poetic form. If you want to go beyond this simple analysis, consider investing in a poetry handbook such as Mary Kinzie's *A Poet's Guide to Poetry* (1999) and a guide to scansion, such as Derek Attridge's *Poetic Rhythm: An Introduction* (1996).

Look back at the poem; identify its basic narrative strategy. Narrative strategy has to do with the way in which the poem presents its ideas. There are five distinct "narrative strategies" poets may use:

Has the poet chosen to tell a story, with a beginning, middle, and end?
Does the poet make an argument, with premises and a final conclusion?
Does the poet describe an experience? If so, is this experience physical or mental? (Does he walk through a garden, or struggle with guilt?)
Does the poet describe a physical place, object, or sensation, and allow this to stand for some other nonphysical reality?
Is the poem evocative of a mood, feeling, idea, or emotion?

Of course, a poet may choose to use a combination of methods, but (especially in a short poem) one is likely to be dominant.

Identify the poem's basic form. *Form* has to do with the way in which a poem is put together. A sonnet can make an argument or describe an experience; an ode can evoke a mood or recount an event. Of the many basic poetic forms, these are the ones you will see most often:

Ballad: Also a narrative, but on a smaller scale, featuring one main character or a small group of characters. Generally, a ballad has two- or four-line stanzas and a repeating refrain.

Elegy: A lament. Greek elegies were not necessarily mournful, but all had a certain meter; modern elegies tend to be laments for dead people or dead times.

Epic: A long narrative tale featuring the great deeds of legendary heroes—deeds with some sort of cosmic significance.

Haiku: This Japanese form, adapted into English, conveys a single impression. Haiku, used by some modern writers, have seventeen syllables, arranged into three lines with the syllable pattern five-seven-five. The haiku begins with an image and then widens its focus, after the fifth or after the twelfth syllable, to a larger idea or spiritual perception connected to the idea.

Ode: In English, a poem of exalted character, often addressing the reader directly ("apostrophe").

Sonnet: A poem of fourteen lines, written in iambic pentameter, with a very particular rhyme scheme.

Petrarchan sonnet: The first eight lines (the *octet*), rhymed *abbaabba*, pose a question, an idea, or an argument; the last six lines (the *sestet*), rhymed *cdcdcd* (or, occasionally, *cdecde*; other variations are also possible) resolve, respond to, or illustrate the idea presented in the first eight lines. Between the octet and sestet is a *volta*, or turning point, where the shift between problem and resolution occurs.

"Shakespearian" or "English" sonnet: The first twelve lines of the poem are divided into three "quatrains" of four lines each, with the rhyme scheme *abab cdcd efef,* and the last two lines of the poem are a rhyming couplet *(gg).*

Spenserian sonnet: This form also contains three quatrains and a couplet, but the rhyming scheme is *abab bcbc cdcd ee.*

Villanelle: A poem with five three-line stanzas and one last four-line stanza. The villanelle only has two rhymes; the first and third lines of the first stanza reappear as an alternating refrain in the following stanzas and appear as the last two lines of the final stanza. (Dylan Thomas's "Do Not Go Gentle into That Good Night" is the best known modern villanelle.)

Examine the poem's syntax.   Find the subjects and verbs in each poetic sentence. Although this seems like a simple exercise, it will immediately show you whether the poet is using natural diction or a heightened, poetic form. In Tennyson's *Idylls of the King*, which uses formal poetic diction, the lines

> Saying which she seized,
> And, thro' the casement standing wide for heat,
> Flung them, and down they flash'd, and smote the stream.

have a subject and verb together ("she seized") but the next verb that goes with the subject "she" ("flung") is separated from the subject by an entire line, where it would be more natural to say, "She seized and flung them through the casement." Separation of subject and verb, or reversal of the two, or an understood ("elided") subject or verb, demonstrates "poetic diction"; a more speechlike pattern is found in Carl Sandburg's "Working Girls": "The working girls in the morning are going to work."

Try to identify the poem's meter (or meters).   There are two major kinds of meter: syllabic meter, which counts the number of syllables in each line, and accentual meter, which only counts the stresses, or strong syllables.

In syllabic meter, each group of syllables is called a *foot*. English verse has five common feet, or patterns:

The *anapest* is two unaccented syllables followed by an accented one (the "limerick" meter):

> There ONCE was a MAN of BlackHEATH,
> Who SAT on his SET of false TEETH.

The *dactyl* is one accented syllable followed by two unaccented ones:

> KNOW ye the LAND of the CEdar and VINE,
> Where the FLOwers e'er BLOSsom, the BEAMS ever SHINE
> —Byron, "The Bride of Abydos"

The *iamb* is an unaccented syllable followed by an accented one.

The *spondee,* two accented syllables together, generally occurs as a variation in a line based on another pattern. The spondee often comes before or after a *pyrrhic foot* (two unaccented syllables).

The *trochee* is an accented syllable followed by an unaccented syllable:

> TYger! TYger, BURning BRIGHT

"Meter" names the number of feet in each line: dimeter (two feet), trimeter (three feet), tetrameter (four feet), and so on up: pentameter, hexameter, heptameter, and octameter (eight). The lines from Byron above are in dactylic tetrameter; there are four dactyls in each line. (Even though there are not four full dactyls in each line, the overall pattern is dactylic.)

In English verse, the most common foot is iambic, and the most common iambic meter is iambic pentameter. Since "iambic" means that the basic poetic unit, or foot, is a set of two syllables, the second of which is stressed:

> Of MAN'S first DISoBEd'ence, AND the FRUIT
> Of THAT forBIDden TREE whose MORtal TASTE

and "pentameter" means that there are five feet in each line, iambic pentameter contains five pairs of syllables. "Blank" means that the lines are unrhymed. Iambic meter becomes trochaic if the weak and strong stresses are reversed, as they are in Edgar Allan Poe's "The Raven":

> ONCE uPON a MIDnight DREAry
> WHILE I PONdered, WEAK and WEARy,
> OVer MANy a QUAINT and CURious . . .

In the first two lines, the voice tends to stress the first (technically unstressed) syllables of each foot rather than the second syllable, which in terms of meaning is less important; this creates a singsong, more proselike meter.

"Accentual verse," practiced by Gerard Manley Hopkins and William Butler Yeats (among others), counts the number of strong or stressed syllables in a line, rather than the total number of syllables. You find a strong syllable by reading the line in a normal voice; you naturally place the accents on the strong syllables. Modern verse tends to combine accentual and syllabic meter.

Examine the lines and stanzas. First, ask yourself, Does each line sound like a whole, or does the line naturally divide into halves (*hemistichs*)? Then find the beginnings and ends of each sentence. Are the sentences and lines identical? Do the sentences run over the ends of the lines (*enjambment*)? If they do, is the enjambment natural, or does the line break come at an awkward place? If the poet chooses a line length that clashes with his sentence length, he has decided to draw attention to one or the other; why?

Then look for stanzas. Stanzas are sets of lines that impose structure on the poet; if she decides to use them, she is making a choice to confine her-self; why? How many lines does each stanza have? Does each stanza follow a similar pattern of rhyme and meter, or does the poet relax the technical confines of the stanza and vary the pattern? Where do the stanzas fall; do they show a change of meaning, a reversal, a further development?

Examine the rhyme pattern. Poetic notation uses a letter of the alphabet for each unique rhyme sound; you can use these to note a rhyme scheme in your journal. "End rhyme" is the most common type of poetic rhyme, but don't forget to also look for internal rhyme or middle rhyme (a rhyme within a line, as in Shelley's poem "The Cloud": "I sift the snow on the mountains below"). Once you've found the rhymes, you can classify them. A feminine rhyme is a rhyme on a last syllable that is unaccented, a mascu-line rhyme is a rhyme on an accented last syllable or a one-syllable word; slant rhymes or near rhymes occur when two syllables have a similar but not identical sound.

Examine diction and vocabulary. Does the poet use allusive, abstract, idea words, or concrete, particular words? Does he prefer rounded, multisyl-labic, Latinate vocabulary, or brief, plain monosyllables? What images are present in the poem? What do these images stand for? What senses do the images appeal to: sight, sound, smell, taste, feel? Does the poet appeal pri-marily to the body, to the emotions, or to the intellect of the reader? If the poem contains explicit similes (using the words *like* or *as*), pay particular attention to both parts of the image: What two things are being compared? How are they alike; how are they different? And is the writer highlighting their sameness—or their distinctiveness?

Look for monologue or dialogue. Is there dialogue between the narrator of the poem and another person? If so, how would you characterize it: hostile, friendly, kind, interrogative? Does the narrator carry on a dialogue with herself? If so, what does this internal dialogue result in—resolution, or a further kind of complication? Does it improve or complicate the poet's relationship with the outside world? Does it improve or complicate the poet's relationship with others?

The Third Level of Inquiry: Rhetoric-Stage Reading

Now you'll need to finish your examination of the poem by asking: What ideas does this poem convey to me—and how is the form of the poem related to those ideas? The answers to the following questions will vary tremendously from poem to poem, but remember: Resist the urge to reduce the poem to a declarative sentence. If the poet had been able to put his ideas into a simple declarative sentence, he'd have had no need to write a poem.

Is there a moment of choice or of change in the poem?   Is the poem set in one unchanged world? Or does a change take place from the poem's beginning to its end? If there is a change, does it happen *to* the poem, or is there a moment of choice for the poet/narrator? (Sometimes this choice is very obvious, as in Robert Frost's famous "Two roads diverged in a yellow wood"; sometimes it is much more subtle.)

Is there cause and effect?   Does the writer link her state of mind or experience to any particular event or cause? If so, does this link resonate for you? Is there causality at all? If there is no causality in the poem, do emotions or events arise for no particular reason?

What is the tension between the physical and the psychological, the earthly and the spiritual, the mind and the body?   Do the objects and physical settings in the poem work for or against the emotions expressed? In the world of the poem, does the physical lead to spiritual enlightenment—or block it? Are mind and body at war? Are earthly and spiritual aspects of the poem in tension? Or is only one of these aspects present? If so . . . where is the other?

What is the poem's subject?   What is the poem *about*? Remember, this doesn't need to be a declarative sentence: you can answer it with a single word. "Grief." "Friendship." "Ireland." What word or phrase seems to name the core around which the poem resolves?

Where is the self?   Is the poet's "self" in the poem? If so, what is the relationship between that self and the subject of the poem?

Do you feel sympathy?   To ask "Do you feel sympathy with this poem?" is to ask, "Do you agree?" Does the poem resonate with you—or is it foreign to your experience? Can you identify which parts of the poem you recognize, and which seem alien?

How does the poet relate to those who came before?   Where does the poet stand in the rhetoric of ideas? In the past, critics have seen younger poets as rebelling against their elders, developing their own poetic styles in reaction to an older generation; or they have viewed younger poets as taking the techniques, themes, and even the language of older poets and incorporating them into new poetic works. Do you recognize either of these relationships among the poetic works that you have read?

THE ANNOTATED POETRY LIST

In the list that follows, poets are organized in chronological order of their birth date. When you read a novel, you read a work; when you read a series of poems, you read a life. So in many cases I have recommended a collected "greatest works" rather than a particular volume published during the poet's lifetime. Because poems are meant not to be read once, but returned to again and again, the list of recommended editions is aimed at helping you build a poetry library. There are many other editions of most of these poets available; I have listed some "Be sure to read" poems so that if you wish to use another edition, you can still experience the poet's most characteristic works.

You can go as far as you please into investigating a poet who seizes your fancy; for the collected poems, I have suggested a brief list of poems that you should be certain to read. If you find this hard going, you don't necessarily need to read on: A poem, like a spice, is not going to suit every taste. The recommended poems are not necessarily the poet's "best" (an impossible judgment by any means). Instead, they have been chosen as that poet's most commonly referred to, criticized, and quoted poems. Reading them will allow you to understand the place the poet occupies in the larger world of poetry.

As with fiction, some of these poem collections are available in much cheaper editions, if you're willing to put up with small print and narrow margins. For ancient works, I suggest that you use the recommended translations, rather than the out-of-date or anonymous versions often used in cheaper paperbacks and low-cost ebook versions.

The Epic of Gilgamesh
(c. 2000 B.C.)

Recommended translations: An excellent, lyrical poetic rendering is the Stephen Mitchell translation, Gilgamesh: A New English Version *(Atria Books, reprint edition, 2006); it is also available on Audible in an unabridged audio reading by George Guidall. David Ferry's 1993 verse translation,* Gilgamesh: A New Rendering in English Verse, *puts the story into anachronistic heroic couplets that are sometimes difficult to read, and makes some imaginative leaps over places where the tablets bearing the Sumerian story were broken or missing, but the story reads as a unified whole. Maureen Gallery Kovacs's* The Epic of Gilgamesh *(Stanford University Press, 1989) is a more scholarly and literal translation that indicates missing text and fragments. Two prose renderings are also available; the well-regarded Penguin Classics translation by N. K. Sandars (1960) and the Benjamin R. Foster translation for W. W. Norton (2001) (this critical edition uses brackets and ellipses for missing text, which breaks the story up).*

Gilgamesh is one of the oldest stories in the world; these collected tales about the legendary king Gilgamesh (probably based on a real king who lived in modern-day Iraq around 3000 B.C.) were told orally for hundreds of years before they were written down. The first written version of the epic seems to date from around 2000 B.C., although the version we have is a later copy from the library of the Assyrian king Asshurbanipal, who began his reign in 669 B.C. Although Asshurbanipal's primary interest was conquest, he bears the distinction of being the world's first librarian; he employed a team of scholars to collect the history, poetry, religious literature, and medical and scientific writings of the surrounding peoples for his library at Nineveh. The *Gilgamesh* we know was translated from some unknown source, probably in ancient Sumerian, into the Akkadian language the Assyrians used, and was copied onto clay tablets in cuneiform script. Asshurbanipal's library was smashed when the Babylonians stormed through the Assyrian capital in 612 B.C., so although several of the tales ("Gilgamesh and the Land of the Living" and "Gilgamesh and the Bull of Heaven") are complete, others ("The Death of Gilgamesh") are fragments of longer texts. "Gilgamesh, Enkidu and the Netherworld" is apparently a tale from a separate tradition that was copied onto the Assyrian tablets with no attempt to reconcile it with the contradictory tales already given. The story of Gilgamesh and the flood probably comes from a later tradition as well, since the story has also been discovered in the Sumerian language starring another hero named Ziusudra; at some unknown point, it was incorporated into the set of Gilgamesh tales as well.

Gilgamesh, part human and part god and supernaturally strong, is the king of Uruk. When he oppresses his people, they call out to the sky god Anu for relief. Anu creates a wild man, Enkidu, and sends him to challenge Gilgamesh's strength. Eventually the two become friends; Enkidu curbs Gilgamesh's excesses, and himself learns how to live among civilized men. The two go on an adventure to kill the demon Humbaba the Terrible, who lives in the Cedar Forest south of Uruk; later they also fight against the Bull of Heaven, who rampages through Gilgamesh's kingdom, killing hundreds of his people. The gods, annoyed by the strength of the two, send sickness to Enkidu. When he dies, the grief-stricken Gilgamesh goes on a quest to find the secret of immortality, held by Utnapishtim, an old and mysterious man who survived the great flood that drowned the world long ago. Utnapishtim tells Gilgamesh how to find the magic plant that will make him live forever, but on his way back to Uruk Gilgamesh loses the plant forever: "For whom have I labored and taken this journey?" he laments. "I have gained absolutely nothing!" Gilgamesh is a tragic hero; although possessing divine blood and strength, he is helpless against death and the passage of time, and suffers from the loss of his friend like any mortal man.

HOMER
the *Iliad* and the *Odyssey*
(c. 800 B.C.)

Recommended translations: There are three excellent translations of Homer available in paperback. The contemporary Robert Fagles translations of The Iliad *(Penguin Classics, 1998) and* The Odyssey *(Penguin Classics, 2006) are energetic, straightforward, clear, and easy to understand, with a good narrative flow. The Robert Fitzgerald translations,* The Iliad *(Anchor Books, 1989) and* The Odyssey *(Farrar, Straus and Giroux, 1998), are several decades older; these translations are more poetic, with echoes of Shakespearean cadences. And yet a third translation, by Richmond Lattimore, has kept its place as a brilliant work of English poetry in its own right:* The Iliad *(University of Chicago Press, 2011) and* The Odyssey *(HarperPerennial Modern Classics, 2007).*

Stephen Mitchell has recently translated both the Iliad *(Atria Books, 2012) and the* Odyssey *(Atria, 2013) into energetic, contemporary poetry. His* Iliad *is based on a Greek text edited by Martin West, who pruned of hundreds of lines that he judged to be later interpolations; as a result it is significantly shorter than the versions above.*

The Fitzgerald, Lattimore, and Mitchell translations of the Iliad *are available unabridged on Audible; the Fagles translation is only available as an abridged version, but since it's read by Derek Jacobi, it's worth a listen anyway. The Fagles translation of the* Odyssey *is read, unabridged, by Ian McKellen; the Fitzgerald* Odyssey *is also available on Audible.*

Both Achilles, the hero of the *Iliad*, and Odysseus, hero of the *Odyssey*, suffer from their own brilliance: Too strong, too influential, too powerful for their own good, they cannot yield to even the slightest public humiliation; jealously guarding their own reputations, they create havoc in the lives of everyone else. The *Iliad* is set in the last year of the ten-year Trojan War; the Greeks, who have sailed across the Aegean Sea to Troy, are camped around Troy in makeshift tents and huts, laying siege to the city. The Greek commander Agamemnon and Achilles, the greatest Greek warrior, quarrel over captive women, and Achilles—publicly humiliated by Agamemnon, but bound in loyalty to his king by an oath—complains to his mother, the sea goddess Thetis. Thetis turns Zeus's wrath against Agamemnon and the other Greeks, and Agamemnon is convinced by a dream to make a disastrous attack on Troy. But when the gods become involved in the battle, it spirals into chaos; eventually Zeus halts the fighting and scolds his divine colleagues for weighing in on the side of the Greeks. When the battle restarts, Zeus himself gives instructions to Hector, the son of Troy's king and the most powerful Trojan warrior, but the sea god Poseidon throws his weight behind the Greek hero Ajax. Hector is wounded and the Trojans are driven back. Hector, bandaged, returns to the fighting; Zeus eventually gives all of the gods permission to reenter the fighting, and the war turns into a two-level fight, between the armies of men on the one hand and the quarreling gods on the other. When Athena, who loves the Greeks, tricks Hector into fighting Achilles, Hector is killed, and Achilles drags his body around the city; but Zeus intervenes again, telling Thetis to instruct her son Achilles to give the body back to Priam, the king of Troy. Priam ransoms his son's corpse from Achilles, and the tale ends with a great funeral.

The *Odyssey* takes place after the end of the Trojan war. Odysseus, a Greek king, sets sail for home; but although the other Greeks return without incident, Odysseus is sidetracked by the hostility of Poseidon, who sends storms to wreck Odysseus' ship and maroon him. Meanwhile his wife Penelope is under intense pressure to remarry; she has stalled her suitors for ten years, but has run out of excuses. Odysseus struggles home; on the way he escapes the land of the Lotus-Eaters (where his men are drugged into sloth when they eat a magic plant), the cave of the one-eyed Cyclops (Poseidon's son; when Odysseus blinds him, Poseidon grows even angrier), the goddess Circe (who turns his men into pigs and seduces Odysseus), and a side journey to Hades. Then he passes the island of the Sirens (who tempt men to their deaths with their song) and survives a journey through a narrow strait between the six-headed monster Scylla and the enormous whirlpool Charybdis, only to land on the shores of an island owned by the sun god, Helios. When his men eat Helios's sacred cows, Zeus kills them all and destroys their ship; Odysseus, fleeing, is sucked into Charybdis and spewed out onto the island of the nymph Calypso, who tries to marry him. Finally he escapes Calypso and returns home just as Penelope is running out of techniques to stall her suitors. When he sees his house filled with hostile warriors who hope to marry his wife, he disguises himself as a beggar until he is able to arrange a shooting contest, the winner to be awarded Penelope in marriage. Bow in hand, he turns on the suitors, kills them all, and reclaims his throne.

GREEK LYRICISTS
(c. 600 B.C.)

Recommended editions (choose one): Greek Lyrics, *trans. Richmond Lattimore, rev. ed. (University of Chicago Press, 1960);* Greek Lyrics: An Anthology in Translation, *trans. Andrew M. Miller (Hackett, 1996); or* Archaic Greek Poetry: An Anthology, *trans. Barbara Hughes Fowler (University of Wisconsin Press, 1992).*

At the very least, be sure to read the poems of Sappho, Pindar, and Solon; this will expose you to a range of poetic styles and themes.

The Greek lyric poems, which exist now only in fragments, were written to be performed onstage to the accompaniment of the lyre. Choral poetry was sung in unison by a trained chorus; monodic poetry was recited by the poet. All Greek lyric poetry was rooted in the worship of the gods, and the poems are almost all framed by invocations to deities and pleas for divine favor. But within that framework, the Greeks wrote poems that range from the passionate pleadings of Sappho, to the religious, impersonal hymnlike choral lyrics of Pindar, to the political and philosophical musings of Solon.

Although the choral lyrics and hymns to the gods are archaic now, the Greek monodic lyrics (which paint a particular moment of time or an instant of emotional experience with great detail, as Sappho does) were startlingly innovative in their day—and remain completely comprehensible to us, centuries later. The epigram, a slightly later form of verse, encapsulated a single mood, experience, or conclusion into a compressed, polished sentence or two. Later English poets borrowed the Greek terms *ode* and *elegy* (names that originally referred to different kinds of meter) for their own poems—and found, in the Greek ability to capture a single vivid impression in verse, a goal for their own poetry.

HORACE
Odes
(65–8 B.C.)

Recommended translations: Odes: With the Latin Text, *trans. James Michie (Modern Library Classics, 2002), a lyrical translation that includes the Latin on the facing page. The translations by David West in* The Complete Odes and Epodes *(Oxford World's Classics, 2008) are also readable and engaging.*

Be sure to read: For a sampling of the best-known odes, try book I, Odes 1–9, 17, and 30; book II, Odes 19–20; book III, Odes 1–6 and 13; book IV, Odes 1 and 7.

Life is brief and death is coming, so enjoy each moment. Horace's odes are organized around this philosophy; they tend to begin with a scene from nature or from society (a great banquet, a drinking party, a forest at dawn) and to progress from this concrete image to a brief argument that explains why (and how) the reader should enjoy what each day brings, without dreading the future. The odes aren't united by any one subject; Horace addresses, in turn, various women, virgin maidens, his friend Septimus, and gods ranging from Calliope to Bacchus. He writes of the weather, nature, farm life ("All the farm beasts on the green ground / Gambol, and with time to spare / The world enjoys the open air"), the meaning of Roman citizenship, festivals, feasts, and love. But his philosophy of *carpe diem* ("pluck the day," seizing whatever it brings without apprehension) shapes every poem. This pragmatic advice is given in full knowledge that death is inevitable, but Horace doesn't see this as cause for mourning. Rather, the unstoppable approach of death becomes a moral center for his work: Accept your mortality and always act in the knowledge that time is short.

Horace's composition of poetry is his own effort to "seize the present moment." In his first ode, he describes the various ways that men choose to "grasp the day"; the charioteer competes for the victory palm, "others the civic crown desire," still others accumulate wealth, or sail abroad for adventure, or fight in wars. "But learning renders me divine," Horace concludes. "If I to lyric fame arise / My brow shall touch the very skies" (translation by Herbert Grant).

Beowulf
(c. 1000)

Recommended translations: Seamus Heaney's translation, Beowulf: A New
Verse Translation *(W. W. Norton, 2001), is head and shoulders above the
rest. Heaney himself narrates an abridged audio version for Audible; it is worth
a supplementary listen. J. R. R. Tolkien's recently published translation,*
Beowulf: A Translation and Commentary *(Houghton Mifflin Harcourt,
2014), completed by his son Christopher, is popular with many readers; it is
an enjoyable version with some wonderful lines, but I find Tolkien's archaisms
("lo, "thou," "spake," "recalleth") unnecessary and distracting. Heaney's work
remains the more lively and energetic read.*

Beowulf, probably composed orally in the eighth century, was written
down near the end of the tenth century in Old English (a Germanic dialect heavily influenced by Icelandic). It bears marks of its oral origin in
its alliterative lines, which contain four stressed syllables, two or three
of which begin with the same sound; and in its use of *kenning*, formulaic hyphenated names that describe people or objects in terms of their
character qualities and provide extra syllables to fill out the meter (so,
when necessary, the sea becomes the "whale-road," a ship's sail becomes
the "sea-shawl," and the monster Grendel is "God-cursed," the "hall-
watcher," the "shadow-stalker" and "terror-monger").

At the poem's beginning, the Danish King Hrothgar has a problem;
he has built a beautiful mead hall on a high, well-lit hill, but a monster, descended from the biblical Cain, stalks through the tangled swamps
below, forever cut off from God and from man. Grendel attacks at night,
eating Hrothgar's men and terrifying his subjects, and no one can defeat
him—until the hero Beowulf travels from Geatland to help. Beowulf
fights Grendel with his bare hands and defeats him. But Grendel's mother,
thirsting for revenge, is twice as evil; Beowulf struggles to defeat her and
eventually is forced to use a magic sword from the days of the giants to kill
her. After his victories, Beowulf inherits the kingdom and rules peace-
fully for fifty years—until a thief, stealing a jeweled cup from a dragon's lair, awakens the dragon. It roams through Beowulf's land, burning
houses and killing his subjects, and the old king arms himself for one last
battle. He defeats the dragon, but dies in the process, and is burned on the
shore as his people mourn.

Beowulf's battles against the three monsters beg for allegorical interpretation. John Gardner suggests that the three foes represent the mal-
function of three different parts of the soul (Grendel represents unreason,
Grendel's mother a lack of moral sense, the dragon a surrender to lust and

greed); many other critics have pointed out that Beowulf is an obvious Christ figure who strides out to meet the Satanic dragon with twelve followers and dies to protect his people; Grendel, the monster from the plains, is the pagan soul cut off from God. Yet these undeniably Christian elements are mingled with a thoroughly un-Christian submission to impersonal fate (*wyrd*), an uncritical acceptance of the warrior ethic that demands revenge for the death of a kinsman, and a fervent belief in spells and ancient demons. Allegorical interpretations aside, the story is just plain good reading; you'll hear it in phrases stolen by later writers, from Tolkien to Conan Doyle, and in Seamus Heaney's hands, the verse ranges from beautiful to downright creepy:

> A few miles from here
> a frost-stiffened wood waits and keeps watch
> above a mere; the overhanging bank
> is a maze of tree-roots mirrored in its surface.
> At night there, something uncanny happens:
> the water burns. And the mere bottom
> has never been sounded by the sons of men.
> On its banks, the heather-stepper halts:
> the hart in flight from pursuing hounds
> will turn to face them with firm set horns
> and die in the wood rather than dive
> beneath its surface. That is no good place.

DANTE ALIGHIERI
Inferno
(1265–1321)

Recommended translations: The Inferno of Dante: A New Verse Translation, *translated by Robert Pinsky (Farrar, Straus and Giroux, 1996). This idiomatic, energetic translation by an American poet has the Italian on facing pages. Anthony Esolen's translation for Modern Library Classics (2005) is a lovely, forward-flowing version that also includes the Italian text; the lines are set in unrhymed iambic pentameter. The Allen Mandelbaum translation,* The Divine Comedy of Dante Alighieri: Inferno, *has been a standard for years and is still widely read; it is less idiomatic and more formal (Bantam Books, 1982).*

On Good Friday, Dante (the narrator of his own poem) becomes lost in a dark wood; uncertain as to whether he is sleeping or waking, he tries to find his path but instead finds wild animals blocking his way. The ghost of the Roman poet Virgil appears, offering to show him the path, which will eventually lead Dante to Heaven and to the spirit of Beatrice, Dante's lost love—but Virgil warns that the path will lead them through Hell first.

The journey through Hell reveals it to be made up of concentric circles, ranging from an outer belt where the least blameworthy reside (this Ante-Inferno contains the souls of those who lived "without disgrace and without praise," worthy of neither heaven nor hell) to the innermost Ninth Circle, which contains those who betray their families, their countries, and their benefactors. At the very center of Hell is Lucifer himself, frozen in ice, and chewing on the three greatest sinners of history: Judas, who betrayed Christ, and Cassius and Brutus, who betrayed Caesar. (The point is the betrayal of a close and trusted friend, not a parallel between Caesar and Christ.) From the First to the Ninth Circle, Dante ranks sins from the least to the most reprehensible and provides a punishment for each. These punishments offer profound insights into the nature of evil, which is portrayed first as a choice, and then as an inevitability that traps its devotees in an eternal, sickening cycle. Sinners in Dante's Inferno spend eternity performing acts that they despise, without any hope of an end.

In writing, Dante had always in mind the fourfold exegesis that Thomas Aquinas had prescribed for the interpretation of Scripture. His journey through hell is a literal adventure, but also an allegorical journey of a soul who glimpses the true nature of Satan's kingdom, and beyond it the beauties of heaven ("My guide and I came on that hidden road," Dante concludes, in Mandelbaum's translation "to make our way back into the bright world . . . until I saw, / through a round opening, some of those things / of beauty Heaven bears. It was from there / that we emerged, to see—once more—the stars"); a tropological journey, showing the inevitable working out of all different varieties of sin; and an eschatological journey as well: it yields a glimpse of final judgment.

Sir Gawain and the Green Knight
(c. 1350)

Recommended translations from the original Middle English: Simon Armitage's excellent Sir Gawain and the Green Knight: A New Verse Translation *(W. W. Norton, 2008) has the original text on facing pages. Marie Boroff's elegant translation, newly revised, is now available in a Norton Critical Edition (2009), edited by Laura L. Howes. Slightly more archaic in its language, but fun to read for echoes of Middle Earth, is the J. R. R. Tolkien translation,* Sir Gawain and the Green Knight, Pearl, Sir Orfeo *(Del Rey, 1979).*

Gawain is a member of Arthur's court, that bright, glittering, Hollywood-shiny palace filled with "the most noble knights known under Christ, / And the loveliest ladies that lived on earth ever." At Christmas, a central feast of the Christian year, a Green Knight rides into Arthur's hall, sneers at the knights ("There are about on these benches but beardless children!" he scoffs) and throws out a challenge: He will allow any knight to strike him with his axe, as long as he can return the blow a year from now. This challenge meets with silence, until Arthur himself stands up to accept it—at which point Gawain, his nephew and kinsman, offers to play the "game" instead. Gawain cuts off the Green Knight's head, but the Knight picks his head up and departs, reminding Gawain to meet him at the "Green Chapel" in a year and a day.

A year passes, and Gawain—bound by his oath—sets out to find the Green Chapel. Lost in a wilderness, he prays to the Virgin Mary for guidance, and immediately sees a castle, where he goes for shelter. The lord and lady of the castle offer him hospitality for three days; each morning the lady tries to seduce him while her husband is out hunting, but Gawain rejects each temptation until the last, when she offers him a green girdle that will magically render him invincible. Gawain takes the girdle and keeps it a secret from the lord of the castle, even though he has promised to give his host anything he acquires during his stay. When Gawain finally does meet the Green Knight, the Knight flourishes the axe at him twice, nicks him once, and then reveals his true identity: He is the lord of the castle, and the nick is punishment for Gawain's weakness in accepting the green girdle and keeping it secret. "True men pay what they owe," the Green Knight remarks, "You lacked, sir, a little in loyalty there." Gawain, ashamed at his failing, wears the green girdle afterward as part of his armor; and his fellow knights of the Round Table adopt the green belt as well, the "sign . . . of cowardice and coveting."

The Camelot of the poem is rich in chivalry, that set of values which encompasses honesty, courtesy, respect for women, unswerving loyalty to leaders, and Christian faith. Yet there is a certain uneasiness at Camelot's core, a doubt about whether this chivalry—the code that replaced the bloody, primitive warrior's code of revenge found in *Beowulf*—is truly a manly substitute. Gawain is able to resist seduction, but in the end his courage fails him.

As you read, look for the poem's characteristic use of the "bob and wheel" form: a stanza of long, alliterated lines, followed by a line with only two syllables (the "bob") that connects the long-lined stanza with the "wheel," a stanza of four short lines rhymed *abab*:

The stout stirrups were green, that steadied his feet. . .
That gleamed all and glinted with green gems about,
The steed he bestrides of that same green
    so bright
        A great horse great and thick;
        A headstrong steed of might;
        In broidered bridle quick,
        Mount matched man aright.
        —trans. by Marie Boroff (New York: W. W. Norton,
           1967), part I, lines 168–178

GEOFFREY CHAUCER
The Canterbury Tales
(c. 1343–1400)

Recommended editions: The Penguin Classics edition, translated by Nevill Coghill (Penguin Books, 2003), and the Oxford World's Classics translation by David Wright (2011) both turn the Middle English verse into vivid, modern English verse. Wright's version is a little more idiomatic and contemporary than Coghill's. If you want to make a run at the Middle English, try the Norton Critical Edition, The Canterbury Tales: Nine Tales and the General Prologue, *edited by V. A. Kolve and Glending Olson (1989); this reader-friendly edition provides plenty of vocabulary notes and explanatory footnotes.*

    Be sure to read: The Prologue, the Knight's Tale, the Miller's Tale, the Wife of Bath's Prologue and Tale, the Pardoner's Tale, and Chaucer's Retraction.

Chaucer's pilgrims set out from London, that secular city, on a journey to Canterbury, the center of the Christian faith in England. The journey, which also has the allegorical significance of man's journey toward heaven, has its oddities: it is at least a three-day trip, but the pilgrims never seem to sleep; the group of pilgrims is impossibly varied, containing a representative of every level of society, from the aristocratic Knight down to the blue-collar Miller.

Around the fire, each pilgrim tells a story—the Canterbury Tales. For these stories, Chaucer uses common medieval literary forms: the *estates satire*, a stereotypical portrait of the vices of a particular social class; the *romance*, a long, serious tale, often historical, told by a serious and trustworthy narrator, usually concerning knights, kings, and other aristocratic personages; the *fabliaux*, a short story featuring low-class characters and obscene humor; the *beast fable*, like Aesop's fables, a moral tale starring talking animals; the *exemplum*, a brief moral tale, a preacher's illustration. Yet he uses each form with a wink and a nudge, parodying the conventions of each; the Tales are no more "real" than are the pilgrims, who (although on a religious journey) spend their time drinking, feasting, singing, and telling dirty jokes. The Knight's Tale, a long (and boring) romance between highborn characters, is immediately followed by the Miller's Tale, which reverses every single convention of the romance by putting lecherous and stupid characters at the center of the plot and which culminates, not in a chaste kiss, but in scatological humor. The Wife of Bath's tale, which (she assures us) will reveal what women *really* want, ends up describing what men really want (a wife who is perpetually young and beautiful and entirely submissive).

At the end of his book, Chaucer primly retracts the Tales along with his other "worldly translations," thus shifting the blame for enjoying them onto the reader. Scholars argue endlessly about this Retraction. Is it genuine, the product of a deathbed repentance? Was it inserted by later scribes? Is it ironic, a jab from the poet at the idea that tales must be "unworldly" to be worthwhile? The last explanation seems most likely; the Canterbury Tales, told by pilgrims who (theoretically) have their minds on higher things, illustrate the impossibility of keeping the imagination on those things rather than on earthly matters.

WILLIAM SHAKESPEARE
Sonnets
(1564–1616)

Recommended editions: Shakespeare's sonnets are available online and in multiple editions, including Complete Sonnets *(Dover Thrift Editions, 1991),* Complete Sonnets and Poems *(Oxford World's Classics, 2008), and* Shakespeare's Sonnets *(Folger Shakespeare Library, 2004).*
  Be sure to read: 3, 16, 18, 19, 21, 29, 30, 36, 40, 60, 98, 116, 129, 130, 152.

Shakespeare's sonnets follow a particular English sonnet form. Each is written in iambic pentameter, a rhythm scheme in which each line has ten syllables; those syllables are divided into pairs, or "feet," known as *iambs*. Each iamb has an unstressed syllable, followed by a stressed syllable; when these are *scanned*, or written in poetic notation, they are noted as u —

first foot	second foot	third foot	fourth foot	fifth foot
u —	u —	u —	u —	u —
My MIS tress' EYES	are NO thing	LIKE the SUN

The sonnets contain fourteen lines of iambic pentameter. The first twelve lines are divided into three quatrains, each containing four lines with the rhyme scheme *abab cdcd efef.* These quatrains are related in meaning; they present three parallel ideas, or build an argument in three points. Or the first quatrain presents an idea and then the next two complicate it or explain it. The final two lines, a rhymed couplet, have the rhyme scheme *gg* (they rhyme only with each other). Although Shakespeare keeps to this rhyme scheme, he occasionally also makes use of the Petrarchan development of meaning, in which the first eight lines pose a problem while the next six solve or react to it. This sonnet form can begin to guide your reading: The sonnets do not convey impressions or moods, or relate stories; they propose problems and search for answers.

Although the sonnets can be read separately (and reams of criticism have been written on every aspect of their construction), they have traditionally also been read as parts of a whole, as one sequence. Read in this way, the poems seem to reveal a "narrator" who is not necessarily Shakespeare himself. The "Poet," as a fictional character, can be discerned behind the sonnets; he is discontented, restless, resisting calmness and repose. Three other characters can also be found in the sonnets. The "Dark Lady" is referred to in Sonnet 127 as a "black beauty"; "My mistress' eyes are raven-black," the Poet explains. The "Dark Lady" is described again in Sonnets 130, 131, and 132, and is referred to elsewhere; a Rival Poet, shows up in nine sonnets (21, 78–80, and 82–86); and a Young Man, addressed in the first seventeen sonnets, is praised for his youth and (fleeting) beauty and is encouraged to marry and pass his beauty on to children: "Then what could death do if thou shoudst depart," the Poet asks in Sonnet 6, "Leaving thee living in posterity?"

JOHN DONNE
(1572–1631)

Recommended edition: John Donne: The Complete English Poems, edited by A. J. Smith (Penguin Classics, 1977). This edition has careful endnotes explaining all of Donne's references and interpreting Donne's conceits. The Modern Library Classics edition, The Complete Poetry and Selected Prose of John Donne *(2001), also includes several of Donne's best-known sermons, a collection of his letters, and other writings.*

Be sure to read: Elegy 1 ("To his Mistress Going to Bed"), Elegy 12 ("Nature's lay idiot"), "The Flea," "Song ['Go, and catch a falling star'],"
"The Sun Rising," "The Canonization," "Air and Angels," "Love's Alchemy," "The Bait," "A Valediction: Forbidding Mourning," "The Ecstasy," and the sixteen-sonnet sequence Holy Sonnets.

John Donne's reputation as a dissolute, poetry-spouting rake who miraculously mutated into a devout priest and dean of St. Paul's Cathedral isn't entirely deserved. True, Donne did spend the first part of his life as a courtier and man about town, and he did carry on an affair with his employer's sixteen-year-old niece, Anne More, when he was himself nearly thirty. But he married Anne (after her father had him jailed) and lived with her faithfully afterward. And although Donne's poetry is traditionally divided into two parts—the earthy love poetry written in the first part of his life, and the poetry of devotion to God produced during his later years—he actually began writing religious poetry years before he became a priest, and was still producing amorous verses two years after his ordination.

John Donne's poetry is marked by the use of the "metaphysical conceit," a device that draws together two unlikely images, objects, or ideas in order to illustrate an unexpected similarity between them (a prime illustration of the new Renaissance belief in the interconnectedness of all things). Probably the most notorious of Donne's conceits appears in "The Flea," which compares sex to a blood-swollen flea which has bitten the two lovers; sex and the flea both mingle the blood of the two into one body. "Mark but this flea," the impatient lover tells his reluctant mistress, "and mark in this, / How little that which thou deny'st me is." She won't sleep with him out of her sense of honor, but—he points out—the flea is already combining their bodily fluids, and no one is suffering from shame. (It is, he adds pathetically, more fortunate than he.)

Donne's *Holy Sonnets*, written later in his life, are Petrarchan sonnets (combining an eight-line octet, rhymed *abbaabba* with a six-line sestet; the sestet's rhyme scheme varies, but the last two lines usually rhyme and provide a conclusion). They make use of less grotesque conceits. "I am a little world made cunningly / Of elements, and an angelic sprite," begins the fifth meditation, continuing on to describe the little world's betrayal to sin and the judgment of fire that must consume it. And Donne's heart becomes first a besieged castle, then an occupied village, and finally a captive maiden in "Batter my heart, three-personed God," which concludes,

> Take me to you, imprison me, for I
> Except you enthral me, never shall be free,
> Nor ever chaste, except you ravish me.

Throughout the *Sonnets*, Donne's poetic persona is capable of no good on his own; he is a helpless slave of sin and Satan, needing violent action on the part of God to rescue him. "Not one hour I can myself sustain," he writes, and concludes "Meditation 2" with a desperate appeal to Christ the Warrior:

Except thou rise and for thine own work fight,
Oh I shall soon despair, when I do see
That thou lov'st mankind well, yet wilt not choose me,
And Satan hates me, yet is loth to lose me.

KING JAMES BIBLE
Psalms
(1611)

*Recommended edition: You can read the Psalms from any "Authorized Text,"
but be careful that you're not reading from the Revised Standard Version,
which is a twentieth-century revision of a British revision of the Authorized
Version, or from a "New King James," which is also a contemporary revision.
Oxford World's Classics publishes a paperback version of the 1611 translation,*
The Bible: Authorized King James Version, *edited by Robert Carroll
and Stephen Prickett (2008). For a 1611 version that preserves the spelling,
original marginal notes, and translators' preface, look for the hardcover* Holy
Bible: King James Version, 1611 Edition *(Hendrickson Publishers, 2006).*

*Be sure to read: Psalms 1,2, 5, 23, 27, 51, 57, 89, 90, 91, 103, 109, 119,
121, 132, 136, 148, 150.*

The "Authorized Version" of the Bible, a translation sponsored by King James
of England, affected the English language for centuries afterward, and the
Psalms—the Bible's book of poems—has colored the language of poets right
through the twentieth century. The translators of this 1611 English-language
version of the Bible intended to make a Bible that was accessible to all readers.
Translation, they wrote in their preface, "openeth the window, to let in the
light . . . breaketh the shell, that we may eat the kernel . . . putteth aside the
curtain, that we may look into the most Holy place . . . removeth the cover
of the well, that we may come by the water." In their attempt to make the
Psalms "open" to seventeenth-century English readers, the translators rendered Hebrew poetry into good English, keeping some Hebrew conventions
and doing enormous violence to others. They faithfully retained the typical
Hebrew structure of a poetic line as involving two (and less frequently, three)
parallel phrases, a structure evident in Psalm 2:1–4.

Why do the heathen rage, and the people imagine a vain thing?
The kings of the earth set themselves, and the rulers take counsel together,
against the Lord, and against his anointed, saying,
Let us break their bands asunder, and cast away their cords from us.
He that sitteth in the heavens shall laugh: the Lord shall have them in derision.

In each line of Hebrew poetry, the first phrase is followed by a second parallel phrase. The second phrase may restate the first in different words (synonymous parallelism); it may contradict the first (antithetic parallelism); it may repeat the first phrase but add to it (repetitive parallelism), or the second phrase may express an effect, of which the first phrase is the cause (causative parallelism):

The Lord is my shepherd, I shall not want.
He maketh me to lie down in green pastures, he leadeth me beside the still waters.
He restoreth my soul, he leadeth me in the paths of righteousness for his name's sake.
Yea, though I walk through the valley of the shadow of death, I will fear no evil,
For thou art with me, thy rod and thy staff they comfort me.
—Psalm 23:1–4

The singsong parallelism of the King James version of the Psalms shows up in the work of later poets, Milton not the least:

> By sudden onset, either with Hell fire
> To waste his whole creation, or possess
> All as our own, and drive as we were driven,
> The puny habitants, or if not drive,
> Seduce them to our party, that their God
> May prove their foe, and with repenting hand. . . .
> —*Paradise Lost,* book II

The connecting "ands" of the King James Bible, a faithful translation of the Hebrew "waw consecutive" which strings Hebrew sentences together, also show up again and again in later poetry, particularly poetry written in a self-consciously biblical mode:

> And are there other sorrows beside the sorrows of poverty?
> And are there other joys beside the joys of riches and ease?
> And is there not one law for both the lion and the ox?
> And is there not eternal fire and eternal chains,
> To bind the phantoms of existence from eternal life?
> —William Blake, "The Vision of the Daughters of Albion"

JOHN MILTON
Paradise Lost
(1608–1674)

Recommended editions: The Oxford World's Classics edition, edited by Stephen Orgel and Jonathan Goldberg (2008), has the explanatory footnotes (extremely helpful, since Milton uses archaic expressions and hundreds of obscure classical references) at the bottom of the page. The Norton Critical Edition, edited by Gordon Teskey (2004), has modernized spelling, explanatory footnotes, and a lot more: essays on sources, backgrounds, reception, and criticism.

Be sure to read: Paradise Lost. No one but Milton scholars ever tackles Paradise Regained.

Milton's fascination with all things classical is partly a manifestation of his love for order and symmetry; in *Paradise Lost*, Milton's retelling of the Genesis 1–3 story of the Fall, Hell is characterized by chaos and pandemonium (a word invented by Milton), while Heaven is a place where everyone speaks in calm voices and moves in preordained patterns. But his sympathy for the ancient epics also stems from his sympathy for the ancient view of man as essentially helpless to change history, able only to act nobly in the face of forces beyond his comprehension or control. In *Paradise Lost*, a "secondary epic" (a written poem that copies the conventions of oral epic), these forces are Christianized; they are represented by God and by Christ, who have a plan, set into place before the foundation of the world, which even includes Satan's temptation and Adam's fall. This plan acts as the organizing backbone of history; Milton promises, in his prologue, that *Paradise Lost* will "justify the ways of God to man," and indeed the poem seems to organize all of existence into a flow chart that accounts for every aspect of the universe. Milton's God is reasonable; his Satan is driven by envy and the lust for revenge, two unreasonable emotions; Eve falls because she allows her sense to triumph over her reason. As the poem progresses, the reader finds much more interest in Satan than in any of the rational, sinless "good guys"; it is difficult to make an emotional connection with Christ's sinless perfection, but relatively easy to identify with gnawing jealousy.

And this, as Stanley Fish notes in his classic study *Surprised by Sin*, is exactly Milton's aim; the poem seduces the reader into reenacting the Fall, allowing emotion and sympathy to triumph over reason and judgment. The true Fall, in Milton's *Paradise Lost*, happens not when Eve chooses to eat the apple—Eve, after all, is a vain creature, driven by sensation, who spends more time gazing at her reflection than working in the garden. It

happens when Adam, realizing that Eve's sin will cause God to destroy
her, *decides* to eat as well so that they can remain together. Milton (in
Fish's words) aims to "re-create in the mind of the reader . . . the drama
of the Fall, to make him fall again exactly as Adam did and with Adam's
troubled clarity, that is to say, 'not deceived.'" In this, Milton demonstrates that for all his love of reason, he too knows its limits; it is perfectly
possible to reason one's way to a logical but devastating conclusion.

WILLIAM BLAKE
Songs of Innocence and of Experience
(1757–1827)

*Recommended editions: Although the poems themselves have been republished
multiple times, you should read them along with the full-color illustrations;
the poems were originally published as companion pieces to Blake's mystical
paintings. Editions with the paintings include* Songs of Innocence and
Experience: Illustrated Throughout in Full Color *(Oxford University
Press, 1977), with an introduction by Sir Geoffrey Keynes;* Songs of Experience: Facsimile Reproduction with 26 Plates in Full Color *(Dover
Publications, 1984); and* Songs of Innocence: Color Facsimile of the
First Edition with 31 Color Plates *(Dover Publications, 1971).*

The poems in Blake's *Songs of Innocence* have darker parallels in *Songs of
Experience*; the enlightened, natural, pure state depicted in the *Innocence*
poems is vulnerable to the corruptions of government, society, and organized religion. "Nurse's Song" in *Songs of Innocence* tells of children playing, unfettered by parental or school authority: The children cry out to
their nurse at bedtime,

> "No, no, let us play, for it is yet day
> And we cannot go to sleep;
> Besides, in the sky the little birds fly
> And the hills are all cover'd with sheep."

> "Well, well, go & play till the light fades away
> And then go home to bed."
> The little ones leaped & shouted & laugh'd
> And all the hills ecchoed.

But the companion piece in *Songs of Experience* shows a warped and
distorted adult, looking back on those children with scorn.

When the voices of children are heard on the green
And whisp'rings are in the dale,
The days of my youth rise fresh in my mind,
My face turns green and pale.

Then come home, my children, the sun is gone down,
  And the dews of night arise;
Your spring & your day are wasted in play,
And your winter and night in disguise.

In Blake's poems, rationality is the straitjacket that reduces the energetic, creative child to a dull, passive adult. An authentic existence is one in which we are free to act on impulse; Energy is Blake's God, and the God of the church (the one whom, as Blake writes, inscribes "Do Not" on the doors of his chapels) is actually the Devil, out to destroy humanity. "Energy is the only life," Blake writes, in *The Marriage of Heaven and Hell*, "and is from the Body; and Reason is the bound or outward circumference of Energy. Energy is Eternal Delight. Those who restrain desire, do so because theirs is weak enough to be restrained. And being restrain'd, it by degrees became passive." Blake's poetry, written in a wild and unfettered mix of rhyme and meter, is exhortation; it aims to set that desire free again.

WILLIAM WORDSWORTH
(1770–1850)

Recommended editions: The Oxford World's Classics edition, William Wordsworth: The Major Works, Including the Prelude, *edited by Stephen Gill (2008), or the Modern Library Classics paperback,* Selected Poetry of William Wordsworth, *edited by Mark Van Doren (2002).*

Be sure to read: "Composed upon Westminster Bridge," "The Idiot Boy," "It Is a Beauteous Evening, Calm and Free," "I Wandered Lonely as a Cloud," "Lines Composed a Few Miles above Tintern Abbey," "Lines Left upon a Seat in a Yew-tree," "Lines Written in Early Spring," "London, 1802," "Lucy Gray," "Ode: Intimations of Immortality," "The Prelude," "She Dwelt Among the Untrodden Ways," "Simon Lee," "The World Is Too Much With Us."

In 1798, Wordsworth and Samuel Taylor Coleridge published together a volume called *Lyrical Ballads*—a collection of Wordsworth's lyrical poems along with Coleridge's mystical *Rime of the Ancient Mariner*. These poems mark, for most critics, the formal beginning of Romantic poetry as a movement. Wordsworth shares Blake's suspicion of rationality, and his conviction that a divine force exists in humans; but, unlike Blake, Wordsworth interprets the divine not as a wild mystic force, but as a gentle enlightening presence that infuses both man and nature. "I have felt," Wordsworth wrote, in "Lines Composed a Few Miles above Tintern Abbey,"

> A presence that disturbs me with the joy
> Of elevated thoughts; a sense sublime
> Of something far more deeply interfused,
> Whose dwelling is the light of setting suns,
> And the round ocean and the living air,
> And the blue sky, and in the mind of man;
> A motion and a spirit, that impels
> All thinking things, all objects of all thought,
> And rolls through all things.

For Wordsworth, the pastoral poem (the poem of nature) is a device which gives him a glimpse of the Sublime, the divine creative force. He can sense the Sublime in "fleeting moods / Of shadowy exaltation" (to quote his long autobiographical poem *The Prelude*). But Wordsworth, like all men, constantly struggles for that sense of the Sublime; it is quickly blotted out by the artificial world, by cities, conventional rules of manners, education, the patter of social conversation. Wordsworth longs to shake free from all of this. He is fond of individuals, but not enthusiastic about society; his heroine is Lucy Gray, who disappears from the middle of a snow-covered bridge, leaving no tracks, and is afterward seen singing a "solitary song" alone on the heath; in "Lines Composed upon Westminster Bridge," he finds the city most majestic when it is empty and sleeping.

In his search for the Sublime, Wordsworth celebrates childhood (a time when man can remember the "clouds of glory" that accompanied his birth, when the "prison house" of education has not yet closed around him) and the natural world; for Wordsworth, the pastoral ("nature") poem is a window into the divine. Yet his musings on nature have an overtone of the tragic; he is constantly aware of his own separation from the glory that infuses the natural world. At best, he can get only a sideways glimpse of truth; he only sees the glory darkly. In Book I of *The Prelude*, he describes such a revelation, which comes after he gazes at a mountain, towering over a lake at sunset:

[A]fter I had seen
That spectacle, for many days my brain
Worked with a dim and undetermined sense
Of unknown modes of being. In my thoughts
There was a darkness—call it solitude
Or blank desertion—no familiar shapes
Of hourly objects, images of trees,
Of sea or sky, no colours of green fields,
But huge and mighty forms that do not live
Like living men moved slowly through my mind.

SAMUEL TAYLOR COLERIDGE
(1772–1834)

Recommended editions: The Penguin Classics paperback, The Complete Poems, *edited by William Keach (1997), or the Oxford World's Classics edition,* Samuel Taylor Coleridge: The Major Works, *edited by H. J. Jackson (2009).*

Be sure to read: "Christabel," "Dejection: An Ode," "The Eolian Harp," "Kubla Khan," "The Rime of the Ancient Mariner," "This Lime-Tree Bower My Prison."

Coleridge, Wordsworth's partner in poetry, shares Wordsworth's view of nature as a place where the divine lives; in "This Lime-Tree Bower My Prison," he writes of the "deep joy" that comes when, "silent with swimming sense," he gazes at sunset "on the wide landscape . . . of such hues / As veil the Almighty Spirit, when yet he makes / Spirits perceive his presence." But while Wordsworth believed that the poet can serve as a prophet, crafting poems that—in their appeal to the imagination—reveal some kind of truth about human existence, Coleridge was less certain.

In his narrative poems ("Kubla Khan," "The Rime of the Ancient Mariner") Coleridge makes myths, like Blake; but he lacks Blake's sublime confidence in his own ability to communicate. The "prophet" of "The Rime of the Ancient Mariner" is unbalanced, if not insane; in "Kubla Khan," the narrator recalls a mythical city with walls and towers; he hears a maid singing verses, and mourns, "Could I revive within me / Her symphony and song . . . I would build that dome in air . . . And all who heard should see them there." But the poem breaks off; the poet cannot construct the dome again; the maid's verses are lost, and so is the city. As Coleridge aged, he had (in Jerome McGann's words) "nightmares: that the love, the knowledge, and the imagination which he has believed in are chimeras, at best momentary defenses against the world's ancestral violence and darkness."[20] Coleridge himself writes, in "Dejection: An Ode," "Afflictions bow me down to earth. . . . Hence, viper thoughts, that coil around my mind, / Reality's dark dream!" He turns to the imaginative faculty, hoping to find relief from the darkness of reality: "There was a time, when . . . Fancy made me dreams of happiness: / For hope grew round me, like the twining vine." But the vine imagery is itself disturbing, implying an ominous stranglehold related to the idea of "hope"; and as the mythical poems reveal, Coleridge's imagination provided him with little relief.

> All in a hot and copper sky,
> The bloody Sun, at noon,
> Right up above the mast did stand,
> No bigger than the Moon.
>
> Day after day, day after day,
> We stuck, nor breath nor motion,
> As idle as a painted ship
> Upon a painted ocean.
>
> Water, water every where,
> And all the boards did shrink;
> Water, water, every where,
> Nor any drop to drink.
> —From "The Rime of the Ancient Mariner"

JOHN KEATS
(1795–1821)

Recommended editions: John Keats: The Complete Poems, *edited by John Barnard (Penguin Classics, 1977), or* Complete Poems and Selected Letters of John Keats, *edited by Edward Hirsch (Modern Library Classics, 2001).*

 Be sure to read: "Endymion," "The Eve of St. Agnes," "Hyperion: A Fragment," "La Belle Dame sans Merci," "Ode on a Grecian Urn," "Ode to a Nightingale," "To Autumn."

---

[20]Jerome J. McGann, *The Romantic Ideology: A Critical Investigation* (Chicago: University of Chicago Press, 1983), p. 99.

Keats, writing a generation after Coleridge and Wordsworth, saw both of these "elder statesmen" of the Romantic movement as hampered by the necessity of *explanation*. The poet's job, Keats wrote, is not to explain; rather, the poet is marked by "negative capability," the ability to hold "uncertainties, Mysteries, doubts" in the mind, without any "irritable reaching after fact & reason." The purpose of the poem is not to search for solutions; the purpose of the poem is *beauty*.

> When old age shall this generation waste,
> Thou shalt remain, in midst of other woe
> Than ours, a friend to man, to whom thou say'st,
> "Beauty is truth, truth beauty,—that is all
> Ye know on earth, and all ye need to know."
> —From "Ode on a Grecian Urn"

The poetry of Keats—and his condemnation of the older Romantics for their "irritable reaching"—reveals the ongoing development of Romantic thought. Where Coleridge and Wordsworth were trying to demonstrate the ways in which man could come into direct contact with the Sublime, Keats took it for granted that the depiction of perfect beauty would reveal the Sublime to man, whether or not he was bothering to search for it. Furthermore, Keats's definition of "beauty" did not have primarily to do with the imagination; it had to do with the senses. Keats's poetry is full of sound, sight, warmth and cold, smell. Physical sensation, not the imagination (which originates in the mind) was the path to the sublime. When Keats accused Coleridge and Wordsworth of laboring too hard over their poetry, he saw them with furrowed brows, trying to *think* their way to the Sublime. Instead, Keats suggested, the poet should cultivate a passive receptiveness to the senses.

> [L]oad and bless
> With fruit the vines that round the thatch-eaves run;
> To bend with apples the mossed cottage-trees,
> And fill all fruit with ripeness to the core;
> To swell the gourd, and plump the hazel shells
> With a sweet kernel. . . .
> Then in a wailful choir the small gnats mourn
> Among the river shallows, borne aloft
> Or sinking as the light wind lives or dies. . . .
> And gathering swallows twitter in the skies.
> —From "To Autumn"

HENRY WADSWORTH LONGFELLOW
(1807–1882)

Recommended editions: The Penguin Classics paperback, Longfellow: Selected Poems, *edited by Lawrence Buell (1988), or* Henry Wadsworth Longfellow: Poems & Other Writings, *edited by J. D. McClatchy (Library of America #118, 2000).*

Be sure to read: "The Courtship of Miles Standish," "Hiawatha's Childhood," "Paul Revere's Ride," "The Village Blacksmith," "The Wreck of the Hesperus."

Longfellow, a staple of school readers, tends to be short-shrifted by critics. Writing at the same time as Dickinson and Whitman, he told stories about the American past while they struggled with the American identity. But those stories are, like Frost's poems, a "momentary stay against confusion"; Longfellow is a poetic conservative, reacting to the uncertainties of the present by building a nostalgic American past. He is the American Milton, finding patterns and writing them overtop of chaos; pouring an orderly foundation underneath a building that already stands. Longfellow has largely been booted out of the academy, partly because he (unlike John Keats) had no interest in literary theory. Longfellow was widely known as a "fireside poet" (which is to say, a poet read for enjoyment). His absence from academic writing on poetry and his ongoing popularity with "regular readers" illustrates the beginning of that split between academic and popular audiences which grew impossibly broad in the early 1990s.

Longfellow's narrative poems use meter to reinforce the spoken, "epic" quality of his stories, and he matches form to content; the triple rhythms of "Paul Revere's Ride":

> ONE if by LAND, and TWO if by SEA,
> and I on the OPposite SHORE will BE

are reminiscent of galloping hooves. In the *Song of Hiawatha* Longfellow uses a "trochaic meter," in which the stress falls on the first syllable of each syllable pair, rather than on the second:

> ON the MOUNtains OF the PRArie,
> ON the GREAT red PIPE-stone QUARry,
> GITche ManiTO, the MIGHty,
> HE the MAST'R of LIFE, deSCENding,
> ON the RED crags OF the QUARry. . . .

This reversal of iambic meter sounds like an Indian drum.

ALFRED, LORD TENNYSON
(1809–1883)

Recommended editions: Alfred Tennyson: The Major Works, *ed. Adam Roberts (Oxford World's Classics, 2009), or* Alfred Lord Tennyson: Selected Poems, *ed. Christopher Ricks (Penguin Classics, rev. ed., 2008). Neither contains the complete* Idylls of the King, *so you may need to add the Penguin Classics edition of the* Idylls, *edited by J. M. Gray (1989).*

Be sure to read: "The Dying Swan," The Idylls of the King, *"In Memoriam," "The Lady of Shalott," "The Lotos-Eaters," "Ulysses."*

Tennyson, like Longfellow, is an orderly poet. In the long literary epic *The Idylls of the King*, Tennyson does for the English past what Longfellow does for the American past: He creates a myth for it, retelling the story of Camelot in blank verse (and creating, almost singlehandedly, the romantic tournaments-and-ladies Camelot that governed English and American imaginations for a hundred years). *The Idylls of the King* lays out an orderly, Miltonic universe, in which Arthur is determined to make his country work by reasonable regulation: "The old order changeth," Arthur declares, as he is crowned king, "yielding place to the new." In Arthur's new Round Table (which he describes, tellingly, as the "Order" which "lives to crush / All wrongers of the realm") every knight who follows the rules is rewarded, and knights who break the rules are punished.

At least until Lancelot comes along. Passion wrecks this Order; good knights die, evil knights triumph, Arthur himself weeps, before the final battle,

> I found Him in the shining of the stars,
> I mark'd Him in the flowering of His fields,
> But in His ways with men I find Him not.
> I waged His wars, and now I pass and die.

The Table has failed; Arthur kills his own son and is borne off into the West, and the order disintegrates into chaos. Was this disintegration inevitable? Tennyson never makes a final judgment; this resistance to a final conclusion marks some of his most famous poetry.

> Flower in the crannied wall,
> I pluck you out of the crannies,
> I hold you here, root and all, in my hand,
> Little flower—but if I could understand

What you are, root and all, and all in all,
I should know what God and man is.
— "Flower in the Crannied Wall"

This seems to express a faith in an order that starts with the smallest element of creation and extends unbroken to the greatest; an Enlightenment-inspired confidence in the ultimate rationality of the universe. Yet the poem does contain an *if*; Tennyson's understanding of God and man depends on his understanding of the flower, and the poem makes no prediction about whether he will ever reach this understanding.

WALT WHITMAN
(1819–1892)

Recommended editions: The Signet Classics paperback, *edited by Peter Davison (2013), or* Leaves of Grass: The "Death–Bed" Edition, *from Modern Library Classics (2001).* Leaves of Grass *was first published in 1855 and was continually revised and republished by Whitman during his lifetime; the Signet and Modern Library editions both offer the final "deathbed" version of the poem, published in 1892. You can also consult* Leaves of Grass: The Original 1855 Edition *(Dover Thrift Editions, 2007). The Norton Critical Edition,* Leaves of Grass and Other Writings, *ed. Michael Moon, reproduces both version of the poem.*

Be sure to read: Leaves of Grass *is less like a book of poems than like one massive poem with multiple parts. However, certain sections of this huge work are more often cited: They are (listed in order of occurrence within* Leaves of Grass) *"I Hear America Singing," "Song of Myself," "I Sing the Body Electric," "Song of the Open Road," "Out of the Cradle Endlessly Rocking," "As I Ebb'd with the Ocean of Life," "The Wound-Dresser," "When Lilacs Last in the Dooryard Bloom'd," "O Captain, My Captain."*

Whitman isn't the first modern poet; he's the last Romantic. Like the English Romantics, he celebrates the immense diversity of human existence; he is convinced that each of us can find sublime knowledge through experiencing the world ("You shall possess the good of the earth and sun," he writes, in "Song of Myself," "You shall no longer take things at second or third hand . . . nor feed on the spectres in books. . . . A morning-glory at my window satisfies me more than the metaphysics of books").

The Romantic poets put themselves squarely into their own poetry, attempting to show readers the Sublime by chronicling their own experiences with it. Whitman takes this Romantic strategy even further. He chronicles not simply his experiences, but *himself*: "I dote on myself," he writes, "there is that lot of me and all so luscious." (Yes, he's serious; Whitman's celebrations of his own body occasionally go over the top.) Like an autobiographer, Whitman creates himself in *Leaves of Grass*, in a compelling and oddly contradictory manner. His purpose is to represent himself, simply, as an American—a "common man" who is, paradoxically, both common and unique. He is both "one of a kind" and representative of all mankind; he is both individual and all men:

> Walt Whitman, a kosmos, of Manhattan the son,
> Turbulent, fleshy, sensual, eating, drinking and breeding,
> No sentimentalist, no stander above men and women or apart from them,
> No more modest than immodest.
> Unscrew the locks from the doors!
> Unscrew the doors themselves from their jambs!
> —From "Song of Myself"

Busy breaking down barriers and opening doors, insisting on the complete equality of all humans, Whitman removes the door of traditional poetic form from its jambs and refuses to walk through it. *Leaves of Grass*, which attempts to capture the natural rhythms of American speech, is mostly without meter or rhythm. (The most notable exception is "O Captain, My Captain," the elegy for Lincoln, which has a more traditional form.) This confident rejection of formal poetics reveals Whitman's complete and total confidence in his own poetry. No Coleridgean dejection for Whitman; he is Blake minus God, confidently sure that poetry can serve as a kind of new Scripture for a new kind of American, set free from superstition and able to shape his or her own life. Whitman never seems to doubt his own authority, and *Leaves of Grass* continually announces its own status as a book of truth for all.

I speak the pass-word primeval, I give the sign of democracy. . . .
Through me many long dumb voices,
Voices of the interminable generations of prisoners and slaves. . . .
Through me forbidden voices,
Voices of sexes and lusts, voices veil'd and I remove the veil,
Voice indecent by me clarified and transfigured. . . .
I believe in the flesh and the appetites,
Seeing, hearing, feeling are miracles, and each part and tag of me is a miracle.
Divine am I inside and out, and I make holy whatever I touch or am touch'd
    from,

The scent of these arm-pits aroma finer than prayer,
This head more than churches, bibles, and all the creeds.
—From "Song of Myself"

EMILY DICKINSON
(1830–1886)

Recommended edition: Final Harvest: Emily Dickinson's Poems, *edited by Thomas Johnson (Back Bay Books, 1976). Dickinson's poems have been published in many different editions, but this is one of the few to maintain Dickinson's own punctuation and capitalization, which make up part of her poetic strategy.*

Be sure to read: "A bird came down the walk," "A narrow fellow in the grass," "A word is dead," "Because I could not stop for Death," "Before I got my eye put out," "Each life converges to some center," "Hope is the thing with feathers," "I died for beauty," "I felt a funeral in my brain," "I had been hungry all the years," "I heard a fly buzz when I died," "I never saw a moor," "I took my power in my hand," "I'm nobody? Who are you?" "Much madness is divinest sense," "Safe in their alabaster chambers," "There is a pain so utter," "The soul selects her own society," "'Twas just this time last year I died."

Dickinson, not Whitman, is the first American modernist. Where Whitman overflows with boundless confidence in the power of poetry, Dickinson remains skeptical; where Whitman sees an America filled with the energetic enthusiasm of the common man, Dickinson sees the inevitability of chaos and decay. She did not deny the possibility of ecstatic experience, but she had no hope that any glory would linger:

> Except the heaven had come so near,
> So seemed to choose my door,
> The distance would not haunt me so;
> I had not hoped before.
>
> But just to hear the grace depart
> I never thought to see,
> Afflicts me with a double loss;
> 'Tis lost, and lost to me.
> —"Except the heaven had come so near" [XXXI]

In her poems, Dickinson (famously remaining in her home in Massachusetts almost all of her life) turns away from the Romantic preoccupation with "encountering the Sublime" and instead attempts to account for a world in which she is constantly confronted with the reality of approaching death. Dickinson's poems have flashes of delight, but joy is not her natural home:

> I can wade grief,
> Whole pools of it,
> I'm used to that.
> But the least push of joy
> Breaks up my feet
> —From "I can wade grief"[IX]

She is not, in the end, on good terms with the world; her experiences in it are always marked by discomfort, by doubt, and by the inability to settle on a definite interpretation of her experiences, one that makes sense of the different parts of her life according to some overall plan. This alienation becomes one of the characteristic marks of modern poetry.

In her poetry, Dickinson seems to battle with the constraints of language—not to rejoice in its expressiveness, as Whitman does. She retains a careful poetic meter, often using a "hymn rhythm" (an alternation of four-beat and three-beat lines):

> Not knowing when the dawn will come
> I open every door
> —From "Dawn" [VII]

> Because I could not stop for Death,
> He kindly stopped for me;
> —From "The Chariot" [XXVII]

or a similar four-line pattern of three/three/four/three beats:

> The bustle in a house
> The morning after death
> Is solemnest of industries
> Enacted upon earth,—
> —From "The bustle in a house" [XXII]

But the regular meters are complicated by her tendency to use irregular stresses, lengthy pauses noted by dashes, and distorted syntax—as though normal English syntax were inadequate for her thoughts. As Dickinson grew older, her use of poetic form became less and less regular; she began to refuse to choose among words, sometimes writing three and four choices in a row without crossing any out. Before her death, she was writing poems in fragments, sideways, on scraps, upside down—straining for a form of expression unbounded by print.

CHRISTINA ROSSETTI
(1830–1894)

Recommended editions: The Complete Poems, *edited by R. W. Crump and Betty S. Flowers (Penguin Classics, 2001), or* Rossetti: Poems *(Everyman's Library Pocket Poets, published by Alfred A. Knopf, 1993).*
  Be sure to read: "A Better Resurrection," "A Birthday," "After Death," "A Christmas Carol," "The Convent Threshold," "De Profundis," "Dream Land," "Goblin Market," "Good Friday," "Maude Clare," "Monna Innominata," "The Prince's Progress," "Remember," "Sister Maude," "The Three Enemies," "Up-Hill," "When I am dead, my dearest."

While only eleven of Dickinson's poems were published during her lifetime, Christina Rossetti gained a fair degree of fame. Rossetti's poetry is preoccupied with the problem of different passions existing side by side: poetry and love, the love of God and the love of men, the love of men and friendship with women, poetry and God. Exploring these tensions, Rossetti always seems to conclude that one passion will have to be renounced so that the other can flourish. In most cases, it is earthly love that proves flawed, or destructive; in her most famous narrative poem, "Goblin Market," she writes of a young (virgin) girl tempted away by goblins who offer her luscious "goblin fruits." She eats them and is immediately addicted. Her innocence and creativity diminish into an obsession with physical satisfaction:

> While with sunken eyes and faded mouth
> She dreamed of melons, as a traveller sees,
> False waves in desert drouth. . . .

But in other poems, Rossetti writes of the equally frightening possibility that no "goblin" will ever offer fruit at all:

> You took my heart in your hand
> With a friendly smile,
> With a critical eye you scanned,

> Then set it down,
> And said: It is still unripe,
> Better wait awhile.
> —From "Twice"

These poems are full, not only of disappointment, but of betrayal; in both the lyric poems and the narrative poems, those who hope to find true fulfillment in love always end up disillusioned.

Rossetti, like her brother Dante Gabriel Rossetti, the poet Charles Swinburne, and the painter William Morris, belonged to an informal circle of artists known as "Pre-Raphaelites," who thought that art and poetry (which they saw as two methods of expressing the same ideas) had been distorted by the Romantics into a preoccupation with beauty instead of a discovery of truth. With the detailed works of medieval artists (those who came before Raphael) as their models, the Pre-Raphaelites set out to discover a new simplicity in the portrayal of people and landscapes. In poetry, this Pre-Raphaelite emphasis appears as close attention to detail and to the senses: sight, sound, color, and taste. In its glorification of the past, Pre-Raphaelite poetry also made heavy use of medieval (or at least medieval-sounding) myths and tales; Rossetti's poetry is a mix of lyric explorations of renunciation and rich, detailed, sensuous narrative fables. Her attention to detail extends to the form of her poems as well; Rossetti pays close attention to meter and rhyme, never writing "free verse" or conversational verse as Whitman does, but often juggling the stresses of her lines, cutting them short or changing her meter unexpectedly:

> "We must not look at goblin men,
> We must not buy their fruits;
> Who knows upon what soil they fed
> Their hungry thirsty roots?"
> "Come buy," call the goblins. . . .
> The customary cry,
> "Come, buy, come, buy,"
> With its iterated jingle,
> Of sugar-baited words . . .
> That goblin cry.

GERARD MANLEY HOPKINS
(1844–1889)

Recommended editions: Gerard Manley Hopkins: The Major Works,
ed. Catherine Phillips *(Oxford World's Classics, 2009), or* Gerard Manley
Hopkins: Poems and Prose, *ed. W. H. Gardner (Penguin Classics, 1953).*
　　Be sure to read: "God's Grandeur," "Pied Beauty," "The Caged Sky-
lark," "The Windhover," "Carrion Comfort," "No worst," *and* "The
Wreck of the Deutschland."

Hopkins's poems are remarkable for two reasons: in them, a genuine and
deep religious faith coexists with an equally genuine and deep despair;
and he manages to express this contradiction in entirely original meters,
rhymes, and even words. Attempting to explain an impossible relationship
between belief and anguish, one which could not be contained within
accepted religious language, he did violence to language itself.

　　Hopkins's poetry is governed by his theory of "individuation": Each
created thing has a beauty that "inheres" in it and makes it distinct.
He coined two terms to help him express this principle: "inscape," the
individual, distinct, "oneness" of each natural thing; and "instress," the
force or unique energy which maintains this individuality. Instress keeps
objects together, but it also makes them distinct to the looker: "Instress,"
to quote W. H. Gardner, is "a sudden perception of that deeper pattern,
order, and unity which gives meaning to external forms."[21] For Hopkins,
instress keeps him from final despair; it shows him, if only fleetingly, the
"deeper pattern" behind the dis-order that threatens to overwhelm him.
The "beauty of inscape," Hopkins wrote in his journal, is "near at hand
. . . if [we] had eyes to see it and it could be called out everywhere again."
In poetry, he attempts to make this beauty clear.

　　To do so, Hopkins makes the poems themselves into unique objects
with their own "inscape." His innovative "sprung rhythm," which he
first used in "The Wreck of the *Deutschland*," is a complicated meter that
(in Hopkins's own words) counts "accents or stresses alone, without any
account of the number of syllables, so that a foot may be one strong syllable or it may be many light and one strong." Each line of the poetry may
be a different length, but each contains the correct number of "strong"
syllables. (It's very difficult to find these syllables without help; Hopkins
used to mark the strong syllables in his poems, but most modern editions

---

[21]W. H. Gardner, introduction to *Gerard Manley Hopkins: Poems and Prose* (New York:
Penguin, 1985), p. xxi.

of his poetry eliminate the marks.) He also used nontraditional rhyming schemes (alliteration, assonance, internal rhymes) along with traditional end rhymes, and makes up his own adjectives (and nouns) whenever existing words seem inadequate:

> I kiss my hand
> To the stars, lovely-asunder
> Starlight, wafting him out of it; and
> Glow, glory in thunder;
> Kiss my hand to the dappled-with-damson west;
> Since, tho' he is under the world's splendour and wonder,
> His mystery must be instressed, stressed;
> For I greet him the days I meet him, and bless when I understand.
> —From "The Wreck of the *Deutschland*"

Hopkins became a Catholic priest, entering a theological world in which the physical always gives witness to God; his days are never "just" days, birds never "just" birds, a field never "just" dirt; God inheres in all of creation.

> All things counter, original, spare, strange;
> Whatever is fickle, freckled (who knows how?)
> With swift, slow; sweet, sour, adazzle, dim;
> He fathers-forth whose beauty is past change:
> Praise him.
> —From "Pied Beauty"

WILLIAM BUTLER YEATS
(1865–1939)

Recommended edition: The Collected Poems of W. B. Yeats, *2nd rev. ed., edited by Richard J. Finneran (Scribner's, 1996).*

Be sure to read: "A Prayer for My Daughter," "The Cap and Bells," "Down by the Salley Gardens," "Easter 1916," "The Coming of Wisdom with Time," "The Lake Isle of Innisfree," "Lapis Lazuli," "Leda and the Swan," "The Magi," "Memory," "Sailing to Byzantium," "The Second Coming," "The Secret Rose," "September 1913," "Three Things," "The Wheel," "When You Are Old," "The Wild Swans at Coole."

Yeats, an Irish Protestant with a mystical bent, constructed his own cosmology; he saw the world as progressing through two-thousand-year cycles, each cycle dominated by one particular civilization and that civilization's set of myths. The close of each cycle is marked by disintegration, chaos, and disorder; this disorder in turn leads to the birth of a new cycle. "The Second Coming" describes the end of the cycle before the coming of Christ, which led in turn to the beginning of Yeats's own age:

> Turning and turning in the widening gyre
> The falcon cannot hear the falconer;
> Things fall apart; the centre cannot hold;
> Mere anarchy is loosed upon the world. . . .
> The darkness drops again; but now I know
> That twenty centuries of stony sleep
> Were vexed to nightmare by a rocking cradle,
> And what rough beast, its hour come round at last,
> Slouches toward Bethlehem to be born?

Yeats, like the other great Modernists, sees chaos, dissolution, and violence in his own age—but unlike later poets, he finds a pattern behind the chaos. The current age, he suggested, was even now decaying downwards to its end, but its death would lead to rebirth. He pictures each two-thousand-year cycle as a "gyre," a spiraling cone of time; each gyre rotates completely around, and as it draws to an end, a new beginning emerges.

> What matter though numb nightmare ride on top. . . .
> What matter? Heave no sigh, let no tear drop,
> A greater, a more gracious time has gone. . . .
> What matter? Out of cavern comes a voice,
> And all it knows is that one word "Rejoice!"
> —From "The Gyres"

These "gyres" reappear, consistently, throughout Yeats's poetry and prose. They represent the connected nature of all time; each cycle appears separate, but if viewed from above (from a God's-eye perspective), they all prove to be part of a single pattern. Disorder always leads to order, death to life, chaos to a new pattern.

Yeats, Irish by birth, made himself into a poet of Ireland and a spokesman for "Irish folk culture"; sympathetic to Ireland's wish for independence from Britain, he became a senator of the Irish Free State at the age of fifty-seven. "Easter 1916," one of his most enduring poems, commemorates the defeat of Irish nationalists by British troops in an Easter uprising in Dublin, and ascribes to the uprising itself a "terrible beauty." But the Protestant Yeats did not share the faith of the Irish Catholic nationalists, and as he grew older he seems to have become increasingly discontented with the violence of the nationalist movement. As the great contemporary Irish poet Seamus Heaney puts it, he was plagued by "self-divisions." "He famously declared," Heaney writes, "that the man who sat down to breakfast was a bundle of accident and incoherence, whereas the man reborn in a poem was 'intended' and 'complete'; one way to see his life's work is as a pursuit of that intention of completeness."[22] Yeats's poetry shows a keen awareness of the struggle between opposing forces that seemed to mark every aspect of life at the beginning of the twentieth century—and also a longing for this struggle to give birth, finally, to peace.

> I will arise and go now, and go to Innisfree,
> And a small cabin build there, of clay and wattles made. . . .
> And I shall have some peace there, for peace comes dropping slow. . . .
> —From "The Lake Isle of Innisfree"

PAUL LAURENCE DUNBAR
(1872–1906)

Recommended edition: The Collected Poetry of Paul Laurence Dunbar, edited by Joanne M. Braxton (University Press of Virginia, 1993).

Be sure to read: "A Negro Love Song," "An Ante-Bellum Sermon," "At the Tavern," "Colored Band," "The Debt," "Douglass," "Little Brown Baby," "Ode to Ethiopia," "The Old Front Gate," "The Poet and His Song," "The Seedling," "Signs of the Times," "Sympathy," "We Wear the Mask," "When Malindy Sings," "When de Co'n Pone's Hot," "When Dey 'Listed Colored Soldiers."

Dunbar's poetry speaks in voices borrowed both from black folk culture and from the educated, white culture of American poetry. Dunbar finds himself balancing between the two, adopting the voice of the poetic mainstream when he writes of ideas:

> I am no priest of crooks nor creeds,
> For human wants and human needs
> Are more to me than prophets' deeds. . . .

[22]Seamus Heaney, "All Ireland's Bard," *Atlantic*, vol. 280, no. 5 (November 1997): 157.

> Go, cease your wail, lugubrious saint!
> You fret high Heaven with your plaint.
> —From "A Creed and Not a Creed"

and the African American folk voice when he writes of experience.

> Fol' yo' han's an' bow yo' haid—
> Wait ontwell de blessin's said;
> "Lawd, have mussy on ouah souls—"
> (Don' you daih to tech dem rolls—)
> "Bless de food we gwine to eat—"
> (You set still—I see yo' feet;
> You jes' try dat trick agin!)
> "Gin us peace an' joy. Amen!"
> —From "In the Morning"

To appreciate Dunbar, you need to make a serious attempt to read his dialect poetry out loud. My own attempts to teach Dunbar to undergraduates have been hampered by the reluctance of readers (particularly white readers) to do this; in the highly politicized university classroom, "mimicking" black speech seems like a risky thing to do. But if you can, do this in private, without worrying about listeners.[23]

Any tension you might feel in reading this dialect out loud would have been fully appreciated by Dunbar himself. In "The Poet," he fretted about his own career:

> He sang of life, serenely sweet,
> With, now and then, a deeper note. . . .
> He sang of love when earth was young,
> And Love, itself, was in his lays.
> But ah, the world, it turned to praise
> A jingle in a broken tongue.

Dunbar divided his own poetic work into "Major Books" and "Minor Books," assigning his dialect poetry to the "Minors," yet critics as prominent as William Dean Howells preferred the dialect: "It is when we come to Mr. Dunbar's Minors that we feel ourselves in the presence of a man

---

[23]To hear the poems read by an expert, go to www.plethoreum.org/dunbar/gallery.asp, which contains audio files of the Dunbar scholar Herbert Woodward Martin performing Dunbar's dialect and nondialect poems.

with a direct and a fresh authority." "Mr. Howells has done me irrevocable harm in the dictum he laid down regarding my dialect verse," Dunbar
retorted, bitterly.[24] He felt trapped not so much by Howells's preference as
by the white critic's insistence that this dialect verse displayed "vistas into
the simple, sensuous, joyous nature of his race." Dunbar—like Dickinson
and Hopkins—struggles with the limitations of language; when he writes
in a "black voice," other readers see simple joyousness and are unable to
peer past their own ideas about the dialect to the more complex experience from which it rises.

ROBERT FROST
(1874–1963)

Recommended edition: The Poetry of Robert Frost: The Collected
Poems, *edited by Edward Connery Lathem, 2nd rev. ed. (Holt Paperbacks,
2002).*

 *Be sure to read: "A Boy's Will," "After Apple-Picking," "Birches," "The
Death of the Hired Man," "Departmental," "Design," "Fire and Ice,"
"Home Burial," "Mending Wall," "Mowing," "The Need of Being Versed
in Country Things," "Nothing Gold Can Stay," "The Pasture," "Putting
In the Seed," "The Road Not Taken," "Stopping by Woods on a Snowy
Evening," "To Earthward," "Trespass," "The Wood-Pile."*

"There are two types of realists," Robert Frost once remarked, "the one
who offers a good deal of dirt with his potato to show that it is a real one,
and the one who is satisfied with the potato brushed clean. I'm inclined to
be the second kind. To me, the thing that art does for life is to clean it, to
strip it to form." Where William Butler Yeats used his poetry to express an
order which he could sense beyond the apparent chaos of the world, Frost
uses the poetry to create order. He writes straightforward scenes: a bird
balancing on a weed, a traveler stopping at a crossroads, a man kneeling
and staring down into a well. In many of the poems, his characters are
solitary:

> Two roads diverged in a yellow wood,
> And sorry I could not travel both
> And be one traveler, long I stood

[24]A fuller account of this exchange between poet and critic can be found in Gregory
L. Candela, "We Wear the Mask: Irony in Dunbar's The Sport of the Gods," *American
Literature*, vol. 48, no. 1 (March 1976): 60–72.

And looked down one as far as I could
To where it bent in the undergrowth;
Then took the other. . . .
—From "The Road Not Taken"

But the straightforward forms of these stories conceal a deeper purpose. The carefully painted scenes have blurred edges; much is left unsaid. William H. Pritchard writes that the proper way to analyze Frost is to say, "We know what this poem is about, we know how it sounds, just so long as you don't ask us to say exactly."[25] Frost himself called his poetry "synecdochic," with *synecdoche* meaning "small points of entry to larger significance."[26] He follows an almost Augustinian poetic, providing a literal meaning (a traveler standing in the wood, a man mending a wall) that serves as a door into another, mystical layer of meaning. This deeper meaning resists being put into words. Frost himself used religious terms to describe it: The first layer of meaning in a poem, he told a group of poets in 1954, is like the hem of a garment; touching the hem of the garment (the reference is to a miracle of Jesus' in the Gospels) leads to a mystical understanding of the whole. The reader can "get the meaning by touch . . . the way the woman did from Jesus. . . . [T]he virtue went out of him. . . . [T]ouching the hem is enough."[27]

So how should you read Frost? Not by reducing the poems to allegory ("The two woods are two kinds of careers, and he chose one instead of the other and always regretted it") but rather by imagining yourself into the scene. What happens then?

Ideally, some mysterious and fleeting connection that Frost himself could not quite describe. In "For Once, Then, Something," the poet is staring down at the water, looking for the picture reflected back at him:

Once, when trying with chin against a well-curb
I discerned, as I thought, beyond the picture,
Through the picture, a something white, uncertain,
Something more of the depths—and then I lost it. . . .
[A] ripple
Shook whatever it was lay there at bottom,

---

[25] William H. Pritchard, "Wildness of Logic in Modern Lyric," in *Forms of Lyric*, ed. Reuben A. Brower (New York: Columbia University Press, 1970), p. 132.
[26] In Gerard Quinn, "Frost's Synecdochic Allusions," *Resources for American Literary Study*, vol. 25, no. 2 (1999): 254–64.
[27] Ibid., p. 255.

Blurred it, blotted it out. What was that whiteness?
Truth? A pebble of quartz? For once, then, something.

CARL SANDBURG
(1878–1967)

Recommended edition: Carl Sandburg: Selected Poems, *edited by George and Willene Hendrick (Harvest Books, 1996).*

Be sure to read: "Chicago," "Cool Tombs," "Elizabeth Umpstead," "Fog," "Grass," "I Am the People, the Mob," "Nocturne in a Deserted Brickyard," "The People, Yes (No. 57)," "Planked Whitefish," "Skyscraper," "Smoke and Steel," "Window."

Sandburg is best known for his "Chicago poems," which celebrate America with a wince. Like Whitman, Sandburg was a journalist before he was a poet, and like Whitman he describes the people of America in careful, journalistic detail:

> The working girls in the morning are going to work—
> long lines of them afoot amid the downtown stores
> and factories, thousands with little brick-shaped
> lunches wrapped in newspapers under their arms.
> Each morning as I move through this river of young-
> woman life I feel a wonder about where it is all
> going, so many with a peach bloom of young years
> on them and laughter of red lips and memories in
> their eyes of dances the night before and plays and
> walks. . . .
> —From "Working Girls"

But unlike Whitman, Sandburg admires America with reservations. All that boundless American energy turned Chicago into an enormous city—but also built the factories and offices that blot every consideration but profit from the minds of Americans. Sandburg is a common-man prophet, avoiding "technique" and refusing to display poetic expertise in favor of run-on lines and the natural rhythms of speech. He protests the shape America has begun to take:

> She and her man crossed the ocean and the years that
> marked their faces saw them haggling with landlords
> and grocers while six children played on the stones

and prowled in the garbage cans.
One child coughed its lungs away. . . .
one is in jail, two have jobs in a box factory
And as they fold the pasteboard, they wonder what the
wishing is and the wistful glory in them that flutters
faintly when the glimmer of spring comes on
the air. . . .
—From "Population Drifts"

Sandburg does sometimes find a sort of stately beauty in industrialism, but the "Chicago Poems" are alarmed more often than celebratory. Where Whitman found immense diversity, Sandburg found an increasing and disturbing sameness—a factory-run country where a colorful, heterogeneous American people was becoming standardized into uniformity.

WILLIAM CARLOS WILLIAMS
(1883–1963)

Recommended edition: William Carlos Williams: Selected Poems, *edited by Charles Tomlinson (New Directions, 1985).*

Be sure to read: "Asphodel, That Greeny Flower," "The Descent of Winter," "Landscape with the Fall of Icarus," "The Last Words of My English Grandmother," "Proletarian Portrait," "The Red Wheelbarrow," "Self-Portrait," "Sonnet in Search of an Author," "Spring and All," "This Is Just to Say," "Tract," "To Elsie."

Williams avoids the stance of prophet as well as the position of storyteller. His lyrics are, instead, influenced by Japanese haiku, which describe a small, vivid physical object and then turn to open out from that object to a larger, cosmic idea. But unlike the haiku, Williams's lyrics don't open out. Williams was skeptical of the mind's ability either to find meaning, or to create it; he was suspicious of logic, which he saw as creating an illusory relationship between cause and effect where none existed; he was suspicious (therefore) of traditional English syntax, since syntax makes rules about the logical connections between parts of speech. "Kill the explicit sentence," he wrote, suggesting instead that poetry should use "verbal sequences. Sentences, but not grammatical sentences." This sort of "verbal sequence" appears at the beginning of "Asphodel, That Greeny Flower," one of his best-known poems.

Williams was willing to accept that words themselves had some kind of value; he saw language itself (although not the rules that govern language) as a kind of material object. For Williams, words are *things*, superior to the untrustworthy and elusive ideas that they are supposed to represent. In his essay "The Embodiment of Knowledge" (1929), he calls words "materials" that "supersede in themselves all ideas, facts, movements which they may under other circumstances be asked to signify." Even the "spaces between the words" are important, as important as words themselves—they are physical objects. Williams writes, famously, that much depends on a wheelbarrow—but does not then tell us *what* depends (or why, or how). "A poem is a small (or large) machine made out of words," Williams wrote. "Prose may carry a load of ill-defined matter like a ship. But poetry is a machine which drives it, pruned to a perfect economy. As in all machines, its movement is intrinsic, undulant, a physical more than a literary character."[28]

EZRA POUND
(1885–1972)

Recommended editions: Selected Poems of Ezra Pound *(New Directions, 1957). This text contains excerpts from* The Cantos, *along with other Pound poems; the entire text of* The Cantos, *an enormous epic poem, can be read in* The Cantos of Ezra Pound *(New Directions, 1998). Or invest in the 1400-page Library of America hardcover,* Ezra Pound: Poems and Translations *(2003).*

Be sure to read: "Canto One," "Canto Two," "Exile's Letter," "In a Station of the Metro," "Mauberly," "The Return," "The River-Merchant's Wife," "The Sea-Farer," "Sestina: Altaforte," "The White Stag."

Pound combines Imagist tendencies (commitment to exactness, to particularity, to "distilled" poetry that avoided cosmic generalities) with classical learning (which lent Greek rhythms and allusions to his lines) and anti-American sentiment. Writing in 1912, he accused the country of wallowing in a spiritual "Dark Age," with all beauty and sensitivity wiped out by the loud, raw, crass, rising tide of capitalism. "Nine out of every ten Americans," Pound sneered, "have sold their soul for a [stock] quotation." Pound's earlier poetry is almost Pre-Raphaelite, borrowing medieval images and archaic language and combining it with precise images:

> See, they return, one, and by one,
> With fear, as half-awakened;
> As if the snow should hesitate

[28]William Carlos Williams, "The Embodiment of Knowledge," in *Selected Essays of William Carlos Williams* (New York: New Directions, 1969), p. 256.

And murmur in the wind,
and half turn back;
These were the "Wing'd-with-Awe,"
Inviolable.
Gods of the wingèd shoe!
With them the silver hounds, sniffing the trace of air!
—From "The Return" (1912)

But Pound's later work breaks away from this Romantic influence; the Greek influences remain, but *The Cantos*, his most massive work, moves away from any coherent narrative line, toward a fragmentized assembly of phrases and pieces, incomplete and rambling sentences that demand hard labor with an encyclopedia and thesaurus. A mere fourteen lines from Canto LXXXI veers between English and Spanish, references Zeus, Ceres, and the English painter Sargent, skates from the Chinese city Taishan to the Greek island Cythera, and records pieces of a conversation between a priest and a communicant over the taking of the Sacrament. This poetic technique abandons, as Williams does, grammatical syntax; it too views words as physical "things" and places them in the poem as objects, without attempting to make clear logical connections between them. It also abandons any attempt to make contact with the "common reader." It is an elitist poetics, one which dazzles the reader with allusion but conveys no single impression.

Pound's other poems tend to fall between these two extremes. The earlier *Cantos* also retell bits of legends and assemble pieces of Pound's reading together into a whole, but the sentences have a more familiar shape; readers can find their way, even without a dictionary of Greek mythology. Even here, though, Pound continually halts the reader's eye with "rapid switches in language and contexts, exclusive private musing, obscure references, multiple allusions"—all techniques to "impede reading."[29] As we read, he reminds us that reading is not likely to yield anything like truth—or even simple coherence.

T. S. ELIOT
(1888–1965)

Recommended edition: The Waste Land and Other Writings, *ed. Mary Karr (Modern Library Classics, 2002).*

---

[29]Margaret Dickie, "The Cantos: Slow Reading," *ELH: English Literary History*, vol. 51, no. 4 (Winter 1984): 819.

Be sure to read: "The Love Song of J. Alfred Prufrock," "The Waste Land,"
"Ash Wednesday," "The Journey of the Magi," "The Four Quartets."

Eliot, Williams, and Pound are the "high modernists" of poetry, marked by their conviction that the world is chaotic and fragmented and their skepticism over the ability of language to convey any truth, in such a disordered universe. The poems of the "high modernists" tend to be more interested in themselves than in the world; the focus of the poetry is often not what is being described but just exactly how the poem is describing it. But while Pound's poetry becomes increasingly more inward focused, commenting on itself rather than on anything outside of its own lines, T. S. Eliot still holds out the possibility of describing the chaos of the world in some meaningful fashion. This may have something to do with Eliot's Anglicanism; his poetry shows a groping for the "still point" of a spiritual life. "At the still point, there the dance is," he writes in Quartet 1, "Burnt Norton": it is the place where the self can make sense out of everything that surrounds it.

Eliot's poetry, like Pound's, is difficult and self-referential ("The Waste Land" carries with it an apparatus of footnotes almost as long as the poem itself, although the footnotes themselves are a sly, tongue-in-cheek wink at the reader's expectations). But the *Four Quartets*, written later in Eliot's life, suggest that the disorder of this life may someday resolve itself into a different existence, outside of time, where we might find "release from action and suffering, release from the inner / And the outer compulsion. "

In Eliot's poetry, it is still possible to glimpse the eternal—and those glimpses are frightening, not (as for the Romantics) warm and glorious. The Magi, visiting the Christ Child in "The Journey of the Magi," find a swaddled child who bears a message, not of comfort, but of "hard and bitter agony." Glimpsing God incarnate, they return to their old lives to find themselves displaced, uneasy, longing for their own deaths to set them free. When the eternal and the earthbound intersect (the rose garden in the *Four Quartets* is another example), we get a glimpse of truth—and are terrified by it.

Although you might expect an Anglican poet to insist that language has some sort of relationship to truth (or at least can make a stab at communicating truth), Eliot isn't quite ready to admit this. Words, he writes in "Burnt Norton," are strained, cracked, broken things, perishable, imprecise, and decaying. But his willingness to put at least a provisional, tentative trust in language appears in the syntax of his poems; even Eliot's obscure sentences tend to have subjects and verbs.

LANGSTON HUGHES
(1902–1967)

Recommended edition: The Collected Poems of Langston Hughes *(Vintage Classics, 1995).*
   Be sure to read: "The Negro Speaks of Rivers," "The Weary Blues," "Montage of a Dream Deferred," "Dream Variations," "I, Too, Sing America," "The South," "Still Here," "Interne at Provident," "Dream Boogie," "Democracy," "The Negro Mother."

Like Dunbar, Langston Hughes struggled with two languages and with a philosophical dilemma: He wrote of the black experience for black readers, yet knew that many of his intended readers would not have the education to understand his more formal verse. "Hughes's poetic practice of social portraiture was one almost entirely unrestricted, imaginatively speaking," writes Helen Vendler. "But this wonderfully inclusive inventory was restricted in another way. . . . [I]t limited itself to language that the most uneducated person could hear and understand. For a man of Hughes's far-ranging mind and reading, that linguistic self-restriction was a sign of unquestioned moral commitment to the black reader."[30] Committed to making his poems accessible to all readers, Hughes has tended to be ignored by critics. And he stands out of the poetic mainstream; in 1929, Hughes wrote in his journal that his "ultimate hope" was to "create a Negro culture in America—a real, solid, sane, racial something growing out of the folk life, *not copied from another,* even though surrounding race."[31]

So rather than using modernist conventions or lyric forms, Hughes's poems draw their idioms from folktales and hymns, songs and ballads. Hughes rooted them not in any idealized rural setting, but in Harlem, and consciously avoided any techniques which might fit into a European, modernist pattern: "The mountain standing in the way of any true Negro art in America," he wrote in the essay "The Negro Artist and the Racial Mountain" is the "urge within the race toward whiteness, the desire to pour racial individuality into the mold of American standardization, and to be as little Negro and as much American as possible."[32]

---

[30] Helen Vendler, "Rita Dove: Identity Markers," *Callaloo,* vol. 17, no. 2 (Spring 1994): 381–98.
[31] Quoted in David R. Jarraway, "Montage of an Otherness Deferred: Dreaming Subjectivity in Langston Hughes," *American Literature,* vol. 68, no. 4 (December 1996): 821.
[32] Langston Hughes, "The Negro Artist and the Racial Mountain," *The Nation,* June 23, 1926.

W. H. AUDEN
(1907–1973)

Recommended edition: Collected Poems: Auden, *edited by Edward Mendelson (Vintage Books, reprint edition, 1991).*

Be sure to read: "As I Walked Out One Evening," "The Common Life," "Compline," "Epitaph on a Tyrant," "The Fall of Rome," "In Memory of Sigmund Freud," "In Memory of W. B. Yeats," "Lay Your Sleeping Head, My Love," "Lullaby," "The More Loving One," "On the Circuit," "Prospero to Ariel," "September 1, 1939," "The Shield of Achilles," "Under Which Lyre," "The Unknown Citizen," "Walk After Dark."

Auden's earlier poetry, like Imagist verse, is concise, condensed, and clipped, but the center of his poetic work is a set of four long poems: "For the Time Being" (a Christmas poem), "New Year Letter" (a reflective poem), "The Age of Anxiety" (an alliterative poem), and "The Sea and the Mirror" (a commentary on Shakespeare's *Tempest*). This reflects Auden's immense range of both technique and topic; he is a political poet, a social poet, a philosophical poet. If there is a unifying theme in his work, it is the possibility that friendship and love can provide that "still place" in the chaotic world that the modernist poets so often seek. Auden's "September 1, 1939," written at the beginning of World War II, reflects this preoccupation: "We must love one other or die," the poem begs, even as the poet himself faces the death, evil, and despair of the coming war.

As he aged, Auden developed an interest in Christianity, which he saw both as the embodiment of his ideal of friendship and as a philosophy which promised equality between all men. You can listen to Auden's own reading of his poems (in New York, March 27, 1972), at an audio archive site archived by the *New York Times*; see http://susanwisebauer.com/welleducatedmind for the link.

After the Modernists

After the modernists, the number of "must-read" poets swells exponentially; time has not yet sorted out the great from the very good. The following poets are worth your further exploration:

PHILIP LARKIN
(1922–1985)

Recommended edition: The Complete Poems, *edited by Archie Burnett (Farrar, Straus and Giroux, 2013).*

Be sure to read: "Annus Mirabilis," "Aubade," "Deceptions," "Essential Beauty," "Far Out," "High Windows," "I Remember, I Remember," "The Importance of Elsewhere," "Is It for Now or for Always," "Long Sight in Age," "Modesties," "The Old Fools," "Story," "Since the Majority of Me," "This Be the Verse," "To Put One Brick upon Another," "Toads," "Why Did I Dream of You Last Night?"

ALLEN GINSBERG
(1926–1997)

Recommended edition: For the "minimal Ginsberg experience," read the Pocket Poets Series edition of his most famous volume, Howl and Other Poems *(City Lights Publishers, 2001); for more Ginsberg, invest in the much larger* Collected Poems 1947–1997 *(Harper Perennial Modern Classics, reprint edition, 2007).*

Be sure to read: All of Howl and Other Poems; *or, in* Selected Poems 1947–1995, *"Metaphysics," "Love Poem on Theme by Whitman," "Howl," "Footnote to Howl," "America," "Kaddish," "Elegy for Neal Cassady," "New York Blues," "Manhattan May Day Midnight," "Do the Meditation Rock," "The Ballad of the Skeletons."*

ADRIENNE RICH
(1929–2012)

Recommended edition: Adrienne Rich's Poetry and Prose, *edited by Barbara Charlesworth Gelpi and Albert Gelpi (W. W. Norton, 1993). Since Rich's poetry has been published in many small volumes, this collection is the best way to read a collection of her most important poems.*

Be sure to read: "Aunt Jennifer's Tigers," "Burning of Paper Instead of Children," "Diving into the Wreck," "I Am in Danger—Sir—," "The Necessities of Life," "Living in Sin," "The Phenomenology of Anger," "Planetarium," "Power," "Shooting Script," "Snapshots of a Daughter-in-Law," "Sources," "Trying to Talk with a Man," "Twenty-One Love Poems."

SYLVIA PLATH
(1932–1963)

Recommended edition: The Everyman's Library Pocket Poets edition, Plath: Poems, *edited by Diane Wood Middlebrook (1998). This volume contains all of Plath's best-known poems. The more extensive* Collected Poems, *edited and annotated by Ted Hughes, contains fifty poems written before 1956 along with all of Plath's work after 1956, including previously unpublished poems (Harper Perennial Modern Classics, reprint edition, 2008).*

Be sure to read: "Two Sisters of Persephone," "Suicide off Egg Rock," "Poem for a Birthday," "Zoo Keeper's Wife," "Barren Woman," "Crossing the Water," "The Bee Meeting," "The Arrival of the Bee Box," "Stings," "The Swarm," "Wintering," "Nick and the Candlestick," "Event," "Ariel," "Child," "Edge."

MARK STRAND
(1934–2014)

Recommended edition: Mark Strand: Selected Poems *(New York: Knopf, 2014).*

Be sure to read: "The Accident," "The Coming of Light," "Eating Poetry," "From the Long Sad Party," "Giving Myself Up," "Keeping Things Whole," "The Mailman," "My Mother on an Evening in Late Summer," "Sleeping With One Eye Open," "The Tunnel," "The Way It Is."

MARY OLIVER
(1935–)

Recommended editions: New and Selected Poems, Vol. 1 *(Beacon Press, reprint edition, 2004) and* New and Selected Poems, Vol. 2 *(Beacon Press, 2007).*

Be sure to read: "The Journey," "Wild Geese," "At Black River," "The Summer Day," "A Thousand Mornings," "Sometimes a Rare Music," "When Death Comes."

SEAMUS HEANEY
(1939–2013)

Recommended edition: Opened Ground: Selected Poems 1966–1996 *(Farrar, Straus and Giroux, reprint edition, 1999).*

Be sure to read: "Blackberry-Picking," "Bogland," "Casualty," "Digging," "Death of a Naturalist," "Field Work," "Hailstones," "The Haw Lantern," "Lightenings," "The Ministry of Fear," "Mossbawn: Two Poems in Dedication," "Personal Helicon," "'Poet's Chair,'" "Squarings," "Tollund."

ROBERT PINSKY
(1940–)

Recommended edition: Selected Poems *(Farrar, Straus and Giroux, 2012).*
  Be sure to read: "Everywhere I Go, There I Am," "The Figured Wheel," "The Ice Storm," "Impossible to Tell," "The Night Game," "Poem with Refrains," "The Refinery," "Shirt," "The Unseen."

ROBERT HASS
(1941–)

Recommended edition: The Apple Trees at Olema: New and Selected Poems *(Ecco, reprint edition, 2011).*
  Be sure to read: "Meditation at Lagunitas," "Songs to Survive the Summer," "Between the Wars," "Faint Music," "Privilege of Being," "Berkeley Epilogue," "Then Time."

JANE KENYON
(1947–1995)

Recommended edition: Collected Poems *(Graywolf Press, 2007).*
  Be sure to read: "Briefly It Enters, And Briefly Speaks," "Depression," "Dutch Interiors," "Eating the Cookies," "February: Thinking of Flowers," "Happiness," "Having It Out with Melancholy," "Let Evening Come," "Otherwise," "Rain in January."

RITA DOVE
(1952–)

Recommended edition: Selected Poems *(Vintage Books, 1993).*
  Be sure to read: "Small Town," "Upon Meeting Don L. Lee, In a Dream," "Agosta the Winged Man and Rasha the Black Dove," "Primer for the Nuclear Age," "Thomas and Beulah."

Chapter 10

The Cosmic Story: Understanding the Earth, the Skies, and Ourselves

CIENCE BEGAN LONG before the first science text, just as storytelling came before the novel, poetic performances before the written poem. Science, says historian-of-science George Sarton, began as soon as humans "tried to solve the innumerable problems of life." Mapping out a journey by the skies, balancing a wheel, building an irrigation canal, mixing herbs to relieve pain, designing a pyramid: this was science.[1]

And it went on for quite a long time before anyone decided to write about it.

Compared with the other genres we've investigated, science books have a much more distant relationship to the actual *practice* of the craft. Made-up stories; stories about the past; stories about ourselves; lyrical outpourings about God, or love, or depression; acting out imagined scenes: all of these existed before novels, histories, autobiographies, poems, and plays took the forms we now know. But all of them had to migrate into written form before they could survive, develop, evolve.

Science is different. Scientific discoveries don't *require* the written word. Many of the most essential insights into the natural world (right triangles exist; electrical current can be channelled through a wire; the atoms of elements can be charted onto a periodic table; antibiotics kill bacteria) have not led to books about them. Science is perfectly capable of continuing independent of written narratives.

But side by side with the actual doing of science, a tradition of science writing slowly evolved: starting, as history did, with the Greeks.

---

[1]George Sarton, *A History of Science: Ancient Science Through the Golden Age of Greece* (Cambridge: Harvard University Press, 1952), p. 3.

A TWENTY-MINUTE HISTORY OF SCIENCE WRITING

The Natural Philosophers

In the fifth century B.C., the physician Hippocrates was struggling with the nature of disease.

He had been trained to practice medicine in a world where the divine suffused everything. Doctors were also priests, and they treated the sick by sending them for a night's vigil in one of the temples of Aesculapius, god of healing. Perhaps the sacred serpents that lived in the temple would lick the patient's wounds and miraculously heal them; or maybe the god would send a dream explaining how the illness should be treated; or, Aesculapius himself might even appear to carry out the cure.[2]

In this world, Hippocrates was an outlier.

He did not think that diseases were caused by angry deities, nor that they needed to be cured by a benevolent one. "I do not believe," he wrote in his treatise about epilepsy, long thought to be a holy affliction sent directly from the gods, "that the 'Sacred Disease' is any more divine or sacred than any other disease, but, on the contrary, has specific characteristics and a definite cause . . . It is my opinion that those who first called this disease 'sacred' were the sort of people we now call witch-doctors, faith-healers, quacks and charlatans . . . By invoking a divine element they were able to screen their own failure to give suitable treatments."[3]

Instead of invoking the gods, Hippocrates looked to the visible world, searching for both "definite causes" and "suitable treatments" in nature itself.

His investigations led him to formulate an entirely secular theory of disease. Four fluids course through the human body, Hippocrates claimed: bile, black bile, phlegm, and blood. When these four fluids ("humors") exist in their proper proportions, we are healthy. But any number of natural factors might throw the fluids out of whack. Hot winds, for example, cause the body to produce too much phlegm; drinking stagnant water can lead to an overabundance of black bile. The recommended treatment? Restore the body's balance. Use purges and bleeds to get rid of excess humors; send sick men and women to different climates, away from the winds and waters that are deranging their harmonies.[4]

---

[2]Plinio Prioreschi, *A History of Medicine, Vol. I: Primitive and Ancient Medicine*, 2nd ed. (Omaha, Neb.: Horatius Press, 1996), p. 42.

[3]Hippocrates, "On the Sacred Disease," qtd. in Steven H. Miles, *The Hippocratic Oath and the Ethics of Medicine* (New York: Oxford University Press, 2005), p. 20.

[4]Lawrence I. Conrad et al., *The Western Medical Tradition: 800 BC–AD 1800* (New York: Cambridge University Press, 1995), pp. 23-25; Pausanius, *Pausanias's Description of Greece,*

The theory was ingenious, convincing, and completely wrong.

It could hardly be otherwise. Hippocrates had no access to the body's secrets; no way to discern what was *really* happening inside the skin. Twenty-three centuries later, Albert Einstein and the physicist Leopold Infeld jointly offered an analogy for Hippocrates's plight. The ancient investigator of the natural world, they wrote, was like

> a man trying to understand the mechanism of a closed watch. He sees the face and the moving hands, even hears its ticking, but he has no way of opening the case. If he is ingenious he may form some picture of a mechanism which could be responsible for all the things he observes, but he . . . will never be able to compare his picture with the real mechanism and he cannot even imagine the possibility or the meaning of such a comparison.[5]

Hippocrates was no more able to peer inside the watch-case than his priest-physician contemporaries. He was not doing science as we would understand it; he was *philosophizing* about nature, attempting to reason his way into a closed system that he could not observe. But Hippocrates and his followers were at least attempting to find natural factors that would help explain the natural world. So the Hippocratic *Corpus*—some sixty medical texts, collected by his students and followers, that neither blame nor invoke the gods—is the first written record of a scientific endeavor.

In the centuries after Hippocrates, other Greek philosophers expanded his way of thinking of to encompass *phusis:* not just man, but the whole of the ordered universe.

Their theories were varied. The monists believed that the ordered universe all began with a single underlying element, one sort of stuff (water, or fire, or some still-unknown material); the pluralists were in favor of multiple underlying elements, most often a four-way assembly of earth, air, fire, and water. And the atomists suggested that all of reality was made up of minuscule elements called *atomoi,* the "indivisibles"—incomprehensibly small particles that clump together to form the "visible and perceptible masses" that make up our world.[6]

This last theory, as we now know, was within stabbing distance of the truth. But the atomists, like the monists and pluralists, were still doing

---

Vol. III, trans. J. G. Frazer (New York: Macmillan & Co., 1898), p. 250; "On Airs, Waters, and Places," in *The Corpus,* p. 117.

[5] Albert Einstein and Leopold Infeld, *The Evolution of Physics* (New York: Cambridge University Press, 1938), p. 33.

[6] Simplicius, *Commentary on the Physics* 28.4–15, qtd. in Jonathan Barnes, *Early Greek Philosophy,* rev. ed (New York: Penguin, 2002), p. 202; Aristotle, *On Democritus* fr. 203, qtd. in Barnes, pp. 206–207.

philosophy. None of these explanations were susceptible to proof. These early "scientists" were theorizing with no way to check their results; the watch case was still firmly closed.

For the philosopher Aristotle—born a century after Hippocrates' death, on the opposite side of the Aegean Sea—the greatest flaw in all of these speculations was their failure to account for *change*. Searching for a quality that all natural things shared, Aristotle pinpointed the principle of development. An animal, a plant, fire, water—none of these things remain the same indefinitely. Each, Aristotle wrote in his great work *Physics,* "has within itself a source of change . . . in respect of either movement or increase and decrease or alteration." A bed, or a cloak, or a stone building—all created by man's artifice—have no such "intrinsic impulse for change."[7]

Watching a sprout grow into a tree, a cub into a lion, an infant into a man, Aristotle wanted an explanation. How do these changes *happen*? In what stages does one entity, one *being,* assume more than one form? What impels the change, and what determines its ending point? And even more, he wanted a reason. *Why* does a kitten become a cat, a seed a flower? What sends it on the long journey of transformation?

The monists and atomists had no answers for him; nor did the pluralists, although he found their theory of multiple elements more convincing. So he began to work his way toward a new set of explanations. To the pluralist sketch of four elements that combine to make up all natural things, Aristotle added a fifth, an imperishable heavenly substance called *aether* that carries the stars. He also proposed that each element has particular qualities (air is cold and dry, water is cold and wet) that interact with each other and produce change (for example, the "dry" in air can expel the "wet" from water, making water cold and dry, and thus converting water to air). Earth is the heaviest of the elements, and so is drawn toward the center of the universe; fire, the lightest, always tends to fly away from the cosmic core.[8]

Most important of all, natural things have within themselves a *principle of motion*: an internal potential for change. Each object and being in the natural world *must* move from its present state into a future, more perfect one. Built into the very fabric of the seed, the kitten, the infant, is the impulse to develop toward a more fully realized end.

[7]Aristotle, *Physics,* trans. Robin Waterfield (New York: Oxford University Press, 2008), II.1

[8]Edward Craig, ed., *Routledge Encyclopedia of Philosophy* (Oxford, U.K.: Taylor & Francis, 1998), pp. 193–194; David Bolotin, *An Approach to Aristotle's Physics, With Particular Attention to the Role of His Manner of Writing* (Albany: SUNY Press, 1998), p. 127; J. Den Boeft, ed., *Calcidius on Demons (Commentarius CH. 127-136)* (Leiden: E. J. Brill, 1977), pp. 19–20.

The *Physics,* widely read in the Greek world, provided a model of the universe that would influence the practice of science for two thousand years. But Aristotle, too, was philosophizing. He could offer no solid proofs of his elements, nor pinpoint the principle of motion within them. And his vision of a driven and purpose-filled world did not go unchallenged.

The atomists were his most vocal opponents; particularly Epicurus, a generation Aristotle's junior, who argued vehemently that there was no purposeful movement in the universe. There were only randomly moving atoms and "the empty"—the place in which atoms rushed about, collided, and intertwined by chance. The world that we see has come into being only because atoms, spinning through the void, occasionally give an unpredictable hop, a random jump sideways, slam into each other, and fortuitously join up to create new objects.[9]

Two hundred years after Epicurus's death, his disciple Lucretius—a Roman educated in Greek philosophy—recast his teachings in a long poem called *De Rerum Natura* (*On the Nature of the Universe* or, more literally, *On the Nature of Things*). The atoms that make up everything, Lucretius writes, are in "ceaseless motion" and vary in size and shape. They created the earth and the human race; there is no design, either natural or supernatural. The soul is not transcendent; like our bodies, it is made up of material particles, of atoms "most minute." Too tiny to comprehend, they disperse into air when the body dies, and so the soul too ceases to exist.

But the most central truth of atomism, as Lucretius explains in Book II, is that all things come to an end. All natural bodies—sun, moon, sea, our own—age and decay. They do not mature into greater and truer versions of themselves. Rather, they are struck again and again by "hostile atoms" and slowly melt away. And what is true of the physical bodies within the universe is true of the universe itself: "So likewise," he concludes, "the walls of the great world . . . shall suffer decay and fall into moldering ruins . . . [I]t is vain to expect that the frame of the world will last forever." Aristotle's teleology was a delusion. The universe will perish, as surely as our own bodies, and come not to fulfillment, but only to dust.[10]

Even more firmly than Hippocrates and Aristotle, Lucretius insisted that *phusis,* the ordered universe, could be explained in purely natural

[9]C. C. W. Taylor, *The Atomists: Leucippus and Democritus, Fragments* (Toronto: University of Toronto Press, 1999), pp. 60, 214–215; Epicurus, "Letter to Herodotus," in *Letters and Sayings of Epicurus,* trans. Odysseus Makridis (New York: Barnes & Noble, 2005), pp. 3–6; Anthony Gottlieb, *The Dream of Reason: A History of Philosophy from the Greeks to the Renaissance* (New York: W. W. Norton, 2000), pp. 290, 303.

[10]Titus Lucretius Carus, *Lucretius on The Nature of Things,* trans. John Selby Watson (London: Henry G. Bohn, 1851), p. 96.

terms: the most central principle of modern science. But like them, he had no way of proving his theories. He could not observe his atoms at work, any more than Hippocrates could view his humors, or Aristotle examine the aether. The "watch case" of nature was still firmly closed; and for the next fifteen hundred years, no one would succeed in popping the lock.

The Observers

In 1491, Nicolaus Copernicus began a new search for the key.

He was eighteen years old, a student of astronomy at the University of Cracow, grappling with his introductory astronomy textbook. The *Epitome of the Almagest,* a standard handbook for beginners, was an abridgment of a much more complex manual: the *Almagest,* assembled by the Greek astronomer Ptolemy in the second century. The *Almagest* assumed that the universe was exactly as Aristotle had described it: spherical, made up of five elements, with the earth sitting at its center. (That was logical enough. The earth is "heavy matter," constantly drawn toward the center of the universe, and it's clearly not falling through space: Q.E.D., it must already *be* at the center.) The stars above the earth, along with the seven independently moving celestial bodies known as the *aster planetes* (the wandering stars), moved around the earth.

But this movement around the earth was far from simple.

According to the *Epitome of the Almagest,* each planet came to a regular stop in its orbit (a "station") and then backtracked for a predictable, calculable distance ("retrogradation"). They also performed additional small loops ("epicycles") while traveling along the larger circles ("deferents"); and the center of the deferents was not the earth itself, but a point slightly offset from the theoretical core of the universe (the "eccentric"). Furthermore, the *speed* of planetary movement was measured from yet a *third* point, an imaginary standing place called the *equant.* (The equant was self-defining—it was the place from which measurement had to be made in order to make the planet's path along the deferent proceed at a completely uniform rate.)[11]

---

[11]Margaret J. Osler, *Reconfiguring the World: Nature, God, and Human Understanding from the Middle Ages to Early Modern Europe* (Baltimore: Johns Hopkins University Press, 2010), p. 15; C. M. Linton, *From Eudoxus to Einstein: A History of Mathematical Astronomy* (New York: Cambridge University Press, 2008), p. 48.

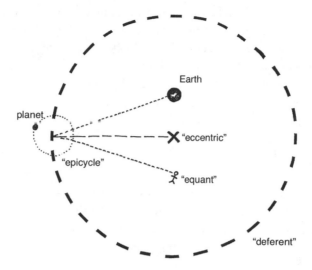

This was a complicated and ugly system—but by measuring from the equant and the eccentric and by building epicycle upon epicycle, students of astronomy could accurately predict the future position of any given star or planet.

In all likelihood, none of them believed that the *Epitome of the Almagest* provided an actual picture of the universe. Ptolemy himself probably did not think that, should he suddenly be transported into the heavens, he would see Jupiter suddenly charge backward into retrograde and then swing around into an epicycle. The mathematical strategies were just that: gimmicks and tricks that yielded the correct results, not realistic sketches.

This was called "saving the phenomena"—proposing geometrical patterns that matched up with observational data. The patterns were reliable enough for the use of navigators and time-keepers, and allowed astronomers to (more or less) accurately chart the heavens. And, since no one had the ability to *look* into the heavens and see what Jupiter was actually up to, the earth-centered orbits were generally accepted.[12]

But from his first introduction to the *Almagest*, Copernicus questioned those elaborate and unwieldy paths. Why, he wondered, should each planet require its own individual set of movements, its own particular laws? It was as if, he later wrote, an artist decided to draw the figure of a man, but gathered "the hands, feet, head and other members for his

---

[12]Norris S. Hetherington, *Cosmology: Historical, Literary, Philosophical, Religious, and Scientific Perspectives* (London: CRC Press, 1993), pp. 74–76.

images from diverse models, each part excellently drawn, but not related to a single body . . . the result would be monster rather than man."[13]

The earth-centered universe of the *Almagest* was, he thought, monstrous: an unwieldy set of awkward mathematical contortions.

Copernicus spent a decade and a half studying the *Almagest* and making his own records of planetary positions. By 1514, he had formulated a more graceful theory. He wrote it out in a simple and readable form, eliminating all of the mathematics involved, and circulated it to his friends. This informal proposal was known as the *Commentariolus*.

"I often considered," it began, "whether there could perhaps be found a more reasonable arrangement of circles." This more reasonable arrangement began with a simple assumption: "All the spheres revolve about the sun as their mid-point, and therefore the sun is the center of the universe." The earth was merely the center of the "lunar sphere," not the entire universe. Furthermore, the earth did not remain motionless; instead, it "performs a complete rotation on its fixed poles in a daily motion." This earthly rotation actually caused the apparent movement of the sun, and accounted for what seemed to be retrograde motion in the planetary paths.[14]

Copernicus spent the next quarter of a century working the *Commentariolus* up into the full-fledged astronomical manual *On the Revolutions of the Heavenly Spheres*, complete with mathematical calculations. "The harmony of the whole world teaches us their truth," Copernicus wrote, "if only—as they say—we would look at the thing with both eyes." That truth was simple: Only the mobility of the Earth, and the sun's position at "the centre of the world," can explain the motion of the stars.[15]

In other words, the heliocentric model was intended to be a *true* picture of the universe, not just a mathematical strategy. Unlike the Greek astronomers, Copernicus clearly believed that, should he suddenly be transported into the heavens, he would *see* the earth tracking faithfully around the sun.

He was moving away from philosophy, toward what we would now think of as a more scientific endeavor: a careful explanation of the physical world based on phenomena, not on *a priori* assumptions. But it was an incomplete journey. Copernicus had no telescope capable of providing

---

[13]Nicolaus Copernicus, Preface, *De Revolutionibus,* qtd. in Thomas S. Kuhn, *The Copernican Revolution: Planetary Astronomy in the Development of Western Thought* (Cambridge: Harvard University Press, 1957), p. 137.

[14]Nicolaus Copernicus, *Three Copernican Treatises,* trans. Edward Rosen (Mineola, N.Y.: Dover Publications, 1959), pp. 57–59.

[15]Copernicus, Preface, p. 18.

visual confirmation of his model; he was a theoretical eyewitness, not an actual one.

And heliocentrism had its problems. For one thing, Copernicus couldn't explain why, if the earth was whirling on its axis *and* sailing around the sun, both of those motions were imperceptible to people standing on its surface. And for another, heliocentrism seemed to contradict the literal interpretation of biblical passages such as Joshua 10:12–13, in which the sun and moon "stand still" rather than continuing to move around the earth.

So when *On the Revolutions* was first printed in 1542, an unsigned introduction was appended to it, explaining that the heliocentric model was merely another mathematical trick, not a real description. "For these hypotheses," the introduction explained, "are not put forward to convince anyone that they are true, but merely to provide a reliable basis for computation."

Copernicus may not even have seen this disclaimer; it is generally thought to have been written by a friend who was overseeing the printing process. Yet it was accepted as genuine by most readers, and for a century, Copernicus's scheme remained merely one among many.

Its ultimate triumph was due to the work of two men: the English philosopher Francis Bacon, and the Italian astronomer and physicist Galileo.

Bacon, born nineteen years after *On the Revolutions* was published, was an ambitious politician and an even more ambitious thinker. While he was busy climbing up the ladder of preferment at the English court, he was also planning out his masterwork. This would be a definitive study of human knowledge called the *Great Instauration*: the Great Establishment, a complete system of philosophy in six volumes that would shape the minds of men and guide them into new truths.

By 1620, he had only completed the first two books, and his time was running out; his position at court had been undermined by his enemies, he was about to be confined in the Tower of London, and he would die of pneumonia in 1626 without returning to his magnum opus. But *Novum Organon* ("New Tools"), published shortly before his death, laid the foundations for the modern scientific method.

Novum Organon (a play on the title of Aristotle's six books on logic, known collectively as the *Organon*) challenged the reliability of deductive reasoning, the Aristotelian way of thinking generally followed by natural philosophers. Deductive reasoning begins with generally accepted truths, or *premises,* and works its way toward more specific conclusions:

MAJOR PREMISE: All heavy matter falls toward the center of the universe.

MINOR PREMISE: The earth is made of heavy matter.
MINOR PREMISE: The earth is not falling.
CONCLUSION: The earth must already be at the center of the universe.

Bacon had come to believe that deductive reasoning was a dead end that distorted physical evidence, and made observation secondary to preconceived ideas. "Having first determined the question according to his will," he complained, "man then resorts to experience, and bending her to conformity . . . leads her about like a captive in a procession."

Instead, he argued, the careful thinker must reason the other way around: starting from specific observations, and building from them toward general conclusions. This new way of thinking—*inductive reasoning*—had three steps to it. The "true method," Bacon explained, "first lights the candle, and then by means of the candle shows the way; commencing as it does with experience duly ordered and digested, not bungling or erratic, and from it deducing axioms, and from established axioms again new experiments." In other words, the natural philosopher must first come up with an idea about how the world works: "lighting the candle." Second, he must *test* the idea against physical reality, against "experience duly ordered"—both observations of the world around him, and carefully designed experiments. These experiments should be carried out with the use of instruments that magnify, intensify, and make clearer the process of nature: "Neither the naked hand nor the understanding left to itself can effect much," Bacon wrote. "It is by instruments and helps that the work is done." [16]

Only then, as a last step, should the natural philosopher "deduce axioms," or come up with a theory that could be claimed to carry truth.

Hypothesis, experiment, conclusion: Bacon had just traced out the outlines of the scientific method. It was not, of course, fully developed. But the *Novum Organum* continued to shape the seventeenth-century practice of science. Finally, a method was in place that would allow natural philosophers to "look with both eyes," as Copernicus had asked, and to come to conclusions based on their observations.

Chief among the "instruments and helps" that made these observations more useful was the telescope: brand new, and under steady improvement even as Bacon was writing. Ten years before the publication of the *Novum Organon,* the Italian mathematician and astronomer Galileo Gal-

[16] Francis Bacon, *Selected Philosophical Works,* ed. Rose-Mary Sargent (Cambridge: Hackett Publishing Co., 1999), pp. 118–119.

ilei had first encountered a telescope on a visit to Venice. This arrangement of convex and concave lenses had been invented the year before by a Low Country spectacle-maker; immediately on returning home, Galileo set to work grinding his own lenses and improving the instrument's refraction.

The original telescope had been only slightly more useful than the naked eye, but Galileo managed to refine the magnification to around 20X. Through his instrument, he saw mountains and valleys on the moon, and many more stars than were visible to the eye alone. He also saw four objects near Jupiter, never before observed. When Galileo first viewed them, he thought they were fixed stars.

But when he looked at them again on the following day, they had *moved.*

And they kept moving, in and out of sight, to the left and to the right of Jupiter itself. Over the course of a week, Galileo was able to sketch out their progression and come to the inevitable conclusion: they were moons, and all four "perform[ed] their revolutions about this planet . . . in unequal circles."

This provided unequivocal proof that not all heavenly bodies revolved around the earth—proof that Galileo published in 1610, in a short work known as *The Sidereal Messenger* ("The Starry Messenger"). A few months later, he used his telescope to observe the changing phases of Venus; inexplicable in the Ptolemaic system, making sense only if Venus were, in fact, traveling around the sun.

These observations did not convince anyone. In fact, the chief philosopher at Padua, an Aristotelian named Cesar Cremonini, simply refused to look through Galileo's telescope. "To such people," Galileo wrote bitterly to the astronomer Johannes Kepler, "truth is to be sought, not in the universe or in nature, but (I use their own words) by comparing texts!" In Galileo's opinion, Aristotle himself would have been happy both to look, and to adjust his physics in response: "We do have in our age new events and observations," he later remarked, "such that, if Aristotle were now alive, I have no doubt he would change his opinion."[17]

An epic battle was shaping up: between ancient authority and present observation, Aristotelian thought and Baconian method, text and eye. Galileo himself had not yet written anything that explicitly supported

[17]David Deming, *Science and Technology in World History,* Vol. 3 (Jefferson, N.C.: McFarland & Co., 2010), p. 165; Galileo Galilei, *Dialogue Concerning the Two Chief World Systems: Ptolemaic and Copernican,* trans. Stillman Drake, ed. Stephen Jay Gould (New York: Modern Library, 2001), pp. 130–131.

Copernicus. But his observations in *The Sidereal Messenger* certainly implied that he accepted heliocentrism, and he had already offered (in an unpublished collection of essays known as *De motu*) a mathematical explanation for why the earth's motion through space was imperceptible from its surface.

In 1616, the cardinal Robert Bellarmine (under orders from Pope Paul V) recommended that *On the Revolutions* be placed on the church's list of condemned texts. He also warned Galileo, in a private but official meeting, to abandon public agreement with Copernicus. Instead, Galileo spent the next sixteen years tackling the remaining problems with the heliocentric model, one at a time.

In 1632, he put all of his conclusions into a major work: the *Dialogue on the Two Chief World Systems, Ptolemaic and Copernican*. In order to sidestep Bellarmine's dictate, Galileo framed the *Dialogue* as a hypothetical discussion, an argument among three friends as to what might be the best possible model for the universe. Two of his characters, charmingly intelligent and sympathetic, agree that the Copernican theory is superior; the third, a moronic idiot named Simplicius, insists on Aristotle's earth-centered system.

The first print run of a thousand copies sold out almost immediately. It didn't take long for churchmen to notice that Galileo was violating Bellarmine's warning; and in 1633, Galileo—now in his seventies, and unwell—was forced to travel to Rome to defend himself against the Inquisition. Threatened with "greater rigor of procedure," a code phrase for torture, Galileo agreed to "abandon the false opinion which maintains that the Sun is the center and immovable." The *Dialogue* was banned in Italy, and Galileo was sentenced to house arrest. He died in 1642, his condemnation still in place.[18]

But outside the reach of the Inquisition, the *Dialogue* continued to circulate: reprinted, read throughout Europe, translated into English in 1661, consulted by astronomers who used ever more powerful telescopes to confirm Galileo's conclusions.

At the same time, the English scientist Robert Hooke took Bacon's recommendations in the other direction; instead of using instruments to examine the distant skies, he looked more closely at earthly objects.

Hooke was an excellent mathematician, an expert at grinding and using lenses, the inventor of a barometer, a competent geologist, biologist, meteorologist, architect, and physicist. In 1662, he was appointed to the post of Curator of Experiments for the fledgling Royal Society of

[18]Deming, *Science and Technology*, pp. 177–178.

London for Improving Natural Knowledge. The Society was a "research club," a regular gathering of natural philosophers who were committed to the experimental method of science; they were all students of the *Novum Organan,* and the Royal Society's dedicatory epistle (written by the poet Abraham Cowley, himself an enthusiastic amateur scientist) was all in praise of Francis Bacon.

From words, which are but pictures of the thought,

Cowley enthused,

> Though we our thoughts from them perversely drew
> To things, the mind's right object, he it brought . . .
> Who to the life an exact piece would make,
> Must not from other's work a copy take . . .
> No, he before his sight must place
> The natural and living face;
> The real object must command
> Each judgment of his eye, and motion of his hand.

This examination of "real objects," when carried out with instruments and helps, was known as "elaborate," and such experiments were done in well-equipped "elaboratories"; Hooke himself had worked, as a young man, in the elaboratory of the chemist Robert Boyle. His training there, along with his wide-ranging skills and interests, made him the perfect choice as Curator of Experiments. He was paid a full-time stipend to do two things: to present a variety of weekly experiments to the gathered Society, explaining and demonstrating as he went; and to assist the Fellows with their own experiments, as needed.

This made Robert Hooke (probably) the first full-time salaried scientist in history. The Royal Society was made up of astronomers, geographers, physicians, philosophers, mathematicians, opticians, and even a few chemists, so Hooke was called on to experiment and research across the entire field of natural philosophy. He conducted demonstrations with pendulums, distilled urine, insects placed in pressurized containers, colored and plain glass, and much more.

But, increasingly, his experimental demonstrations involved the microscope.

Microscopes had improved as telescopes had grown more powerful. In 1663, the minutes of the Royal Society note, Hooke demonstrated the microscopic structures of moss, cork, bark, mold, leeches, spiders, and "a curious piece of petrified wood." This puzzled him greatly, but he suggested perhaps it had "lain in some place where it was well soaked with water . . . well impregnated with stony and earthy particles," and that the stone and earth had "intruded" into it.[19]

Hooke had described, for the first time the process of fossilization. And he had gone beyond observation with instruments to something new: the establishment of a new physical process which he had not (and could not) see, but which he was able to *deduce*.

In 1664, the Royal Society formally requested that Hooke print his micrographical observations. On top of his other competencies, Hooke was a skilled draughtsman and artist. Rather than merely describing his discoveries in words, or commissioning nonscientists to produce his drawings, he made his own: large, exquisitely detailed, and perfectly clear. The resulting work, *Micrographia,* was published in 1665.

The eye-grabbing pictures attracted the most attention. But even more notable is that, throughout, Hooke uses his newly extended senses to build new theories. After carefully examining the colors and layers of muscovite ("Moscovy-glass") he goes beyond his observations to suggest nothing less than a theory of how light works: it is, he speculates, a "very short vibrating motion" propagated "through an Homogeneous medium by direct or straight lines." It was not enough merely to extend the senses by way of instruments; the reason must follow the path laid by these observations, interpret them, and then check itself again.

And again, and again, and again. Hooke and the members of the Royal Society were committed to Baconian thinking, but they were also cautious, reluctant to draw conclusions without exhaustive proof—an attitude that soon drove a wedge between the Society and its newest member, one "Mr. Isaac Newton, professor of mathematics in the university of Cambridge."

Isaac Newton, twenty-nine years old when he joined the Society in 1672, was a student of the experimental method and an enthusiastic user of artificial helps (his most recent work was with prisms). But when he shared his most recent "philosophical discovery"—that all light is made up of a spectrum of rays, and that "whiteness is nothing but a mixture of all sorts of colours, or that it is produced by all sorts of colours blended together"—the Society greeted him with skepticism. Hooke objected

[19]Robert Hooke, *Micrographia* (1664), Preface; David Freedberg, *The Eye of the Lynx: Galileo, His Friends and the Beginnings of Natural History* (Chicago: University of Chicago Press, 2002), p. 180; Thomas Birch, *The History of the Royal Society of London,* Vol. 1 (London: A. Millar, 1756), pp. 215ff.

that he could think of at least two other "various hypotheses" that could equally well explain Newton's results, and the other members of the Society recommended that many more experiments should be made before any universal conclusions were drawn.[20]

These experiments dragged on for the next three years, with much correspondence flying back and forth between Newton's Cambridge elaboratory and the Society's London headquarters. Newton became increasingly frustrated. "It is not number of experiments, but weight, to be regarded," he complained in 1676, "and where one will do, what need many?" Gradually, he withdrew from participation in the Royal Society, and devoted himself instead to his own research: not only light and optics, but also the orbits of the planets, and the celestial mechanics that might explain them.

In 1687, he published his first major work: *Philosophiae Naturalis Principia Mathematica,* or "Mathematical Principles of Natural Philosophy." It was intended to solve the biggest problems that still plagued the heliocentric model. For one thing, calculations based on perfectly circular orbits didn't match up with the exact position of the planets. Galileo's friend and colleague Johannes Kepler had proposed laws for *elliptical* orbits; this yielded much better results, but neither Kepler nor Galileo had been able to explain *why* the orbits should be elliptical rather than circular.

Newton had a possible solution. Planets circled the sun, he suggested, not because they were mounted on some sphere, but because the sun was exerting a force on them. Planets exerted the same force on moons that surrounded *them*. This force he called *gravitas*.

Galileo, like Aristotle, had believed that objects fell because of an inherent quality within them, an intrinsic "weightiness." Newton argued that objects fell because the earth's *gravitas* drew them toward it. But the strength of this force did not remain the same over distance. It *changed*. As the planets moved further from the sun, the force that pulled on them weakened: thus, the ellipse.

In order to fully explain the laws governing this new force, Newton had to come up with an improved mathematics, capable of accounting for continual small changes. This new math was a "mathematics of change," able to predict results in a setting where the conditions were constantly shifting, forces altering, factors appearing and receding.[21]

So the *Principia* performed two groundbreaking tasks simultaneously.

---

[20]Thomas Birch, *The History of the Royal Society of London,* Vol. 3 (London: A. Millar, 1757), pp. 1, 10.
[21]Ron Larson and Bruce Edwards, *Calculus* (Independence, Ky.: Cengage Learning, 2013), p. 42.

It explained the *why* behind the ellipses of the planets—and in doing so, revealed for the first time a new force in the universe, the force of gravity. And it introduced an entirely new branch of mathematics, which became known as *calculus* (from the Latin word for "pebble," the tiny stones used as arithmetical counters).

None of this was easy going. The *Principia* is, deliberately, composed of impenetrable mathematical explanations; William Derham, Newton's longtime friend and colleague, later explained that since Newton "abhorred all Contests," he "designedly made his Principia abstruse" in order to "avoid being baited by little Smatterers in Mathematicks." (This drove off quite a few academics as well; a frustrated Cambridge student famously remarked, as Newton passed him on the street, "There goes the man who has writt a book that neither he nor any one else understands.")[22]

But at the beginning of Book 3, Newton abandoned his dense formulaic prose in order to write clearly.

The "Rules for the Study of Natural Philosophy" that begin Book 3 are, in a way, his final response to the Royal Society's unending demands for proof. Newton was aware that the conclusions of the *Principia* could be dismissed by the literal-minded as "ingenious Romance"—mere guesses. After all, he had not actually spun planets at different distances from the sun to observe the rate of their orbit. Instead, he had taken the results of experiments with weighted objects carried out on earth, and had extrapolated their results into the heavens.[23]

The Rules explain why Newton's conclusions about the planetary orbits, while not experimentally proven in the way that would make the Society happy, are nevertheless reliable—as the first three Rules make very clear.

1. Simpler causes are more likely to be true than complex ones.
2. Phenomena of the same kind (e.g., falling stones in Europe and falling stones in America) are likely to have the same causes.
3. If a property can be demonstrated to belong to all bodies on which experiments can be made, it can be assumed to belong to all bodies in the universe.

[22]James L. Axtell, "Locke, Newton and the Two Cultures." In John W. Yolton, ed., *John Locke: Problems and Perspectives* (New York: Cambridge University Press, 1969), pp. 166–168.
[23]Barry Gower, *Scientific Method: A Historical and Philosophical Introduction* (New York: Routledge, 1997), p. 69.

This is Bacon's inductive reasoning, always progressing from specifics to generalities, based on observation—but now extended by Newton to breathtaking lengths.

Across, in fact, the entire face of the universe.

The Historians

For nearly two centuries, the universe would remain Newtonian.

His laws always seemed to work, in every place. Gravity functioned in the same way in every corner of the universe. Time passed everywhere at the same rate. The universe was static and infinite, and it went on forever.

But this did not mean that the *earth* was static and unchanging, or that the living things upon it had always been the same. And Newton's Rules made it possible for observations about the present to be extrapolated back into educated guesses about the past.

For one thing, how long had the earth been around?

Newton himself speculated that the earth might originally have been a molten sphere. In that case, it would have taken at least 50,000 years for it to cool to its present temperature—although he refused to offer this as an actual *theory,* since he didn't feel he had the experimental proof to back it up. His colleague and sometimes competitor, the German mathematician Gottfried Wilhelm von Leibniz, offered a similar speculation—that the earth had once been liquified, like metal, and had cooled and hardened over time. This had produced large bubbles; some of them calcified into mountains, others shattered and disintegrated, producing valleys.[24]

Questions about the age of the earth and its past history became suddenly more fraught in 1701, when the the Bishop of Winchester, William Lloyd, inserted a creation date of 4004 B.C. to the marginal notes of the newest version of the 1611 Authorized Version of the Bible. This date had first been proposed by the Irish bishop and astronomer James Ussher a half century before; Ussher had combined the study of biblical chronology with his own astronomical observations, and had concluded that the earth could not be more than six thousand years old.

The Authorized Version of the Bible was the most widely read and influential English translation in print. From this point on, proposing an age of more than six thousand years for the earth would carry with it the slur of denying Scripture—and not just in English-speaking countries. In

[24]Isaac Newton, *Mathematical Principles of Natural Philosophy*, trans. Andrew Motte (Daniel Adee, 1848), p. 486; G. Brent Dalrymple, *The Age of the Earth* (Stanford, Calif.: Stanford University Press, 1991), pp. 28–29.

1749, the French naturalist George-Louis Leclerc (usually known by his title, the Comte de Buffon) estimated the age of the earth at 74,832 years, and privately thought that an even longer time frame was probable—perhaps as long as three billion years (not so far off from the contemporary estimate of 4.57 billion). His theories drew the attention of the Faculty of Theology in Paris, which carried on a long and suspicious correspondence with him over his understanding of Genesis. But Buffon dug in his heels, refusing to yield the point.[25]

He was not alone in his insistence. Despite theological opposition, a growing cadre of scientists was coming to the conclusion that the scientific method and Newton's Rules, exercised together, yielded a long, long history for the earth. In 1785's *Theory of the Earth,* the Scottish-born James Hutton argued that the continents had been formed, over vast amounts of time, by the exact same cycles of erosion and buildup, ebb and flow, that still operate today. And the measurement of those present processes suggested that change happened *very, very slowly.*

So slowly, in fact, that Hutton could not wrap his head around the amount of time needed. "[T]he production of our present continents must have required a time which is indefinite," he wrote. ". . . The result, therefore, of this physical inquiry, is that we find no vestige of a beginning, no prospect of an end." Geological time—what John McPhee would later label "deep time"—was so different from the time of human experience that Hutton could barely even use the measure of years to express it.[26]

In 1809, the French zoologist Jean-Baptiste de Monet—better known as the Chevalier de Lamarck—suggested that the living creatures on the earth's surface had a history almost as long. Before Lamarck, most natural historians had treated animals and plants as coming late to the surface of the globe, arriving more or less already in their present forms. But Lamarck's *Zoological Philosophy* married the history of life to the history of the globe: As it altered, so did the creatures on its surface. "With regard to living bodies . . . nature has done everything little by little," he wrote. "[S]he acts everywhere slowly and by successive stages."[27]

[25]Dalrymple, *The Age of the Earth,* pp. 29–30; Jacques Roger, *Buffon: A Life in Natural History,* trans. Sarah Lucille Bonnefoi (Ithaca: Cornell University Press, 1997), pp. 187–193.
[26]Dennis R. Dean, *James Hutton and the History of Geology* (Ithaca: Cornell University Press, 1992), pp. 17, 24–25; James Hutton, "Theory of the Earth," in *Transactions of the Royal Society of Edinburgh,* Vol. I (J. Dickson, 1788), pp. 301, 304.
[27]M. J. S. Hodge, "Lamarck's Science of Living Bodies," in *The British Journal for the History of Science* 5:4 (December 1971), p. 325; Martin Rudwick, *Bursting the Limits of Time: The Reconstruction of Geohistory in the Age of Revolution* (Chicago: University of Chicago

Unfortunately, Lamarck couldn't really come up with a defensible theory as to *how* living creatures altered. The best he could do was to offer
a "principle of use and disuse," which suggested that when the environment changed, living creatures found themselves using some organs more
(leading to greater "vigour and size" in those parts) and other organs less
(causing them to "deteriorate and ultimately disappear"). This was impossible to demonstrate experimentally and the principle was widely scorned
by other scientists: "Something that might amuse the imagination of a
poet," sniffed Lamarck's contemporary, the naturalist Georges Cuvier.[28]

But despite Lamarck's shortcomings, he and his predecessors had managed to establish a firm working principle: Both the earth, and the living
creatures who occupied it, had an unimaginably long history. It was a
principle that gave birth to the foundational works of modern biology and
geology.

The first among these was written by Georges Cuvier himself. In his
twenties, Cuvier had been given the job of organizing and cataloguing
the massive collection of fossil bones piled haphazardly in the storage
rooms of Paris's National Museum of Natural History. It seemed clear to
Cuvier that some of these fossil skeletons—particular two that he labeled
as "mammoth" and "mastodon"—were not simply variations on present-
day animals; they were something else, species that no longer existed.

Eventually, Cuvier identified, in the museum stockpiles, twenty-three
species that appeared to be extinct. Trying to figure out why they had
disappeared, Cuvier turned to the rock layers in which the fossils had
been found. He and his colleague, the mineralogist Alexandre Brongni-
art, identified six distinct layers in the rock strata around Paris: six different eras in the earth's past, each with its own population of plants and
animals, some now extinct. Before long, Cuvier extrapolated these discoveries into an earth-wide theory. In 1812, he published this theory as
the preface, or "Preliminary Discourse," to his collected papers on fossils
(*Recherches sur Les Ossemenes Fossiles de Quadrupeds*, an assembly of all of
the different studies he had presented and published since 1804).

The earth, Cuvier argued, had undergone six separate catastrophic
changes. Its layers changed suddenly and distinctly, not gradually and by
degrees; therefore, it seemed clear that a series of nearly worldwide disasters had wiped out various populations of flora and fauna. "Thus, life

---

Press, 2005), p. 390; J. B. Lamarck, *Zoological Philosophy,* trans. Hugh Elliot (London:
Macmillan & Co., 1914), pp. 12, 41, 46.
[28]Robert J. Richards, *Darwin and the Emergence of Evolutionary Theories of Mind and Behavior* (Chicago: University of Chicago Press, 1987), p. 63.

on earth has often been disturbed by terrible events," Cuvier concluded. "These great and terrible events are clearly imprinted everywhere, for the eye that knows how to read."[29]

For a time, Cuvier's catastrophism was the most widely accepted model for the past—until the geologist Charles Lyell proposed a different version of the past.

Catastrophe, Lyell argued, wasn't *necessarily* the cause of past phenemona. "It appears premature," he wrote in the London journal *Quarterly Review,* "to assume that existing agents could not, in the lapse of ages, produce such effects." Extraordinary, earth-wrecking disasters *could* have produced the specimens in Cuvier's collections. But it was equally possible that the "existing agents" still at work in the world—plain old erosion, the common rise and fall of temperatures, the regular wash of the tides— might be responsible instead.[30]

Which was Lyell's distinct preference. He was convinced that catastrophism was a dead end for science. If one-time past events were responsible for the current form of the earth, there was no way that the past could be understood through the exercise of reason. The natural philosopher could always haul in a disastrous flood, or a passing giant comet, or some other event that could never be experimentally reproduced, to explain the planet.

Instead, Lyell argued, every force that has operated in the past can be observed, still acting, with the same intensity, in the present: a principle now known as *uniformitarianism.* The title of his 1830 natural history made this commitment perfectly clear: *Principles of Geology, Being an Attempt to Explain the Former Changes of the Earth's Surface, by Reference to Causes Now in Operation.*

Uniformitarianism made catastrophes unfashionable, global floods and divine intervention unnecessary. Uniformitarianism also made the unimaginably long time frame first proposed by Hutton completely necessary. "Existing agents" such as tides and erosion could have shaped the world into its present form, but it would take them a really, really long time.

The year after the *Principles of Geology* was published, a young Charles Darwin put it into his luggage before setting off on the HMS *Beagle* for what would become a five-year journey of exploration: from Plymouth Sound to the South American coast, then to the Galápagos Islands, Tahiti,

---

[29]Martin Rudwick, *Georges Cuvier, Fossil Bones, and Geological Catastrophes* (Chicago: University of Chicago Press, 1997), p. 190.
[30]Charles Lyell, *Principles of Geology* (New York: Penguin, 1998), p. 6.

and Australia, circling the globe before returning home. "[Lyell's] book was of the highest service to me in many ways," he later wrote. He was struggling with the problem of *species* (where did they come from? what accounted for the differences between them?) and he found Lyell's long-and-slow philosophy of change entirely convincing. "Natura non facit saltum," Darwin concluded: *Nature does not make sudden jumps.* Whatever mechanism had produced the difference between species, it had taken a very long time to work.

He also read Lamarck, but disagreed vigorously with the principle of use and disuse. "It is absurd!" he scribbled in the margin of the *Zoological Philosophy*. Instead, Darwin found the key to the species question in Thomas Malthus's bestselling *An Essay on the Principle of Population*, which had been first published in 1798. The future of the human race, Malthus argued, was shaped by two factors: Humanity has an innate drive to reproduce, which means that the population constantly increases. But because the food supply does not increase as rapidly as the population, a large percentage of those born will always die of starvation.

"It at once struck me," Darwin later wrote, "that under these circumstances favourable variations would tend to be preserved and unfavorable ones to be destroyed. The result of this would be the formation of new species." He had found, he believed, the key to the species problem; but he drafted and redrafted his thoughts for over a decade before finally publishing *On the Origin of Species by Means of Natural Selection, or the Preservation of Favoured Races in the Struggle for Life* in 1859.[31]

The book laid out a series of arguments in support of Darwin's main conclusion: Life, like the earth itself, is changing constantly, and natural causes *alone* account for that change. And different species of animals have not always existed; new species appear when *previous* species develop variations, and those variations prove helpful in the fight for survival. In 1864, the well-known biologist and philosopher Herbert Spencer used the phrase "survival of the fittest" to described Darwin's theory; although it never appears in *The Origin of Species* itself, the phrase soon became inextricably entwined with Darwin's own work.

A major stumbling block remained. Although Charles Darwin was quite sure that variations were passed from parent to child, he had no idea how this worked.

"The laws governing inheritance are quite unknown," he lamented, in the second chapter of *The Origin of Species*. "No one can say why a pecu-

---

[31]Charles Darwin, *Charles Darwin: His Life Told in an Autobiographical Chapter* (London: John Murray, 1908), p. 82.

liarity . . . is sometimes inherited and sometimes not so." Nine years after *Origin of Species* was first published, he suggested that inheritance could be explained through the existence of "minute particles" called *gemmules,* which are thrown off by every part of an organism, accumulate in the sex organs, and are then passed on to offspring. The strongest argument for this theory was simply that he couldn't think of anything better. "It is a very rash and crude hypothesis," he wrote to his friend T. H. Huxley, "yet it has been a considerable relief to my mind, and I can hang on it a good many groups of facts."[32]

He never came up with a better explanation, although the key to the truth was literally under his own roof.

At Darwin's death in 1882, his library contained unopened copies of a short paper in German by the Austrian botanist (and Augustinian friar) Gregor Mendel, describing Mendel's nine-year experiments with sweet peas. Interbreeding thirty-four different varieties, Mendel had discovered a series of laws that seemed to govern how their characteristics (shape and color of the seeds and pods, position of flowers, length of stem) were passed on.

Clearly, the characteristics were carried from parent pea to offspring pea by the egg and pollen cells, so (Mendel proposed) those cells must contain discrete units, or *elements,* with each element carrying a particular characteristic within it. The proper manipulation of those elements could change the characteristics of the next generation—and, Mendel speculated, might be able to eventually mutate one species into another.[33]

Mendel wasn't able to identify exactly what the elements of heredity were, or *where* in the cell they might be. But a series of biological experiments to pinpoint them was already underway.

The German biologist Ernst Haeckel, a generation younger than Darwin (and originator of the catchy phrase "ontogeny recapitulates phylogony")[34] proposed that inheritance might be controlled by something in the nucleus of a cell. He didn't have the equipment to prove it, but in the early 1880s, Haeckel's countryman Walther Flemming made use

---

[32]Charles Darwin, *The Variation of Animals and Plants Under Domestication,* Vol. II (New York: D. Appleton & Co., 1897), p. 371; P. Kyle Stanford, *Exceeding Our Grasp: Science, History, and the Problem of Unconceived Alternatives* (New York: Oxford University Press, 2006), p. 65; Darwin, *The Origin of Species,* p. 13.

[33]Gregor Mendel, *Experiments in Plant Hybridisation* (New York: Cosimo Classics, 2008), pp. 15, 21ff., 47.

[34]The development of a living creature, from egg/embryo to adult ("ontogony") goes through the same series of steps as the evolution of a living creature from a primitive to a modern state (phylogeny). The theory was wildly popular in the late nineteenth and early twentieth centuries, but now has been thoroughly discarded by biologists.

of much-improved microscopic lenses and better staining techniques to observe minuscule, thread-like structures in cells that had begun to divide (mitosis). His colleague Wilhelm Waldeyer suggested that these should be named *chromosomes,* a name which simply described their ability to soak up dye (*chrom,* color; *soma,* body).

In 1902, the German biologist Theodore Boveri discovered that sea urchin embryos need exactly 36 chromosomes to develop normally—which strongly suggested that each chromosome carried a unique and necessary piece of information from parent to child. Simultaneously, an American graduate student named Walter Sutton realized from his experiments with grasshoppers that chromosomes carry the "physical basis of a certain definite set of qualities." The Danish botanist Wilhelm Johannsen gave this unit of heredity, the carrier of information from one generation to the next, its name: the *gene.* This was Darwin's missing puzzle piece, the mechanism that transformed organic life from one form into another.[35]

A decade and a half later, a German astronomer named Alfred Wegener stumbled across the other major missing mechanism: the one that had transformed the inorganic surface of the globe.

"Anyone who compares, on a globe, the opposite coasts of South America and Africa," Wegener wrote, in his 1915 book *The Origin of Continents and Oceans,* "cannot fail to be struck by the similar configuration of the two coast lines." The jigsaw match suggested to him that the continents had once been a single mass, a giant supercontinent that he labeled Pangea; long, long ago, Pangea had broken up and drifted apart. This required him to provide an explanation for how solid earth could "drift." So he proposed that the earth was not actually solid. Instead, it consisted of a liquid core, surrounded by a series of shells that increased in density as they got closer to the surface.[36]

It was a simple, elegant explanation, and accounted for almost all the factors that puzzled geologists: odd similarities between fossils found in far distant places, the apparent interlocking fit of the continental coastlines, the origin of mountains (which, according to Wegener, sprang up where the drifting pieces collided and overlapped). The problem was the absolute absence of any physical evidence. Wegener could not demonstrate the existence of a liquid core; nor could he supply a reason why Pangea didn't simply remain in one supercontinent.

[35]J. A. Moore, *Heredity and Development,* 2nd ed. (New York: Oxford University Press, 1972), p. 74.
[36]Alfred Wegener, "The Origin of Continents and Oceans," in *The Living Age,* 8th Series, Vol. XXVI (April, May, June 1922), pp. 657–658.

But Wegener believed that the explanatory power of his theory trumped his lack of explicit proof. He argued that, after all, the earth "supplies no direct information" about any part of its history: "We are like a judge confronted by a defendant who declines to answer," he wrote, "and we must determine the truth from the circumstantial evidence. . . . The theory offers solutions for . . . many apparently insoluble problems."[37]

Thirteen years after the original publication of *The Origin of Continents and Oceans,* the naval astronomers F. B. Littell and J. C. Hammond compared the longitudes of Washington and Paris in 1913 and in 1927. Their readings revealed that the distance between the two cities had increased by 4.35 meters—a creep of .32 meters per year.

Given that Paris is some six thousand kilometers from Washington, it would have taken over 18 million years for the two cities to move that far apart. But the drift was measurable, beyond a doubt. The continents were indeed drifting—and had been doing so for a very long time. They, like the living creatures on them, had a history; and the basic time line of that history had now been put into place for both.

The Physicists

While historians of life were working out a narrative for the past, physicists were puzzling out the present—and discovering that time, space, and matter itself were not nearly as straightforward as Newton, Bacon, and their heirs had once thought.

Ten years before the publication of *The Origin of Continents and Oceans,* the patent examiner and physicist Albert Einsten had completed five papers in a single year, all dealing with problems in electricity, magnetism, and related issues of space, time, and motion. One of the papers proposed that the conversion of energy into mass could be expressed as

$$E = mc^2$$

which became the most familiar formula of the twentieth century.

But Einstein thought another of the papers, "On the Electrodynamics of Moving Bodies," even more important. It was, he told a friend, an out-and-out "modification of the theory of space and time": his first exploration of what would later be known as the *special theory of relativity.*

The paper set out to reconcile two apparently contradictory principles

---

[37]Alfred Wegener, *The Origins of Continents and Oceans,* trans. John Biram (New York: Dover Publications, 1966), p. viii.

of physics. The first concerned the speed of light. Since the early 1880s, physicists had agreed that light traveling through a vacuum always has the exact same velocity ("c = 300000 km/sec.").

The second was the *principle of relativity,* a cornerstone of the Newtonian universe, which decrees that a law of physics must work in the same way across all related frames of reference.

Imagine, Einstein later wrote, that a railway car is traveling along next to an embankment at a regular rate of speed. At the same time, a raven is flying through the air, also in a straight line relative to the embankment, and also at a steady rate of speed. An observer standing on the embankment sees the raven flying at a certain rate of speed. An observer standing on the moving railway car sees the raven flying at a *different* rate of speed. But although the speed changes, relative to the observer, both watchers *still* see the raven flying at a constant rate of speed, and in a straight line. The principle of relativity dictates that the raven cannot suddenly appear to be accelerating, or traveling in zigzags.

Now, imagine that a vacuum exists above the railway tracks, and that a ray of light travels above it, in the same direction as the raven. The principle of relativity says that light too will travel at a constant rate, and in a straight line. But it *also* implies that an observer on the embankment and an observer on the railway car will see the light traveling *at two different speeds*—which means that the speed of light is *not* constant.

Most physicists dealt with this problem by abandoning the principle of relativity. But Einstein argued that *neither* law needed to be given up—as long as we are willing to adjust our ideas about time and space.[38]

Both observers measure the speed of light per second; perhaps, Einstein

[38] Albert Einstein, *Relativity: The Special and General Theory,* trans. Robert W. Lawson (New York: Pi Press, 2005), pp. 25, 28; Galison et al., p. 223; Jay M. Pasachoff and Alex Filippenko, *The Cosmos: Astronomy in the New Millennium,* 4th ed. (New York: Cambridge University Press, 2014), pp. 239–240, 271–272.

suggested, what was changing was not the speed per second, but the *second itself.* Time itself was slowing down as the observer moved faster. For the observer who was moving, a second was actually . . . *longer.* Time was not, as had always been thought, a constant.

Instead, Einstein concluded, time was a fourth dimension that we move through—a dimension that changes as we travel in it. The "special theory of relativity" had redefined the nature of time.

In 1916, Einstein redefined space as well.

Building on the work of the nineteenth-century mathematician Bernhard Riemann, Einstein proposed that space is just as relative to the observer as time (the "general theory of relativity"). The presence of massive objects, Einsten argued, actually *bends* space. Since we (the observers) are *within* space, we cannot see the curves—but objects traveling *through* space are affected by the bends.

This theory could be checked against effects caused by the sun, the most massive object nearby. If Einstein was correct, light from stars, traveling through space, would move along curved space as it neared the sun. The starlight would then appear to be "pulled" toward the mass of the sun; starlight would be, observably, bent by the sun's mass.

This could only be observed during a total solar eclipse, and it was another three years before the British astronomer Arthur Eddington was able to take the necessary measurements. His calculations, made during a solar eclipse in 1919, showed that the starlight passing by the sun had shifted, to the exact degree that Einstein had foreseen.

In *Relativity: The Special and General Theory,* Einstein laid out his conclusions about time and space for general readers. Neither, it turned out, was what it seemed. Baconian observation had its limits; common sense can lead the observer astray.

Meanwhile, a small handful of Einstein's colleagues were doing equally revolutionary work on a much smaller scale: on the atom itself. By the end of the nineteenth century, physicists had come to believe that atoms— Lucretius's "indivisible" particles—were, in fact, made up of smaller particles carrying a negative electrical charge; these were labeled *electrons* by the Irish physicists George Stoney and George Fitzgerald. Early in the twentieth century, the young German physicist Hans Geiger and his elder colleague Ernest Rutherford theorized that these electrons were orbiting a central mass, a "nucleus." It was an elegant, intuitive model; electrons spun around the nucleus like planets around the sun, the smallest particles in the universe mirroring the heavens.[39]

[39]Ernest Rutherford, *The Collected Papers of Lord Rutherford of Nelson,* Vol. 2 (New York: Interscience Publishers, 1963), p. 212.

But the orbits of those electrons posed a problem.

The "Rutherford model" imagined electrons to be something like satellites circling the earth. If a satellite orbiting the earth lost some of its energy, it would spiral down and crash. But when an atom emitted energy (as, for example, hydrogen atoms did, giving off light particles that some physicists had labeled *photons*), it remained stable. The orbits of the electrons did not seem to decay.

In 1913, the Danish physicist Niels Bohr proposed a solution. Electrons, he suggested, don't orbit in continuous smooth circles, like planets or satellites. Instead, they *jump* from discrete spot to discrete spot. When a hydrogen atom emits a photon, the electron loses energy, but it doesn't spiral down; it "leaps" to a lower orbital path, one which is stable but takes less energy to maintain.

These jumps were known as *quantum jumps*. A few years earlier, the physicist Max Planck had discovered that he could only predict the behavior of certain kinds of radiation if he treated energy, not as a wave (radiating out smoothly and evenly, as was the accepted model) but as a series of chunks: separate particles, pulsing out at intervals. Planck called these hypothetical energy particles "quanta," and he wasn't happy with them. They were, he told a friend, a "formal assumption," a mathematical hat trick, a way of "saving the phenomenon." "What I did can be described as simply an act of desperation," he explained. "It was clear to me that classical physics could offer no solution to this problem . . . [so] I was ready to sacrifice every one of my previous convictions about physical laws."[40]

But then Einstein himself found that treating light as if it were made up of quanta, rather than waves, helped explain some previously perplexing properties. And now, Bohr had solved an atomic-level problem by proposing that an electron's path was quantized. Quantum theory, announced Max Planck in his Nobel Prize Address of 1922—a clear and interesting summary of the field's development—had the potential "to transform completely our physical concepts" of the universe.[41]

Yet its implications became increasingly odder. For example: in the new "Bohr–Rutherford model" of the atom, an electron performed a "quantum leap" between orbits, rather than gliding smoothly through

---

[40]Bruce Rosenblum and Fred Kuttner, *Quantum Enigma: Physics Encounters Consciousness,* 2nd ed. (New York: Oxford University Press, 2011), pp. 59–60; M. S. Longair, *Theoretical Concepts in Physics: An Alternative View of Theoretical Reasoning in Physics,* 2nd ed. (New York: Cambridge University Press, 2003), p. 339.

[41]Max Planck, *The Origin and Development of the Quantum Theory,* trans. H. T. Clarke and L. Silberstein (New York: Clarendon Press, 1922), p. 12.

consecutive space. This implied that, while *making* the leap, the electron was . . . nowhere.

It was also impossible to predict, with certainty, where the electron would reappear at the end of its jump. The best physicists could do was predict its *probable* place of reappearance. The theoretical physicist Werner Heisenberg, who worked extensively on this problem, pointed out (reasonably enough) that the uncertainty is *infinitesimal* once physics moves into the realm of objects larger than a molecule; an electron orbiting the nucleus of a hydrogen atom might make an unexpected leap, but a goat grazing on a hillside isn't going anywhere unpredictable at all.

But other scientists found it maddening to be pushed into the realm of probabilities, rather than measurable certainties. "If we are going to have to put up with these damn quantum jumps," the Austrian physicist Erwin Schrödinger complained to Niels Bohr, "I am sorry that I ever had anything to do with quantum theory." Even Einstein, who had a high capacity for startling new ideas, objected that quantum theory was "spookish." ("I cannot seriously believe in it," he wrote to his friend Max Born, not long before Born won the Nobel Prize for his work in quantum mechanics.)[42]

Yet quantum theory continued to solve problems, despite the massive disturbance it had caused in the world of physics.

The Synthesists

Meanwhile, Darwinian evolution had begun to lose its grip on the scientific imagination.

Since Darwin had created the grand narrative of evolution, individual researchers in widely separated fields had been slotting new details into place: the existence of chromosomes, the laws of heredity, the presence of deoxyribonucleic acid (DNA) within the nucleus of cells. Better instruments, more data, and improved research techniques were yielding discoveries thick and fast, many of them (in new fields of study: cytology, biometry, embryonics, genetics) filling in the empty fretwork of Darwin's overarching structure.

But these studies were clogged with technical language, published in narrowly focused professional journals with tiny specialist audiences. There was, in Ernst Mayr's words, "an extraordinary communication gap" between the sciences. Genetics had nothing to do with anthropology, or

---

[42]Quoted. in Franco Selleri, *Quantum Paradoxes and Physical Reality: Fundamental Theories of Physics* (Dordrecht: Kluwer Academic Publishers, 1990), p. 363.

paleontology with biochemistry. Each researcher, viewing his (rarely *her*) own brick in the wall, had lost sight of the the whole building. "The theory of evolution," concluded the director of the National Museum of Natural History in Paris, in 1937, "will very soon be abandoned."[43]

Yet individual discoveries in the life sciences were confirming, again and again, that natural selection *did* explain the present form of organic life. A defense of Darwin was needed: a defense which would connect the highly meaningful dots, explaining the ways in which the grand theory and specific discoveries acted together.

In 1937, the Russian entomologist Theodosius Dobzhansky published the first attempt to do just that: *Genetics and the Origin of Species.* The book was a synthesis of his laboratory experiments in genetics, his field observations on fruit fly inheritance, and his work in the mathematical field of population genetics. In the next decade, a handful of well-regarded biologists followed his lead. George Gaylord Simpson's *Tempo and Mode in Evolution,* Bernhardt Rensch's *Evolution above the Species Level,* and Ersnt Mayr's *Systematics and the Origin of Species, from the Viewpoint of a Zoologist* all made the same argument: Darwinian natural selection *did,* indeed, account for the existence of species.

In 1942, yet another work on the topic appeared: *Evolution: The Modern Synthesis,* by the English biologist Julian Huxley (grandson, as it happened, of one of Darwin's most ardent contemporary supporters, Thomas Huxley). Julian Huxley was not only a well-regarded biologist, but a skilled popular writer; a decade before, he had collaborated with the novelist H. G. Wells on a best-selling popular history of biology.

Evolution: The Modern Synthesis was a sprawling, multifaceted book. It covered, in turn, paleontology, genetics, geographical differentiation, ecology, taxonomy, and adaptation—but clearly, readably, without jargon. It was an instant success: "The outstanding evolutionary treatise of the decade, perhaps of the century," exclaimed one of the most important journals of the field. From 1942 on, the ongoing attempt to connect specialized laboratory discoveries with the larger world of natural history, all in support of the Darwinian scheme, would take its name from Huxley's book: the modern synthesis.[44]

Two years later, Erwin Schrödinger—still struggling with those damn quantum jumps—published another kind of synthesis. *What Is Life?*

[43]Ernst Mayr and William B. Provine, *The Evolutionary Synthesis: Perspectives on the Unification of Biology* (Cambridge: Harvard University Press, 1998), pp. 8, 282, 315, 316.
[44]Julian Huxley, *Evolution: The Modern Synthesis: The Definitive Edition* (Cambridge: MIT Press, 2010), pp. 3, 6–7.

dealt with the overlap between quantum physics and biology, the common ground between the study of ourselves and the study of the cosmos. Using quantum theory to account for the behavior of orbiting electrons, Schrödinger showed how this behavior affected the formation of chemical bonds, and how those chemical bonds then affected cell behavior, genetics, evolutionary biology itself.

The success of *What Is Life?* as a synthesis can be measured by the number of physicists who were inspired, after reading it, to migrate over into biological research. "No doubt molecular biology would have developed without *What Is Life?*" writes Schrödinger's biographer, Walter Moore, "but it would have been at a slower pace, and without some of its brightest stars. There is no other instance in the history of science in which a short semipopular book catalyzed the future development of a great field of research."[45]

Semipopular: the word is a signpost, pointing out a shift in scientific writing.

What Is Life? was, first and foremost, written for other scientists. A biologist had once been able to glance over an entire kingdom. Now, it was a full-time job to keep up with discoveries in a single subspecies: epigenetics, population genetics, genomics, phytochemistry, phylogenetics, and many more. The study of physics—the behavior of the universe—had increasingly focused itself on smaller and smaller segements of the cosmos, each requiring more and more specialized instrumentation: optics, photonics, particle physics, radio astronomy, quantum chemistry. New theories were written up for academic journals with very narrow audiences. The articles made use of technical vocabulary and arcane mathematical notation, inaccessible to nonspecialists—and even more so to the general public.

As discoveries multiplied, audiences shrank. Yet translating those discoveries for the wider reading public—the interested, intelligent layperson—turned out to be a fraught activity.

The Popularizers

A faint line had been already traced between professional and popular science writing.

In 1894, Julian Huxley's grandfather had complained about the unwillingness of scientists to write plainly for the lay reader, for fear of lowering their prestige in their own fields: "[They] keep their fame as scientific

---

[45] Walter J. Moore, *Schrödinger: Life and Thought* (New York: Cambridge University Press, 1992), p. 404.

hierophants," T. H. Huxley grumbled, "unsullied by attempts—at least of the successful sort—to be understood of the people." As the twentieth century wore on, the line between popularizers and academic scientists darkened. Best-selling books on science were widely scorned by professional researchers, and to be labeled a "mere popularizer" was death to an academic career.[46]

Simultaneously, the public thirst for science was growing greater and greater. The first daily science feature to run in a newspaper ("What's What with Science," by journalist Watson Davis) appeared in the *Washington Herald* in the 1920s; in the 1930s, the National Association of Science Writers (journalists, not professors) took shape. The end of World War II whetted interest in atomic science, and the startling launch of *Sputnik* by the Soviet Union in 1957 sparked a general demand for information about space.

Yet scientists were slow to feed this public appetite. "For better or worse, whether scientists like it or not," mourned the *Bulletin of the Atomic Scientists* in 1963, "the public today gets its image of science, its information about science, and its understanding of scientific concepts largely from these nonscientists, the science writers." Why not join the ranks of science writers themselves? Because most scientists believed themselves to be objective, unbiased, clearsighted hunters of truth. The "science writer," on the other hand, "works in the world of journalism and is subject to its pressures, its traditions and conventions, and its biases."[47]

Given this deepening hostility toward "popular" science, it is hardly surprising that the next influential science book to hit the shelves was written by a (female) outsider: Rachel Carson, a talented biologist who ran out of money after completing her M.A. in 1932, and was never able to complete her Ph.D. or gain an academic position. Instead, she wrote about science: first, for the *Baltimore Sun,* and then for the U.S. Fish and Wildlife Service. Her second book, 1951's *The Sea Around Us,* was a best seller and National Book Award winner. But sales of her third book, *Silent Spring,* left it in the dust.

"There are very few books that can be said to have changed the course of history," writes Carson's biographer, Linda Lear, "but this was one of them." *Silent Spring* began with a dreadful warning: "For the first time in

[46]Peter J. Bowler, *Science for All: The Popularization of Science in Early Twentieth-Century Britain* (Chicago: University of Chicago Press, 2009), pp. 5–6; William Jay Youmans, ed., *Popular Science Monthly* XLVI (New York: D. Appleton & Co., November 1894–April 1895), p. 127.
[47]Pierre C. Fraley and Earl Ubell, "Science Writing: A Growing Profession," *Bulletin of the Atomic Scientists* (December 1963), pp. 19–20.

the history of the world, every human being is now subjected to contact with dangerous chemicals, from the moment of conception until death." The book went on to attack Western governments, the chemical industry, and the farming industry for the indiscriminate use of pesticides.

Silent Spring was not only a massive work of synthesis (between chemistry and biology, laboratory science and public policy, academic research and citizen activism, the study of man and the study of man's entire world) but popular science at its best: well-informed and dramatic, a gripping blend of statistic and story, affecting *every human being*. Carson had demonstrated just how powerful popular science could be; and in the next two decades, an unprecedented raft of academic scientists defected to the popular fold.[48]

Life scientists led the pack. In 1967, the zoologist Desmond Morris teased out the full implications of Darwinian evolution for human behavior in *The Naked Ape,* an interpretation of man's cultural behavior through the lens of biology: one of the first works of sociobiology. The following year, James Watson published an account of his work with Francis Crick on DNA. That odd little substance in the nucleus of the cell had been identified as the carrier of genetic information from one generation to the next, and in 1953, Crick and Watson together had proposed a double helix structure for DNA that made sense of the mechanism. Their model, which would not actually be observed for some decades, was chemically sound, tested worldwide, and soon accepted by biologists everywhere. Watson's 1968 bestseller, *The Double Helix: A Personal Account of the Discovery of the Structure of DNA,* mixed science with memoir, and made DNA a household word.

In 1976, Oxford biologist Richard Dawkins took the story of DNA further in *The Selfish Gene,* which offered a comprehensive explanation for all organic life, including ours. "Intelligent life on a planet comes of age when it first works out the reason for its own existence," Dawkins begins, and the reason he has worked out is a simple one: we eat, sleep, have sex, think, write, build space vehicles and war machines, sacrifice ourselves or others, all in order to preserve our DNA. Natural selection happens at the most basic level, the molecular; our bodies have evolved to do nothing more than protect and propagate our genes, which are ruthlessly selfish molecules working to ensure their own survival.[49]

This was not a comforting view of human nature, but popular science

[48]Rachel Carson, *Silent Spring,* anniversary edition (Boston: Houghton Mifflin, 2002), pp. xii–xiv, 15; Linda J. Lear, "Rachel Carson's 'Silent Spring,'" in *Environmental History Review* 17:2 (Summer, 1993), p. 28.

[49]Richard Dawkins, *The Selfish Gene* (New York: Oxford University Press, 1976), p. 1.

was proving a perfect vehicle for scientists to make the sort of sweeping conclusions (about human existence, all of culture, the cosmos itself) that scientific papers and journal articles rarely contained.

In 1977, Steven Weinberg's smash hit, *The First Three Minutes* leapt directly from physics to metaphysics. Weinberg explained the so-called "Big Bang," the expansion of the entire universe from an original super-dense point known as a singularity—and then went further:

> It is almost irresistable for humans to believe that we have some special relation to the universe . . . that human life is not just a more-or-less farcical outcome of a chain of accidents reaching back to the first three minutes. . . . The more the universe seems comprehensible, the more it also seems pointless.

That conclusion (one that certainly reaches beyond the Baconian project) leads him to an even broader statement about the purpose of human existence. "If there is no solace in the fruits of our research," Weinberg concludes, at the very end of the book, "there is at least some consolation in the research itself. . . . The effort to understand the universe is one of the very few things that lifts human life a little above the level of farce, and gives it some of the grace of tragedy."[50]

Popular science was itself evolving. It was more than information, more than entertainment, more than a call to activism. It offered scientists a chance to make broader conclusions about human life: to explain not just *what,* but *who* and *why* we are.

In some ways, popular science *did* succumb to the "traditions and conventions" of the marketplace, as the *Bulletin of the Atomic Scientists* had gloomily foretold. Scientists were forced to write in ways that would grab, and keep, their readers; witness the fairy-tale opening of *Silent Spring* ("Some evil spell had settled on the community . . . Everywhere was the a shadow of death"), the vivid analogies of *The First Three Minutes* ("If some ill-advised giant were to wiggle the sun back and forth, we on earth would not feel the effect for eight minutes, the time required for a wave to travel at the speed of light from the sun to the earth"), and the epic first chapter of Walter Alvarez's *T. rex and the Crater of Doom,* which is titled "Armageddon" and begins with an epigraph from the *Lord of the Rings.*

The hostility between popular and academic science grew more nuanced and complex, but didn't go away. "Popularization," concluded a

---

[50]Steven Weinberg, *The First Three Minutes: A Modern View of the Origin of the Universe,* 2nd ed. (New York: Basic Books, 1993), p. 153.

1985 study of the relationship, "is traditionally seen as a low-status activity
. . . something external to research which can be left to non-scientists,
failed scientists, or ex-scientists." Among scientists, the Oprah Effect
became known as the Sagan Effect, "whereby one's popularity and celeb-
rity with the general public were thought to be inversely proportional to
the quantity and quality of real science being done."[51]

Science writing, increasingly, traveled down two different paths: one
broad and well-trodden, the other narrow and high-walled. New discoveries and groundbreaking theories were first floated to the scientific
world in journals, articles, and conference talks, and slowly disseminated
through the scientific world. Only then did they take book form and enter
the general consciousness. James Gleick's best-selling *Chaos: Making a New
Science* came out in 1987, twelve years after the mathematicians Tien-Yien
Li and James A. Yorke used the term *chaos theory* in their technical paper
about nonlinear equations, and twenty-four years after Edward Lorenz
had first described the phenomenon. And Stephen Hawking's cosmology
overview *A Brief History of Time,* published in 1988, sold over 10 million
copies—but contained nothing revolutionary at all.

T. rex and the Crater of Doom, Walter Alvarez's widely read account of his
detective work in finding tracks of the asteroid that (theoretically) wiped
out the dinosaurs, came out in 1997, seventeen years after Alvarez and his
colleagues first published their theory as an academic paper ("Extraterrestrial Cause for the Cretaceous-Tertiary Extinction"). Alvarez's dramatic
scenarios ("Doom was coming out of the sky . . . Entire forests were
ignited, and continent-sized wildfires swept across the lands . . . [A] wall
of water . . . towered above the shorelines") were immediately incorporated into the movies *Deep Impact* and *Armageddon,* sparking an entire sub-
genre of films about the end of the earth—and also gave rise to academic
conferences (such as 2009's "Near-Earth Objects: Risks, Responses and
Opportunities," hosted by the University of Nebraska–Lincoln) and at
least one multinational committee tasked with "establishing global frame-
works to respond to NEO threats." Popular science writing had not only
grasped the public imagination; it had altered public policy—and even
turned back to shape the academy.[52]

[51] Carson, *Silent Spring,* p. 2; Weinberg, *The First Three Minutes,* p. 8; Michael B. Shermer,
"This View of Science: Stephen Jay Gould as Historian of Science and Scientific Historian, Popular Scientist and Scientific Popularizer," in *Social Studies of Science* 32:4 (August
2002), pp. 490, 494.
[52] "Apollo 9 astronaut to kick off conference on 'Near-Earth Object' risks." Released
April 9, 2009, by UN-L. Accessed September 29, 2014, at http://newsroom.unl.edu/

HOW TO READ SCIENCE

All of the books on the annotated list can be read by nonspecialists, but be prepared to take some time. As you'll see from the steps listed below, science should be approached with a slightly different attitude than the other books we've discussed. Your first read-through is where the really hard work happens; understanding the context and content of the text is the greatest challenge (which is why this chapter has a much longer "history of" section, and much shorter "how to read" assignments). Don't rush the first read-through, and make use of any reference works or guides necessary.

Keep your purpose in mind, though. You aren't trying to master physics, or genetics, or biochemistry. You are attempting to learn something about the development of human understanding, the ways in which we have used our reason and our senses to comprehend the world. As Mortimer Adler wrote, over forty years ago, "As a layman, you do not read the classical scientific books to become knowledgeable in their subject matters in a contemporary sense. Instead, you read them to understand the history and philosophy of science." That task is well within the ability of any serious reader—even if you don't remember anything about your college survey course in cosmology.[53]

The First Level of Inquiry: Grammar-Stage Reading

Read a synopsis.   Before this point, you've always started with the book itself. But when you're reading science—particularly the pre–twentieth century works—your chances of understanding the book on your first read-through will be much improved if you have some idea of what it's about before you crack it open. Unlike history, which is about human *experience* (something you have firsthand knowledge of), science is about a *construct*: an interrelated set of ideas and theories that you might not be at all familiar with. Reading a summary of Aristotle's *Physics* or the *Commentariolus* of Copernicus will introduce you to the construct and give you some sense of the book's structure.

---

releases/2009/04/09/Apollo+9+astronaut+to+kick+off+conference+on+'Near-Earth+Object'+risks.

[53] Mortimer J. Adler and Charles Van Doren, *How to Read a Book: The Classic Guide to Intelligent Reading* (New York: Simon & Schuster, 1972), p. 251.

If the book contains an introduction written by an expert in the field, that introduction probably contains a brief summary of the book's content. If the book itself doesn't contain a synopsis, look online. Searching for "aristotle physics synopsis," for example, brings up summaries at Sparknotes and the Stanford Encyclopedia of Philosophy (both reliable sources), as well as multiple summaries written by university instructors and posted on course websites. A search for "stephen hawking brief history of time summary" brings up several reviews from reputable papers that include a survey of the book's content, as well as a number of reader-generated guides and a Wikipedia entry. These are perfectly acceptable—you're going to read the book yourself, after all, so you'll discover any inaccuracies as you go. Your goal with this step is simply to put yourself into the same frame as the book: to acquaint yourself with the context in which the author was writing, the primary arguments made, and any concepts central to the book's development.

Look at the title, cover, and table of contents.   As you did with your histories, note down the title, the author's name, and the original publication date. Read through the table of contents to get a sense of the topics the author will cover.

Define the audience and its relationship to the author.   Who is the author, and for whom is he or she writing? A scientist writing primarily for other scientists, as Julian Huxley did? A scientist writing for laypeople? A nonscientist digesting technical information for other nonscientists? The cover copy, back cover summary, and introduction, preface, or foreword of the book can point you toward the answers.

Keep a list of terms and definitions.
Now, start reading.
As you read, look for technical terms and their statements of definition. Write them in your journal for reference.
For example, in the first chapter of Steven Weinberg's *The First Three Minutes,* you will encounter the "electron, the negatively charged particle that flows through wires in electric currents and makes up the outer parts of all atoms and molecules" and the "positron, a positively charged particle with precisely the same mass as the electron." The beginning of James Lovelock's *Gaia* offers, "An aeon represents 1,000 million years," "A supernova is the explosion of a large star."
These are fairly straightforward (and if you already understand a technical term, you don't need to write it down). But a statement of definition can also be a little more complex. On the first page of Galileo's *Dialogue Concern-*

ing the Two Chief World Systems, for example, the character Salvati observes that there are in nature "two substances which differ essentially. These are the celestial and the elemental, the former being invariant and eternal; the latter, temporary and destructible." This is a statement of definition; the terms "celestial" and "elemental" will be important as Galileo's argument develops, so you will want to write these terms in your notebook as

> *two substances in nature*
> *celestial: unvarying and eternal*
> *elemental: temporary and destructible*

If you're having trouble locating the statements of definition, keep a look out for sentences which take the form *noun* [the term being defined], *state of being verb/linking verb,* and then *description* OR *predicate nominative.*

| | | *linking* | *predicate* |
| *noun* | | *verb* | *nominative* |

"The second motion, which is peculiar to the earth, is the daily rotation on the poles . . . from west to east."   (Nicolaus Copernicus, *Commentariolus*)

> *second motion of the earth: daily rotation on poles from west to east*

| | *state of being* | |
| *noun* | *verb* | *definition* |

"The pair-formation stage . . . is characterized by tentative, ambivalent behaviour involving conflicts between fear, aggression and sexual attraction."   (Desmond Morris, *The Naked Ape*)

> *pair-formation stage: tentative ambivalent behavior, conflict of fear, aggression, attraction*

Whenever you run across an italicized or bold word or phrase, be sure to find its definition. In many cases, these have been set off because they come at the *end* of a longer, somewhat complicated paragraph (or paragraphs) of definition. For example, in Chapter Five of *The Origin of Species,* Darwin writes:

> Hence, when an organ, however abnormal it may be, has been transmitted in approximately the same condition to many modified descendants, as in the case of the wing of the bat, it must have existed, according to our theory, for an immense period in nearly the same state; and thus it has come not to be more variable than any other structure. It is only in those cases in

which the modification has been comparatively recent and extraordinarily great that we ought to find the *generative variability,* as it may be called, still present in a high degree.

"Generative variability," it turns out, is the term he has decided to assign to a type of modification that he's been describing over the previous two pages. Looking back, I can paraphrase the (somewhat convoluted) explanation as:

> *generative variability: when very rapid and recent changes in a species means that not all members of the species have a particular variation*

It's absolutely OK to "cheat" in order to find definitions. Science writers do not always provide the clearest possible definitions for their terms, and even after rereading the text I'm not entirely sure that I understand what Darwin means. If I do an online search for "generative variability + Darwin," I mostly end up with reprints of the *Origin of Species* text, but if I search for "generative variability is," I find the following explanation:

> Generative variability is variation manifest in structures that have recently experienced rapid and considerable evolutionary change. Darwin envisions this as a dynamic process. Given enough time—after the structure has reached its maximum extent of development—selection weeds out most of the deviations and the trait ends up fixed. (James T. Costa, *The Annotated Origin,*Harvard University Press, 2009, p. 154)

Any time you can't quite figure out the meaning of a term, use reference tools to sharpen your understanding.

The more unfamiliar terms a book contains, the longer it will take for you to do your first reading. Don't lose heart. For science books, the first reading is the hardest; your second and third levels of inquiry will go much more quickly (and smoothly) if you take the time now to understand exactly what the book is saying.

Mark anything that still confuses you and keep reading.   You will probably find that some pages, sections, or even entire chapters of these books still confuse you. Don't get stalled. Take a reasonable amount of time to look up definitions, and then, if you remain puzzled, bookmark or turn down the page and keep going.

Your primary goal, on this first read-through, is to get through to the end. In most great books of science, the last chapter is the clearest and most straightforward, because the author—having done the difficult and painstaking work of laying out the evidence and drawing conclusions from it—is free to explain what it all *means.* Not only is the conclusion (usually) easier to read, but it tends to illuminate everything that came before: once you know where the book is heading, it's much simpler to make sense of the details that line the path.

The Second Level of Inquiry: Logic-Stage Reading

Go back to your marked sections and figure out what they mean. Once you've reached the last page, you're ready to go back and reread those confusing sections.

Are they *technically* confusing? If you simply don't understand the concepts, bring in some other experts to help. Do an online search for explanations; look for university websites and excerpts from published books, as these tend to be more reliable than personal websites or blogs. Or consult an encyclopedia of science such as James Trefil's *The Encyclopedia of Science and Technology* (Routledge, 2014) the *McGraw-Hill Concise Encyclopedia of Science and Technology* (6th ed., McGraw Hill, 2009), or the hyperbolically titled *Science Desk Reference: Everything You Need to Know about Science, From the Origins of Life to the Ends of the Universe,* ed. John Rennie (Scientific American/John Wiley, 1999).

Are they *linguistically* confusing? Try rewriting the section in your own words. Begin with a sentence-by-sentence paraphrase, and then attempt to summarize your paraphrase in a single paragraph.

A related method that some readers find helpful is to outline the text in question instead. Try to identify the main topic of each paragraph; assign that topic a Roman numeral (I, II, III . . .). Then, ask yourself: What are the most important pieces of information *about* this idea? Assign capital letters (A, B, C . . .) to those ideas. If necessary, you can then identify details about each idea and list them with Arabic numerals (1, 2, 3 . . .).

Define the field of inquiry. What set of phenomena, exactly, is the writer *studying*? And to what field of science do they belong? Aristotle's *Physics* is an attempt at a unified theory of the universe, encompassing astronomy, cosmology, physics, biology, and mathematics; Galileo's *Dialogues* brings physics as well as astronomy to the table. Walter Alvarez's *T. rex,* the latest book on the annotated list, is rooted in Alvarez's training as a geologist, but paleontology plays a large role in Alvarez's investigations, and Alvarez himself now teaches a course in cosmology ("Big History").

First, locate the work within one of the major divisions of science: earth science, astronomy, biology, chemistry, physics. Then, spend some time investigating the sub-branches of each. For this purpose, Wikipedia can be very useful, as it offers multiple charts and ways of connecting the sciences; you can also make use of one of the science encyclopedias listed above, or do an online search for "branches of science."

Now try to identify the subfields of science that the work in question encompasses. You can spend as much or as little time on this project as you find helpful; draw diagrams or branch charts of your own, if useful; read up a little on the kinds of work done in the fields; or simply identify them and move on. Each scientific field has its own conventions; each has its own history, rooted at a particular point in time; each prioritizes a certain kind of evidence, which leads to the next step . . .

What sort of evidence does the writer cite?   Are the writer's conclusions based on observations, such as Hooke's microscopic studies, or Darwin's notes on species seen in the Galápagos Islands? If so, how were those observations made? In person? Gathered from the works of others? What helps and instruments were used? Did those instruments introduce any distortion into the observation? What kind of distortion?

Are the conclusions experimental, set up in a laboratory and carried out in order to test a particular hypothesis? Where were the experiments done, and by whom? How many times were they repeated? Have they been confirmed by other scientists? (You might have do a little external research to answer that question.)

What part does anecdote play? Rachel Carson's *Silent Spring* offers both observational and experimental evidence to demonstrate the destruction caused by pesticides, but she also relies on a series of stories, such as those told by the residents of southeastern Michigan about a 1959 spraying for Japanese beetles. ("A woman . . . reported that coming home from church she saw an alarming number of dead and dying birds . . . A local veterinarian reported that his office was full of clients with dogs and cats that had suddenly sickened.")

Identify the places in which the work is inductive, and the areas where it is deductive.   Does the writer begin with a "big idea" and then work down to specifics, as Aristotle and Alfred Wegener do? This is the inductive method: beginning with a large concept or overall theory, and then looking for pieces of evidence to support it. Or, does the writer start out with individual observations, inconvenient facts, experimental results that can't be explained under current theories, and then generalize to a larger hypothesis? If so, the work is primarily deductive in nature.

Despite the elevation of deductive thinking in modern science, almost all researchers also make use of inductive thinking, and the relationship between the two is complex. Walter Alvarez found iridium where it should not have been; this led him to theorize that perhaps a comet or asteriod had struck the earth (deductive). If the comet struck the earth, there should be an impact crater; so he then spent years searching for the impact crater. This search led him to interpret the sediment layers on the Yucatán peninsula in reference to impact, which in turn led him to the conclusion that he had discovered the crater. This is induction: beginning with the assumption that the crater existed, and then looking for the evidence to support it.

Flag anything that sounds like a statement of conclusion. "I believe," writes Darwin, as he rejects Lamarck's theory of use and disuse in favor of his own variation by natural selection, "that the effects of habit are of quite subordinate importance to the effects of . . . natural selection."

Darwin helpfully precedes many of his statements of conclusion with "I believe," but the statement of conclusion can take a number of forms. "The universe will certainly go on expanding for a while," writes Steven Weinberg. "It obviously follows that if we are to gain scientific knowledge of nature," Aristotle concludes, "we should begin by trying to decide about its principles." And James Lovelock tells us, "The theory of Gaia has developed to the stage where it can now be demonstrated, with the aid of numerical models and computers, that a diverse chain of predators and prey is a more stable and stronger ecosystem than a single self-contained species, or a small group of very limited mix."

Look for the following markers:

Therefore . . . [or *thus,* or other related words; Darwin is fond of "hence"]
It is clear that . . .
I believe . . .
We now know . . .
It can be demonstrated that . . .
Certainly . . .
It is obvious that . . .
It follows that . . .
Scientists now agree that . . .

Once you've located the conclusions, jot them down (in your own words, if you prefer) in your journal.

Now, you're ready to move on to the final level of inquiry.

The Third Level of Inquiry: Rhetoric-Stage Reading

For nonscientists, it isn't easy to answer the most basic question of the rhetoric stage: *Do you agree?*

You can certainly attempt to evaluate the connection between evidence and conclusion, making use of the techniques suggested on pages 198–206 of my chapter on history. But science writing, particularly in the twentieth century and beyond, often cites evidence that is impossible for the lay reader to evaluate. If you're determined to test Galileo's conclusions, you can drop two different weights off your second-floor deck and watch them strike the ground; but most of us are not going to have much luck reproducing the quantum leap of a decaying atom, or the nonlinear equations of a chaotic system.

So the final stage of reaction to each text needs to be slightly more philosophical. When Steven Weinberg tells us that the present universe "faces a future extinction of endless or intolerable heat," non-physicists are obliged to take him at face value. But when he adds that "working out the meaning of the data" accumulated by science is "one of the very few things that lifts human life a little above the level of farce," we should feel free to argue back.

Consider asking two large questions of each work.

What metaphors, analogies, stories, and other literary techniques appear, and why are they there?   The first chapter of *The First Three Minutes* begins, rather unexpectedly, with the Viking origin myth found in the Edda: the universe emerged as a cosmic cow began to devour a salt-lick. This is more than an engaging, reader-friendly opener—as Weinberg's conclusion ("Men and women are [no longer] content to comfort themselves with tales of gods and giants") makes clear. Weinberg isn't just writing about the first three minutes; he's providing an alternative origin story, one that can take the place of religious explanation.

Metaphors and narratives, in other words, give clues to the science writer's basic argument. The opening scene of Rachel Carson's *Silent Spring* immediately sets up a contrast between the good life of the rural past, and the world of the chemical companies—a commercial, industrial, unnatural society. Even Albert Einstein's opening metaphor in *Relativity: The Special and General Theory* points the reader toward Einstein's underlying theory of knowledge: "In your schooldays," he writes, "most of you who read this book made acquaintance with the noble building of Euclid's geometry, and you remember— perhaps with more respect than love— the magnificent structure, on the lofty staircase of which you were chased about for uncounted hours by conscientious teachers." Staircases lead to upper levels, *magnificent* ones: mathematics is the ladder that we climb to find truth.

Find the metaphors, or stories, or narratives. Ask yourself: Why *this* metaphor? Why this particular story? What does it tell me about the writer's assumptions?

Are there broader conclusions? Isaac Newton famously remarked that, while he could explain *what* gravity was, he felt no need to explain *why*. He did not intend to explain the nature of the cosmos. He simply wanted to discover its laws.

He was in the minority. Many of the books on the annotated list go well beyond the boundary Newton erected—from Lucretius's insistance that all religious belief darkens the mind, to Stephen Hawking's speculation that a unified theory of physics might actually answer "the question of why it is that we and the universe exist."

Which texts make sweeping statements about the nature of man, the ultimate purpose of our existence, the *why* of the cosmos? What are those statements? Do you agree with them? If so, is it because the writer has convinced you that those broader statements arise logically out of the evidence presented? And if you disagree, why?

THE ANNOTATED SCIENCE LIST

The following books are chosen, not to give you a comprehensive overview of the greatest discoveries in science (that would require a much longer list) but to highlight the ways in which we *think* about science. It is a reader's list for nonspecialists, so important books that are highly technical and equation-heavy (Euclid's *Elements*, for example) are not on it.

It isn't necessary to read every word of the older texts. Dipping into Hippocrates will give you a good sense of his method; Aristotle's *Physics* certainly doesn't have to be mastered in every detail before you move on; and if you examine a few of the illustrations in *Micrographia,* you'll be perfectly well equipped to understand Robert Hooke's revolutionary ideas.

From *Silent Spring* on, many of the books are available as unabridged audios. But almost all of these books contain graphs, illustrations, and charts that will help your understanding—so consider the audio versions supplemental.

HIPPOCRATES
On Airs, Waters, and Places
(460–370 B.C.)

Best translations: The nineteenth-century Francis Adams translation, still readable, is widely available online. It is included in several printed collections simply titled The Corpus; *editions include paperback reprints by Kessinger Legacy (2004) and Kaplan Classics of Medicine (2008). A more modern translation is included in the Penguin Classics paperback,* Hippocratic Writings, *trans. G. E. R. Lloyd, John Chadwick, and W. N. Mann (1983). The sentence structure is slightly easier to follow, but the two translations are very similar.*

The neuroscientist Charles Gross once characterized Hippocratic medicine as combining "absence of superstition, accurate clinical description, ignorance of anatomy, and a physiology that is largely an absurd mixture of false analogy, speculation, and humoral theory."[54] All four of those characteristics are on full display in "On Airs, Waters, and Places."

"Whoever wishes to investigate medicine properly," the essay begins, "should proceed thus: in the first place to consider . . . the winds . . . the qualities of the waters . . . and the grounds." The cures for mankind's various bodily ills will not be found in prayer, but in a better understanding of the natural world.

So the physician must understand his patients' surroundings: winds, waters, temperatures, and elevations of particular cities shape the health of their inhabitants. Each place has its own peculiar kind of air and water, so each also has its own kind of diseases. A city that is exposed to hot southern winds, for example, will be filled with flabby men and women who don't eat and drink much and suffer from too much phlegm; babies are subject to convulsions and asthma, and the most the common diseases are dysentery, diarrhea, chronic winter fevers, and hemorrhoids. By contrast, cities which are sheltered from hot southern breezes but open to northern winds have hard, cold water. Their inhabitants suffer from a *lack* of correct bodily fluids; the men are prone to constipation, the women often have trouble nursing their babies, and everyone is subject to nosebleed and

---

[54]Charles G. Gross, *Brain, Vision, Memory: Tales in the History of Neuroscience* (Cambridge: MIT Press, 1999), p. 13.

stroke. To treat his patients, the physician must first analyze the natural surroundings, and then shift the sick from one climate to another in order to encourage production and balance of the appropriate humors.

Salted into this theorizing are some perfectly valid observations; for example, that "marshy, stagnant" waters with "a strong smell" are unwholesome and will cause illness. Hippocratic medicine chalked this unwholesomeness up to humoral imbalance: bad-smelling waters produce too much bile, which makes those who drink it sick. This was, of course, the wrong explanation. But the Hippocratic physician could at least *see* the connection between foul water, and the subsequent stomach upset in his patient. In seeking to connect natural causes to natural effects, the Hippocratic approach took the first huge step away from magical thinking.

ARISTOTLE
Physics
(c. 330 B.C.)

Best translations: Robin Waterfield's translation for Oxford World's Classics (1999) is clear and fluid. In addition, the R. P. Hardie and R. K. Gaye translation, done as part of a forty-year effort to translate Aristotle into a standard English version (the "Oxford Translation"), is widely available and is still very readable; a good edition is the Clarendon Press Physics *(1930), available as a free ebook.*

The *Physics* is divided into eight books, but the first two are the most important. Book 1 establishes Aristotle's scientific method: He recommends beginning with our general understanding of the universe ("the things which are more knowable and obvious to us") and proceeding from these general ideas to the specific examination (always shaped by our previous understanding) of specific things, or phenomena ("clearer and more knowable by nature"). This is deductive reasoning (starting with a general truth and reasoning your way to logically necessary conclusions) rather than inductive reasoning (beginning with individual observations and reasoning your way toward a general explanation that accounts for them). Modern science relies on inductive reasoning, but not until the sixteenth century would deductive reasoning give way to its rival.

Book 2 defines "nature" in terms of the principle of internal change: Natural things contain within themselves a principle of motion, while things constructed by men ("art") do not. A sapling grows into a tree because of its intrinsic principle of motion; a house or a bed, although made of wood, never grows into anything else; it is a work of art, and remains a house or a bed. The principle of motion is purposeful: motion propels natural things, inexorably, toward an end which is predetermined.

Throughout the *Physics*, Aristotle assumes that the world is evolving toward something better. This is, of course, not exactly what we mean by evolution today: modern biological evolution has no predetermined goal, no overall design. Aristotle's science on the other hand, is *teleological*, firmly convinced that nature is developing, purposefully, toward a more fully realized end. But this end was not (as medieval science, baptized into Christianity, would assume) set into place by a Creator. A sprout becomes a tree because its *treeness* is already inherent in it. For Aristotle, teleology is not an external guiding force, but an internal potentiality.

LUCRETIUS
On the Nature of Things (De Rerum Natura)
(c. 60 B.C.)

Best translation: Lucretius wrote in Latin verse: the scientific prose of the ancient world. Ronald Melville's translation On the Nature of the Universe *(Oxford University Press, 2009) is a clear and elegant poetic version; if you'd rather have Lucretius in prose, try Ronald E. Latham's translation for Penguin Classics (rev. ed., 1994).*

Lucretius lays out three key positions. First, religion is mere superstition: "We start then from [Nature's] first great principle," he writes, "that nothing ever by divine power comes from nothing" (1.148–149). Belief in the gods darkens the mind, making it unable for thinkers reach any true or accurate understanding of the world. Book One opens with a paean to Epicurus, the first man who dared to teach that the gods did not control daily life, and continues to develop a philosophy of complete materialism. Doing away with belief in the divine, Lucretius argues, opens the mind's eye: "The terrors of the mind flee all away," he explains, in Book Three, "the walls of heaven open, and through the void/ Immeasurable, the truth of things I see" (3.16–17).

Second, a degenerative principle is at work in the universe. All things are continually struck by an ongoing hail of atoms, which wears away at them; eventually, everything in the cosmos will decay ("So shall the ramparts of the mighty world / Themselves be stormed and into crumbling ruin / Collapse") (2.1145–1147). Book Two is one of the earliest written attempts to lay out a philosophy of entropy.

Third: there is no plan in the universe. All that is has come from a chance collision of the atomic particles which make up the world. Book Five explains all of human history as the result of randomness: "For sure," Lucretius sums up, "not by design or intelligence / Did primal atoms place themselves in order" (5.419–420). No other explanation accounts for the random aspects that Lucretius sees in the world around him: a place of inhospitability, ill fortune, and death.

NICOLAUS COPERNICUS
Commentariolus
(1514)

Best translation: The Commentariolus *is included, along with a summary of Copernicus's work written by his champion Rheticus (the* Narratio Prima*) and a letter written by Copernicus disproving the calculations of the astronomer Johannes Werner (the* Letter against Werner*), in the paperback* Three Copernican Treatises, *translated by Edward Rosen (2nd rev. ed., Dover Publications, 2004). If you feel adventurous, you can tackle* On the Revolutions of the Heavenly Spheres *itself. The early twentieth-century translation by Charles Glenn Wallis has been reprinted in paperback by Prometheus Books (1995) and by Running Press (2002, with notes by Stephen Hawking).*

The *Commentariolus* begins with a brief statement of the presenting problem: even with the employment of eccentrics, epicycles, and equants, planets do not move with "uniform velocity." The problem can be partially solved, Copernicus explains, if the sun is at the center of the universe.

Much of the *Commentariolus* is devoted to explaining this new universe, but Copernicus also tackles the movement of the earth, which is threefold: it "revolves annually in a great circle about the sun," it rotates on its own axis, and it also tilts from side to side, over the course of the seasons. These movements cause "the entire universe" to appear to "revolve with enormous speed" around the earth, but this, Copernicus concludes, is merely illusion: "The motion of the earth can explain all these changes in a less surprising way."

Throughout, the *Commentariolus* is dedicated to finding the simplest explanation. Yet, as Copernicus goes on to investigate the motion of each planet, he finds himself building more and more shells around the sun, an increasingly complex interlocking series of spheres. His simple explanation eventually wraps him into a ridiculously complicated final statement: "Altogether," he concludes, "thirty-four circles suffice to explain the entire structure of the universe and the entire ballet of the planets."

FRANCIS BACON
Novum Organum
(1620)

Best translations: The nineteenth-century translation by James Spedding and Robert Ellis remains readable. It is still the most commonly reprinted and can be read in multiple free ebook versions, such as The Philosophical Works of Francis Bacon, *trans. and ed. James Spedding and Robert Ellis, Vol. IV (Longman & Co., 1861). A more recent translation with introduction, outline, and explanatory notes is* The New Organon, *ed. Lisa Jardine and Michael Silverthorn (Cambridge University Press, 2000). The notes are useful, but the translation, while more contemporary, is not always clearer.*

Since Aristotle, deductive reasoning had ruled the practice of science; Bacon sets out to overthrow it. On the cover of the first edition of the *Novum Organum*, Bacon placed a ship—his new inductive method—sailing triumphantly past the Pillars of Hercules: the mythological pillars that marked the furthest reach of Hercules's journey to the "far west," the outermost boundaries of the ancient world, the greatest extent of the old way of knowledge.

Book I begins with "Aphorisms," brief independent statements that lay out Bacon's objections to the current methods in use in natural science. Deductive reasoning, Bacon objects, tends to reinforce four inaccurate ways of thinking. He calls these the "Idols of the Tribe" (general assumptions that all of society accepts as common sense and no longer questions), the "Idols of the Cave" (assumptions that seem natural to individual thinkers because of their own peculiar education, or experience, or inborn tendencies), the "Idols of the Marketplace" (the careless assumption that words and definitions carry the same meaning to every listener), and the "Idols of the Theatre" (assumptions based on philosophical systems handed down from ancient times). In Section 82, he lays out his alternative proposal for finding knowledge, the three steps that (eventually) developed into the modern scientific method.

Book II expands on Bacon's central theme: if men could only "lay aside received opinions" (all those idols), and "refrain the mind for a time from the highest generalizations," the "native and genuine force of the mind" will impart understanding. It isn't necessary to read all of Book II, which dissects various physical processes in order to prove Bacon's point and ends with Bacon's attempt to divide the study of natural history into categories.

GALILEO GALILEI
Dialogue Concerning the Two Chief World Systems
(1632)

Best translation: The most readable is Stillman Drake's, originally published in 1953 and now available in a nicely revised and annotated edition from the Modern Library Science Series: Dialogue Concerning the Two Chief World Systems: Ptolemaic and Copernican *(2001).*

By the time Galileo published the *Dialogue,* Cardinal Bellamine was dead; but the Inquisition was still alive and active, so the *Dialogue* is framed as a hypothetical discussion among three friends as to whether the heliocentric, geokinetic model could, theoretically, prove to be the best possible picture of the universe.

The Copernican model is defended by the thoughtful and intelligent characters Salviati and Sagredo; all Inquisition-approved opinions are voiced by the least sympathetic character, the clearly ignorant and incompetent Simplicius, blindly loyal to Aristotle, willing to check his reason at the door. The ruse was sufficient to get the *Dialogue* past the initial censor, the Dominican theologian Niccolo Riccardi, although Riccardi insisted on a preface that recognized the Church's objections to heliocentrism as perfectly valid. He also wanted a disclaimer at the end, cautioning that the tides could be understood without recourse to a moving earth.

Galileo promply supplied a highly sarcastic preface ("Several years ago there was published in Rome a salutary edict which, in order to obviate the dangerous tendencies of our present age, imposed a seasonable silence upon the . . . opinion that the earth moves"), and placed in Simplicius's mouth an ending assertion that God, "in His infinite power and wisdom," was probably causing the tides to move "in many ways which are unthinkable to our minds." This temporarily satisfied the censor, but didn't fool any of Galileo's scientific colleagues.

The *Dialogues* are divided into four books of discussion, each taking place over the course of a day. The discussions of the First and Second Days are the most central; the Third and Fourth Days expand on the problems of motion laid out in the first two parts.

ROBERT HOOKE
Micrographia
(1665)

Best editions: Although multiple reprints of the Micrographia *are available, few of them reproduce Hooke's groundbreaking illustrations at the original size or with decent detail. The best way to view the illustrations is in the Octavo CD, which offers clear scans of the actual pages of the original book, in PDFs that can be magnified, rotated, and viewed in color or black and white (Octavo Digital Rare Books, CD-ROM, 1998). However, the text itself, complete with unmodernized spelling, is extremely difficult make out in the Octavo scans. Consider turning to one of the free ebook versions (such as that found at Project Gutenberg) or a paperback reprint (Cosimo Classics, 2007) in order to read Hooke's accompanying essays.*

First, read the Preface, in which Hooke explains the relationship between the senses and the faculty of reason. Then, take some time to examine Hooke's prints. The first fifty-seven illustrations and observations are microscopic; the last three, of refracted light, stars, and the moon, are telescopic.

Throughout *Micrographia*, Hooke uses his close observations—the extension of the senses through artificial means—as the launching place for new ways of thinking. Ultimately, his instruments augment human *reason*, not just human senses. Close observation leads to new theories; new theories lead to new paradigms.

Using William Harvey's circulatory system as his analogy, Hooke explains in the *Preface* that true natural philosophy

is to begin with the Hands and Eyes, and to proceed on through the Memory, to be continued by the Reason; nor is it to stop there, but to come about to the Hands and Eyes again, and so, by a continual passage round from one Faculty to another, it is to be maintained in life and strength, as much as the body of man is by the circulation of the blood through the several parts of the body, the Arms, the Feet, the Lungs, the Heart, and the Head. If once this method were followed with diligence and attention, there is nothing that lies within the power of human Wit . . . Talking and contention of Arguments would soon be turned into labours; all the fine dreams of Opinions, and universal metaphysical natures, which the luxury of subtle brains has devised, would quickly vanish, and give place to solid Histories, Experiments and Works. And as at first, mankind fell by tasting of the forbidden Tree of Knowledge, so we, their posterity, may be in part restored by the same way, not only by beholding and contemplating, but by tasting too those fruits of natural knowledge, that were never yet forbidden.

Instruments and helps are no longer merely extensions of the senses; they become, for Hooke, the Tree of Knowledge, the path to perfection.

ISAAC NEWTON
"Rules" and "General Scholium"
from *Philosophiae Naturalis Principia Mathematica*
(1687/1713/1726)

Best translations: Selected excerpts from the Principia *(including the "Rules" and "General Scholium") can be found in the Norton Critical Edition of Newton's work:* Newton: Texts, Backgrounds, Commentaries, *ed. and trans. I. Bernard Cohen and Richard S. Westfall (W. W. Norton, 1995). The entire* Principia *has been translated by I. Bernard Cohen and Anne Whitman in the massive (950-page) paperback* The Principia: Mathematical Principles of Natural Philosophy: A New Translation *(University of California Press, 1999). A simpler way to read the entire book is to search for the public domain 1729 translation by Andrew Motte, which is not significantly more difficult to read.*

The four books of the *Principia* lay out the rules by which gravity functions. Throughout, Newton establishes and makes use of three principles ("Newton's Laws of Motion"). The Law of Inertia states that objects in motion remain in motion, and objects at rest remain at rest (unless an outside force is applied). The Law of Acceleration states that, when a force is applied to a mass, acceleration results; the greater the mass, the greater the force needed to produce acceleration. And the Law of Action and Reaction states that, for every action, there is an equal and opposite reaction. Books I and II establish these laws of motion, both in the abstract (without any friction present) and in the presence of resistance; the remainder of the *Principia* deals with gravity as a universal force.

The Rules of Reasoning explain why Newton can be sure that these laws function everywhere in the universe. He was concerned that his critics might accuse him of offering a mere "ingenious Romance," rather than a reliable hypothesis. So, in the Rules, Newton sets out to show that experimental conclusions can be generalized to reach beyond the scope of individual experiments.

Then, in the General Scholium (which also contains a famous discussion of the place of God in natural philosophy) Newton places limits on the method. Gravity, Newton explains, is a force

> that penetrates as far as the centers of the sun and planets without any diminution of its power to act, and that acts not in proportion to the quantity of the *surfaces* of the particles on which it acts . . . but in proportion to the quantity of *solid* matter, and whose action is extended everywhere to immense distances, always decreasing as the squares of the distances.

But, he cautions, "I have not yet assigned a cause to gravity." He could deduce the laws of gravity from his experiments on earth, but the *reason* for gravity lay beyond his grasp. Nor did he feel it was necessary for him to explain *why* it existed: "It is enough," he concludes, "that gravity really exists and acts according to the laws that we have set forth and is sufficient to explain all the motions of the heavenly bodies and of our sea." In extending the reach of the experimental method across the universe, he had also been careful to erect a boundary fence on the other side: Science can tell *what,* but it has no responsibility to tell *why.*

GEORGES CUVIER
"Preliminary Discourse"
(1812)

Best translations: Martin J. S. Rudwick's, in Georges Cuvier, Fossil Bones, and Geological Catastrophes: New Translations & Interpretations of the Primary Texts *(University of Chicago Press, 1998). The "Preliminary Discourse," titled "The Revolutions of the Globe" (the title often given the discourse when published separately), is found in Chapter 15. There is no need to read all of Rudwick's preface, which is almost as long as the discourse but less elegantly written. You can also search for Robert Jameson's 1818 translation, published under the title* Essay on the Theory of the Earth, *which is archaic in spots but still perfectly readable.*

The "Preliminary Discourse" arose out of Cuvier's commitment to the Baconian method. Sorting through the National Museum's "charnel house" of fossils, he found species that no longer existed. He had no explanation as to *why* they had died out, no grand overarching theory of life; instead, he examined each specific fossil and the strata in which it was found. Increasingly, these led him to believe that "the globe has not always been as it is at present." The strata were a book of the earth's past that could be read by the perceptive, and Cuvier's reading led him to a series of propositions:

Life has not always existed.

There have been several successive changes in state, from sea into land, from land into sea.

Several of the revolutions that have changed the state of the globe have been sudden.

Using only the evidence before him, Cuvier had moved from observation to hypothesis: The past is punctuated by a series of catastrophic disasters.

CHARLES LYELL
Principles of Geology
(1830–1832)

Best editions: The original 1830 text, published by John Murray, can be read online or downloaded as a PDF from multiple sources. Penguin has also produced a high-quality paperback, edited by James A. Secord (1997).

Most available editions of the *Principles of Geology* contain all three volumes, written between 1830 and 1832. Originally, Lyell had planned to write just two volumes, one dealing with his overall principles (Volume 1), and the second marshaling more specific geological proofs (now Volume 3). Eventually, though, he realized that he had to give some accounting for the fossil record, so interposed a new volume (the current Volume 2) between. You only need to read Volume 1, which lays out Lyell's basic principles; the specific observations in Books 2 and 3 have been thoroughly superseded.

In the twenty-six short chapters of Volume 1, Lyell lays out three interlocking principles for geology, now generally known by the names *actualism, anti-catastrophism,* and (more awkwardly) *the earth as a steady-state system.*

Actualism: Every force that has acted in the past is still acting (and can be observed) in the present.

Anti-catastrophism: Those forces did not act with more intensity in the past; their *degree* has not changed.

The earth as a steady-state system: The history of the earth has no direction or progression; all periods are essentially the same.

Lyell refused to entertain the idea that any extraordinary events played a part in the history of the earth—not flood, or comet, or asteroid, or even heating or cooling beyond what can be observed in the present day. *"No causes whatever,"* he wrote, "have, from the earliest time to which we can look back, to the present, ever acted, but those *now acting*; and . . . they never acted with different degrees of energy from that which they now exert."

Two years later, the English natural philosopher and clergyman William Whewell gave Lyell's principles the label by which they have been known ever since: *uniformitarianism.*

CHARLES DARWIN
On the Origin of Species
(1859)

Best editions: The Origin of Species *is widely available in many different editions and formats. Check the textual notes; the original 1859 text is the clearest, most succinct, and most easily grasped by the general reader. The Wordsworth Editions Ltd. reprint (1998) reproduces both the 1859 text and the essay that Darwin added to the third (1861) edition, "Historical Sketch of the Progress of Opinion on the Origin of Species," which lays out his intellectual debt to Lyell, Lamarck, and others.*

Charles Darwin's five-year journey on the HMS *Beagle* began in certainty: "When I was on board the *Beagle*," he later wrote, "I believed in the permanence of species." Different kinds of animals, he assumed, had always existed. But as he took notes on the vast variations of living creatures he now encountered, his puzzlement grew. What *was* a species? Where did they come from? Why did different species arise? As he prepared his notes for publication (1829's *Journal and Remarks,* now generally known as *The Voyage of the Beagle*), he became convinced that "many facts indicated the common descent of species."

He was still working on the problem in 1858, when he received a letter from the British explorer Alfred Russel Wallace, fourteen years his junior. Wallace had collected his own observations on tens of thousands of different species and had come to the conclusion that species change, or evolve, because of environmental pressures. "On the whole," Wallace wrote "the best fitted live."

From the effects of disease the most healthy escaped; from enemies, the strongest, the swiftest, or the most cunning; from famine, the best hunters or those with the best digestion; and so on. Then it suddenly flashed upon me that this self-acting process would necessarily improve the race, because in every generation the inferior would inevitably be killed off and the superior would remain—that is, the fittest would survive.[55]

Wallace had enclosed his essay, "On the Tendency of Varieties to Depart Indefinitely From the Original Type," in his letter to Darwin, asking him to pass it on to any natural philosophers who might find it interesting.

Darwin had independently come to exactly the same conclusion. He sent Wallace's letter on to the Linnean Society of London, a century-old club for the discussion of natural history, along with an abstract of his own conclusions; in August of 1858, Wallace's and Darwin's theories were published side by side in the Linnean Society's printed proceedings.

The following year, Darwin, energized by Wallace's co-discovery of the principle of natural selection, finally published his entire argument. This first edition—*On the Origin of Species by Means of Natural Selection, or the Preservation of Favoured Races in the Struggle for Life,* immediately sold out. Over the next two decades, he revised *The Origin of Species* six times. Even in his final revision, he did not take his theory to its logical end; but he had already privately concluded that his principles of natural selection applied to the human race as well. "As soon as I had become . . . convinced that species were mutable productions," he wrote in his later *Autobiography,* "I could not avoid the belief that man must come under the same law."

GREGOR MENDEL
Experiments in Plant Hybridization
(1865)

Best translation: Mendel's paper was translated into English by the Royal Horticultural Society of London in 1901; this clear and succinct translation remains the standard. W. P. Bateson's republication of the entire English-language paper in his 1909 book Mendel's Principles of Heredity *is widely available online; Cosimo has also republished it in a high-quality paperback with all formulae and diagrams included (2008).*

Gregor Mendel spent nearly a decade interbreeding sweet peas, in an effort to confirm—or disprove—the most widely accepted nineteenth-century model of inheritance. This was called "blending," and proposed that the characteristics of both parents somehow passed into their offspring and melded together to create a happy medium: a black stallion and a white

[55]Alfred Russel Wallace, *Infinite Tropics: An Alfred Russel Wallace Anthology,* ed. Andrew Berry (New York: Verso, 2002), p. 51.

mare should have a gray foal, a six foot father and five foot mother should produce a child who would mature at five foot six.

There were two problems with this. First, it was (often) demonstrably untrue. And second, blending was completely incompatible with the theory of natural selection: blending tended to remove all variations, not preserve the most favorable ones.

Mendel discovered that some of the characteristics of the peas were *always* passed on to the next generation; he called these "dominant" characteristics. Other aspects seemed to disappear in the offspring, but then would sometimes reappear several generations on; these, Mendel termed "recessive." The painstaking cross-fertilization of generation after generation of sweet peas allowed Mendel to work out a series of formulas for the passing on of these dominant and recessive characteristics. And as he did so, he realized that blending did not explain his sweet-pea variations. Rather, there must be separate units of inheritance that pass from one plant to the next.

Over time, this could indeed transform one species into another:

> If a species *A* is to be transformed into a species *B,* both must be united by fertilisation and the resulting hybrids then be fertilised with the pollen of *B*; then, out of the various offspring resulting, that form would be selected which stood in nearest relation to *B* and once more be fertilised with *B* pollen, and so continuously until finally a form is arrived at which is like *B* and constant in its progeny. By this process the species *A* would change into the species *B*.

ALFRED WEGENER
The Origin of Continents and Oceans
(1915/1929)

Best translation: John Biram's 1966 translation, made from the fourth German edition of 1929, has been reprinted by Dover Publications (1966).

Alfred Wegener came up with his theory of continental drift not based on evidence, but because the most widely accepted explanation for the presence of ocean basins and continental masses had been cast into doubt.

Following a theory of Isaac Newton's, many geologists believed that the earth had once been molten. As it cooled, it contracted and its crust wrinkled, sinking in some places, rising up into continents and mountains in others. In that case, the earth must still be cooling. But discoveries in radiation at the turn of the century made it clear that certain atoms generated *more* heat over time. This didn't fit at all with the idea that a uniformly hot earth was now cooling; or, as Wegener himself put it in *The Origin,* "The apparently obvious basic assumption of contraction theory, namely that the earth is continuously cooling, is in full retreat before the discovery of radium."

Instead, Wegener came up with his theory of continental drift, laid out in *The Origin of Continents and Oceans.* Don't look for proofs; this was a grand theory in the Aristotelian tradition. Wegener came up with the huge overarching explanation first, and defends it entirely on its internal consistency. "The theory offers solutions for . . . many apparently insoluble problems," he concludes.

Most geologists disagreed. The hypothesis gained very slow acceptance over time; the measurements of Littell and Hammond in 1929 helped, but not until the discovery of mantle convection currents in the 1960s was the mechanism for continental drift finally understood.

ALBERT EINSTEIN
The General Theory of Relativity
(1916)

Best translation: Robert W. Lawson's 1920 translation into English is widely available; most editions include Einstein's summary of his findings on the special theory first. Read both, since the general theory builds on the special. An excellent edition is Relativity: The Special and the General Theory, *trans. Robert W. Lawson, with introduction by Roger Penrose, commentary by Robert Geroch, and historical essay by David C. Cassidy (Pi Press, 2005).*

"The present book is intended, as far as possible," Einstein's 1916 preface begins, "to give an exact insight into the theory of Relativity to those readers who, from a general scientific and philosophical point of view, are interested in the theory, but who are not conversant with the mathematical apparatus of theoretical physics." In other words, with a little persistance, you too can follow Einstein's arguments. Einstein worked at the end of an era; he was one of the last great scientists to bring his most groundbreaking discoveries directly to the general public.

MAX PLANCK
"The Origin and Development of the Quantum Theory"
(1922)

Best translation: The original English translation by H. T. Clarke and L. Silberstein is widely available online (The Clarendon Press, 1922), as well as in a paperback reprint by Forgotten Books (2013).

Planck's brief essay, the written version of his Nobel Prize address, provides a fascinating glimpse into the development and early direction of quantum theory. By 1922, the contradictions inherent in quantum mechanics were already clear. Don't try to follow all the details of Planck's address; instead, pay special attention to pages 10–11. Look for the promise that he believes quantum theory will fulfill—and the possible consequences that Planck fears.

JULIAN HUXLEY
Evolution: The Modern Synthesis
(1942)

Best edition: The MIT Press version, The Modern Synthesis: The Definitive Edition *(2010).*

"The death of Darwinism has been proclaimed not only from the pulpit, but from the biological laboratory," Huxley begins, "but, as in the case of Mark Twain, the reports seem to have been greatly exaggerated, since to-day Darwinism is very much alive." And his first chapter lays out his intentions:

> Biology in the last twenty years, after a period in which new disciplines were taken up in turn and worked out in comparative isolation, has become a more unified science. It has embarked upon a period of synthesis, until to-day it no longer presents the spectacle of a number of semi-independent and largely contradictory sub-sciences, but is coming to rival the unity of older sciences like physics, in which advance in any one branch leads almost at once to advance in all other fields, and theory and experiment march hand-in-hand. As one chief result, there has been a rebirth of Darwinism. . . . The Darwinism thus reborn is a modified Drawinism, since it must operate with facts unknown to Darwin; but it is still Darwinism in the sense that it aims at giving a naturalistic interpretation of evolution. . . . It is with this reborn Darwinism, this mutated phoenix risen from the ashes of the pyre . . . that I propose to deal in succeeding chapters.

It was a sprawling, multifaceted task, but the clarity of Huxley's style and the down-to-earth, jargon-free presentation of technical ideas made *Evolution: The Modern Synthesis* both readable and popular. The book went through five printings and three editions; the latest, in 1973, included a new introduction co-authored by nine prominent scientists, affirming the overall truth of the synthesis and updating its data.

ERWIN SCHRÖDINGER
What Is Life?
(1944)

Best edition: The standard edition is published by Cambridge University Press as What Is Life? The Physical Aspect of the Living Cell with Mind & Matter and Autobiographical Sketches *(1992).*

What Is Life? begins with an introduction to classical, Newtonian physics; continues, in the second and third chapters, to sum up advances in genetics; and then brings quantum mechanics into the picture. Schrödinger's goal is to offer a single coherent explanation, drawing on physics, chemistry, *and* biology, for the ways in which life is sustained and passed on: "The obvious inability of present-day physics and chemistry to account for such events," he begins, "is no reason . . . for doubting that they *can* be accounted for by those sciences." Schrödinger was the first to propose that *chemistry* could explain how inheritance functioned. There must be, he argued, a "code-script" that could be chemically analyzed and passed on; life was not a mysterious "vital force," but an orderly series of chemical and physical reactions.

A young James Watson happened on *What Is Life?* and was immediately hooked: "Schrödinger argued that life could be thought of in terms of storing and passing on biological information," Watson later wrote. "Chromosomes were thus simply information bearers . . . To understand life . . . we would have to identify molecules, and crack their code." *What Is Life?* created the new field of biochemistry, and led directly to the discovery of DNA.

RACHEL CARSON
Silent Spring
(1962)

Best edition: Houghton Mifflin (1994), with a new introduction by Al Gore.

From its first lines, *Silent Spring* shows itself to be a new kind of science book: one that is intended to grasp the imagination as well as the brain, emotion as well as reason. "There was once a town in the heart of America, where all life seemed to live in harmony with its surroundings," Carson begins, and goes on to sketch an idyllic portrait of white-blooming orchards in spring, scarlet and gold leaves in the fall, wildflowers, birds soarching in a blue sky, fish leaping in clear ponds, herds of deer "half hidden in the mists." And then a "strange blight" creeps in, an "evil spell" that sickens livestock, kills birds, strikes down children while at play and causes them to "die within a few hours."

This morality tale is a prediction: what will happen to organic life if the use of chemicals is not regulated. *Silent Spring* is a story of failure on the part of government, blind greed on the part of corporations, silence on the part of science: Pesticides, unregulated and unexamined, have the power to wipe out the complex ecosystem around us. Man, Carson says, has "written a depressing record of destruction, directed not only against the earth he inhabits, but against the life that shares it with him."

Silent Spring was brilliantly successful. Called to testify before Congress about the dangers of unregulated pesticides, Carson was greeted by one senator with the words, "Miss Carson, you are the lady who started all this." *All this:* the regulation of pesticides, the creation of the EPA, and the beginning of the modern environmental movement.[56]

DESMOND MORRIS
The Naked Ape
(1967)

Best edition: The Naked Ape: The Controversial Classic of Man's Origins *(Delta, 1999).*

Both Charles Darwin and Erwin Schrödinger had edged up to the implications of their discoveries, and then sidled away. Darwin had declined to tease out the full implications of his theory of origins, even though (as he later wrote) he "could not avoid the belief that man must come under the same law" as every other species: man, too, was mutable. *What Is Life?* had concluded that life is chemical, but ended with a final epilogue, "On Determinism and Free Will," in which Schrödinger attempted to hold on to the uniqueness of the human experience.

"I am a zoologist," Desmond Morris begins, in *The Naked Ape*'s Introduction, "and the naked ape is an animal. He is therefore fair game for my pen and I refuse to avoid him any longer because some of his behavior patterns are rather complex and impressive." In the chapters that follow, Morris attempts to explain almost every aspect of human existence, from origin to romantic love, from feeding patterns to maternal and paternal love, as survival mechanisms. Everything we do, from getting our hair styled to laughing at a joke, has a biological and chemical explanation.

It was, at the time, shocking: "Zoologist Dr Desmond Morris has

[56]Carson, *Silent Spring,* p. xix.

stunned the world by writing about humans in the same way scientists describe animals," marveled the BBC. But Morris's study, boosted by an approachable prose style and a canny amount of space devoted to sex, was translated into twenty-three languages and sold over ten million copies. It was the first popular work in a field which would become known as *sociobiology*: the investigation of human culture as, no less than human inheritance, shaped and determined by physical and chemical factors.

JAMES D. WATSON
The Double Helix: A Personal Account of the Discovery of the Structure of DNA
(1968)

Best editions: Watson's original text is available as both a paperback reprint and an ebook from Touchstone (2001). A more elaborate edition, containing editorial annotations, historical background, excerpts from personal letters, and additional illustrations, is The Annotated and Illustrated Double Helix, *ed. Alexander Gann and Jan Witkowski (Simon & Schuster, 2012).*

"Science seldom proceeds in the straightforward logical manner imagined by outsiders," remarks Watson, near the beginning of *The Double Helix;* and his account of the "discovery" of DNA by himself and his British colleague Francis Crick is filled with false starts, stolen research, territorial jousts between scientists, and misogyny ("The best home for a feminist," Watson remarks, in one of his less charming moments, "was in another person's lab").

Despite its title, Watson's memoir isn't about a "discovery": it is about the construction of a theoretical structure. Crick and Watson, determined to come up with a model that would 1) be consistent with the chemical and structural properties of the nucleic substance known as deoxyribonucleic acid, and 2) allow it to pass information along, came up with the idea of a double helix. In April of 1953, Watson and Crick proposed this model in a short article published in the journal *Nature,* concluding with a brief sentence (composed by Crick) suggesting that the double helix would allow nucleic acids to form hydrogen bonds—which meant DNA could reproduce itself. "It has not escaped our notice," Crick wrote, in the paper's conclusion, "that the specific pairing we have postulated immediately suggests a possible copying mechanism for the genetic material."

The model was convincing: consistent with observed properties of DNA, and clearly able to replicate itself. It was elaborated upon by such biochemical luminaries as Frederick Sanger, George Gamow, Marshal

Nirenberg, and Heinrich Matthaei. By the time James Watson published *The Double Helix: A Personal Account of the Discovery of the Structure of DNA* in 1968, the double helical structure of DNA and its role in reproducing life was accepted as gospel (although Crick objected to the memoir, pointing out a number of places where his recollection didn't match up with Watson's story).

But not until the late 1970s would scientists have the technical tools to produce a truly detailed map of DNA. Neither Watson nor Crick had "discovered" DNA. Like Copernicus, they had instead built a convincing theory that accounted, very neatly, for decades of observable phenomena.

RICHARD DAWKINS
The Selfish Gene
(1976)

Best editions: The first edition (1976) can be easily located secondhand, but the third edition, The Selfish Gene: 30th Anniversary Edition *(Oxford University Press, 2006), contains updated bibliography and a new introduction.*

The Selfish Gene took Desmond Morris's conclusions to the molecular level; Morris had explained human culture in terms of the organism's will to survive, but Dawkins argued that that organism itself (animal, or human) will had nothing to do with it. The gene *itself,* he concluded, will preserve itself at all costs.

Dawkins had not "invented the notion . . . that the body is merely an evolutionary vehicle for the gene" (as one science book claims), any more than Watson and Crick had "discovered" DNA. In fact, in 1975, the year before *The Selfish Gene* was published, the biologist E. O. Wilson had concluded (in the first chapter of his text *Sociobiology*) that "the organism is only DNA's way of making more DNA." But Dawkins was a good writer and a capable rhetorician, and *The Selfish Gene* managed to spell the implications of this idea out with particular clarity, accessible both to lay readers and to students of the life sciences. In the words of evolutionary biologist Andrew Read, a doctoral candidate when the book came out, "[T]he intellectual framework had already been in the air, but *The Selfish Gene* crystallized it and made it impossible to ignore."[57]

Read the whole book, but note especially Chapter Nine, where Dawkins discusses the ways in which cultural as well as biochemical informa-

[57]Matt Ridley, *The Red Queen: Sex and the Evolution of Human Nature* (New York: Harper Perennial, 2003), p. 9; Alan Grafen and Mark Ridley, eds., *Richard Dawkins: How a Scientist Changed the Way We Think* (New York: Oxford University Press, 2007), p. 7.

tion is transmitted from generation to generation. Looking for a name for a "unit of cultural transmission" (Dawkins offers, as examples, "tunes, ideas, catch-phrases, clothes fashions, ways of making pots or of building arches"), Dawkins abbreviated the Greek word *mimeme* to *meme,* thus contributing a brand-new (and now common) word to the English language.

STEVEN WEINBERG
The First Three Minutes:
A Modern View of the Origin of the Universe
(1977)

Best edition: The 1977 text, which has never gone out of print, has been published in a second updated edition, with a new foreword and an even more recent afterword, by Basic Books (1993).

By 1977, physicists were largely in agreement: the universe had once been a singularity, a super-dense, molten, "primeval atom" that somehow contained all matter now in the universe, and had expanded outward. It was, in fact, *still* expanding steadily outward; the expansion, seen as the steady distancing of distant nebulae from our vantage point, had been measured. Originally a theoretical construct proposed by the Belgian astronomer Georges Lemaître, the so-called "Big Bang" (a name given by the theory's opponents) was not an explosion, but a steady expansion outward over inconceivable amounts of time. Its supporters suggested that the enormous heat of this original super-dense starting point would still be radiating around the universe as residual microwave radiation; when this radiation was first measured, in 1965, even skeptical physicists began to agree that, yes, the singularity had once indeed existed at the center, or beginning (the two were identical) of the cosmos.

It took the general public a few more years to sign on. The expansion of the universe from a singularity was both technical and counterintuitive. It needed a popularizer, and Steven Weinberg—a theoretical physicist from New York who won the Nobel Prize two years after publishing *The First Three Minutes*—was able to convey highly technical content in a clear and simplified way. *The First Three Minutes* clearly lays out background information about the expansion of the universe, runs through the historical development of various explanations (including steady-state theory), and shows the necessity of cosmic microwave radiation; it was the first widely read explanation of the Big Bang, and the catalyst for a explosion of books for lay readers on cosmology and theoretical physics over the next decade.

Yet, as groundbreaking as it was, *The First Three Minutes* shares the drawbacks of all origin stories. It demands a leap of faith about the beginning of the universe: "There is an embarrassing vagueness about the very beginning," Weinberg wrote, in his introduction, "the first hundredth of a second or so . . . we may have to get used to the idea of an absolute zero of time—a moment in the past beyond which it is in principle impossible to trace any chain of cause and effect." And Weinberg also is unable to avoid speculating about the end. The universe, Weinberg writes, must, ultimately, stop expanding; it will either simply cease, fading away into cold and darkness, or else "experience a kind of cosmic 'bounce,'" and begin to re-expand, in "an endless cycle of expansion and contraction stretching into the infinite past, with no beginning whatever."

E. O. WILSON
On Human Nature
(1978)

Best edition: Hardcover copies of the first edition (Harvard University Press) are widely available. The 2004 revision, On Human Nature: With a New Preface *(rev. ed., Harvard University Press), contains a useful foreword by Wilson, reflecting on the public reception of the original book.*

On Human Nature, Wilson's most widely read work, assumes that human behavior rests on chemistry. Wilson's philosophy is one of *disciplinary reductionism*; insights from physics and chemistry, demonstrable through experimentation, able to be confirmed by calculation, are the bedrock of all human knowledge. Biology rests on this bedrock; biological laws are directly derived from physical and chemical principles. And the social sciences—psychology, anthropology, ethology (natural animal behavior), sociology—float above, entirely dependent upon the "hard" sciences beneath.

Wilson's first work was done on ant societies. His 1975 text *Sociobiology: The New Synthesis*, argued that human behavior, no less than ant action, results from nothing more transcendent than physical necessity. Even seemingly intangible feelings and motivations (hate, love, guilt, fear) are

constrained and shaped by the emotional control centers in the hypothalamus and limbic system of the brain. . . . What, we are then compelled to ask, made the hypothalamus and limbic system? They evolved by natural selection . . . [T]he hypothalmus and limbic system are engineered to perpetuate DNA. We are flooded with remorse, or the impulse to altruism, or despair, only because our brains (independent of our conscious knowledge) are reacting to our environment in the way that will best preserve our genes.

"Sociobiology," then, was the attempt to understand human society solely as a product of biological impulse.

All of *Sociobiology* except for the last chapter was based on animal research; *On Human Nature,* published three years later, focuses in more closely on *human* data. "The human mind," Wilson argues, "is a device for survival and reproduction, and reason is just one of its various techniques." He then explains how each of our most treasured attributes arise from our genes (so, for example, "The highest forms of religious practice . . . can be seen to confer biological advantage," not to mention "Genetic diversification, the ultimate function of sex, is served by the physical pleasure of the sex act").

Like James Watson and Richard Dawkins, Wilson proved to be a talented writer, with a knack for powerful metaphors. *On Human Nature* was praised, excoriated, and read; it was an instant best seller, and in 1979 won a Pulitzer Prize.

JAMES LOVELOCK
Gaia
(1979)

Best edition: The Oxford University Press reprint, Gaia: A New Look at Life on Earth *(2000).*

James Lovelock picks up Rachel Carson's themes, exploring the interrelationship between human beings and the planet by envisioning the entire related system as a single symbiotic "being." This is not, he hastens to explain, a *literal* being, a sentient creature of some kind: rather, "the entire surface of the Earth, including life, is a self-regulating entity, and this is what I mean by Gaia." (The name was suggested by his neighbor William Goldman, author of *The Princess Bride.*)

With this as his central construct, Lovelock—an environmentalist and inventor who did his graduate work in medicine—explores the interrelationship of the biosphere (the "region of the Earth where living organisms" exist) and the surface rocks, air, and ocean. It is, he argues, a tightly organized interlocking system, with pollution or sickness in one part forcing the entire "super-organism" to adapt.

Like his fellow popularizers, Lovelock then progresses to conclusions about human existence. He explains the human sense of beauty ("complex feelings of pleasure, recognition, and fulfillment, of wonder, excitement, and yearning, which fill us") as a biological response that has been "programmed to recognize instinctively our optimal role" in relationship to the earth. "It does not seem inconsistent with the Darwinian forces of evolutionary selection," he concludes, "for a sense of pleasure to reward us by encouraging us to achieve a balanced relationship between ourselves and other forms of life."

STEPHEN JAY GOULD
The Mismeasure of Man
(1981)

Best edition: Paperback copies of the original 1981 edition can easily be located secondhand. The original publisher, W. W. Norton, put out a revised and expanded edition of the title in 1996; it includes Gould's updated defense of his argument and his interaction with biological determinism in the years since original publication.

Stephen Jay Gould believed that Morris and Wilson were oversimplifying. In *The Mismeasure of Man,* he argues against what he calls "Darwinian fundamentalism"—the use of natural selection to explain the totality of human experience. Instead, Gould writes, there are multiple overlapping factors (all of them natural, but the sum total too complex to be reduced to DNA) that determine human behavior.

The Mismeasure of Man was (like Wilson's own book) aimed at a general readership. It was a focused and powerful refutation of *one* specific instance of what Gould saw as "fundamentalist": the "abstraction of intelligence" as a biochemically determined quality, its "quantification" as a number (thanks to the increasing popularity of IQ tests), and "the use of these numbers to rank people" in a biologically determined "series of worthiness."

The argument was intended to play a much larger role than simply debunking IQ tests: Gould hoped to refute the disciplinary reductionism so prominent in Wilson's works. "*The Mismeasure of Man* is not fundamentally about the general moral turpitude of fallacious biological arguments in social settings," he wrote, in his introduction. "It is not even about the full range of phony arguments for the genetic basis of human inequalities" (a clear shot at *Sociobiology*). Rather, "*The Mismeasure of Man* treats *one particular form* of *quantified* claim about the ranking of human groups: the argument that intelligence can be meaningfully abstracted as a single number capable of ranking all people on a linear scale of intrinsic and unalterable mental worth."

Like Wilson, Gould was assailed by some ("More factual errors per page than any book I have ever read," snapped the prominent psychologist Hans Eysenck, himself a believer in the genetic basis of intelligence) and praised by others (the book won the National Book Critics Circle award in 1982).[58]

JAMES GLEICK
Chaos: Making a New Science
(1987)

Best edition: Gleick's original 1987 text (Viking) is still available secondhand; a slightly revised and updated second edition was published in by Penguin Books in 2008.

Unlike the other authors on this list, James Gleick is not a scientist; he is a journalist (and English major). But in *Chaos,* he was able to digest and re-present a series of highly technical research articles so clearly that chaos theory became a household name (and ended up in the movies.)

Chaos theory was born in 1961, when the American mathematician Edward Lorenze was tinkering with metereology. Lorenz had written computer code that should have taken various factors (wind distance and speed, air pressure, temperature, etc.) and used them to predict weather patterns. He discovered, accidentally, that tiny variations in the factors entered—changes in wind speed, or temperature, so small that they should have been completely insignificant—sharply changed the predicted patterns.

In 1963, he published a paper suggesting that, in some systems, minuscule changes could actually produce massively different results. In 1972, he followed up with another, called "Predictability: Does the Flap of a Butterfly's Wings in Brazil Set Off a Tornado in Texas?" It was the first time that a butterfly's wing was used as an analogy for one of those tiny starting changes: the first use of the "butterfly effect." In 1975, two other mathematicians, Tien-Yien Li and James A. Yorke, published a paper that first gave this phenomenon a name. They called it chaos: an immensely powerful word for most English-speaking readers who, even by 1975, knew something of its biblical use: utter formlessness, confusion, disorder.

Chaos theory was still in its early adolescence when Gleick—a *New York Times Magazine* columnist and freelance essayist—chose it as the sub-

[58]Hans. J. Eysenck, *Intelligence: A New Look* (New Brunswick, N.J.: Transaction Publishers, 2000), p. 10.

ject of his first book. Peppered with vivid metaphors, *Chaos* gripped the popular imagination. The "Butterfly Effect" became a household phrase, especially once Jeff Goldblum's rock-star scientist character in *Jurassic Park* gave worldwide audiences the shorthand version ("A butterfly can flap its wings in Peking, and in Central Park, you get rain instead of sunshine . . . Tiny variations . . . never repeat, and vastly affect the outcome").

But the word *chaos* is misleading. *Chaos* here means "unpredictability"—and not even ultimate, intrinsic unpredictibility (as in, "No matter how much we know, we will not be able to predict the end result") but, instead, a contingent, *practical* unpredictibility ("This system is so sensitive to microscopic changes in initial conditions that we are not, at the moment, capable of analysing those initial conditions with the accuracy necessary to predict all possible outcomes").

STEPHEN HAWKING
A Brief History of Time
(1988)

Best edition: A Brief History of Time: Updated and Expanded Tenth Anniversary Edition *(Bantam Books, 1998).*

A Brief History of Time was not the first popular physics best seller ("Surely not another book on the Big Bang and all that stuff," physicist Paul Davies remembers thinking when he first saw Hawking's tome), but it outdid all the rest. Hawking's modest goal is to use physics to answer a series of questions: "What do we know about the universe, and how do we know it? Where did the universe come from, and where is it going? Did the universe have a beginning, and if so, what happened *before* then? What is the nature of time? Will it ever come to an end?" The answers garnered a readership of over ten million readers in thirty-five languages—making *A Brief History of Time* one of the most popular science books ever written.

WALTER ALVAREZ
T. rex and the Crater of Doom
(1997)

Best edition: The Princeton University Press paperback (2008).

Finding a strange abundance of the element iridium in a layer of Italian rock where it had no business being, Walter Alvarez—taught, by his scientific training, to prefer uniformitarianism over catastrophe—began to suspect that a huge catastrophe had, in fact, once struck the earth. The rock in question was at the so-called "K-T" boundary, a strata of rock where geologists had long noted a discontinuity in the fossil record. Before the K-T boundary, dinosaurs and ammonites abounded; after it, they disappeared.

Together, Alvarez and his father, physicist (and Nobel Prize winner) Luis Alvarez, theorized that the iridum might come from an asteroid collision with the earth. In 1980, Alvarez proposed in the journal *Science* (in a paper co-authored by his father, along with fellow scientists Frank Asaro and Helen Michel), that the "KT boundary iridium anomaly" might well be due to an asteroid strike. Furthermore, this impact might explain the fossil discontinuity:

> Impact of a large earth-crossing asteroid would inject about 60 times the object's mass into the atmosphere as pulverized rock; a fraction of this dust would stay in the stratosphere for several years and be distributed worldwide. The resulting darkness would suppress photosynthesis, and the expected biological consequences match quite closely the extinctions observed in the paleontological record.[59]

What was missing was the impact crater. Eleven years later, Alvarez and his colleagues found traces of a crater 125 miles across, concealed by millennia of accumulated sediment, on the Yucatán coast. The impact of a striking object large enough to make such a crater would have vaporized crust, set forests on fire, sent tsunamis ripping through the oceans, and thrown enough debris into the atmosphere to block the sun's rays and create storms of poisonous acid rain. The impact, Alvarez concluded, changed the face of the planet—and wiped out the dinosaurs.

In 1997, Alvarez published his account of the hypothesis's formation in *T-Rex and the Crater of Doom.* For the most part a carefully written, precise account of the clues that led Alvarez and his team to their conclusions, the book begins with a first chapter called "Armageddon," a quote from *The Lord of the Rings,* and a dramatic account of what the impact must have looked like. ("Doom was coming out of the sky . . ."). Popular science writing had hit its zenith: "Suddenly," says science writer Carl Zimmer of Alvarez's book, "the history of life was more cinematic than any science fiction movie."

---

[59] Alvarez et al., "Extraterrestrial Cause for the Cretaceous-Tertiary Extinction," p. 1095.

Index

Page numbers in **bold** refer to main discussions of topics.